READINGS IN MANAGEMENT CONTROL

ADMINISTRATION SERIES

Eugene E. Jennings, *Editor*

Basic Computer Programming
Decima M. Anderson

Cases in Personnel Management and Supervision
Richard P. Calhoon

Personnel Management and Supervision
Richard P. Calhoon

The Organization Makers
Orvis Collins, David G. Moore

Readings in Business Policy
Edmund R. Gray

Executive Success
Eugene E. Jennings

Organization Renewal
Gordon L. Lippitt

Readings in Management Control
Robert J. Mockler

Management in International Perspective
S. Benjamin Prasad

Research and Development Management
Daniel D. Roman

Measuring Executive Effectiveness
Frederic R. Wickert, Dalton E. McFarland

Business Policies and Decision Making
Raymond J. Ziegler

Edited by

Robert J. Mockler

READINGS IN MANAGEMENT CONTROL

New York

APPLETON-CENTURY-CROFTS
Educational Division
MEREDITH CORPORATION

To my wife

760–1

Library of Congress Card Number: 73–116565

PRINTED IN THE UNITED STATES OF AMERICA

390–64439–0

CONTRIBUTORS

Lee Adler
The Interpublic Group of Companies

Robert N. Anthony
Harvard Graduate School of Business Administration

E. Leonard Arnoff
Ernst & Ernst

Joseph I. Barnett
Standard Program Corporation

Charles J. Berg, Jr.
John B. Joynt & Associates

Rudolf Borchardt
Spartans Industries

Edwin T. Boyle
Governing Council, American Institute of CPA's

Warren B. Brown
Indiana University

Stanley E. Bryan
Michigan State University

Neal J. Dean
Booz, Allen & Hamilton

A. Fendrock
Air Reduction Company

Joseph Freitag, Jr.
Hughes Aircraft Company

John T. Garrity
McKinsey & Company, Inc.

Friedhelm Goronzy
Louisiana State University

Ernest I. Hanson
University of Wisconsin

Herbert G. Hicks
Louisiana State University

Colin Hill
Pressed Steel Fisher Ltd.

Walter E. Hoadley
Armstrong Cork Company

Richard A. Johnson
University of Washington, Seattle

Fremont E. Kast
University of Washington, Seattle

E. N. Khoury
Burroughs Corporation

Harold Koontz
University of California at Los Angeles

Karl E. Korn
Western Electric Company, Inc.

Philip Kotler
Northwestern University

Allen I. Kraut
International Business Machines Corporation

James H. Lamb
Western Electric Company, Inc.

J. K. McConnell
Air Products and Chemicals, Inc.

Robert J. Mockler
Management Consultant

Thomas B. Neff
I.T.T. de Mexico

H. Wayne Nelson
Burroughs Corporation

M. J. Netzorg
Ernst & Ernst

Sidney I. Neuwirth
Lybrand, Ross Bros. and Montgomery

Maurice S. Newman
Haskins & Sells

Ray M. Powell
University of Notre Dame

James E. Rosenzweig
University of Washington, Seattle

Harold M. F. Rush
National Industrial Conference Board

John B. Scott
Peat, Marwick, Mitchell & Company

Donald L. Shawver
University of Missouri

Max S. Simpson
Mobil Oil Company, Inc.

Milton H. Spencer
Wayne State University

Alexander L. Stott
American Telephone & Telegraph Company

James W. Taylor
Booz, Allen & Hamilton

Arthur B. Toan, Jr.
Price Waterhouse & Company

Bayard E. Wynne, Jr.
Arthur Andersen & Company

McCready S. Young
Peat, Marwick, Mitchell & Company

Joel Zelnick
Auerbach Corporation

PREFACE

Readings in Management Control gives a comprehensive review of management control theory and principles, describes the major tools and techniques used in management control, and explores ways in which these principles and techniques can be applied to specific business problems.

Part I of the book concerns theory and principles. The first article develops an outline of the science of management control. This is the structure upon which the book is built. Further perspectives on the subject are then presented by other authorities in the field. Part II of the book covers seven basic areas of control technology. Part III concerns the application of this theory and technology to business decision making.

The scope of management control, as developed in this book, is considerably broader than that found in other studies of the subject. This is mainly because *Readings in Management Control* for the first time brings together in one work both management control theory and the many techniques used in performing the management control function, while at the same time attempting to relate these aspects of control to actual business problems.

Readings in Management Control is intended for anyone who wants to learn more about business control. The book was an outgrowth of the author's forthcoming text *The Management Control Process,* and has been used both alone and in conjunction with the textbook in business control courses. *Readings in Management Control* should prove useful in control-related courses such as finance, accounting, systems, operations research, and general management principles.

I wish to thank the authors and publishers of the articles reprinted in this book for their permission to use the material. In addition, I am indebted to my series editor, Eugene Jennings, and to my students for their helpful comments. Lastly, I want to thank my research assistant, Thomas Deely, for his untiring efforts in helping build the book, and my wife, without whom the book would never have come into print.

Robert J. Mockler

New York City

CONTENTS

B New Scientific Tools and Techniques

C Electronic Data Processing

D The Behavioral Sciences

E Economic Planning and Forecasting

F Finance and Accounting

INTRODUCTION

There are several reasons for the increasing interest in developing the theory and principles of management control in a more orderly and scientific manner. In the past—and even today in many areas of business—control was considered the special province of the controller, accountant, or financial officer. As a result, little attention has been paid to the management control function as it might be practiced by any manager, in any functional area, in any business. Emphasis on the controller's viewpoint has also led to a tendency to stress the compliance aspects of control—setting standards, checking conformity to them, and correcting deviations from them. This in turn has led to some stifling of the drives for creativity, innovation, and change within an enterprise.

Modern management control theory, principles, and practice strive to break this restrictive mold, and to help improve both the overall control of business operations and the performance of the control function by individual managers. Management control shows a manager how he can apply the basic problem-solving process to control problems in his own operating area. It gives him principles and techniques he can personally put into practice to improve his management performance. And it develops a more fruitful balance between compliance and stimulation throughout a corporation's operations and tries to channel, not restrict, the forces of innovation and progress in the business enterprise.

Another reason for the increasing interest in the study of management control can be found in the explosion of new control technology in the areas of systems, operations research, and electronic information processing. The complexity of these areas and the speed with which they have expanded have created a compelling need for new methods of explaining this technology and putting it to work for the firm in the most effective way possible. Modern management control provides such a framework to help a manager better understand and use the corporate control tools and processes which are available throughout the business enterprise.

As Jerome points out, there has never been a time when a fully developed science of management control was more needed in business.[1] The complexity and rapid rate of change in the present social and political environment, and the resulting demands on business to deal with this complexity and change, require that a fresh look be taken at management control. The restraints of compliance control need to be broken and new and more sophisticated management control theories, principles, and techniques developed. Equally important, these new theories, principles, and especially techniques need to be developed within a single, simplified, and unified scientific framework if busy managers are to be able to grasp them and put them to use.

Readings in Management Control attempts to present such a unified scientific framework.

THE HISTORY OF THE STUDY OF BUSINESS CONTROL

The study of business control has had a long history, starting with the early works of the general management theorists. In 1916, for example, in one of the earliest efforts to develop a science of management, Henri Fayol gave the following definition of management control: "Control consists of verifying whether everything occurs in conformity with the plan adopted, the instructions issued and principles established. It has for object to point out weaknesses and errors in order to rectify and prevent recurrence."[2] Fayol was thinking mainly in terms of financial control, and this viewpoint prevails in his discussion of the various processes and tools needed for controlling a business operation effectively and efficiently.

A review of the studies of general management theory and practice that followed Fayol reveals both a continuing interest in the subject and an ever-increasing awareness of the importance of control to successful business management.[3] In their definitions of the control process, the authors of these studies continue to stress the compliance aspects of

[1] Wm. Travers Jerome III, *Executive Control—The Catalyst* (New York: John Wiley & Sons, Inc., 1961), Chapter 1.

[2] Henri Fayol, *General and Industrial Management,* trans. Constance Storrs (New York: Pitman Publishing Corp., 1949), pp. 107 ff.

[3] The following are some of the better-known studies to appear (or reappear) during the last eight years: William H. Newman, *Administrative Action: The Techniques of Organization and Management,* 2nd ed. (Englewood Cliffs, N.J.: Prentice-Hall, Inc., 1963), Chapters 24–26; George R. Terry, *Principles of Management,* 4th ed. (Homewood, Ill.: Richard D. Irwin, Inc., 1964), Chapters 26–30; Justin G. Longnecker, *Principles of Management and Organization Behavior* (Columbus, Ohio: Charles E. Merrill Books, Inc., 1964), Chapters 24–26; Harold Koontz and Cyril O'Donnell, *Principles of Management: An Analysis of Managerial Functions,* 3rd ed.

control. And like Fayol, in their discussions of control tools and techniques, these authors for the most part concentrate on over-all company financial controls.

Although useful, these studies of management control leave much to be desired. First, because they are brief, they do not cover the wide range of problems encountered in management control decision making by both individual managers and corporate control departments. Second, because they have a limited perspective, they do not explore the subject in depth and so do not provide a broad conceptual basis for developing a distinct and unified science of management control. Third, because these studies concentrate on the compliance aspects of control, they neglect other positive aspects of management control.

Prior to 1960 very little effort was made to study management control as a separate discipline—as a distinct decision-making process that could be used by any manager in any functional area. In *Top–Management Organization and Control* (1941 and 1951), Holden, Fish and Smith concentrated on explaining the control techniques used in their day in such areas as organization, costs, salaries and wages, product lines, and the quality of key personnel.[4] Outside of a few pages on the process of control, however, the book contains no discussion of the fundamental theory and principles of management control. Rose and Farr attempted much more in *Higher Management Control* (1957).[5] After defining control, the authors describe their experiences in setting up control systems for management operations. However, the emphasis of this book is still on the techniques used in the early 1950's by a controller or a control department in a corporation, not on the control function performed by all managers at all levels of management. Neither of these texts, therefore, meets the needs of today's executives.

In 1957 the Financial Executives Institute sponsored a study of the installation of a new system for budgetary control at the H. J. Heinz Company.[6] Although the study primarily concerns the internal control

---

(New York: McGraw-Hill Book Company, 1964), Chapters 28–31; Ernest Dale, *Management: Theory and Practice* (New York: McGraw-Hill Book Company, 1965), Chapter 26; Max D. Richards and Paul S. Greenlaw, *Management Decision Making* (Homewood, Ill.: Richard D. Irwin, Inc., 1966), Chapter 12; William H. Newman, Charles E. Summer, and E. Kirby Warren, *The Process of Management: Concepts, Behavior, and Practice,* 2nd ed. (Englewood Cliffs, N.J.: Prentice-Hall, Inc., 1967), Chapters 27–30.

[4] Paul E. Holden, Lounsbury S. Fish, and Hubert L. Smith, *Top-Management Organization and Control: A Research Study of the Management Policies and Practices of Thirty-One Leading Industrial Corporations* (New York: McGraw-Hill Book Company, 1941, 1951).

[5] T. G. Rose and Donald E. Farr, *Higher Management Control* (New York: McGraw-Hill Book Company, 1957).

[6] *Management Planning and Control: The H. J. Heinz Approach, a Case Study in Management Planning and Control Objectives, Organization and Methods with Particular Emphasis on the Part Played by the Comptroller's Division in this Work* (New York: Controllers Institute Research Foundation, Inc., 1957).

problems faced by the corporate controller, it contains a significant departure from the viewpoint that prevails in compliance-oriented, internal control studies. In the Heinz study the authors emphasize how the control process can be used to stimulate creativity, innovation, education, and coordination—all of which tend to be de-emphasized in studies of internal corporate control, where compliance to standards is emphasized.

The Financial Executives Institute has also sponsored a number of other studies in the control field, but these deal almost exclusively with techniques and tools of control from the controller's or financial officer's viewpoint.[7]

There are a number of studies dealing with control tools in the accounting area, whose authors attempt in various ways to relate their fields to management control. These include: Anthony, *Management Accounting Principles* (1965); Keller and Ferrara, *Management Accounting for Profit Control* (1966); Heckert and Willson, *Business Budgeting and Control* (1967); Korn and Boyd, *Accounting for Management Planning and Decision Making* (1969); Flink and Grunewald, *Managerial Finance* (1969); and Norbeck *et al., Operational Auditing for Management Control* (1969).[8] *Management Controls* (1964),[9] edited by Bonini, Jaedicke, and Wagner, presents a series of papers on current management control techniques in such areas as simulation, accounting, economics, and the behavioral sciences. While some attempt is made in all of these studies to explore the broader aspects of management control, their major focus is still on accounting or financial control tools.

Management control also makes use of tools drawn from the operations research and statistical areas. The use of operations research and

[7] *Planning, Managing and Measuring the Business: A Case Study of Management Planning and Control at General Electric Company* (New York: Controllers Institute Research Foundation, Inc., March 1961); Michael Schiff and Martin Mellman, *Financial Management of the Marketing Function* (New York: Financial Executives Research Foundation, 1962); Raymond Villers, *Research and Development: Planning and Control* (New York: F.E.R.F., 1964); David Solomons, *Divisional Performance: Measurement and Control* (New York: F.E.R.F., 1965); Glenn A. Welsch and Burnard H. Sord, *Management Planning and Control* (New York: F.E.R.F., 1968); Robert K. Mautz, *Financial Reporting by Diversified Companies* (New York: F.E.R.F., 1968).

[8] Robert N. Anthony, *Management Accounting Principles* (Homewood, Ill.: Richard D. Irwin, Inc., 1965); I. Wayne Keller and William L. Ferrara, *Management Accounting for Profit Control,* 2nd ed. (New York: McGraw-Hill Book Company, 1966); J. Brooks Heckert and James D. Willson, *Business Budgeting and Control,* 3rd ed. (New York: Ronald Press Company, 1967); Solomon J. Flink and Donald Grunewald, *Managerial Finance* (New York: John Wiley & Sons, Inc., 1969); S. Winston Korn and Thomas Boyd, *Accounting for Management Planning and Decision Making* (New York: John Wiley & Sons, Inc., 1969); Edward F. Norbeck *et al., Operational Auditing for Management Control* (New York: American Management Association, 1969).

[9] Charles P. Bonini, Robert K. Jaedicke and Harvey M. Wagner, eds., *Management Controls: New Directions in Basic Research* (New York: McGraw-Hill Book Company, 1964).

statistics in business decision making is explained in detail in: Schlaifer, *Probability and Statistics for Business Decisions* (1959); Miller and Starr, *Executive Decisions and Operations Research* (1969); Bierman *et al., Quantitative Analysis for Business Decisions* (1965); Hillier and Lieberman, *Introduction to Operations Research* (1967); Brabb, *Introduction to Quantitative Management* (1968); and Hough, *Modern Research for Administrative Decisons* (1970).[10] While these control tools are used in the performance of management control today, none of these books explores at any length the basis of management control theory and principles underlying the development and use of these tools.

Since 1960 there have been a number of books on the business information systems used in planning and control. These include: Forrester, *Industrial Dynamics* (1961); Anthony, Dearden and Vancil, *Management Control Systems* (1965); Young, *Management: A Systems Analysis* (1966); Glans *et al., Management Systems* (1968); Cleland and King, *Systems Analysis and Project Management* (1968); and Rudwick, *Systems Analysis for Effective Planning* (1969).[11] Although the subject of these studies is business information systems, the authors devote some time to discussing basic management control concepts.

Many books on other control tools in the area of electronic data processing, reporting, organizational behavior, and finance, have also touched upon the subject of management control. As Robert N. Anthony points out, however, the field of management control currently has "scarcely any generally accepted principles, and everyone in the field, therefore, works by intuition and by folklore."[12] In his *Planning and*

[10] Robert Schlaifer, *Probability and Statistics for Business Decisions: An Introduction to Managerial Economics under Uncertainty* (New York: McGraw-Hill Book Company, 1959); David W. Miller and Martin K. Starr, *Executive Decisions and Operations Research,* 2nd ed. (Englewood Cliffs, N.J.: Prentice-Hall, Inc., 1969); Harold Bierman, Jr. *et al., Quantitative Analysis for Business Decisions,* rev. ed. (Homewood, Ill.: Richard D. Irwin, Inc., 1965); Frederick S. Hillier and Gerald J. Lieberman, *Introduction to Operations Research* (San Francisco: Holden-Day, Inc., 1967); George J. Brabb, *Introduction to Quantitative Management* (New York: Holt, Rinehart and Winston, Inc., 1968); Louis Hough, *Modern Research for Administrative Decisions* (Englewood Cliffs, N.J.: Prentice-Hall, Inc., 1970).

[11] Jay W. Forrester, *Industrial Dynamics* (Cambridge, Mass.: M.I.T. Press, 1961); Robert N. Anthony, John Dearden, and Richard F. Vancil, *Management Control Systems: Cases and Readings* (Homewood, Ill.: Richard D. Irwin, Inc., 1965); Stanley Young, *Management: A Systems Analysis* (Glenview, Ill.: Scott, Foresman & Company, 1966); Thomas B. Glans, Burton Grad, David Holstein, William E. Meyers, Richard N. Schmidt, *Management Systems* (New York: Holt, Rinehart & Winston, Inc., 1968); David I. Cleland and William R. King, *Systems Analysis and Project Management* (New York: McGraw-Hill Book Company, 1968); Bernard H. Rudwick, *Systems Analysis for Effective Planning: Principles and Cases* (New York: John Wiley & Sons, Inc., 1969).

[12] Robert N. Anthony, *Planning and Control Systems: A Framework for Analysis* (Boston: Division of Research, Graduate School of Business Administration, Harvard University, 1965), p. vii.

Control Systems: A Framework for Analysis (1965), Anthony attempted to lay the groundwork upon which a science of management control could be built.

A few years earlier, in *Executive Control—The Catalyst* (1961), William Travers Jerome III had also begun to break ground for a science of management control when he said that control is "a subject area with its own distinctive concepts and precepts."[13] In his study Jerome attempted to develop a scientific framework for management control, and explored at length its theory and principles. He paid particular attention to developing the creative, educational, and coordination aspects of control, which lead to innovation, change, and progress.

Two additional research studies, which explore the subject of management control in depth, were conducted under Anthony's direction: Robert Deming's *Characteristics of an Effective Management Control System in an Industrial Organization* (1968) and James S. Hekimian's *Management Control in Life Insurance Branch Offices* (1965).[14] Both studies involve detailed examinations of existing control systems at major corporations, and both give interesting insights into the various levels of control within a company and the variety of ways control is exercised. These studies, however, were designed only to test Anthony's conceptual framework, and not to develop a new concept of management control.

Four recent works which study various kinds of control problems are also indicative of the increasing interest in developing a unified concept of a control science. Earl P. Strong and Robert D. Smith, in *Management Control Models* (1968), study the different control tools used in business today as part of a single control discipline. However, while the study has a brief introduction on what control is, like so many earlier works its focus is on tools and their applications. In contrast, a major part of Marvin Mundel's *A Conceptual Framework for the Management Sciences* (1967) not only deals with the concept of control but also explores at length the ways in which that concept is applied in the production, financial, and sales areas. Arnold S. Tannenbaum's book of readings, *Control in Organizations* (1968), also treats control as a unified concept, but he deals only with the behavioral science aspects of control. Paul M. Stokes's *A Total Systems Approach to Management Control* (1968) gives a concise overview of control for top corporate management, covering the development and use of controls and control standards in eight critical performance areas: finance; operations; productivity; market position; service relations; public, customer, and government re-

[13] Jerome, *Executive Control,* p. 27.

[14] Robert H. Deming, *Characteristics of an Effective Management Control System in an Industrial Organization* (Boston: Division of Research Graduate School of Business Administration, Harvard University, 1968); James S. Hekimian, *Management Control in Life Insurance Branch Offices* (Boston: Division of Research, Graduate School of Business Administration, Harvard University, 1965).

lations; employee relations and development; and ownership and member relations.[15]

While Anthony, Jerome, and the others cited above made major contributions to the development of the science of management control, none of these authors claimed to be making any more than a beginning. The state of the science of management control today is similar to the state of the science of corporate long-range planning a decade ago. In 1958, David Ewing put together a book of readings on corporate planning which was to give focus and impetus to the study of planning.[16] While some work on this subject had been done prior to Ewing's book, only after 1960 did major works on the theory and principles of corporate long-range planning appear and a science of corporate long-range planning develop. Hopefully, within the next decade management control will also develop into a well-defined area of management science.

A NEW APPROACH TO BUSINESS CONTROL

In addition to the books cited above, many articles have been written on the subject of management control. *Readings in Management Control* brings together the most significant articles which have appeared in recent years and organizes them within the framework of the science of management control.

The concept of management control, as developed in Part I of the book, goes beyond the controller's, the accountant's, or the financial officer's viewpoint and covers the following areas:

1. General problem-solving techniques and their applications to control problems in any area of business.
2. General management control theories and principles of action.
3. Tools of mathematics and logic used in control problem solving.
4. Newly developed tools in the behavioral sciences and electronic data processing fields which are used in control.
5. Traditional control tools in the accounting and financial areas.
6. The application of this body of theory, principles, and tools to the marketing, production, financial, and accounting areas of business operations.

[15] Marvin E. Mundel, *A Conceptual Framework for the Management Sciences* (New York: McGraw-Hill Book Company, 1967); Earl P. Strong and Robert D. Smith, *Management Control Models* (New York: Holt, Rinehart & Winston, Inc., 1968); Arnold S. Tannenbaum, ed., *Control in Organizations* (New York: McGraw-Hill Book Company, 1968); Paul M. Stokes, *A Total Systems Approach to Management Control* (New York: American Management Association, 1968).

[16] David W. Ewing, ed., *Long-Range Planning for Management* (New York: Harper & Brothers, 1958).

Part I of the book is designed to give the reader a comprehensive outline of the science of management control, within which the various aspects of management control tools and techniques can be interrelated and so more easily understood. The first article of Part I develops a framework for understanding management control (1) by defining management control, (2) by describing the processes followed in solving management control problems and in performing management control, and (3) by giving some principles of action. The other articles in this part give further perspectives on the theory and principles of management control.

Part II contains seven sections which cover the basic tools and techniques used in performing effective management control: the systems approach; mathematical, model-building, and statistical techniques; electronic data processing; the behavioral sciences; economic forecasting; finance and accounting; and reporting.

The systems approach, Section A, includes articles which provide a conceptual basis, as well as principles and guidelines, for establishing a more efficient information system for planning and control within a business.

The articles in Section B concern new scientific tools and techniques used for control decision making. The quantitative control tools currently being used and developed fall generally within the category of operations research. As defined by Miller and Starr in *Executive Decisions and Operations Research,* "operations research is a scientific method of providing executive departments with a quantitative basis for decisions regarding operations under their control." [17] In addition to mathematical model-building techniques, the readings in this section cover descriptive, analytical, or simulated model-building techniques, and the use of statistics in business decision making. Techniques such as PERT, CPM, and decision trees are also included in this section, since they are important tools in developing management control systems and in making management control decisions.

Section C, Electronic Data Processing, concerns the control tool that has had the most dramatic effect on management control thinking in recent years. Basic to an understanding of this newly developing control tool is the distinction between an information system and an electronic data processing system. An information system involves all the flows of information within a business enterprise which are needed for decision making. Some parts of this system will be manual, some mechanical, and some electronic. Viewed in this context, the electronic data processing system is seen as a subsystem within the total information system, and this is the perspective within which management control views electronic data processing. The articles in Section C explore some of the ways in

[17] Miller and Starr, *Executive Decisions and Operations Research,* p. 104.

which management control attitudes and viewpoints have been affected by the growth of electronic data processing, and some of the ways in which management can deal with the problems and opportunities presented by the computer.

Sections D, E, F, and G of Part II concern traditional management control tools. The articles in these sections deal with some of the new attitudes and techniques that are developing in these areas.

Part III explores selected ways in which management control theory and principles, and tools and techniques, can be applied in actual business situations. The ultimate test of any body of applied science is whether or not it is effective in practice. The articles in this section are part of the growing body of literature which shows how management control theory can be applied successfully to improve business operations.

The rapid growth of control technology has made it difficult for the average executive or business student to keep up with the new developments and apply this technology to his business problems. This book gives both executive and the business student a review of these new technological developments and a framework for understanding them, by interrelating them within a single scientific discipline—management control.

I

THE NATURE OF MANAGEMENT CONTROL

The articles in this part explore various aspects of the concept of management control. Each author attempts to develop a comprehensive framework for the science of management control, in order to provide the reader with an overview of the management control function. While there are differences in the authors' approaches, a common thread of management control theory and principles of action runs through all the articles.

Since the articles are largely exploratory treatments of the subject, none of them can be considered to be the final word on management control. The articles do, however, make an important contribution to the management field, for they are part of the investigation, research, and trial-and-error that are necessary preliminary steps in the development of a scientific discipline for management control.

The author discusses the basic concept of management control, the relation of control to planning, the control decision-making process, principles for exercising control, and modern control technology.

1

DEVELOPING THE SCIENCE OF MANAGEMENT CONTROL

Robert J. Mockler

In spite of the fact that management control is one of the basic management functions, there is no comprehensive body of management control theory and principles to which business executives can turn for guidance in performing their management control functions.

Management planning was in a similar state a decade ago, when David W. Ewing first put together his book of readings on the subject in 1958.[1] Only after 1960 did major works on the theory and principles of corporate planning begin to appear in sufficient numbers to suggest that a science of management planning was at last beginning to develop. Hopefully, within the next decade management control will also develop into a well-defined area of management science.

The purpose of this article is to describe the science of management control as we know it today. The article does not cover all aspects of management control; rather, it is intended to be only an introduction to the discipline. It is designed both to provide the business executive with guidelines that will help him control his operation more effectively and to give the student of management a framework within which the study of management control theory can be explored further and upon which a more complete science of management can be built.

Reprinted from *Financial Executive,* December 1967, pp. 80–93, by permission of the publisher.

[1] David W. Ewing, ed., *Long-Range Planning for Management* (New York: Harper & Brothers, 1958).

DEFINING MANAGEMENT CONTROL

Management control can be defined as a systematic effort by business management to compare performance to predetermined standards, plans, or objectives in order to determine whether performance is in line with these standards and presumably in order to take any remedial action required to see that human and other corporate resources are being used in the most effective and efficient way possible in achieving corporate objectives.[2]

All control starts with an enterprise's plans and expectations for the future because the objectives and standards against which performance is measured are based on those plans and expectations.

In an operational control situation, a means of obtaining accurate and up-to-date information about current performance must be developed next. The actual is then compared with the expected. Depending upon the evaluation of the meaning of any variation from standard, some sort of action is then taken.

In those situations that involve developing controls for planning decisions—an aspect of management control frequently overlooked—a realistic means of quantifying possible future events must be developed, so that all alternatives can be stated in comparable terms. These projections of performance can then be compared with the predetermined performance requirements set for the company or operation involved, and a choice can be made among alternative courses of action.

SOME DISTINGUISHING CHARACTERISTICS

While management control has characteristics common to all forms of control, it also has a number of distinguishing characteristics.

[2] This definition of management control is an extension, based on the author's experience, of the definition given by Jerome and Anthony:

> Wm. Travers Jerome III, *Executive Control—The Catalyst* (New York: John Wiley & Sons, Inc., 1961), p. 24: "Some sort of systematic effort to compare current performance to a predetermined plan or objective, presumably to take any remedial action required."
>
> Robert N. Anthony, *Planning and Control Systems: A Framework for Analysis* (Boston: Division of Research, Graduate School of Business Administration, Harvard University, 1965), p. 17: "The process by which managers assure that resources are obtained and used effectively and efficiently in the accomplishment of the organization's objectives."

Other definitions of control can be found in Anthony, *ibid.*, pp. 129–147; Chris Luneski, "Some Aspects of the Meaning of Control," *Accounting Review*, Vol. 39. No. 3 (July 1964), pp. 591–597; and Peter F. Drucker, "Controls, Control and Management," *Management Controls: New Directions in Basic Research*, eds. Charles P. Bonini, Robert K. Jaedicke, and Harvey M. Wagner (New York: McGraw-Hill Book Company, 1964), pp. 286–296.

First, management control refers specifically to the control functions within a business enterprise. Second, it concerns the business manager's control functions. Third, it is control designed to help a business enterprise reach its over-all objectives, and it is always viewed as an extension of a company's long-range plan. In other words, management control is another means managers have to achieve corporate objectives more effectively, whether it be at the staff, management, or operational level, whether the controls are used to protect assets or to stimulate creative use of those assets, or whether the controls are used to maintain production efficiency or to make decisions to purchase equipment.

The widely accepted description of management functions as planning, organizing, staffing, directing, and controlling [3] is much too general. In practice there is no clear distinction between these functions: control and planning are effective means of coordination, a good plan has good controls built into it, sound planning techniques are needed in planning for control, and directing really embraces all the other functions. In addition, definitions of management control such as, "Control . . . measures performance, corrects negative deviations, and assures the accomplishment of plans," [4] are much too negative and narrow and fail to distinguish business control from other types of control.

These generalized descriptions of management, and of the functions necessary to manage well, are of little value to the practitioner. Instead, the business executive needs a systematic body of knowledge that contains the following:

- Definitions that relate the concepts involved to business management problems.
- Guidelines for applying management control theory to practice.
- Specific tools which enable the executive to control better his particular business operation.

Only when such a comprehensive, systematically organized body of theories, principles, and techniques is developed will there be a science of management control.

MANAGEMENT CONTROL AND PLANNING

Because management control is designed to help a corporation reach its long-term objective, management control begins with corporate planning.

[3] For example, Harold Koontz and Cyril O'Donnell, *Principles of Management: An Analysis of Managerial Functions* (3rd ed.; New York: McGraw-Hill Book Company, 1964), p. 1.

[4] *Ibid.*, p. 41.

Corporate planning is an intellectual process which requires analysis of future circumstances, both external (environmental) and internal (company), and the development of an objective, policies, and programs within the context of that future.[5] The type of business planning defined here is always done within the framework of the entire corporation's long-term future, whether the plan itself is for one or ten years, and may be either for the corporation as a whole or for only one of its major operations. In most instances the corporate planning process includes the creation of an intermediate or long-range plan for a business enterprise.

Management control is an extension of the corporate planning process, for a good plan should have controls built into it. And a management control system cannot be developed, nor can management control be exercised effectively, unless the company has a specific objective and over-all plan for reaching that objective. For example, in building a control system, one must know not only what kind of business the company is in now, but also the kind of business it plans to be in three, five, or even ten years from now. Nor can one establish standards for measuring performance without knowing the company's expectations for the future.

By definition, therefore, management control is always exercised within the perspective of the over-all corporate plan, although the two functions are distinct: the management planning process leads to the creation of a corporate plan; the management control process controls performance within the framework of that corporate plan.

In order to understand just how performance is controlled and control decisions are made, it is necessary to examine in detail the two major management control processes. The first is the process followed in solving control problems and in setting up effective controls or a system for effective control. The second is the process of controlling the operation and making decisions once the controls or control system have been developed.

[5] This definition of planning is based upon the work of many authorities on planning. A review of definitions of planning for a corporation is found in Anthony, *Planning and Control Systems,* pp. 129–147. Further references to works on planning can be found in Melville C. Branch, *Selected References for Corporate Planning* (New York: American Management Association, 1966), and *Management Planning and Control: An Annotated Bibliography* (New York: Controllership Foundation, 1955).

While this definition is limited to corporate planning, such planning has much in common with public planning (city planning, domestic government planning, and international development planning) and military planning. The relationship between corporate planning and planning in other areas is discussed by Neil Chamberlain, *Public and Private Planning* (New York: McGraw-Hill Book Company, 1965) and Melville C. Branch, *Planning: Aspects and Applications* (New York: John Wiley & Sons, 1966).

THE PROCESS FOLLOWED IN SOLVING CONTROL PROBLEMS AND SETTING UP CONTROLS

The approach to solving management control problems closely parallels the fundamental approach to problem solving/decision making.

The steps in the problem-solving/decision-making process, as outlined by Peter Drucker, are as follows: [6]

1. Diagnose the situation and review all of the facts in order to find and define the problem.
2. Examine the problem and review the facts in order to find the key factors affecting the problem and its solution. This step is sometimes referred to as premising.
3. Develop alternative solutions to the problem.
4. Test and evaluate the alternatives to determine the best solution.
5. Construct a clear statement of the solution selected, and convert the decision into a plan of action.

The following is an outline of how this process can be applied to management control problems:

1. *Diagnose the situation in order to find and define the control problem.* The investigation should result in definitions (i.e., simple statement) of:
   - The control problem which must be solved.
   - The scope of the problem, its management implications, and tangential areas related to the control problem.
   - The extent of the solutions needed and the method to be used in solving the problem.

2. *Examine the control problem and review the facts in order to find the key factors affecting the problem and its solution.* The principal areas of investigation would be:
   - Corporate planning factors, such as the nature of the company's

[6] These steps are given in Peter Drucker's *The Practice of Management* (New York: Harper and Row, 1954), pp. 351–359, and in H. Igor Ansoff's *Corporate Strategy* (New York: McGraw-Hill Book Company, 1965), pp. 1–11. For other discussions of problem-solving/decision-making theory, see C. T. Hardwick and B. F. Landuyt, *Administrative Strategy and Decision Making* (2nd ed.; Cincinnati, Ohio: South-Western Publishing Company, 1966); Manley Howe Jones, *Executive Decision Making* (Rev. ed.; Homewood, Ill.: Richard D. Irwin, Inc., 1962); Charles H. Kepner and Benjamin B. Tregoe, *The Rational Manager: A Systematic Approach to Problem Solving and Decision Making* (New York: McGraw-Hill Book Company, 1965); Charles E. Summer, Jr. and Jeremiah J. O'Connell, *The Managerial Mind: Science and Theory in Policy Decisions* (Homewood, Ill.: Richard D. Irwin, Inc., 1964); and Max D. Richards and Paul S. Greenlaw, *Management Decision Making* (Homewood, Ill.: Richard D. Irwin, Inc., 1966).

business, the company's objective and major policies, the timing of major steps in the plan, and other factors related to the corporate long-range plan.

• The nature of the control problem being solved or of the operation for which the controls or control system is being created. For example, the problem could be an information system, capital equipment acquisition, production, inventory or other operational control, or any of a wide range of control situations.

• The purpose for which the controls or control system is being developed.

• The standards or criteria against which performance will be measured or compared.

3. *Develop alternative solutions.* The areas covered would be:

• Mechanics. The specific tools of analysis or the actual control system to be used. These would include the reporting forms needed and the precise information wanted on these forms, a design for the information system proposed and the organization needed, the mathematical and analytical models which will be used, and the assumptions to be used for quantifying risk and uncertainty.

• Implementation. The way to put the new solution (if one is proposed) into operation.

• The exercise of control. Where the controls or control system are automatic, this step in solving the control problem would be included as part of the mechanics. If executive judgment and action are required, principles of action and attitude and procedures must be spelled out. How control is exercised and how decisions are made on the basis of the control information developed are discussed below in the section on "Exercising Control."

4. *Test and evaluate these alternatives* to determine the best control tools, techniques, or system, how they can best be put into operation, and how they can be used most effectively by managers to achieve over-all corporate objectives.

5. *Prepare a written statement of the solutions selected in all major areas and proceed to carry it out.*

The apparent simplicity of this statement of the management control process is deceptive, for although the process is simple to define, it is difficult to apply in practice. The statement of the process is in reality no more than a descriptive checklist, an artificial breakdown of the process into its components. While this breakdown is useful for understanding the process, it is an incomplete guide for solving an actual control problem. In practice one discovers that the "steps" given are not steps at all, but merely the areas which must be covered to solve the control problem.

Rather than being an orderly and sequential series of steps, the process involves much overlapping and back-and-forth movement among the different parts of the outline, many of which must be performed simultaneously.

A detailed examination of how a control system is actually determined (see Step 3 above) illustrates the complexities of the management control process. Contrary to what is implied by the outline, the "development of alternative solutions" phase is never completed once and for all at Step 3. This phase is stated subsequent to the "finding key factors" phase merely because the key factors given in Step 2 ultimately control the development of the alternative solutions presented in Step 3, and so it is best to present the two steps in this order in a final report which details the control solution.

The actual intellectual activity is quite different from the outline. During the preliminary review of the situation, the executive solving the control problem is likely to form some vague and generalized ideas of what his system will be. For example, he may think he needs a system which will use an IBM 360 computer but not be at all sure how much it will be able to do, whether it will be worth the cost, and what all his alternatives are.

As the analysis of the situation proceeds, he develops tentative alternative solutions to assist in testing and checking the feasibility of certain courses of action. For example, he may first examine the various alternative computerized information systems. After investigating each of these alternatives, he may come to the conclusion that a computerized information or control system is too costly, and that a combined manual and punched card processing system will be best for his operation. At this point he will develop additional alternatives.

As the analysis progresses further, therefore, revised solutions are usually developed. This is the phase during which the executive has the opportunity to correct, adjust, or confirm the earlier solutions in the light of subsequent analysis and evaluation.

Lastly, he develops final solutions. This is the stage during which the solutions are stated in the formal written plan presented to management.

This same process is at work in Step 2 of the management control process when the executive is seeking, defining, and quantifying the over-all key factors affecting his solution. For example, while it is important to know that standards must be established, the executive's real job is to develop the specific standards and the format in which they will be presented. Such questions as how those using the standards will respond to them and use them and whether the standards are a true reflection of the corporation's long-term goals are crucial to the success or failure of the control system. Constant probing, testing, and hypothesizing are necessary before a clear definition of the most relevant key factors can be formulated.

The process is repeated again when developing plans for putting the new system into operation, when, for example, developing ways to get operating managers to accept a new control system. And nothing can be done to by-pass or simplify this continual process of investigation and evaluation so necessary for successful management control.[7]

The existence of these difficulties and complexities does not mean that management control is not a science, for underlying the back-and-forth intellectual searching described above are the familiar steps of problem definition, premising, and developing, testing, and implementing the solution.

What the complexities do mean is that knowing management control theory is only a small beginning. Adapting that theory to solving the problem at hand is the art of management control, which complements the science. It is an art which is critical to the successful application of the science of management control in a business situation. It is an art which requires considerable experience and judgment, and so is learned principally by doing.

EXERCISING CONTROL

Once a control problem has been resolved and a new control tool or system developed, then the question of how to use the system or tool most efficiently for controlling and making control decisions must be explored. In many instances control is exercised automatically—performance is checked and adjustments are made by automated equipment. A home-heating system is an example of this type of automated control,[8] as are many modern chemical plant operations.[9]

[7] Only a few writers have attempted to describe the intellectual process involved in solving a problem and in making a decision. One of the best descriptions of this subject is Jones, *Executive Decision Making,* which provides additional insight into the complexities of solving a management control problem.

Jones traces how one searches for the key factors or premises affecting a decision. While searching, one is constantly developing tentative courses of action. As one subsequently evaluates alternatives, he frequently uncovers key factors which have an important bearing on the decision but which he failed to recognize in the earlier analysis.

The intellectual interplay which Jones describes parallels very closely that involved in developing solutions to management control problems. As a result, in the management control process (as in the problem-solving process) the key factors (or premises) are always stated in their clearest form only after the control system or controls (or solution) have been developed.

[8] Arnold Tustin, "Feedback," *Automatic Control* (A Scientific American Book) (New York: Simon and Schuster, Inc., 1955), pp. 10–23.

[9] Eugene Ayres, "An Automatic Chemical Plant," *Automatic Control* (A Scientific American Book) (New York: Simon and Schuster, Inc., 1955), pp. 41–52.

The type of control being discussed here is not, however, automatic control, but the type of control that involves executive judgment and executive action in using the control tools or system to achieve broad corporate objectives.

Above all, management control requires that a balance be maintained between compliance and stimulation in exercising control. For example, when variances from budget occur, what balance can be struck between criticizing operating personnel for noncompliance and taking constructive steps for educating them in corporate goals? Or how much use can be made of the discussions of the variances to better coordinate functional operations, such as production and marketing, without at the same time destroying the system's value in maintaining compliance?

In exercising control, the executive can limit himself merely to insisting upon compliance—protecting assets, policing, checking accuracy, gathering more information, reprimanding, and the like. However, this is too restrictive a viewpoint.

Management control dictates that the executive strive to attain more positive goals in exercising control. The primary aim of management control is to stimulate better use of assets, create new ways to do business, better coordinate the efforts of individual operating departments, educate operating personnel so that their efforts are more closely geared to accomplishing specific corporate objectives—in short, to create an enabling atmosphere, whose vistas are broadened, not narrowed, by the controls.

A study of the introduction of a new control system at H. J. Heinz, Inc., in the mid-1950s illustrates this point.[10] At Heinz the development of the new control system started with long-range planning. The six development steps were:

1. Establishing the goals of the business.
2. Forecasting conditions.
3. Developing plans.
4. Preparing and scheduling estimates.
5. Controlling commitments and expenditures.
6. Reporting and appraising results.[11]

The organization for control was then established and the responsibility for introducing new controls was fixed.

While on the surface the steps appear to lead to a system emphasizing compliance, a number of precautions were taken to guard against this. A clear distinction was drawn between line and staff functions.

[10] Controllers Institute Research Foundation, Inc., *Management Planning and Control: The H. J. Heinz Approach* (New York: Controllers Institute Research Foundation, 1961).

[11] *Ibid.*, p. viii.

It was "a very challenging problem to get competent staff and special study groups to make effective analyses and give sound advice without assuming (or giving the impression of assuming) any part of line authority and without attempting to take personal credit for successful programs carried through by the line organization." [12]

In introducing the new program, time and money were allowed for education and training all those involved in the new system. Suggestions for improvements were sought from all those involved. This education program was not stopped once the new system was introduced, and a "continuing learning program" was undertaken.[13]

Both initially and as the program continued, those responsible for performance originated standards used within the new control system. These standards could be changed when circumstances changed.

In analyzing operating variances from standards, the main emphasis was on finding and correcting the causes of variances in order to improve future performance. The creative emphasis led to the analysis of favorable as well as unfavorable variances. As explained by the company,

> The line of thinking, of course, is that something caused the favorable variance—either unexpected effectiveness of factors of production or some reduction in standard cost which needs re-examination. If the causes of improvement are positive and can be identified, their possible permanence can be appraised; and if the development, whatever it is, can be passed on to other factories or departments, it will improve the over-all company profit picture. There are frequent improvements in the company's products, recipes, processes, and costs, and some of these are directly traceable to properly investigated variances from standards and budgets.[14]

The primary purpose of the profit planning department was to coordinate and consolidate the various division plans.[15] At Heinz the plans themselves were not as important as the planning process, which helped coordinate the operating divisions. Profit planning was "not a course in 'forward accounting' but a system whereby business plans are screened, evaluated, and reduced to realistic, attainable objectives in a well-coordinated program of action—and the responsibility of their attainments is then specifically delegated to those most logically responsible for results—and, it should be emphasized—*to those who have had an opportunity to participate in the planning and development of these activities.*" [16]

Thus, Heinz strove to emphasize the creative, educational, and coor-

[12] *Ibid.*, pp. 30–31.
[13] *Ibid.*, p. 4.
[14] *Ibid.*, p. 55.
[15] *Ibid.*, p. 59.
[16] *Ibid.*, pp. 73–74.

dination benefits of their new control system rather than the compliance aspects. In this way they were able to use the system for "management" control instead of limiting it to "accounting" control.

In management control, the educational and coordination benefits of an operating control system are as important as meeting any specified budgets. Controls can highlight problems for management and lead them to more creative solutions to these problems. When, as was done at Heinz, operating personnel are brought into control development and participate actively in the control process, especially in setting standards and reviewing performance, they are educated in over-all corporate directions and self-checks, and balances are built into individual operations.

Achieving the balance between the compliance and creative uses of controls is not an easy task. Jerome points out the difficulty of finding this balance:

> I want to refer again to the basic dilemma faced by any management in its attempt to achieve a controlled operation. This is the dilemma of attempting to achieve a workable balance between creativity and conformity. Or, expressed somewhat differently, this is the problem of encouraging initiative on the part of subordinates by keeping operations flexible, and minimizing the chances of error by keeping operations standardized.[17]

This capacity of executive control for motivating constructive action, developing initiative, and generating progress is, according to Jerome, "by all odds its most important characteristic." [18]

Considerable tact and judgment and a high degree of regard for the individual are required to exercise management control effectively. The principles of exercising control outlined in this section can at times seem inefficient, since they often involve lengthy discussions with individuals, exploring the causes of problems and developing a true understanding by the individual of the management implications of the problems. In the long run, however, following such principles can lead to more efficient use of corporate resources.

A second aspect of exercising management control, which has not been touched upon, is the executive judgment involved in giving weight to nonquantitative factors affecting a management control decision. For example, in an equipment acquisition decision, the calculations of return on investment (ROI) can be run out so that the executive has certain control tools to work with. But his decision does not hinge solely on these quantitative factors; it is affected by other factors, such as what weight he gives to possible obsolescence, competitive market position, possible political developments, and the like, before making his decision.

[17] Jerome, *Executive Control,* p. 75.
[18] *Ibid.,* p. 34.

Statisticians such as Robert Schlaifer have made some effort to quantify judgmental factors through Bayesian statistics,[19] but no complete substitute has yet been found for decision-making experience and the intuitive insights developed from that experience. And it is unlikely that any complete substitute for them will ever be found. The success of all management control decision making will always ultimately depend in some degree on the maturity of the decision-maker's experience and judgment.

MANAGEMENT CONTROL AND NEW TECHNOLOGY

One of the principal roadblocks to mastering management control has been the rapid development of new control technology. The list of new developments is a long one and includes such areas as systems, linear programming, sampling, operations research, decision theory, game theory, simulation, waiting-line theory, managerial economics, statistical theory, and electronic data processing. Techniques in such traditional areas as accounting and finance extend even further the field of technical knowledge which can be used in effective management control.

The wide range of available management control tools places a great burden on the executive not directly concerned with control administration. For he must learn enough about each area of new technology to understand how it works, what it can and cannot accomplish, and how it can be used to help him manage better.

Because of the complexities of the new technology, two self-defeating approaches are sometimes taken: to ignore developments simply because they are too complex and time-consuming to master; and to become immersed in the mechanics of the new technology and lose perspective on their primary purpose—helping the executive manage better. Those concerned with the installation of new computers frequently fall into this latter category.

Both pitfalls must be avoided. This is difficult, if for no other reason than the realistic limits of the manager's available time. In spite of these difficulties, however, each executive must manage his time in such a way as to maintain a balance between knowing enough about control technology to use it for control and still to retain the over-all management control perspective. If he does not do this, he will be managing less efficiently than he should and not achieving the profits that are possible for the corporation.

[19] Robert Schlaifer, *Probability and Statistics for Business Decisions: An Introduction to Managerial Economics under Uncertainty* (New York: McGraw-Hill Book Company, 1959).

LOOKING BEHIND FIGURES AT ASSUMPTIONS

In solving management control problems and exercising management control, the perspective is always that of a business manager. A manager looks at how and why controls are developed, the reasoning behind a control system, the ways to use the control tools to manage better, and other management implications of the control question at hand. Although some knowledge of basic control tools, such as operations research, information systems, automated data processing, accounting, managerial economics and statistics is necessary, the executive does not limit himself to developing the techniques or tools needed to solve the control problem.

Management control requires looking behind the figures at the assumptions, the purpose of the system, the objectives of the corporation, the basis of the standards, and the methods used in collecting and disseminating information. If presented with figures, a manager must be skeptical. He never assumes that the accountants, statisticans, economists, operations researchers, or systems analysts will present solutions designed specifically for his control purposes.

In subsequent exercising control, an executive does not confine himself merely to maintaining compliance. He looks beyond compliance at the many constructive ways in which the control tool or system can be employed to improve the use of corporate resources.

Management control principles can be applied in all control areas, even in specific operational control situations.[20] Its principles are also useful in the financial, accounting, and information handling areas, since, like operational control, these areas are important tools for management control.

[20] As Anthony, *Planning and Control Systems,* pp. 17–18, points out, management and operational control can be distinguished: "Operational control is the process of assuring that specific tasks are carried out effectively and efficiently" and "management control is the process by which managers assure that resources are obtained and used effectively and efficiently in the accomplishment of the organization's objectives." While these two can be distinguished, however, management control thinking should nonetheless pervade all control areas.

The author formulates a working philosophy of management control.

2

PRINCIPLES OF MODERN MANAGERIAL CONTROL

Ray M. Powell

Experienced business executives fully realize that the economic, social, and political structures under which their businesses operate today have become tremendously complex. Certainly a difficult task is placed before those at the helm in American businesses who are charged with directing material and human resources in economic, social, and political environments which are not only changing in their complexity, but which in the future will be changing more drastically and with greater rapidity.

Fortunately, business executives have available instruments of direction and control which are vastly superior to those which their predecessors had as well as personnel who are increasingly better educated and more highly trained. These improvements in techniques and resources serve to diminish the work load for top management. Nevertheless, there remain the responsibilities for selecting the objectives toward which their organizations will work; for organizing, motivating, and equipping the human resources through which these objectives will be reached; for coordinating the diverse responsibilities of individuals and controlling their performance. All of these functions are more critical than in the past. The "payoffs" for successful management are greater today, but the penalties are more drastic and far more sudden. In this country it formerly took a generation for a poorly controlled firm to go out of existence, often measured from the time its founder passed it on to his heirs. Today, with

Reprinted from *Financial Executive,* April 1966, pp. 54–60, by permission of the publisher.

the accelerating rate of change we are experiencing, the founder of a business is now able to be present at its dissolution.

Today's managers benefit from the fact that the philosophy and practice of management control are being subjected to continuous and constructive critical analysis, which is developing the scientific aspects of managerial control. Managerial control will become more professionalized and productive; already it is realized that efficiency in management control is an important factor in the success or failure of the individual firm as well as in the operation of our national economy.

There is reason to expect continued refinement in the many aspects of management control: more intelligent planning, better coordination of resources, more accurate measurement of those facets of business which can be measured, and an increased appreciation for the non-quantifiable aspects of management.

Within the broad field of management control, important changes are occurring which require the thoughtful attention of everyone in a managerial position—as well as anyone who aspires to such a position. The purpose of this discussion, in addition to stressing that each such individual must give substantial thought to developing his own philosophy of managerial control, is to offer some comments upon what such a philosophy might include.

CONTROL VERSUS CONTROLS

Let us first consider the literature on management control. Application of the concept of management control requires as a minimum the following:

1. identifying key factors in the business operation which need to be controlled in order to achieve a given over-all result;
2. specifying the basis for establishing standards of performance for each control factor, such as forecasts, budgets, standard costs, turnover ratios, and lead times;
3. defining the information—accounting and operating data and statistics—that must be accumulated to measure status and performance;
4. establishing a reporting structure that identifies performance in each control area, relates causes and effects, signals trends, and identifies results by responsibility under the plan of organization.[1]

The development of such a management control system requires careful study of the total enterprise and its separation into controllable

[1] Gordon L. Murray, partner, Haskins & Sells, "Current Targets for Management Attention." Speech before the Beta Gamma Sigma alumni of New York City, March 1963.

components. A close scrutiny must also be made of each component in terms of its operational characteristics.

What has been so far stated represents "received doctrine," recognizing that, although some firms incorporate such measurements and information into their control systems, most of them do not. But we must go beyond the minimum steps outlined for developing a philosophy of control. As Peter F. Drucker explains, "We are recently acquiring a great capacity to design 'controls' in businesses, based upon a great improvement in techniques, especially in the application of logical and mathematical tools to business data, and in the ability to process and analyze large masses of data very fast." [2]

Drucker then raises the question: "What do these improved techniques mean for control?" . . . Might we simultaneously be enlarging the *means* to control (that is, the measurement and information systems) without achieving the *end results* of control which we seek? This may well be the case, because in too many instances the measurements and information pertain to historical data; yet the most effective controls are known to deal with the future, about which we know far too little. Frederic G. Donner, chairman of the board of General Motors, for example, points out that he spends far more time contemplating forecasts of future conditions than reviewing financial data of past operations. Management has at its disposal three positive actions by which control can be exercised:

1. planning ahead;
2. day-to-day scheduling, direction, and supervision;
3. after-the-fact response to data systems feedback.

Any present or prospective controller considering his own philosophy of control would do well to bear in mind one distinction: we may find ourselves with too many controls and too little control. The individual in a firm who is most directly charged with producing the means to control (information and measurement systems) is the "controller." Most knowledgeable executives, controllers included, quickly agree that it would be a gross mistake for controllers to use the controls to exercise personal control in the business. As staff executives, controllers must recognize that line executives at the various levels in administration determine whether the firm can truly be said to be "in control." A further distinction has been made by the Financial Executives Institute: the functions of controllership include establishing, coordinating, and maintaining an integrated plan for the control of operations, *through authorized management.* According to James L. Peirce, vice president-finance of

[2] Peter Drucker, "Controls, Control and Management," in *Management Controls: New Directions in Basic Research* (New York: McGraw-Hill Book Company, 1964), p. 286.

A. B. Dick Company, these last three words need emphasis if such a plan is to become operational.[3]

Because we deal with human beings in the conduct of business enterprises, effective control cannot be achieved unless measurement and information systems allow latitude for personal accomplishment and contribution. Therefore, a valid philosophy of managerial control utilizes the premise that even the most complete system of *quantitative* control must be consonant with the *qualitative* control provided by the human organization.

Four additional factors stated by Drucker [4] which operate to affect the managerial philosophy are:

1. Measuring business data interferes with the data measured.
2. Measures of business data must be appropriate.
3. There are diminishing returns on internal management controls.
4. Business is a unique control situation.

These factors warrant consideration at this point.

1. *Measuring business data interferes with the data measured.* In the physical sciences, measurement is an objective process: it changes neither the object measured nor the individual making the measurement. In business, however, as in many other areas of the social sciences, quite often the act of measuring interferes with the event being measured. The mere fact that an item (such as return on investment, inventory, turnover, or sales revenues) has been selected for measurement attaches an undesirable bias and lack of objectivity to the item. We are aware that the item has been selected for measurement and control—therefore it *must* be important!

Actions may be taken which are irrational in over-all company terms in order to "window dress" the item being measured. Executives who have operated under budgetary control may over-emphasize the need to stay within the budget, often losing sight of what should be their goal: economical and profitable operations. Changed circumstances may well justify deviation from the original budget, but even then, only an experienced executive willingly abandons the carefully prepared budget target.

What, then, should we measure in our control system?

We should measure those events and results which managers at various levels believe are of over-all importance as well as critical in their own areas of supervision.

Unless executives in a company satisfactorily determine what should

[3] James L. Peirce, "The Planning and Control Concept," *The Controller,* XXII, 9 (1954), pp. 403–6, 422, 424–25.

[4] Drucker, *op. cit.,* pp. 288–94.

be measured, the measurement and information systems they design will make the business even more difficult to control. The manager will all too soon be buried in controls which do not effectively provide control.

2. *Measures of business data must be appropriate.* Drucker cites as an example a report of an industrial relations department which showed grievances from the working force were running one-half of one percent (.005) or "five grievances per thousand employees per month." On the surface this appeared minimal, because most managers in business implicitly apply a normalization concept which interprets this to mean that one department with 200 employees had one grievance on the average. The fact was that one department with 20 employees had had all five of the experienced grievances!

Similar non-normalized statistics reflect that "10 percent of the inventory items account for 75 percent of the dollar value of inventories held," or "90 percent of the dollar volume of business is usually represented by less than 5 percent of the number of products a company handles." There are certainly implications here for *what* the manager needs to control, as well as for the nature of the measurement and information systems and how they should reflect such data for him.

These are isolated illustrations of the kind of measurements on which many managers must rely. The traditional measurement systems, accounting included, too often conceal rather than highlight most of the truly significant data needed by managers.

A critical need in management is to increase the ability to perceive the essential items in a given situation and to direct attention to them, for proper identification of the problem and its essential elements often provides the solution to the problem. An information and measurement system which would focus attention only on crucial events and results would give any manager much more aid and would result in much better performance than we have any right to expect under typical reporting systems.

3. *Diminishing returns on internal management controls.* The last two decades have witnessed concentration on internal operating efficiencies. In many industrial firms today further substantial internal operating economies may no longer be reasonably expected. Although it is perfectly logical to continue to monitor through internal control devices a firm's processes and operations to assure their continuation in a "state of control," nevertheless the highest "payoffs" from *additional* control efforts lie outside the firm. Using an example from industry, it may be argued that the 50 percent of the consumer's dollar which is typically expended in the distribution process (after the product is physically completed) offers far greater opportunities for added control benefits. But,

at present, little of the total control effort is being expended outside of the producing firm.

Admittedly the information and measurements in our control systems are more readily adaptable to internal rather than external monitoring; but the greatest opportunity lies outside the firm. One aspect of this control system should be evaluation of outside earnings possibilities. Diversification and merger studies have made substantial advances in recent years, yet the external facets of control have been barely explored by most companies. The whole field of entrepreneurship offers an opportunity for control systems applications. Drucker [5] pointed as an example to the field of electronic data processing, which he believes offers proof that, because the basic idea of electronic data processing was sound, IBM's internal efficiency was irrelevant for over a decade. They *were* efficient internally, but the opportunities external to the firm in this field were so massive that they overshadowed the internal aspects. As the EDP industry matures, this imbalance may disappear, but the point remains that the great opportunity for profits at the time was external.

4. *Business is a unique control situation.* We have seen many control applications transferred to business almost intact from the physical sciences. In many cases such applications have been highly successful. But should not the business field be regarded as a separate, meaningful sphere or human endeavor which is subject to control? Business certainly presents a unique appearance to those interested in controls and in control. Unlike all natural or mechanically operated systems, it exhibits a wide range of events and results that are of profound importance to its successful operation, but which *cannot easily be quantified* within existing systems of measurement.

Business may well be the only system possessing such a wealth of both quantifiable and non-quantifiable results and events of primary importance to successful control. This offers a unique opportunity for controls if we are but cognizant of the non-quantifiable as well as the quantifiable results and events. Management scientists in particular, having a background in physics or engineering, have had difficulty in realizing that practically every definition underlying measurement of accounting data (accounting entities, accrual accounting, conservatism, consistency, cost, going concern, disclosure, matching cost against revenue, materiality, objectivity, realization, stable measuring unit, and uniform accounting period) is based on assumptions and practices which were not always easily rationalized and cannot presently be physically verified. We have defined the concepts—and then measured. Only within very rigid limitation are accountants permitted to change the definitional ground rules as they operate in areas where they have been bold enough to attempt

[5] Drucker, *op. cit.*, p. 292.

measurements of business data. Certainly these conventions and practices have facilitated measurement of many business data, but we need to extend the areas where measurement can be achieved. As an accountant, it worries me that far too many of the measurements in accounting are the recorded facts about *past* events. Unfortunately, accountants seem to be too little concerned about the "facts" of the *future*. And, as we have pointed out, too great a preponderance of the measured facts of the past concern internal, rather than external, events and results.

For these two reasons, important developments on the outside—especially as they pertain to the future—are not measurable until it is too late to exercise control. It follows that we are whipsawed by day-to-day events and results outside our control. A balance between the measurable and non-measurable—between the past and the future, and between the internal and the external—will remain for some time as a crucial problem facing those concerned with management control.

Where does this leave us in our search for a philosophy of control? Accountants, more than most professional men, recognize that a business is a separate entity and at the same time realize that this is a legal "fiction," in more ways than one. A business is presumed to possess its own resources and objectives; on the other hand, a business is comprised of persons, each with his own purposes, ambitions, ideals, and needs. Successful businesses satisfy the ambitions and needs of their members, as individuals, and do so through systems of incentives, rewards, deterrences, and penalties. Here lies the real regulatory control of business: people at work.

Approached with a proper appreciation for the ultimate control which lies in decisions by "people harmoniously at work" at all levels of the organization, the "received doctrine" of managerial control can be effective to the degree with which it:

1. identifies key factors needing control;
2. establishes standards for measuring achievement;
3. defines measures of status and performance;
4. reports and analyzes accomplishment by responsibility:
5. controls before-the-fact through preplanning;
6. highlights critical data for managers;
7. increasingly seeks to monitor events *external* to the firm, even though in the past they may have been regarded as non-quantifiable.

The author defines and discusses the management control process and its relation to strategic planning and technical control.

3

FRAMEWORK FOR ANALYSIS

Robert N. Anthony

Since dogs and humans are both mammals, some generalizations that apply to one species also apply to the other. It is for this reason that some new surgical techniques can be tested on dogs before being risked on humans. But dogs and humans differ, and, unless these differences are recognized, generalizations that are valid for one species may be erroneously applied to the other. For example, canine behavior can be largely explained in terms of conditioned reflexes, but human behavior is much more complicated. Similarly, some generalizations can be made about the whole planning and control process in a business; however, there actually are several quite different types of planning and control processes, and mistakes may be made if a generalization (principle, rule, technique) valid for one type is applied to the other.

The purpose of this article is to suggest a classification of the main topics or "species" that come within the broad term, Planning and Control Systems, and to suggest distinguishing characteristics of each. Hopefully, this will lead to a sorting out and sharpening of principles and techniques applicable to each species.

The particular classification chosen has been arrived at after careful analysis of how well various alternatives match statements made in the literature and, more important, what is found in practice. It is, however, tentative. Better schemes may well be developed, and we expose this one primarily in the hope that discussion of it will lead to agreement on *some* scheme, not necessarily this.

Reprinted from *Management Services,* March–April 1964, pp. 18–24, by permission of the publisher.

In this article, we shall focus on a process labeled *management control.* We shall describe its main characteristics, and distinguish it from processes labeled *strategic planning* and *technical control.* (Two other processes, *financial accounting* and *information handling,* are also relevant, but space does not permit a discussion of them here.)

Obviously, we do not assert that these processes can be separated by sharply defined boundaries; one shades into another. Strategic planning sets the guidelines for management control, and management control sets the guidelines for technical control. The complete management function involves an integration of all these processes, and the processes are complementary.

We do assert that the processes are sufficiently distinct so that those who design and use planning and control systems will make expensive errors if they fail to take into account both the common characteristics of a process and the differences between processes. This article will deal with these similarities and differences and point out some of the errors that are made when they are not recognized.

MANAGEMENT CONTROL

Management control is the process of assuring that resources are obtained and used effectively and efficiently in the accomplishment of the organization's objectives.

Management control is a process carried on within the framework established by strategic planning. Objectives, facilities, organization, and financial factors are more or less accepted as "givens." Decisions about next year's budget, for example, are limited by policies and guidelines prescribed by top management. The management control process is intended to make possible the achievement of planned objectives as effectively and efficiently as possible within these "givens."

The purpose of a management control system is to encourage managers to take actions which are in the best interests of the company. For example, if the system is structured so that a certain course of action increases the reported profits of a division, and at the same time *lessens* the profits of the company as a whole, there is something wrong. Technically, this purpose can be described as *goal congruence.*

"Total" System Necessary

Psychological considerations are dominant in management control. Activities such as communicating, persuading, exhorting, inspiring, and criticizing are an important part of the process.

Ordinarily, a management control system is a *total* system in the sense that it embraces all aspects of the company's operation. It needs to be a total system because an important management function is to assure that all parts of the operation are in balance with one another, and, in order to examine balance, management needs information about each of the parts.

With rare exceptions, the management control system is built around a *financial* structure; that is, resources and outputs are expressed in monetary units. Money is the only common denominator by means of which the heterogeneous elements of output and resources (e.g., hours of labor; type of labor; quantity and quality of material; amount and kind of products produced) can be combined and compared. (Although the financial structure is usually the central focus, nonmonetary measures such as time, number of persons, and reject and spoilage rates are also important parts of the system.)

The management control process tends to be *rhythmic;* it follows a definite pattern and timetable, month after month and year after year. In budgetary control, which is an important part of the management control process, certain steps are taken in a prescribed sequence and at certain dates each year: the dissemination of guidelines, the preparation of original estimates, the transmission of these estimates up through the several echelons in the organization, the review of these estimates, final approval by top management, dissemination back through the organization, operation, reporting, and the appraisal of performance. The procedure to be followed at each step in this process, the dates when the steps are to be completed, and even the forms that are to be used can be, and often are, set forth in a manual.

Interlocking Subsystems

A management control system is, or should be, a *co-ordinated, integrated* system: that is, although data collected for one purpose may differ from those collected for another purpose, these data should be reconcilable with one another. In a sense, the management control system is a *single* system, but it is perhaps more accurate to think of it as a set of interlocking subsystems. In many organizations, for example, three types of cost information are needed for management control: (1) *costs by responsibility centers,* which are used for planning and controlling the activities of responsible supervisors; (2) *full program costs,* used for pricing and other operating decisions under normal circumstances; and (3) *direct program costs,* used for pricing and other operating decisions under special circumstances, such as when management wishes to utilize idle capacity. ("Program" is here used for any activity in which the organization engages. In industrial companies, programs consist of products or product lines, and "product costs" can be substituted in the above statements.)

Line managers are the focal points in management control. They are the persons whose judgments are incorporated in the approved plans, and they are the persons who must influence others and whose performance is measured. Staff people collect, summarize, and present information that is useful in the process, and they make calculations which translate management judgments into the format of the system. Such a staff may be large in numbers; indeed the control department is often the largest department in a company. However, the significant decisions are made by the line manager, not by the staff.

STRATEGIC PLANNING

Strategic planning is the process of deciding on changes in the objectives of the organization, in the resources that are to be used in attaining these objectives, and in the policies that are to govern the acquisition and use of these resources.

The word *strategy* is used here in its usual sense of deciding on how to combine and employ resources. Thus, strategic planning is a process having to do with the formulation of long-range, strategic, policy-type plans that change the character or direction of the organization. In an industrial company this includes planning that affects the objectives of the company; policies of all types (including policies as to management control and other processes); the acquisition and disposition of major facilities, divisions, or subsidiaries; the markets to be served and distribution channels for serving them; the organization structure (as distinguished from individual personnel actions); research and development of new product lines (as distinguished from modifications in existing products and product changes within existing lines); sources of new permanent capital; dividend policy; and so on. Strategic planning decisions affect the physical, financial, and organizational framework within which operations are carried on.

Irregular in Nature

Briefly, here are some ways in which the strategic planning process differs from the management control process.

A strategic plan usually relates to some part of the organization, rather than to the totality; the concept of a master planner who constantly keeps all parts of the organization at some co-ordinated optimum is a nice concept but an unrealistic one. Life is too complicated for any human, or computer, to do this.

Strategic planning is essentially *irregular*. Problems, opportunities, and "bright ideas" do not arise according to some set timetable, and they have to be dealt with whenever they happen to be perceived. The appropriate analytical techniques depend on the nature of the problem being analyzed, and no over-all approach (such as a mathematical model) has been developed that is of much help in analyzing all types of strategic problems. Indeed, an overemphasis on a systematic approach is quite likely to stifle the essential element of creativity. In strategic planning, management works now on one problem, now on another, according to the needs and opportunities of the moment.

The estimates used in strategic planning are intended to show the *expected* results of the plan. They are neutral and impersonal. By contrast, the management control process, and the data used in it, are intended to influence managers to take actions that will lead to *desired* results. Thus, in connection with management control, it is appropriate to discuss how "tight" an operating budget should be: Should the goals be set so high that only an outstanding manager can achieve them, or should they be set so that they are attainable by the average manager? At what level does frustration inhibit a manager's best efforts? Does an attainable budget lead to complacency? And so on. In strategic planning, the question to be asked about the figures is simply: Is this the most reasonable estimate that can be made?

Strategic planning relies heavily on *external information,* that is, on data collected from outside the company, such as market analyses, estimates of costs and other factors involved in building a plant in a new locality, technological developments, and so on. When data from the normal information system are used, they usually must be recast to fit the needs of the problem being analyzed. For example, the current operating costs of a plant that are collected for measuring performance and for making pricing and other operating decisions usually must be restructured before they are useful in deciding whether to close down the plant.

Communications Are Limited

Another characteristic of the relevant information is that much of it is imprecise. The strategic planner estimates what *will* happen, often over a rather long time period. These estimates are likely to have a high degree of uncertainty, and they must be treated accordingly.

In the management control process, the communication of objectives, policies, guidelines, decisions, and results throughout the organization is extremely important. In the strategic planning process, communication is much simpler and involves relatively few persons; indeed, the need for secrecy often requires that steps be taken to inhibit communication. (Wide communication of the *decisions* that result from strategic planning is obviously important, but this is part of the management control process.)

Strategic planning is essentially applied economics, whereas management control is essentially applied social psychology.

Both management control and strategic planning involve top management, but middle management (i.e., operating management) typically have a much more important role in management control than they have in strategic planning. Middle managers usually are not major participants in the strategic planning process and sometimes are not even aware of the fact that a plan is being considered. Many operating executives are by temperament not very good at strategic planning. Also, the pressures of current activities usually do not allow them to devote the necessary time to such work. Currently, there is a tendency in companies to set up separate staffs which gather the facts and make the analyses that provide the background material for strategic decisions.

These and other differences between management control and strategic planning are summarized in Exhibit 3–1.

EXHIBIT 3–1

SOME CONTRASTS

	STRATEGIC PLANNING	MANAGEMENT CONTROL
Person primarily involved	Staff and top management	Line and top management
Number of persons	Small	Large
Mental activity	Creative; analytical	Administrative; persuasive
Variables	Complex; much judgment	Less complex
Time period	Tends to be long	Tends to be short
Periodicity	Irregular, no set schedule	Rhythmic; set timetable
Procedures	Unstructured; each problem different	Prescribed procedure, regularly followed
Focus	Tend to focus on one aspect at a time	All encompassing
Source of information	Relies more on external and future	Relies more on internal and historical
Product	Intangible; precedent setting	More tangible; action within precedent
Communication problem	Relatively simple	Crucial and difficult
Appraisal of soundness	Extremely difficult	Much less difficult

Strategic planning and management control activities tend to conflict with one another in some respects. The time that management spends in thinking about the future is taken from time that could otherwise be used in controlling current operations, so in this indirect way strategic planning can hurt current performance. And, of course, the reverse also is true.

More directly, many actions that are taken for long-run, strategic reasons make current profits smaller than they otherwise would be. Research and some advertising expenditures are obvious examples. The problem of striking the right balance between strategic and operating considerations is one of the central problems in the whole management process.

CONSEQUENCES OF CONFUSION

Following are statements illustrating some of the consequences of failing to make a distinction between strategic planning and management control.

"We should set up a long-range planning procedure and work out a systemized way of considering *all* our plans similar to the way we construct next year's budget." (A long-range plan shows the estimated consequences over the next several years of strategic decisions already taken. It is part of the management control process. Although it provides a useful background for considering strategic proposals, it is not strategic planning. Strategic proposals should be made whenever the opportunity or the need is perceived in a form that best presents the arguments.)

"The only relevant costs are incremental costs; pay no attention to fixed or sunk costs." (This is so in strategic planning, but operating managers are often motivated in the wrong direction if their decisions are based on incremental costs; for example, in intracompany transactions.)

"We may be selling Plant X some day. We should therefore set up the operating reports so that management will have at its fingertips the information it will need when it is deciding this question. For example, we should show inventory and fixed assets at their current market value." (Operating reports should be designed to assist in the management of current operations. Special compilations of data are needed for such major, nonroutine actions as selling a plant. Collection of such data routinely is both too expensive and likely to impede sound operating decisions.)

"Our ultimate goal is an all-purpose control system—integrated data processing—so that management will have all the data it needs for whatever problem it decides to tackle. We should collect data in elemental building blocks that can be combined in various ways to answer all conceivable questions." (This is an impossible goal. Each strategic proposal requires that the data be assembled in the way that best fits the requirements of that proposal. No one can foresee all the possibilities. The "building block" idea is sound within limits, but the limits are not so broad that all problems are encompassed.)

"All levels of management should participate in planning." (All levels of management should participate in the planning part of the management control process, but operating managers typically do not have the time, the inclination, or the analytical bent that is required for formulating strategic plans. Furthermore, such plans often must be kept highly secret.)

TECHNICAL CONTROL

Technical control is the process of assuring the efficient acquisition and use of resources, with respect to activities for which the optimum relationship between outputs and resources can be approximately determined.

The definition of technical control refers to outputs and resources. *Outputs* are the accomplishments of the organization, what it does, and *resources* are the inputs which the organization consumes. For a whole business, the outputs are the goods and services sold, which are measured by revenues earned, and the inputs are costs and expenses incurred. In rough terms, "output" equals "results," and "resources" equals "cost."

One of the important tasks in an organization is to seek the *optimum* relationship between outputs and resources. For some activities, this optimum relationship is fairly easy to establish: To manufacture a given part should require such-and-such labor, a certain sequence of machine operations, and so on. For other activities, there exists no "scientific" (even in the loose sense of this term) way of establishing the optimum relationship; for these activities, decisions as to what costs to incur depend on human judgment.

The term "managed costs" is a descriptive one for those types of resources for which an objective decision as to the optimum quantity to be employed cannot be made. An important management function is to make judgments as to the "right" amount of managed costs in a given set of circumstances. These are, by definition, subjective judgments.

Management control applies to the whole of an organization, and to any parts of the whole in which managed costs are significant. Technical control applies to those activities, and only to those activities, in which there are no significant elements of managed cost. Or more simply, in the management control process, management judgment is an important element; in the technical control process, the technique itself is dominant.

As an example of technical control, consider inventory control. If the demand for an item, the cost of storing it, its production cost and production time, and the loss involved in not filling an order are known or can be reasonably estimated, then the optimum inventory level and the optimum production schedule can both be calculated, and reasonable men will agree with the results of these calculations.

In other than exceptional circumstances, these calculations can determine the actions that should be taken. Management intervention is necessary only when these exceptional circumstances arise.

Some Areas Can't Be Measured

By contrast, consider the legal department of a company. No device can measure the quality, or even the quantity, of the legal service that constitutes the output of this department. No formula can show the amount of service that should be rendered nor the optimum amount of costs that should be incurred. Impressions as to the "right" amount of service, as to the "right" amount of cost, and as to whether the relationship between the service actually rendered and the cost actually incurred was "right" are strictly subjective. They are judgments made by management. If persons disagree on these judgments, there is no objective way of resolving the disagreement. Yet the legal department as a part of the whole organization must be controlled; the chief counsel must operate within the framework of policies prescribed by top management. The control exercised in this situation is management control.

Examples of activities that can be subjected to technical control are: automated plants, such as cement plants, oil refineries, and power generating stations; the direct operations of most manufacturing plants (but often not the overhead expense items); production scheduling; inventory control; the "order-taking" type of selling activity; and order processing, premium billing, payroll accounting, check handling, and similar paperwork activities.

Examples of activities for which management control is necessary are: the total activities of most manufacturing plants, which include such "judgment" inputs as indirect labor, employee benefit and welfare programs, safety activities, training, and supervision; most advertising, sales promotion, pricing, selling (as distinguished from order taking) and similar marketing activities; most aspects of finance; most aspects of research, development, and design; the work of staff units of all types; and management activity itself.

The control appropriate for the whole of any unit which carries on both the technical and the management types of activities is management control. The control of the whole accounting department is management control even though technical control is appropriate for certain aspects of the work, such as posting and check writing.

Some people believe that the distinction between the two classes of activities described above is merely one of degree rather than of kind; they say that all we are doing is distinguishing between situations where control is "easy" and "difficult," respectively. We think the distinction is more fundamental than that, and hope this will be apparent from the following brief list of characteristics that distinguish management control from technical control.

Management control covers the whole of an organization. Each technical control procedure is restricted to a subunit, often a narrowly circumscribed activity.

Just as management control occurs within a set of policies derived from strategic planning, so technical control occurs within a set of well-defined procedures and rules that are derived from management control.

Control is more difficult in management control than in technical control because of the absence of a "scientific" standard with which actual performance can be compared. A good technical control system can provide a much higher degree of assurance that actions are proceeding as desired than can a management control system.

Rules Can Be Programed

A technical control system is a *rational* system; that is, the action to be taken is decided by a set of logical rules. These rules may or may not cover all aspects of a given problem. Situations not covered by the rules are designated as "exceptions" and are resolved by human judgment. Other than these exceptions, the application of the rules is automatic. The rules can in principle be programed into a computer, and the choice between using a computer and using a human being depends primarily on the relative cost of each method.

In management control, psychological considerations are dominant. The management control system at most assists those who take action; it does not directly or by itself result in action without human intervention. By contrast, the end product of an inventory control system can be an order, or a decision to replenish a certain inventory item, and this order may be based entirely on calculations from formulas incorporated in the system. (The formulas were *devised* by human beings, but this is a management control process, not a technical control process.)

In a consideration of technical control, analogies with mechanical, electrical, and hydraulic systems are reasonable and useful, and such terms as feedback, network balancing, optimization, and so on, are relevant. It is perfectly appropriate, for example, to view a technical control system as analogous to a thermostat which turns the furnace on and off according to its perception of changes in temperature. These analogies do not work well as models for management control systems, however, because the success of management systems is highly dependent on their impact on people, and people are not like thermostats or furnaces; one can't light a fire under a human being simply by turning up a thermostat.

A management control system is ordinarily focused on a financial structure, whereas technical control data are often nonmonetary. They may be expressed in terms of man-hours, number of items, pounds of waste, and so on. Since each technical control procedure is designed for a limited area of application, it is feasible to use the basis of measurement that is most appropriate for that area.

Approximations Meet Data Needs

Data in a technical control system are in real time and relate to individual events, whereas data in a management control system are often retrospective and summarize many separate events. Computer specialists who do not make such a distinction, dream about a system that will display to the management the current status of every individual activity in the organization. Although this *could* be done, it *should not* be done; management doesn't want such detail. Management does not need to know the time at which lot No. 1007 was transferred from station 27 to station 28; rather, it needs to know only that the process is, or is not, proceeding as planned, and, if not, where the trouble lies.

Similarly, technical control uses exact data, whereas management control needs only approximations. Material is ordered and scheduled in specific quantities, employees are paid the exact amount due them, but data on management control reports need contain only two or three significant digits and are therefore rounded to thousands of dollars, to millions of dollars, or even (in the U.S. Government) to billions of dollars.

A technical control system requires a mathematical model of the operation. Although it may not always be expressed explicitly in mathematical notation, there is a decision rule which states that given certain values for parameters $a, b, \ldots n,$ action X is to be taken. Models are not so important in management control. In a sense, a budget or a PERT network are models associated with the management control process, but they are not the essence of the process.

The formal management control *system* is only a part of the management control *process,* actually a relatively unimportant part. The system can help motivate the manager to make decisions that are in the best interests of the organization, and the system can provide information that aids the manager in making these decisions; but many other stimuli are involved in motivating the manager, and good information does not automatically produce good decisions. The success or failure of the management control process depends on the personal characteristics of the manager: his judgment, his knowledge, his ability to influence others.

Technique Is All-Important

In technical control, the system itself is a much more important part of the whole process. Except in fully automated operations, it is an exaggeration to say that the system *is* the process, but it is not much of an exaggeration. The technical control system ordinarily states what action should be taken; it makes the decisions. As with any operation, management vigilance is required to detect an unforeseen "foul-up" in the operation, or a change in the conditions on which the technique is predicated. And management will be seeking ways to improve the technique. In general, however, the degree of management involvement in technical control is small, whereas in management control it is large.

As new techniques are developed, there is a tendency for more and more activities to become susceptible to technical control. In the factory, the production schedule that was formerly set according to the foreman's intuition is now derived by linear programing. And, although not too long ago it was believed that technical control was appropriate only for factory operations, we now see models and formulas being used for certain marketing decisions, such as planning salesmen's calls and planning direct mail advertising. This shift probably will continue; it is a large part of what people have in mind when they say, "management is becoming increasingly scientific."

Following are statements illustrating the consequences of failing to make a distinction between management control and technical control:

"Computers will make middle management obsolete." (Although

computers can replace human beings in technical control, they are not a substitute for the human judgment that is an essential part of the management control process.)

"Business should develop a management control system like the SAGE and SAC control systems that work so well for the military." (The military systems mentioned are technical control systems. They are not related to the management control problem in the military, let alone that in business.)

"The way to improve the management control process is to develop better management decision rules." (This implies that mathematics, rather than human beings, is the essence of management control.)

"Transfer prices should be calculated centrally." (This gives no recognition to negotiation and the exercise of judgment by divisional managers.)

"If you follow the planning and control techniques described in this book, your profits are a near predictable certainty." (This implies that the technique, rather than the quality of management, is the principal determinant of success.)

SUMMARY

We have described several subsystems that come under the general heading, "planning and control systems." Although related to one another, they have different purposes and different characteristics; different ways of thinking about each of them are therefore required. Generalizations about the whole area are, if valid, so vague as not to be useful. By contrast, useful generalizations, principles, and techniques can be developed for each of the subsystems. Mistakes are made when those valid for one subsystem are applied to another.

The author, in an effort to establish a scientific foundation for management control, discusses its relation to other management functions and formulates control principles in three areas: the nature and purpose of control, the structure of control, and the process of control.

4

MANAGEMENT CONTROL: A SUGGESTED FORMULATION OF PRINCIPLES

Harold Koontz

Although the need for improving management in all kinds of enterprise is widely recognized, and although much inquiry into management and the training of managers is being undertaken, there is serious question that enough attention is being given to formulating a conceptual framework from which to approach these important tasks. Much of both research in management and training of managers seems to have been proceeding from the questionable premise that exchange of experience and emphasis on technique are adequate to meet the widely recognized need for improving the quality of management.

One cannot deny the importance of analyzing experience through case study or research, or of giving managers lessons in "how-to-do-it" as indicated by experience. But particular techniques of dealing with problems must be passed on with care since these are not always transplantable from one manager to another or from one enterprise to another. What can be transferred, however, are the generalizations that can be distilled from specific situations. Generalizations—or principles, which can be applied in certain areas and which have a predictive value in guiding thought and action in these areas, can be a practical means of understanding and improving management. And if these principles can be

Reprinted from the *California Management Review*, Vol. 1, No. 2, Winter 1959, pp. 47–55.

arranged logically in a conceptual scheme, they can furnish the elements of a useful theory of management.

Control is one of the most widely discussed and studied areas of management. Yet it is a functional area in which little attempt has been made to formulate principles that might be useful to practicing managers, helpful in training them, and suitable for guiding research. Considerable attention has been given to organization principles, and the basics of formal organization have been so well recognized and explained that most research and practice in organization show a clear awareness of theoretical implications, an awareness which may account for the relative effectiveness of most managers in organizational matters. Some attention has been given to the codification of principles of planning.[1] But rather little has been given to formulating and codifying principles of control, staffing, or direction.

This is not to say that principles of control cannot be found. A number of profound inquiries have been made in this area, many basic truths have been highlighted, and great contributions made, but they lack the refinement, completeness, and codification found in organization. In other words, while many individual principles of control have been recognized by such scholars as Frederick Taylor, Henri Fayol, Chester Barnard, Billy Goetz, Lyndall Urwick, and Joel Dean as well as by many practicing business managers, the entire area has been inadequately reviewed and summarized.

The development of such activities as medicine, dentistry, engineering, music, and agriculture has characteristically been towards the evolution of a science, a systematized body of knowledge dealing with a given area and formulated with reference to principles and laws. A mature field of management cannot be developed without a scientific foundation, and a framework of principles appears to be a proper starting place. As Talcott Parsons, himself a scholar in another "young" science, puts it:

> It is scarcely too much to say that the most important index of the state of maturity of a science is the state of its systematic theory. This includes the character of the general conceptual scheme in use in the field, the kinds and degrees of logical integration of the different elements which make it up, and the ways in which it is actually used in empirical research.[2]

[1] See, for example, the author's "A Preliminary Statement of Principles of Planning and Control," *Journal of the Academy of Management,* I, 1 (April 1958). In this paper, originally given before the Academy of Management in 1956, only four principles of control were identified and it was felt that the managerial function of control was largely a technical matter about which few generalizations could be made. Further study and reflection have indicated that this position was incorrect.

[2] *Essays in Sociological Theory, Pure and Applied* (Glencoe, Ill.: Free Press, 1949), p. 17.

In the rapidly evolving programs of management research and training, there is often so much recounting of experience—without reflecting on what is fundamental in the job of management and without expressing this experience in these terms—that findings tend to contribute only a hodge-podge of structureless facts. If research efforts were realigned to broaden knowledge of principles and to interpret this research in the light of principles, more progress could surely be made towards the development of scientific foundations for management.

Apart from its necessity as a guide for research and for the development of scientific management, a framework of principles is important in training managers. Principles describe the nature of the managerial job, crystallize the purpose of management, and act as a kind of checklist for the manager to follow in practicing the art of management. In doing so, they furnish the basis for seeing the manager's job as a whole and become the cornerstone upon which the training of managers can be undertaken.

Early students of management—eminently practical scholars such as Henri Fayol, Chester Barnard, Lyndall Urwick, and Alvin Brown—felt strongly the need for a body of theory in the teaching of management. For example, in his great classic published originally in 1916, Fayol bemoaned the absence of management teaching in the vocational schools and ascribed it to the lack of theory since, as he said, "Without theory no teaching is possible." [3] Similar observations have been made by those now teaching management.[4]

Principles, or theory, and art are not, of course, mutually exclusive. As principles are formulated, verified, and applied in solving problems, they become the working rules of an art. While management will always be an art and perhaps will depend largely on know-how, improvements in the art of management, as in the art of bridgebuilding or missile design, can come from an understanding of principles.

As the working rules of an art, principles can, then, increase managerial efficiency. Probably no task is more complex or has a greater number of variables than that of the manager. The application of principles to this job should facilitate reasoned decisions, might make unnecessary much laborious research and trial-and-error operation, and could show the way to understanding many of the complexities of the task. But unless these principles are clearly related to the job of management and logically organized, their usefulness to the manager and to the researcher will be limited.

[3] *General and Industrial Management* (New York: Pitman Publishing Corp., 1949), pp. 14–15.

[4] See, for example, Leon C. Megginson, "The pressure for Principles: A Challenge to Management Professors," *Journal of the Academy of Management,* I, 2 (August 1958), 7–12.

CONTROL AS A FUNCTION

In order to see the managerial function of control in proper perspective, it must be regarded in the light of the other functions of the manager. In my opinion, control is one of five major functions of the manager at any level of an enterprise—whether president or foreman—and in every organized enterprise—whether business, government, education, church, or other kind. These functions, all of which are necessary to the job of getting things done through people and all of which differ from those of the engineer, accountant, machinist, or personnel expert, may be summarized as follows:

A. *Planning*—the selection from among alternatives of enterprise objectives, policies, procedures, and programs.

B. *Organizing*—the grouping of activities necessary for accomplishing enterprise objectives and the assignment of these groupings to a manager with the necessary authority for undertaking them and with provision for vertical and horizontal coordination of the authority relationships.

C. *Staffing*—the selection and training of subordinates.

D. *Directing*—the guidance and overseeing of subordinates.

E. *Controlling*—the measurement and correction of activities of subordinates to make sure that plans are transformed into action.

It will be readily seen that all of the functions of the manager are so closely interrelated that it is difficult in practice to ascertain where one function ends and another begins. Indeed, in practice these functions tend to coalesce because the operating manager performs all of them virtually at the same time. Planning and control are particularly closely related since the purpose of control is to make sure that plans are accomplished. Any attempt to control without planning would be meaningless since no one can tell whether his subordinates are doing what he wishes them to do unless he first knows what his wishes are. As Goetz has put it, "Managerial planning seeks consistent, integrated and articulated programs," while "management control seeks to compel events to conform to plans."[5] Plans thus furnish the criteria for control.

Similarly, since the manager accomplishes enterprise or department goals through people and since events can only be made to happen by people, control and organization are closely intertwined. For, just as

[5] *Management Planning and Control* (New York: McGraw-Hill Book Company, 1949), p. 2.

planning furnishes the criteria for control, so organization defines who must be controlled. Without the assurance that subordinates who are expected to accomplish tasks hold the necessary and coordinated authority, no manager can properly carry out the function of control.

Given the prerequisites of integrated and clear plans and sound organization, the control process is the same wherever it is applied. Whether the manager wishes to assure quality of product, availability of necessary cash, orderly production, a desired level of inventories, or any other planning goal, the control process involves three steps: (1) the establishment of standards; (2) the appraisal of performance against these standards; and (3) the correction of deviations.

It should be noted that the third control step overlaps other managerial functions. Deviations from plans may, of course, be corrected through additional planning, through better direction, through selecting someone else to do it, through a program of subordinate training, or through reorganization.

CLASSIFICATION OF PRINCIPLES

One of the major purposes of a theory is to explain the nature of a subject by presenting a clear and systematic view of it. With this in mind, it appears that managerial control can be analyzed by placing the basic principles of control into the categories of (1) those dealing with the nature and purpose of control, (2) those having to do with the structure of control, and (3) those explaining the process of control.[6] (The same classification of principles could, no doubt, be used for the managerial functions of organizing and planning, and perhaps also for staffing and direction.)

In placing the principles which I believe to be basic to managerial control within this framework, I must emphasize that this classification is tentative. The classification does appear to have the merit of being widely applicable to all functions of management and it does appear to deal with those facets of management important to the practicing manager. Disagreement as to the classification is expected [7] and it is probable that

[6] The author used a similar classification in his suggested principles of planning. See "A Preliminary Statement of Principles of Planning and Control" (Note 1).

[7] For example, Urwick, who has perhaps done more than anyone else to develop a systematic theory of management, has classified principles of control (as other principles of management) in a logical scheme based upon the premise that every problem area or subject has an underlying principle, which in turn has a process, and an effect. In turn, each of these has its principle, process and effect. See Lyndall F. Urwick, *The Pattern of Management* (Minneapolis: University of Minnesota Press, 1956), Chap. 5. As Urwick has often pointed out, this logical scheme was borrowed from Mooney and Reilly, who, in turn, borrowed it from the German logician, Louis F. Anderson. While this system, which leads to neat

others would identify principles other than those stated in each classification.

Most of these principles are not, of course, original. As will be noted, many of them have been referred to in almost the same language by others who have attempted to dissect the job of the manager.

NATURE AND PURPOSE OF CONTROL

The nature and purpose of managerial control seem to be reflected in five principles, which may be summarized as follows:

1. *Principle of Assurance of Objective:* Controls must contribute to the accomplishment of group objectives by detecting deviations from plans in time and in a manner to make corrective action possible.

It is obvious that the purpose of all organized enterprise is the accomplishment of group objectives, ends which cannot be accomplished by individuals acting alone. This essential fact has been recognized in many analyses of management.[8]

For example, a company's objective in instituting a new product program may be to maximize return on investment; but if, as the program proceeds, a forecast of revenues and expenses indicates that the program (perhaps because of a competitor's action) will yield a negative or a negligible return, control should make it possible to reconsider the original decision and modify or replace the program before it is too late. If a control were designed to show only the state of progress in the development of the product itself, the company might find itself with a fully developed, but relatively unprofitable new product which had already absorbed its resources.

Therefore, controls must have as their essential reason the attainment of objectives or goals, just as the other functions of the manager must have as their *raison d'etre* the accomplishment of objective. In the case of control, this purpose can only be accomplished if the techniques used make it possible to detect failures in plans. This is a simple truth, but one which often is overlooked by the practicing manager.

---

groups of nine principles, has a certain graphical charm, it does not appear to be as useful or understandable as the one adopted here.

[8] As Barnard, in his *The Functions of the Executive* (Cambridge, Mass.: Harvard University Press, 1938) pointed out (p. 23), "Cooperation justifies itself, then, as a means of overcoming the limitations restricting what individuals can do" and (p. 82) "An organization comes into being when (1) there are persons able to communicate with each other (2) who are willing to contribute action (3) to accomplish a common purpose."

2. *Principle of Efficiency of Control:* Controls are efficient if they effectively detect deviations from plans and make possible corrective action with the minimum of unsought consequences.

Chester Barnard has very clearly pointed out the applicability of the scientific concepts of effectiveness and efficiency to systems of human co-operation.[9] A control may be effective in the sense that it does assure the attainment of objectives, but it is inefficient if it does so at unnecessarily high cost in dollars, hours, lost morale, or individual dissatisfaction.

Techniques of control have a way of becoming costly, complex, and burdensome. It is entirely possible for a manager to spend considerably more than it is worth to detect deviations from plans. And such costs go beyond dollars. For example, a control technique so vigorous and thorough that it negates authority delegations or seriously impairs the morale of those who must execute plans can easily result in costs beyond any possible value it might have. Among the countless instances of costly controls found in practice are complex engineering procedures and controls which hamstring creativeness and human efficiency, detailed budget controls which place a strait jacket on the manager, and purchasing controls which not only delay deliveries but involve costs beyond the value of the items purchased.

3. *Principle of Control Responsibility:* Control can be exercised only by the manager responsible for the execution of plans.

The principle follows logically from the two preceding it. If the organization structure, through its delegation of authority and assignment of tasks, gives a manager responsibility for the accomplishment of certain plans or portions of plans, this responsibility cannot be waived without changing the organization. It is logically and practically inconsistent to expect a manager to make and accomplish plans and not to expect him to exercise control to make sure that these plans are being accomplished. Yet this principle is sometimes misunderstood in practice. Some managers expect control to be exerted only from some top point in an enterprise, or they wait to be told from above what controls to exercise and when.

The principle of control responsibility also appears to clarify the often misinterpreted role of controllers and centralized control units. Although these agencies may, in a staff or service capacity, assist the manager by furnishing him information needed to control his department, they cannot assume the part of actually exercising these controls without destroying the unity and meaning of the manager's job.

[9] Barnard, p. 19.

4. *Principle of Future Controls:* Effective control should be aimed at preventing present and future deviations from plans.

It has sometimes been said that planning is looking ahead and control is looking back. This seems to be a distorted view of control. Just as planning must be forward looking, so must control. Since the manager cannot possibly control the past, and too seldom can move fast enough to detect and correct current deviations from plans, his controls should be aimed at the future.

The tendency to regard control as looking back has arisen largely because managerial control has been so dependent upon accounting and statistical data instead of forecasts and predictions. In the absence of any means to look forward, reference to history, on the assumption that what is past is prologue, is admittedly better than not looking at all. But this principle does point to the need for more control information based on forecasts.

One can hardly deny that the alert manager would prefer a forecast of what *will* happen in the execution of a given plan, even though this projection has a margin of error in it, to a decimately accurate report of the past, about which he can do nothing. Of course, what a manager would probably like best of all is a system of control that would operate with instantaneous feedback, like the servo-system of an automated machine tool, so that deviations might be corrected before they occur by means of correcting tendencies to stray from desired performance.

That managers are increasingly looking ahead for purposes of control is apparent from the greater attention being given to expense and revenue projections and the forecasting of cash. Well managed companies always forecast cash requirements carefully for periods varying from four to twenty-four months in advance. By seeing their cash needs well ahead of time, they are usually able through careful planning to provide for them *before* cash stringencies occur. On the other hand, many companies have found themselves in desperate circumstances by suddenly awakening to the fact that they do not have the cash to meet commitments. And it is almost a tradition that cash is difficult to get in emergencies, but easy to obtain if arranged for well ahead of needs.

5. *Principle of Direct Control:* The most effective technique of control in an enterprise is to assure the quality of subordinate managers.

Most controls used by managers are actually indirect controls because they are based on the need to keep subordinates, particularly managerial subordinates, from making mistakes. Unquestionably, the best and most direct kind of control is to assure the best possible quality of managers. Able and well trained managers plan well and thoroughly, delegate authority, assign tasks, and do the most effective job of selecting, training, and directing subordinates. They make fewer mistakes and require fewer indirect controls.

THE STRUCTURE OF CONTROL

A second group of three principles are significant for the structure of control techniques, particularly in their relation to plans, organization, and the managerial incumbent.

6. *Principle of Reflection of Plans:* Controls must be designed so as to reflect the character and structure of plans.

This principle underlines the fact that controls must be tailored to individual plans. Thus, if the control of costs is the aim, the control technique used must be based on planned costs of a definite and specific type. If one would control inventory, clearly the controls must take into account and follow those plans which influence inventory; and true inventory control must be based upon the entire program of production planning and scheduling, purchasing, shipping, warehousing, sales, and finance. Too often, in these and similar cases, the manager deceives himself by thinking he is controlling an aspect of operation when his control technique is not designed to reflect the pertinent plans involved.

7. *Principle of Organizational Suitability:* Controls must be designed to reflect organization structure.

Since managers and their subordinates are the means through which the events of planning must be accomplished, it follows that effective controls must be applicable to a manager's authority area and must therefore reflect the organization structure. Consequently, any device of control must be tailored to the manager and his position in the organization, and information to appraise performance against plans must be suitable to the manager who is to use it. Urwick has expressed this as the principle of uniformity and has emphasized that "all figures and reports used for purposes of control must be in terms of the organization structure." [10]

As can be readily seen, this principle is similar to the principle of control responsibility outlined above. The principle of control responsibility, however, emphasizes that control of events can be exercised only through people, with the manager the focal point of control. But

[10] Lyndall F. Urwick, *Elements of Administration* (New York: Harper & Brothers, 1943), p. 107.

control techniques must be structured so that a certain manager can be held responsible. This can only be done by making the controls consistent with organization structure. It does no good to hold a manager responsible for costs, for example, if the cost reports do not pinpoint which manager in an organization position is responsible. In other words, one principle has to do with the personal responsibility for control, the other with the orientation of control information to the organization structure.

8. *Principle of Individuality of Controls:* Controls must be designed to meet the personal needs of the individual manager.

An important factor in any system of control is the fact that people do vary in terms of personal biases, training, and ability to comprehend information. No matter how much a statistician, mathematician, or accountant might like to mold a manager into his own image, it is a fact of life that what a manager cannot understand or will not understand cannot be useful to him for control. What might be a delight to the figure-minded treasurer might be abhorrent to the plant superintendent. What might be meaningful to the chief engineer might be incomprehensible to the sales manager. Some managers may like reports, others tables, some charts, and still others mathematical formulae or curves. Control devices and information are important enough that they should be tailored to these needs.

THE PROCESS OF CONTROL

In the operation of controls, there appear to be six principles which point to the most effective possible techniques of control. To be sure, control, being so much a technique, rests heavily on the art of management, on "know-how" in a given instance. But experience in control yields certain benchmarks which no manager should overlook in practice.

9. *Principle of Standards:* Effective and efficient control requires objective, accurate, and suitable standards.

Standards are authoritative criteria by which performance can be measured. The principle of standards implies that every plan must have measures of effectiveness which are as specific and simple as possible and which accurately measure whether a planned program is being accomplished.

Not only are such standards highly desirable from the standpoint of giving the manager a precise measurement of operations in relation to plans, but they are desirable because events are controlled through people.

Actual performance is sometimes camouflaged from the manager by a subordinate's sparkling or dull personality or by his ability to "sell" a deficient performance. Thus measurements of performance that are not objective can often be wrong. Moreover, good standards objectively applied as a measure of a subordinate's performance are most likely to be accepted by the subordinate as fair and reasonable.

10. *Principle of Strategic Point Control:* Effective and efficient control requires that attention be given to those factors which are strategic to the appraisal of performance.

It is ordinarily wasteful and unnecessary for a manager to follow every detail of the execution of plans. What he must know is that plans are being executed in such a manner that their goals can be accomplished. He should, therefore, concentrate his attention on selected parts of performance which will indicate whether significant deviations in the total plan are occurring or will occur.

There are no easy guidelines which might be applied by a practicing manager to determine the strategic points he should watch, since the selection of these is predominantly a matter of the managerial art. Perhaps the manager can reach his own solution to the problem by asking himself what things in *his* operations will show *him* best whether the plans for which he is responsible are being accomplished.

11. *The Exception Principle:* Efficiency in control requires that attention of the manager be given primarily to significant exceptions.

This principle, which was pointed out many years ago by Frederick Taylor,[11] is sometimes confused with the principle of strategic point control. But they are essentially different concepts even though both have to do with the utilization of standards. Strategic point control refers to the selection of certain key factors which determine whether performance conforms with plans, while the exception principle has to do with watching for (and taking action with respect to) significant deviations at these points.

The difference between the exception principle and the principle of strategic point control can be illustrated by the techniques a sales manager might employ to control field sales. He might select as critical points to watch such items as sales per salesman, sales by products and by territories, or gross profits from sales by product. However, in watching these critical points, he would see no need for action unless he detected deviations beyond limits which he regarded as normal, that is, deviations which constitute noteworthy exceptions.

[11] *Shop Management* (New York: Harper & Brothers, 1919), pp. 126–127.

The exception principle is often quoted as an essential requirement of managerial control efficiency. However, the manager who first chooses the fewest practicable strategic points to watch, and then concentrates on exceptions increases his efficiency markedly. The necessary number of strategic points to be watched will depend upon the importance of the plan and the extent to which strategic points showing progress under the plan can be found or devised. This difference might be illustrated by practices in quality control. It may be important to test carefully every part of a missile guidance and control system and hold each part to close performance tolerances; but in the missile fuselage shell there might be only few points to be checked, and the allowable tolerances might be relatively broad.

12. *The Principle of Flexibility of Controls:* Controls should incorporate sufficient flexibility to remain effective despite the failure of plans.

Stated negatively, this principle, first given clear form by Goetz,[12] means that controls should not be so inextricably bound into a particular plan that, should unforeseen events or shifts in goals make the plan unworkable, all control is lost. This principle is best illustrated by the considerations which led to the flexible, or variable, budget. Such budgeting, which provides for budgets to be changed quickly and virtually automatically if the business outlook changes, arose from fears that under fixed budgets control might be lost through continuation of managerial authority to spend at a level determined by previous sales forecasts but not justified by actual sales volume.

While this principle is difficult to implement in practice, the manager should be aware of the desirability of such flexibility. Otherwise, the manager may go along blithely thinking that he has proper control of the execution of a plan, only to find that the situation for which the plan was tailored has been changed. Many managers tend to lose control over the costs of new product programs when the unforeseen difficulties of such ventures cause costs to mount—while the elusive rabbit of completion seems to be around one more corner.

13. *Principle of Review:* The control system should be reviewed periodically.

Because of the dynamics of enterprise and the environment in which it operates, not only should controls be kept flexible but the system and techniques of controls should periodically be reviewed. Controls, like

[12] Billy E. Goetz, *Management Planning and Control* (New York: McGraw-Hill Book Company, 1949), p. 229.

plans, are never final. Just as the manager should continually re-evaluate his plans and take navigational readings to see if he is on course, so should he periodically and systematically review his controls to make certain that the standards used, the strategic points selected, and the tolerances permitted are consistent with his plans and goals.

14. *Principle of Action:* Control is only justified if measures are undertaken to correct indicated or experienced deviations from plans through appropriate planning, organizing, staffing, and directing.

Control is meaningless and wasteful and the application of the principles above a fruitless exercise unless action is taken to correct deficiencies detected. These corrections may be in the form of revised or new plans, new or different delegations of authority and assignments of tasks, better training or selection of subordinates, or a better order of counseling and guidance by the manager.

This principle not only underscores the action aspect of control but also the fact that control tends to coalesce with the other functions of the manager. It emphasizes the basic unity of management and the essential fact that control functions cannot be delegated, cannot be centralized in a staff or department which does not have the authority to execute a plan, and cannot be taken away from the manager without destroying managership itself.

The authors explain how to avoid pitfalls in setting standards for control and how to use standards more effectively for control.

5

NOTES ON THE NATURE OF STANDARDS

Herbert G. Hicks
Friedhelm Goronzy

Standards give a common frame of reference; they permeate human civilization. For example, communication is based on more or less standard meanings of words and symbols. However, universal or absolute standards or constants, such as the most celebrated, the velocity of light, are scarce.[1] Most standards are to some degree arbitrary; many even are determined accidentally. Even poor ones, however, frequently are used for long periods.

THE EFFECTS OF CULTURE ON STANDARDS OF SCIENTISTS

Every human activity requires a value judgment. Science—physical and human—is no exception. Scientists who investigate every physical and human field of knowledge rank objectivity high, but culturally-determined values strongly influence the rate of scientific progress.

Learning of science usually starts in grade schools with the acceptance of established doctrines. In a university the student probably continues to learn textbook truth until he achieves some mastery of the subject. But he also begins to learn the basic features of scientific judgment and

Reprinted from *Academy of Management Journal,* December 1966, pp. 281–293, by permission of the publisher.

[1] S. B. Littauer, "On Some Aspects of Technological Measurement," *Management Technology* (January 1960), p. 36.

experimental proof.[2] This whole process may be viewed as learning by acceptance of authority.[3] As the student progresses he relies less on authority, and follows more and more his own judgment. Striving to be a scientist himself, he will take unto himself part of the function that authority previously served.[4] When this process matures, the student has reached independence.

Modern scientists are not universalists. Often an individual scientist understands expertly only a small fraction of his specialty. Therefore, scientists rely on communication as the invisible hand that coordinates their activity.

The merit of a communicated scientific contribution commonly is evaluated by three interrelated standards: (1) plausibility, (2) scientific value, and (3) originality.[5]

1. *Plausibility.* The ideas advanced must conform sufficiently with current scientific opinion. Plausibility insures scientists that they are not plagued with "great discoveries" of laymen who would like to contribute to a subject matter they do not understand.

2. *Scientific value.* The accuracy of the findings, their systematic importance and the intrinsic interest of the subject matter determines their scientific values. The findings communicated should be related to the current interest of the scientific community and help others to benefit from the knowledge presented.

3. *Originality.* Do the ideas forwarded shed new light on the problems under study by other investigators? In what way do the findings deviate from currently accepted scientific truths?

For the typical scientist these three standards have become part of himself as he progressed from student to independent scholar. Each standard has its own distinct influence on the rate of progress. Relying on these standards, scientific contributions are evaluated by comparing with existing knowledge. This evaluation procedure has been described as follows:

> Each scientist watches over an area comprising his own field and some adjoining strips of territory, over which neighbouring specialists can also form reliable firsthand judgments. Suppose now that work done on the specialty of B an be reliably judged by A and C; that of C by B and D; that of D by C and E; and on. If then each of these groups of neighbours agrees with re-

[2] Michael Polanyi, *Science, Faith, and Society* (Chicago: The University of Chicago Press, 1964), p. 43.

[3] *Ibid.*, p. 46.

[4] *Ibid.*, p. 45.

[5] Michael Polanyi, "The Republic of Science: Its Political and Economic Theory," *Minerva* (Autumn 1962), pp. 57–58.

spect to their standards, then the standards on which A, B and C agree will be the same on which B, C and D agree, and on which also C, D and E agree, and so on, throughout the whole realm of science.[6]

The relative strength of the three cited standards has an important influence on the pace of progress. The standards of plausibility and scientific value encourage conformity, and the standard of originality encourages dissent. The first two standards appear to serve as minimum criteria in the sense that any scientific contribution has to be of a certain quality to merit scientific recognition. But simultaneously these criteria set an upper limit to progress.

Recent studies have indicated that conformity and resistance to change is more prevalent among scientists than commonly expected.[7] Many may accept textbook truth without much questioning. Thus, scientists become committed to a paradigm—the currently accepted conceptual model. They may largely cease to explore the unknown, but prefer to concretize the known. Only when research conducted under the old theories begins to give wrong results—according to the theory—do the theories begin to be questioned. A paradigm change then may begin to take place.

Bernard Barber [8] reported some findings illustrating that commitment to a paradigm can be very strong. He pointed out that scientists are only human with minds that often may prefer static conditions. New ideas that do not conform with currently accepted scientific opinions are often objects of fear and may be met with repulsion. Seniority, professional recognition, and other tangible or intangible vested interests often are threatened by the new. This may especially be true of outsiders who intrude the field with new methodological concepts. For example, older botanists objected to the introduction of mathematics into botany because they were not familiar with mathematics as a tool. And finally, good scientific theories might obstruct the introduction of better ones. Thus, the open-mindness of scientists is probably more a wish than an actuality. The great physicist Max Planck once remarked sadly that new ideas do not triumph because they are convincing, rather, the opponents eventually die.

The foregoing indicates that the forces of conformity in science may be somewhat stronger than usually assumed. Thus, it can be tentatively concluded that standards of the scientific community foster progress by requiring a minimum performance. At the same time, however, they tend

[6] Michael Polanyi, *Personal Knowledge* (Chicago: The University of Chicago Press, 1958), p. 217.

[7] Thomas S. Kuhn, "The Function of Dogma in Scientific Research," *Scientific Change,* ed. A. C. Crombie (New York: Basic Books Inc., 1963), pp. 347–369.

[8] Bernard Barber, "Resistance by Scientists to Scientific Discovery," *Science* (September 1, 1961), pp. 596–602.

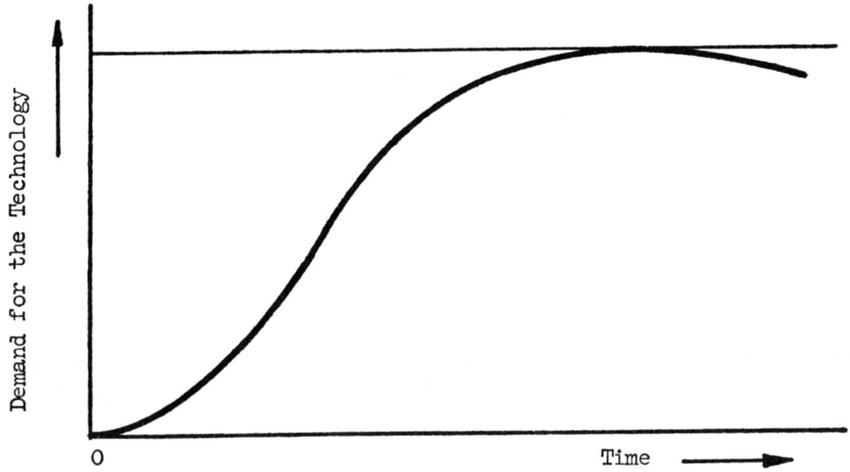

Graph 5–1. Demand for the technology through time

to retard progress by forcing scientists to accept a considerable amount of conformity, thereby discouraging originality.

STANDARDS AS MEASURES OF PROGRESS

In a competitive economic system, the profit motive may be responsible for innovation. An entrepreneur seeking pure profits has to find a way to achieve lower costs or to develop a presently unavailable product or service that will be accepted by the market. Such a change can be called an innovation.

One can distinguish three kinds of innovations: (1) new products and services, (2) new skills and ways of producing, and (3) new concepts and definitions. Conceptual innovations have become increasingly important and often precede the first two.[9]

An innovation has to be substantial enough to overcome the environmental threshold—the resistance to change. However, once this threshold is overcome there can be rapid acceptance of the innovation, and pure profits may accrue to the innovator. Pure profits attract followers who want to share the fruits of the invention, but who eventually bid away the pure profits.

The improvement or acceptance curve of an innovation is "S" shaped, as shown in Graph 5–1. Immediately after the initial discovery, improve-

[9] J. W. Cook, "Innovation and Progress," *Commercial and Financial Chronicle,* June 14, 1962, pp. 2779–2780.

ments and acceptance are rapid. But through time the curve approaches the horizontal. Incremental improvements then are slow and costly because the technological potentialities become almost completely exhausted; only a new breakthrough—another innovation—promises significant advances. This is the point when another breakthrough can be most expected.[10] If a new innovation indeed does occur, the demand for the old technology begins to decline.

THE EVOLUTION OF STANDARDS

Observations of the development of new innovations or technologies suggest that progress is measured by similar sets of standards. Four distinctly different sets of standards appear to accompany each innovation:

1. Using the performance of the old, replaced method as the criterion.
2. Comparing different uses or versions of the innovation with each other.
3. Measuring the present state of the innovation against its theoretical limits.
4. Measuring the highly-perfected innovation against a replacing technology or an ideal method of accomplishing the work.[11]

To illustrate the four sets of standards we consider an inventory control application handled by machines. We regard punched card machines as the old method, ordinary electronic computers as the current method, and real-time systems as a replacing technology.[12] We relate these methods to the four sets of standards for technologies.

1. *Using the performance of the old, replaced method as the criterion.* Punched card machines are frequently considered as the forerunners of computers. Their work is based on the unit record system. Each bit of information is recorded on a separate record, the punched card. Once the information is punched into the card, this same card can be used many times for a number of calculations and analyses.

Each punched card machine can perform only a limited number of operations; special machines are required for such jobs as keypunching, sorting, collating, and tabulating. The tabulator is usually regarded as the

[10] A. Zvorikine, "Technology and the Laws of its Development," *Technology and Culture* (Fall 1962), p. 450.

[11] Herbert G. Hicks and Friedhelm Goronzy, "A Procedure for Development of Performance Standards for Data Processing Installations," *Management International* (forthcoming).

[12] Much of the following discussion is based on William H. Desmonde, *Computers and Their Uses* (Englewood Cliffs, N.J.: Prentice-Hall, Inc., 1964), 296 pp. and William H. Desmonde, *Real Time Data Processing Systems: Introductory Concepts* (Englewood Cliffs, N.J.: Prentice-Hall, Inc., 1964), 186 pp.

mainframe of the installation because it can add, subtract, and print lists of subtotals and totals. Although punched card machines save many hours of labor and some kind of analyses are only possible because of them, they have some distinct limitations. For example, the tabulator can execute only one operation at a time, and each operational sequence requires a separate pass through the machine. These limitations require human intervention after the execution of each operation. Thus, the sequence of the operations—the program—is executed manually by the machine operator. These deficiencies in punched card machines led to the next logical development, the stored-program machine that eliminated the need for human intervention after completion of each program step.

Computers are stored-program machines, with radically new capabilities when compared with punched card machines. The memory of a computer makes the storage of intermediate results possible; instructions for a large sequence of different operational steps can be stored internally; and thus a wide variety of operations can be executed.

In the first phase of their development computers were compared to punched card machines, the technology they replaced. No other standard has as much relevance.

Computers gained an enormous popularity because they represented a great advance when compared to the old punched card technology. But even in the computer there are some inherent limitations. Memory capacity is limited, making it necessary that the bulk of relevant information still be stored on unit records. Further, computational speed is limited by a number of technological factors. In the course of time, the limits of the machines have become known and felt. Computers will no longer be compared as much with punched card equipment but more often with each other.

2. *Comparing different uses or versions of the innovations with each other.* Computer installations have been so widely accepted that comparing with punched card equipment has become increasingly less meaningful. A better set of standards for measuring computer achievements has become desirable.

A study was undertaken by the authors to determine an approach for developing comparative standards for different computer applications.[13] It was hypothesized that the time, and consequently the monthly rental cost, that firms allocate to a computer application is a function of the number of accounts processed for that particular application. Statistical analysis of the reported data revealed that such a relationship apparently does indeed exist. Graph 5–2 illustrates the fundamentals of this procedure—it shows how much rent per month different firms allocated to their payroll accounting function. The relatively high correlation coefficient

[13] Hicks and Goronzy, *op. cit.*

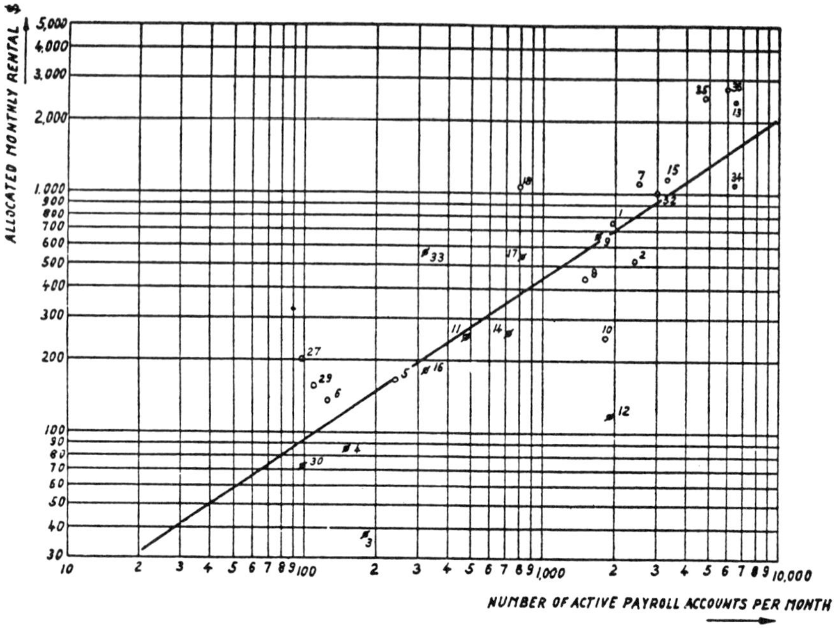

Graph 5–2. Payroll accounting

Legend: o—Computer; ɸ—Tabulating Machine; Form of Regression Line: $y = 4.15 \times x^{.66}$; Correlation Coefficient: $r = .83$; t—Test of significance at the $p = .01$ probability level: $t^{.01} \times 2.797 < t = 7.3$; correlation is significant.

Source: Herbert G. Hicks and Friedhelm Goronzy, "A Procedure For Development of Performance Standards for Data Processing Installations," *Management International* (forthcoming).

and the t-test indicate a highly significant relationship. Investigations of accounts receivable, accounts payable, cost accounting, and inventory control revealed similar relationships, although with somewhat lower coefficients of correlation.

This second period of growth and development in the electronic data processing field measures accomplishments of different applications of computers with each other. Comparisons with the old method, punched card machines, becomes obsolete. Computer technology is presently (1966) well into this second stage, but in practice, computer work standards often are still based on the obsolete standards of the first, introductory period described above.

3. *Measuring the present state of the innovation against its theoretical limits.* This standard becomes appropriate when an innovation approaches maturity. A typical innovation, such as the computer, will have not one theoretical limit, but several. For example, the limits on the

computational speed are for the most part negligible in computer applications for business problems, but limitations on memory capacity are important.

Business information is usually contained on printed documents maintained in files. Even when the data are transferred to unit records, the problem of storing and maintaining the files remains. Great electronic computational speed is of little help if the results have to be punched or printed with relatively slow electromechanical devices. The separation of computer and printer is an improvement, but it does not eliminate the problem. Similarly, the transformation of card files to paper or magnetic tapes improves accessibility and eases updating information, but the information handling problem remains. Thus, the typical computer is limited by capacity of its memory. Although memory is usually large enough to accommodate even complex business computer programs, it is not large enough to contain the vast information files required in large businesses. A storage large enough to hold all data electronically would overcome this disadvantage.

This third stage in the development of computers is characterized by standards that compare the performance of the innovation with its theoretical limits.

4. *Measuring the highly-perfected innovation against a replacing technology of an ideal method of accomplishing the work.* We have considered data processing applications that are based on in-putting data on unit records, such as cards or data that may already be stored on paper or magnetic tapes. Output consists of printed pages or tape for further processing or filing. Such data processing has several limitations. Processing is done in batches because the machine is programmed to receive it that way. Information has to be accumulated for some period before it is processed in the machine. Hence, there is always some time lag between organization and processing. Consequently, decisions based on output are founded in past information. And this method of data processing is inherently dependent on the manual maintenance of files. In many applications—including inventory control and banking—it would be of great advantage to update the files immediately after the occurrence of an event and to simultaneously have fast random access to the files. Conventional computers, because of their limited memory, do not provide such a potentiality.

Computers that can store and recall instantly vast amounts of information at random are called real-time systems with random access memories. The random access memories are auxiliary units with storage capacities of many millions of characters. Thus real-time systems may make ordinary computer installations obsolete because they eliminate manually maintained files. For certain business applications this opens up entirely new potentialities for handling information. Real-time systems can truly be called a breakthrough.

As the use of real-time computer systems becomes more widespread, the progress of the current technology—ordinary electronic computers—will be measured in terms of the capabilities of real-time systems.

During the introductory period of computers the performance of the new computers was compared to that of punched card machines. Because of their advantages, computers made fast inroads into the former applications of punched card machines. As more and more firms acquired computers, comparison with an outdated method was of little value. Relative standing to other users became the basis of standards. As computer technology matured, its inherent limitations became apparent. Attention then focused on the best use of the technology, considering only its limitations. Finally, the desire to be free of the limitations of the then present technology led to a new criterion—comparing the perfected technology with a replacing one. Thus we see through an example that the relevant performance standards have continually changed as the technology progressed.

IMPLICATIONS OF INNOVATIONS

A certain technology can be improved up to the inherent limit of this technology. Further advances require entirely new concepts. However, new advances do not necessarily appear in sequence; new breakthroughs do not depend necessarily on the perfection of the old method. Different technologies, each in different stages of perfection, can exist side-by-side. This concept is illustrated with Graph 5–3.

What happens if a firm fails to progress after the introduction of an innovation? Its fate is obvious; advancing technology adopted by competitors will bring pressures on the firm. Thus, in the case of computers, the job is not done merely by introducing computers. They have to be constantly made to work on new applications. Garrity [14] found that simple introduction of computers (just replacing the old method) usually brings small gains when compared with the potential gains that can be obtained by further development and top management attention to this problem.

QUANTITATIVE PERFORMANCE STANDARDS

Many quantitative performance standards may exist in a business enterprise: for example, sales quotas, material usage, overhead cost, and

[14] John T. Garrity, *Getting the Most Out of Your Computer* (New York: McKinsey and Company, Inc., May 1963), 20 pp.

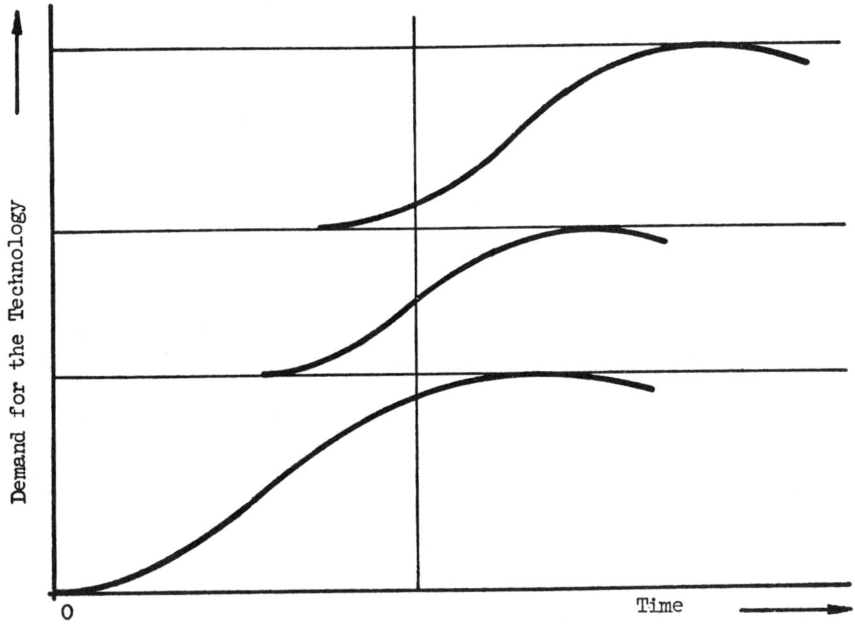

Graph 5–3. Overlapping of several related technologies

labor time for each operation. For the purpose of this paper we will investigate only time standards and their implications on the welfare of the company.

The first requirement for establishing effective standards is that the best practice or methods attainable with the present technology should become the basis for any standard. In undertaking work measurement, one has to separate the work situation into two components: (1) man himself, and (2) the environment or machine.[15] Thus, operations in a work situation are usually man-controlled and machine-controlled. Man-controlled operations are decisively influenced by behavioral factors, and can show large variations in the measuring process. On the other hand, machine-controlled operations usually have a much smaller range of variations. Because of human factors, it is doubtful that work measurement can ever be purely objective.[16]

Although beset with many problems of measurement, both management and unions make standards the basis for their decisions. What are the advantages of standards, and what are the disadvantages? Compared to an hourly rate, it has been shown that a bonus rate will likely yield higher output; a piece rate based on a time standard may yield an even

[15] Adam Abruzzi, *Work, Workers, and Work Measurements* (New York: Columbia University Press, 1956), p. 14.

[16] *Ibid.*, p. 13.

higher output.[17] Time-work standards also may be the basis for predicting and planning performance as expressed in an annual budget.[18]

Standards and budgets enable a firm to operate under the management-by-exception principle. When performance falls short of expectations, management steps in and takes corrective action to remedy the situation. If over-performance occurs, management also seeks to determine the causes. If the cause is improved technology, standards may be reset to conform to the new technology. This view about the resetting of obsolete standards, however, disregards one of the important factors in today's work situation—labor unions.

Time studies frequently are a conceptual framework for bargaining.[19] Certain aspects, for example, the worker's individual performance, cannot be measured, and are subject to judgment rating. The influence of such a value judgment can completely overshadow the most objective part of the study, the actual time measurement.[20]

It has been argued that one of the most powerful reasons for organization of labor into unions is the desire for standards that cannot be changed easily. Often organized labor also demands a voice in setting time standards. The assurance of some co-determination in these matters seems to be an essential ingredient of the security package that an individual receives through belonging to a union.[21]

The bargaining or standard-setting process is a rather unique "game." During the first round—the actual time measurement—workers may attempt to introduce a bias in their favor into the operations. The industrial engineer tries to eliminate this bias through his rating of performance. The second round in the process begins after the standard is established. A lenient standard usually is accepted; a tight standard is often challenged by demanding a restudy. This process often leads to a less tight standard.[22] Because uniformity may be more desirable than a few tight standards mixed in with many loose standards the result often is an over-all loose rate structure.[23] This observation is not new and not solely an outcome of modern bargaining procedure.[24]

Thus, standards cannot be changed easily even when advancing

[17] Morris and Viteles, *Motivation and Morale in Industry* (New York: W. W. Norton and Company, 1953), p. 130.

[18] Ralph C. Davis, *Fundamentals of Top Management* (New York: Harper and Brothers, 1951), p. 35.

[19] Abruzzi, *op. cit.*, p. 19.

[20] *Ibid.*, p. 26.

[21] Walter P. Reuther, "Labor Uses Standards," *National Standards in a Modern Economy*, ed. Dickson Reck (New York: Harper and Brothers, 1956), p. 303.

[22] Abruzzi, *op. cit.*, p. 19.

[23] Davis, *op. cit.*, p. 41.

[24] H. S. Person, ed. (The Taylor Society), *Scientific Management in American Industry* (New York: Harper and Brothers, 1929), p. 196: "A Standard is usually dependent on other standards and the maintenance of all is essential to the maintenance of any one. . . . It should be noted that it is practically impossible to maintain high standards in juxtaposition to poor standards. Throughout an industrial

technology actually warrants a change. Well-meant suggestions about periodically revising standards to reflect the present technology often are not only meaningless; they may be outright misleading. The idea that a standard should act like a ratchet wheel preserving progress, and periodically be updated is not very much in touch with reality.[25]

Now the questions arise, what are the implications of relatively fixed standards, especially in the long run? Once a standard is accepted, minimum performance is more or less guaranteed. But what about performance above standard? It is very unlikely that workers, once they have obtained standards on a bargaining basis, will produce very much above the standard. Extensive experience indicates that although production goes up with the introduction of standards and incentive systems, workers make sure that production will never go up too far.[26] Hence standards set a floor—a minimum performance—but simultaneously they set a ceiling as well.

IMPLICATIONS OF RELATIVITY FIXED TIME STANDARDS AND TECHNOLOGICAL IMPROVEMENT

Progress in a given technology continues indefinitely.[27] Improvements take place because of learning and technical innovations. Learning depends on the labor content of the job and the level of skills required. In the air frame industry where labor is a significant factor, it has been found that learning is sufficiently regular to be predictable.[28] Technical improvements are largely transformations of manual operations into machine operations. Both factors cause the direct man-hours per unit constantly to go down as long as production continues. The improvement curve is a negative exponential function; the time required for the ith unit is only some fraction of the first.[29]

$y_i = y_1 i^b$

y_i = time required for the ith unit

y_1 = time required for the first unit

b = rate of time reduction from unit i to $i + 1$

---

establishment there is always a leveling tendency with respect to standards—a Gresham's Law. The association of high standards with low standards has much more tendency to pull down the high standards than raise the low."

[25] Davis, *op. cit.,* p. 41.

[26] Abruzzi, *op. cit.,* pp. 292–293.

[27] Efficiency within the technology continues even if the technology is in less demand.

[28] Richard Conway and Andrew Schultz, "The Manufacturing Progress Function," *Journal of Industrial Engineering* (January–February 1959), p. 39.

[29] *Loc. cit.*

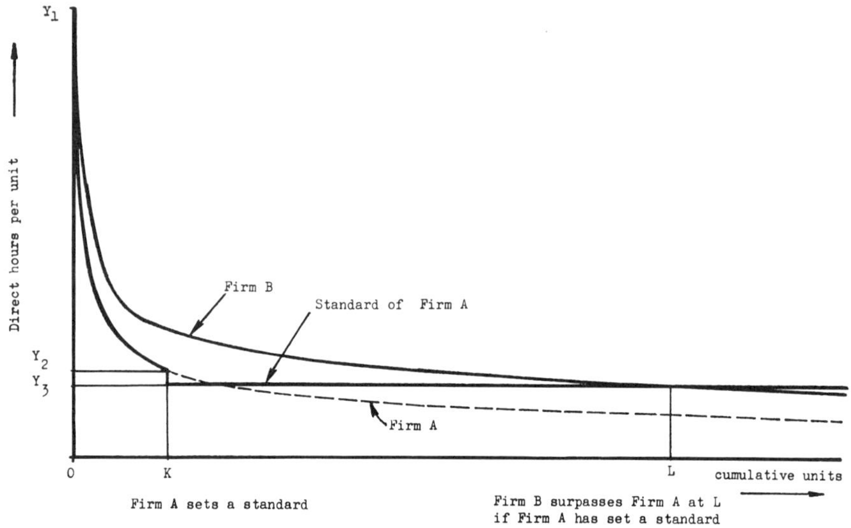

Graph 5–4. Reduction of direct hours per unit as a function of cumulative number of units produced

In the production of aircraft, it was found that "thc fourth plane required only 80% as much direct labor as the second; the eighth plane only 80% as much as the fourth, the one hundredth, only 80% as much as the fiftieth; and so on."[30] There are, of course, curves with rates of improvement other than 80%.

Usually it is said that time study should only be undertaken after the activity to be studied has reached "stability." As we saw above, because of continuous technological improvement, real stability is never reached. Thus, setting a standard may cause the firm to forego substantial benefits from future progress. Graph 5–4 illustrates the possible consequences of such a practice. In Graph 5–4, Firm A and Firm B both produce the same product. We assume that both firms start production of the product at the same time. Firm A requires Y_1 direct man hours to produce the first unit of the product. Thereafter the time required per unit declines steadily. After a cumulative production of K units, production has become fairly stable. This is the point when a standard is introduced. Often the standard will not be set at Y_2 but rather below the improvement curve at Y_3, leading to immediate short-term gains. These short-term gains, however, can have severe long-run disadvantages.

Firm B also needs Y_1 direct man hours per unit for the first unit. However, its improvement function is less steep than that of Firm A.

[30] Winfred B. Hirschmann, "Profit from the Learning Curve," *Harvard Business Review* (January–February 1964), p. 125.

Under ordinary circumstances Firm B always would be at competitive disadvantage because it is less efficient than Firm A. However, Firm B does not set a standard. Consequently, it begins to out-produce Firm A after a cumulative production of L units. Firm B can then undersell Firm A, perhaps forcing Firm A to drastic measures.

These grave consequences of standards that cannot be changed have been illustrated by examples furnished by Adam Abruzzi.[31] He pointed out that standard setting is not scientific, but is a process of accommodation. If in the long run standards cannot be changed, the entire rate structure tends to become "loose." Inefficient performance in the firm drives out good performance. As long as the firm holds some kind of monopoly in the market, the problem may not be acute. When, however, other firms attracted by profits begin to enter the market, serious survival problems begin to develop. Attempts to "restudy" the rate structure are very expensive and usually not possible because of labor objections. Workers often will not accept changed rates except in some desperate conditions. As a consequence some firms have had to close plants and move into a different geographical area, or change to an entirely new product or technology. Thus, we see that time standards in the long run can contribute to the stagnation or failure of the firm.

SUMMARY

This paper has investigated three points concerning the nature of performance standards. First, in the scientific community that works for progress in both technical and behavioral fields, cultural standards exert subtle but extremely powerful influences on the rate of advancement of knowledge. Second, performance standards are relative; the appropriate standards for a particular time depends upon the stage of development of the technology. Third, performance standards can be a mixed blessing. They do set minimum levels of acceptable performance, but in the long run they can cause an organization to stagnate at a fixed performance level. A knowledge of these aspects of standards can help one to avoid their pitfalls and to use them more effectively.

31 Adam Abruzzi, "The Quest for Certainty," *Journal of Industrial Engineering* (September–October 1958), pp. 452–459.

II

MANAGEMENT CONTROL TOOLS AND TECHNIQUES

The study of management control inevitably involves the executive in a number of highly sophisticated areas of specialization. Seven of these areas are covered by the articles in this part.

The articles in Sections A, B, C, and D of Part II deal with relatively new areas of business technology important to management control: systems theory and its applications; model building, and mathematical and statistical techniques; electronic data processing; and the behavioral sciences. The technology within each of these areas is advancing rapidly and is by nature complex and difficult to master. In spite of the difficulties and complexities, however, the manager must understand and know how to use the technology in each, if he is to exercise effective management control.

Selected aspects of three other, more traditional areas of management control tools and techniques, with which the manager should also be familiar, are discussed in Sections E, F, and G: economic planning and forecasting; new developments in the overall directions and attitudes of financial and accounting management; and reporting.

A

Systems Theory and Its Applications to Management Control

The authors give a detailed description of what systems theory is and how it can be effectively applied to business management.

6

SYSTEMS THEORY AND MANAGEMENT

Richard A. Johnson
Fremont E. Kast
James E. Rosenzweig

INTRODUCTION

The systems concept can be a useful way of thinking about the job of managing. It provides a framework for visualizing internal and external environmental factors as an integrated whole. It allows recognition of the proper place and function of subsystems. The systems within which businessmen must operate are necessarily complex. However, management via systems concepts fosters a way of thinking which, on the one hand, helps to dissolve some of the complexity and, on the other hand, helps the manager recognize the nature of the complex problems and thereby operate within the perceived environment. It is important to recognize the integrated nature of specific systems, including the fact that each system has both inputs and outputs and can be viewed as a self-contained unit. But it is also important to recognize that business systems are a part of larger systems—possibly industry-wide, or including several, maybe many, companies and/or industries, or even society as a whole. Further, business systems are in a constant state of change—they are created, operated, revised, and often eliminated.

What does the concept of systems offer to students of management

Reprinted from *Management Science,* January 1964, pp. 367–384, by permission of the authors and the publisher.

and/or to practicing executives? Is it a panacea for business problems which will replace scientific management, human relations, management by objective, operations research, and many other approaches to, or techniques of, management? Perhaps a word of caution is applicable initially. Anyone looking for "cookbook" techniques will be disappointed. In this article we do not evolve "ten easy steps" to success in management. Such approaches, while seemingly applicable and easy to grasp, usually are shortsighted and superficial. Fundamental ideas, such as the systems concept, are more difficult to comprehend, and yet they present a greater opportunity for a large-scale payoff.

SYSTEMS DEFINED [1]

A system is "an organized or complex whole; an assemblage or combination of things or parts forming a complex or unitary whole." The term system covers an extremely broad spectrum of concepts. For example, we have mountain systems, river systems, and the solar system as part of our physical surroundings. The body itself is a complex organism including the skeletal system, the circulatory system, and the nervous system. We come into daily contact with such phenomena as transportation systems, communication systems (telephone, telegraph, etc.), and economic systems.

A science often is described as a systematic body of knowledge; a complete array of essential principles or facts, arranged in a rational dependence or connection; a complex of ideas, principles, laws, forming a coherent whole. Scientists endeavor to develop, organize, and classify material into interconnected disciplines. Sir Isaac Newton set forth what he called the "system of the world." Two relatively well known works which represent attempts to integrate a large amount of material are Darwin's *The Origin of Species* and Keynes's *General Theory of Employment, Interest, and Money*. Darwin, in his theory of evolution, integrated all life into a "system of nature" and indicated how the myriad of living subsystems were interrelated. Keynes, in his general theory of employment, interest, and money, connected many complicated natural and man-made forces which make up an entire economy. Both men had a major impact on man's thinking because they were able to conceptualize interrelationships among complex phenomena and integrate them into a systematic whole. The word system connotes plan, method, order, and arrangement. Hence it is no wonder that scientists and researchers have made the term so pervasive.

The antonym of systematic is chaotic. A chaotic situation might

[1] For a more complete discussion see: Johnson, Kast, and Rosenzweig [3], pp. 4–6, 91, 92.

be described as one where "everything depends on everything else." Since two major goals of science and research in any subject area are explanation and prediction, such a condition cannot be tolerated. Therefore there is considerable incentive to develop bodies of knowledge that can be organized into a complex whole, within which subparts or subsystems can be interrelated.

While much research has been focused on the analysis of minute segments of knowledge, there has been increasing interest in developing larger frames of reference for synthesizing the results of such research. Thus attention has been focused more and more on over-all systems as frames of reference for analytical work in various areas. It is our contention that a similar process can be useful for managers. Whereas managers often have been focusing attention on particular functions in specialized areas, they may lose sight of the over-all objectives of the business and the role of their particular business in even larger systems. These individuals can do a better job of carrying out their own responsibilities if they are aware of the "big picture." It is the familiar problem of not being able to see the forest for the trees. The focus of systems management is on providing a better picture of the network of subsystems and interrelated parts which go together to form a complex whole.

Before proceeding to a discussion of systems theory for business, it will be beneficial to explore recent attempts to establish a general systems theory covering all disciplines or scientific areas.

GENERAL SYSTEMS THEORY

General systems theory is concerned with developing a systematic, theoretical framework for describing general relationships of the empirical world. A broad spectrum of potential achievements for such a framework is evident. Existing similiarities in the theoretical construction of various disciplines can be pointed out. Models can be developed which have applicability to many fields of study. An ultimate but distant goal will be a framework (or system of systems) which could tie all disciplines together in a meaningful relationship.

There has been some development of interdisciplinary studies. Areas such as social psychology, biochemistry, astrophysics, social anthropology, economic psychology, and economic sociology have been developed in order to emphasize the interrelationships of previously isolated disciplines. More recently, areas of study and research have been developed which call on numerous subfields. For example, cybernetics, the science of communication and control, calls on electrical engineering, neurophysiology, physics, biology, and other fields. Operations research is often pointed to as a multidisciplinary approach to problem solving. Information theory is another discipline which calls on numerous subfields. Organization theory embraces economics, sociology, engineering, psychology, physiology, and anthropology. Problem solving and decision making are becoming focal points for study and research, drawing on numerous disciplines.

With these examples of interdisciplinary approaches, it is easy to recognize a surge of interest in larger-scale, systematic bodies of knowledge. However, this trend calls for the development of an over-all framework within which the various subparts can be integrated. In order that the *interdisciplinary* movement does not degenerate into *undisciplined* approaches, it is important that some structure be developed to integrate the various separate disciplines while retaining the type of discipline which distinguishes them. One approach to providing an over-all framework (general systems theory) would be to pick out phenomena common to many different disciplines and to develop general models which would include such phenomena. A second approach would include the structuring of a hierarchy of levels of complexity for the basic units of behavior in the various empirical fields. It would also involve development of a level of abstraction to represent each stage.

We shall explore the second approach, a hierarchy of levels, in more detail since it can lead toward a system of systems which has application in most businesses and other organizations. The reader can undoubtedly call to mind examples of familiar systems at each level of Boulding's classification model.

1. The first level is that of static structure. It might be called the level of *frameworks;* for example, the anatomy of the universe.

2. The next level is that of the simple dynamic system with predetermined, necessary motions. This might be called the level of *clockworks.*

3. The control mechanism or cybernetic system, which might be nicknamed the level of the *thermostat.* The system is self regulating in maintaining equilibrium.

4. The fourth level is that of the "open system," or self-maintaining structure. This is the level at which life begins to differentiate from not-life: it might be called the level of the *cell.*

5. The next level might be called the genetic-societal level; it is typified by the *plant,* and it dominates the empirical world of the botanist.

6. The animal system level is characterized by increased mobility, teleological behavior, and self-awareness.

7. The next level is the "human" level, that is, of the individual human being considered as a system with self-awareness and the ability to utilize language and symbolism.

8. The social system or systems of human organization constitute the next level, with the consideration of the content and meaning of messages, the nature and dimensions of value systems, the transcription

of images into historical record, the subtle symbolizations of art, music and poetry, and the complex gamut of human emotion.

9. Transcendental systems complete the classification of levels. These are the ultimates and absolutes and the inescapables and unknowables, and they also exhibit systematic structure and relationship.[2]

Obviously, the first level is most pervasive. Descriptions of static structures are widespread. However, this descriptive cataloguing is helpful in providing a framework for additional analysis and synthesis. Dynamic "clockwork" systems, where prediction is a strong element, are evident in the classical natural sciences such as physics and astronomy; yet even here there are important gaps. Adequate theoretical models are not apparent at higher levels. However, in recent years closed-loop cybernetic, or "thermostat," systems have received increasing attention. At the same time, work is progressing on open-loop systems with self-maintaining structures and reproduction facilities. Beyond the fourth level we hardly have a beginning of theory, and yet even here system description via computer models may foster progress at these levels in the complex of general systems theory.

Regardless of the degree of progress at any particular level in the above scheme, the important point is the concept of a general systems theory. Clearly, the spectrum, or hierarchy, of systems varies over a considerable range. However, since the systems concept is primarily a point of view and a desirable goal, rather than a particular method or content area, progress can be made as research proceeds in various specialized areas but within a total system context.

With the general theory and its objectives as background, we direct our attention to a more specific theory for business, a systems theory which can serve as a guide for management scientists and ultimately provide the framework for integrated decision making on the part of practicing managers.

SYSTEMS THEORY FOR BUSINESS

The biologist Ludwig von Bertalanffy has emphasized the part of general systems theory which he calls open systems [1]. The basis of his concept is that a living organism is not a conglomeration of separate elements but a definite system, possessing organization and wholeness. An organism is an open system which maintains a constant state while matter and energy which enter it keep changing (so-called dynamic equilibrium). The organism is influenced by, and influences, its environment and reaches a state of dynamic equilibrium in this environment. Such a description

[2] Boulding [2], pp. 202–205.

of a system adequately fits the typical business organization. The business organization is a man-made system which has a dynamic interplay with its environment—customers, competitors, labor organizations, suppliers, government, and many other agencies. Furthermore, the business organization is a system of interrelated parts working in conjunction with each other in order to accomplish a number of goals, both those of the organization and those of individual participants.

A common analogy is the comparison of the organization to the human body, with the skeletal and muscle systems representing the operating line elements and the circulatory system as a necessary staff function. The nervous system is the communication system. The brain symbolizes top-level management, or the executive committee. In this sense an organization is represented as a self-maintaining structure, one which can reproduce. Such an analysis hints at the type of framework which would be useful as a systems theory for business—one which is developed as a system of systems and that can focus attention at the proper points in the organization for rational decision making, both from the standpoint of the individual and the organization.

The scientific-management movement utilized the concept of a man-machine system but concentrated primarily at the shop level. The so-called "efficiency experts" attempted to establish procedures covering the work situation and providing an opportunity for all those involved to benefit—employees, managers, and owners. The human relationists, the movement stemming from the Hawthorne-Western Electric studies, shifted some of the focus away from the man-machine system per se to interrelationships among individuals in the organization. Recognition of the effect of interpersonal relationships, human behavior, and small groups resulted in a relatively widespread reevaluation of managerial approaches and techniques.

The concept of the business enterprise as a social system also has received considerable attention in recent years. The social-system school looks upon management as a system of cultural interrelationships. The concept of a social system draws heavily on sociology and involves recognition of such elements as formal and informal organization within a total integrated system. Moreover, the organization or enterprise is recognized as subject to external pressure from the cultural environment. In effect, the enterprise system is recognized as a part of a larger environmental system.

Since World War II, operations research techniques have been applied to large, complex systems of variables. They have been helpful in shop scheduling, in freightyard operations, cargo handling, airline scheduling, and other similar problems. Queuing models have been developed for a wide variety of traffic-and service-type situations where it is necessary to program the optimum number of "servers" for the expected "customer" flow. Management-science techniques have undertaken the solution of many complex problems involving a large number of variables. However, by their very nature, these techniques must structure the system for analysis by quantifying system elements. This process of abstraction often simplifies the problem and takes it out of the real world. Hence the solution of the problem may not be applicable in the actual situation. Simple models of maximizing behavior no longer suffice in analyzing business organizations. The relatively mechanical models apparent in the "scientific management" era gave way to theories represented by the "human relations" movement. Current emphasis is developing around "decision making" as a primary focus of attention, relating communication systems, organization structure, questions of growth (entropy and/or homeostasis), and questions of uncertainty. This approach recognizes the more complex models of administrative behavior and should lead to more encompassing systems that provide the framework within which to fit the results of specialized investigations of management scientists.

The aim of systems theory for business is to develop an objective, understandable environment for decision making; that is, if the system within which managers make the decisions can be provided as an explicit framework, then such decision making should be easier to handle. But what are the elements of this systems theory which can be used as a framework for integrated decision making? Will it require wholesale change on the part of organization structure and administrative behavior? Or can it be woven into existing situations? In general, the new concepts can be applied to existing situations. Organizations will remain recognizable. Simon makes this point when he says:

> 1. Organizations will still be constructed in three layers; an underlying *system* of physical production and distribution processes, a layer of programmed (and probably largely automated) decision processes for governing the routine day-to-day operation of the physical *system,* and a layer of nonprogrammed decision processes (carried on in a man-machine system) for monitoring the first-level processes, redesigning them, and changing parameter values.
>
> 2. Organizations will still be hierarchical in form. The organization will be divided into major subparts, each of these into parts, and so on, in familiar forms of departmentalization. The exact basis for drawing departmental lines may change somewhat. Product divisions may become even more important then they are today, while the sharp lines of demarcation among purchasing, manufacturing, engineering, and sales are likely to fade.[3]

We agree essentially with this picture of the future. However, we want to emphasize the notion of systems as set forth in several layers.

[3] Simon [4], pp. 49–50. (Italics by authors.)

Thus the systems that are likely to be emphasized in the future will develop from projects or programs, and authority will be vested in managers whose influence will cut across traditional departmental lines. This concept will be developed in more detail throughout this article.

There are certain key subsystems and/or functions essential in every business organization which make up the total information-decision system, and which operate in a dynamic environmental system subject to rapid change. The subsystems include:

1. A *sensor subsystem* designed to measure changes within the system and with the environment.
2. An *information processing subsystem* such as an accounting, or data processing system.
3. A *decision-making subsystem* which receives information inputs and outputs planning messages.
4. A *processing subsystem* which utilizes information, energy, and materials to accomplish certain tasks.
5. A *control component* which ensures that processing is in accordance with planning. Typically this provides feedback control.
6. A *memory or information storage subsystem* which may take the form of records, manuals, procedures, computer programs, etc.

A goal setting unit will establish the long range objectives of the organization, and the performance will be measured in terms of sales, profits, employment, etc., relative to the total environmental system.

This is a general model of the systems concept in a business firm. In the following section a more specific model illustrating the application of the systems concept is established.

AN ILLUSTRATIVE MODEL OF THE SYSTEMS CONCEPT

Traditionally, business firms have not been structured to utilize the systems concept. In adjusting the typical business structure to fit within the framework of management by system, certain organizational changes may be required. It is quite obvious that no one organizational structure can meet operational requirements for every company. Each organization must be designed as a unique system. However, the illustrative model set forth would be generally operable for medium- to large-size companies which have a number of major products and a variety of management functions. The primary purpose of this model is to illustrate the application of systems concepts to business organizations and the possible impact upon the various management functions of planning, organizing, communication and control. The relationships which would exist among the top management positions are shown in Figure 6–1.

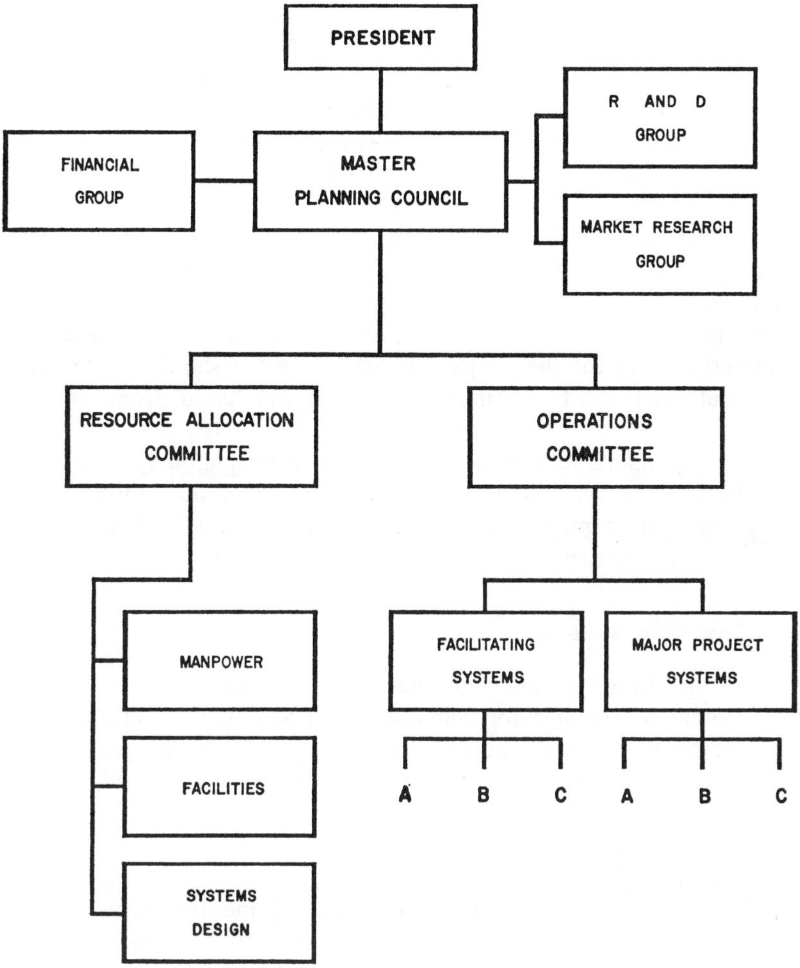

Figure 6–1. The systems model: top management

The master planning council would relate the business to its environmental system, and it would make decisions relative to the products or services the company produced. Further, this council would establish the limits of an operating program, decide on general policy matters relative to the design of operating systems, and select the director for each new project. New project decisions would be made with the assistance and advice of the project research and development, market research, and financial groups. Once the decision was made, the resource allocation committee would provide the facilities and manpower for the new system, and supply technical assistance for systems design. After the system had been designed, its management would report to the operations committee as a major project system, or as a facilitating system.

Facilitating systems would include those organized to produce a service rather than a finished product. Each project system would be designed toward being self-sufficient. However, in many cases this objective may not be feasible or economical. For example, it may not be feasible to include a large automated mill as a component of a major project system, but the organization as a whole, including all of the projects, might support this kind of a facility. A facilitating system, would be designed, therefore, to produce this kind of operating service for the major project systems. The output of the facilitating system would be material input for the project system and a fee should be charged for this input, just as if the input had been purchased from an outside source.

A soap manufacturer could have, for example, major project systems in hand soap, laundry soap, kitchen soap, and tooth paste. A facilitating system might be designed to produce and *sell* containers to the four project systems.

Operating Systems

All operating systems would have one thing in common—they would use a common language for communicating among themselves, and with higher levels of management. In addition, of course, each system designed would be structured in consideration of company-wide policies. Other than these limits, each operating system would be created to meet the specific requirements of its own product or service. A model of an operating system is shown in Figure 6–2.

Figure 6–2 illustrates the relationship of the functions to be performed and the flow of operating information. The operating system is structured to (1) direct its own inputs, (2) control its own operation, and (3) review and revise the design of the system as required. Input is furnished by three different groups: technical information is generated as input into the processing system, and in addition, technical information is the basis for originating processing information. Both technical and processing information are used by the material input system to determine and supply materials for processing. However, corrective action, when necessary, would be activated by input allocation.

This model can be related to most business situations. For example, if this represented a system to produce television sets, the technical information would refer to the design of the product, processing information would include the plan of manufacture and schedule, and the material input would pertain to the raw materials and purchased parts used in the processing. These inputs of information and material would

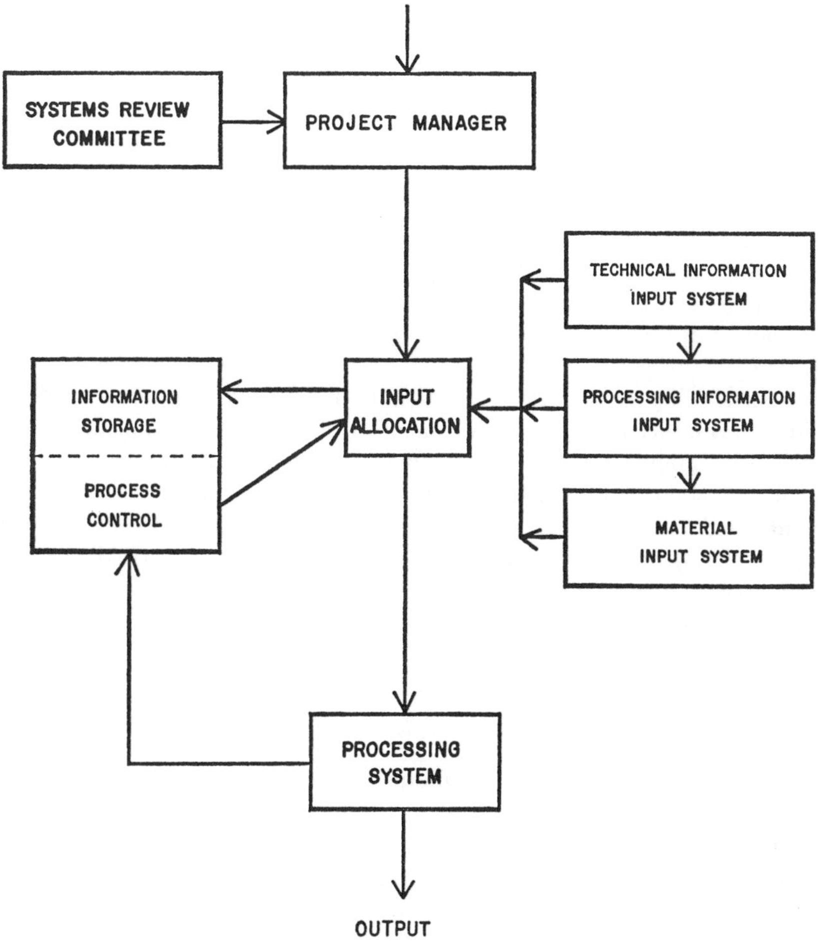

Figure 6–2. An operating system model

be processes and become output. Process control would measure the output in comparison to the standard (Information Storage) obtained from input allocation, and issue corrective information whenever the system failed to function according to plan. The design of the system would be reviewed continually and the components rearranged or replaced when these changes would improve operating efficiency.

Basically, the operating systems would be self sustaining with a high degree of autonomy. Therefore, they could be integrated into the over-all organizational structure (Figure 6–1) with a minimum of difficulty.

SYSTEMS CONCEPTS AND MANAGEMENT

Managers are needed to convert the disorganized resources of men, machines, and money into a useful and effective enterprise. Essentially, management is the process whereby these unrelated resources are integrated into a total *system for objective accomplishment*. A manager gets things done by working with people and physical resources in order to accomplish the objectives of the system. He coordinates and integrates the activities and work of others rather than performing operations himself.

Structuring a business according to the systems concept does not eliminate the need for the basic functions of planning, organization, control, and communication. However, there is a definite change of emphasis, for the functions are performed in conjunction with operation of the system and not as separate entities. In other words, everything revolves around the system and its objective, and the function is carried out only as a service to this end. This point can be clarified by reviewing each of the functions in terms of their relation to the model of the systems concept illustrated previously.

Planning

Planning occurs at three different levels in the illustrative model. These levels are shown in Figure 6–1. First, there is top level planning by the master planning council. Second, the project and facilitating systems must be planned and resources allocated to them. Finally, the operation of each project and facilitating system must be planned.

The master planning council establishes broad policies and goals and makes decisions relative to the products or services the company produces. It decides upon general policy matters concerning the design of the operating systems and selects the director for each new program. It is the planning council which receives informational inputs from the environmental and competitive systems. It combines these inputs with feedback information from the internal organizational system and serves as the key decision-making center within the company. Much of the decision making at this level is non-programmed, unstructured, novel, and consequential. While some of the new techniques of management science may be helpful, major reliance must be placed upon mature assessment of the entire situation by experienced, innovative top executives.

Once these broad decisions have been made, the planning function is transferred to the resource allocation and operating committees. They plan and allocate facilities and manpower for each new system and supply technical assistance for individual systems design. At this planning level it is possible to utilize programmed decision making—operations research and computer techniques.

The third level, planning the operations of each project or facilitation system, is concerned primarily with the optimum allocation of resources to meet the requirements established by the planning council. This planning can most easily be programmed to automatic decision systems. However, the project director would still have to feed important non-quantifiable inputs into the system.

Under the systems concept of planning there is a direct relationship between the planning performed at each of the three levels. The first planning level receives informational inputs from the environment and competitive system and feedback information from within the organization. It translates this into inputs for the next planning level which in turn moves to a more detailed level of planning and provides inputs for the third or project level. One of the major advantages of this systems model is to provide a clear-cut delineation of the responsibility for various types of planning.

This concept facilitates integrated planning on a systems basis at the project level within the organization. Given the inputs (premises, goals, and limitations) from the higher levels the project managers are delegated the function of integrated planning for their project.

Organization

Traditional organization theory emphasized parts and segments of the structure and is concerned with the separation of activities into tasks or operational units. It does not give sufficient emphasis to the interrelationships and integration of activities. Adapting the business organization to the systems concept places emphasis upon the integration of all activities toward the accomplishment of over-all objectives but also recognizes the importance of efficient subsystem performance.

The systems basis of organization differs significantly from traditional organization structures such as line and staff or line, staff, and functional relationships. As shown in Figure 6–1, there are three major organizational levels, each with clearly delineated functions. The master planning council has broad planning, control, and integrative functions; the resource allocation committee has the primary function of allocating manpower and facilities, and aids in systems design for the facilitating or project systems. One of the major purposes of this type organization is to provide an integration of activities at the most important level—that is the individual project or program.

Staff specialization of skills is provided for the master planning council through such groups as financial, research and development, and market research. Their activities, however, are integrated and coordinated by the planning council. There are specialists at the operating level who are completely integrated into each project system. Thus, the activities of these specialists are geared to the effective and efficient performance of the individual project system. This type organization minimizes a major problem associated with staff and functional personnel—their tendency to associate their activities with specialized areas rather than with the optimum performance of the over-all operation. Yet, under the model the importance of initiative and innovation are recognized. In fact, the major function of the master planning council is planning and innovation. Specific provision for receiving information inputs from product and market research are provided in the model.

There are other advantages of the systems concept. Business activity is dynamic, yet the typical organization is structured to perpetuate itself rather than change as required. There is generally resistance by the various specialized functions to change in order to optimize organization performance. For example, Parkinson's Law states that there is an ever increasing trend toward hierarchies of staff and functional personnel who are self-perpetuating and often do not contribute significantly to organizational effectiveness, or in extreme cases may be dysfunctional. In contrast, a system is designed to do a particular task. When the task is completed, the system is disbanded.

Systems are created from a central pool of resources. Facilities, machines, and manpower are assigned to specific projects or programs. The approach is to create and equip the project system with a complete arrangement of components to accomplish the job at hand. This may result in the duplication of certain activities in more than one operating system; however, this disadvantage is not as serious as it may seem. For example, it may be more efficient to have several typewriters assigned to each system rather than a center pool of typewriters. In the first instance, the typewriters may be utilized less than 100 percent of the time, but the problems of scheduling the work at the central pool, delays, accountability, measurement of contribution, etc., would soon offset the advantages of centralizing equipment. Too much effort may be spent in creating processing information which accomplishes no objective other than keeping the machines utilized. A reasonable amount of redundancy or extra capacity will provide more flexibility, protect against breakdowns, reduce flow time, require less planning, eliminate many problems associated with interdepartmental communication, and reduce the amount of material handling.

Obviously, there are situations when it is impractical to decentralize a particular facility, because individual systems cannot utilize it sufficiently to warrant its incorporation into each separate operation. In these instances, a facilitating system would be created which would sell its services to any or all of the major project systems. These service systems would have to justify their existence and compete with outside vendors as suppliers to the major project system.

One of the great advantages of the systems concept for organizing pertains to the decentralization of decision making and the more effective utilization of the allocated resources to the individual project system. This has the merit of achieving accountability for performance through the measurability of individual systems of operation.

Control

The systems concept features control as a means of gaining greater flexibility in operation, and, in addition, as a way of avoiding planning operations when variables are unknown. It is designed to serve the operating system as a subsystem of the larger operation. Its efficiency will be measured by how accurately it can identify variations in systems operation from standard or plan, and how quickly it can report the need for correction to the activating group.

We must conclude that error is inevitable in a system which is subject to variations in input. When the lag in time between input and output is great, more instability is introduced. Feedback can reduce the time lag; however, corrective action which is out of phase will magnify rather than overcome the error. Every system should be designed to make its own corrections when necessary. That is, a means should be provided to reallocate resources as conditions change. In our model the Systems Review Committee (see Figure 6–2) should be aware of any change in operating conditions which might throw the system "out of control." Replanning or redesign may be required.

In controlling a system it is important to measure inputs of information, energy, and materials; and outputs of products and/or services. This will determine operating efficiency. In addition it may be important to establish points of measurement during critical or significant stages of processing. Such measurements would be used principally to help management analyze and evaluate the operation and design of individual components. The best approach is to spotlight exceptions and significant changes. Management can focus their attention on these areas. One important thing to remember is that the control group is not a part of the processing system—it is a subsystem, serving the operating system. Cost control can be used as an example to illustrate this point. The cost accountant must understand that his primary objective is to furnish managers with information to control costs. His task is to inform, appraise, and support; never to limit, censure, or veto. The same principle applies to every control group serving the operating system.

Communication

Communication plays a vital role in the implementation of the systems concept. It is the connecting and integrating link among the systems network. The flow of information, energy, and material—the elements of any processing system—are coordinated via communication systems. As shown in the model (Figure 6–2) the operating system requires information transmission to ensure control. Communication systems should be established to feed back information on the various flows—information, energy, and material. Information on the effectiveness of the planning and scheduling activities (as an example of information flow) would be helpful in adjusting the nature of this activity for the future. Similarly, reports on absenteeism are examples of communication concerning the energy flow (the people in the system) to the processing activity. Information on acceptance inspection is an example of information stemming from the material flow aspect of an operating system. All of these feedback communication systems provide for information flow to a sensor and a control group. Comparison between the information received and the information stored (the master plan for this particular operating system) would result in decisions concerning the transmission of corrective information to the appropriate points.

Relationships within and among various project systems and between the levels of the system as a whole are maintained by means of information flow which also can be visualized as a control device. Moreover, any operating system maintains contact with its environment through some sensory element. Referring to Figure 6–1, the sensory elements in this case are the groups reporting to the master planning council. The master planning council makes decisions, concerning the product or service the organization will produce, based on information gained from market research, research and development, and financial activities. In a sense, these activities function as the antenna of the organization, maintaining communication with the external environment. The master planning council melds the information received through these activities with other premises covering the internal aspects in order to make decisions about future courses of action. Here again, communication or information flow can be visualized as a necessary element in controlling the course of action for the enterprise as a whole. Based on the feedback of information concerning the environment in general, the nature of competition, and the performance of the enterprise itself, the master planning council can continue its current courses of activity or adjust in light of developing circumstances. Thus, communication or information flow facilitates the accomplishment of the primary managerial functions of planning, organizing, and controlling.

Communication by definition is a system involving a sender and a receiver, with implications of feedback control. This concept is embodied in the lowest level projects or subsystems, in all larger systems, and in the system as a whole. Information-decision systems, regardless of formal charts or manuals, often flow across departmental boundaries and are often geared to specific projects or programs. The systems concept focuses on this approach and makes explicit the information-decision system which might be implicit in many of today's organizations.

The systems concept does not eliminate the functions of management, i.e., planning, organizing, control, and communication. Instead, it integrates these functions within a framework designed to emphasize their importance in creating more effective systems. Because of the great diversity of operations and environments, particular missions of organizations differ and each system must be unique or at least have some unique elements. Nevertheless, the illustrative model and its application to the management functions of planning, organizing, controlling, and communication can serve as a point of departure in systems design.

PERVASIVENESS OF SYSTEM CONCEPTS

Many of the most recent developments in the environment of businessmen and managers have involved systems concepts. For example, the trend toward automation involves implementation of these ideas. Automation suggests a self-contained system with inputs, outputs, and a mechanism of control. Yet the concept also recognizes the need to consider the environment within which the automatic system must perform. Thus the automated system is recognized as a subpart of a larger system.

The kinds of automation prevalent today range in a spectrum from sophisticated mechanization to completely automatic, large-scale production processes. Individual machines can be programmed to operate automatically. Large groups of machines also can be programmed to perform a series of operations, with automatic materials-handling devices providing connecting links among components of the system. In such a system, each individual operation could be described as a system and could be related to a larger system covering an entire processing operation. That particular processing operation could also be part of the total enterprise system, which in turn can be visualized as a part of an environmental system.

Completely automated processing systems such as oil refineries are also commonplace today. In such cases the entire process from input of raw material to output of finished products is automated with preprogrammed controls used to adjust the process as necessary, according to information feedback from the operation itself.

The systems concept is also apparent in other aspects of automation. The above examples deal with physical processing; another phase which has been automated is information flow. With the introduction of large-scale, electronic-data-processing equipment, data-processing systems have been developed for many applications. Systems concepts are prevalent, with most applications built around the model of input-processor-output and with feedback control established within the instructions developed to guide the processing of data. Here again, there is an entire spectrum of sophistication leading from simple, straightforward data-reduction problems to elaborate, real-time data-processing systems.

Physical distribution systems have received increasing attention on the part of manufacturers and shippers. The concepts of logistics, or materials management, have been used to emphasize the flow of materials through distribution channels. The term *rhochrematics* has been coined to connote the flow process from raw-material sources to final consumer.[4] In essence, these ideas embrace systems concepts because emphasis is placed on the total system of material flow rather than on functions, departments, or institutions which may be involved in the processing.

In recent years increasing attention has been focused upon massive engineering projects. In particular, military and space programs are becoming increasingly complex, thus indicating the need for integrating various elements of the total system. Manufacturing the product itself (a vehicle or other hardware) is quite complex, often involving problems of producibility with requirements of extremely high reliability. This is difficult to ensure for individual components or subsystems. In addition, each subsystem also must be reliable in its interrelationship with all other subsystems. Successful integration of subcomponents, and hence successful performance of a particular product, must also be integrated with other elements of the total system. For example, the functioning of the Nike-Zeus antimissile missile must be coordinated with the early warning system, ground facilities, and operating personnel. All elements must function as an operating, integrated whole.

The previous discussion has emphasized the mechanistic and structural aspects of the systems concept. Yet, we cannot forget that business organizations are social systems; we are dealing with man-made systems. Obviously, a great deal could be said about the possible consequences of applying systems concepts to human relationships, but such a task is beyond the scope of this article. However, in discussing the impact of the systems concept it should not be assumed that people basically resist systems. Much of man's conscious activities since the dawn of history has been geared to creating system out of chaos. Man does not resist systema-

[4] Rhochrematics comes from two Greek roots; rhoe, which means a flow (as a river or stream), and chrema, which stands for products, materials, or things (including information). The abstract ending -ics has been added, as for any of the sciences.

tization of his behavioral patterns per se. Rather, the normal human being seeks satisfactory systems of interpersonal relationships which guide his activities. Without systematization, behavior would be random, non-goal-oriented, and unpredictable. Certainly, our complex, modern, industrial society demands more systemized human behavior than older, less-structured societies. A common characteristic in a rapidly advancing society is to make systems of interpersonal relationship more formal. While many of these systems have been implicit in the past, they are becoming more explicit. This remains one of the basic precepts of our systems model; systematic interpersonal relationships are necessary for accomplishing group objectives and an effective organizational system should be designed to meet this need.

SUMMARY

General systems theory is concerned with developing a systematic, theoretical framework for describing general relationships of the empirical world. While a spectrum, or hierarchy of systems can be established over a considerable range, the systems concept is also a point of view and a desirable goal, rather than a particular method or content area. Progress can be made as research proceeds in various specialized areas but within a total system context.

The business organization is a man-made system which has a dynamic interplay with its environment—customers, competitors, labor organizations, suppliers, government, and many other agencies. In addition, the business organization is a system of interrelated parts working in conjunction with each other in order to accomplish a number of goals, both those of the organization and those of individual participants. This description parallels that of open systems in general which maintain a constant state while matter and energy which enter them keep changing; that is, the organisms are influenced by, and influence their environment and reach a state of dynamic equilibrium within it. This concept of the organization can be used by practicing managers in order to integrate the various ongoing activities into a meaningful total system. Regardless of specific adjustments or organizational arrangements, there are certain subsystems or essential functions which make up a total information-decision system. However, the exact form utilized by a particular organization may depend upon the task orientation. We have presented a generalized illustrative model which indicates an approach that may be appropriate for a large segment of modern business organizations.

Managers are needed to convert disorganized resources of men, machines, and money into a useful, effective enterprise. Essentially, management is the process whereby these unrelated resources are integrated *into a total system for objective accomplishment.* The systems concept provides no cookbook technique, guaranteed to provide managerial success. The basic functions are still planning, organization, control, and communication. Each of these activities can be carried out with or without emphasis on systems concepts. Our contention is that the activities themselves can be better accomplished in light of systems concepts. Furthermore, there can be a definite change in emphasis for the entire managerial process if the functions are performed in light of the system as a whole and not as separate entities.

The business organization as a system can be considered as a subsystem of a larger environmental system. Even industry or inter-industry systems can be recognized as sub-elements of the economic system, and the economic system can be regarded as a part of society in general. One of the major changes within business organizations of the future may be the breakdown of traditional functional specialization geared to optimizing performance of particular departments. There may be growing use of organizational structures designed around projects and information-decision systems. The systems concept calls for integration, into a separate organizational system, of activities related to particular projects or programs. This approach currently is being implemented in some of the more advanced-technology industries.

The breakdown of business organizations into separate functional areas has been an artificial organizational device, necessary in light of existing conditions. Management-science techniques, computer simulation approaches, and information-decision systems are just a few of the tools which will make it possible for management to visualize the firm as a total system. This would not have been possible two decades ago; it is currently becoming feasible for some companies; and it will become a primary basis for organizing in the future.

REFERENCES

Bertalanffy, L. von, "General System Theory: A New Approach to Unity of Science," *Human Biology,* December 1951, pp. 303–361.

Boulding, K., "General Systems Theory: The Skeleton of Science," *Management Science,* April 1956, pp. 197–208.

Johnson, R. A., Kast, F. E., and Rosenzweig, J. E., *The Theory and Management of Systems,* New York, McGraw-Hill Book Company, 1963.

Simon, H. A., *The New Science of Management Decision,* New York, Harper & Brothers, 1960.

The author outlines the basic elements of systems theory and studies its applications to both organizations and decision-making processes within organizations.

7

SYSTEMS, BOUNDARIES, AND INFORMATION FLOW

Warren B. Brown

THE SYSTEMS CONCEPT

We will first briefly establish some concepts and vocabulary about systems since these will provide us with some tools. Although any definition of a particular system is somewhat unique and arbitrary, various definitions of the general systems concept itself will invariably contain many common elements that can be applied to all types of systems.

Some System Characteristics

Here we use the term system to refer to a group or complex of parts (such as people, machines, etc.) interrelated in their actions towards some goals. Typically it is the interrelationships among these system elements, and between them and their environments, that is of most interest in system design both for human organizations and for purely physical systems. Although these interrelationships often are difficult to describe fully and precisely for human organizations, we nonetheless can anticipate that a systems approach will provide a useful framework for examining organizational phenomena, and allow us to fill in whatever detail we find appropriate.

In our attempts to obtain a good description of how a system oper-

Reprinted from *Academy of Management Journal,* Vol. 9, No. 4, December 1966, pp. 318–327, by permission of the publisher.

ates, we shall use a variety of system characteristics. The first three [1] are rather broad but useful; these are: (a) flows (of information, materials, money, etc.); (b) structure (referring to physical and geographic aspects, organizational design, etc.); and, (c) procedures (the pre-planned activities which affect the flows and structure). Interest here focuses on complex, formal organizations, where the structure and flows in the organization are purposeful and planned, i.e. rational systems as opposed to self-organizing or natural ones. Organizational change and adaptation, of course, are not ruled out.

Another general system characteristic is that of control. This centers on the prevention and correction of deviations in a system's behavior from those standards which are specified at a given time.

Closed and Open Systems

In a self-regulating system, the key element for a control procedure is feedback. This refers to a circularity of the flows among two or more parts of the system structure such that the output of the system (or subsystem) is maintained at a desired level. Typically this procedure involves a constant monitoring of the system output, a comparison of the output values with the standards, evaluation of any discrepancies, and a flow of information concerning the degree of deviation back to the other elements in the system structure so that the procedures may be changed if necessary.

Example of a closed-loop system with feedback:

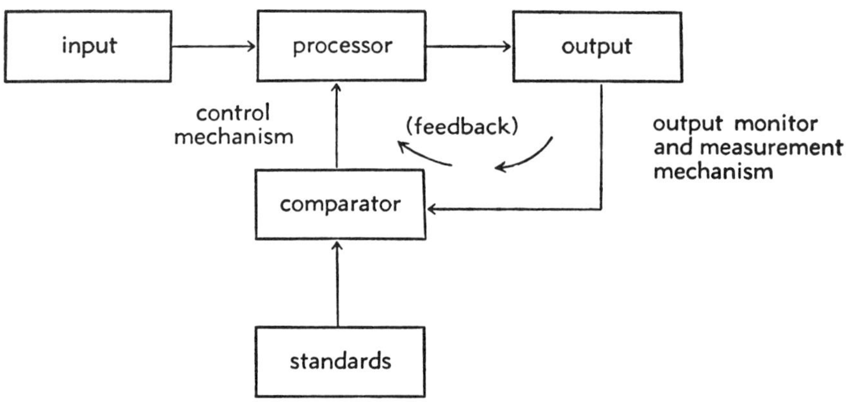

For fully mechanistic systems, with only deterministic elements in the structure and with all control procedures consisting of direct coupling and feedback mechanisms, we can obtain complete automation. Human organizations of course present more variability.

Systems are also characterized as closed or open. A closed system, as

[1] R. C. Hopkins, "A Systematic Approach for System Development," *IRE Trans. on Eng. Mgt.*, EM-8 (June 1961).

indicated in the above sketch, is called information-tight.[2] This means that the information loop is closed, and that the control mechanism has the capability to affect the processor so that the desired output is achieved. Commonly used examples are the Watts governor for the control of engine speeds, and the household thermostat for temperature. We should note that information-tight systems may be open in terms of other flows, such as materials and energy, through the input-output processes.

Open systems do not have the information-tight control units which are characteristic of closed systems. Instead, the relations among the elements of the system, and between the system and its environment are often unknown, and the precise causes of system changes may be a mystery. Examples are an individual's behavior, a nation's economy, and a rocket system where there is no further control once the rocket has been fired.

However, even where one does not have complete knowledge or control of the internal workings of a system, it often still is possible to make many inferences about the interrelationships of the system elements. The technique used is called the "Black Box" approach,[3] wherein the system analyst tries to deduce the nature of the internal workings by manipulating the inputs to the system and observing the consequent outputs. For large, complex systems this approach obviously presents many practical difficulties.

Example of an open system:

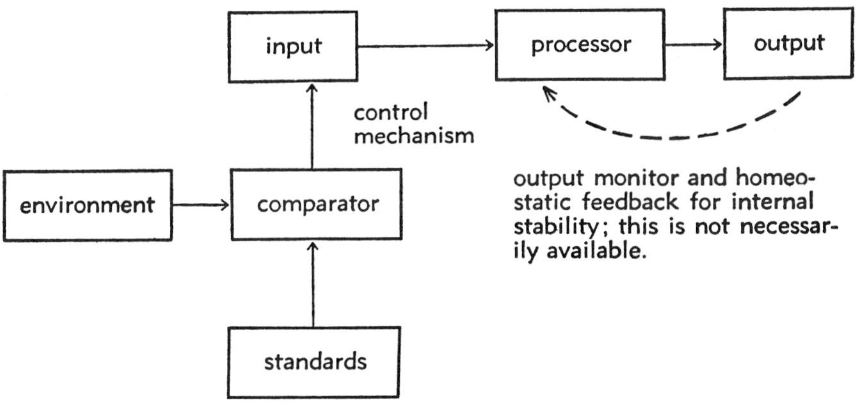

Our interest focuses on human systems that are open to their environments. Such systems are capable of bringing in resources by which they can modify their own internal flows, structures, and procedures.

This behavior prevents the entropic process which is well known in

[2] W. R. Ashby, "General Systems Theory as a New Discipline" in *General Systems Yearbook,* Vol. 3 (1958).

[3] For a good discussion of this concept see S. Beer, *Cybernetics and Management* (New York: John Wiley & Sons, 1959), Ch. 6.

physical and biological systems: if there are no counteracting forces, entropy (a measure of the unavailable energy in a system) increases toward a maximum, and the system elements become more randomized and less differentiated.[4] The result of the entropic process is that the system runs down and achieves an equilibrium at the most probable distribution of the elements.

Open systems counteract this phenomenon by obtaining from their environments more energy and resources than they expend in their operations. They can store resources for possible future crises, and otherwise utilize these additional resources for deliberate system changes, such as adaptation and growth, which are in accord with the system goals.

Open systems also have the characteristic of striving to maintain a dynamic balance (homeostasis).[5] As the environment changes, an open system will receive signals to this effect, and then try to adapt itself to the change in keeping with its character and goals. We note that over time this is a dynamic balance, rather than a static one.

ORGANIZATIONAL BOUNDARIES

Once we have described a system, we necessarily have separated those elements belonging to the system from other elements in its environment. However, the separation is rarely absolute, i.e. some of the elements in the system typically will interact with the system environment. For human organizations the amount of interaction can be thought of in terms of the permeability of the organization's boundaries. This refers to the flow of both people and information across the boundary; these two factors may be interrelated or separate. The degree and kind of permeability will affect the adaptation of the organization to its environment.

Permeability of Boundaries

Some organization boundaries are easily penetrated,[6] for example those of voluntary civic organizations and political groups. With these rather extreme boundary conditions, persons can enter or leave such organizations largely at their own will, and consequently boundary control of membership is minimal. The other extreme occurs when a person has no choice about his membership in an organization, for example when a citizen is drafted by a society into its army. Business firms tend to lie between these extremes, with an individual's hiring and firing often occurring in a semi-voluntary manner due to practical complications like union restrictions, seniority rights, and so on.

[4] D. Katz and R. L. Kahn, *The Social Psychology of Organizations* (New York: John Wiley & Sons, 1966), p. 21.

[5] Katz and Kahn, *op. cit.*, pp. 23–4.

[6] Katz and Kahn, *op. cit.*, pp. 59–62, 122–124.

Since people and information coming into an organization will bring knowledge and values from the external environment, the relative permeability of an organization's boundaries affects the degree to which the organization's members are exposed to such influences. If the boundaries effect a tight screening of both information and individuals so that only those people and pieces of information which reinforce the current internal values are allowed in, then the organization may facilitate internal agreement among its members. However, at the same time it may lose its position in its environment, such as when a firm gets into a rut with its technology and product line. An alert management often can select the degree of boundary permeability which seems to best fit the needs of the organization.

Impact of Environmental Factors

As an aid in understanding the impact of environmental factors on behavior in organizations, Dill [7] has argued that the environment can be conceptualized as the flow of information which crosses the organizational boundaries. This study illustrated how differences in autonomy exercised by various high-level management groups resulted from the different environments that they faced. One interesting factor concerned the reception points for information crossing the boundary. Those who had relatively exclusive access to pertinent inputs were better able to manipulate the information flow to their peers or other organization members, thus gaining a measure of internal control. Such a position can further be used to avoid unsolicited advice which otherwise could be pressed in an informal manner to affect their decisions.

While the focus in Dill's study was on rather high-level decision makers, the activities of many other organization members of course may also involve the crossing of organizational boundaries. For example, persons concerned with the sales and purchasing functions in business firms routinely will deal with outsiders.

Three Levels of Decision-Making

However, before we examine another organizational level in this regard, we will first distinguish among three traditional levels of decision-making in organizations: [8,9] (a) the institutional level for strategic planning, i.e. those concerned with general company objectives and the broad

[7] W. R. Dill, "Environment as an Influence on Managerial Autonomy," *Administrative Science Quarterly* (March 1958); reprinted in *Comparative Studies in Administration,* ed. J. D. Thompson *et al.* (Pittsburgh: University of Pittsburgh Press, 1959).

[8] T. Parsons, *Structure and Process in Modern Societies* (New York: Free Press, 1960).

[9] R. N. Anthony, *Planning and Control Systems* (Boston: Division of Research, Harvard Business School, 1965).

problems of the position of the organization in its environment; (b) the managerial level which focuses on the gathering, coordinating, and allocating of resources for the organization, e.g. planning budgets, formulating personnel practices, and deciding on routine capital expenditures; and, (c) the technical level, involving the acquisition and utilization of technical knowledge for operational controls, e.g. production scheduling, inventory controls, and decisions concerning the measurement of workers' efficiency. Although some descriptions regarding the levels of decision-making are more restrictive, here we will argue that all three basic levels involve boundary-spanning activities.

In a descriptive study of purchasing agents, Strauss [10] found that they too were concerned with controlling information flows across organizational boundaries in order to enhance their influence. He found that many of their tactics involved influence based on information exchanges, though of course other techniques also were used, such as an imaginative interpretation of the rules, and the involvement of allies both within and outside the organizational boundaries to bolster their positions.

In a broader analysis, Thompson [11] has examined face-to-face interactions across organizational boundaries and set them into four types of transaction structures, involving two dichotomized dimensions: (a) the specificity of organizational control over members; and, (b) the degree of non-member discretion.

The first of these dimensions is of particular interest; it refers to the degree to which the behavior of an organization member at the boundary is pre-set by standard operating procedures. At one extreme the member performs highly routine (or programmed) activities, while at the other end of this dimension a member's activities are guided only by general guidelines or heuristics. The programmed positions involve routine flows of information, e.g. data concerning current deliveries of raw materials, while the non-programmed activities often involve special information searches. Within a business organization the less programmed activities generally are associated with higher positions in the authority hierarchy, i.e. with those who set corporate policies and long-range strategies, though this is not always true.

INFORMATION FLOWS

The manner in which an organization determines the kind and amount of information allowed to cross its boundaries can be thought of as a coding

[10] G. Strauss, "Tactics of Lateral Relationship: The Purchasing Agent," *Administrative Science Quarterly* (September 1962).

[11] J. D. Thompson, "Organizations and Output Transactions," *American Journal of Sociology*, No. 3 (November 1962).

process. This process refers to both mechanical and human transmission of information, and it reflects the norms, values, and subculture of the organization. Those persons who have accepted membership in an organization presumably accept the coding process—indeed they are part of it—and consequently they will perceive and interpret various pieces of information differently from non-members. While many factors affect one's perceptions,[12] we simply note that a coding process can (and often does) lead to distortions, elaborations, and other transformations of the information. Further, such effects occur not only when the information crosses an organization's boundaries, but also when it is passed among various members with differing organizational roles.

Adjustment Processes for Overload

It is not only the coding process that can lead to problems in information transmission across organization boundaries, but also the adjustment processes that an organization can evoke when its information system is overloaded. This condition occurs when a system which is rationally designed to operate effectively under certain fairly constant conditions suddenly is hit by changes in its inputs. Such unanticipated changes tend to overload one or more parts of the total system.

Organizational responses to such overload conditions are quite varied. Miller [13] has classified them into seven categories: (1) omission, simply not processing the information; (2) error, processing information correctly and not making necessary adjustments; (3) queuing, delaying responses during peak demand periods and catching up during lulls; (4) filtering, systematic omission of certain categories of information according to some priority scheme; (5) approximation, less accurate responses because there is no time to be precise; (6) multiple channels, using parallel transmission subsystems that can do comparable tasks at the same time as in the special case of decentralization; and, (7) escape, leaving a situation entirely or effectively cutting off the flow of information.

A similar listing of adjustment processes has been noted by Meier,[14] based on his study of an undergraduate university library during a period when there was an increasing demand for books. Briefly, his listing includes: queuing; priorities in queues; destruction of low priority inputs (filtering); omission; reduction of processing standards (approximation); decentralization; formation of independent organizations near the periphery (multiple channels); mobile reserves (multiple channels); rethinking

[12] S. S. Zalkind and T. W. Costello, "Perception: Some Recent Research and Implication for Administration," *Administrative Science Quarterly* (September 1962).

[13] J. G. Miller, "Information Input, Overload, and Psychopathology," *American Journal of Psychiatry* (116), 695–704. Cited in Katz and Kahn, *op. cit.*, p. 231.

[14] R. L. Meier, "Information Input Overload: Features of Growth in Communications—Oriented Institutions," *Libri*, Vol. 13, No. 1, pp. 1–44.

procedures; redefining the boundaries of the system, e.g. instituting customer self-service; escape; retreat to formal, ritualistic behavior; and lastly, the possibility of dissolving the larger system with salvage of its assets into several new, smaller units.

As science and technology constantly change the environments of many organizations, this problem of information overloads and changing inputs will probably become more common. However, we must note that in the lists above, the responses vary considerably in long-range usefulness. Some, (e.g. the error response), are simply very temporary and often costly adaptations. Other responses, such as decentralization, may involve the deliberate restructuring of the organization on a long-range basis. Similarly, queuing and filtering can become a deliberate feature of the organizational coding process which can be routinely evoked whenever an overload condition seems imminent.

Choice of Appropriate Response

The particular selection of one or more of these responses depends at least in part on the perceived costs to the organization. The costs will involve factors such as the availability of necessary or desirable resources; time constraints; survival threats; and the like. These costs will be weighed against the amount of resources stored or readily available (the negative entropy in the system). Then the rational organization will strive for a response suitable to the organization's objectives, and which also maintains its dynamic balance.

A dynamic system also must have mechanisms for obtaining from the environment the various kinds of information it needs to maintain both its internal operations and its position of dynamic balance within its environment. Commenting on organization controls, Roberts [15] has stated, "The boundaries of a management control system design study must not be drawn to conform with organizational structure merely because of that structure. System boundaries cannot ignore vital feedback channels of information and action if the system is to be effective." Consequently, in terms of our earlier comments, the organization's boundaries deliberately must be made permeable to facilitate the flow of a variety of information into the organization.

Levels and Kinds of Information

Although there are several ways of classifying information needed by organizations,[16] we use here a scheme of separating the information

[15] E. B. Roberts, "Industrial Dynamics and the Design of Management Control Systems," *Management Controls,* ed. Bonini, Jaedicki, and Wagner (New York: McGraw-Hill, 1964), p. 124.

[16] For example, see D. R. Daniel, "Management Information Crisis," *Harvard Business Review* (September–October 1961).

according to the level of decision-making for which it is needed, i.e. strategic, managerial, and technical.

Strategic information refers to such knowledge as environmental trends concerning political, economic and social factors, and the impact of the organization on its environment. Managerial information is typically used to focus on an evaluation of the organization's activities, assessing the effectiveness of the institution's past performance, and programs against other similar—possibly competing—organizations. Technical or operational information is primarily obtained for use with organizational control functions, and consequently it becomes the critical feedback needed for small closed-loop sub-systems within the total organization. If this activity is highly programmed, then there may be little new information flow across the organization boundary. However, even seemingly specific functions at the organization's boundary can be greatly modified by the role occupants, thus stimulating additional information flow as we noted earlier in the example of the purchasing function.

Related Intelligence Mechanisms

The need for these three basic kinds of information necessitates a corresponding need for three intelligence structures whereby an organization can regularly search its environment for new information. Each intelligence structure must also provide an appropriate coding procedure, since most information channels are not multi-purpose. For example, an information channel constructed to handle technical data will not be useful for transmitting information about new companies entering a firm's traditional markets, or community relations, or about new tax laws affecting business which are proposed in the state legislature.

We shall call these three types of intelligence mechanisms filters, screens, and sieves. In general, the filters are to provide the technical information from the environment, the screens will bring in managerial level information, and the sieves should provide information for the strategy or policy-making level. We must note in passing that although such information nets can be made virtually identical with an organization's authority structure, for most complex organizations specialized structures are evolved for both the authority and information flows.[17]

Each of these intelligence mechanisms must be allocated enough organizational resources to carry out its own function. If the intelligence function is assigned as a secondary mission to a sub-part of the organization, it is not surprising if much relevant information never gets into the appropriate channel. For example, if a market research group is assigned

[17] H. Guetzkow, "Communications in Organizations," *Handbook of Organizations*, ed. J. G. March (Chicago: Rand McNally, 1965).

the additional responsibility of giving to management an over-all evaluation of the firm's environment, it is not likely to provide an adequate substitute for the sieve function mentioned above. Such a group may well generate a thorough evaluation of consumer reactions to the firm's current products, but it probably will not have the resources or expertise to evaluate such things as the impact of new technical developments upon the organization's formal and informal structures.

Proposed Information Agency

In addition to the three kinds of intelligence mechanisms, we propose the creation of an information agency which would formally be placed in the information flow pattern. This group, providing a kind of clearing house for information flows, would have representatives from all major divisions of the organization. It would have as its primary responsibility the integration, evaluation, and comparison of the various kinds of information coming into the organization.

In discharging this responsibility, the agency will have its main impact in its recommendations to the policy level of the firm, though it would not be restricted to communications at that level. In fact, it is important that it have access to all three basic levels of information flow and decision-making if it is to carry out its mission effectively. While processing the selected parts of the total information inputs, this agency also can provide an anti-bias function by making adjustments in its evaluations based on the perceived distortions existing at the various levels in the coding processes.

Further, such an information agency would aid in providing standards concerning the operations of the filter, screen, and sieve functions, e.g. stating the desired specificity of an individual's behavior when it involves boundary-spanning activities. When overload problems occur, the type of action taken by the organization would also be determined by this group. In addition, this agency would be intimately concerned with the kinds of information that the intelligence mechanisms are generating; if some types of information for evaluations appear to be lacking, this agency could suggest an appropriate change in the search and coding processes for that level. Conceivably it could have the formal authority to enforce such changes, though basically it serves in an advisory capacity.

In the power structure of the organization we suggest that this group be placed between the policy and managerial levels. It is not meant to replace decision-making at these levels by the regular persons involved, but to aid their efforts and thus provide a vital link for an open, human system in its efforts to maintain a dynamic balance vis-à-vis its environment.

Some selected aspects of information flows:

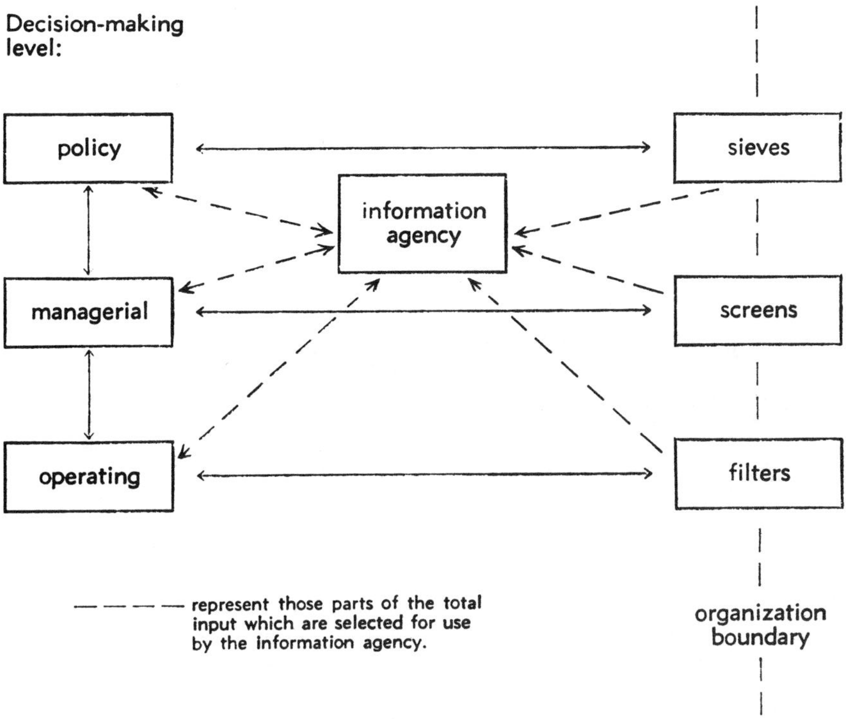

CLOSING COMMENT

This discussion was designed to indicate the usefulness of a systems framework as an aid in analyzing at least some types of organizational problems. Specifically, we focussed on problems related to the flow of information across organizational boundaries, where the boundaries involve both human and physical variables that buffer the organization's interaction with its environment. After noting several types of problems we evolved a general, three-level scheme for bringing various kinds of information into the organization, based on a classification of decision-making within the firm. In addition, we proposed an internal information agency, and explained its functions.

As a final note we want to add that for specific companies and specific formats of information flow, there are good possibilities of using a computer to simulate these organizational properties. In this manner a company could test out in advance the impact of proposed changes in its information channels, as well as testing the efficiency of any particular pattern over a range of possible demands on the system.

The author, in giving five steps to be followed in systems analysis and development for a business enterprise, stresses the importance of developing systems within the framework of overall corporate objectives and policies.

8

ANALYZING AN OVERALL SYSTEM

Charles J. Berg, Jr.

The most powerful computers and the most advanced analytical techniques can cost money instead of saving it if they are not properly applied in a basically sound overall system. This presentation will concern itself with the assistance the systems function renders to line management in improving systems and methods, and in the application of new techniques to the solution of business problems.

In this presentation you will hear the terms "business systems," "integrated system," and "integrated data processing." Perhaps you are not completely sure of the definition of these terms. It would be surprising, indeed, even if you felt sure you knew the definitions that you would agree on them. The trouble is that these terms mean different things to different people, a situation that illustrates a common difficulty in communication among people on any subject.

So, since systems education, training and communication are all basic responsibilities of the systems function, let's start with a few definitions and illustrations so that we can communicate better with each other.

First, what is a business system?

A business system is a set of policies, rules, and procedures which defines the actions, responsibilities, and authorities of all elements of a business organization in the day-by-day conduct of its normal activities.

Reprinted from *Systems and Procedures Journal,* November–December 1963, pp. 38–41, by permission of the author and the publisher.

A business system has as its objective the coordination of actions involving people, equipment, time and money. Its input is information in the form of customer orders, sales forecasts, planning and control data and the like. Its product should be *sound operations,* and the specifications of a good business system are that it:

1. Improves decision making
2. Increases management effectiveness
3. Improves productivity
4. Eliminates all non-essentials
5. Reduces cost
6. Provides for sound planning

A *sound* business system is one which: establishes the objectives, clarifies the understanding, and specifies the responsibilities of all participants; delineates actions, simplifies decisions, and provides management with standards of performance to be used in evaluating productivity. These factors must be present for it to qualify as *sound.*

Why should we be concerned about this? Well, if we look at what has been happening in business, we find that in many companies growth has been very great over a relatively short period of time. Many more products are now produced, volume of billings has greatly increased, number of employees has increased substantially; facilities have expanded widely to cover the country coast to coast, and competition and government regulations have increased materially. With this growth has emerged an ever-increasing growth of the data required to manage operations properly and to satisfy the ever-increasing demand for information and reports.

To illustrate some of the business data we now are required to process, think of market data, sales analyses, personnel information, expense breakdowns, capacity and loading data, material status, cost analyses, money availability and many more types of information considered necessary to properly perform all functions. All of these actually detract from the speed and economy with which we must do business; each is creating more and more paperwork.

All of our past efforts such as supervisory work simplification, methods analysis and standards, and mechanization, have enabled us to just hold the line on managed costs (other than direct labor and fixed costs). But there has been no significant breakthrough in these costs, and today we find ourselves facing higher managed costs and increased customer demands for services, information, shorter delivery dates and reduced prices.

We must attune our thinking to the needs of the new decade. And we should be looking for ways of achieving accurate control data, fast information flow, economical data processing and increased productivity of employees. This brings us to the concept of an *integrated system* and the term *integrated data processing.*

Our attention in the past has been directed toward systems improvement on a *functional perfection* basis. We in systems are not opposed to functional perfection, if it can be achieved, but what is really needed is a *breakthrough* in data processing and hence in managed costs. The key word for systems improvement in the future must be *integration*—with emphasis on integrating the activities of all functions and operations concerned with the processing data.

Our integrated data system must be based on a total system analysis in which we analyze the input into the system and use it most efficiently to yield the maximum output. Reprocessing of the same data in every department must be avoided. The objective is to deliver a finished product to those departments in the form of reports and summaries, ready for *evaluation, decision,* and *action.* It is important to emphasize that in a good system study, consideration is given to every means of processing the data, starting with integrated data processing through manual methods and advancing to justification and use of electronic equipment. Integrated data processing *does not* necessarily imply the use of computers.

To illustrate in oversimplified fashion one of the management tools for an integrated systems concept at the plant operating level, see the exhibits on the next three pages.

The point we wish to make here is that the large masses of input and output data required to run today's businesses represent an area of large potential improvement. This sample system advocates a series utilization of the information so that it is not reused or "messaged" unnecessarily.

As mentioned earlier, this is an oversimplified example and pertains only to the finished goods inventory type of business; however, our advocations are that similar concepts be applied to all types of products and all types of manufacture. It should be mentioned that while this type of approach is adaptable and compatible with computerization, this is not a system requirement; that is, the system can be operated using manual means if this is the most economical thing to do.

The principal use of this example is to devise a long range plan for effectively controlling the business. The purpose of this plan is to give us an objective which will reduce managed costs and improve profitability. It also gives us a step-by-step program for our day-to-day actions which ultimately will achieve the plan which we have devised for ourselves. Once the direction and specific objectives are established, there are other techniques which can be used to implement the program.

We generally advocate a five-step analytical technique for defining our present position and for use as a systems reference point. Step One is the use of the conventional flow chart of the existing system, with

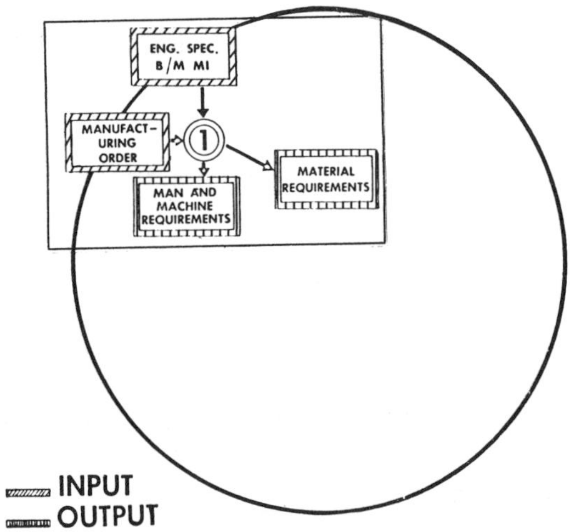

One: If you have a manufacturing order and this is combined with an engineering specification, bills of material and manufacturing information, these can be combined and materials information, manpower and the facilities required can be determined.

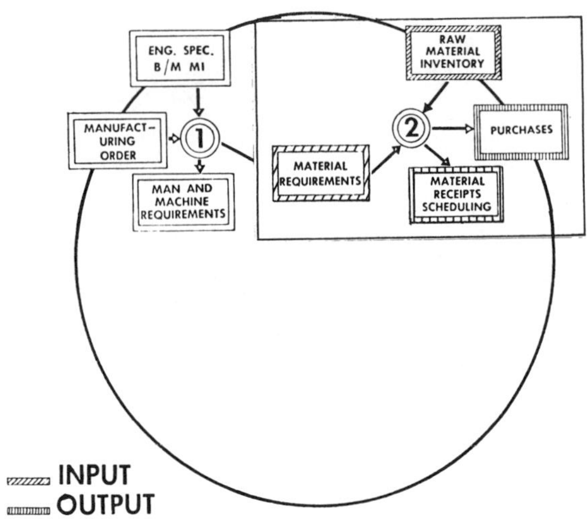

Two: With material requirements being compared to raw material inventories, purchases and material receipts schedules can be derived.

each step analyzed and measured showing the amount of time, money and physical distance required in each processing component. It is not unusual to find at this stage that unnecessary transportation, time and money are incorporated into the system. Step Two relies on the information previously produced, but it is a modified form of the same

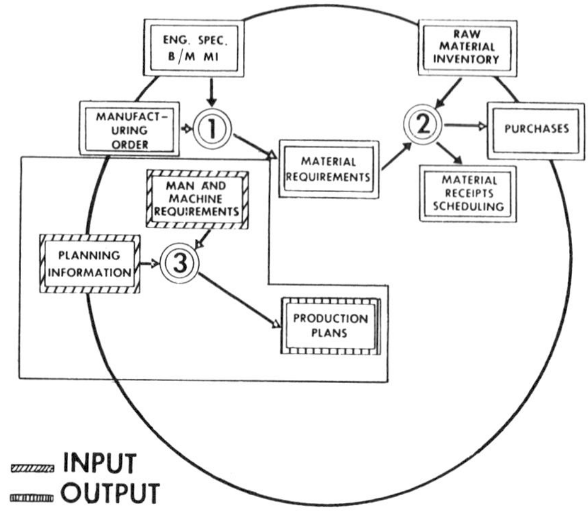

Three: Returning now to the manpower and facilities requirements, combining and comparing this with planning information, we can evolve specific production plans.

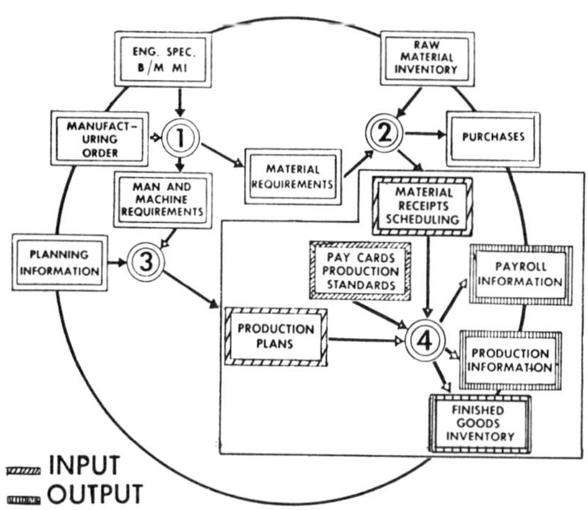

Four: Material receipts schedules and pay cards, along with production standards and the production plans, can be integrated to produce payrolls, production data and finished goods inventory.

information. This is the input-output analysis chart. This technique clearly depicts the multitudinous uses of various data. Generally it can be stated that where many inputs are used to devise many outputs, potential systems improvements are of a high order. Step Three is to relate the present system as described in steps one and two above into financial terminology.

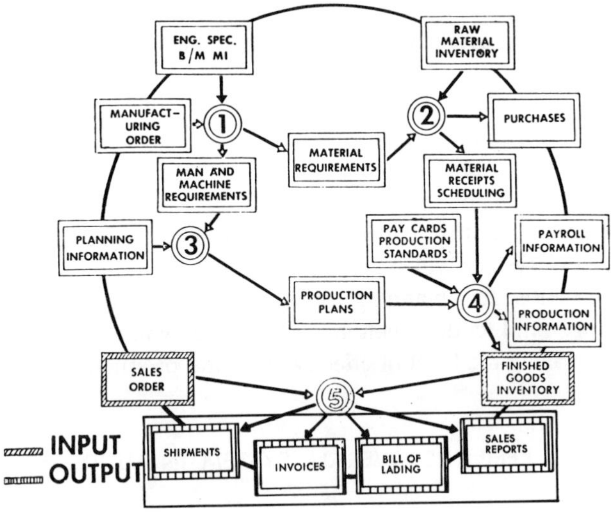

Five: Coordinating the information of a sales order with that of the finished goods inventory, we can produce shipments, invoices, bills of lading and sales receipts.

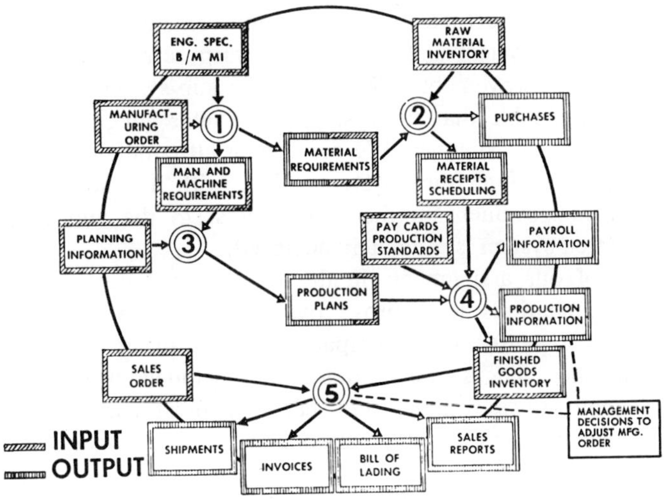

Six: Finally, we can build management decisions into the system which are necessary to operate it most effectively.

What lines on the statement are affected and what are the potential improvements available? Step Four is the allocation of people responsibility for the planned systems improvement, along with specific financial objectives to be attained. Step Five is to accomplish the improvements resulting from the analysis of the above information.

The output of the system is information in the form required by the various functional departments for immediate action without further processing.

This total system has been a build-up of many clerical operations. To attain the maximum effectiveness and economy, each operation must integrate with the others and be well-planned, measured and continuously controlled and evaluated.

What effect will this concept have on the technique of managing? Such a business system will result in optimum utilization of skills, freeing management skills for planning purposes, sales and engineering skills for producing. And under such a system, we would expect to be continuously improving the level of effectiveness and productivity.

KEEP THE OVERALL SYSTEM IN MIND

This brings us to a discussion of a basic systems policy: *In each company, program and achieve current and long range improvement objectives in the systems function.*

In all our work with companies, our fundamental approach is first to help them appraise the overall system as an entity, even though we may be directly concerned with the improvement of a specific and limited part of the system at the time. The purpose of this approach is to assure that the improvements effected in the sub-system we are directly working on will enable that sub-system to be later integrated with others in a logical, workable manner. We are urging all companies to develop a master, long-range, integrated systems plan, with a schedule of accomplishment of improvement in the sub-systems, to the end that a completely integrated system is ultimately achieved.

Typical of our assignments in this work is a recent project to develop recommendations to improve overall marketing effectiveness and reduce related expenses in a company manufacturing refrigerators and washing machines. The scope of this study included all phases of marketing this company's product and parts. Typical survey areas were: analysis of the business system components of the primary accounts in the sales, order service and warehousing budgets; analysis of marketing reports from the viewpoint of providing management with required information at optimum speed; analysis of the information transmission system between the manufacturing, warehousing and sales locations of the company; and analysis of the existing order and distribution systems including the feasibility of expanding the use of mechanical, electronic data processing and communications equipment. This assignment was a cooperative effort of a five-man consulting team, two from our company and three from the client's systems department. Throughout the study, the feasibility of the sub-system from the standpoint of its ultimate integration into a master system for the entire company was given major consideration.

TRAINING AND DEVELOPING SYSTEMS PERSONNEL

And now let's discuss two more policies, also related to long-range improvement of the systems function in each company. *Have management personnel with ability and experience. Continually improve the caliber of systems personnel through recruitment, training, development and advancement.*

This portion of the presentation will concern itself with the functions of recruitment and educational assistance to client companies' systems personnel.

Also, we will try to answer the question, "How can companies take advantage of these concepts and the services available to them from the consultant?

With the growing importance and expanding horizons of the electronic data processing, office systems and methods, and other forms of business analysis, it becomes increasingly important that you concern yourselves with the future progress of men qualified to move into more complex work in the business systems field. This requires not only that you have a long-range plan for training and development of systems personnel, but that you have the means for recognizing exceptional ability where it exists.

In personnel selection, your sights must be clear on the need for men with analytical, creative, and sales abilities as well as a high potential for advancement.

Stress must be placed on planned training and development, and continuous evaluation and follow-up to insure progress and guarantee a contribution to the reduction and control of managed cost.

GUIDANCE IS AVAILABLE

Training embraces formal training in equipment and techniques, offered periodically by computer manufacturers and by various management and technical societies and associations, suggested courses of self study at universities, suggested reading lists, rotational training of men from company divisions to headquarters and vice-versa, and regular staff and regional meetings.

If a company is to move ahead in this work, considerable attention must be directed toward developing promising young men for the large job before us.

Guidance is available from the consultant in the form of services to companies in problems involving application of techniques or equipment. Also, we undertake periodic dissemination of information of value to all systems personnel. Finally, direct service is available in application of these concepts and techniques to those smaller businesses that cannot justify having their own systems personnel.

The author presents the basic concepts and requirements for successfully establishing a management information and control system in a business enterprise.

9

HOW TO INSTALL A MANAGEMENT INFORMATION AND CONTROL SYSTEM

Joseph I. Barnett

The decision to establish a formal management information and control system (MICS) becomes almost inevitable in today's business climate. The accelerating needs for uniform, concise and timely information by all levels of management dictate the establishment of such a system. The results can be better control of and greater profitability from the enterprise.

Essentially, the functioning of a MICS involves transmission of all pertinent data necessary to the conduct of a business to one or more management information centers, where it is maintained and then disseminated in discrete form to all levels of management.

This description provides no reference to computers or any other specific type of data processing equipment. This is to emphasize that possession of data processing equipment is not a prerequisite for a MICS. Computers, punched card equipment, data collection and transmission equipment, etc., are excellent tools that can, if costs and volume warrant, be extremely useful in a MICS program.

Reluctance of many managements to undertake a MICS program can be traced to the confusion and lack of understanding surrounding the subject of information systems, and how they can be effectively in-

Reprinted from *Systems and Procedures Journal,* September–October 1966, pp. 10–14, by permission of the author and the publisher.

stalled. Contributing to this confusion are accounts, such as those below, that relate the experience of others who have undertaken such a program.

1. Associates in other companies either praising or condemning the results of similar programs undertaken by their companies. This contradiction becomes more confusing when the reasons given for success or failure differ from person to person.
2. Internal line and staff management personnel stating the absolute necessity for, or violent objection to, such an undertaking with each endorsement or objection supported with valid proof.
3. Presentations by experts in the information processing field pointing out the simplicity or extreme complexity of such an undertaking.
4. The sudden appearance of excessive costs, during or following installation, that were not considered at the time of the original estimates.
5. Underlying fear of personnel that installation of a MICS will uncover weak spots in the organization that could lead to changes affecting them.

In order to dispel this confusion and lack of understanding surrounding MICS, this article presents in clear and specific terms the basic concepts and requirements for undertaking and achieving success for such a program. The specifics of running committees, designing systems, writing procedures, etc., are left to the specialists assigned these tasks, who hopefully are adept at their particular skills.

WHY UNDERTAKE MICS?

Management is continuously faced with the frustrations of receiving inadequate, incorrect or untimely information. As a result the validity of management decisions and actions based on this type of information is at times questionable. Timely, adequate and correct information—the means through which management can effectively monitor, control, and plan—is becoming increasingly elusive as businesses grow in size and complexity.

Progressive companies recognizing this situation are at various stages of development and installation of MICS. In many cases the management of these companies, although disillusioned at times with the progress, costs and results achieved, still continues on the path toward MICS. The reasons for this continued determination on the part of management to pursue MICS can be found in its desire to achieve a stage in information storage, use and handling that will achieve:

Uniformity of Information—with a single source generating the required information.

Reliability of Information—resulting from adequate controls established and constantly monitored on all input and output of the system.

On Time Response—communication of established information needs as often and as quickly as desired.

As these items are achieved the benefits resulting from an MICS become evident: the potential for achievement of substantial reductions in operating costs, information that management can refer to quickly and simply to assist in its decision process, and a smoother more efficient organization that can supply the information when needed. With these benefits available, management can realize such basic contributions to cost reduction and higher profits as improved sales forecasting and production control, increased inventory turnover rate, increased productivity of all facilities, etc. The realization and extent of any savings is completely dependent upon management's ability to understand and effectively utilize the information generated by the system.

An additional cost savings aspect of installing MICS is achieved through the elimination, modification and/or combination of systems and procedures previously used by the organization. These more immediate savings can be impressive, but not nearly as much as the potential long range savings that can be achieved once the system is installed. Management should also realize that both short and long range savings can start being attained without waiting for the installation of the entire system.

Following is a representative listing of the type of information that can be made available to management from a well designed and installed MICS. The ability of the system to produce this type of information on time and in a usable form depends on the means employed to design and install the system.

- Sales status by product, territory, salesman, etc., with variances.
- Cash position.
- Inventory position in units and/or dollars—comparison to budgeted.
- Inventory items not meeting minimum turnover rate for an established period.
- Profit position—by profit centers for an established period.
- Production status—by product, plant, etc., including orders not on time and reasons for variances.
- Projection of inventory and sales position using a simulation model.
- Budget variances of expenses, capital expenditures, projects, etc., by budget centers.
- Personnel skills inventory of all company employees.

PREREQUISITES TO UNDERTAKING MICS

Once management has agreed to consider MICS, but prior to the commitment of any company facilities, it is necessary to review certain aspects of the organization to make sure that MICS will be built on a firm base. This base is composed of the prerequisites described below. These prerequisites are all related to people—the key factor in the design, installation and continued growth and success of MICS. Until management feels that these items are in place, or can readily be achieved, it would be best to delay the start of company involvement in MICS.

1. Adequate corporate discipline so that common inter-functional procedures can be implemented.

2. Documentation of potential savings anticipated from installation of MICS. This documentation must include reasonable supporting data to substantiate the savings, and to justify the investment of company facilities for such an undertaking.

3. A relatively stable management, especially at the policy-making level. A company undergoing continual reorganization at this level does not have an environment conducive to effective systems design and installation of this nature. Paradoxically, an MICS, if properly designed, will help stabilize an organization as a result of the well defined responsibilities and controls required for such a system.

4. Management that is willing to commit its own time and interest to understand the various plans, techniques and equipment associated with the proposed system. This understanding should be in sufficient detail to enable intelligent monitoring of the costs and progress of the system.

5. The willingness of management to start acquiring and training a core of experienced systems personnel. This core can range in size from one man in a small company to a full staff of 20 or more in a major corporation.

6. The presence within the organization of operational personnel who are knowledgeable in depth concerning the information requirements, methods, procedures and techniques within the functions they are associated with. These personnel will play a major role in the design and implementation of such a system. Management must be willing to relinquish considerable time from the regular duties of these personnel since they will become members of the design and installation committee discussed later.

KEY STEPS REQUIRED

Companies with success in undertaking the installation of MICS have found the following key steps vital to their installation plans. These steps are listed in the required sequence, but in many cases it is not necessary to await the total completion of one before starting on the next. This overlapping can best be illustrated by use of the flow chart shown on page 122. This chart is a modification of a PERT chart and can be, with the necessary elaboration, used as an effective tool for the planning and control of this program.

Design and Installation Committee

Members appointed to this committee will be responsible for the complete design and installation of the system; therefore extreme care should be exercised in choosing members. Committee members should be chosen by top management from the various line functions that will be directly affected by the system. Appointments should be made on a full-time basis since the responsibility of committee membership in terms of vital contributions in knowledge and time warrants full-time participation.

Members should hold positions at a reasonably high level within their function to ensure their equal status with other committee members and to be assured that they speak with authority on matters concerning their function.

The committee should have at least one member who is experienced in the techniques of systems analysis and design. The time saved, as well as the reliability achieved, with this type of experience available would be considerable. The committee must be given authority to solicit assistance from any segment of the organization when needed.

MICS Steering Committee

The steering committee, composed of top management personnel, with the president as chairman (if practicable), will have the basic responsibility of reviewing all major recommendations and proposals presented by the MICS design and installation committee as well as monitoring the progress and costs of the system design and installation.

The steering committee is in the best position to insure that all recommendations, designs and costs are consistent with the established policies and goals of the company.

Policies and Decision Rules

The basic guidelines and parameters of the system are determined by the design and installation committee subject to review and approval

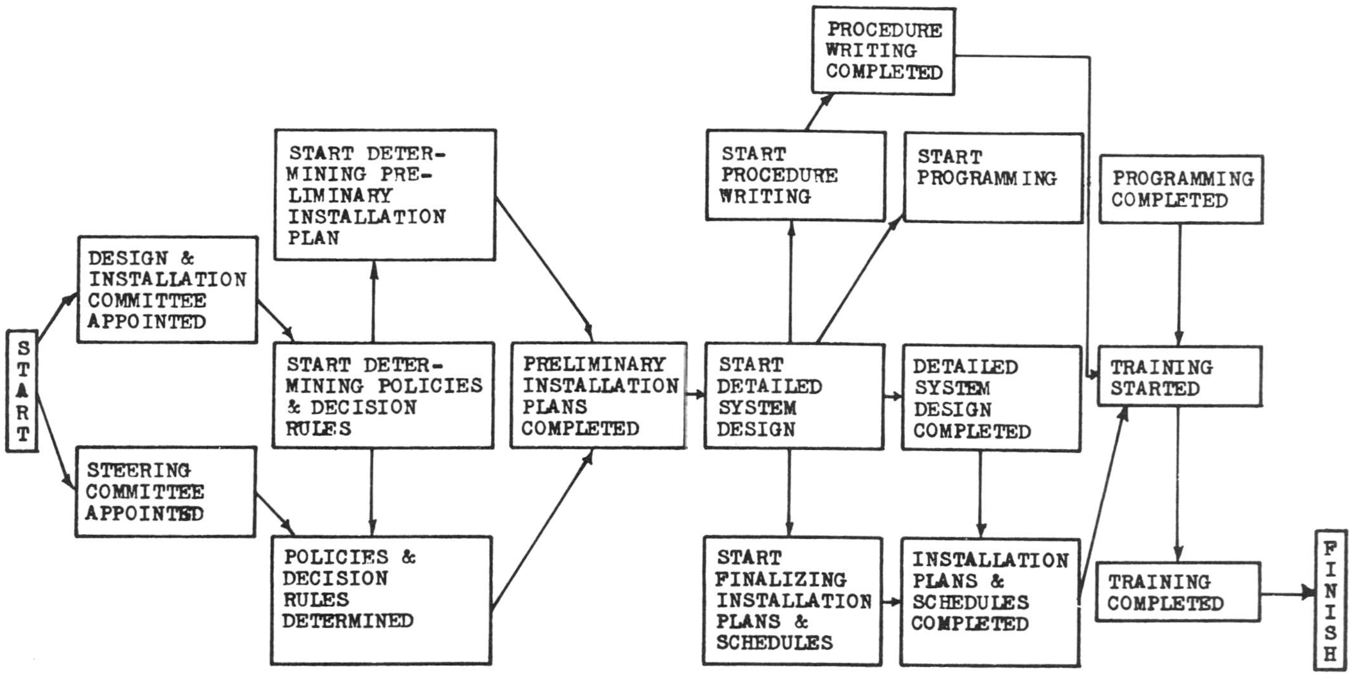

Steps required for a successful MICS installation

This modified PERT chart can, with the necessary elaboration, be used as an effective tool for the planning and control of steps vital to installing an MICS.

of the steering committee. All policies and rules must be compatible with the established long and short range plans and objectives of the organization. These policies and decision rules should basically be concerned with the following aspects of the organization:

1. The functional areas of the organization to be included in the system and their priority during design and implementation.
2. The degree of centralization of the system, especially in a multi-division or multi-plant organization.
3. Criteria for establishing the type and frequency of reporting.
4. The universal information requirements of all functions in the system.
5. Establishment of standards for measuring trends and budgets against actual performance.

Determination of this information by the design and installation committee should be made on a scheduled basis with specific assignments for each member.

The Preliminary Installation Plan

With the knowledge gained by members of the design and installation committee from the previous step, the development of a preliminary installation plan should be developed at this point by the committee. The plan should include:

1. A listing of all steps needed for installation of the system in each functional area of the organization, the estimated time to accomplish each step and the persons responsible for its successful completion.
2. Manpower requirements for achieving full installation.
3. Any equipment requirements and estimated funds needed for their acquisition.

This data should be thoroughly documented and submitted to the MICS steering committee for approval. Once approved, this data will form the basis for monitoring the program. Because of the tentative nature of any schedules and requirements developed at this stage, it becomes extremely important to establish effective communications between the two committees. Progress review meetings and appropriate progress reports must be established on a scheduled basis.

Detailed Systems Design Specifications

This step produces the complete details required by the design and installation committee for completing the installation plan and schedule. In addition to detailed specifications produced at this point will be used by programmers, procedure writers and training personnel for preparing their output.

Any system specification for which use of data processing equipment appears feasible should be submitted to selected equipment manufacturers for purposes of soliciting proposals. The submitted proposals should be reviewed with each manufacturer by members of the design and installation committee. The procurement or rental of data processing equipment should be approved by the steering committee.

The detailed systems specifications, written and documented, should include:

1. Input Specifications—including form content, form design, means of preparation and transmission, current and anticipated volumes, etc.
2. Output Specifications—including content and format, distribution, frequency, current and anticipated volumes, etc.
3. Processing Requirements—defining in detail what is required to be done with the input to achieve the required output.
4. File Descriptions—the detailed contents and volumes (present and anticipated) of all files needed for the system.
5. Control Requirements—all controls necessary to ensure accuracy of input and output.

Documentation of these specifications should be under the direction of a senior systems designer who is thoroughly trained and experienced in this type of effort. Line personnel members of the design and installation committee will play a major role by contributing the necessary detailed operating information and systems design suggestions in this step.

The Final Installation Plans and Schedules

At this point the design and installation committee should establish the final installation plan as a result of the detailed data generated from the systems design specifications. Before starting installation of any part of the system, the following must be considered.

Preparation of a detailed installation plan and schedule for each segment of the system should be accomplished through the joint effort of the design and installation committee and operating personnel of the functions involved. The plan should include the means of phasing in the new procedures and phasing out the old (if any exist). For each installation step, assignment of responsibilities to a specific individual must be made, and detailed instructions for accomplishing each installation step must be written. This will lessen the possibility of error or misunderstanding. Training for those involved in any special tasks required for installation should be instituted when necessary.

Programming

If data processing equipment will be used by the system, the design specifications described previously are furnished to trained programmers who are responsible for the documenting of instructions (programs) that will enable the equipment to efficiently process the input and produce the required output. In addition, the testing of the program to insure reliability and accuracy in meeting the systems design specifications is included as part of the task required to complete this step.

Procedure Writing

There are two types of procedures required at this stage in system installation. Both types should be written and maintained on a permanent basis.

1. Standard Operating Procedures (S.O.P.'s) cover in detail the specific duties and responsibilities of each person assigned to perform a job within the system. This type or procedure should include the detailed actions to be taken under varying conditions, relationships with other functions, etc. These procedures will form the basic curriculum for the training programs to follow.
2. Policies and procedures are applicable to interfunctional information flow. Included should be specified control requirements and control points, assignment of responsibilities, etc.

Training

The training program is intended for all personnel whose positions expose them to the new system, even indirectly, and is composed of two segments.

1. A description of the total system to indicate in general terms the relationships and responsibilities of each function to the whole system.
2. A detailed description of a segment of the system to be performed by specific operating personnel, e.g., order processing. In this segment training should cover the step-by-step duties and responsibilities of each person. The use of S.O.P.'s and policies and procedures as training tools is a necessity.

Members of the design and installation committee should assist the training staff in all phases of the training program.

GENERAL COMMENTS

In addition to the steps discussed above, the following comments related to a MICS installation are presented because of their importance.

1. During and following installation of any portion of the system, the need for changes in the design will become evident. Causes for

changes can range from some overlooked piece of information required by a function to a major reorganization of a department. The design and installation committee must, therefore, have the ability to react rapidly to such causes in order to determine the system changes required and to modify installation plans to reflect these changes.

2. The need for adequate planning and control of all installation steps has been mentioned before. PERT or CPM techniques have been used with great success in this area, and the writer strongly recommends the use of similar techniques for the planning and control of any MICS installation.

3. The impact on personnel of a company undertaking such a program as MICS can be significant, either positively or negatively, depending upon the means employed by management to acquaint personnel with their role in the system. There is no doubt that the key to success of an undertaking such as MICS rests to a considerable extent on the amount of understanding and support of the system engendered in company personnel by management. To achieve positive reactions, management must be willing to undertake an educational program that is comprehensive enough to overcome the ever present (but usually unjustified) fear created by a pending change in the manner of doing things. This is especially true when the employment of computers and other data processing equipment is anticipated by the company.

4. The committees described should not be considered luxuries that can be afforded only by the larger company. These committees can be informal and small, e.g., in some small companies two or three men could perform the duties of the design and installation committee. The larger and more complex the company, the greater the representation should be.

5. The need for a detailed written description of all information that is produced during the design and installation of the system is absolutely necessary. This is especially true of all completed procedures, policies, programs, specifications and operating instructions. Many information systems have been documented assuming that any detailed information can be obtained from the system designers, machine operators, programmers, etc., when needed. This approach is an invitation to potential disaster, since there never is a guarantee that these personnel will be available when needed.

SUMMARY

Attaining the goal of a successfully installed MICS requires the same types of techniques and know-how that are needed for any corporate undertaking that involves the commitment of the company's resources:

1. Making certain that all aspects of the business are ready for such an undertaking.
2. Planning all steps of the program with time and responsibilities assigned to each step.
3. Monitoring progress to make certain committed resources are being utilized efficiently.
4. Training all personnel to make certain that there is complete understanding of their role in the program.
5. Establishing controls within the program to enable rapid adjustment to new or changing conditions.

The result of this planned approach doesn't guarantee success, but will at least enable management to know when and why delays to a successful installation occur.

The results obtained from successful installation of such a program—timely, adequate and correct information if utilized properly—will more than compensate for the expenditure of resources involved.

B

New Scientific Tools and Techniques

The author discusses the theory of quantitative model building and its usefulness in solving a wide variety of business problems.

10

QUANTITATIVE MODELS IN BUSINESS – AN AID TO MAKING DECISIONS

Donald L. Shawver

During the 1930's and 1940's two significant developments in business management were the widespread acceptance of statistical techniques as an aid in analyzing business problems, and the rapid technological progress associated with these statistical techniques. Hypothesis testing, correlation analysis, and scientific sampling—to mention only a few—developed rapidly during these two decades, and today have achieved a significant and accepted place in business management.

Interest in quantitative models in business developed somewhat later than did that in statistical analysis. Only in the last decade has continuous interest been expressed in the use of mathematics and programming techniques for the solution of business problems. Progress has been extremely rapid. Today, one hears much of Linear Programming and Operations Research as aids to management in making decisions. The advent of the electronic digital computer since about 1954 has had a revolutionary effect on the general movement toward quantitative analysis.[1]

Reprinted from *University of Missouri Business and Government Review,* Vol. 5, No. 6, November–December 1964, pp. 5–13, by permission of the author and the publisher.

This article is based substantially on Chapter 14 of the new book by Dwight L. Gentry and Donald L. Shawver, Fundamentals of Managerial Marketing (New York: Simmons-Boardman Publishing Corporation, 1964). Special acknowledgement is made to Professor Gentry of the University of Maryland and to Mr. Russell F. Moore of Simmons-Boardman for permission to include certain copyrighted material.

[1] See C. Orville Elliott, "Using Computers in Business," *Business and Govern-*

Since 1954, the concurrent development of electronic computers and applied mathematics has given impetus to use of quantitative models in business. The purpose of this article is to examine quantitative models as an aid to management in making decisions—particularly with respect to marketing problems.

CHARACTERISTICS OF MODELS

Any model can be looked upon as an attempt to simplify a phenomenon belonging to the real world through a process of abstraction. The objective of model-building is to learn more about the operating characteristics of the real world.

Models range from the very simple to the highly sophisticated. A model airplane, for example, might be a child's toy or it might be a carefully scaled replica constructed by an aircraft engineer for a wind-tunnel test. Even though scale models may "look like the real thing;" they should not be confused with the real world since scale models may have a considerable amount of abstraction. The scale model may be made of plastic, whereas the real airplane is built of aluminum and steel and rubber. Thus, though measurements of length and breadth correspond to the real world, characteristics relating to weight do not.

Models should be judged according to their usefulness; however, if one model is more sophisticated than another, that does not necessarily enhance its usefulness. A mockup of an automobile braking system, for example, may not "look like the real thing," and might well be in two dimensions instead of three. Yet, such a model is highly useful in explaining such things as the operation of valves or the flow of hydraulic fluid. Similarly, a road map can be a very simple scale model and highly useful.

It is not the purpose of the model to represent the entire phenomenon in all of its complexity. The unique value of a model lies primarily in the quality of its abstractions. This means that the model-builder must decide which attributes of the real world are pertinent to his problem and which can be eliminated.

Models, particularly mathematical models, are frequently criticized because their resemblance to the real world is not apparent. It is true that a stringent set of assumptions is needed to go from the real world to an abstract model. Naturally, these assumptions do not describe the real world—if they did, there would be little purpose in making them

---

ment Review, March–April 1964, pp. 15–22, and Roy F. Keller, "Computer Research Center at University of Missouri," *Business and Government Review,* September–October 1961, pp. 16–25.

at all. A model should first be examined to see if it is consistent with the assumptions made. Its usefulness, then, depends on whether the results which it gives will hold when the assumptions underlying it are modified to fit the many facts existing in the real world.

Quantitative models are the most abstract of all. Unlike physical or symbolic models, they initially appear to have no relationship to the real world. Yet, after careful scrutiny, they can be viewed as simply a more sophisticated abstraction than other models.

RELATED ACTIVITIES

Three related activities are ordinarily associated with quantitative models in business:

1. Mathematical Model-Building

The basic approach is that of establishing a mathematical representation with subsequent determination as to whether suitable data and methods of solution are available. An alternative approach is to take data from the real world and develop a theoretical model which will explain the data. These two ways of building marketing models have been labeled *abstraction* and *realization*.[2]

At present many of the mathematical models pertaining to marketing are conceptual models rather than operational ones. Hopefully, in the future, more models will be developed where the business manager can "plug in" data and use the model as an operational device. The development of conceptual mathematical models is, in itself, a substantial contribution.[3] These models relate to the real world somewhat as a topcoat fits a man. On occasion, there is almost perfect fit, but at times room for improvement.

The use of mathematical models has some definite advantages for the decision maker. First, in going from a verbal description to such models, a certain rigor is necessary since models demand precise definitions. Second, analyses that are not possible through verbal models may be advanced through mathematical ones.

2. Simulation

In this area, one embraces the electronic computer enthusiastically and proceeds to construct detailed models for which data are available.

[2] William Lazer, "The Role of Models in Marketing," *Journal of Marketing*, April 1962, pp. 9–14.

[3] For a selective review and explanation of several models, see Frank M. Bass, Robert D. Buzzell, et al. (eds.), *Mathematical Models and Methods in Marketing* (Homewood, Illinois: Richard D. Irwin, Inc., 1961).

Ordinarily, the mathematics is simple, but the number of variables is large, and the entire operation is so detailed that only a computer can do the work.

Simulation has recently been used with varying degrees of success in a number of the social sciences. An excellent pioneering study of interest to students of marketing is that recently completed by Balderston and Hoggatt. This study simulated the patterns of trade and business operations among lumber manufacturers, wholesalers, and retailers on the U.S. Pacific Coast.[4]

The Balderston-Hoggatt model contained about 16,000 variables—a number so large that even the capacity of a giant computer was taxed for the simulation. Through simulation, behavior of the market system associated with different values of the parameters was observed. For example, the behavior of the market system was recorded for unit message costs of 0, 12, 48, and 192.[5]

A great many marketing problems do not lend themselves to analytical solutions. Some are characterized by a complex system containing feedbacks, distributed lags and/or uncommon probability distributions. In fact, an analytical solution may not even exist. Some observers believe that simulation offers an acceptable solution to problems of this nature.[6]

It may be that the business manager would like to anticipate the behavior of a particular business system before making decisions which bring the system into being. Suppose, for example, that a firm has a system consisting of a number of factories and a number of warehouses. What would happen to the system if new warehouses were built at numerous points around the country?

It might be that management could arrive at an analytical solution by using Linear Programming techniques. But, in some instances no analytical solution may be available. By simulating the system, either with or without a computer, and by making repeated trials, management might obtain a better location solution than by using intuition and judgment. A solution thus obtained through simulation is not necessarily *optimal.* However, if done carefully, it approximates one closely enough.

3. Decision Theory

The business executive is interested in formulating decision rules for the commitment of resources under conditions of certainty, risk, and uncertainty. Decision theory attempts to explain how *optimal* decision rules can be developed.

[4] Frederick E. Balderston and Austin C. Hoggatt, *Simulation of Market Processes* (Berkeley: Institute of Business and Economic Research, University of California, 1962).

[5] *Ibid.,* p. 15.

[6] Philip Kotler, "The Use of Mathematical Models in Marketing," *Journal of Marketing,* October 1963, pp. 31–41.

Under conditions of certainty, the decision maker knows which events will occur after his decision has been made. For example, in arranging a shipping schedule, he knows if he ships from Point *A* to Point *B*, the cost will be exactly *k* dollars per unit.

Under conditions of risk, the decision maker knows the probabilities of events which could affect the results. To illustrate, in making the decision to stock exactly *r* units of product *S*, the probability distribution of calls for product *S* might be known.

Under conditions of uncertainty, the decision maker is aware of the *states of nature;* however, he is not able to compute probabilities for the *states*. For example, the addition of a product to an existing product line may be done under conditions of uncertainty. Management is well aware that success depends upon certain outside factors—say the action, or lack of action by competitors. However, probabilities associated with future acts of competitors are not known and management must act under conditions of uncertainty.

Decision theory deals with an explanation of how *optimal* decision rules should be made. The usual method of choosing the best strategy (making a decision) is to assign values for each strategy and *state*. The executive next assigns subjective probabilities to the *states* and proceeds to select an *optimal* strategy.[7]

So far as business managers are concerned, the term decision theory refers to a study of the structure of quantitative decisions abstracted from any specific problem. It deals with analytical techniques by which complex problems can be reduced to a limited number of simpler problems. The chief technique involves what is popularly called "Bayesian Decision Theory."

The Bayesian approach is characterized by the decision maker's use of subjective probabilities—even when there is no history on which to base them. These subjective probabilities can be interpreted as the decision maker's betting odds or the way he feels about future events. Once the executive has identified each relevant *state of nature* and placed a subjective probability on its occurrence, he determines a consequence or "payoff" associated with each possible strategy and *state of nature*. If the decision maker gains further information, say from market research, the probabilities assigned are modified—ordinarily by the use of Bayes' Theorem. Finally, the decision made is governed by some criterion, perhaps maximum expected value, which depends in part on the personal philosophy of the decision maker.[8]

[7] The pioneering work in this area is Robert Schlaifer, *Probability and Statistics for Business Decisions: An Introduction to Managerial Economics Under Uncertainty* (New York: McGraw-Hill Book Company, Inc., 1959).

[8] See the two related articles: Harry V. Roberts, "Bayesian Statistics in Marketing," *Journal of Marketing*, January 1963, pp. 1–4, and Paul E. Green, "Bayesian Decision Theory in Pricing Strategy," *Journal of Marketing*, January 1963, pp. 5–14.

There is considerable controversy among scholars relating to the Bayesian approach. Critics object to the decision maker placing subjective probabilities on *states of nature*. Many mathematicians argue that these numbers are not probabilities at all. Further, the decision maker must not only place subjective probabilities on a number of different states, but he must also determine the payoffs associated with each state and each strategy. This is an extremely difficult task.

At the very least, however, Bayesian decision making forces a more rigorous approach to problems. Moreover, defenders of the Bayesian approach contend that it is analytically sound. The question arises as to what alternatives are available. If a better decision is possible through the use of Bayesian techniques, then it can be argued that they should be used.

AN ELEMENTARY MODEL

To illustrate the type of thinking that might occur in establishing a mathematical model, consider one well-known in marketing literature and called variously Reilly's Law, Converse's Law, or The Law of Retail Trade Movement.[9]

Suppose the Law of Retail Trade Movement did not exist, and it was advantageous to discover it. First of all, think about two cities attracting trade from a town located somewhere between them and ponder on what causes one city to attract more trade than the other. If the market is observed long enough, it might be suspected (a hypothesis drawn) that the larger a city, the more trade attracted by it from an intermediate town. Further observation might lead to a second hypothesis that a city draws more trade from nearby towns than it does from distant ones.

Now there are two propositions going at once. There exists a positive factor—the size of a city is measured by population—which attracts trade to that city. Also there is a negative factor—the distance which must be traveled by shoppers to trade in a city—which limits trade. It might be further theorized that it is really the breadth of the assortment of goods offered to the customer by a city that is the positive factor and that population is a good index to this assortment. It might be hypothesized further (as did Reilly) that a city's outside trade *decreases* faster than distance from the city *increases*. The question is: "How much faster?"

It might help to construct a schematic model first. Let A be the larger city, B the smaller city, and I the intermediate.

[9] For a recent application of Reilly's Law see Francis L. Stubbs, "Missouri Economic Centers and Areas," *Business and Government Review*, July–August 1963, pp. 38–48.

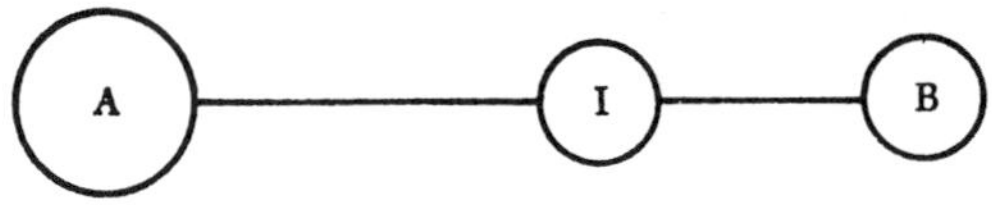

Figure 10–1. A schematic model

Next, a mathematical model of retail trade movement is constructed. The statement: "The bigger the city, the more outside trade it will draw," means that the amount of outside trade enjoyed by a city increases directly in proportion to some *power* of the population. And when it is suggested that a city's outside trade decreases faster than distance from the city increases, it is meant that the amount of outside trade varies inversely in proportion to some *power* of the distance of the town from the city.

A more elaborate set of symbols is useful:

Let T_a be the dollars of trade going from I to A
T_b be the dollars of trade going from I to B
P_a be the population of A
P_b be the population of B
D_a be the distance from A to I
D_b be the distance from B to I

Then mathematically:

$$\frac{T_a}{T_b} = \left(\frac{P_a}{P_b}\right)^x \left(\frac{D_b}{D_a}\right)^y$$

which is a very abstract mathematical model indeed. The resemblance to the real world is not readily apparent, and even our elementary model has a certain amount of sophistication!

We now have one mathematical formula in two unknowns: x and y. Knowledge of mathematics indicates that the exponent x reveals the rate at which outside trade drawn by a city increases as its population increases. The exponent y denotes the rate at which the outside trade decreases as the distance from the city increases. After a precise mathematical representation has been realized, the next step is to try and obtain values for the two unknowns. Experimenting mentally might result in a number of different values, or the model might be adjusted to the real world.

A Refined Model

Reilly believed that the number 1 should be arbitrarily assigned to x and then empirical data could be used to solve for y. Assigning the number 1 to x, in effect states that the relationship between size of city and attraction of trade is *linear*. That is, if city A is twice as large as B, it will (other things being equal) attract twice the trade. If city A is three times as large as B, it will attract three times as much trade.

If one is willing to do so and has the funds, it is quite possible to make field studies and determine the T's in the equation. Since the P's and D's are known, there is only one unknown *y* remaining in the equation. Reilly made such studies and found that the value of *y* varied within the range of 1.5 and 2.5. He decided to use 2 for the value of *y*. The Law of Retail Trade Movement as formulated by Reilly in 1931 became:

$$\frac{T_a}{T_b} = \frac{P_a}{P_b}\left(\frac{D_b}{D_a}\right)^2$$

Thus, the model here has been adjusted by using data from the real world. Although it is now a refined model, it is still an abstract mathematical one. Since mathematics is a language, it is possible to translate mathematics into English. If one prefers, the Law of Retail Trade Movement can be stated as: "Two cities attract retail trade from an intermediate town in the vicinity of the breaking point, approximately in direct proportion to the populations of the two cities and in inverse proportion to the square of the distances from these two cities to the intermediate town." [10] Distances are measured on improved automobile highways, and the breaking point is defined as that point up to which one city dominates retail trade movement, and beyond which the other city dominates.

An Illustrative Case

The model discussed here is not only interesting from the academic and historical point of view, but it can also be an operational model. Automobiles and highways have changed since 1930, and it might be desirable to "plug in" travel times instead of distances and number of retail stores in lieu of population. It might also be contended that the model applies only for shopping goods and should not be used in a situation where A is considerably larger than B. In any event, data from the real world can be utilized to see if the model presented here helps explain retail trade movement.

Suppose A has a population of 30,000; B population of 10,000; and that town I is located 20 miles from A and 10 miles from B. Then:

$$\frac{T_a}{T_b} = \frac{30,000}{10,000}\left(\frac{10}{20}\right)^2 = \frac{3}{4}$$

This is interpreted as follows: city A attracts $3 of trade from town I for each $4 of trade attracted by city B. Another interpretation is that city A

[10] William J. Reilly, *The Law of Retail Gravitation* (New York: William J. Reilly, 1931), p. 9.

attracts about 45 percent of the total trade lost from town I to cities A and B. These estimates can be checked out, of course, by making an empirical study of the residents of town I. It can be reasoned that city A has a larger population, hence assortment, than does city B. But A is much further away; in fact, it is so far away in relation to B that the residents give B $4 of trade for every $3 that goes to A.

The Breaking Point

An interesting property of a mathematical model is that once set up it can be manipulated. Suppose one is interested in finding the breaking point between two towns (the 50 percent point)—that point from which half the trade from an intermediate town goes to A and half goes to B. How does one proceed?

Assume we are interested in the distance from B (the smaller city) to the breaking point. Let $D_b{}^*$ be the distance from the breaking point to B, and $D_a{}^*$ be the distance from the breaking point to city A. Let $D = D_a{}^* + D_b{}^*$. The problem is to find $D_b{}^*$ such that $T_a = T_b$.

After algebraic manipulations we find:

$$D_b{}^* = \frac{D}{1 + \frac{\sqrt{P_a}}{\sqrt{P_b}}}$$

This formula can be used for finding the breaking point between the two cities, provided the distance between the two and their populations are known. It is a highly operational model and can be readily used by a retailer to bound his trading area.

The procedure of finding the breaking point illustrates a unique advantage of mathematical models. They can be manipulated, and the result is sometimes quite different from the original. Frequently, the outcome is something not obvious in the minds of most men.

Let us put the formula to work. Recall the previous example where city A had a population of 30,000 and city B a population of 10,000 and the cities were 30 miles apart. We have:

$$D_b{}^* = \frac{30}{1 + \sqrt{\frac{30{,}000}{10{,}000}}} = 11 \text{ miles}$$

In other words, the breaking point between A and B is about 11 miles from B and, of course, 19 miles from A. If desired, the theoretical results can be checked empirically by going out and surveying people with respect to their shopping habits.

ECONOMIC ORDER QUANTITY

The objective of inventory management is to have the right amount of stock on hand at all times and at minimum cost. This means the business executive attempts to order an economic quantity, one which results in ample inventory but not in an excessive number of orders per time period.

Basically two different kinds of costs are associated with inventory management—Procurement Costs and Carrying Costs. Procurement Costs include costs associated with replenishment studies, invoice routines, receiving and inspecting stock and the routine of paying invoices. Carrying Costs include such items as interest, storage, and costs associated with risks due to obsolescence and deterioration. Procurement Costs vary directly with the number of orders placed and inversely with the dollar investment in inventory. Conversely, Carrying Costs vary directly with inventory investment and inversely with the number of orders. Thus, a decrease in Procurement Costs causes an increase in Carrying Costs and *vice versa.* The business executive is interested in balancing one cost against the other, and attempts to order an economic quantity which will minimize Total Costs.

How does the executive proceed? One alternative is to use intuition and judgment and hope that his solution is close to *optimal.* The other alternative is to build a mathematical model and use it as an aid to his judgment.

To go from the real world to the model, certain simplifying assumptions are needed. The following is assumed:

—demand is known with certainty

—the rate of demand is constant and continuous throughout all time periods

—no time lag exists in placing and receiving an order.

It is known that the real world does not operate in a manner consistent with the assumptions presented here, but these simplifications are needed if the model is to be built. We proceed:

Let D be the number of units demanded during 1 year
Q be the number of units to be ordered in each lot
K be the Procurement Cost per order
C be the Carrying Cost per unit per year.

Then D/Q is the number of orders per year and DK/Q is total Procurement Costs. To obtain total Carrying Costs, the average inventory must be computed. The number of units in stock varies over time and we have schematically:

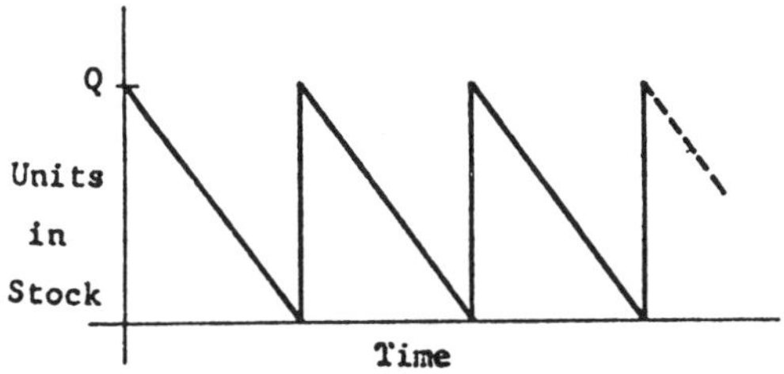

Figure 10–2. Sawtooth inventory model

It can be seen (as well as proven mathematically) that in this model the average inventory is Q/2. Total Carrying Costs, of course, are QC/2.

Now Total Costs in a function of Q. Total Costs depends on the number of units ordered in each lot. We have: $f(Q) = DK/Q + QC/2$. If it is assumed that this function is continuous and differentiable, the following can be found: $f'(Q) = -DK/Q^2 + C/2$. Setting $f'(Q) = O$, it can be shown that $DK/Q^2 = C/2$ and the optimal Q or $Q^* = \sqrt{2DK/C}$.

For those not well versed in the calculus, Q* can be developed differently. Intuitively, it would appear that the optimal conditions occur at that point where Procurement Costs are exactly equal to Carrying Costs. This is at the point where $DK/Q = QC/2$. If this equation is solved algebraically for Q, we have again $Q^* = \sqrt{2DK/C}$.

An Example

Suppose that 300 units are demanded during the year, and that it costs $5.00 for each order placed. Suppose further, that it costs $7.50 to carry one unit of stock 1 year. What is the optimal economic order quantity?

One method of solution might be to make computations similar to those shown in Table 10–1. Total Costs appears in the right hand column. We observe that as Q (the lot size) is increased, Total Costs at first declines and then increases. From Table 10–1, it can be seen that a Q of 20 results in Total Costs of $150 and we suspect Q* is equal to 20.

The data in Table 10–1 can be used to prepare Fig. 10–3 which illustrates graphically what is taking place. We observe that the low point on the Total Cost curve is associated with the intersection of the Procurement Cost curve and the Carrying Cost curve. The minimum point of the Total Cost curve is at (20, $150), or where Q* (lot size) is 20 and f(Q*) (total costs) is $150.

Of course, it is much quicker to use our mathematical model for finding the optimal Q. We "plug in" the values and find that

$$Q^* = \sqrt{\frac{2(300)\ (5)}{7.5}} = 20$$

TABLE 10–1

LOT SIZE AND TOTAL COSTS ASSOCIATED WITH INVENTORY

Lot Size Q	Average Inventory Q/2	Carrying Costs QC/2	Orders per Year D/Q	Procurement Costs DK/Q	Total Costs QC/2 + DK/Q
10	5	$37.50	30	$150	$187.50
15	7.5	56.25	20	100	156.25
20	10	75.00	15	75	150.00
25	12.5	93.75	12	60	153.75
30	15	112.50	10	50	162.50
35	17.5	131.25	9	45	176.25
40	20	150.00	8	40	190.00
45	22.5	168.75	7	35	203.75
50	25	187.50	6	30	217.50
.					
.					
.					
75	37.5	281.25	4	20	301.25
.					
.					
.					
150	75	562.50	2	10	572.50

D = 300 units
K = $5.00
C = $7.50

Recalling that 300 units will be needed throughout the year, this means that the business executive arranges for 15 orders of 20 units each. Further, it is observed that $f(Q^*) = f(20) = 300\ (\$5)/20 + 20(\$7.50)/2 = \$150$.

It is difficult for most men to "intuit" about the square roots of ratios. One can see that the optimal Q is proportional to the square root of twice the unit sales times the ratio of Procurement Costs to Carrying Costs. This is a perfectly valid verbal model! But it is suggested here that our mathematical model is highly useful and helps management make better decisions.

The example has dealt with a simple inventory model. However, it may be observed that inventories lend themselves to "model" control with computer calculations—particularly when purchases or sales are for more than one item, and where a firm operates more than one warehouse from which customers may be served.

AN EVALUATION

The business manager finds frequently that his intuition and judgment are limited in making decisions. Certain classes of decisions can be made

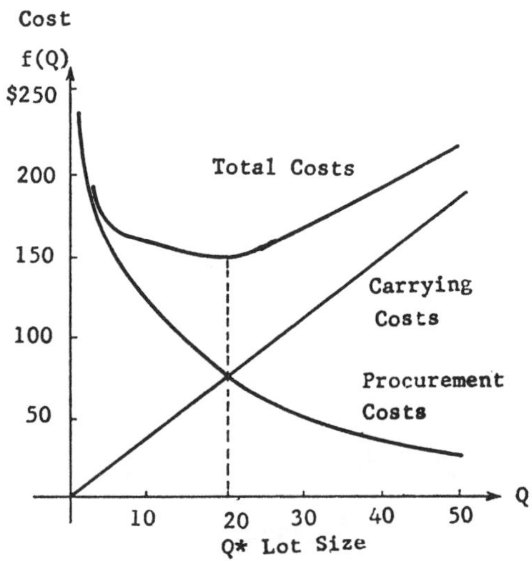

Figure 10–3. Costs and lot size

logically if, and only if, intuition and judgment are aided through use of quantitative methods of analysis. If a problem lends itself to quantification, certain rigorous methods of analysis become available. Hopefully, the executive will use quantitative analysis properly, and better decisions will result.

In the last decade much interest has developed, and there has been rapid growth in use of quantitative models in solving business problems. Nevertheless, the use of such models is still in the stage of infancy, and much fruitful work remains to be done. Observers speculate that the importance of quantitative models, as well as the extent of their use, will continue to grow.

A distinct possibility exists that the potential usefulness of the quantitative approach has been oversold. However, there also exists the intriguing possibility that a real and substantial contribution may be forthcoming. With general availability of electronic digital computers and the concurrent growth of applied mathematics, the business manager has the opportunity to attempt solutions of business problems not possible heretofore.

The author defines the concept of risk and the concepts of decision making under certainty and uncertainty, and explores their relevance to management decision making.

11

THE FRAMEWORK OF MANAGEMENT DECISION MAKING

Milton H. Spencer

On August 2, 1954, an unusual article appeared in *Life* magazine. Written by Branch Rickey, one of baseball's most brilliant managers, the article dealt with the subject of baseball as a science. To most people it probably conveyed the impression of being a lesson in mathematics, but to some readers it undoubtedly posed the interesting question of whether the game of baseball might not someday be played on electronic computers and the outcome predicted before the players get onto the field.

Branch Rickey was interested in the question of whether a team's strengths and weaknesses could be measured so that its efficiency could be improved. Accordingly, he gathered statistics and took them to mathematicians who, upon analyzing the data, established that a team's standing over a season could be closely approximated by taking the difference between its average runs and the average runs of its opponents. But what are the elements that determine the scoring of runs? After setting down the factors that seemed most important, Rickey developed a mathematical formula for measuring a team's efficiency.[1] The formula itself is unimportant for our purposes, but for the benefit of curious readers it is presented, with a few slight changes in symbols, in footnote 1.

At this point one may ask, what do baseball and business have

Reprinted from *MSU Business Topics,* Summer 1963, pp. 33–47, by permission of the publisher, the Bureau of Business and Economic Research, Division of Research, Graduate School of Business Administration, Michigan State University.

[1] Let T_e denote team efficiency; H = number of hits; B = number of bases on

in common, other than their initials, and what is the purpose of starting a discussion of decision making with a short discourse on the science of competitive sports? The answers to these questions can be derived from a study of the literature which comprises the subject known as *decision theory.* In the paragraphs below, our interest centers on sketching quickly and broadly, in a brief and intuitive way, a few of the main outlines of that field. As we shall see, this framework and presentation permit the development of concepts which have long been overlooked in much of the traditional literature of administration and management. In essence, therefore, this discussion is intended to provide a broad conceptual groundwork for the more detailed study of managerial decision processes, and a basis for appreciating to a fuller extent much of what now appears in the modern technical literature of management theory. Against the background of the ideas presented here, we shall conclude with some suggestions for a new way of viewing management—one which is in harmony with the spirit of modern management thinking and research, as contrasted with the more descriptive and anatomical view of the traditionalist schools of management thought.

Before proceeding, it may be noted that although the discussion is conducted primarily in terms of management decision making, the underlying concepts are equally applicable to the decision processes of consumers, households, and other organisms acting in a socio-economic environment.

CLASSIFICATION

It is customary to classify decision making according to (1) the people who make the decisions, and (2) the conditions under which the decisions are made. Each of these may then be further partitioned, if desired, into subsets of the following nature.

The first classification has to do with whether the decision maker is an individual or a group. This distinction is important for obvious reasons: a decision made by an individual whose motivations are based on unitary or integrated considerations may take one form; a decision

---

balls; A_b = times at bat; H_p = hits by pitcher; T_b = total of bases; R = number of runs; H_b = hits by batsmen; E_r = earned runs; S = strikeouts; and F = fielding. Then

$$T_e = \left[\frac{H + B_b + H_p}{A_b + B_p + H_p} + \frac{3\,(T_b - H)}{4A_b} + \frac{R}{H + B_b + H_p}\right] - \left[\frac{H}{A_b} + \frac{B_b + H_b}{A_b + B_b + H_b} + \frac{E_r}{H + B_b + H_b} - \frac{S}{8\,(A_b + B_b + H_b)} - F\right]$$

where the first set of brackets represent the offense, and the second set, the defense.

made by a group whose multiple motivations are resolved by conflict or compromise may take quite a different form.

The bulk of the literature of decision theory has concentrated on the former type of situation. In such cases a set of individuals comprising an organization, such as a department or a business firm, are considered as a single entity in conflict with other single entities for analysis purposes. On the other hand, in the study of group as compared with individual decision making, a chief task is to develop compromise preference patterns from the dissimilar and sometimes discrepant preference patterns of members. From the viewpoint of democratic theory, this involves the interesting question of how to arrive at "fair" methods of amalgamating individual choices into optimum preference or social arrangements. Hence it is a problem which has intrigued many economists, psychologists, and sociologists, as well as political scientists.

The second classification refers to the particular state of knowledge under which a decision is made. In making decisions and in formulating plans for the future, a business manager, for example, is confronted with three types of outcomes: *certainty, risk* and *uncertainty.* Businessmen are prone to think of all types of outcomes that may result in losses as risks, but there are some technical distinctions between these three concepts that are fundamental for purposes of analysis. Thus we have decision making under condition of:

1. *Certainty,* where each alternative is known to result invariably in a specific outcome.[2]
2. *Risk,* where each alternative results in one of a set of possible specific outcomes, and the probability of each outcome is known.
3. *Uncertainty,* where one or more alternatives results in a set of possible specific outcomes, but where the probabilities of the outcomes are neither known nor meaningful.

According to the above definitions, certainty is seen to be a special (i.e., degenerate) case of risk in which the probabilities are 0 and 1. Also, by utilizing experimental evidence within the framework of modern statistical inference, a fourth partition resulting in a combination of both risk and uncertainty is feasible. In any case, each of the above classifications is important enough to warrant a brief but separate discussion of its overall scope and nature. As implied above, we shall deal primarily with decision making in the individual rather than group sense, although the distinction between the two is generally clear from the context.

[2] In some of the behavioral science literature, such words as "act," "action," "prospect," or "stimulus" are used, whereas in business and economic literature the term "alternative" is employed. See R. Duncan Luce and Howard Raiffa, *Games and Decisions.* New York: Wiley, 1957, pp. 12–23, 275–78, 324–26.

THE CONCEPT OF CERTAINTY

Certainty has been defined as a state of knowledge in which the decision maker knows in advance the specific outcome to which each alternative will invariably lead. How realistic is this type of situation? Are there many examples of decision problems that could logically be placed in this category? At first thought there is often a tendency to suspect that this state of affairs is "theorectical and impractical" and therefore only of academic interest. Actually, however, the opposite is generally the case.

Types of Problems

Decision making under certainty includes most of the problems and theories of choice that arise in the economic and behavioral sciences. Specifically, business administration, economics, and psychology abound with examples involving decision making under certainty. Thus, problems requiring the maximization of production functions, profit functions, and utility functions, and situations dealing with the minimization of cost functions and disutility functions, have long been familiar. The mathematical tools most frequently used for maximizing and minimizing have, for static types of problems, traditionally been those of elementary calculus. For problems in "dynamic programming" where the objective may be to maximize or minimize performance over time, the calculus of variations has been employed. In any event, these problems relate to traditional types of situations which have been typical of decision making under certainty—situations in which the alternatives are known, and the problem is to optimize (i.e., maximize or minimize, as the case may be) some given index such as profits, costs, or utilities.

In contrast to these traditional procedures, newer classes of problems have arisen which are conveniently discussed under the heading of linear programming. In general terms, linear programming problems deal with the optimum allocation of scarce resources, such as men, materials and machines. However, one or more restrictions on utilization of the resources may exist. Then, whenever the particular performance measure to be optimized can be stated as a linear function of the controlling variables, and the restrictions can be expressed as a system of linear equations or inequalities, the problem is one of linear programming. Extensive applications of linear programming techniques have been made, some of the more famous ones being:

• the diet problem, in which prescribed nutritional needs are established at minimum cost,

- the personnel assignment problem, in which people are matched or assigned to jobs so as to achieve maximum total output,
- the traveling salesman problem, in which an individual minimizes the total distance he must cover in visiting a number of scattered cities.

The mathematical tools employed in linear programming may include those of the calculus; however, the theory of convex bodies has been of major importance.

Selecting the Appropriate Index

As pointed out above, decision making under certainty is typified by problems which can be expressed in the following form: *given a set of possible alternatives, to choose one or more that will maximize (or minimize) a particular index.* But which index? This is often the most difficult part of the problem. In cases of an economic and business nature, quantities such as profit, sales, production, or cost are usually suitable indices, but in many problems of a behavioral nature a desired index is not readily available. In such situations, how can a decision maker select an index function so that his choice is then reduced to that of finding the alternative with the maximum index?

Psychologists and economists have long been interested in this question, and a considerable body of literature on the problem now exists. It is normally treated under the general heading of "utility"—a topic which is actually the basis of this and many other problems in modern decision theory. For our purpose at this time, however, it can be simply stated that the individual might index his choices in an ordinal or ranking manner from most to least preferred. Then, if he were confronted with any pair of choices, he would always select the one with the higher rank or index. This assumes, however, that the individual's preferences satisfy the very important condition of *transitivity:* if the decision maker is confronted with all possible triples of alternatives A, B, and C, and if he prefers A to B in the paired comparison (A, B), and B to C in the paired comparison (B, C), then he always prefers A to C in the paired comparison (A, C).

The importance of this concept of transitivity as a cornerstone of modern decision theory cannot be overemphasized. The notion itself has some connection with many comparisons we make in our day-to-day activities: if A is larger than B and B is larger than C, then A is larger than C. Instead of larger, we can substitute other words such as "stronger" or "lighter." The point to be emphasized at this time is that this method of ranking permits an ordering of alternatives, or an *ordinal* preference pattern, to be established, as distinguished from a *cardinal* preference pattern based on the amount by which one alternative is preferred to another. On this basis, economists after World War I developed the theory of demand in terms of indifference curves, thereby breaking away from the necessity of postulating an underlying cardinal utility function as done earlier by Alfred Marshall and the neoclassical school of economic thought. And psychologists also found a vast new field within which to roam. Both groups have conducted many interesting experiments in attempts to predict decision making activities and to explore the role of ordinal and cardinal utility in decision processes.

THE CONCEPT OF RISK

Risk has been defined as a state of knowledge in which each alternative leads to one of a set of specific outcomes, each outcome occurring with a probability that is known to the decision maker. Risk may therefore be regarded as the quantitative measurement of an outcome, such as a loss or a gain, in a manner such that the probability of the outcome can be predicted. Thus among the central ideas in the concept of risk are measurement and prediction, their purpose being to estimate the likelihood of an eventuality of contingency. Let us note briefly, in an intuitive and conceptual manner, how this is accomplished.

Methods of Estimating Risk

There are two approaches that can be used in arriving at a probability measure or risk: one of these is *a priori,* by deduction; the other is *a posteriori,* by empirical measurement. Both methods provide the information needed in predicting outcomes.

In the a priori method, a decision maker can compute with certainty the probability of an outcome without the necessity of relying on past experience. Deductions are made on the basis of assumed principles, provided that the characteristics of the eventuality are known in advance. Thus it is not necessary to toss a coin a large number of times in order to discover that the relative frequency of a heads (or tails) approaches ½, or one out of every two tosses. Likewise, it is not necessary to make a continuous drawing of cards from a poker deck containing 52 cards in order to conclude that the probability of drawing any particular card is 1/52. And with continuous rolls of a perfect die, it can be predicted with certainty that over the long run any given number, say four, will turn up one out of six times, so the probability can be written as 1/6 or 0.17.

Are probability statements such as these intended to predict a particular outcome? The answer is no. They merely state that in a large number of cases this is the only outcome that will be realized with certainty. It follows, therefore, that the habitual gambler who entertains himself with organized games of chance such as those encountered in

"Lost Wages," Nevada, is faced with risks (not with uncertainty as we shall see below), and the only thing that is certain is that he must lose over time.

Many practical decision problems do not involve a priori probability. Nevertheless, this method of prediction is useful in deriving and illustrating theoretical concepts. Alternatively, a common method of predicting outcomes is by empirical measurement, because the results are based on actual experiences recorded in the form of past data.

The use of historical data for predicting the future assumes, roughly, that past performances were typical and will continue in the future. In a stricter sense, this has traditionally meant, in the literature of statistics, that in order to establish a probability the number of cases or observations must be large enough to exhibit stability, they must be repeated in the population or universe, and they must be independent.[3] Given these conditions, the statistical probability of an event can be computed and the likelihood of the outcome can be classified as a risk. Thus, insurance companies predict with a high degree of certainty the probability of deaths, accidents, fire losses, etc., and thereby make decisions about premium levels and rates. Though they cannot establish the probability that a particular individual will die or that a particular house will burn, they can predict with small error how many people will die next year or how many houses out of a given number will burn.

For eventualities or outcomes that involve risks, a primary task of professional decision makers, e.g., managers, is to develop techniques that will enable them to calculate and subsequently minimize the risks inherent in a particular problem. The method used to accomplish this is to construct a frequency or probability distribution of outcomes, as in Figure 11–1. On the vertical axis the probability scale must range from 0 to 1, since the proportion of outcomes can never be negative and since it can also never exceed 100 percent, or a relative frequency of 1.00. That is, a probability must always lie between 0 and 1. A probability of 0 means that the event is not expected to occur; a probability of 1 means that the event is expected to happen all of the time. (These two degenerate cases of risk were discussed in the previous section as decision making under certainty.) Values in between denote degrees of certainty.

On the horizontal axis, the outcomes being analyzed are scaled off. These might be wheat yields per acre, glass breakage in restaurants, or some other variable under consideration. A frequency or probability distribution of outcomes is then plotted, which in Figure 11–1 is in the form of a standard normal curve. The parameters of the distribution should also be established for purposes of analysis. That is, a measure

[3] Independency means that the observations are distributed in the manner of a stochastic variable, i.e., at random.

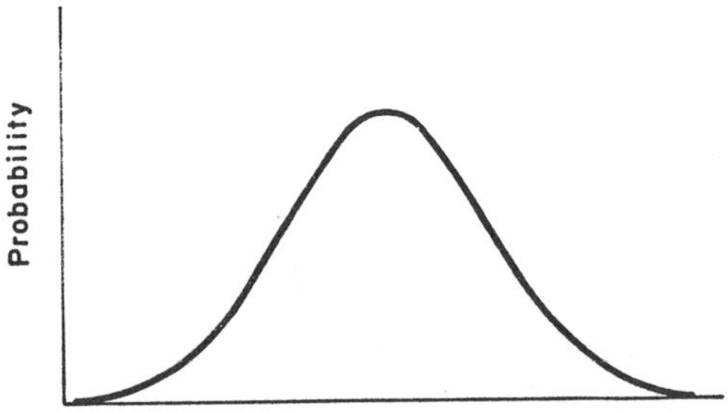

Figure 11–1. Normal frequency or probability distribution

of central tendency is needed, such as the mean, median, or mode, to describe the typical size of the distribution; a measure of dispersion, such as the standard deviation, variance, or moments, to establish the scatter; a measure of skewness to denote the degree of symmetry; and a measure of kurtosis, or degree of peakedness of the distribution. These measures can be established with an empirical probability of 1 (certainty) for the distribution as a whole. Risk would be present when the outcomes can be predicted over a period of years, in terms of these measures, as well as the number of years in which the outcomes will fall.

Risk Planning and the Cost of Risk

Two aspects of the theory of risk deserve some brief comments. One of these involves the notion of self-insurance or intrafirm risk; the other pertains to the idea of risk-shifting or interfirm risk. Both of these are intimately related to the general problem of *planning for risk.*

In its capacity as a decision maker and planner, management's activities are essentially forward looking in nature. Plans are made in the present based on expectations of the future. Since it is a characteristic of risk that the parameters (mean, variance, skewness, etc.) of the frequency distribution of outcomes can be estimated statistically, the expected losses or gains can be incorporated in advance into the firm's cost structure. This is true whether the risk is of an intrafirm nature, or interfirm nature, as explained below.

Intrafirm risk occurs when management can establish the probability of loss because the number of occurrences within the firm is large enough to be predicted with known error. For example, a factory may experience a loss of about 2 machine-hours out of every 100 machine-hours due to equipment breakdown. It might seem that management should protect itself against this type of loss through the purchase of insurance, but such is not the case. In reckoning profits, the cost of the production lost can be added to the cost of the production resulting from the remaining

98 machine-hours, and the profit rate will be altered accordingly by the revision in the cost structure. In other words, where the mean expected loss for the company can be predicted for the coming period, the loss can be "self-insured" by treating it as a cost of doing business, and hence no insurance from outside sources to cover the loss is even necessary. In short, the probable future cost of the loss can, in such cases, be planned in advance of the company's fiscal period, thereby facilitating the decision processes of management. Thus, small-loan companies expect a certain percentage of defaults, banks charge off regularly a portion of their loans, and many companies have attempted to institute self-insurance programs for various kinds of risk to which they are subject, and which they feel they can prepare themselves against through proper reserve accounting. These are only a few of many familiar examples that can be given to show how businessmen adjust to, or plan for, intrafirm risks.

Interfirm risk occurs when the number of observations or cases is not large enough within any one firm for management to feel that it can predict the loss with reasonable confidence. However, when many firms are considered, the number of observations becomes numerous enough to exhibit the necessary stability for prediction. Examples of such risks are losses caused by floods, storms, fires, etc. Since managers are unable to predict such losses for themselves, they are able to shift the burden of the risk to insurance companies whose function it is to establish the probability of such losses based on a large number of cases. Under such circumstances, the probability of loss for a specific firm cannot be predicted, but the probability of loss covering many firms can definitely be established with a small amount of error. It follows, therefore, that since the insured pays a risk premium for insurance, this can also be recognized for purposes of planning future costs.

THE CONCEPT OF UNCERTAINTY

Uncertainty has been defined as a state of knowledge in which one or more alternatives result in a set of possible specific outcomes, but where the probabilities of the outcomes are neither known nor meaningful. Unlike risk, therefore, uncertainty is not objective and does not assume complete knowledge of alternatives. Uncertainty is a subjective phenomenon: no two individuals will view an event and necessarily formulate the same quantitative opinion. This is due to a lack of knowledge or of sufficient historical data on which to base a probability estimate, which in turn is caused by rapid changes in the structural variables or "states of nature" that determine each economic or social environment.

Under uncertainty conditions, decision makers must make choices in an environment of incomplete knowledge; they may do so by forming mental images of the future, or of outcomes, that cannot be verified in any quantitative manner. It follows from this that uncertainty is not insurable, and cannot be integrated within the firm's cost structure as can risk. The parameters of the probability distribution cannot be established empirically, because all predictions are subjective and within the framework of each manager's own anticipations of the future. At best, it may be possible to assign subjective probabilities to these anticipated outcomes, but the distribution of expectations resulting therefrom cannot be established with objective certainty.

Strategies and States of Nature

One of the first tasks to be accomplished in decision making under uncertainty is to identify the relevant structural environments or states of nature that may exist. For example, in marketing a new product, the decision may depend on whether management anticipates a period of prosperity, recession, or normality. These, then, represent the states of nature. The returns of payoffs that will result from a decision to market it will clearly depend on which state of nature is eventually realized.

As another example, the decision of a government to encourage the use of its limited resources for the production of "guns vs. butter," so to speak, may depend on whether it anticipates a state of nature in the form of war, or a state of nature in the form of peace. Of course, it may anticipate *both* states of nature with varying degrees of uncertainty. Thus, it may feel that there is a 70 percent chance of peace and, therefore, a 30 percent chance of war, or perhaps an equal or 50–50 chance of each. In any event, each act or strategy may be associated with each state of nature, and an expected return or payoff thereby established. The techniques of constructing or arraying the various payoffs—or, more generally, the methods of developing formal guides for making optimum decisions in problems such as these, is beyond our scope at this moment. Suffice it to say that such procedures do exist, but at present our interest centers on the development of the broad concept of uncertainty as a background and framework for certain classes of decision-making problems.

Degree of Uncertainty

Since expectations are subjective in nature, there will be degrees of uncertainty on the part of decision makers. Two businessmen, for example, may view the same event, but each will establish his own expectations with greater or less confidence than the other. What are the different ways in which decision makers might view the uncertain outcome of an event? In answering this question, we begin by assuming that there is a true state of nature which is unknown to the decision maker at the time of choice. Three classes of uncertainty situations, complete knowledge, complete ignorance, partial ignorance, may then be distinguished.

Complete knowledge (or perfect knowledge) occurs when there exists an a priori probability distribution over the states of nature—that is, a *distribution which the decision maker regards as meaningful.* When this type of uncertainty situation exists, the problem can be transformed to one of decision making under risk and can be handled by specific analytical tools designed for such purposes. Notable among these is the notion of *expected value*—a weighted average of outcomes in which each outcome is weighted (multiplied) by its probability of occurrence and the resulting products are summed. The act or course of action which yields the largest index would then be chosen as the "best" strategy to adopt—best, that is, in the sense that it is the optimal course of action against the given a priori probability distribution.

Complete ignorance about the "true state" is the opposite situation of complete knowledge. In this case there is no assumption or knowledge on the part of the decision maker as to the probabilities of the various states of nature. Accordingly, he may use any one of a number of rational criteria for decision making. For instance, in the case of a business venture, the decision maker may adopt a pessimistic or conservative outlook. In that event he might examine the minimum outcomes or profit expectations of each combined strategy and state of nature, and then choose the strategy which yields the maximum of these minimum profits. Hence this is called the "maximin criterion." Alternatively, he may adopt an optimistic and speculative outlook. In that case he might examine the maximum profit expectations of each strategy and associated state of nature, and then choose the strategy which yields the maximum of these maximum profits. Hence this is called the "maximax criterion." Other criteria have also been established to meet the particular needs of decision problems under uncertainty where complete ignorance or complete lack of knowledge is the prevailing condition.

Partial ignorance occupies the intermediate ground between complete knowledge and complete ignorance. Much of the pioneering research on decision theory in this area was done by the noted statistician L. J. Savage. In his monumental treatise, *The Foundations of Statistics* (1954), he develops a procedure for generating an a priori probability distribution over the appropriate states of nature in a decision problem. In this manner the decision problem is reduced from one of uncertainty to one of risk, with the a priori probability distribution called a *subjective* probability distribution. Since a great many decisions in the social sciences and business administration are made on the basis of partial ignorance or incomplete knowledge of the facts, a brief intuitive sketch of the notion of subjective probability distributions should be of interest.

Subjective Probability Distributions

Degrees of uncertainty may be illustrated by the set of probability or frequency distributions of expectations shown in Figure 11–2. Expected outcomes, such as profits, sales, GNP, etc., are plotted horizontally, while the subjective probability of the outcome is measured off vertically.

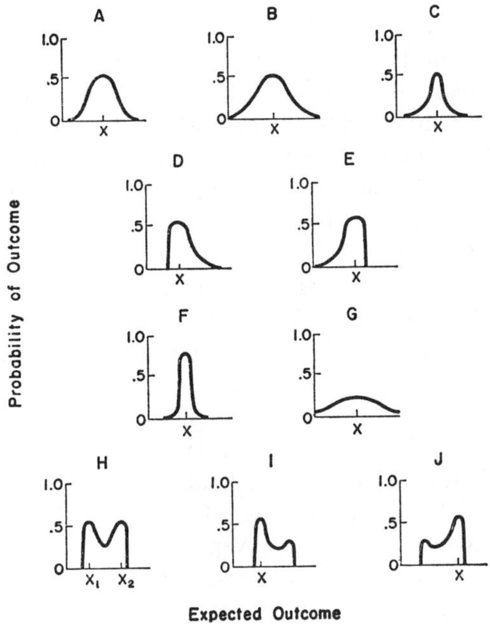

Figure 11–2. Subjective probability distributions

In the top panel of Figure 11–2 there are three normal distributions, but only A is of unit or standard normal form. In contrast with B and C (all of which are plotted in the same units), A represents greater uncertainty than C. This is due to the variance or spread of the distributions. If X is taken as the modal or most frequent outcome, the greatest variation in expectations (or greatest uncertainty) occurs in B because it has the widest spread; the least variation or uncertainty is in C because it has the least spread. Thus, as an indication of the degree of uncertainty, a measure of the *dispersion* of expectations such as the range, the standard deviation, or the variance could be used. The degree of uncertainty could be said to vary directly with the dispersion: a dispersion of zero would mean "perfect certainty," or a single-valued expectation; a larger dispersion would indicate greater uncertainty or mutlivalued expectations.

In Figure 11–2, D and E illustrate the significance of *skewness.* Compare these curves with the normal curve of A, where the expected outcomes are arranged symmetrically about the modal outcome. In A, there is an even chance that a deviation from the most probable (modal) outcome will be greater or less than the mode. In D, a deviation from the mode *X* will most probably be in the direction of higher values, while in E the most probable deviation is toward lower values. Thus, a measure of skewness, since it describes the lopsidedness of the distribution, is a further indication of the degree of confidence or uncertainty.

A comparison of F and G reveals still further characteristics. The degree of peakedness of a distribution, called *kurtosis,* in statistical terminology, is yet another indication of uncertainty. In F the probability of the particular modal outcome *X* is greater than for any other distribution shown. In G, however, where the distribution is relatively "flat topped," the subjective probability of the modal outcome is only slightly greater than outcomes higher or lower. In F, the decision maker is relatively certain of the modal outcome; in G, his expectations cover a wide area of almost equal probabilities, and he would find it difficult to formulate plans based on the modal outcome or on outcomes higher or lower than *X*.

Finally, H, I, and J represent a different pattern of distributions. The U-shaped distribution of H implies high, equal probabilities for outcomes whose values are either large or small, and a low probability for outcomes in between. The J-shaped curve of J shows a high probability of higher-valued outcomes, while the reverse-J curve of I implies a high probability for the lower-valued outcomes. These latter two curves have statistical connotations similar to those of E and D, respectively.

It may be noted that, technically, there has sometimes been a disagreement among theorists as to whether the mode or the mean should be used as the "expected value" for prediction purposes. One group has contended that the mode is preferable as the most probable value because it is more realistic: a decision maker is unlikely to calculate the mean of a probability distribution whose shape may not be clear-cut to begin with. Another group has favored the mean value because it is the theoretically correct one from which to compute the standard deviation as a measure of dispersion for the distribution. In any event, it is beyond our scope to go into the ramifications of these arguments. What concerns us most is the development of a conceptual orientation—a way of thinking about the nature of uncertainty—that forms a basis for scientific decision making and planning in modern management theory.

Economic Insurance and the Socio-Economics of Uncertainty

It is interesting to inquire why insurance against the uncertainty of losses has never been instituted in the business world. Enough has already been said to distinguish risk from uncertainty, and it should be clear that insurance can only be a response to the former rather than the latter. However, some further comments on the subject may be of interest here.

Fundamentally, there is no means known by which uncertainties can be isolated and generalized to the point where they can be classified as objective risks. Marketing researchers, for example, have yet to discover the economic laws (if any) that govern consumer behavior, and economists have yet to reduce to precise mathematical formulas the forces determining business cycles and the losses resulting therefrom. In short, there are simply too many imponderables to take into account in arriving at an exact method of prediction. Further, the creation of an adequate insurance program, if such were possible, would probably have to be based on long-run changes in prosperity and depression.

During prosperity periods when most companies are profitable and losses are at a minimum, the total amount of insurance premiums paid should exceed the total amount of losses incurred. Conversely, in depression periods losses are more general and should exceed the premium payments. Over the long run, therefore, the insurance company's profit during prosperity would presumably be balanced by its deficits during depression. But this would assume that the amplitude and frequency of business fluctuations could be forecast with accuracy, which they cannot, and this is precisely the problem at hand. Moreover, if such accurate forecasts of depressions were possible, insurance would be unnecessary; action could be taken instead to avoid the setback, thereby eliminating the need for insurance.[4]

Uncertainty vs. Security. The role of uncertainty also manifests itself with respect to income and employment. Broadly, as certainty increases in industries because of improved human ability to predict, incomes there will tend to decline in the long run relative to the more uncertain fields of employment. At least this is true to the extent that individuals choose and train for occupations on the basis of their probability estimates of future earnings. The greater the uncertainties of the future in an occupational line, as indicated by the dispersion of earnings probabilities, the more attractive is the drive for security (in return for lower incomes) in the more certain fields of employment. Witness the fact that employees in civil service, banks, and public utilities generally earn less than their colleagues in the more uncertain though similar lines of

[4] "It is fascinating to contemplate political or social institutions in a perfectly certain world. Policemen would be needed only at the moment of crime, firemen only at the time of fire; laws could be more pointed to cover precisely the specific objectionable future occurrence, etc. The mere knowledge of future developments would not always be sufficient to prevent anti-social outbreaks, for some of them may not always be amenable to advance control." (S. Weintraub, *Price Theory*. New York: Pitman, 1949, p. 349.)

activity in other industries. Admittedly, these monetary differentials may be somewhat compensated by nonmonetary factors (longer vacations, shorter hours, retirement benefits, etc.). But the fact remains that coal miners earn more than ditch diggers, window washers in skyscrapers command a higher wage than dishwashers in restaurants, and college professors earn less than corporation executives, though they may live longer. The clash between uncertainty and security can manifest itself in many ways. The removal of uncertainty, if that were possible, would serve to modify the structure and pattern of resource allocation and income distribution, and would create a type of economy substantially different from that which currently prevails.

It is probably fortunate, all things considered, that insurance of the type discussed is nonexistent. When managers have less reason to fear the possibility of loss due to a wrong decision because such loss will be largely protected, the incentive for greater efficiency and improved planning is substantially weakened. Uncertainty has created a venturesome spirit as the essence of American capitalism and free enterprise, and it seems neither possible nor desirable that this be sacrificed for an organized scheme of profit protection.

THE ANALYTICAL APPROACH

To what extent have the formal theories of risk and uncertainty influenced the development of management as a science? In the light of the foregoing discussion, the stage is now set for development of a concept of management which reflects the trend in much of modern managerial theory and research. But first, a contrast between the old and the new should help sharpen this distinction.

The Traditional Concept

The traditional approaches to the study of management have been largely descriptive, and have emphasized the anatomy rather than the physiology of the managerial process. For example, consider the following two typical definitions of management which can be found in many standard textbooks and articles on the subject:

- "Management is getting things done through people."
- "Management is the process of organizing, staffing, leading, directing, planning, and controlling."

The first is sufficiently general to be practically meaningless. The second is an excellent example of the anatomical approach, as exemplified by many textbooks in the field which tend to be completely organized and written in terms of detailed descriptions of these managerial functions.

Actually, the second definition amounts to the statement that management is largely concerned with the allocation of resources. But the science of optimal resource allocation has always been a paramount concern of economics—and of psychiatry too, for that matter, since people go to psychiatrists when they are unable to allocate their own resources in a manner which they regard as optimal. Hence, *the above definitions do not meet the requirements of a good definition as far as logical criteria are concerned: at best, they are mere descriptions (rather than definitions) of various phases of human activity; at worst, they are ambiguous generalities and redundancies which could just as well be discarded without serious loss.*

A Modern Coordinative Concept

Instead of trying to define management in terms of routine functions such as organizing, planning, controlling, etc., we can think of it instead as an integrated activity in which these functions are *not* separated. This is a more abstract approach, but it permits a classification of managerial activities in terms that are far more useful for many conceptual and analytical purposes.

The functions of managers may be classified for purposes of analysis into two distinct levels of activity: one is *coordination,* the other is *supervision.* The coordinative function is that of decision making—the process of selecting an action from alternative courses of action. The need for this function is universal, since it arises in environments of risk and uncertainty, that is, in situations where decisions must be made and plans formulated on the basis of expectations. The other phase of management, that of supervision, involves the fulfillment of plans already established, and hence requires little if any coordination of a decision-making nature. It is management in the coordination sense which is now recognized by many modern scholars as a central concept of management theory. This classification of management functions may be somewhat different from, but is not in fundamental disagreement with, the analyses underlying the distinguished contributions to modern management theory by such writers as Andreas Papandreou, Herbert Simon, James March, Richard Cyert, and others.

The justification for viewing management in a coordinative or decision-making sense is easily established. All human behavior involves, by conscious or unconscious means, the selection of particular actions out of all those that are available to the individual and to those over whom he exercises influence and authority. The process of making selections has been called decision making. Behavioral scientists have shown that selections may themselves be the product of complex chains of activities which the traditional writers referred to above have called organizing, staffing, leading, etc. If these activities are true descriptions of the managerial process, then it follows that decision making is the core of that process. Thus, major advancements in management research in such areas as organization, leadership, planning, communication, control, etc., have been and are now being made by focusing on central concepts of decision making and decision theory. Many of these developments are emerging not only in the fields of operations research or management science where the impetus has perhaps been strongest, but in the fields of business, economics, and the behavioral sciences as well.

The fundamental role of the coordinating unit—management in its true sense—is that of choosing between alternatives. Problems of choice arise because the material and human resources available to an organization, such as capital, land, labor and other inputs, are limited and can be employed in alternative uses. The executive function from the coordinative standpoint thus becomes one of making choices or decisions that will provide the optimum means of attaining a desired end, whether the end be the preservation of the existing situation between the organization and its competitors, or the long-run attainment of domination, or any other objective. But regardless of the goal, managers may classify outcomes as risks or as uncertainties. If knowledge of the future were perfect, decisions could be made and plans could be formulated without error and hence without need for subsequent revision. In many cases, however, the time involved precludes perfect knowledge. Thus decisions and plans are made at one point in time that are based on current knowledge, in anticipation of results that will be forthcoming at future points in time. As more facts become known, new decisions may have to be made and old plans may have to be revised as new courses of action are adopted in order to achieve desired objectives. Managers are thus engaged in the continuous process of charting such new courses of action into hazy horizons.

CONCLUSION

The above ideas constitute the essence of the coordinative function, and hence the bare elements of the concept of management under risk and uncertainty. There is a fundamental point in all of this that is worth reiterating: *an organization* (as distinguished from a mere physical producing plant), *or management in the coordination sense* (as distinguished from management in the supervisory sense), *exists largely as a device for adjusting to risk and uncertainty.* If the future were completely known, management in the coordination sense would be needed for the most part only at the start or initial phase of an investment in order to formulate a plan for the future; thereafter, management in the supervisory sense would be all that is needed for the purpose of administering or carrying out the plan. Apparently, since risk and uncertainty constitute the environment in which businessmen operate, planning, organizing, controlling, directing, etc. are actually inseparable activities of coordinative management. *Hence, the traditional classification and description of managerial functions along these lines is of doubtful value both on logical and operational grounds, as pointed out above.*

To what extent do managements—at least "progressive" managements—think in terms of the concepts presented above? An indication is perhaps given in the following copy from an advertisement by Celanese, a major producer of chemicals, fibers, plastics and polymers, which appeared in various magazines in April, 1963.

Probability

At the very heart of free enterprise is the element of risk. It is the willingness of industry to back its judgment with the fruits of past labor—*and possibly to lose*—that is the moral basis of profit.

It follows that successfully building a company is a matter of influencing the "odds," of "managing the probabilities." At Celanese we try to surround each project with all the research techniques, marketing methods and organizational patterns available to help assure success. As these techniques become more scientific, the odds in favor of success improve.

And it is further the mark of a well-run company that it can take an occasional loss without losing its corporate courage.

The authors show how this war-born technique—when properly understood and applied—can give the decision maker a scientific basis for solving a wide variety of business problems.

12

OPERATIONS RESEARCH—THE BASICS

E. Leonard Arnoff
M. J. Netzorg

It is a cliché that the problems confronting business decision makers today are more complex in nature and more far-reaching in scope than ever before. Fortunately, new methods, techniques, and tools are also making decision making easier—for the executive who is able and willing to use them.

One of the most important of these new techniques is operations research. For orientation of businessmen and consultants who have not yet had personal experience with its use, this article describes operations research—what it is, where it originated, how it is used in problem solving, and where it has been applied in industry.

WHAT OPERATIONS RESEARCH IS

Operations research (commonly referred to as OR) is the systematic, method-oriented study of the basic structure, characteristics, functions, and relationships of an organization. Such study is intended to provide the executive with a sound, scientific, and quantitative basis for decision making.

Reprinted from *Management Services,* January–February 1965, pp. 42–51, by permission of the authors and the publisher.

Operations research is based on the fact that in economic systems, just as in the physical world, there is a great deal of orderliness, even where this is not readily apparent. Thus, OR is concerned with determining (1) how a system behaves under a wide range of conditions, (2) the relationships which explain why the system behaves in this manner and, finally, (3) the manner and timing through which this behavior should be changed so as to best achieve the organization's goals.

Operations research is concerned with the relationships of the activity under study to all other *pertinent* elements of the system. It is also concerned with evaluation of the host of possible alternative courses of action open to the decision maker.

The roots of operations research are as old as science and the management function. OR uses techniques adapted from many fields, such as physics, psychology, industrial engineering, and—most particularly—symbolic logic, mathematics, probability, and statistics. In addition, new methods, techniques, and tools have been developed or adapted specifically for OR-type problems. Many of these developments are of recent origin —within the past five to ten years—so that one can now solve scientifically a host of important problems that were heretofore handled on a judgmental basis.

The capabilities, flexibility, speed, and scope of usefulness of electronic computers have aided in the growth of operations research. They have made possible the study and solution of problems of a complexity that was previously beyond the time limits that confront any feasible number of individuals, no matter how competent. Some operations research techniques require the use of computers, but in a number of areas highly effective work can be accomplished with little or no use of computer time. Under no circumstances is the computer a substitute for intelligence, thought, business imagination, and acumen.

The results of successful operations research, for the decision maker, are these:

1. Assistance in substantially improving the operations under his control and better achieving the goals of the organization
2. Increased knowledge and insight into the basic facts, characteristics, and relationships of the business
3. More effective, more responsive, and broader control
4. Better, more timely, and more quantitative information
5. A reduction of the time and effort required for routine decisions ("management by exception")
6. More time for planning and managing.

OR-TYPE PROBLEMS

Operations research has become increasingly useful to management, especially for solving those problems which affect more than one functional unit (division, department, section, etc.) within a firm. Such problems involve conflicts of interests, where a policy most favorable to one unit is rarely most favorable to the others. These conflicts of interest must be resolved to determine those policies and decisions that will maximize the effectiveness of the organization as a whole.

These problems have been called "executive-type" problems. They have arisen as a direct consequence of the functional division of labor in business enterprises—brought about by the rapid growth, diversification, and decentralization of industry. With the increased segmentation of the management function came increased attention of applied scientists to problems generated in the various functional units. From their efforts emerged a number of branches of applied science—including chemical, industrial, and mechanical engineering; industrial psychology; statistical quality control; industrial economics; and others. As each functional unit developed and better achieved its own objectives, executive-type problems increased in frequency and importance.

The solution of executive-type problems demands a highly refined balance of departmental objectives and over-all corporate objectives. *Operations research is devoted to the solution of executive-type problems—to provide management with a scientific basis for solving problems involving the interaction of functional units of the organization in terms of the best interest of the total organization.*

To illustrate an executive-type problem, consider briefly some of the objectives and conflicts involved in the inventory decisions of a firm:

Manufacturing seeks to minimize the unit costs of production (including set-up costs); hence, it favors long, uninterrupted production runs. This would result in large inventories composed of relatively few products.

Personnel is also interested in inventories. It wishes to stabilize labor and minimize the costs of hiring and layoff as well as employee discontent. This can be achieved by producing to finished inventory during times of slack customer demand.

Sales seeks to give outstanding service to customers and, hence, wishes to maintain a large inventory of a wide variety of products readily accessible in many locations. Further, it wishes manufacturing to be flexible and able to fill special orders on short notice.

Finance generally seeks to minimize the capital tied up in inventory and, hence, wishes a high rate of inventory turnover, that is, low inventory levels.

Other departments are also seriously affected by the production and inventory plan that is selected.

These objectives are, of course, in conflict with each other. The problem here is to determine the inventory policy which is best for the organization as a whole. Almost every managerial position is affected by the operating plan that is chosen and how well it is executed. However, because of the diverse objectives, and especially because of the conflicts among the objectives, choosing a plan is a controversial executive problem. Where the decision is made through negotiation and depends on the relative powers of persuasiveness of the individual departmental or divisional executives concerned, the outcome can easily be a plan of action that is far afield from what would best serve the company's overall interest.

It is under such circumstances that operations research is of highest value. It is a highly useful means by which to clarify and simplify decision making in the face of business uncertainties and risks, such as incomplete knowledge of future sales volumes and of the plans of competitors; in the face of a multiplicity of alternative courses of action; and in the face of conflicts of interest within the company.

Another type of situation where operations research is highly useful is under conditions where conflict of interest may be secondary in importance but where there are a great number of factors to be considered, highly complex interactions, and a sheer bulk of data.

Since operations research is a relatively new discipline, let us discuss its origin and development and how it works—and give a brief description of a few of the hundreds of decision areas in which it has been successfully applied.

ORIGIN OF OPERATIONS RESEARCH

Operations research's development began in the United Kingdom in 1939 when a group of scientists was assigned to the Operational Staff in Britain's military organization. This group of scientists included physicists, psychologists, engineers, mathematicians, and others. The group was divided into teams to study large-scale military problems. The inclusion of several disciplines on a team was found to lead to gratifying results in that the interplay among the scientists often yielded new and successful approaches to complicated problems. Outstanding contributions to the war effort included the effective use of radar, the allocation of British Air Force planes to missions, and the determination of the best patterns to be used in searching for submarines.

The dramatic success of these first efforts led to the formation of more such groups in the British armed services and in all branches of the United States military organization. Today, a substantial number of operations researchers are engaged in military operations research.

Immediately after World War II the methods and techniques so successfully applied by the military were adapted to business and industry. Further developments, many of them along new lines, have also been successful. It is this rapidly increasing body of knowledge—methodology, techniques, and special analytic approaches—that gives strength to operations research as it exists today.

HOW OR WORKS

Operations research, like all scientific research, is based on scientific methodology, which proceeds along the following lines:

1. *Analysis of the system*—to determine the objectives of the study and the specifications, form, and characteristics of the solution to the problem. Before this can be done, there must be a good, unbiased working knowledge of the existing system. (This is materially assisted through flow charting the relevant parts of the business under study). Basic to this stage is identification of decision points, plus determination of relevant factors and the extent to which they are subject to control. The eventual solution, accordingly, is conditioned by restrictions as to what must be done and what must not be done, as well as by consideration of limiting values and expressions of management policies.

It is at this stage that the general approach is established and the problem is formulated and often partitioned into interconnected subproblems. It is at this stage that broad appraisal is made as to both the cost and the pay-off value of a successful study and estimates are made of the required time and effort. This, combined with an appraisal of the difficulty of the study and the probability of its success, determines whether it is worthwhile (feasible) to undertake an operations research study—and, if so, in what scope and depth.

This first stage, as described above, is commonly referred to as an *orientation-feasibility study*. An important product of the orientation-feasibility study is a detailed research plan which sets forth the one or more phases of the study in such a manner that, phase by phase, results can be implemented and benefits achieved without awaiting the completion of the full study.

2. *Construction of a representation of the system*—a "model"—that has sufficient likeness to the real situation so that the model, rather than the system, can be munipulated meaningfully. The formal model is usually a mathematical representation of the system under study, designed in such a way as to facilitate the most effective evaluation of the influence of the various factors that affect the decisions.

3. *Testing the model.* The model must reflect those (and only those) real world conditions that are pertinent to problem solution. Collection and analysis of pertinent data then lead to appropriate modification and refinement of the model.

4. *Solving the model.* The model is then solved; that is, for any given set of conditions within stated policies and restrictions, the model is used to establish recommended courses of action. The analyst also calculates the effect of relaxing or tightening restrictions or of changing one or more policies.

5. *Controlling the model and solution.* At this point, controls must be established to indicate the limits within which the model and its solution can be considered as sufficiently reliable and to indicate under what future conditions and in what manner either the model or solution will have to be modified.

6. *Implementing results.* Finally, when the research is at an appropriate stage of progress, steps must be taken to put its findings to work.

The use of a model is commonplace; for instance, every factory schedule is a model. The accounting system of a firm is also a model, and often a very complex one. The power of operations research model building is that it is able to encompass a multitude of factors and a multitude of yardsticks and, hence, to resolve highly complex problems. A schedule is a model whose primary yardstick is time, with money important but secondary. An accounting system turns all the variables to money values, so that all other variables play a secondary role. The operations research approach typically involves a delicate weighting and balancing along interlocking measurement scales.

The use of an operations research model is especially important and advantageous in that it permits experimentation "on paper," without manipulation of the actual system. In using the model, one can assess the *sensitivity* (response) of the system to a wide variety of conditions—without requiring either the time, expense, or risks associated with experimenting with the system itself (if such experimentation would, in fact, be possible and meaningful). The appropriate transition from one set of conditions to another set of conditions can also be determined. Hidden relationships can be brought to light and brought to bear upon decisions and control of activity. Accordingly, operations research is particularly advantageous in dynamic (changing) situations.

The operations research approach to a problem gives consideration to the practical solution, as contrasted to the purely mathematical, or theoretical, solution. Analyses are performed to determine when further research or refinement will be more costly than the potential savings. Alternative solutions, indicating the cost of deviations from the computed optimal solution, are also derived and presented to management, thus giving management a better basis for selecting from among a group of alternative courses of action.

The use of operations research assures a sufficiently complete solution to a problem rather than a "patchwork" solution. The tendency in industry and business today is to be in a continual state of fire-fighting, treating the *symptoms* of problems rather than the true *causes*. Furthermore, the best solution for a particular component of a system when studied in isolation may be quite different from the solution when the over-all system is studied. For example, the stockage policies at a group of warehouses will generally be different when each warehouse is considered individually than when the total warehousing system is considered.

Since operations research is frequently involved in research, as contrasted to the application of previously developed techniques, there always exists the possibility of not being able to arrive at a full solution. However, the methodology of operations research provides an approach to problem solution that maximizes the probability of success in accomplishing the research objectives.

In summary, operations research, when applied to suitable problems by competent practitioners, leads to proper solution of problems—problems that could not be so clearly and decisively understood, stated, or handled by any other means.

Operations research has been applied in virtually every kind of business and industry. Among others, it has been used extensively in the petroleum, paper, chemical, metal processing, aircraft, rubber, transport and distribution, mining, and textile industries. Operations research has been very successful in aiding executives in solving problems in such areas as these:

Production

- Planning and scheduling
- Purchasing—materials and supplies
- Raw material and in-process inventory management
- Make or buy decisions
- Allocation of fixed facilities and manpower
- Equipment and materials utilization
- Maintenance and replacement of equipment and facilities

- Waiting lines (bottlenecks)
- Plant location

Marketing and Distribution

- Allocation of sales effort
- Salesmen's compensation plans
- Allocation of advertising dollars
- Evaluation of advertising effectiveness
- Product mix
- Finished goods inventory management
- Pricing and bidding strategy
- Forecasting (demand, supply, price)
- Warehouse location
- Centralization vs. decentralization
- Transportation
- Warranty
- Customer service

Investment and Finance

- Facilities planning
- Selection of process and equipment
- Replacement policy
- Diversification and acquisition
- Budgeting
- Portfolio selection
- Sampling in accounting
- Financial planning and control
- Financial forecasting

Organization

- Organization structure
- Centralization vs. decentralization
- Communication
- Long-range planning
- Organization of problem-solving groups
- Stockholder control

Others

- Evaluation of problem-solving groups
- Research and development expenditure
- Design of experiments
- Urban planning and area redevelopment
- Various uses of sampling
- Credit analysis (e.g., credit card accounts)
- Benefit plans—executives and employees
- Decision-oriented management information systems

The following brief descriptions give further indication of the immense range of problems and situations where operations research has been successfully applied. While reference is made to studies in specific industries, the problems involved often have basic underlying structures that conform to general types. So the solutions that were obtained could be paralleled in many industries, with those modifications required to take full account of the individuality that gives truth to the saying . . . "but my business is different."

The design, development, and implementation of an optimal production and inventory management system—in a machine-tool company. This application covered the planning and control of the ordering; scheduling; sequencing; dispatching; machine loading; warehousing; assembly; and raw, in-process, and finished goods inventory functions. Included also were analyses and appropriate changes in data collection, generation, and processing (computers and *decision-oriented* management information systems) and in forecasting. Decision rules and procedures were developed for both day-to-day operation and long-range planning.

Production planning and labor stabilization—in the rubber industry. In an industry where demand is highly seasonal, factory production rates and manpower levels were determined so as to minimize the sum of the costs of (1) hiring and layoff of personnel, (2) carrying inventory, and (3) overtime.

Planning and scheduling of materials, processes, manpower, and facilities—in a refinery complex. A method was developed for determining the selection and use of resources so as to maximize profit. Price-volume relationships were analyzed, and optimum product mixes were established for market planning. (This is an extension of optimum blending procedures for gasolines, middle distillates, and heavy fuel oils.)

The selection and scheduling of research and development projects—in the pharmaceutical industry. The estimated pay-off, cost, effort, and likelihood of success were determined for each potential research project. Available funds, manpower, and skills were then allocated so as to determine an over-all research program with greatest profit potential.

Maintenance and replacement program—in a trucking company. The study determined the optimum preventive maintenance and replacement program. The structure of the system was analyzed for a variety of basic alternative policies. Included in the analyses were the costs of maintenance and road failures.

Group replacement vs. individual replacement—of light bulbs in manufacturing companies and municipalities. For items that do not deteriorate with age or with use but which ultimately fail, the determination is made whether or not to replace in a group and, if so, when to do so. This problem arises since the cost per unit for group replacement (before failure) is less than the cost per unit for individual replacement (after failure).

The maintenance of mechanical equipment—for large, world-wide governmental agencies. These studies were concerned with the optimum number and location of maintenance shops, personnel requirements, stockage policies at depots and in the field, and the question of assembly vs. component part replacement.

The determination of optimum reserve generating capacity—in the electric utility industry. An analysis was made of shortage policies, maintenance programs, customer demand, and interconnections—to determine when to add generators and of what size. A major task here was the determination of the probabilities of equipment breakdown (forced outages) for the total system.

The determination of warehouse dock facilities—for a department store. Variations in the number and time of daily truck arrivals, the servicing times (loading and/or unloading), restrictions on the parking facilities, and customer and company truck waiting times were taken into account in determining the dock requirements for a warehouse which was to replace three existing warehouses.

The determination of facility requirements (cranes, docks, etc.) to accommodate the expected volumes and mixes of ores and coal received at a port. Factors considered included (1) the characteristics of ships arriving at the docks, (2) the effects of these characteristics on unloading rates and dock space, (3) limitations on the number of ships that can wait in the harbor, and (4) the cost associated with ships delayed in unloading due to insufficient facilities versus (5) the cost of idle unloading facilities.

Establishing, monitoring, and updating master plans for urban renewal and city planning. This requires integrated analyses of growth patterns (population and industry); the resulting effects on city income; and the sociological implications of various housing, recreational, office, and transportation systems.

The allocation of salesman effort—for a light-bulb manufacturer. This study involved determining the number of salesmen needed, sales territory boundaries, and the number of sales calls to make on each type of dealer so as to maximize the total profitability of the sales effort.

The establishment of an optimal distribution system—for a bulk-chemical producer. Optimum product mix, product reorder levels and order quantities, number and location of warehouses, the assignment of customers to warehouses, and the assignment of warehouse facilities to production plants were determined. Storage, transportation, and production costs, as well as customer service levels, were considered.

The selection of coal for coke plants. The objective of this study was to minimize the total cost of a given amount of coke. The costs of transportation, mining, and conversion (coal to coke) were included, along with consideration of the availability of coal at each mine and the capacity of each coke plant.

Planning for seasonal retail sales. Sales patterns for numerous products—sold by approximately 10,000 dealers with different geographical locations, types of stores, and sales volumes—had to be considered in developing a sampling plan for estimating end-user purchases. The results were then used to develop production, distribution, and marketing programs in a highly seasonal business.

The determination of an optimal warranty system—for a durable goods manufacturer. This study included the evaluation and change of settlement policies; where and by whom the claims should be settled; optimum produce quality level; and how product problems can be quickly detected, evaluated, and corrected.

The development of bidding strategies for obtaining leases for oil exploration. Included in this study were the development of a predictor of future production for a given lease and an analysis of the relationship between the amount bid and the likelihood of obtaining the lease for that bid.

THE OR APPROACH

Great care must be taken to assure that the right problem is being formulated and then solved—in its proper scope. As noted earlier, the use of an operations research model is especially advantageous here, inasmuch as it permits assessing the response, or sensitivity, of the system to a wide variety of conditions. In particular, it enables the analyst to determine the sensitivity of the solution to individual factors and, in turn, to determine the importance of such factors in obtaining still further improvements in the system.

A study conducted for an airline illustrates the operations research approach in assuring a complete, yet practical, solution:

A commercial airline sought to determine (1) how frequently it should conduct classes for the training of stewardesses, and (2) the size that these classes should be. This rather limited problem was formulated precisely, and a decision rule was obtained for administering the school so as to minimize the sum of the costs involved.

In the course of solving the problem, the operations research team discovered that the effectiveness with which the school was operated was very sensitive to the number of stewardesses required by the airline. Consequently, an investigation was undertaken as to how these requirements were determined at each base and, hence, for the total system.

This led, in turn, to the development of a procedure for minimizing the number of stewardesses (including reserve stewardesses) required at each base. This step required developing (1) new procedures for the preparation of individual flying assignments ("bids," prepared monthly) and (2) new provisions for "makeup" flying whenever flying assignments were missed (due to cancelled flights, etc.).

However, this investigation revealed that a base's requirements for staffing were sensitive to the assignment of flights to that base and that the total system's staffing requirements were sensitive to the number and location of bases and the assignment of flights to each of them.

A study was therefore undertaken to determine (1) how many bases there should be, (2) where the bases should be located, and (3) how the flights should be assigned to each base in order to yield the best possible performance of the total system.

However, since flights could not be assigned to bases without considering the male crews (the male crews and stewardesses flew the same monthly "bids"), the study was finally generalized to consider the total crew.

Once each of these aspects of the system's operations had been analyzed, the results of the several phases were synthesized and over-all planning procedures for training and utilization of personnel were developed.

Further studies of utilization of aircraft, maintenance policies, etc., were also suggested by the study, because of relationships which were revealed. These studies were subsequently undertaken. In addition, the study and its corresponding model put the company on a better basis for conducting its negotiations with the flight personnel unions, inasmuch as the implications of new contract terms could be determined in advance.

In this example, the "symptoms" were not indicative of the true problem; it was the over-all approach that eventually indicated the total problem that had to be solved. However, the intermediate steps were so conducted that the solution was optimized each time, subject to the constraints imposed by the rest of the system.

It is important to note that the benefits obtained from solving the over-all problem were substantially greater than those that would have been obtained by solving the limited problem originally stated.

ORGANIZING FOR AN *OR* STUDY

For each specific project, an OR task force should be formed consisting of qualified operations researchers as well as personnel directly involved with the subject area under study. These latter personnel will supply necessary technical know-how and experience, will assist in collecting and generating data, and will also assist in working out the details of implementation.

The joint task force should, in turn, report to a steering committee consisting of the managers (or representatives) of those functions of the company most vitally connected with, and affected by, the study.

The steering committee should usually consist of three to five members, although at times it is desirable to have additional representation. The task force should meet regularly with the steering committee, approximately two to four times per month, and with individual members of the committee even more frequently.

In turn, the task force and the steering committee should meet with a top management committee—typically every six to ten weeks. Ordinarily, the top management committee for the OR study is a regularly functioning committee already in existence. This committee is usually a fairly large one including representation from each and every major function of the company. In many instances, members of the steering committee are also regular members of the top management committee.

In some instances the nature and scope of the problem, as related to the company structure, are such that only a single management committee is needed, usually consisting of three to ten members.

The use of the operations research task force, a steering committee, and a top management committee yields many important benefits—so important, in fact, that it is safe to assert that *an operations research study will seldom be effective unless such committees are used.* With proper use of the committees, the benefits include the following:

1. These committees serve as filters for the research, help prevent errors of both commission and omission, provide additional know-how, and generally guide the team *during* the study, thereby increasing the chances of success. (In particular, interactions among functions are uncovered where they might otherwise be missed.)

2. Since the committees represent the areas affected by and involved in the study, the OR team is not put in the position of an outsider (e.g., staff) trying to tell others (e.g., operating personnel) what to do. Everyone has a sense of participation and contribution and also a much better opportunity for discussion and, hence, understanding, thereby increasing chances for acceptance and successful implementation. Furthermore, implementation can then be carried out more readily and quickly.

3. Several levels of management and operating personnel are thereby educated in the nature of operations research, making them more aware of its potentialities and its limitations.

The success of operations research in any company often depends as much on management as it does on the operations research staff. Hence, wherever possible, the informal discussions on operations research at the committee meetings should be supplemented by a series of formal sessions on OR—designed to develop a better understanding by management. Such sessions have been conducted—with great success—in a large number of companies.

4. Further OR projects will usually be suggested by these committees,

thereby inducing a better acceptance of and environment for operations research at all levels of the company.

WORDS OF CAUTION

Whenever operations research is mentioned, executives are likely to express some bewilderment over the fact that results have ranged all the way from limited success to the highest usefulness and profitability.

So far, this article has discussed the steps, the procedures, the attitudes, the probings, and the methodology—which are a minimal basis upon which to build toward success. In so doing, the positive side has been accentuated. However, there is also a need to point out the negative side. Certain common traps and pitfalls can easily be, and have been, the ruination of otherwise good work. Some of these pitfalls are fairly obvious, while others are so subtle and deeply hidden that unless careful heed is taken their presence is not even suspected.

At the very outset of problem solving—the problem selection and formulation phase—a number of pitfalls can and do arise. Here, the executive and the operations researcher have the joint task of selecting the right problem and of defining it completely and accurately. Is the right problem being solved? Is the problem being considered in its proper scope, or will the gains be localized and at the expense of other parts of the organization ("suboptimization")? Will the solution pertain to the actual system under study and properly reflect the goals of the organization as well as the imposed restrictions? Are appropriate measures of performance being used? The problem formulation phase is probably the most important and most difficult part of the entire study. Deliberate and skillful planning is especially required here.

Data gathering can represent a very large part of the time and cost of an operations research study. Hence, an early analysis of the sensitivity of the solution to the input data should always be made, since it will save gathering unneeded data and will often indicate the areas in which measurement and control (and, hence, better data) are most important. Fortunately, a system reasonably close to optimum usually gives excellent results. Hence, rough, order-of-magnitude estimates will often give considerable insight into system behavior and results.

Solving the problem also contains some potential dangers. Not the least of these is over-concern with the elegance of the solution, which can lead to an elaborate and correct answer that may be too late or too complex to be used. It also can lead to "over-optimization," that is, attempting to obtain the last few percentage points of improvement by a detailed and expensive analysis. A less complicated model will often yield most of the potential gain, at considerably less cost and with much greater likelihood of success; in fact, the cost of any further gain may well exceed the gain itself.

Other pitfalls in problem solving include (1) taking a "cookbook" approach when a custom design is needed (as, for example, precipitous use of standard lot-size formulas), (2) warping the problem to fit an available model, technique, or tool, (3) substituting high-speed, brute force computer groping for sound analysis, (4) failing to test the model and the solution adequately prior to implementation, and (5) failing to establish proper controls on the results.

Estimating benefits from system improvements requires a word of caution, in that theoretical benefits are usually not completely achieved and potentials must be discounted in order to give realistic, practical expectations of accomplishments. The disappointment of not fully achieving a potential gain can overshadow the benefits that are actually attained, even when such benefits are sizable.

A number of operations research studies have not realized great potential because the results were not fully accepted. Many of these studies were technically sound, but the operations researcher failed to communicate properly with management. It is the operations researcher's responsibility to translate his highly specialized and technical thoughts, concepts, and ideas into the realm of experience of the executive and into the language of the business and to translate complex solutions and formulas into tools and procedures that can be readily used. Further, it is essential that the operations researcher determine and develop the procedures necessary for smooth transition from the original system to the new system.

One further word of clarification is that, in fact, a truly optimum solution is never achieved. Rather, what is called an optimum solution is such only for the problem as specifically stated, the area covered, and the conditions that existed at that point in time. However, the fact that a solution may not be truly optimum does not mean that substantial gains cannot be achieved.

Finally, what may appear to be a pitfall is the fact that a good operations research study may raise more questions than it answers. However, this can lead to a more penetrating inquiry into the operation of the system and what it is intended to do—with the ultimate result of greater insight into the system and even more far-reaching benefits and improvements. This inquiring aspect of operations research is one of its strongest attributes.

The author outlines the operations research approach, discusses its application to six types of business problems, and defines the major OR techniques.

13

PROBLEM SOLVING WITH OPERATIONS RESEARCH

A. Fendrock

You are the chief executive of a several million dollar a year company. The company has ten plants throughout the country making two basic products that are sold directly to customers from the plants and through a complex of 80 warehouses and distributors. Each plant has a different manufacturing cost and production capacity. The products may be delivered in various size vehicles and containers, each of which has a different distribution cost and payload. During recent years the company has experienced a profit squeeze—prices are deteriorating and costs are rising . . .

Marketing and Sales insist that prices must remain competitive and costs reduced to make a profit. Manufacturing and Distribution state that costs cannot be further reduced—the products are highly seasonal, and work force and equipment must be retained to meet the peak requirements . . .

Sound familiar? This is a usual business problem—the type of problem which lends itself to analysis and "solution" with the use of mathematical models. In fact, operations research techniques have been used to "find a better" way for some time.

Reprinted from *Systems & Procedures Journal,* May–June 1967, pp. 34–38, by permission of the author and the publisher.

WHAT IS OPERATIONS RESEARCH?

Operations research may be defined as the application of *scientific/mathematical* methods, techniques and tools to the solution of operating business problems. Operations research is concerned primarily with operating business problems, and this is the area in which the greatest degree of success has been achieved. The problem may be any system, not necessarily an emergency situation, such as the loss of a plant or facility. The following may be considered as problems:

- Inventory systems.
- Warehousing.
- Production/distribution.
- Competitive situations, e.g., how will competition react to the raising or lowering of prices?
- How to blend raw materials to produce products to specifications at least cost.
- Evaluation of investment opportunities.

Inventory systems are perhaps the one business problem in which most O.R. work has been done. These range from simplified hard goods inventory level problems through complex order receiving, distribution, manufacturing, economic lot size determination and warehousing problems. Essentially, this type of model answers the questions "what to stock?", "where?" and "in what quantities?" such that the sum total of order processing, manufacturing and distribution costs are minimized.

Consider the problems of a manufacturer who has four plants with approximately 35,000 items (from raw materials to finished goods) and approximately 650 distribution points (including the plants, warehouses and distributors). The products are shipped prepaid to customers throughout the country. Orders are sporadic and replacement parts must be kept in stock. Some of the plants manufacture the same products, and costs at these plants vary. Simulation of the order entry, manufacturing and distribution system, using various inventory stocking and manufacturing lot size formulae, can minimize the sum total of the manufacturing and distribution costs.

To give a brief explanation of why operations research techniques and the concomitant use of computers for the solution of problems is necessary, let's consider another brief illustration.

The formula for determining the number of ways in which things may be combined is:

$$(2^n - 1)$$

If we wanted to find the number of ways one item can be stocked in three warehouses, it would be as follows:

$$(2^3 - 1) = 7$$

Admittedly, this is a small problem, and it would be very unusual if a business situation involved only three factors in combination. It is not unlikely that we would be looking at 20 or 30 items in combination. As you can see from the following, this represents a calculation of considerable magnitude:

$$(2^{20} - 1) = 1{,}048{,}575$$

This is the number of combinations involved in the equivalent of up to two plants serving up to ten warehouses

$$(2^{40} - 1) = 1{,}099{,}511{,}627{,}775$$

This is the number of combinations involved in the equivalent of up to five trucks serving up to eight customers

These problems can be solved only with the use of the most advanced operations research techniques and fastest and most modern computing equipment. They are beyond the reach of ordinary manual methods in terms of both time and economic value.

OPERATIONS RESEARCH APPROACH

Business organizations consist of various functional units, each having individual objectives. Often, these units have conflicting short-range goals. For example, consider the inventory problem. Marketing ideally would like to have every product on the doorstep of the customer. Production would want a steady level of production with a few large lots to minimize set-up costs and to make the most efficient utilization of men and equipment. Financial would want to keep inventories low to minimize carrying costs and the investment in inventories.

The operations research approach to the solution of these conflicts attempts to look at the total problem—to evaluate the combined impact on the performance of the organization as a whole and not merely an individual functional unit. This is contrary to what might be considered a conventional approach to problem solving; namely, cutting the problem down to size or considering the problem from one functional unit's point of view. The total solution to the problem indicates a course of action best for the organization as a whole.

Operations research employs scientific/mathematical methods, techniques and tools. The methods used in operations research are best described as follows:

1. Analysis of the problem.
2. Identification of objectives.
3. Development of specific measures of performance.
4. Identification of relevant factors.
5. Identification of significant relationships.

Analysis of the Problem

All problems have two aspects:

1. "Content"—substance of the matter with which the problem is concerned.
2. "Form"—structure of principle.

Many problems, while different in content, may be similar in form. For example, an inventory problem dealing with hardgoods has the same basic form as cash in banks or the deployment of airline stewardesses. These are all inventory problems in form, although the content of these problems differs. A basic difficulty of an operations research study is to attempt to abstract the form from the content for the solution of business problems. Unfortunately, most business problems are not that easily defined and, in fact, may have many forms.

In the analysis of the problem, it is essential to employ a combined effort of the managements of the various functional units involved and the operations research group. As a matter of fact, we would like to think of the solution of operations research problems being the responsibility of the division for which services are being performed, rather than the operations research group. The organizations for which the studies are performed supply the necessary knowledge, insights, and inter-relationships of their activities, while the operations research group adapts the real business situation and applies the operations research tools and techniques.

All data must be analyzed, tested, revised and refined. For example, the identification of fixed and variable costs for accounting purposes may not be suitable for an O.R. study. In fact, it may be desirable, and perhaps necessary, to revise the accounting treatment of fixed and variable cost if variable budgets are to be developed and O.R. studies in the future are to be able to use accounting data without refinement.

Identification of Objectives

Since many functional units are involved for the total solution of a problem, the objectives of the organization as a whole must be identified. This can best be accomplished by the team approach described above —continually questioning, interpreting the answers to questions and their implications, relating values, etc.

It is not unusual that an objective, as stated, is not the objective at all. "What vehicles do I need at location X to minimize distribution costs" may not be the problem at all. The broader question "What types, sizes and numbers of vehicles, from a limited fleet of vehicles, should be deployed at each location such that customer service can be maintained at some given level and distribution costs minimized?" is the one which must be asked.

Measures of Performance

Some measurements of the performance of the present operations must be made in order that any revised method of operations can be evaluated against it. Have costs in fact been reduced or profits increased? The results of the study must be consistent with the objectives of the organization. Further, it must reflect the relative importance of, and conflict between, the diverse objectives of the different functional units.

A comparison between budget or operating costs and costs predicted by the solution of the mathematical model serves very well as a measure of performance. Conversely, if a profit model is used, then a comparison between the forecast or actual profits and profits predicted by the model will serve as a measure of performance.

Identification of Relevant Factors

The factors involved compose the problem content. These factors influence the problem areas, and must be identified with their parameters (limits) whether they are controllable or uncontrollable, and can be identified only by the joint efforts of both the managements of the various functional units and the operations research group.

Depending upon the problem, factors, such as special customer requirements (delivery between certain hours, need for trailer equipped with power, limited warehouse facility, etc.), product characteristics (limited shelf life, special handling and storage, etc.) must be identified and the mathematical model restricted accordingly.

Identification of Significant Relationships

The relationships of the significant factors must be determined in order that the results can properly be evaluated. We must be sure that too much weight is not given to one factor—and too little to another—which will distort the performance of the system and produce erroneous results.

In an inventory model, for example, overestimating or "padding" purchasing or manufacturing lead times will result in higher inventories.

The proper employment of these methods leads to the successful representation of the business situation in a mathematical model.

MODEL FORMULATION AND USE

A model may be defined as a mathematical, economic, or statistical description of a business system. In fact, it should be a representation of the system in quantitative terms. While it bears a similarity to the real system, it also has a nonidentity with the system, in that it is not a real system. It is obtained by abstracting the form (or structure) of the problem from the combined statements of the problem (content). It includes a measure of performance and the relationships between all significant factors and their interactions.

A model is used for prediction in that it permits the evaluation of a system. It also permits operation under various policies, procedures and conditions that could not be carried out in the real world. Therefore, a model permits prediction of how changes in policies, procedures and conditions would work in the real system. Obviously, many different policies and procedures could not be carried out in the real system, because they would take too much time, cost too much money and could cause an adverse reaction.

In order to develop a model, it is not unusual that hundreds of hours of work may be required, and this work is principally done by the managers of the activities under study. In preparing for a model, one must gather data, prepare data and test the model against specific measures of performance. The model must contain a sensitivity analysis; that is, how much are model outputs affected by small changes in input data?

Suppose, for example, that some fixed costs were inadvertently included in the manufacturing costs of products. An immediate determination must be made with regard to the effect on the results. Must the costs be purged? Would the results be biased toward purchasing a product rather than manufacturing in house? Would territorial boundaries for areas serviced by the plant be drastically revised? What is the effect of climate on the shelf life of the product? Is it different for different areas of the country?

It should also identify what penalties may result (additional costs or less profit) for implementing a "nonoptimal solution." The model also determines over what range the present solution is valid, and what changes in the solution are associated with changes in conditions.

The model must be evaluated by the analysis of the outputs obtained from its use. These results must be interpreted in terms of the system under study to determine their validity. The process of problem analyzing, identifying objectives, determining measures of performance, identifying factors, sensitivity analysis and evaluation may be repeated many times in order to obtain satisfactory results.

OPERATIONS RESEARCH TECHNIQUES

In the discussion of techniques we will limit consideration to the six better known operations research techniques. These are as follows:

1. Linear programming
2. Inventory theory
3. Simulation
4. Dynamic programming
5. Decision theory
6. Queuing theory

In the discussion of the techniques we will attempt to show the kinds of problems to which they may apply.

Linear Programming

Linear programming is a mathematical technique for directing the most efficient use of raw materials, manpower, tools of production or capital toward an objective, such as maximizing profit or minimizing costs. Several different means are used to describe this technique. A transportation model is a form of linear programming, depending on the extent to which the linear programming (mathematical formula) has been developed. Linear programming may also be called by terms such as simplex method, revised simplex method, ALPAC, etc. Characteristics of a linear programming problem are the following. There must exist:

1. A set of "constraints"—where limitations or minimum requirements must be met.
2. "Choice" or "choices" within alternative courses of action.
3. A "best" answer—optimization.

Typical examples of where linear programming may be used are on many "allocation" problems. These are characterized by the requirement to perform a set of jobs with not enough resources to do each job best. Basically, the problem is how to assign resources to the job. Production/distribution problems, transportation, production mix and blending problems fall into this category. The production/distribution problem in the opening part of this article falls into this category.

Inventory Theory

Inventory type problems are identified by idle resources (inventory in storerooms) and two types of costs:

a. An ownership cost; that is, cost which increases as inventory increases.

b. Acquisition and shortage costs; that is, costs which decrease as inventory increases.

The inventory problem attempts to determine the frequency of order and quantity to be ordered to minimize the sum of the costs. Some examples of this type of problem are the conventional inventory problem, capital and assignment of airline stewardesses.

Simulation

Some problems are too complex, badly behaved, etc., for tractable, mathematical optimization. Also, not every real problem consists of a single basic form. Many consist of a combination of problems, yet the application of a combination of techniques is not possible and one must resort to simulation. Simulation means the duplication of the essence of the system or activity without actually attaining reality itself.

Two basic types of simulation are:

1. Enumeration—determination of all possible outcomes (and probabilities) for each set of operating policies.
2. Monte Carlo—experimentation with model using chance to determine inputs for outcomes which are not known with certainty.

Examples of simulation use include continuous process plant operations, the manufacturing process of hardgoods, operation of carbide and steel and alloy furnaces. The order processing/inventory problem previously described is this type.

Dynamic Programming

The essential characteristics of the dynamic programming problem form involve multistage decision processes wherein decisions can be made sequentially. It is desirable to have sequence of decisions optimize some objective function, such as reducing costs or increasing profits. Examples are truck routing problems, sequencing problems, such as some production line problems, and the replacement of machines or facilities.

Decision Theory

The essential characteristic of decision theory is that the consequences of any course of action are not known with certainty. In this instance, probabilities are used. Decision theory is used in competitive type problems, such as bidding, pricing and some marketing problems.

Pricing policies are very good examples of this application. The effect of raising or lowering prices, probabilities of increasing or losing a share of the market, probable competitive reaction, effect on profits, etc., can be tested in this manner.

Queuing Theory

The essential characteristic for queuing theory is that arrivals into the system must be serviced at a service facility. If the service facility is busy, then a queue (or waiting line) results, and a queuing discipline (service in a specified order) must be established. Queuing theory will attempt to minimize the sum of the costs of supplying service and of customers waiting.

Well-defined mathematical techniques of probability theory are used for the solution of this type of problem. Examples of this technique are scheduling or line balancing problems, such as in a manufacturing process, unloading docks or order processing.

Of course, the benefits to be derived from any of these techniques are in proportion to the detail which goes into their preparation.

RESULTS OF OPERATIONS RESEARCH

Results, or what operations research can do for you, can consist of the following:

The solution of a model provides procedures capable of optimal solutions under any set of conditions; that is, decision rules. It also provides procedures for detecting changes in conditions and permitting adjustments of the solution.

A better insight or understanding of some of the relationships which affect the operation of the system is obtained, and O.R. also identifies areas for further study in that the study itself may uncover other problem areas.

SUMMARY

Operations research is a tool, aid, or guide to supplement business judgement—not supplant it. It is not a cure-all. O.R. is most effective when used as a planning tool—a guide to the most efficient use of present resources and for future planning—an operating guide for foreseeable changes in conditions and not a day-to-day decision maker.

Can improvement be made without operations research? Probably yes. But this is like comparing riding horseback to California or taking a jet. Factors such as speed, safety, comfort, and cost are equally important.

Management's responsibilities are:

1. To familiarize itself with operations research methods and techniques.
2. Recognize areas for application.
3. Provide the necessary resources; that is, personnel necessary to work on an operations research team.

Where a proper rapport has been established between management and the O.R. group, the results of an O.R. study can be extremely useful. The author's firm has found that the cooperative efforts of both operating management and the O.R. group are the key to the successful completion and implementation of the results of an O.R. study.

BIBLIOGRAPHY

Ackoff, Russell L., *Progress in Operations Research,* Vol. I, New York, John Wiley & Sons, Inc., 1961.

Ackoff, Russell L., and Rivett, Patrick, *A Manager's Guide to Operations Research,* New York, John Wiley & Sons, Inc., 1963.

Bellman, Richard E., and Dreyfus, Stuart E., *Applied Dynamic Programming,* Princeton, N.J., Princeton University Press, 1962.

Bowman, Edward H., and Fetter, Robert B., *Analyses of Industrial Operations,* Homewood, Ill., Richard D. Irwin, Inc., 1959.

Bowman, Edward H., and Fetter, Robert B., *Analysis for Production Management,* Homewood, Ill., Richard D. Irwin, Inc., 1961.

Churchman, C. West, Ackoff, Russell L., and Arnoff, Leonard E., *Introduction to Operations Research,* New York, John Wiley & Sons, Inc., 1957.

Dantzig, George B., *Linear Programming and Extensions,* Princeton, N.J., Princeton University Press, 1963.

Duckworth, W. E., *A Guide to Operational Research,* London, Methuen & Company, Ltd., 1962.

Fetter, Robert B., and Dalleck, Winston C., *Decision Models for Inventory Management,* Homewood, Ill., Richard D. Irwin, Inc., 1961.

Garvin, Walter W., *Introduction to Linear Programming.* New York, McGraw-Hill Book Company, Inc., 1960.

Gass, Saul I., *Linear Programming,* New York, McGraw-Hill Book Company, Inc., 1958.

Hertz, David B., and Eddison, Roger T., *Progress in Operations Research,* Vol. II, New York, John Wiley & Sons, Inc., 1964.

Magee, John F., *Production Planning and Inventory Control,* New York, McGraw-Hill Book Company, Inc., 1958.

McMillan, Claude, and Gonzalez, Richard F., *Systems Analysis,* Homewood, Ill., Richard D. Irwin, Inc., 1965.

Miller, David W., and Starr, Martin K., *Executive Decisions and Operations Research,* Englewood Cliffs, N.J., Prentice-Hall, Inc., 1960.

Mills, Edwin S., *Price, Output, and Inventory Policy,* New York, John Wiley & Sons, Inc., 1962.

Morse, Philip M., *Queues, Inventories and Maintenance,* New York, John Wiley & Sons, Inc., 1958.

Raiffa, Howard, and Schlaifer, Robert, *Applied Statistical Decision Theory,* Boston, Harvard University, 1961.

Schlaifer, Robert, *Probability and Statistics for Business Decisions,* New York, McGraw-Hill Book Company, Inc., 1959.

Schlaifer, Robert, *Introduction to Statistics for Business Decisions,* New York, McGraw-Hill Book Company, Inc., 1961.

Starr, Martin K., and Miller, David W., *Inventory Control: Theory and Practice,* Englewood Cliffs, N.J., Prentice-Hall, Inc., 1962.

Wagner, Harvey M., *Statistical Management of Inventory Systems,* New York, John Wiley & Sons, Inc., 1962.

The authors explain what PERT is, how it works, and ways to apply it to solve specific business problems.

14

AN INTRODUCTION TO PERT

Sidney I. Neuwirth
Joel Zelnick

INTRODUCTION

Although PERT (Program Evaluation Review Technique) is a relatively new technique, it has gained considerable acceptance. For the most part, this recognition is due to its successful application to diversified projects. For example:

- A major metals manufacturer schedules its around-the-clock mining operations with this new approach—and saves money by cutting time for maintenance and repairs.
- One of the largest chemical producers employed PERT methods to mastermind the multimillion-dollar move of an entire division of the company from one city to another.
- A large construction company has used a PERT variation for more than 50 projects; on one job alone it sliced 25 percent from the estimated cost.

The novelty of PERT lies in the graphic and conceptual integration of all components of a project into a network. In PERT, a detailed breakdown is made of all elements or activities in a project, with associated completion times and costs. Their interrelationship is then graphically portrayed in a flow chart, and an analysis of all network sequences

Reprinted from *The Journal of Accountancy,* Vol. 115, No. 5, May 1963, pp. 83–87, by permission of the publisher.

establishes the sequence of activities in which no delay can occur without delaying the total project. This sequence of activities is known as the "critical path," and its determination identifies for management those activities that require priority attention in case of delay, so that manpower and other resources can be rescheduled (usually from peripheral events) to minimize the effect of the delay on the entire project.

PERT's ancestry might be said to go back to the development of the Gantt Chart. Introduced about 1914, the Gantt Chart is a recognized management tool for which many uses have evolved over the years because of its applicability to projects having or requiring an orderly sequence of events, e.g., to set up control systems for planning and monitoring production. Revisions were made to production plans, as indicated by such control systems. In some cases, these revisions were made manually, in others they were accomplished via a computer program. Such systems were already an incipient PERT technique, but with the increase in detail associated with the administration of governmental and industrial projects, more refined techniques than the Gantt Chart were urgently needed to plan and control them. About 1958, PERT emerged to assist in the planning and control of these projects, and at about the same time, another scheduling technique known as the Critical Path Method (CPM) also came into being.

In contrast to CPM, which requires only one time estimate, PERT requires three time estimates for completion of an activity: optimistic time, most likely time, and pessimistic time. These three estimates are combined mathematically to produce the expected completion time of an event.

Do three time estimates provide better results in terms of meeting schedules than one estimate? Currently, insufficient data is available to answer this question. Tentatively, however, certain factors seem significant. A preliminary study has indicated that three estimates result in a more pessimistic schedule than one estimate only. Consequently, the use of three estimates forces a tightening of internal schedules to meet projected target dates. Further, by using three estimated time values, probabilities can be determined by means of which the *degree of uncertainty* associated with the completion of the project can also be determined. These two factors would seem to verify the value of PERT's three time estimates per activity, but it cannot yet be said that they materially compensate for the uncertainty of subjective judgments.

TERMINOLOGY

A new language has emerged with PERT. Below is a list of terms used in PERT analysis:

1. *Activity.* An activity is a time-consuming element in any project, and is usually represented on a network by an arrow. It is determined by events that precede and succeed it.

2. *Activity time.* Activity times are time estimates for completion of an activity. In PERT there are three activity times for each event:

a. Optimistic time. Assuming unusually favorable conditions, it will be the shortest time required to perform a given task. It is given the symbol "a."

b. Most likely time. This time is the most realistic estimate for the completion of a given project. It is given the symbol "m."

c. Pessimistic time. Assuming the most unfavorable conditions for the completion of a project, it is the longest time the activity should take. It is given the symbol "b."

3. *Network.* A diagram of events, activities, and time estimates, which constitutes a pictorial representation of a project.

4. *Event.* A specified part of a project, which is represented on the PERT diagram or network by a circle.

5. *Critical path.* The sequence of interrelated events between the beginning of a project and its completion date that will require the longest time to complete.

6. *Expected completion time for an event.* The expected completion time for an event is a weighted mean of its three estimated activity times: optimistic, most likely, and pessimistic.

$$t_e = \frac{a + 4m + b}{6}$$

7. *Preceding event.* An event that must be completed before the following activity can begin.

8. *Succeeding event.* An event that cannot be started until the preceding event is completed.

9. *Latest allowable time.* The latest allowable time of any event is equal to the latest allowable time of the succeeding event, less the expected event time of the activity joining these two events. It is given the symbol "T_L."

10. *The earliest expected time.* The earliest expected time of the last event is equal to the sum of the expected times of the preceding events, beginning with the start event. It is given the symbol "T_E." In the case of parallel paths, the largest sum only is considered.

11. *Slack.* The difference between the latest and expected completion times for an event. It is positive when the expected date is less than the latest completion date, and it is negative when the expected date is greater than the latest date.

RULES FOR ESTABLISHING NETWORKS

Network construction is fundamental to PERT. Basically, an activity is described by an arrow diagram. The conventions for depicting such activities are:

1. Each arrow should represent only one activity.
2. The length of the arrow is determined only by convenience and clarity, and is not related to the time needed for that activity.
3. Each activity except the first must have an activity preceding it.
4. Each activity except the last must have an activity following it.
5. For any activity to begin, all preceding activities must be completed.
6. No two activities can have the same origin and ending.

Another symbol used in a PERT network is a node or small circle. Conventions for the use of nodes are:

1. The event title is inscribed in a circle called a bubble. The arrows joining the bubbles denote event sequence.
2. A common practice when drawing a network where many activities are started concurrently is to start with a base line rather than a start bubble or node. Thus, a beginning network could be represented as:

3. The event title must be unequivocal and must explicitly denote either the beginning or the ending of an activity. For example:

Acceptable	*Not Acceptable*
Start test	Test
Test completed	

4. In order to handle events in computations, each bubble should be numbered. For example:

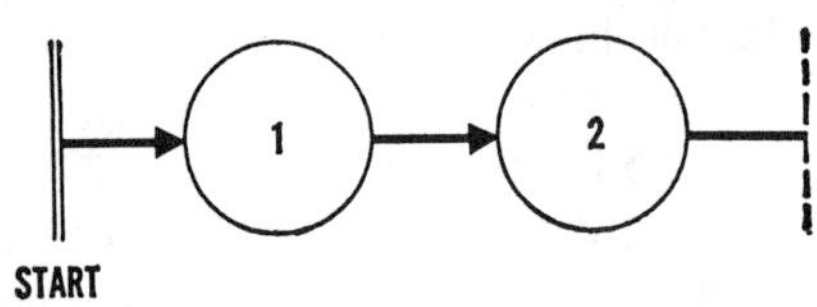

START

CASE STUDY

PERT network for the installation of a new organizational structure. The new organizational structure for a company had to be installed. Management wanted to know how long it would take for them to install their new organization. Since a reorganization can cause a great deal of personnel problems if it is not installed properly, it was decided to use PERT to insure a smooth installation of reorganization.

The first step was to appoint an analyst to (1) co-ordinate the development of the PERT network; (2) to keep all concerned fully informed; and (3) to prepare and issue revised networks and plans as often as necessary. To do this, the rules below were used:

1. Specify all "events" necessary to accomplish the over-all objective (Figure 14–1). These events should be expressed in terms of completed action, such as "Personnel evaluations updated."

No.	
0	Reorganization approved
1	Administrator's appointment announced
2	Progress reporting system installed
3	Personnel evaluations updated
4	New position descriptions completed
5	New personnel specifications completed
6	New salary classifications determined
7	Manpower forecasts completed to 1962
8	Manpower forecasts completed to 1967
9	Recruitment program launched
10	Organization costs estimated
11	Procedural system started
12	Existing procedures documented
13	Essential new procedures documented
14	First stage completed

Figure 14–1. Listing of events

2. Prepare a schedule in which each of these events is given a serial number and shown in terms of sequence, namely, that event 6 can be completed only after event 5 is completed.

3. From this schedule, draw a network in which each event is represented as a number in a circle, with arrows connecting it with the events that *must* precede it and that *must* follow it.

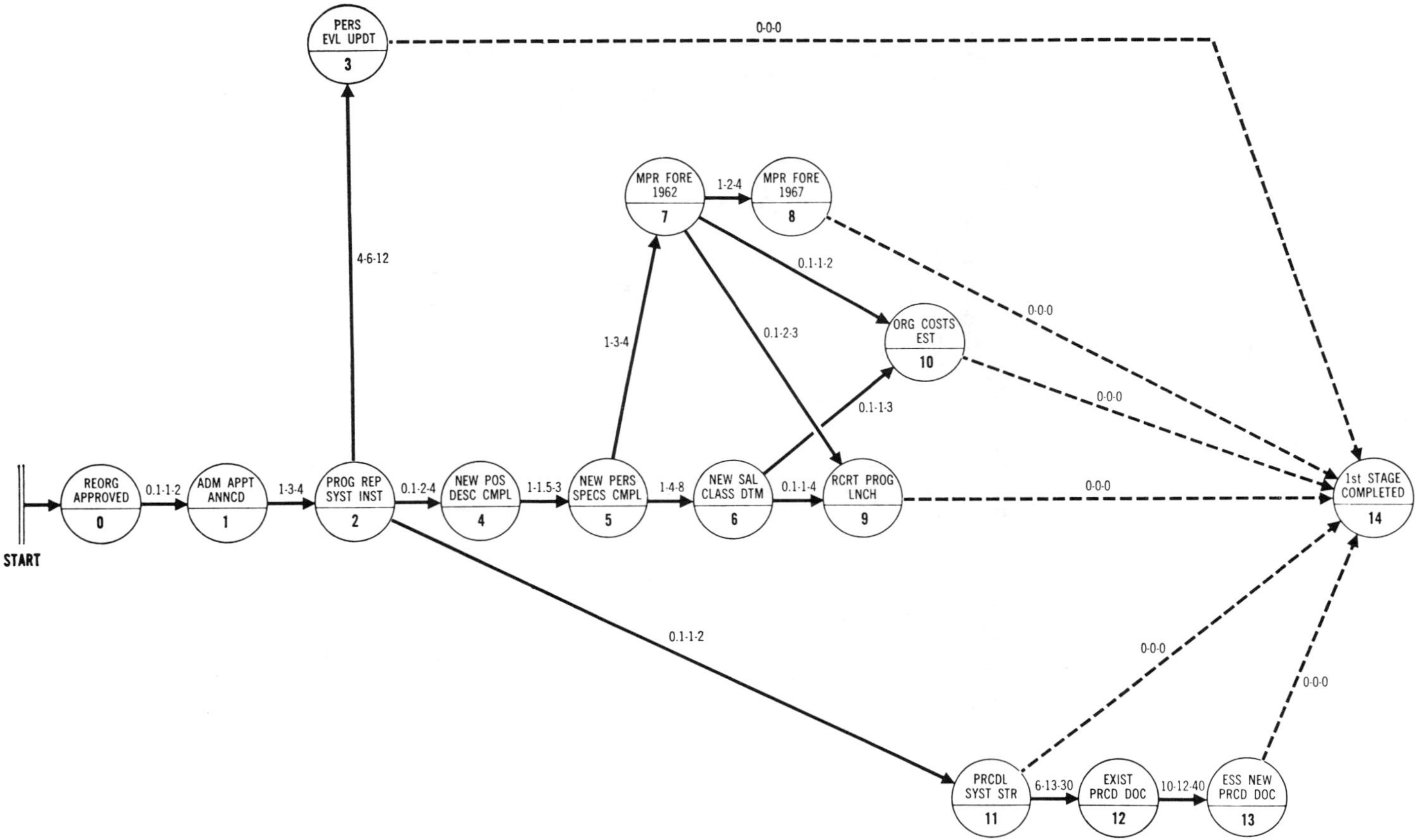

Figure 14–2. The PERT network

4. Based on the network, draw up a work sheet itemizing the events in the time sequence deduced from the network.

5. Determine the time required for movement from each event to the next following event. This is done by discussing with the people most likely to be able to provide reliable estimates:

- the most optimistic time expected—referred to as "a"
- the most reasonable time expected—referred to as "m"
- the most pessimistic time expected—referred to as "b."

6. Chart the network (Figure 14–2).

7. Perform the necessary calculations and determine the critical path (Figure 14–3). Map in the critical path on the network (Figure 14–4).

8. On completing the network and calculations with proper explanatory data to all concerned, publish it. From the network, management knew that the project would take 36 days if there were no slippages.

9. With regard to progress reports:

a. They should be kept as brief as possible.

Event	*Preceding Event*	*Optimistic Time "a"*	*Most Likely Time "m"*	*Pessimistic Time "b"*	*Expected Time te*	*Earliest Expected Time Te*	*Latest Allowable Time T_L*	*Slack T_L-T_E*
1	0	0.1	1.0	2.0	1.0	1.0	1.0	0*
2	1	1.0	3.0	4.0	2.8	3.8	3.8	0*
3	2	4.0	6.0	12.0	6.7	10.5	35.8	25.3
4	2	0.1	2.0	4.0	2.0	5.8	28.7	22.9
5	4	1.0	1.5	3.0	1.7	7.5	30.4	22.9
6	5	1.0	4.0	8.0	4.2	11.7	34.6	22.9
7	5	1.0	3.0	4.0	2.8	10.3	34.8	24.5
8	7	1.0	2.0	4.0	2.2	12.5	35.8	23.3
9	6	0.1	1.0	4.0	1.3	13.0	35.8	22.8
9	7	0.1	2.0	3.0	1.9	12.2	35.8	23.7
10	6	0.1	1.0	3.0	1.2	12.9	35.8	22.9
10	7	0.1	1.0	2.0	1.0	11.3	35.8	24.5
11	2	0.1	1.0	2.0	1.0	4.8	4.8	0*
12	11	6.0	13.0	30.0	14.7	19.5	19.5	0*
13	12	10.0	12.0	40.0	16.3	35.8	35.8	0*
14	9	0	0	0	0	12.2	35.8	23.6
14	10	0	0	0	0	12.9	35.8	22.9
14	11	0	0	0	0	4.8	35.8	31.0
14	13	0	0	0	0	35.8	35.8	0*
14	3	0	0	0	0	10.5	35.8	25.3
14	8	0	0	0	0	12.5	35.8	23.3

Notes: Time is given in days.
Events on critical path are starred in Slack column.

Figure 14–3. Calculation sheet

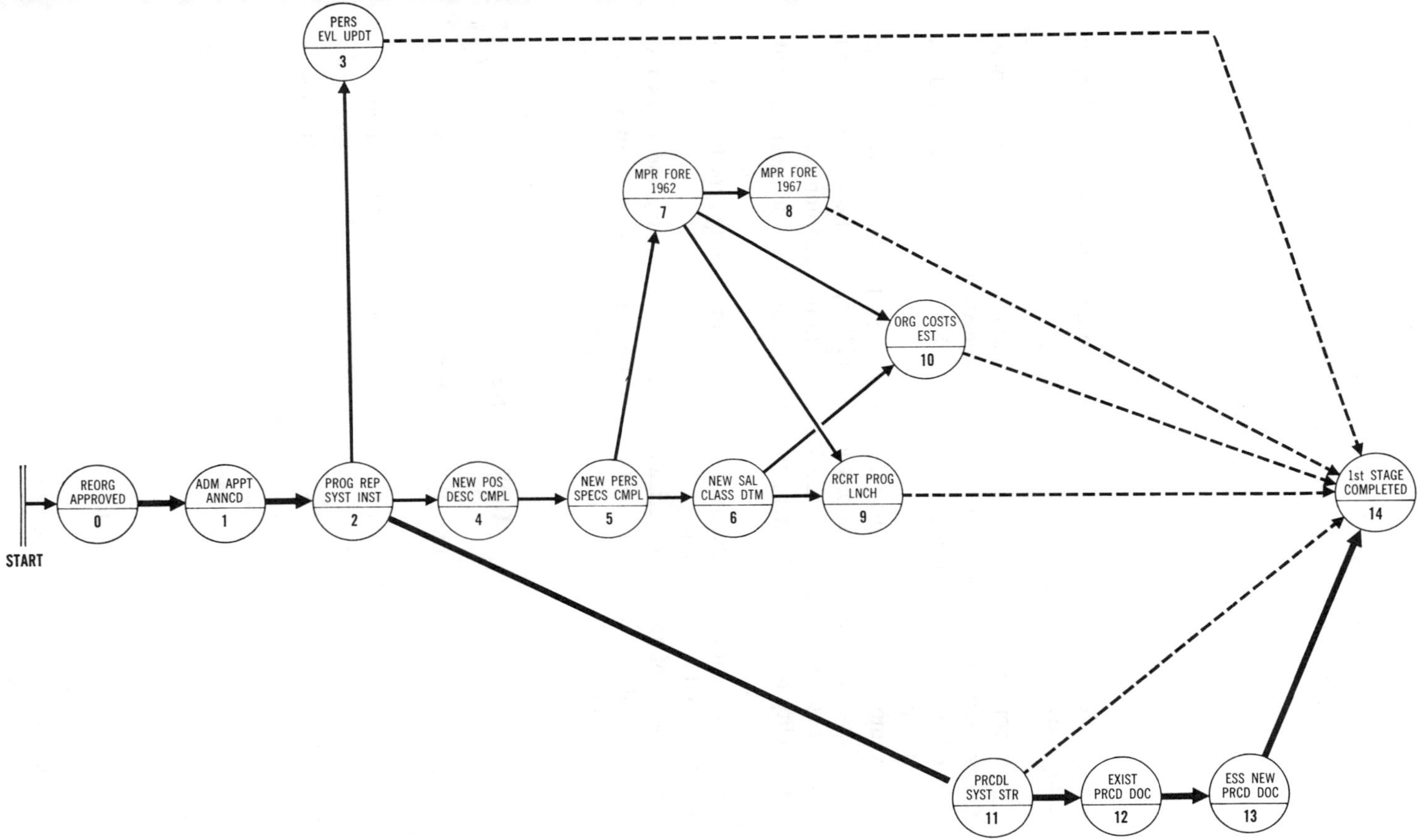

Figure 14–4. The critical path

b. Reporting should be on an exception basis.
c. Slippage should be dealt with promptly and thoroughly.

Periodically, the progress of the project should be reviewed and, if revisions are necessary, the network should be updated accordingly.

ADVANTAGES

It is not difficult to account for PERT's acceptance. It has some distinct advantages over its predecessors:

- A concept inherent in the new technique, which was not a part of earlier planning and control systems, is the definition of the "critical path," and the consequent degree of control that can be concentrated on the activities associated with it.
- A more carefully defined understanding of a given project than would ordinarily be available is provided by PERT, because of the amount of detail necessary to define the PERT network in the planning stage.
- Ability to reschedule manpower and resources in the most efficient way is provided.
- Early warning of potential trouble spots in meeting scheduled completion dates and costs is given.
- Because of the computerization of networks, management has the ability to simulate different networks and, on the basis of these simulations, select the network of optimum effectiveness.

LIMITATIONS

The above does not mean that PERT is without limitations. Major ones are:

Reliance on subjective estimates. PERT relies upon the same subjective judgments necessary in earlier scheduling techniques. Consequently, the computer can check only the consistency of the network; it cannot indicate to management when improper and inaccurate judgments are part of the input to the network.

A tendency to incur high operating costs. Several factors will tend to force costs up:

1. The amount of planning necessary to implement the program
2. The necessity of training, or possibility of hiring, a specialist to direct the establishment of the scheduling system
3. Computerization of the system
4. Necessity for frequent updating

Thus, in any consideration of the use of PERT, the cost of implementing an application should be recognized, defined, and weighed against the potential benefits to be derived.

SUMMARY

PERT is still relatively young. It is an amalgam of many techniques and new tools, and it is inevitable that in any such amalgam a certain number of errors will be made at the start and a certain number of unforeseen events will occur which require sustained experience to be solved. It would be a disservice to regard PERT as a crystallized technique with static advantages and limitations. Some characteristics may prove to be inherent; others will be susceptible of correction.

The author briefly defines CPM, and then discusses the ways it can be applied to improve management decision making.

15

CPM: AN EFFECTIVE MANAGEMENT TOOL

Bayard E. Wynne, Jr.

Financial executives and accountants have a desire to relate the time and cost measures for the performance of corporate efforts. Similarly, these executives recognize that the time-cost relationship would be most useful if it were valid through each of the management phases: Planning, control and analysis. Critical Path Method (CPM) provides a basis for such comprehensive measures. This article describes how CPM may be applied when responsible management and competent professional personnel work together.

Numerous recent articles in business publications have been devoted to the Project Evaluation and Review Technique (PERT). A brief comparison of PERT and CPM will serve to illustrate why executives should seriously consider application of CPM in their operations.

CPM and PERT are basic procedures for estimating the time required to complete activities which may be defined as projects. PERT had its origin in the Navy's Special Project Office while CPM was developed in an industrial atmosphere. Du Pont, with the aid of Remington Rand, evolved CPM as a means for improving planning and cost control for maintenance projects.

One other point of difference between the methods should be noted. PERT was created for application to research and development projects, specifically, bringing new weapons systems into operational status. A high

Reprinted from *The Controller,* June 1962, pp. 258–264, by permission of the publisher.

degree of uncertainty normally exists as to the period of time required to achieve new technological steps in the development of a weapons system. For this reason, the PERT system was designed to accommodate time estimates for individual activities within the project. With this sort of input information the PERT system can be used to estimate the likelihood of completing a project by specific dates.

CPM, on the other hand, was developed for application to projects in which the elapsed time required to perform individual project activities could be estimated quite closely from prior experience. Since time estimates were comparatively certain, the CPM techniques were designed to deal with project costs in addition to project times.

Both methods were initially applied about five years ago. Both have enabled significant improvement in the planning and control of project activities. Today there are many advocates of both systems. Heavy continued application and associated further development of both systems have resulted in fewer significant differences between them. However, at the present time, the CPM techniques are stronger tools for relating project cost to project duration.

CONCEPTS BASIC TO CPM

The first basic concept of CPM requires that the project at hand be definable in terms of individual steps or activities. Typically, an activity is a small enough portion of the project where responsibility for accomplishment of the activity can be assigned to an individual or group leader. For each such activity, two questions must be answered:

What other activities must be completed just prior to the start of this activity?

What other activities can only be started when this activity has been completed?

When the total effort necessary to accomplish the project has been defined in the form of activities and the sequence of activities has been established, the initial project-planning is largely completed.

The second concept basic to CPM comes into play at this point. The planning or organizing of the sequence of activities defines how to perform the entire project. The second concept requires that the time element be considered only after the planning is complete. Competent estimating personnel furnish the elapsed time required to perform each individual activity. Then well-defined procedures, manual and computer, are used to compute the earliest possible project completion time and schedule.

Exhibit 15–1 illustrates the CPM analysis as discussed above. The example project consists of 12 activities, each represented by an arrow.

EXHIBIT 15–1

ARROW DIAGRAM (for delayed starts)

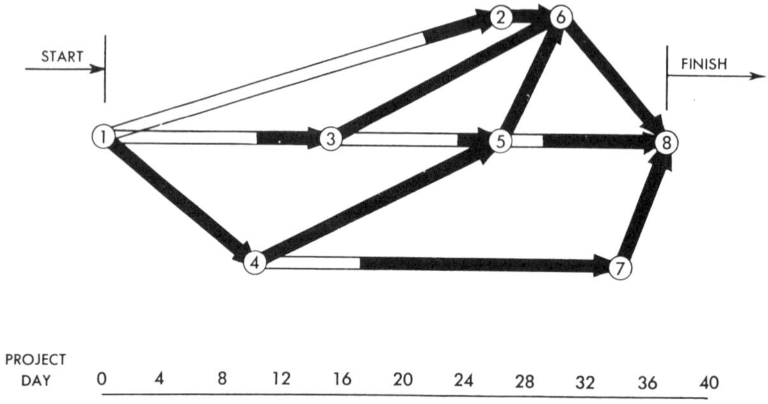

The head-to-tail connections among arrows are in accordance with the sequence relationships determined in the planning cycle. In this diagram the horizontal scale represents elapsed time on the project. The heavy portion of each arrow represents elapsed activity time as specified during the scheduling cycle. For example, the lowest activity, (4)–(7), in the diagram is scheduled to take place between the project days 17 and 34.

The sequence of four activities along the path (1)–(4)–(5)–(6)–(8) shows each succeeding activity starting as soon as possible. Every other path from the beginning to the end of the project has some period during which no effort is scheduled. The path (1)–(4)–(5)–(6)–(8) is the *critical path.* Any delay in performance of activities on this critical path will result in an equal delay in total project completion. All other sequences of activities have *float* which is represented by the outline portion of their respective arrows in Exhibit 15–1. Examining the lowest activity in the arrow diagram, we see that it could have started as early as project day 10.

The first major advantage of CPM is that the scheduling provides a routine way of identifying the critical path as well as the amount of scheduling freedom or float available to noncritical activities.

CPM TREATMENT OF COSTS

Each of the individual activities in a project can be performed more rapidly or more slowly than assumed in the standard elapsed time initially assigned. When an activity is performed during the shorter period, the total direct cost increases. Conversely, when an activity is performed over a longer period the total direct cost decreases. For example, it may take five men eight days to complete a task, whereas ten men could achieve the same results in five days. The three-day reduction in task duration required twice as much manpower.

EXHIBIT 15–2

TIME & COST RELATIONSHIP
FOR INDIVIDUAL ACTIVITY

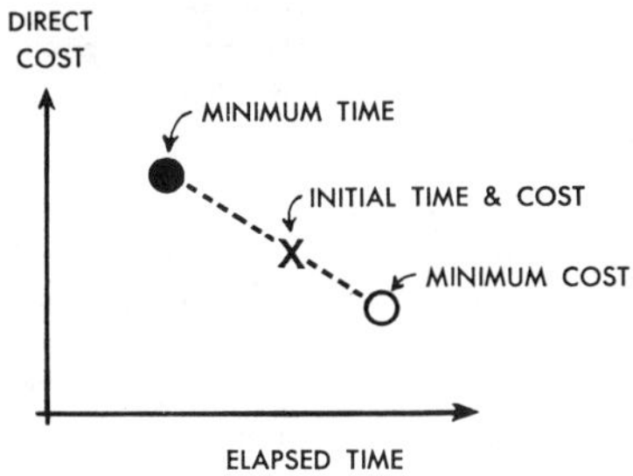

Activity Definition	*Elapsed Time*	*Assigned Manpower*
•	5 weeks	10 men
x	8 weeks	5 men
o	11 weeks	3 men

Exhibit 15–2 portrays this relationship of elapsed time and direct cost. The initial cost-time definition for the activity is represented by the X. The two dots represent practical extremes. The solid dot on the upper left represents the minimum time definition, while the dot in the lower right represents the minimum cost definition.

In general, each of the activities in a project can be performed at lesser cost *or* in less time than specified in their initial definition. Because the total project is the sum of the individual activities, the total project has this same time-cost characteristic.

Exhibit 15–3 deals with our example project in this fashion. Point A is the initial definition, point B is the minimum time definition, achieved by performing all activities as rapidly as possible, and point C is the minimum cost solution, achieved by performing all activities at their respective minimum costs.

Now a second major advantage of CPM can be seen. Point B assumes that all activities are performed in minimum time, which also means that they are performed at minimum cost. However, it is not necessary

EXHIBIT 15–3

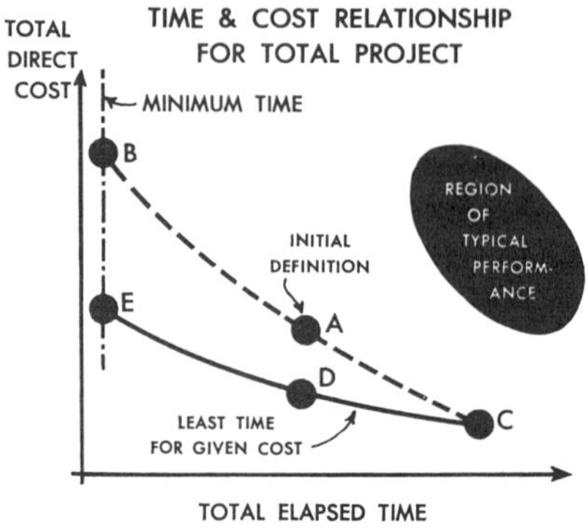

Project Definition	*Total Time*	*Total Cost*	*Project Definition*	*Total Time*	*Total Cost*
C	18 mos.	$600,000	B	9½ mos.	$900,000
A	14 mos.	$700,000	E	9½ mos.	$725,000
D	14 mos.	$640,000			

to perform noncritical activities in this high-cost manner. Their scheduling freedom can be used to perform the activities at a more leisurely pace with less direct costs. The minimum direct cost solution for the minimum project time is shown by point E.

Similarly, the time performance implied by point A can be achieved at an associated minimum cost. A schedule for this solution is implied by point D. The curve CDE represents an entire series of schedules. Any one of these schedules is the least-cost plan for a specified total project time. These schedules may also be regarded as the least-time plan for an authorized project budget. CPM procedures permit direct creation of any of these schedules.

The curve CDE, representing minimum project cost and time, appears again in Exhibit 15–4. The line OS brings in the other cost elements of the project. Costs not directly associated with individual activities, or this particular project, are represented by line OS as time-dependent costs. The *total project cost* is the sum of cost CDE and OS and is shown at the top of Exhibit 15–4. Project management personnel now have a firm basis for selecting the "best" project schedule.

If there are no other significant factors involved in project-planning, management may specify that the project be performed to minimize the total cost. The vertical dotted line defines the elapsed project time associated with minimum total cost. If other factors are significant in the timing of the project, management has a tool which defines the project cost increase incurred to accommodate these other factors.

EXHIBIT 15–4

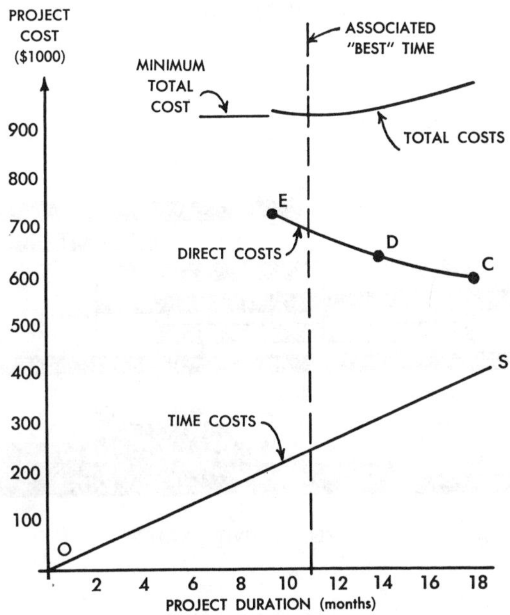

One example of where other factors might suggest the use of a nonminimum cost solution may serve to illustrate this point. Firm A contracts to perform a task for firm B at a fixed cost by a specified date. CPM analysis of the task indicates that the minimum cost solution can be followed without violating the delivery date. Normally this path would be taken.

However, firm B could realize an additional $100,000 profit if delivery were made three months in advance of the agreed date. Firm A, through reanalysis by CPM, finds that its costs would increase by $40,000 in order to compress the schedule eight weeks to meet the new completion date. By arranging an equitable sharing of the $60,000 both firms stand to gain by departing from the original minimum cost solution.

OTHER APPLICATIONS OF CPM

Critical path method can be used in an attempt to meet alternate financial management objectives. Manpower leveling, cash flow and investment minimization are briefly noted here.

Manpower leveling is often important. Short duration peaks in the number of applied project personnel can be expensive. The fixed cost associated with acquiring or releasing employes is unnecessarily incurred.

EXHIBIT 15–5

(See Exhibit 15–7 also.)

ALTERNATE MANPOWER DIAGRAMS

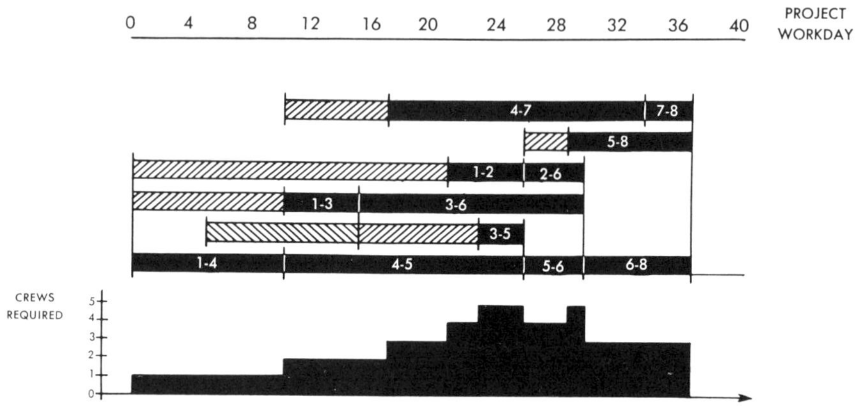

DELAYED ACTIVITY STARTS

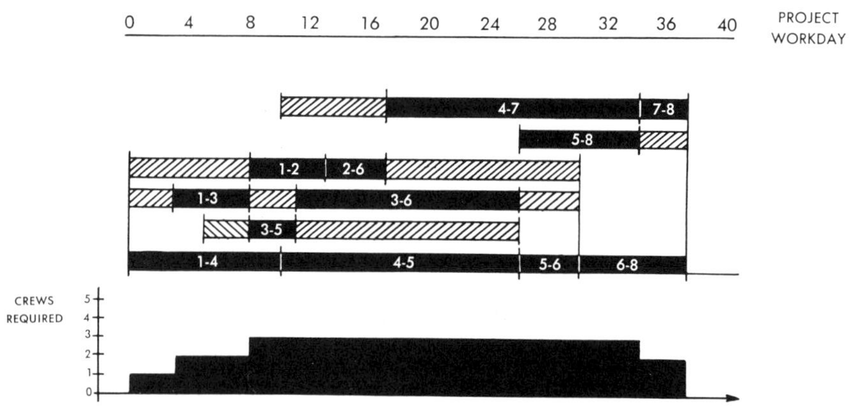

EFFICIENT MANNING

Further, these additional employes are not on the payroll long enough to attain the efficiency of the basic work force.

Exhibit 15–5 contains two conventional bar charts from which manpower requirements can be derived. The upper bar chart corresponds to the schedule of delayed activity starts shown in Exhibit 15–1. Activities are again indicated by shaded bars. Float or scheduling freedom for each related sequence of activities is indicated by a slashed bar.

Manpower requirements are read visually. For example: On project workday 16, two crews would be needed—one crew for activity (3)–(6) and one crew for activity (4)–(5). The manpower requirements thus derived from the upper bar chart indicate that the number of employees is changed seven times during the project, and, further, that a peak of five crews is required on two separate occasions.

The lower bar chart of Exhibit 15–5 corresponds to a project schedule in which efficient manning is planned. In this case, the work force is changed only three times and the peak requirement of three crews exists only once. This is achieved while using the same number of man-days and contemplating the identical project completion date as in the delayed activity start case.

The procedure for changing a schedule into one based upon efficient manning is quite simple in principle. In the top chart of Exhibit 15–5, activities (1)–(2) and (2)–(6) are scheduled to be performed concurrently with activity (4)–(7). In the lower chart (which reflects efficient manning) activity (4)–(7) is started after completion of activity (2)–(6). This is accomplished by shifting activities (1)–(2) and (2)–(6) within the limits of their indicated float or scheduling freedom. A similar shift in activity (1)–(3) allows one crew to perform, in sequence, the activities (1)–(3), (1)–(2), (2)–(6), (4)–(7), and (7)–(8). The actual method of solution when many manpower categories are involved is more complex, but is workable. (See also Exhibit 15–7.)

Cash flow can be programmed because material and labor dollars of known quantity are associated with each activity. Each activity has specified beginning and ending dates. Therefore, the cash requirements of the project can be readily established. As in other applications, float can be used to adjust this initial set of cash requirements. These adjustments could be used to delay input in tight cash months and permit early performance in periods when idle funds exist.

Investment minimization is a variant of the cash flow application. In Exhibit 15–6 a cumulative project investment curve, OXT, is shown. This curve could result from the project plan represented in Exhibit 15–1. The arrow diagram of Exhibit 15–1 shows all activities performed as late as possible. (The arrow diagram of Exhibit 15–8 has the same over-all cost-time definition as that of Exhibit 15–1, but all activities are performed as early as possible.) This project plan could result in the cumulative project investment curve, OYT. Compare the total expenditures at project day 20. When scheduling individual activities as late as possible only 34 percent of project expenditures would be incurred by project day 20. If individual activities were scheduled as early as possible, 64 percent of the project expenditures would be incurred by project day 20. The carrying costs associated with curve OYT exceed those of curve OXT. Under certain conditions this can be important.

EXHIBIT 15–6

ILLUSTRATION OF TIMING PROJECT INVESTMENT

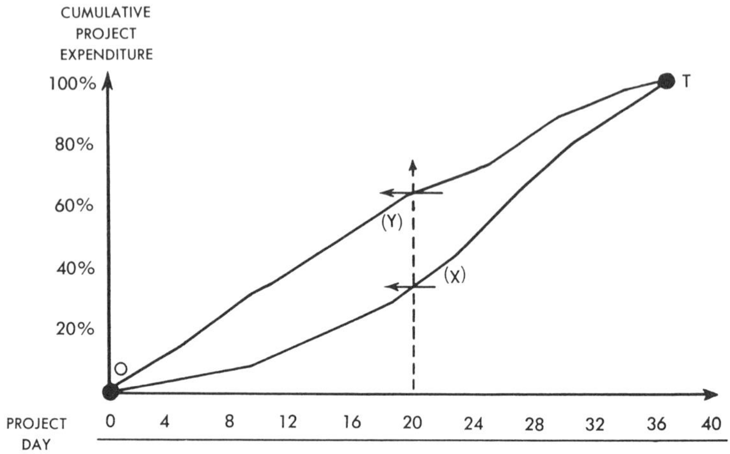

EXHIBIT 15–7

(See Exhibit 15–5.)

ARROW DIAGRAM (for efficient manning)

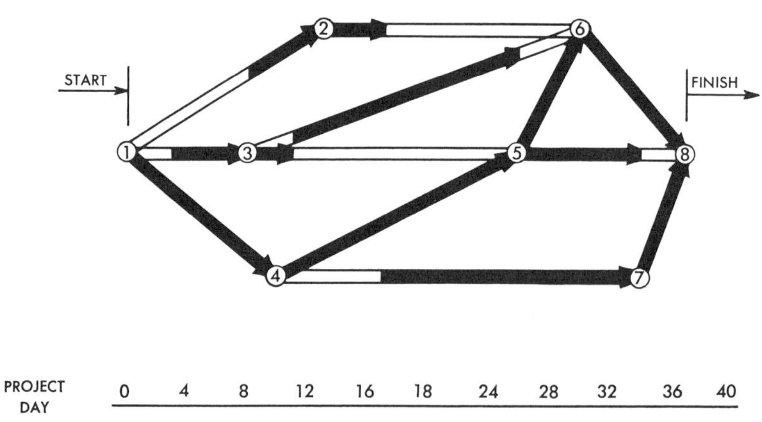

EXHIBIT 15–8

ARROW DIAGRAM (for early finishes)

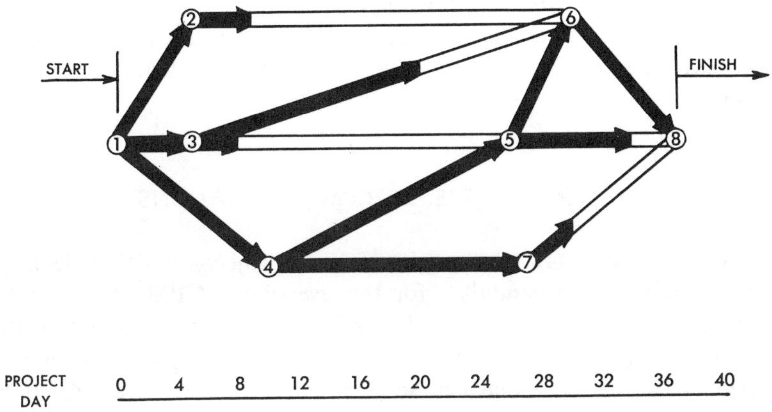

CONTROL AND ANALYSIS WITH CPM

Regardless of the specific application, all the preceding discussions have related to initial project-planning. But CPM is useful in two other phases of project management.

Current control of projects becomes meaningful under CPM. At intervals within the project some completed activities will have taken shorter or longer to perform than originally anticipated. Better knowledge of remaining activities may dictate significant changes in estimated times. Since scheduling under CPM is a routine procedural task, these changes can be rapidly incorporated into periodic schedule revisions.

This ability to react rapidly to changing conditions means that emergencies can be overcome in the most efficient manner. Suppose that a key material shipment is delayed in delivery to the site of the project—CPM can be used to generate a recovery plan which makes the best use of available resources. The same thing would apply to other activity interruptions and delays. The ease with which project plans can be generated carries over into routine reporting:

What progress has been made in the latest period?
Does physical progress coincide with expenditures to date?
Which activities must receive close attention in the immediate future?

These and similar management problems can be dealt with in a system based upon CPM.

Analysis of projects is also simplified through the CPM tools. The project effort, defined as specific individual activities, is more amenable to management-oriented cost accounting. Precise increments of work are accounted for quite easily. Individual responsibility is pinpointed. Cost information is generated that is more useful when estimating and budgeting subsequent projects. Each of these points can be crucial to generation of profit.

CURRENT STATUS OF CPM APPLICATIONS

Any activity which may be thought of as a project—a definable beginning and ending—is a candidate for the use of the CPM tools. Looking into the near future, a significant breakthrough can be outlined. Instead of dealing only with the cost-time trade-off or manpower leveling or utilization of funds, someone will set forth a CPM format which enables overall cost optimization. The sum of direct costs, manpower inefficiency, losses and imputed interest charges will be minimized and a schedule will be generated on this basis.

Countless buildings, many industrial plants, some dams, bridges and tunnels have been managed through the use of CPM in the construction phase. The construction industry will probably continue to lead in applications. The methods and some of the underlying assumptions are particularly well suited to that industry. Current experience, however, shows that many industries can successfully use CPM tools to improve project management.

SUMMARY AND CONCLUSIONS

CPM is a young but proven set of valuable management and accounting tools. Few companies have derived the full benefit currently available from application of these tools. All organizations should consider application of existing CPM tools and keep abreast of extensions to CPM resulting from continuous research efforts.

Financial managers and executives can play a key role in extracting the benefits of CPM. First, reporting systems (of which CPM is only one) are usually designed and operated by accounting departments. Second, the cost-time version of CPM, with or without cost accounting, will only be achieved with the cooperation of all accounting and financial personnel.

By whatever means CPM finds its way into individual firms, most executives will welcome the tools, for they are truly a basis for "management by exception."

BIBLIOGRAPHY

Backer, F. Jr., Barkson, A. W., and Frishberg, M. C., "Least-Cost Estimating and Scheduling," *The Oil and Gas Journal,* November 13, 1961.

Fondahl, J., *A Noncomputer Approach to the Critical Path Method for the Construction Industry,* Stanford, California, Stanford University, 1961.

Fulkerson, D. R., "A Network Flow Computation for Project Cost Curves," *Management Science,* January 1961.

Malcolm, D. G., Roseboom, J. H., Clark, C. E., and Fazar, W., "Application of a Technique for Research and Development Program Evaluation," *Operations Research,* September–October 1959.

C

Electronic Data Processing

While computers serve a useful record-keeping and data-processing function, the authors believe that they can also be of great help in applying scientific model-building and mathematical techniques to management decision making.

16

THE CHALLENGE TO ELECTRONIC DATA PROCESSING

John B. Scott
McCready S. Young

Electronic data processing has had a decade of intensive development and has achieved general acceptance by the business world. It has brought into existence a completely revised concept of record-processing; a concept which is based on common language, integrated operations, routine decision-making, and virtually unlimited ability to provide report data. It has created a new profession, altered the organization charts of companies which use it and forced revision of the accepted techniques of internal control.

Equipment is available on the market today which is capable of meeting almost every requirement for gathering, recording, processing, communicating, and reporting business data. Processing speeds are virtually supersonic, storage capacity is unlimited, input and output capabilities exceed the ability of man to create the source data or to digest the results. In short, the limitations on application of electronic equipment are governed only by the ability of the programmer or systems engineer to utilize them, and management to afford them. Systems can be designed to meet every challenge. There is little doubt that future adaptations of electronic data processing techniques to new problems can and will be successful.

Reprinted from *Financial Executive,* February 1964, pp. 25–31, by permission of the publisher.

SUCCESS IN COMBATTING RECORDKEEPING VOLUME

However, the results achieved by electronic data processing in the past ten years have been most successful in a rather limited area of business operations. That is the area of tangible cost savings. Reduction in out-of-pocket clerical or mechanical data-processing cost has been the most effective entree for introducing electronic equipment into the functions of business operations. The approach taken has been a well and frequently used one. It is the same approach taken by manufacturers of adding, calculating, and typewriting equipment in the years before electronics. It is aimed at eliminating slower, more costly methods.

Allied to this approach is a variant with a similar goal. Experience has shown that, while machines may not always produce a savings, they can produce results in far less time than can clerks. To the company which has in its immediate future ever-mounting paperwork and record-keeping problems, this time-saving is potential cost-saving and is sufficient justification for accepting electronic processing.

The servicing of recordkeeping volume was one of two directions in which the electronic data-processing equipment industry could progress. It served the accounting function in its historical role of providing management with data required for operating and for management control of the business. This responsibility has produced an operating center around which all the data procedures, collection, recording, processing, and reporting has revolved. The result of this figure-processing originally was purely financial. As businesses grew, the financial results were gradually supplemented with more and more statistical, analytical, and operating data.

This has been no slight aid to business. Today, it is imperative that even the smallest business utilize some management control reporting. The larger the company, the more such reporting becomes a basic economic necessity. Because of the relationship between financial results, the accounting system, and internal management control reporting, the responsibility for these functions has continued to be assigned to the accounting or finance departments. Hence, the controller or other chief accounting officer has acted as a catalyst in joining the growing demand for management control data with the availability of electronic data-processing techniques. Today these two areas are still joined in the minds of business management and the electronic data processing industry as the prime field of application of the equipment.

FAILURE IN PROMOTING THE PROBLEM-SOLVING APPLICATIONS

But there is another area of application of electronic data-processing equipment. It was pioneered by the newcomers to the industry and a whole reservoir of new techniques, new approaches, and radically different applications. As these manufacturers were more familiar with scientific and engineering problem-solving, their language sounded strange to the business executive. The reception they were accorded was cool and their proposals were passed from function to function within the company without acceptance.

Why was this? The approach of the newcomers was directed toward utilizing scientific and mathematical techniques for achieving maximum profit with minimum capital investment and operating cost. Such techniques (the use of mathematical models) were not new in the scientific and engineering field, but they were considered too radical for business use. The final, and concrete, argument against business use of these techniques was based on a dollars-and-cents consideration. The results envisioned were intangible and the out-of-pocket costs connected with them were quite real.

The electronic equipment available at the start (analog computers) was more adaptable to this approach—problem-solving—than to the recordkeeping function. Effectively utilized in the scientific fields, it was a proven means of producing high-speed, accurate evaluation of the known and unknown, of the constant and variable factors of the total business operation.

However, because of the built-in resistance of management and the lack of communication on both sides, the scientific approach went by the boards. The newcomers either departed from the scene or directed their efforts toward the more conventional data-processing problems.

HOW THINGS STAND: THE SMALL COMPANY

The solution of conventional data-processing problems was, itself, not simple. The electronic data-processing equipment available was more applicable to mathematical problems than to business, clerical and accounting problems. The need was for adequate data storage, high-speed output, and simple programming. The obstacles were overcome. The determined and sometimes costly struggles of the early exponents of electronic data processing are now a matter of recorded business history. Out of their efforts came two results:

1. Currently available equipment is adaptable to the accounting-oriented requirements of the business world.

2. Equipment is available to meet every requirement of data processing from preparation of source documents, through communication transmission of recorded data, to programmed output of required reports and records.

Unfortunately the increased demand for electronic equipment has created a competitive condition not conducive to meeting the requirements of smaller companies. Equipment is becoming more complex, more integrated, and increasingly more costly. Electronic data processing is oriented to the volume user. The emphasis is on speed, capacity, and integration. The large company is receptive. The smaller company does not have the necessary volume and cannot meet the cost.

The adaptation of electronic equipment to the processing needs of the small and medium-sized business is a major problem yet to be solved. Provision must somehow be made for utilization of integrated electronic processing systems by these companies at a reasonable cost. Once this has become a reality, the management of every company, large and small, can join in challenging manufacturers, managers, and technicians of electronic data-processing equipment to solve the paramount problem facing business and industry today. This problem is the scientific management control of the total business entity.

SCIENTIFIC CONTROL: LIMITS OF ACCOUNTING

The electronic data-processing equipment industry must soon face the challenge of business management to attempt to provide equipment not simply arithmetical in character but which is advanced enough to aid in scientific direction of business operations. The scientific approach, the first direction of the electronic equipment industry, has returned to become the basis for management to challenge the data-processing manager, his equipment and techniques.

How did this situation come about? It was not through acceptance of electronic processing alone, certainly not through the efforts of the manufacturers of electronic equipment or familiarity of management with scientific business techniques: it came about through a combination of other factors. Among these were:

1. The growth and expansion of company operations.

2. The problems of centralization or decentralization of management functions.

3. The expanding width and depth of management communication requirements.

4. The trends toward functional organization.
5. The need for prompt measurement of operating results in terms of planned objectives and functional responsibility.
6. The need for evaluation of business potential, responsibility, capacity, and efficiency in relation to the sales market, competitive factors, and products.
7. The effect of competition.

Historically, these factors have been supported through data processing and reporting in the accounting function, and on the basis of financial data. Rarely have analysis techniques been built into the accounting system except through historical comparison. This means that the requirements of accounting and those of management for objective operating data have followed diverging paths for many years. For the accountant, the requirements of balancing and complete accuracy have governed the establishment of reporting objectives.

Unfortunately, the use of monthly or quarterly reports as a means of measuring current business operations and efficiency, and for providing a foundation for developing new objectives, has proven to be an unsatisfactory arrangement. Too much time elapses between samplings; too much time elapses between changes in objectives; too much time elapses before corrective action can be taken to safeguard profits and exploit the capacity of the business.

While necessary to the business entity, accounting operations are most effective when limited to the financial reporting function and when used as a means of post-auditing the standards, factors, and elements in the management control function. Accounting operations cannot be used effectively for management control reporting because accounting results:

1. Are usually far removed in time from the acts being reported.
2. Must be as exact as it is reasonably possible to make them.
3. Are usually confined to account-periods. Attempts to break into the routines of gathering and processing accounting data between periods can cause additional reporting delays, inaccuracies, and processing control problems.

REQUIREMENTS OF MANAGEMENT CONTROL

The management control function can be organized in many different combinations. It should be directed at one objective—to make the most of the company's assets (personnel, equipment, facilities, and financial capital) for developing maximum penetration into the product market, at the lowest cost, and with the maximum profit permitted by the economic factors involved.

The term, "management control," has gained acceptance in modern business language. It has been used to describe every systems concept from daily activity reports to financial reporting. It has come to mean a great many different things. Its principal objective is the development of data pertinent to the effective management of the business enterprise. Even this definition can be interpreted in a variety of ways. In order to clarify the approach, the following requirements for the management control function are submitted:

1. A simple, logical, straight-line flow of data from source to report within the smallest practicable time period.
2. Functional reporting based on defined and controllable management responsibilities.
3. A supporting means of measuring, evaluating, and correcting results, beginning with the first-line management function and without interrupting the straight-line flow. In short, a set of standards or norms for performance comparison.
4. Integration with the accounting system to provide a means of internal or post-audit control of reporting accuracy within the established data-reporting tolerances.
5. Continual data reduction at each management level to reduce the quantity of information reported, preferably omitting detail which falls into the tolerance areas.
6. An over-all system concept that permits evaluating factors outside the business structure itself, such as people, events, social changes, trends, etc.

One of the most important of these requirements from the management standpoint is the establishment and maintenance of standards. The term, "standards," is not used here in the sense of time-studied standards. It is used to mean relative measurement of performance, based on acceptable limits for that performance. Effective standards for total business operation are possible today. Electronic data-processing equipment is capable of:

1. Evaluating known facts and conditions.
2. Evaluating unknown facts and conditions in relation to those that are known.
3. Establishing a path for the future in terms of the most effective combination of operating factors.
4. Comparing the planned operation in relation to actual performance.
5. Providing the requirements for corrective action.
6. Re-evaluating the total plan in terms of current gains and losses from good or bad performance.
7. Performing these functions on a continuous basis from results of straight-line data flow.

One can almost count on the fingers of both hands the companies which are actually practicing this approach in planning, scheduling, and evaluating their operations. This condition does not exist because the equipment is not available, nor because techniques cannot be developed. Both are available to a degree sufficient to permit effective results. It exists because electronic data-processing activity is more concerned with data reduction and elimination of clerical effort than it is in providing management with a fully integrated planning and information system.

Under the present generally accepted concept of the management control function as an integrated part of the accounting function, only limited results can be expected. Under the concept being developed here, the accounting function is integrated into the management control function. The results, for accounting, must still balance but, in the management control area, there can be approximations if we understand the tolerance and if exactness is not pertinent to the result in terms of action.

Management control requirements are based on the business as a unit and the relationships among all its functions. When we introduce the intangible relationships among the familiar areas of sales, marketing, distribution, production, research and development, and then expand the relationships to include competitive factors, industry trends, customer habits, population trends, etc., we have risen far above the purely arithmetical requirements of conventional data processing.

The real test, therefore, is not in "nailing down" company history and using it to plan the future but in nailing down the future so that, when it becomes history, it is not the result of coincidence or accidents but of intelligent, scientific planning. In short, we are back to the scientific and mathematical techniques advanced more than ten years ago, and in storage since then. The business world is in need of these techniques. Management control requirements have reached the stage where conventional methods are inadequate.

THE CHALLENGE TO ELECTRONIC DATA PROCESSING

In view of the urgent need for effective control of every factor affecting business operations, management challenges electronic data processing to provide the answer. This challenge is directed first to the equipment manufacturers. They must develop the basic techniques for analog measurement of business operations, progress made, and the potential of the future on a basis consistent with the scope of responsibility of every level and function of management. They must also provide the orientation, training, and education of management personnel in the application and use of the techniques involved.

The challenge is directed also at the data-processing manager. No longer is it enough to supervise a production shop for processing accounting and statistical data. The demands of the future will place this function on the management level as the interpretive step between planning and operations, on one hand, and measurement and evaluation on the other. The demands on the data-processing manager will include expanded and thorough knowledge of company operations and the necessary processing techniques (electronic, mathematical, and even scientific) which will be required to provide an effective control system for these operations. He must have ability to develop in the entire management group the acceptance and understanding of the system and work with management personnel for the effective utilization of results.

THE CONTROLLER IS THE KEY MAN

Finally, the challenge is directed at the controller. He must once again become the catalyst necessary to bring this new concept into practical use. The controller's role in the management control system is one of planning, direction, and interpretation. The validity of the entire program is in his hands. Integration of accounting, statistics, and control techniques will be his greatest challenge. This will include correlating the electronic data-processing function with the management control requirements in terms of management needs, applying the principles of accounting and auditing as a means of quality control over the results, ensuring the efficiency and effectiveness of the entire system, and assisting every management area in solving its control problems.

Management challenges electronic data processing to devise different techniques, unearth new applications, develop new responsibilities and apply revised concepts of data-collecting, recording, processing, evaluating, and reporting to achieve the basis for scientific business management. The equipment is available; many of the required techniques exist; the personnel are available; and management is receptive. In spite of this, existing problems are becoming larger and new problems requiring study and solution are arising every day.

Meeting this challenge is vital to the growth and future of every business existing today and to the growth of the national economy. If we are truly in the electronic era, we must utilize the advantages of electronic data-processing capabilities where those advantages can really pay off.

The author shows how computer usage can be extended beyond mere information processing, record keeping, and financial and accounting reporting, by studying the information needs of all the decision-making systems within a business.

17

THE MANAGEMENT INFORMATION DREAM: THE END OR A NEW BEGINNING?

John T. Garrity

"After six years of heavy investment in computers, I can't say that they are helping me personally to do a better job." The speaker was a division general manager of a major company that had invested upwards of $4 million in a computer system supposedly geared to provide management with more, better, and faster information for decision-making. His comment was echoed time and again in McKinsey & Company's recent major survey of computer systems. Despite improvements in information to lower-level management and functional management (production planners, market researchers and the like), the computer has generally proved a disappointment when it comes to facilitating top-management decision-making and control.

Ironically one of the main reasons why business executives a decade ago hailed the introduction and development of computers was that they saw in computer-based systems new hope for real help in the increasingly complex task of planning, decision-making, and control. Virtually every early computer justification was at least partly predicated on the assumption that the computer would provide top management with more, better and faster information. Indeed, in many companies the prospect of better information was the principal justification for acquiring the computer. The computer systems unit accordingly was christened with

Reprinted from *Financial Executive,* September 1964, pp. 11–16, by permission of the publisher.

some such name as the Management Services Department or the Management Information Section.

Undeniably, the growth of American business, the increasing corporate complexity, the moves towards diversification, decentralization, and divisionalization, and the rising risk associated with basic business decisions have created a great and growing need for improved executive information. But despite this need—and despite management's high hopes for filling it—little real help has come from the computer. At least in the typical company, computers have done little in the past five years to improve the quality and quantity of information that top management really needs for setting corporate goals and strategy; developing longer-range, integrated plans; directing basic commitments of money and manpower; and coordinating corporate effort, measuring performance, and exercising over-all control.

Even more disturbing than the lack of progress to date is a growing feeling that computer systems will not—indeed cannot—contribute to improved executive decision-making and control. Said one survey executive vice president, "Better information from computers? That was just another management dream. Sure, computers can probably help regional sales managers and plant superintendents, and that's important. But I don't think they'll ever have much of a bearing on my job. As I see it, I'm not paid to wade through piles of detailed reports—and that's about all computers can do with reports, isn't it?"

The point deserves some serious thought. Where *do* we stand in the development of computer-based management information systems? Have we come to the end of the management information dream—or can we make a new beginning? What, if anything, can be done to bring computer systems to bear on the top-management process?

No one has a more immediate stake in the answers than the financial executive. Whether or not he is administratively responsible for the computer, the financial executive's management information responsibility remains clear and unchanged. He is the man who must provide the leadership to make the management information dream a reality. To do so, he must first face up to some basic questions raised by management's failure to date to realize that dream through the computer.

ACHIEVEMENTS TO DATE

First, can computer-based systems really contribute to improved top-management information? On a practical basis, the answer is "yes." In a few situations, computer-based systems have already made a significant contribution to better management information.

In conjunction with PERT and critical path techniques, computer systems are providing top management with far better means for directing large-scaled, complex projects. Thanks to computers, top management can now measure cost, time and technical performance on an integrated basis, and can better assess the trade-offs involved in putting an "off plan" project back on the track. This management information tool has been most widely used in the aerospace industry. But it is also being applied in a variety of other industries for construction management, complex research efforts, product development and introduction. It is even used for the implementation of large-scaled computer systems.

In many companies, computer-based real-time systems are providing top management with new kinds of useful information. For example, one manufacturer of a broad line of style merchandise is now able to track product movement not merely to the factory shipping dock but right down to the retail level. For this manufacturer, the need for speed (badly overrated in most situations) is really crucial. Faster information—"market place" information—is helping management make better top-level manufacturing decisions and improving its profit results in this fast-moving industry.

Besides more up-to-date information, computers are giving management, through more advanced forecasting techniques, a more reliable picture of the future. In conjunction with their routine order-processing, for example, several companies are making weekly—and in some cases even daily—projections of demands for a host of product items produced at, and distributed from, many supply points. This clearer picture of the future is making for sharper decisions today.

Another information technique made practical by the computer is simulation. Once an economic and operating model has been developed, the likely future impact of alternative courses of action can be tested through computer simulation. This technique is increasingly being used as a guide to facilities-planning, setting inventory levels, and testing out basic distribution patterns.

Risk analysis, a somewhat similar computer-based technique, enables management to evaluate a decision on the basis not of a single projection of the most likely set of occurrences, but of a range of probable events. Companies are showing increasing interest in this technique as an aid to decision-making. They are using it in capital expenditures, evaluation of acquisition opportunities, and the like.[1]

Where more detailed analyses are needed for sound executive decision-making, computer systems can help to provide them. For example, one major appliance manufacturing company, plagued by stagnant profits and market share, undertook a basic review of its position. A major element in this review was an exhaustive analysis of profit contribution by

[1] See David B. Hertz, "Risk Analysis in Capital Investment," *Harvard Business Review,* January–February 1964.

product, by manufacturing and shipping point, and by channel of distribution. This depth analysis, carried out with a computer, led to major changes in the company's product line, production pattern, and marketing and distribution strategies.

Companies have not used computers solely to produce more information; some successful companies are using them to produce less. One company with hundreds of retail outlets is reporting to marketing management only on outlets whose performance is out of line. Along with this move to exception reporting, the company developed—again with the help of the computer—new, more meaningful performance measures.

Clearly, computer systems can make significant contributions to better management information. They also promise an even wider contribution to better management information in the future.

If the potential is there, why has so little been accomplished to date? The reasons are many. Not all of them are under the financial executive's control. In many companies, where the computer system's effort is still relatively young and immature, management has had to gain computer experience in the more straight-forward, routine applications before taking on the demanding information job. Lack of experience, however, is becoming less and less a valid reason for marginal results. Major management information improvements should come about over the next five years.

FACTS BEHIND THE FAILURES

Based both on our survey experience and our work with clients, I would suggest four basic reasons why most companies have failed to realize the potential management information improvements from computer-based systems have for them.

1. *Inadequate effort on the part of top management.* Over the years many executives have been complaining about their management information rather than doing much to improve it. Only infrequently, in my experience, do top executives take the time to work on this problem. Yet management information needs are intimately interwoven with the requirements of the management process, and any information system must to some extent be adapted to the personality, background and training of the executive it is designed to serve. It is hard to see, therefore, how we can hope to develop more meaningful management information without major executive involvement in the design process.

To be sure, much more can be done to stimulate executive interest and participation. But unless, and until, the corporate executive sees management information improvement as an important and valuable use of his time, he will have to be content with his old reports, inadequate to his real needs though they are likely to be.

2. *Limitations in management's approach to developing better management information.* The second obstacle to improved information is the traditional tendency to focus on "scrubbing up" the information already being provided. The typical information-improvement effort starts by compiling all the reports currently being issued, checking them for duplication, and culling out obviously needless detail, with the object of providing management with fewer, more streamlined reports. Again, it is common practice under this "scrub-up" method to ask the key recipients of the reports whether they really need the data—or else to discontinue some reports without asking, until the recipients complain loudly enough to get them reinstated.

With or without a computer, this scrub-up approach can produce only marginal results at best. Since it is limited to reports already in existence, it cannot fill in major information gaps nor remedy fundamental inadequacies in the existing system.

Most management information studies fall short in another respect: they concern themselves almost exclusively with financial information and reports generated by the accounting system. By definition, however, the accounting system is concerned only with dollar results, with past events, and only with what has taken place inside the business organization. Hence, it can supply only part—and not always the most important part—of management's information needs.

Consider the kind of information top management requires to carry out one of its principal functions, the setting of corporate objectives. To do this well, management needs a wealth of data on conditions external to the company—such matters as the outlook for the economy, market trends, and competitive strengths and weaknesses. By definition, this external information falls outside the periphery of the accounting system. The same applies to the information management needs for decisions in launching new ventures, and undertaking new departures.

Effective top-management control, moreover, requires a much more sensitive measure of performance than dollars-and-cents results. By the time financial reports indicate that sales in an important market are declining, it is probably too late to halt the gradual erosion. Effective control requires management to stay abreast of those factors—such as customer service, price, and product performance—upon which sales and competitive position ultimately depend.

This type of information is typically not available from the accounting system. If the control effort is really to be effective, management must become aware of these critical situations long before its financial reports start signaling the loss of sales and profit position.

3. *Failure to make most appropriate use of the computer's capabilities.* In bringing computers to bear on the management information problem, most companies have been fascinated with the computer's speed and its ability to handle large volumes of information. Accordingly, the information design effort has typically concentrated on getting out reports earlier and on providing management with more detailed information. The consequences have often been disastrous—for most management information situations speed is of marginal value and volume is a downright menace.

To be sure, the fresher the information is, the greater its value will be. Senior management, however, is not expected to make, and should not become involved in, day-to-day decisions. At the top-management level, therefore, the value of speedy information is apt to be more psychological than practical. As for volume, more reports added to the busy executive's already staggering load is likely to confuse rather than enlighten, to inhibit rather than foster meaningful action. Yet, in the McKinsey survey, company after company exhibited voluminous reports that looked like little more than machine "run outs." They told us proudly that management was getting these more detailed reports days earlier.

One of the real keys to getting better management information from computer-based systems is a better appreciation of just what the computer has to contribute to better information. Consider the examples of information improvements discussed earlier.

Speed is obviously an important computer attribute. Yet in only one special situation (style merchandise) was speed important at the top-management level. In this particular situation it was the new market place information—rather than reporting speed alone—that spelled the big information difference.

Another important capability is the computer's basic efficiency. Once information is reduced to machinable form, the computer can run countless complicated analyses at little or no additional cost. Thus, it is possible to use the computer to analyze trends and develop projections, to run simulations, and develop correlations at little or no cost. It is this economy of scale, if you will, that makes possible a whole range of management intelligence not practically available in the past.

Another attribute of the computer is its ability to compare. Thus, if we build into the computer program performance tolerance limits, the computer will report out only significant, out-of-control situations and not minor variations. By screening out extraneous information, it can save a busy executive's time. More importantly, it can focus his attention on areas where his action is needed. Thus, in the appliance manufacturer's exhaustive profit analysis, the computer worked over far more information than could have been processed manually. But it reported out only summaries of these analyses, though the detail was available as required.

4. *A fundamentally wrong approach in designing the computer-based management information system.* The last and perhaps most important reason for failing to produce better management information is that most companies have gone about designing computer-based information systems in the wrong way. In our experience, most companies approach it as a by-product of their administrative data-processing system design work. They aim to capture all the information they need to carry out such administration routines as payrolls, billing, inventory record keeping, fixed assets accounting, and the like. Out of this mass of administrative data, they plan to extract the information that should be supplied to management.

This by-product approach has its appeals. It can lead to somewhat lower costs both in design and in operation of the system. And, certainly, any system that has all the details on each transaction in every administrative system must contain the seeds for growing management reports.

Yet, appealing as it sounds, in our experience this approach rarely leads to improved management information. There are three basic reasons. First, the information design criteria are wrong. For administrative needs the computer system must provide penny accuracy, it must comprehend every possible exception to the normal routine. It must do its job at low cost. But these are not the proper criteria of management information, the cost of which is incidental to its potential value, and the accuracy of which—in detail, at least—is of little or no consequence. Moreover, administrative systems, like accounting systems, focus on internal information and past events. Management, in contrast, needs intelligence dealing with external conditions and with the future.

Second, the "audience" is wrong. Under the by-product approach, the systems designer must typically spend the bulk of his time with clerical supervision, tracing the detailed ins and outs of every business transaction. He has little time to spend with top management, identifying the key decisions they make and the kind of information they require to help them reach better judgments. In the nature of things, it is far easier to spot a poor administrative system than an inadequate management information system. Thus, the less important areas get the most attention.

Finally, under the by-product approach, the wrong kind of manpower is assigned to system design. To design an administrative system requires an analyst who can devise a tight, trouble-free, technically sound set of procedures. The analysts who are most skilled in this painstaking and demanding work are typically not equipped either by training or temperament to recognize top-management problems, or work with executives at the top-management level. In these situations, with this kind of staff assigned to the task, top management is understandably reluctant to invest the time and thought needed to achieve information improvements.

In short, unless improved information for top management is recognized as a major and unique opportunity, and approached from that point of view, computer systems will never produce the management information improvements of which they are capable.

STEPS TO IMPROVEMENT

What, then, can we do about the disappointing performance of computer systems, to date, in producing better management information? To my mind, there are six steps we can take:

1. *Recognize management information improvement as a unique opportunity, distinct from the task of developing computer-based administrative systems.* This is the way to focus on the right problems and opportunities, to be sure we are dealing with the right audience, and to ensure that we assign the right people to the job—people with management information competence rather than people with detailed computer "know-how" and nothing more.

2. *Secure top-management interest and involvement.* This is more easily said than done, but executive management is showing a greater interest, and a greater willingness, to invest the time needed to bring about improvements. We can foster this interest by assigning broad-gauged, knowledgeable, mature manpower to the information improvement effort.

3. *Try to break up the total job into manageable pieces.* One of the barriers to launching a major information project is the sheer size of the undertaking. One solution to this problem is to concentrate on a few critical information areas instead of trying to mount a frontal attack on every aspect of the business. For example, a pharmaceutical company where manufacturing economy is not a key profit determinant might by-pass the production area in favor of research, new product development, and market analysis—all areas decisive to its profit and competitive position. Once a company has identified the requirements for success in its industry, its strengths and weaknesses relative to competition, its dollar expenses, and the decisions and actions that really determine its success, it has the criteria of an information system of real value to top management. Top management is primarily concerned with these key conditions. An effective management information system must reflect this concern.

4. *Start the information improvement program by developing information for planning purposes rather than by working on control information.* In most companies, the planning information system is the best place to start. By focusing on the planning process, we are more likely to be concentrating on the areas of primary management interest, and less likely to become immersed in the details of the control process. In most companies, moreover, the control information system has been studied more often in the past. Thus, the chances of achieving substantial improvements are less likely than in the planning areas, where most companies still have a long way to go.

5. *After assessing basic information needs, make a comprehensive review of existing information.* This analysis will provide further insight into information needs. It will also help to size up the improvement potential. To guard against an outlook limited by the present body of management information, this review should be made only after assessing the fundamentals of the business and the management process.

6. *Don't sell the computer short.* In other words, do not become preoccupied with the computer's speed and its ability to process large volumes of data. More important is the computer's ability to provide more *significant* information, thereby reducing the actual volume of data that management must review. It is a tool that will not only report on the past but also project and test out the future.

Computers can and will have a dramatic and increasing effect on management information. There *is* substance to the management information dream.

Through a survey the authors found that well-managed companies were using their computers more and more as an aid in performing multiple planning and control functions and in solving a wide variety of operational problems.

18

MANAGING TO MANAGE THE COMPUTER

James W. Taylor
Neal J. Dean

It has taken me two months to determine that last year we spent a total of $3.7 million on our computer efforts. Now I am being asked to approve an 18% increase for next year. Is this too much? Is it enough? Should we keep expenditures as a constant percentage of capital investment or of sales, or of some other bench-mark figure?

Is too much—or too little—of our computer investment going into new hardware? Should we be investing more—or less—of our money in developing our systems or our software? If we do invest more, how much of it should I regard as a current operating expense, and how much should I consider as an investment in future operating improvement?

We are applying our computer mostly to accounting and paperwork activities, but we are not using it very much in our other operations of the business. I hear that other companies are accomplishing marketing miracles with computer-based information. Are we applying the computer where it can do us the most good? What percent of their computer effort are other companies applying to various applications?

Who should be in charge of our expanding computer effort? I hear that some companies are looking for men with operating experience to head up their computer effort. What success are they having, and how effective are they in

Reprinted from *Harvard Business Review,* September–October 1966, pp. 98–110, by permission of the publisher.

Authors' note: Major contributions to the project were made by Robert C. Stender and Robert J. Osterhus, who conducted the field research, and by the Management Research Departmnet of Booz, Allen & Hamilton.

breaking down the barrier between technical specialist and line operating people?

I hear and read a great deal about the trend toward centralization of computer-based systems and "total information systems." How much of this is "Cloud 9" thinking? How much of it is presently practical? Should we be moving more rapidly toward this kind of structuring of our company? Or, should we be biting off pieces of the problem and integrating just some of our separate computer activities?

These are the kinds of questions top executives in U.S. industry are asking with increasing frequency. To seek out sharp, definitive answers to such questions, and to gain a clearer insight into the current and future management implications of the computer, Booz, Allen & Hamilton recently completed a year-long study. In this study we have reviewed in depth the ways in which outstandingly successful U.S. manufacturing companies are using computers. We have sought to find out what these companies have learned from their past experience, and what plans they have made for the use of computers in the near- and long-term future. Our findings will be summarized in this article.

EMPHASIS OF STUDY

It is well known that management reaction and response to the computer runs across the full spectrum of effectiveness and utilization—not only in the degree of management involvement, but also in the scope and sophistication of computer applications. There are obvious advantages to getting a fix on one's own position in this broad spectrum of the state of computer art—if for no other reason than to establish one's relationship with the competition. As one executive puts it, "Our real goal is to make sure that we achieve more benefits from computers than our competitors do."

That this spectrum is broad, even among superbly managed companies, can scarcely be denied. Examples of extremes are legion and fast becoming legendary. Management involvement ranges from those companies that have put all senior executives through one or more computer courses to at least one company which has its secretaries retyping computer printouts to fit the management report formats its executives are accustomed to! Computer applications themselves range from concentrating massive attacks on large-volume clerical operations to developing sophisticated applications in such areas as advertising effectiveness and consumer motivation.

These examples are atypical and of interest only because of the extremes that they represent. Our study showed that well-managed companies have unquestionably mastered the elementary cost-cutting applications of the computer. They are no longer asking whether the computer is paying its way. They know the answer. Instead, they are taking a much broader look at furthering the management potential of the computer. Virtually all such companies are increasing expenditures on computer-related systems to make them more profitable and more responsive, particularly in the operational areas of marketing, production, and distribution.

In this article we shall concern ourselves not with statistics as such, but with the management implications of the performance of successful companies; we shall try to provide executives with benchmarks to use in evaluating their progress. Both the sample of companies studied and the research approach were carefully designed to provide this kind of information.

Research Approach

Since the primary purpose of the study was to examine the ways in which exceptionally well-managed companies are using computers, leadership in profit and growth were the basic criteria of sample selection.

The sample was drawn from manufacturing firms—one or more from each of the major SIC classifications (#20 to #39). The 33 companies included were all at or near the top of their particular industry in profit and growth performance. To obtain the sample, we ranked all companies in each SIC classification in order of performance in average return on investment for the previous 5 years and by rate of growth. Equal weight was given to each ranking, and the top firms in each category were invited to participate. There was a gratifying proportion of acceptances from the top-ranking companies, particularly in view of the management time and effort required to participate in the study. Multiple companies were included in each SIC category, although some were used only as a control to verify the validity of the sample.

By interviewing 1 to 3 men in the top management of each company, up to 4 men in operating management, the executive in charge of computers, and also up to 5 technical personnel concerned with computers, the researchers were able to cover 90 separate areas of interest in depth and from different points of view.

To ensure uniformity of data, a single research team thoroughly knowledgeable in usage of computers was assigned to conduct the depth interviews. The findings of the field survey were analyzed and interpreted by the field research team and another team experienced in general management, operational management, and computer technology. Each company was rated in two respects:

1. Overall relative effectiveness in relating the computer to the particular needs of the company and its business requirements.
2. Relative effectiveness of current applications in each of six

different areas (listed in the box on computer applications) regardless of their appropriateness to most important company needs.

Computer Applications

What are the management implications of the computer? To answer this question, 33 outstandingly successful manufacturing companies were studied, and their computer applications were analyzed according to this classification:

CATEGORIES	EXAMPLES
1. *Financial and administrative*	Financial reporting & analysis, accounting, payroll, invoicing, billing.
2. *Management planning and control*	Capital investment analysis, resource allocation.
3. *Marketing operations*	Sales forecasting, sales analysis & control, market research, sales order processing.
4. *Distribution operations*	Warehouse operations, shipment order processing, traffic, inventory control.
5. *Factory operations*	Materials control, production scheduling, quality control.
6. *R & D/engineering*	Product test, engineering, research, product design and evaluation.

The rating was based on the allocation of computer resources—hardware, software, and personnel—and on how well they were applied to the critical needs of the business. Consideration was given only to each company's individual operating needs and those specific applications in each area which were appropriate and technically feasible for the company.

The companies in the sample ranged in size from 1 with sales of less than $100 million to 8 with annual revenues of over $1 billion. Although a computer installation was not a prerequisite in selecting the sample, all the companies had computers—ranging from only 1 to 120. Only 6 companies in the sample had less than 5 years' computer experience, and as many as 7 had been using computers for 10 years or more.

USE AND EXPENDITURE

The 33 companies in our study are heavy users of computers. Individually, they spend from 0.13% to 1.33% of their annual revenues on computer activities (machine rental or the equivalent, operating costs, staff systems planning, design, and programming), with the average at 0.54%

EXHIBIT 18–1

RELATIONSHIP OF COMPUTER EXPENSE TO SALES VOLUME OF 33 COMPANIES

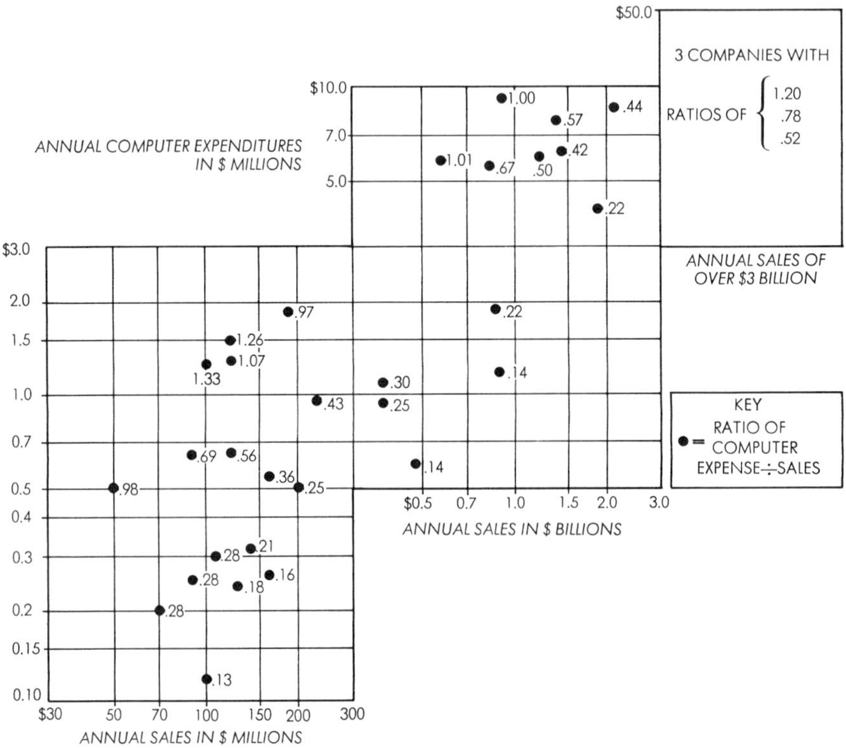

of sales. In all, these companies spend a total of $185 million a year on their computer-based activities. As Exhibit 18–1 indicates, computer expenditures by company size vary widely. Such disparities usually can be traced to the type of industry involved and the maturity of the installation, which determine the extent and type of applications.

Is there any relationship between the amount of a company's expenditures on the computer and its effectiveness in managing it (as rated by our team of analysts)? There is some correlation, but it is not a strong one. The companies with the highest effectiveness rating spend an average of 1.0% of sales on computer activities, and the lowest rated companies average 0.23% of sales. However, there are enough exceptions to indicate that dollars spent are not a major criterion of usage effectiveness. There are examples of companies with high expenditures and low effectiveness in applying the computer to critical areas of their business.

As noted in Exhibit 18–2, average computer expenditures for the

EXHIBIT 18–2

COMPOSITION OF COMPUTER EXPENSES FOR 33 COMPANIES

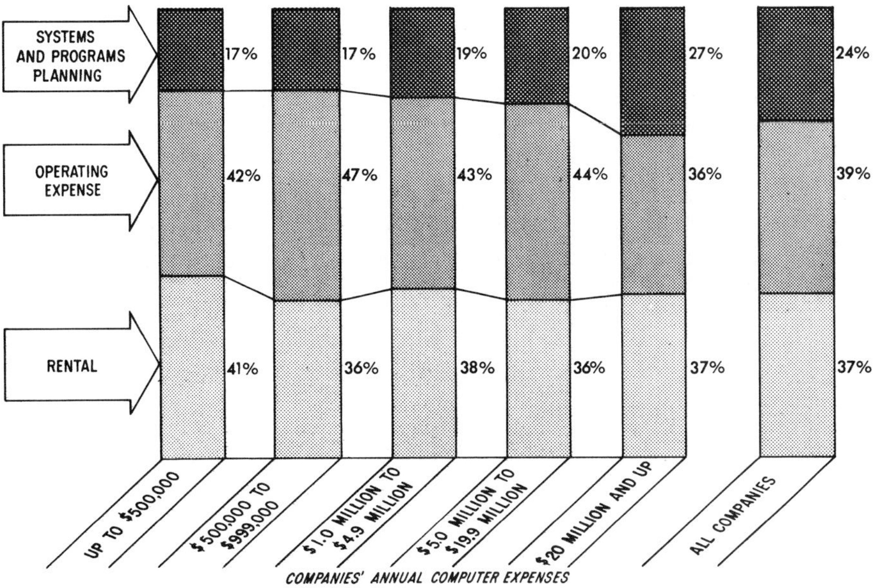

total sample break down to 39% for operating expenses (viz., costs to process data in any of the six categories of applications listed in the box), 37% for rental of hardware, and 24% for systems planning and design. The companies with the largest computer budgets spend more proportionately on systems planning. In most cases, this is a reflection of their maturity as computer users and of their increased emphasis on systems design to implement the new, more complex operating applications which are characteristic of these experienced companies.

As a range, from 25% to 50% of the companies computer budgets are spent on equipment. From 31% to 60% of their expenditures go to operations (i.e., materials, computer operating staff, program maintenance). Systems and programs planning, which is primarily aimed at future applications, accounts for 7% to 31% of computer budgets. It accounts for 20% or more of expenditures for those companies which we judge to be most concerned with continuing progress in their computer efforts.

In the main, the company executives interviewed are fully aware of what the computer is costing them. As one executive said:

> One out of every 16 of our employees is directly involved with data processing in one way or another. Our expenditures on data processing and communications equal nearly 10% of our income after taxes.

Growth with Time

The study clearly indicates that relatively new computer users should be prepared for increasing costs in the future. Companies that have been computer users for more than 10 years spend, on an average, 0.68% of sales on computer applications, while those with under 5 year's experience spend 0.31% of their sales dollar in this way. All but two of the companies are anticipating increasing their level of computer expenditures in the near future.

Thus, after the computer is introduced in a company, it tends to pervade more and more functions and operations, becoming an increasingly important cost factor in company operations. For example, a company with $100 million of sales and 5 years' computer experience can expect costs to increase from $310,000 a year to $680,000 over the next 5 years.

CRITICAL APPLICATIONS

The companies apply computers to critical parts of their businesses with considerable skill. Every company has plans to improve its applications, extend them, and integrate them in digestible bites. Top management is pushing computers with all deliberate speed into all operating areas of the business—factory production, marketing, and distribution functions in particular.

Quite obviously, the relative importance of these operating applications varies widely among individual companies in the sample. In a number of companies, marketing and distribution efforts are most critical; in others, factory operations are more important. Exhibit 18–3 shows the percentages of computer and systems effort going into different applications today—and the distribution of effort planned for the future. As can be seen, few companies are moving computers significantly into the areas of top management decision making by generating new information in new forms for planning and control.

The present concentration of computer activity in financial and administrative functions comes as no surprise, even among these highly successful and sophisticated computer users. In each company, these areas received the first computer applications. Although few companies intend to reduce their efforts in finance, all intend to increase their computer efforts in operational areas, thus reducing the *proportion* of computer effort in finance and administration.

Desire for Improvement

Many executives interviewed commented directly on their efforts to apply computers with more consistent success in the various areas of

EXHIBIT 18–3

ALLOCATIONS OF COMPUTER AND SYSTEMS EFFORT TO DIFFERENT FUNCTIONS

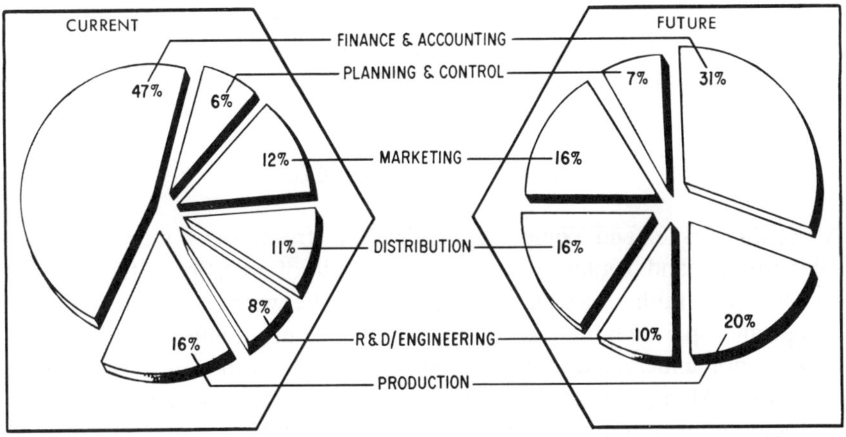

operations. Many feel they still have a long way to go. These comments are illustrative:

> To date, our computer has paid for itself primarily through reduced administrative and clerical staff and reduced credit float. We have just started to use computers in operating areas where the eventual benefits are much larger.—*Vice president, manufacturer of soft goods*
>
> Computers have contributed a great deal to research and development, process control, and accounting. However, we've overcomputerized our business data processing, and consequently we're churning out much useless paper primarily because our applications have not been well coordinated.—*Vice president, chemical company*

As stated earlier, each company's effectiveness with the computer was rated individually, with no attempt to use standards that applied across the board. (Even within a company, differences in operations are so great as to make comparability difficult.) Regarded in this way, the need for improvement seems great. Only 1 company in the study—a large, highly diversified manufacturing company—is currently considered to have an excellent correlation between computer effort and criticalness of applications. The research team rates the effectiveness of 8 other companies as close to, but not quite, excellent; 14 are rated as average; and 10 are rated below average or in the lowest rated group. Clearly, even in these well-managed companies, there is ample room for progress. Bear in mind, however, that even the companies which are rated below average would be rated very high in any analysis of the *total* universe of computer users.

Nearly all companies in the study have plans underway that will result in a much better matching of their computer effort to critical areas of their business. If these companies carry out the plans they now have, 26 of them should have excellent or very good effectiveness correlations by 1970 (in the judgment of our researchers). If the computer provides the benefits expected to result from such plans, these already tough competitors are likely to be a lot tougher in the next few years!

ORGANIZATION STRUCTURE

As companies extend computer applications from areas they now consider proven and routine into new areas full of questions, the stage is set for a "faith-and-understanding gap" between computer-oriented groups and operating managers who must utilize new methods and controls they do not understand. Handled poorly, situations like this could prove disastrous. Managing the computer effort properly involves linking the computer more intimately with the activities to which it is applied. And the link is not electronics; it is human.

In all the companies studied, the computer was brought in under the control of the financial or special computer staff. From this, one might expect a predominance of accounting and systems people in positions of top responsibility for the computer. This is not so in fact. We find that 24 of the 33 companies have men with extensive operating experience in charge of computers—even though, in a majority of cases, the computer operation reports to financial management. (Financial management has the responsibility in 62% of the cases, administrative services in 22% of the cases, and a separate staff in 16% of the cases.) Companies tend to put operating people in charge because it is believed easier to educate them about computers than it is to teach systems specialists about a business.

Problems and Solutions

But having operating men in charge does not necessarily solve all problems. The unevenness with which the companies have applied computers to their various activities attests to that. Is there a relationship between the functional area through which the computer has entered a company and the effectiveness of computer applications in that and other critical areas?
computer is best managed in the function of the business through which
As expected, our study team has found that, without exception, the
it entered. Obviously, longer experience accounts for much of this difference—but not all of it. What does seem to make the real difference is

the background of the computer staff. Most of these people were recruited because of their competence in the original area of application; but when the computer was applied to new areas and operations, people with different capabilities and experience were not brought in.

The better managed companies are well aware of this problem. Some have already taken action, and most have it high on their priority list. Occasionally, corrections require fairly drastic action. For example:

One company had its financial and accounting operations under excellent control. However, its computer systems, though technically good, were rather inefficiently managed in the production and research areas. In trying to force-fit the coordination of computer efforts under financial administration, three eminently qualified systems men failed, one after the other.

Top management's solution was to take one of the top operating executives in the company and put him in charge of data processing as corporate vice president of administration. Onto this executive's staff came the financial men who had previously worked with the computer. But they no longer monopolized the group. The executive salted the staff liberally with men from various plant and division computer groups. The coordination problem, which represented mostly a faith-and-understanding gap, simply vanished.

Many companies have been pushing operating people into computer activities regularly. As one executive vice president said:

We've spent a lot of effort over the last two years infusing a line orientation into our computer activities. We did it by having the computer activities report to the executive vice president of operations for about a year. We also put line managers into the key positions in data processing, including the controller's position. Now our centralized computer activities are back under the controller, and he has a much strengthened information system and data processing operation.

Some companies keep operations separate in the manner described by this machinery company executive:

We have two major systems groups—one in finance and one in manufacturing. Eventually, we may merge the two if we decide to go the integrated systems route, but both groups are well loaded with work for the foreseeable future. The financial staff members are mostly data processing specialists who have learned a fair amount about our business, while the manufacturing staff members are mostly out of manufacturing.

Still other companies use a combination approach. According to one computer executive:

Our computer staff is in our financial organization, but has been built up internally primarily with operating people. We don't seem to have any unusual planning or communications problems. The bargaining over design and application of our systems occurs in close interaction between my systems people and our operating people. Often, during the implementation stage, we interchange people.

Decentralization Issue

Much, perhaps too much, attention has been given to the advantages of centralization as opposed to decentralization of computer activities. Our study has produced no evidence of a relationship between effectiveness of computer usage and centralization or decentralization. Both approaches seem to be able to concentrate the computer effort where it is needed. In companies where the normal management structure is highly centralized, a basically centralized computer system works best. Likewise, in decentralized companies, decentralized computer activities appear to work best. Managements have wisely sought to organize the computer function in much the same manner as they do other key operations of the business.

It is important to distinguish management of the overall computer effort from management of the subfunctions, i.e., computer operations or computer systems and planning. Keeping this distinction in mind will avoid much possible confusion. For instance, in most of the companies, *overall* computer management is centralized; but in almost two thirds of them, computer *operations* are *de*centralized. These facts are detailed in Exhibit 18–4.

With whom is the centralized responsibility for planning and coordination placed? In centralized companies, the executive in charge is typically the man at headquarters with line responsibility for computer activities. In decentralized companies, the responsible person is normally a staff executive at headquarters with a charter from top management to see that the various groups are effectively coordinated.

Evaluating Performance

Less concerned with the technical complexities than with overall performance, management is turning its attention to the major problems of systems organization and control. An extreme case, but illustrative of the growing realization that simplistic cost-reduction approaches are not the answer to corporate needs, is this comment from the chairman of a major company:

> We have an extreme diversity in our products, markets, and product and production technologies. Consequently, we have developed a decentralized, profit-center form of organization. From the outset a decade ago, we've encouraged our division and operating managers to use computers. As a consequence, we have a very decentralized computer structure under what we consider to be adequate corporate minimum standards and objectives. One computer expert told me we could save 30% of our equipment rental if we

EXHIBIT 18–4

Basic patterns of computer organization structure for 33 companies

KEY TO COMPUTER ORGANIZATION STRUCTURE: ● CENTRALIZED ▲ DECENTRALIZED

BASIC COMPANY STRUCTURE		OVERALL MANAGEMENT	SYSTEMS & PLANNING	COMPUTER OPERATIONS
10 CENTRALIZED COMPANIES	1	●	●	●
	2	●	●	●
	3	●	●	●
	4	●	●	●
	5	●	●	●
	6	●	●	●
	7	●	▲	▲
	8	●	▲	▲
	9	●	▲	●
	10	●	●	▲
23 DECENTRALIZED COMPANIES	1	●	▲	▲
	2	●	▲	▲
	3	●	▲	▲
	4	●	▲	▲
	5	●	▲	▲
	6	●	▲	▲
	7	●	▲	▲
	8	●	▲	▲
	9	●	▲	▲
	10	●	▲	▲
	11	●	▲	▲
	12	●	▲	▲
	13	●	▲	▲
	14	●	▲	▲
	15	●	●	●
	16	●	●	●
	17	●	●	●
	18	●	●	●
	19	▲	▲	▲
	20	▲	▲	▲
	21	▲	▲	▲
	22	●	●	▲
	23	●	●	▲

went to a highly centralized computer structure. I expect he might be right. But that saving would be a fraction of 1% of our business volume. While we may do some selective geographic consolidation of computer operations to obtain economics, we are certainly not going to change our basic management approach to computers to achieve that level of savings.

Quite obviously, this senior executive is using a broader view of computer performance than the narrow approach of dollars spent measured against cost reduction obtained. Unfortunately, some studies have sought to measure the efficiency of computers by just such narrow measures. It is an ineffective yardstick on two counts:

(1) Most companies are at an early stage in the learning process, and a good part of their corporate expenditure for computers is still going into an investment in techniques and applications that can only be expected to pay off at some future date.

(2) Cost accounting may have been relevant to the computer when most of its applications were devoted to financial and accounting applications in which clerical cost reduction was the major consideration; but now—as the computer moves out into operating areas—other virtues such as production efficiency, inventory balance, customer service, and other difficult-to-quantify advantages become important. These are the benefits of the computer which provide the most significant competitive advantages to the company.

One manager summed it up rather neatly when he said, "I feel strongly that *good* management will have much more effect on computer usage than good computer usage will have on management practices."

CURRENT EFFECTIVENESS

Contrary to what might be expected, companies which have been expanding their computer effort into other applications, and which have been dealing with the management problems this expansion presents, run routine computer applications equally as well as do those companies that have restricted their efforts to polishing up the more proven computer uses. More specifically:

- As many as 9 out of the 10 companies rated high or above average in efforts to extend the computer to critical areas of the business were also ranked highest in computer application efficiency.
- Of the 10 companies ranked lowest in such efforts, 8 were rated below average or low in efficiency of application.

This finding leaves little comfort for anyone who has been content with the status quo and is convinced his effectiveness in current computer effort is paying unusual dividends. Chances are his competitor who is extending his computer effort is doing just as well in the same areas and getting returns from other applications to boot.

Exhibit 18–5 gives the research team's evaluation of both current and anticipated future effectiveness after planned improvements have been implemented. (Bear in mind, again, that all companies in the sample are successful, and that the least effective company here would surely be rated as highly effective if compared with all U.S. industrial computer users.)

EXHIBIT 18–5

RATED EFFECTIVENESS OF PRESENT AND FUTURE COMPUTER APPLICATIONS

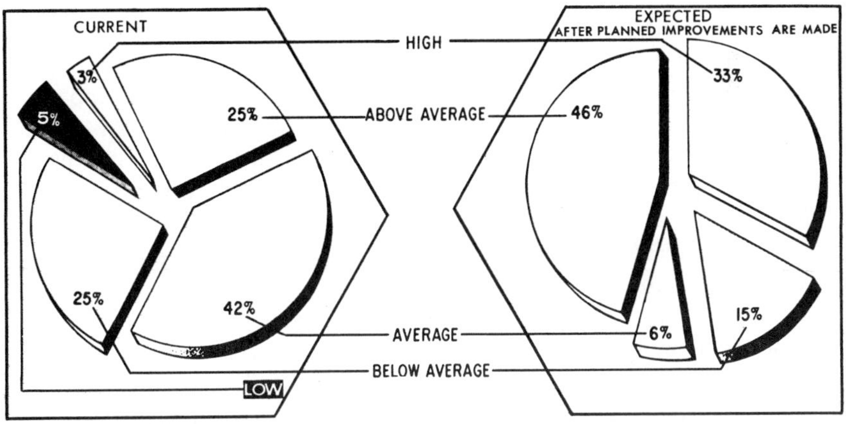

There are numerous examples of inconsistency in effectiveness within an individual company. This might be expected in an evaluation by functional area because, as previously stated, the computer is invariably best used in the area of entry—usually finance and accounting. What is surprising is the great difference in effectiveness noted among various operating units of multidivisional companies. This is readily understandable in those companies that integrate relatively recent acquisitions. But it is much less comprehensible in a number of other companies. In their cases, inconsistency in effectiveness suggests "people problems"—especially, lack of understanding and support on the part of managers who have stayed aloof from electronic data processing.

From the earliest days of the computer, studies of its impact on business have tended to conclude with the warning that the involvement of top executives and operating management is essential. This advice has apparently been heeded by many executives in the companies studied. Time and again, one would begin with the words, "I don't know much about computers, but . . ."—and then proceed to show astounding sophistication and knowledge about what the computer was and was not contributing to his business, and how he planned to use it in the future!

PLANNING AND CONTROL

What new activities in a company could be served well by a computer? What present computer applications need to be improved? How should changes be made, and in what sequence? These are questions with which most of the companies surveyed are greatly concerned. And they are *not* answering the questions in old-fashioned ways.

The historical practice of approving proposed new applications of computers on the basis of clerical or other cost-reduction potential is not the primary basis for approval in most of the companies. Indeed, 12 of the companies use a formal return on investment analysis comparable to that used for other types of proposed new activities. Another 8 companies approve proposed new applications either on the basis of expected operating improvement or return on investment analysis where applicable. Significantly, the companies evaluating potential applications on the basis of return on investment tend to be the same ones rated highest in applying the computer to their most important needs.

Most of the companies have plans that provide general guidance in deciding on new applications of the computer. But only one has analyzed and evaluated prospective applications so specifically that proposals can be compared definitively in the light of them. In this company, the proposed applications can be checked against the plan in terms of both type and expected benefits.

To whom does top management look for initiation of new computer applications? In general, the corporate computer staff is the most important source of proposals. The direct participation of either top management or operating management in determining new applications tends to have a direct influence on how effectively the computer is used.

Auditing Procedures

All but two of the companies have established a regular procedure for auditing their computer activities. There is a significant correlation between poor auditing practice and less-than-optimum computer systems performance. Auditing practices vary from rather informal reports to management on an annual basis to regular quarterly or semiannual audits documenting return on investment, cost reduction, and operating improvement. Here are the highlights of this part of the study:

In 20 companies, the audit is the responsibility of the corporate staff. In 9, it is the combined responsibility of the corporate staff and operating management. In 2, operating management alone is responsible.

Generally speaking, the companies with corporate staff and operating management cooperating on audits seem to be doing the most effective job, although much depends on the individual quality of the auditing procedure. Significantly, the company with the highest rating on computer effectiveness has regular audits in which computer staff and operating management co-operate in reviews of all the computer activities of the company.

Only 13 of the companies in the sample audit and review all activities, while 18 restrict their audits to new and/or critical applications.

This auditing procedure seems to perform the ancillary function of educating management about the computer. It does this better, perhaps, than any other method. It is also apparent that most of the companies intend to take steps to improve their auditing procedure and to make it more objective by involving more members of management not directly concerned with the computer effort. This practice should spread familiarity with computer techniques further throughout management. And that is not the only benefit, as the following example shows:

One company has just completed a comprehensive audit over a period of eight months that required a total of eight man-years of effort. The audit covered all aspects of computers—from retail credit operations through production scheduling, process control, and the use of computers by overseas affiliates. The job required eight subcommittees with memberships from all interested operating elements.

This massive audit, besides yielding a plan for a continuing monitoring system, drew attention to critical manning requirements, necessary standards, and produced the basis for blocking out a basic systems concept for the company that will cover such questions as:

- What type and degree of control should technical groups have over the computer facilities?
- How much geographical consolidation of computing activities can be achieved and at what rate?
- What standards should be set for equipment selection, systems design, programming documentation, and programming languages?

Audits of this scope not only provide an excellent picture of how well the computer is doing, but they also yield a useful perspective on how well the company as a whole is operating.

ULTIMATE GOALS

One of the most controversial questions involving computers has to do with the concept of the "total integrated management information system";

that is, a computer complex that serves all needs for data in executive decision making. Our study throws some light on this issue.

Gradual Integration

Virtually all of the companies in the sample express intentions to gradually integrate subsystems (see Exhibit 18–6). They are interlinking logically related specific applications into larger units. So far, 11 of the companies have made considerable progress in integrating the distribution function; in the next 4 years, another 13 will have distribution functions fairly well integrated. Only 5 companies have made much progress in integrating factory operations, but by 1970, 21 additional companies plan to have computer applications in their factory operations well interlinked and coordinated.

EXHIBIT 18–6

PLANNING FOR INTEGRATION

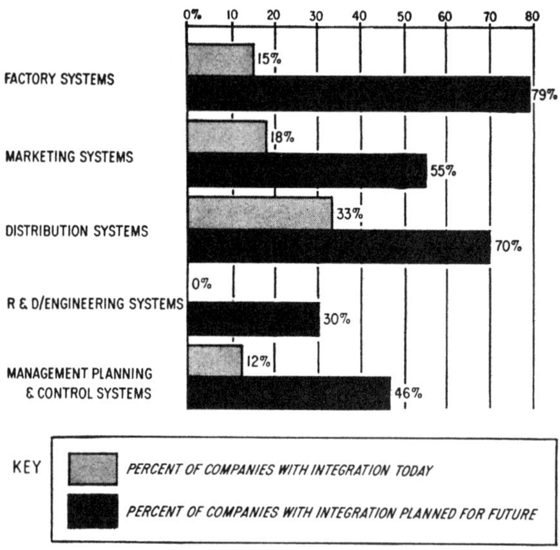

Generally, the attitude toward integration of applications is conservative. Here are typical comments:

> We're interested in—and are pursuing—integration of applications wherever it makes good economic sense. But we have some real opportunities left in rather straightforward applications, particularly in production scheduling, production control, transportation, and distribution.—*Computer executive in petroleum company*

We've just started to realize the real benefits from computers as we're trying to develop significantly integrated factory systems to provide tight control on order status, inventory, and delivery. The preeminent benefit from this is the greatly increased understanding of our business that we are developing. —*Steel company executive*

Judging from evidence like this, the so-called total integrated management information system, the "board-room computer," or the total command and control center in the president's office is a great deal closer to science fiction than to fact. Indeed, not one of the companies in the study regards the total system as a near-term goal. A comment from an executive vice president of a large food company is typical:

We've discussed total management information systems, and have had some interesting ideas and outline schemas. But we're going ahead with the many obviously good applications and have not yet settled firmly on the structure of our systems. Until we learn how to define information needs of key individuals at all decision-making levels and to produce tailored reports of composite information, we're not ready to settle on structure or organization. With this big reservation, we are taking gradual steps toward a multitiered, integrated management information system concentrating on critical areas, especially marketing, first.

The computer executive of a machinery manufacturer defines the problem as follows:

Since we have decided basically on a decentralized but unified corporate information system, we have mounted a massive standardization program aimed at reducing duplication, transferring programs and people where they are most useful, and upgrading installations to the level of our best. Fortunately, since we have been using computers in most of our operations for many years, we have lived through the pains of establishing data codes and numbering systems. However, to develop a unified, decentralized system employing data transmission, we'll have to standardize further on equipment, systems concepts, programming languages, documentation, and operations as a basis for measuring progress and efficiency.

Conflicting Needs

For most top management men and operating executives, the total system is well beyond the horizon. However, it is frequently discussed and considered a distinct possibility for "sometime in the future" for most companies. As such, it does affect current planning. No one wants to set up a system that would make a total system impossible to implement. Hence most companies are establishing plans for central direction and policy control in order to ensure that standards and practices are not conflicting within the company. They want the pieces of the jigsaw to fit as the integrated system—in total or in part—becomes a reality.

Characteristically, the firms which are closest to integrated systems are those highly centralized companies with relatively short product lines and marked geographic concentration.

One company in the sample was found to be actually *de*-integrating its computer setup. It had found that its relatively highly integrated data processing system worked fine when it worked. However, as the controller said, "When any part of the system failed, everything shut down including the shipments." The company is now in the process of modularizing its system and building redundancy into it to reduce the consequences of failure.

All 33 companies have generally defined their objectives for the ultimate total system concept or are in the process of doing so. The 27 companies already having a defined ultimate concept envision some form of close integration of applications—if not in a totally integrated system, at least in integrated modular units. Most of the companies intend to preserve their present basic approach of positioning the computers in the operating unit. In addition, they will link them together through centralized coordination and control to ensure compatible systems design. They recognize the real-world problems of living with today's needs while trying to peer down the murky, poorly defined road of tomorrow's technology.

The balanced approach is not easy, however. The truth of this is best demonstrated by a company that is thoroughly enmeshed in the difficulties of making a relatively simple systems conversion. At the same time, it has untouched plans and charts on file for a highly integrated, total management information system—one that is designed to produce instant profit and loss statements.

CONCLUSION

Unquestionably, the very successful manufacturing companies in our sample have learned to manage their computers. Sensibly, they have achieved their success to date by managing their computer systems in much the same fashion as they control other complex parts of their business. No longer awed by the genies that live in the boxes in the computer room, their managers are learning (though sometimes at considerable expense) that systems men with Ph.D.'s and skilled programmers are still people, and that they do tend to respond to sound managerial approaches.

Management's growing familiarity with the general world of information technology—gained to a large extent through its participation in audits and planning sessions—has resulted in clearing the lines of communication as well as instilling much greater sophistication concerning the computer at all levels of operation.

Pattern of Success

Clearly identifiable patterns of success emerge from this study. As a composite of effective management practices, they offer guidelines for every computer user. These characteristics may be best stated in terms of a hypothetical company which is a composite of the 33 used in the research project:

- The company has followed the same basic pattern in organizing its computer operations as it has followed in other company operations.
- Overall management responsibility for company computer operations is retained at the top corporate level, but apparently in no greater degree than for other vital company activities.
- The company has positioned overall top responsibility for computer activities under the financial executive, but may quite likely be considering moving this responsibility out from under him.
- Any repositioning of overall responsibility for computer activities most likely will occur as the need for or implementation of nonfinancial applications becomes more important.
- Ultimately, computer operations are likely to be directed by a top corporate-level executive who has a broad administrative/management services responsibility.
- The interrelationship of computer activities with other administrative services—particularly as operations research, general business systems, and new management information and control techniques emerge—will influence thinking about the need to position computer responsibilities as part of a broadened top corporate functional area.
- The company's top executive exerts a type and degree of influence and impact on computer activities consistent with the importance and effectiveness of computer usage in company operations.
- Management has placed and will continue to place increasing emphasis on experience with and knowledge of the company and its operations when staffing the key computer-management jobs.
- The company has general plans for future use of the computer and probably is in the process of refining them to meet specific applications, timetables, and other planned needs.
- The computer staff is being looked to for formulation of both general and specific plans, but increasing emphasis is being placed on operating management to accept equal or full responsibility for planning computer applications.
- Applications are planned and approved, and computer perform-

ance is evaluated, on the same basis as other actions involving increased expenditures and investment—if not through return on investment analysis, at least on the basis of judgment of the value of the improvements expected.

- A regular audit of computer applications is conducted both to control and evaluate their effectiveness, and to determine improvement needs.
- The company looks to operating management to audit computer activities if the computer staff has responsibility for planning applications, or to the computer staff to do the audit if operating management is responsible for planning applications.
- The regular audit process covers all applications deemed by management to be of critical importance, but progress is being made toward including all applications and all installations.

The companies are not resting on their laurels; they are not complacent. Typical is this comment by one group vice president:

> Clearly, in our industry, computers have become essential to survival. We've reduced our clerical and administrative costs. We're running with close to 20 annual turns on raw materials and an average of about 10 turns on finished goods inventory. We've leveled out many of the swings and oscillations in our manufacturing operations. And as far as I can see, we've about stayed even with our competitors.

As the computer becomes more imbedded in the fabric of business, as management molds these general-purpose machines to the configuration of individual corporate goals and objectives, it becomes increasingly dangerous to look to industry averages for guidance in proportioning computer effort. The alert management group will find useful guidelines in the experience of other organizations. But it will be the company that shapes the computer to its own destinies—influenced perhaps but not awed by the practices of others—that will find itself most competitive and best prepared to meet the challenges of the future.

D

The Behavioral Sciences

The author describes in simple terms what behavioral science is and what it can do for business managers.

19

WHAT IS BEHAVIORAL SCIENCE?

Harold M. F. Rush

"Nothing is permanent except change," contended Heraclitus back in the sixth century B.C. Succeeding generations have echoed this sentiment, especially in this century of unprecedented change. The business world has taken on so completely new a face in so relatively short a time, that the business manager often finds it difficult to keep abreast with the ever-increasing developments in his field. He may even find that the management concepts he has put into practice for most of his working life are under re-examination.

The conscientious manager who prides himself in being conversant with newer trends probably hears or reads a lot about the widening interest of businessmen in behavioral science. And he may be even a little embarrassed that he isn't quite sure what it's all about. Well, in the most elementary terms, what is it?

A good starting point is to examine the word "behavior." Webster defines it as: "Mode of conducting oneself; the way in which an organism, organ, or substance acts, especially in response to a stimulus."

Behavioral science is interested in studying behavior, specifically human behavior, in response to various stimuli—internal and mental or external and physical. The term came into popular usage because men working in the field considered it more descriptive than the formerly used "social science." The word social, they felt, was associated too much in the layman's mind with sociability, and, possibly more to the point, social science was often confused with socialism.

Reprinted from *The Conference Board Record,* September 1965, pp. 35–41, by permission of the publisher.

Behavioral science connotes all the factors that go into man's fundamental personality—his needs, his emotions, his thinking, his ability to relate his thoughts and feelings. His actions are a result and a composite of all these factors.

WHO IS A BEHAVIORAL SCIENTIST?

The group of academic disciplines which constitute the behavioral sciences is large. In one sense, any person who engages in the study of human behavior is a behavioral scientist; but so broad a definition could be carried to the absurd. (An internal auditor is interested in how people spend money. Is he, then, a behavioral scientist?) A behavioral scientist is simply someone whose *primary* concern is the study of how and why people behave as they do.

The first profession that comes to mind when considering the role of the behavioral scientist is psychology. By definition, psychology is concerned with the study of the mind and its inter-relation with an *individual's* behavior. The second profession is sociology. Sociology is concerned with the evolution of society, or the forms, institutions, and functions of human *groups*. In the study of groups, these two areas, for example, overlap so much that it is sometimes difficult to ascertain which of the two disciplines does what. It would be unprofessional to call these situations jurisdictional disputes; but, as an example of overlap, there is an area of specialization within psychology that is interested in groups also. This is called social psychology. The essential difference between a social psychologist and a sociologist is that the former is primarily interested in studying the behavior of an individual as he relates to, or is affected by, the groups in which he lives and functions, while the latter is more concerned with the group as a whole and one group's relationships with another. When directed to "work situations," the efforts of both the psychologist and the sociologist have applicability to the business world.

The behavioral scientist label also has been applied, under certain circumstances, to the economist, the political scientist, the human engineer (who seeks to adapt the work environment to the man), and to a host of other specialists. What the person is called is of less importance than what he does. Social psychologists, industrial psychologists, industrial sociologists, labor economists, educators, physicians, anthropologists, and many more professionals came under the umbrella of behavioral sciences because all are concerned, to varying degrees, with human behavior.

WHAT DOES HE DO?

In its raw form "science" refers to knowledge obtained by study and practice or to any department of systematized knowledge. By this definition the behavioral scientist is a scientist, although his counterparts in the natural or physical sciences sometimes may balk at the use of the term as applied to psychologists, sociologists, cultural anthropologists, *et al.* Strictly speaking, the behavioral scientist works within the framework of scientific method, and he applies tests of statistical and clinical validity to the evidence he collects. He approaches a problem in much the same way as the physical scientist: he does basic research by measuring and counting and by observing existing phenomena; he performs experimental work based on a given thesis and postulates a system or approach based on the evidence he gleans. In describing his basic methodology he borrows the language of the physical scientist. He speaks in terms of research, development, and application. But his data, unlike those of the physical scientist, can rarely, if ever, meet the criterion of indisputable universality: he cannot work in the perfectly controlled environment of a laboratory; he cannot extrapolate with rigid authority; he does not deal with properties and conditions that remain constant; he cannot control the quality or quantity of his variables. In short, the properties he is working with are the most complex of all organisms, physically, mentally, and emotionally—people.

Even the most scientifically oriented behavioral scientist recognizes that his field is not at this point an exact science. Still, through adherence to principles of scientific method, through constant observation of his subjects, and thorough validation of his findings, he attempts to predict what is likely to happen to a given person or groups of persons within a given situation.

Most behavioral scientists recognize that they may never reach the point of axiomatic certainty—the variables and complexities of people are great. But their efforts have already produced considerable knowledge about how and why people behave as they do, how their strengths and weaknesses can be evaluated, what their needs and wants are.

There are even persons working within the framework of behavioral research (and particularly as it applies to the business world) who do not follow strict rules of scientific method and inquiry. Many businessmen feel, however, that their theories or philosophies have contributed much to the understanding of people at work and generally of the management process.

Some of the disciplines that are lumped together as behavioral sciences are relatively young; psychology as a modern system was still considered to be an embryo as late as the beginning of this century, for example. But the studies, major ones, have been made possible by an increasing level of sophistication over the past couple of decades. As techniques become refined, many expect that a more finite contribution will be made by the behavioral scientist, particularly to the world of work.

WHO IS INTERESTED IN HIS WORK?

There has been a recent surge of interest in behavioral science on the part of people in business. But the question may arise: "After all, hasn't industry managed to survive and even thrive without behavioral science in the past?" Business *has* survived and thrived, but not without behavioral science in some form.

Human behavior and its effects upon productivity have been the interest of management for a long time—long before anyone coined a term for the study of this subject. From the early studies on employee learning, in the 1890's, to the first time-and-motion studies, to the development of tests and a more sophisticated approach to employee selection, to on-the-job training, to supervisory training, and on to the advent of management development, companies have become more and more sensitive to how the employee acts and reacts, how he functions in various situations, how his innate abilities can be matched with the job requirements, how to create a work environment conducive to job satisfaction, harmonious relations, and a higher level of production.

Most earlier behavioral scientists were concerned with the physical factors that make for higher levels of production (well designed machines and work areas, healthy working conditions, illumination, temperatures at the work place, job analysis and selective placement, use of color and music to induce efficiency). They were also interested in keeping the employee loyal and content (rates of pay, paid vacations, insurance benefits and pensions, recreation, coffee breaks, etc.). Broadly speaking, they were interested in manipulating the tangible and/or material environment; and they were, in the main, interested in the rank-and-file worker. Some modern behavioral scientists contend that these earlier studies were concerned with man as an adjunct to a machine, and thus may not be considered behavioral research at all.

It is doubtful whether all of the interest of business in its employees, even in the earlier stages, was initiated out of altruistic concern. Many social pressures, the rise and power of organized labor, the employer's obligation under workmen's compensation laws, and the ever-increasing industrial competition all may have had a part in "forcing" many companies to take a closer look at their relations with their workers. Outside pressures and influences aside, management began to realize that in a competitive free-enterprise economy its only permanent advantage lies in its human resources. With this growing realization, management has intensified its inquiry into the how and why of human behavior.

In this perspective the current activity in behavioral research is, for all practical purposes, a continuation of earlier studies with a new dimension added: the scope of concern.

Whereas early behavioral research concerned itself with workers *en masse,* today's focus is more on the manager and the management process. In the family-owned company the owner did the "hiring and firing," and frequently he kept in close touch with the actual manufacturing operation. In the large modern corporation the head of the company necessarily has a group of technical and administrative specialists who do the jobs the owner-manager used to perform. It has been demonstrated that a good machinist doesn't automatically make a good manager of a machine shop; a crack salesman doesn't necessarily make a good marketing manager. Successful managers need training and special experience in the administration of material and human resources. This need has given rise to the professional manager. The manager of today is rarely the "working group leader." Thus, more than ever, he must depend upon his subordinates to get the work done. Yet, he is accountable to the company for the work output, morale, and performance of those in his unit.

Other factors also have contributed to the change of emphasis. Some of them are: increasing automation; finer distinctions in occupational specialization; refinement of scientific and technical capabilities of the corporation; and the unparalleled affluence of the populace. Society is rapidly becoming one in which the emphasis is shifted from work done by hand to work done by the mind. In this computer age the human mind becomes a more valuable commodity. As machines do the work previously done by men, the professional manager makes his greatest contribution mentally: decision making and management of human resources.

The key to the performance of a manager and to that of his employee is "motivation," a point which is being stressed increasingly by the behavioral scientist in the university and by the businessman. Business has long been concerned about motivation but, for the most part, the interest has been confined to consumer motivation. Researchers have begun to move in their studies from motivation to buy to motivation to work.

What is this thing called motivation? Motivation is defined as a drive within the individual, rather than without, which incites him to action. What the behavioral scientist is interested in is *what* motivates the individual. What are the factors conducive to motivation?

What is involved—or the total concern—can be illustrated by the old saw "You can lead a horse to water but you cannot make him drink." In this folk proverb all the elements are present—you, the horse, the leading, and the water. These are all the external, physical, and material factors. The element missing is the thirst, or the need—or desire—for the water. While modern behavioral scientists recognize that man is infinitely more complex than a horse, the same principle applies. And some behavioral scientists contend that business has for too long tried to do the leading (or actually *has* been leading) without allowing the individual to aspire to or to satisfy his own needs in order to achieve self-realization.

What can the behavioral scientist do about it? For one thing, he can look for the factors that are conducive to motivation. For another, and this, perhaps, is more important, he can determine what the individual's needs *are.* It is an accepted maxim that man is forever a goal-seeking animal, and if it can be determined what those goals *are* and *why* he seeks them, society—or business for that matter—may not only be better equipped to help him reach them, but may also find itself better off.

Some established beliefs about what motivates a person on the job are now being questioned—for example, the long-held assumption that money paid for services is enough to keep a person happy and productive. With high employment and growing affluence, money seems to have lost much of its power as a motivator. Money obviously can be a stimulus to motivation if a man is unemployed and hungry, but it is not a motivator in the real sense. The motivation for the unemployed man is to feed, clothe, and shelter himself, so even then money becomes a means to an end. Some behavioral researchers have shown that above a certain level of responsibility compensation is not a motivating factor at all. If a manager is paid $20,000 annually, for example, it does not necessarily follow that he is more strongly motivated to do a good job if he is raised to $30,000. The salary he receives may make him more *satisfied* with the job, but it won't necessarily make him more highly motivated. A substantial amount of research indicates that compensation, at best, can provide satisfaction only *off* the job.

A prevailing trend in behavioral research as related to human motivation assumes that, in order to reach his inner-directed goals, a man must first know himself and be able to find an outlet for his needs. The atmosphere in which he lives and works must be one that encourages self-expression and self-realization. Furthermore, it is believed that a person's concept of himself determines his attitude toward his contemporaries and the groups in which he functions, because he looks at his world through the only eyes he has—his own. But objectivity about oneself is very difficult to achieve. For this reason much of the behavioral research conducted today is concerned with finding ways to help man know himself, his capabilities, his limitations, and his abilities to relate what is inside him to the external world. Part of his world is composed of the groups in which he moves: his community, his family, and his world of work. His world of work is made up of groups; it is made up of individuals, who make up groups and subgroups. The contemporary manager must communicate with, and work with and around a variety of persons with a wide range of personalities and skills.

WHAT'S HE WORKING ON NOW?

Many behavioral scientists, sensitive to the personal and social needs of the individual, are engaged in research on the nuances of human relationships and interrelationships. As indicated earlier, they are trying to find the elements that create an environment conducive to personal growth and self-realization. Much of their research is designed to elaborate and elucidate on the individual and the group. A few current concerns with special interest for the business world include:

• *Communication.* Upward, downward, and lateral communication within an organization; keeping channels of communication open for flow of accurate and useful information; formal and informal methods of communication; improvement of personal skills in written and oral communication; verbalization of internal needs; "feedback" and effects of communication efforts within the organization.

• *Decision Making.* Development of skills in handling "open-ended" or problematic situations; degree of participation at various levels of the organization; rational versus impulsive (or intuitive) approaches; boundaries or "risk-taking."

• *Innovation and Change.* Effecting technological, managerial, and organizational change within an organization; implementing change when indicated and gaining acceptance of novel situations; barriers to innovation; effect of change on productivity and morale; innovation through high motivation.

• *Conflict.* How it arises in an organization; interpersonal and interdepartmental hostility and conflict; optimum resolution of conflict; effect on organizational goals and the group's ability to function under stress.

• *Leadership.* Qualities of effective leaders; development of leadership ability; relative effectiveness of "permissive," "supportive," and "autocratic" approaches to management of an organization; entrepreneurship.

• *Authority and Accountability.* Limits of power; relation of responsibility and authority; span of control, reaction to authority from peer, subordinate, and superior groups; degree of accountability; delegation of responsibility and authority.

• *Learning, Perception and Creativity.* Measurement of learning capacities; individuals and groups as perceived by other individuals and groups within the organization; development of potentialities; refinement of existing skills; creation of climate for personal growth and creative expression; personal creativity within the larger organization's goals and structures.

The above represents only a most cursory overview of the facets of human composition and behavior that occupy the professional behavioral researcher these days. Not only do these capsule listings comprise but a few examples of the topics that might be identified with contemporary behavioral research, but also within the topics there is much overlap.

HOW'S HE DOING?

With these interests, how is the behavioral scientist doing? At least, how is he doing in terms of the three stages of scientific inquiry, that is research, development, and application? All three warrant comment on the state of the art.

Research is defined as "diligent and systematic inquiry or investigation into a subject in order to discover facts or principles." The research stage seems to be the most active. There are foundations and other philanthropic organizations whose chief activity is the support of research in human behavior. Their encouragement (and their funds) is being used by an ever-growing number of behavioral scientists to do fundamental research in behavior of individuals and groups, increasingly aimed at the business environment. Some well-known social psychologists, sociologists (and a few political scientists and economists) have begun adapting older theories about intergroup behavior—previously concerned mainly with community, educational, and ethnic groups—to the world of work.

Aside from the intensive research in the departments of social science at major universities, there can hardly be found a respected business school without a division that is performing behavioral research of some sort, and there are springing up inter-disciplinary centers which surmount departmental boundaries for concerted effort in behavioral research.

Research is also being performed by the military services, either directly or through contract with behavioral science institutes, on many of the same problems that confront the business world, e.g., leadership, communications, etc. This reflects the growing realization that group problems are group problems—regardless of where they exist.

Basic research is apparently thriving, judging from the outpouring of books on behavioral research and the numerous research reports in scientific and management journals.

This research most often takes place on the university campus or at some other place where the subjects can be observed closely and where data can be verified with a considerable degree of accuracy. The subjects are often students who contribute time to the experiments and then return to their regular work. Sometimes the subjects are businessmen, but the major extent of their participation is a laboratory session for a specified time away from their places of work. Occasionally behavioral research is conducted in an actual work setting, but most frequently the work force sample is small or restricted to companies whose orientation is in favor of behavioral research to the extent that some researchers question the validity of the findings of these experiments performed with "preconditioned" subjects.

EARLY APPLICATION

If one accepts the premise that earlier research in physical factors that affect productivity was actually behavioral research, then the application phase is widespread and evident in modern business. Changes in the work environment and production processes that were considered radical innovations a few years ago are now accepted practice.

Another example of popular acceptance and application of behavioral science is the use of employee selection aids, particularly psychological tests, the structured interview, and the weighted application form.

There is some evidence that business is applying the additional findings of the modern group of behavioral researchers. Consumer motivation studies were cited earlier, but perhaps a more significant trend is the acceptance of work-motivation theories by some companies, noticeably in the management development area. Instances of full-scale adoption of current motivational theories are rare, but a few companies have changed complete organization structures in order to put into use some of the more recent theories. And a growing number of companies are enlisting the aid of the behavioral scientist to conduct "laboratory" sessions within the organization, all aimed at achieving a higher degree of communication and motivation among their executives.

While both development and application require removal "from the laboratory to the world," they are sometimes confused. Development implies further research and follow-up, always with the thought in mind that the thing being tried is still research, while application is the putting into practical use a principle or law which is accepted as a concrete phenomenon.

There are those, including some behavioral scientists, who decry application of theories about interpersonal and intergroup relationships until they are more fully developed. One psychologist asserted, "There are a handful of companies that are so concerned about their executives' mental health and performance that they are ready to embrace any new theory put forth. . . . They seem all too willing to try putting into practical application every new fad that comes along. . . . What we need is more developmental research."

Development means "to bring out the capabilities or possibilities; cause to grow or expand into a more advanced or effective state." Development for behavioral scientists, as for physical scientists, involves taking a piece of pure or theoretical research which has been refined in the laboratory and putting it through further tests in a given situation where the variables are not as strictly controlled. In other words, development is an expansion of a piece of basic research to see if it is pragmatic.

For the behavioral researcher concerned with people at work, it means trying out a theory in an actual work setting with constant observance, measurement, validation, and recording of data, with the hope that he will achieve universality.

THE NEED FOR DEVELOPMENT

The development stage is noticeably missing in the largest segment of business. Development often is indicated for a particular piece of research that already has had some development and application, because conditions for a specific company or type of business may not be the same as for business as a whole. An example of application without appropriate development may be found in the use of psychological tests for screening of employees. Some tests have gained so much in popularity that they have become the *sine qua non* for employment throughout the organization, even though the accepted scores have not been validated for the particular industry, the particular company, and the particular jobs under consideration. To ensure that "cut-off" scores are realistic for the situation in which they are used, development research is indicated in many cases.

Carrying this example further, some companies have begun to stress validation of employment tests. For the most part, however, these validations lack desirable accuracy. The usual procedure in validating a given test is to follow up on the work performance of people after they are employed. It is expected that persons scoring 90, for example, will turn out to be better workers than those scoring 70. In most validation efforts, however, an arbitrary "cut-off" score, say 50, is established, and applicants scoring below that point aren't hired. If the scores established for employment, and taken as an indicator of job success, are to be developed and validated fully, the company would have to hire some people who score in the lower percentiles as well as those who achieve a score in the upper percentiles. Then, the job success of those who scored 10 or 20 could be compared with the higher achievers. Even among those scoring in the upper ranges, the person with a 70 score may show more job success than the person with a 90, if they are in different jobs. If psychological tests are to be given much credence, the need for developmental research is apparent.

For another example of application without thorough development the businessman needs only to look at methods of performance appraisal as they are popularly and widely used. A great deal of basic research has been performed on systems of evaluating an employee's success on the job. The fundamental research showed that such reviews were desirable because they left both the superior and the subordinate with a sense of sympathetic understanding. It was further shown that mutual confidence and trust resulted from the feeling that both parties knew fully what the job required and what was expected of the subordinate in meeting the job's objectives, as well as what he could expect from his superior.

So, a major segment of the business community installed performance appraisals throughout their respective companies at all levels of responsibility.

Did anyone stop to ask: "What effect, if any, does the performance appraisal have on subsequent work performance?" There may have been questions in the minds of some businessmen, but only recently did a large multiplant company, working in collaboration with behavioral scientists from a leading university's school of business, decide to take a look at the effect of those frank, free-communication appraisals on the performance of the employee afterwards. (Incidentally, at least in the study cited, the effect of performance appraisals on subsequent work performance had a *negative* correlation.)

Employment tests and performance appraisals are only two examples of the work of behavioral scientists which has been accepted and put to use without adequate development. Much more fundamental research is at the stage where development is indicated and needed, if the knowledge gained through the basic research is ever to be meaningful for the business world. Why, then, is this developmental research not being conducted?

There are many reasons why the gap exists. Managements' (or organizations') resistance to change has been offered as one reason. Also, relatively few companies have been in a position to provide a climate conducive to behavioral research. Therefore, the developmental research has been restricted, almost exclusively, to a few large corporations with a management that is more likely to be sensitive to new concepts and trends, and with the funds to sustain a staff to carry out the studies. In the main, these efforts have been further restricted to the corporate offices where product output and manufacturing schedules aren't paramount. Occasionally, development research in human behavior is conducted by smaller companies—usually very small companies dealing in services, rather than material products, where communication channels are relatively close and controllable.

The reluctance of most companies to participate in behavioral research may be understandable, even to the behavioral scientists, for many developmental projects can (and do) involve a complete rearrangement of interpersonal and intergroup relationships and functions. For this reason, many businessmen have been hesitant to "play around with profits" by encouraging innovation and change in the organization's structure. Granted that increased productivity and harmonious relations are still the goals of behavioral research as it relates to business, these changes may not be observable immediately. For men accustomed to thinking in terms of manufacturing schedules and year-end profits truly innovative experiments have often been shunned in favor of the "tried and true."

The behavioral scientist may feel, on the other hand, that he has produced theories which have been tested and worked out to their optimum in the atmosphere of fundamental research. It is, therefore, the hope of behavioral scientists that more and more companies will appear upon the scene with both the willingness and the desire to "pick up the ball" and develop the findings of this basic research. On the strength of their experience during the past few years, they feel that their optimism is justified.

The author explores the contributions the behavioral sciences can make to better management.

20

BEHAVIORAL SCIENCE IN MODERN INDUSTRY

Allen I. Kraut

In the past few decades, the behavioral sciences have taken on a growing importance in industry. Why this shift? I think it is largely because the critical problems in modern industry tend to be more and more human problems.

As organizations grow and become more complex, technical problems form a smaller share of difficulties faced by management. At the same time, the social complexity of large organizations leads to an increase in the rate and proportion of "people" problems.

Also, as one moves up the management hierarchy, there is an increasingly greater requirement for human relations skills as opposed to sheer technical skills. The behavioral sciences have grown in importance because they help us to understand and solve the problems involved in social relationships. This paper will illustrate and discuss the range of problem-solving applications being made by the behavioral sciences in industry today.

Perhaps the most important *general* contribution the behavioral sciences can make to better management is the application of scientific method to phenomena that are usually handled on the basis of intuition and subjective feeling. Through the application of scientific method, management's knowledge and understanding of human behavior can go be-

Reprinted from *Personnel Administration,* May–June 1967, pp. 32–37, by permission of the publisher.

yond merely intuitive judgments. Important decisions which must weigh human factor can be based on more objective and reliable grounds.

The behavioral disciplines can precisely measure different aspects of human behavior and objectively quantify them. The data accumulated, over many situations, through such methods can be systematically organized (i.e., cast in a theoretical framework) to provide a powerful set of tools to understand why people behave the way they do. This set of tools can help us solve many of the problems daily faced in the management of industrial organizations.

I would like to present some instances of how the behavioral sciences can and are being applied to *a wide variety of organizational problems*. The areas we will look at are typical organizational concerns, running the gamut of recruitment, selection, training, motivation, promotion and demotion. Many of these applications have been made within IBM (but I claim no originality or superiority in IBM's applications).

RECRUITMENT

The initial job of any management is to bring the required people into the organization. This can be a major problem when a company is growing rapidly and when it needs people who are in short supply. IBM's recruiting efforts have been helped by studies of graduating seniors (mostly engineers) at schools where a lot of recruiting is done. The studies probe the career goals of young people, their knowledge about the company, and their ideas about what a job with it would mean to them. The findings have been helpful in doing a better recruiting job. We found that some of the students' ideas were quite different from what we expected or desired to find. As a result, IBM modified its campus advertising and other communication efforts.

As an adjunct to this program, we have done *studies* to determine why some college graduates reject job offers. This work has tried to clarify the differences between men who accept IBM's offers and those who reject them. This type of investigation explores the job seeker's work goals and opinions about the company, his evaluation of his pre-employment interviews and the position offered to him. This approach has been successful with several occupational groups.

TESTING

An illustration of the application of the behavioral sciences that is well-known is the use of selection testing to raise "the batting average" in hiring men who will be successful on the job. Properly done, selection testing is a very valuable tool. For years IBM has used many different tests for many occupations, but with mixed success. On more than one occasion, we have had the sobering experience of conducting a follow-up study and finding that tests being used for selection were virtually worthless. Over time, we have come to the recognition that selection testing is an activity that requires professional attention on a sustained basis.

Tests cannot be merely introduced into the hiring process and then forgotten. Tests must first be validated. That is, they must *prove* that they actually do help select better people. The use of tests should be based on a scientific determination of their worth and not on a testimonial or a feeling of faith in their effectiveness.

Even where tests have once been validated, management must recognize that the jobs (for which people are being tested) change, the populations from which people are recruited also change, and these differences can be enough to make a test worthless.

TRAINING

Training requirements also expand as product lines become more sophisticated, varied or broader. For example, the initial training of IBM's office products salesmen (they market electric typewriters, dictation equipment and related supplies) has expanded, during the last 6 years, from one week of formal training to 5 weeks now spent in school. Working with psychologists in the company, our training people have developed programmed instruction to achieve some of this formal instruction more effectively. In fact, a full week of formal training for these sales trainees is almost entirely taken up by programmed instruction.

Well-developed programmed instruction covers a given amount of material in a shorter time than does conventional instruction, and it frees the teacher for other work. It is most useful for basic introductory materials, especially those taught to a large number of students. For certain subject matter, programmed instruction results in greater student retention of the material covered and more favorable student attitudes toward the training.

This move toward greater use of programmed instruction in IBM was made after an initial study established that programmed instruction resulted in greater gains than the conventional classroom method. In one study, customer engineers using programmed instruction to learn repair of IBM 7070 computers showed a learning gain of 10 percent over conventional instruction while using 47 percent less training time (Hughes, 1961).

We are now introducing other training innovations such as closed circuit television and home-sized television cameras. This latter device, utilizing videotape, records simulated sales calls and is played back so that the sales trainee can see himself as others see him. Such a playback gives the student greater insight into his own behavior during a sales call and should improve his field performance. It can also permit students, working at a pace most suitable to themselves, to "tune in" prerecorded lectures whenever they are ready for them—and to repeat them if necessary.

OPINION SURVEYS

Opinion surveys are frequently used to look at employee attitudes on a wide variety of job-related topics. The information gathered is very helpful to management in understanding employees' motivation and work goals and how these change over time. Surveys tap feelings about pay, promotion, co-workers and the work itself. Surveys also provide data for fundamental investigations of organizational behavior.

In one major study using a survey questionnaire, we explored the effects of role conflict among more than 800 salesmen (Kraut, 1965). We found that salesmen who experience role conflict (i.e., disagreements between the man and his manager on how he should be doing his job) are more likely to report dissatisfaction with the job, the company and especially the manager. Such salesmen are also more likely to experience job related tension, including psychosomatic symptoms. These adverse effects are magnified if the salesman *feels* a conflict is present, regardless of the level of objectively determined conflict.

However, the man's sales performance was unaffected by the degree of role conflict. This study points out that certain kinds of job problems do not show up in the salesman's quota performance, even though they make the job less fun—as reflected by attitudes of dissatisfaction and increased tension.

PROMOTION AND DEMOTION

Modern industry must promote the most able people to management. To this end, behavioral scientists have developed the Assessment Center method, pioneered by the American Telephone and Telegraph Company (Campbell and Bray, 1967) and now spreading in use. In this method, candidates are rated by trained observers as they undergo a rigorous series of individual and group exercises. Follow-up studies show that the high-rated candidates later chalk up much better management performances.

Just as promotion is a major concern of management, demotion is also of major importance for organizational effectiveness. Professor Fred

Goldner of Columbia's Graduate Business School recently (1966) reported on a study of demotions among management personnel in a large organization. If an organization is to maintain its vigor, he says, demotions must prune away dead wood and provide mobility opportunities for younger men. But demotions must be made with care not to have an adverse effect on the organization.

Several techniques seem to be useful in maintaining a high level of motivation among the men who move down. Goldner notes the maintenance of some degree of ambiguity in personnel moves, as well as frequent use of lateral movements. Relocation and company-paid trips as "consolation prizes" are suggested, along with opportunity to move back up in the management hierarchy. These devices are also useful because they don't create an atmosphere where managers will be afraid to innovate and take risks. Professor Goldner's work is a very keen sociological analysis of the functions and repercussions of demotion in maintaining an effective organization.

MOTIVATION

Perhaps the most difficult job of management is motivating the people in an organization. This topic has been a major research area for behavioral scientists at the University of Michigan's Institute of Social Research. Professor Rensis Likert, Director of the Institute, summing up 15 years of rigorous investigation in 1961, proposed that industry modify its traditional patterns of management to achieve startling gains in effectiveness.

His research found that managers of high producing units as compared to managers of low producing units spent more time in supervisory activities, were people-oriented rather than production-oriented, and solicited employees' suggestions and ideas about their work. Managers of high producing organizations link noneconomic motives to economic motives rather than apply direct pressure for production. These managers have high goals, but they use group methods of supervision and are more supportive in their relationships with their men.

A SYSTEM APPROACH

Likert's contributions are different in a fundamental way from the behavioral science applications we have previously mentioned. Instead of changing the kind of people who enter and are moved within the organization, he proposes to modify the organization itself. The essence of an organization is *not* the sum of the boxes and lines drawn on an organization chart. Essentially, the organization is the system of social relationships in which members of the organization are engaged, and it is just this system of social relationships that Likert wants to change.

In the long run, the most fundamental and far-reaching contributions of the behavioral sciences will be those that influence the form and functioning of organizations. They will affect the system and not just the individuals in it. The behavioral sciences have failed to give sufficient attention to such applications. I am sure this will change drastically in the near future and think the signs of such change can be seen even now.

The need for us "to be as inventive about organizational matters as we have been about hardware" has been very well put by Dr. John Gardner, formerly President of The Carnegie Foundation and now Secretary of the Department of Health, Education and Welfare.

> It is essential that in the years ahead we undertake intensive analysis of the impact of the organization on the individual. We must examine the conditions under which organization is a threat to the individual, the kinds of organization patterns that are the greatest threat and the safeguards that can be built into organization to minimize the threat. We must discover how to design organizations and technological systems in such a way that individual talents are used to the maximum and human satisfaction and dignity preserved. We must learn to make technology serve man not only in the end product but in the doing.

SCIENTIFICALLY UNSOPHISTICATED MANAGEMENT

Most management people, because of their sensitivity to the importance of human relationships, are very receptive to the potential contribution of the behavioral sciences. Unfortunately, most of the same executives have only the vaguest idea of what a scientific approach is, or should be, to problems of human behavior.

In my experience, most marketing executives are extremely capable people and quite bright intellectually. But they are remarkably unsophisticated about scientific method, particularly as applied to the study of human behavior. In their eagerness to "run with the ball," they sometimes overlook, and more often are unaware of, the need for careful measurement and controls. Fortunately, the same executives are very quick to understand when the reasons for such precautions and rigors are explained.

An illustration of the importance of using the scientific method took place in a recent study in which I was involved (Kraut, 1967). Our management was interested in knowing how Negro salesmen in our company were getting along. The first thought of our management was merely to call in and interview men from the nearby New York metropolitan area. As we explored the whys and hows of this project, it became clear that the desired objective was to make some judgment about Negro salesmen throughout the country and not just in this area. Furthermore, we recognized the importance of comparing their experiences against those of white salesmen in order to understand which experiences if any, were really different for Negroes than for whites.

As a result, a study was designed that randomly sampled Negroes from throughout the country. In addition, each man chosen was matched to a white salesman hired at about the same time in the same office, thereby controlling in some degree for the socio-economic climate and the particular manager. Thus we learned that our sales managers give all new salesmen a great deal of help but tend to give some extra help to Negroes in the first few weeks, if only to assure themselves of the new man's success. Incidentally, we found that Negroes are very well accepted in this traditionally "sensitive" direct contact sales occupation. In fact, the reaction from customers and fellow employees was much better than had been expected by either the sales managers or the Negroes themselves. The application of scientific method to this inquiry gave us much better answers to the questions with which management was concerned than we otherwise would have had.

A CHALLENGE TO BUSINESS SCHOOLS

I see this *lack of sophistication* in science that I have just referred to as *a major liability for modern executives.* In an increasingly complex world, there are simply too many limits on the extent and value of so-called common sense. This lack of sophistication represents, I think a major challenge to graduate business schools and other "molders" of our executive talent.

I believe more of the curriculum should be devoted to acquainting future executives with the requirements and methods of scientific inquiry. Business schools need not and should not try to produce future scientists. They must and should try to produce managers who are familiar with the desirability and operation of the scientific approach.

Most executives are quite aware of the need for greater knowledge about human behavior. I believe they are open to learning more about how the behavioral sciences can contribute to this knowledge. The behavioral scientists who are working in industry are already filling some of this need by spending time in "educational" activities (although this is often done in a very informal way). Management development activities, both in-company and out-company training, are also improving executives' knowledge in the behavioral sciences.

Modern executives must know the actual and potential applications of the behavioral sciences, and they should know a great deal about the scientific method itself. With greater knowledge, management can more fruitfully work with behavioral scientists to solve the human problems of today's organizations.

REFERENCES

Campbell, R. J., and Bray, D. W., "Assessment Centers as an Aid in Management Selection," *Personnel Administration,* March–April 1967.

Gardner, J. W., *Self Renewal: The Individual and the Innovative Society,* New York, Harper and Row, 1963.

Goldner, F., "Demotions in Industrial Management," *American Sociological Review,* 1965.

Hughes, J. L., *A Study of Programmed Instruction for Customer Engineer Training on the IBM 7070 Computer,* IBM Applied Personnel Research, Internal Report, 1961.

Kraut, A. I., *The Relationship of Role Conflicts to Job Satisfaction, Tension and Performance,* unpublished doctoral dissertation, University of Michigan, 1965.

Kraut, A. I., *A Study of Negroes Entering Traditionally "Sensitive" Occupations,* in preparation, 1967.

Likert, R., *New Patterns of Management,* New York, McGraw-Hill, 1961.

E

Economic Planning and Forecasting

The author describes seven areas in which the economist can provide meaningful information on external factors that influence management decision making and control.

21

THE ECONOMIST'S CONTRIBUTION TO MANAGEMENT PLANNING

Walter E. Hoadley

United States private business managements usually take a rather flexible attitude toward planning, in contrast to more formal and rigid plans developed elsewhere by some government and business planners. This does not mean any less interest among U.S. business leaders in forecasting and preparing carefully for the future. Rather, it reflects a keen awareness, rooted in experience, that dynamic market conditions often will render too detailed or extended plans ineffective and can actually cause some new opportunities to be missed.

My thesis can be rather simply stated: the increasing complexity of management decision-making requires an ever-expanding degree of specialized skill and knowledge, an important part of which the professional economist can provide effectively to the extent that he is able to win full status on a business management team in an atmosphere in which his services are welcomed and used.

Measured in historical terms, the period in which professional economists have served business organizations, at least in the United States, has been relatively short. Economists have moved into active roles in corporate planning in this country really during the last 30 to 40 years, and in many respects have assumed important responsibilities only since the end of World War II.

Reprinted from *Financial Executive*, December 1963, pp. 25–31, by permission of the publisher.

Most very large United States companies now employ one or more professional economists, but the number serving the entire private business field is probably less than 500, almost exclusively men. Numerous other individuals without formal training, however, carry out the economist function of analysis and forecasting in companies of all sizes. The considerable number of attractive openings currently available for qualified candidates is evidence that management interest in economists continues to rise. Unfortunately, the supply of suitable economists to assist managements in planning is limited, and definitely lagging behind demand. As a consequence, just because a management now recognizes a need for a professional economist does not mean that the need can be quickly met merely by announcing that a job opening exists. There may be a number of applicants, but in practice only a limited number seems to have the well-rounded training and aptitudes to succeed in working closely with business executives on policy matters. So, careful selection is essential if the newly hired economist is to make an important contribution to his management.

In virtually all instances, the success or failure of the economist in private business can be traced not only to his basic ability, training, and experience, but also to his personality and related skills in winning continuing support for himself and his professional ideas. The economist's contribution to management planning, in short, seems to depend heavily upon his ability to "sell" himself and his creative ideas, which at times may well be at variance with the thinking of senior members of management.

To many business executives the economist is still a luxury or perhaps even a necessary evil, but quite expendable in any period of cost reduction. It is not surprising, therefore, to find that while the general status of the business economist is rising in the United States and elsewhere, the individual economist may still be quite insecure in companies today. Nevertheless, there is a strong trend to use more economists for the very basic economic reason that, on the average, they can contribute to the profits of their companies.

To explore more specifically how the economist can contribute to management planning, let us now consider four related questions:

1. What particular management problems lend themselves toward solution through economic analysis?

2. In what ways can the economist best serve management?

3. What is management's specific responsibility in seeking to use an economist? and

4. What is the outlook for the economist's contribution to management planning?

MANAGEMENT PROBLEMS LENDING THEMSELVES TO ECONOMIC SOLUTIONS

Broadly speaking, most management decisions directly or indirectly involve some economic considerations. The economist, therefore, can be expected to be helpful in guiding many decisions, but satisfactory solutions usually are not made on economic grounds alone. Political and psychological factors also frequently can and do exert powerful influences upon areas of management responsibility and action, and both the successful business executive and economist must make appropriate allowance for them.

The most important management decisions necessarily concern the future. Some executives, of course, tend to ridicule forecasting as mere crystal gazing, and claim that no human can honestly claim to know what lies ahead. While this may be perfectly true, it still does not provide any basis for rejecting forecasting. In fact, no management can escape from forecasting. This is because every business decision necessarily rests upon some forecast of future conditions. Not to forecast, therefore, is really to assume or forecast indefinite continuation of the status quo. To expect or forecast no change in these days of dynamic change seems very shortsighted and unrealistic. Thus, the principal question which management faces is not—Shall we forecast?—but rather—How can we improve our forecasting? In my judgment, the services of a competent economist can be one means of such improvement.

Policies necessarily must be formulated in the present, but their ultimate wisdom will only be known as the actual results unfold in the future. Consequently, the principal objective of any management in its decision-making process is to determine the key influences which will impinge upon the business over the period ahead. In general, such influences can be divided into (1) those which lie outside the realm or control of management because they are external to the firm, and (2) those which are more immediately within the control of management because they lie within the internal scope and operations of the firm. As will be seen, the economist tends to be most useful to management in forecasting and in providing information and perspective on the principal external influences affecting the company's operations and profits.

With this background, we can now turn to some illustrative management questions or problems involving external influences which can be critical in planning and which lend themselves to economic analysis:

1. What is the outlook for the national economy? What are the most important local, regional, or worldwide economic trends? What phase of the business cycle lies immediately ahead?

2. What are the demand prospects in new as well as established markets?

3. Where are market and customer opportunities likely to expand most rapidly?

4. Will the availability and cost of credit tend to expand or depress buying? Are "tight" money or "easy" credit conditions ahead?

5. What is ahead for prices of raw materials and finished products as well as for costs of other goods and services?

6. Is the economic strength of competition likely to intensify or diminish?

7. What is the outlook for government economic policies and regulations?

Countless other economically oriented management problems or questions could be cited, but these are probably sufficient to indicate some of the areas of potential contribution of the effective business economist. Reasonably accurate answers to these and similar inquiries should enable managements to plan more wisely both in the scope and direction of their specific programs and in the timing of their actions.

Before leaving the general subject of management problems which lend themselves to economic analysis, it should be noted that the qualified economist also can often be helpful to management in guiding decisions which concern more immediate internal company policies. For example, a broad economic point of view can be quite relevant in establishing sales and profit budgets, determining appropriate levels of production and inventories, framing wage and price policies, and refining procedures for estimating cash and credit requirements.

HOW CAN THE ECONOMIST BEST SERVE MANAGEMENT?

If it has now been established that there are significant opportunities for an economic analyst to contribute to management planning and decision-making, then it is important next to ask how the economist actually can render the greatest possible assistance. Experience has shown that mere employment of an economist is not necessarily a guarantee of satisfactory results. First, the economist must recognize thoroughly that he has a number of major responsibilities and obligations, and second, as we will discuss later, management has some clear-cut responsibilities, too, if the economist is to succeed in his work in a business company.

Nothing may be more important to the potential contribution of the economist than to have a complete understanding by all concerned at the outset that he does not have an infallible method of forecasting. This should be obvious, but at times professional economists without much practical experience tend either to refuse to concede error or to shy from accepting responsibility for forecasting. Truthfully, the only certainty about most forecasts is that they will be wrong to some degree, but reasonable accuracy is all that is required in most practical circumstances. The alternative, as seen, is really not to avoid forecasting but to assume dangerously that no changes will occur, with a much greater potential error.

The successful economist usually sets his goal to minimize surprises for management from general economic and market developments. His analysis of trends and cycles, however, should enable him to alert his management group to business developments which are foreshadowed, to some degree at least, in the trail of economic data recorded and available on a regular basis. Frequently an economist can be as helpful in reassuring management that an important trend will persist as in pointing out the probabilities of a turning point in some activity of interest to the company. While it is too much to expect that anyone, including the economist, can eliminate surprise, it is reasonable to expect that a competent economist can minimize economic surprises, so that management can pursue a more orderly course of planning than otherwise would be the case.

The professional economist is a technically trained individual. During the past decade in particular, formal economic instruction has become considerably more technical with heavy emphasis upon mathematics, econometrics, and the application of electronic computers in data processing and analysis. Traditionally the field of economics has been noted for its wealth of varying and complex theories relating to such matters as competitive conditions, the role of money and credit and other influences upon the course of general business and the individual firm, and the most appropriate public and private economic policies to achieve maximum growth and profits.

To these techniques and theories must be added huge quantities of economic statistics, with inevitable inadequacies and gaps, which are the raw material for the economist. Analysis and synthesis of theory and data provide the means by which the economist can bring a penetrating perspective to management problems. However, he must guard against using his technical terminology in communicating with his management executives. For, it is well known that what management does not understand, it will almost automatically reject.

The economist, in short, has a major responsibility not only to interpret complex economic developments in the business environment, but also to make his observations relevant to his company's policies and objectives and meaningful to management.

Traditionally, economics has been labeled the "dismal science" because of the great stress which has been placed upon such historical economic problems as shortages of money and materials, business cycle crises, and the ravages of inflation and deflation. Professional economist training emphasizes analysis and problem detection. While this is really no different from the diagnostic approach in other sciences, it does tend to make many economists somewhat cautious and reluctant to express positive opinions unless there is more than ample evidence at hand to support their views. As a result, a conflict may arise between the innate optimism of some management personnel and what may seem to be a pessimistic or cautious bias on the part of the economist.

The economist must not necessarily apologize for his cautious attitude because his view may serve a useful purpose in tempering less carefully considered opinions. In many instances, however, chronic pessimism can make the work of the economist rather ineffective. Accordingly, he can serve management best if his inevitable forecasting errors tend to be distributed on the optimistic as well as the pessimistic side.

Within any management organization there is, of course, a wealth of knowledge, training, and experience which enables the company to progress. It follows, therefore, that the economist will be most helpful if he can supplement existing management know-how rather than engage primarily in intellectual competition with the other members of management. This, of course, does not mean that he should not challenge what he believes to be erroneous information or interpretation by his colleagues, but indicates that he should endeavor principally to bring new data and ideas into management's discussions and decision-making.

It follows that the economist must establish and maintain many contacts with individuals and data sources which would not be immediately available to the other members of management. Complete familiarity with reference source materials is essential, but it is still more important that the economist know individuals who are specialists in particular fields of interest to his work. A strong basis of mutual understanding and confidence must be developed between the economist and his professional colleagues and contacts outside the company, and this cannot be accomplished in a short time. One of the best means of determining the caliber of an economist may well be to check his ability to obtain information quickly by phone or cable rather than by lengthy research from either readily available or obscure reference sources.

As previously suggested, it is essential that the economist in business recognize his responsibility to build a reputation as a successful forecaster. This simply means that he must be willing to make considered but fairly positive statements about impending economic developments, based upon the best possible information and analysis, and stake his reputation upon his judgment. Nothing will build management confidence in an economist more quickly and thoroughly than a record of successful forecasts, well documented in advance and modestly evaluated when the actual results become available.

As a corollary it should be emphasized, however, that the economist also has a major responsibility to alert management at the earliest possible moment that he detects an error in his forecast. By calling attention to changes in forecast conditions, he will not only assist management in making appropriate adjustment in policies, but strengthen his own position as a member of the management team, by keeping his fingers on the economic pulse of the business.

Finally, the economist can serve management best only if he never loses sight of the principal objective of his company, namely, to make a profit on its invested capital. The academic training of the economist, as well as critical comments of leaders outside the field of business, may cause an economic analyst to adopt an apologetic or defensive attitude toward profits. Once this is detected by management, the effectiveness of the economist is almost certain to be lost. Consequently, no economist can expect to succeed in serving management unless he has a strong conviction that profits are essential and that his chief obligation is to help increase the profitability of the company.

The foregoing may seem to be a rather formidable array of requirements for an economist who seeks to serve management well. Admittedly this is so, but unless the economist frankly recognizes his obligations and the never-ending need for him to "sell" himself and his ideas, he had better not accept employment in private business.

Many economists may find a place on a large-scale corporate payroll, but if they are to be helpful in influencing management planning and in contributing significantly to company policymaking, they must be prepared to earn the necessary status for doing so. The economist who contributes most to management, in my judgment, does an outstanding job of research and analysis and preparing and delivering reports. But he goes still further. His purpose becomes dynamic as he seeks to be a fully recognized contributor to profits and not merely someone who fills an obscure position in the management hierarchy.

MANAGEMENT'S RESPONSIBILITIES IN USING THE ECONOMIST

Mention was made at the outset that many management people are concerned about the multitudinous problems involved in managing complex businesses in these dynamic times. In these circumstances the suggestion is frequently made in high levels of corporate management—"Let's hire an economist. He should be able to tell us what to do."

As seen, there is a strong case to be built for the contribution which an economist can make to management, but management must do its part to make this contribution possible. More often than not, the management which employs an economist almost as a last resort or for principally defensive reasons is doomed to disappointment.

The first responsibility of management, therefore, is to set forth as clearly as possible what it expects the economist to do and not to do.

Merely to expose a new economist to a management organization is not enough. It must be recognized that someone within the organization has previously performed some of the general functions of the economist even though these may not have been fully recognized as such. Accordingly, there must be some general agreement as to areas of specific responsibility so as to avoid friction and conflicts between the economist and other members of management. Many ranking executives resent an economist because they feel he is trying to tell them how to run their business, whereas he is really seeking to help the executive reduce the probability of errors in policy decisions. The economist makes no final decisions.

The economist should be held accountable for a contribution to profits. While this is not easily measured, some general guidelines of performance can be linked to forecasting accuracy as well as to the significance of his new ideas and analytical interpretations and recommendations. Along with accountability, there must, of course, be adequate compensation and sufficient stature within the company to enable the economist to perform his function. If the economist is to make an important contribution to management, he must be permitted and encouraged to meet directly with the principal members of management. Preferably he should report to a senior officer, if not the chief executive officer. Unless he has this rank, many of his reports and observations will never reach top management, where they should be most effectively used.

The economist must be in a position to have fairly complete knowledge of management's thinking on particular problems, which he is asked to help solve. He must not be placed in the impossible position of being asked to make a contribution without having at least as much internal corporate information as he may require. Unless management has sufficient confidence in the economist to discuss problems quite frankly with him, it should anticipate only limited help from him.

Management has an important responsibility to work closely with the economist especially during the early period of his tenure. Some important adjustments by the economist are inevitable as well as by management having an economist as a key member of the organization. Above all, management must be willing to evaluate the economist's contribution regularly so that he knows fairly clearly where he stands and how he can improve his efforts on behalf of the company's profitable growth. Executives must give the economist some reaction to his reports and recommendations because no experience is more frustrating to an economist or any other individual than to submit findings without ever receiving comments.

When management recognizes that the principal function of the economist is to bring new and important "external" information into company deliberations, it follows that it must encourage the economist to travel outside the company. This is essential not only to get information at the moment, but also to establish contacts to provide further data in the future. There is simply no substitute for personal acquaintanceship and conversation in developing information. Obviously the utmost discretion must be used by the economist in establishing contacts which are legally appropriate and in accordance with the principles of his management.

In short, the economist must be continually in a position to know what other professional economists are thinking and to be abreast of economic research developments pertaining to his company's fields of interest. To accomplish this end will require an adequate travel and expense budget and management agreement that these outside activities are an essential part of his job. Unless this point is really understood, there is grave danger that some members of the management organization will misconstrue the economist's absences from the company as wasteful and unproductive. Needless to say, the economist must prove this is not the case.

Finally, management has a responsibility to treat the economist as it would any other member of the organization by giving him an opportunity to advance in the company, to the extent that his particular abilities and qualifications warrant. In numerous organizations in the United States and elsewhere, men who have been employed as economists have not only made a contribution in this capacity, but have used their talents to serve in still higher positions of responsibility. In employing any economist, therefore, it is important that he be prejudged not only on the grounds of how well he may serve as an economist, but whether he has the potential to climb still further on the management ladder.

OUTLOOK FOR THE ECONOMIST'S CONTRIBUTION TO MANAGEMENT PLANNING

The outlook seems clearly for an increasing number of economists to be employed as aides to management in the United States and in many other countries. The need for more economic guidance in business planning is definitely growing. The principal problem may well be to find sufficient qualified applicants to fill the demand.

Nevertheless, the function of the economist in management—including forecasting and interpretation of "external" economic trends and developments—must and will be performed. The key uncertainty is how well will it be performed?

As scientific and technical advances multiply, it seems almost inevitable that managements will either have to become more technically minded or surround themselves with more technically trained personnel, or both. The economist himself is becoming more technically equipped, and forward strides are being made in refining many management techniques into a management science.

There is some danger, however, that overemphasis upon science and techniques will lead to a sense of false security in management planning. In my opinion, forecasting and all its uncertainties will always remain an integral part of the manegement decision-making progress. Hence, there can be no substitute in the final analysis for individual judgment. The objective of economic analysis is to limit the range of uncertainty within which such judgment must be exercised.

Whatever the future rate of scientific progress—and it seems almost certain to accelerate—major and basic economic problems will persist. Managements will have to pay more attention, not less, to their economic environment and the political and psychological changes constantly disrupting plans and expectations. Only by focusing attention on fundamental economic trends, especially with the help of the economist, will it be possible to minimize many potential dislocations in company operations and profits.

Present tendencies strongly suggest, for example, that international trade and payments problems will persist, if not intensify, over the years ahead. The allowable margin of error for management decision-making seems likely to become even smaller as national and international competition grows. Financial liquidity and credit problems at the national, international, and local level certainly cannot be expected to disappear during the years ahead. Market conditions are shifting drastically all over the world as incomes and living standards rise and nationalism asserts itself. The life cycle of products is shortening noticeably as the pace of research and development quickens. What management of any fairly substantial business can ignore these prospects or rely upon superficial knowledge about them as a basis for planning?

Perhaps the most sobering note for many business executives now is that the sphere of government economic influence and control is rising at a marked rate in many countries. One of the basic tenets of economics is that supply and demand forces are relentless and in due course will overpower all efforts to control them. Managements, in my judgment, now have a responsibility to assert their leadership in economic affairs. They cannot do so without a good understanding of the economic forces at work and the consequences of expedient economic policies in the individual firm as well as any economy.

The professional economist may not be the man of the hour or of destiny, but given management support, can make a major contribution to profitable growth and human welfare over the years ahead. He can offer no panaceas or foolproof answers to management's planning problems, but in my judgment the solutions will be much more sound with his help than without it.

The author discusses the nature of planning and forecasting, the usefulness of forecasting in management planning, forecasting techniques, and the application of these techniques to the automobile industry's planning problems.

22

INTRODUCTION TO PLANNING AND FORECASTING

Colin Hill

THE PURPOSE OF PLANNING

The purpose of planning in a business is much the same as planning for a summer holiday in that it sets out to answer:

Where have we been?
Where are we now?
Where do we want to go?
How do we get there?

Most people plan for something. Consciously or unconsciously we all ask the question, where do we want to go and how do we get there? Our shorter term plans are more definite than our longer term ones, but both are plans—the marshalling of certain facts, the formulation of certain assumptions and the drawing up of alternative plans of action to reach predetermined goals.

Let us pursue the summer holiday analogy. Where we have been determines to some extent where we want to go. So does where we are now. Suppose that for the last twenty years or so we have worked in Birmingham and spent our holiday in a cottage in North Wales. And suppose that our firm has now transferred to a development area and we live in Glasgow. Some external influence has changed our environment. We are now in a different place from this time last year.

Reprinted from *Management Accounting* (United Kingdom), May 1967, pp. 171–180, by permission of the publisher, The Institute of Cost and Works Accountants, and the author.

We may have liked the type of holiday so much that we try to repeat it by taking a cottage in the Trossachs. In other words we try to attain a similar objective without increasing the resources of time and money necessary to reach it. We might however say that it was not the surroundings, it was the people that made the holiday. We must go back to Wales whatever the expense. We maintain our existing plans and accept the increased drain on resources which are a consequence of this decision. Or we may say that things have changed a lot in the last twenty years and cottages in the country aren't what they were. Let us try a holiday camp in the South of France.

All conscious decisions require a set of concrete plans to implement them whether or not we are conscious either of the factors which caused us to make the decision or of the factors going in to the planning process.

Our decision has been either:

A similar objective within a maintained cost structure.
The same objective within an increased cost structure.
A dissimilar objective within a changed cost structure.

FORECASTS AND PLANS

This, in brief, is our holiday planned within the framework of changed external circumstances. But let us first take a look at what led up to those plans. We had to do some forecasting. For example, we had to forecast the weather in Scotland against that in Wales or the South of France. If we were wise we looked up some records of past performance and did not simply rely on memory or on old wives' tales. Now we did not plan the weather. We forecast that the probability is that the weather would be worse, about the same or better in the alternative locations than in the original one. We made a forecast about the number of people likely to be in the area, the cost of living and so on. We made a forecast about our bank balance, which in turn depended upon all sorts of other forecasts about factors extraneous to the holiday.

We then made a plan based on forecasts and probabilities. The plan said we would arrive at Loch Lomond Cottage by car about 6 p.m. on Saturday 23 June and would stay for two weeks. Our forecast said that we could expect about five days of sunshine, two days rain and seven days of indeterminate weather, that the area would not be overcrowded, but that traffic on the road home would be much denser than on the way up, because it would be both later in the day and later in the season.

Of course our forecasts can be wrong and our plans can go astray but in an audience such as this I suppose there are few who would deny the wisdom of making some type of forecast of the cost of the holiday and some sort of plan to keep the cost within available resources.

I hope that this analogy has helped to show the essential nature of planning, how it differs from forecasting, how the latter is an essential component of the former and how even in the simplest situation both are necessary.

THE ELEMENTS OF RISK

They are necessary because in nearly every business situation there is an element of risk. Whatever our business we have to exercise managerial judgment about the balance between risk of losing our shirts and winning a fortune. If you bet on certainties you don't make much money. If you put everything on outsiders all of the time it won't be very long before you have to go out and do an honest day's work for your living.

Risk analysis is something which the computer has opened up for us tremendously; I do not want to discuss methods of risk analysis, but rather try to spell out the types of risk which all of us face whenever we try to forecast. These risks may broadly be divided into five groups.

First, there is the risk arising from inadequate market data, or misinterpretation of it—the domestic appliance market is a good example.

Second, there is risk arising from incorrect technical or financial analyses of the project—most of the national aerospace projects seem to come into this category.

Third, the spread of risk may be narrow—a narrow product range may not give sufficient cushion against market fluctuations.

Fourth, there is the risk of unforeseen external changes—such as natural or induced changes in taste. Holidays in Spain may become more "with it" than new motor cars.

Finally, in each of these four categories, but worth mentioning on its own as a separate item, is the risk of bias in the individuals contributing the assessments whether they be salesmen, production engineers, purchasing officers, financial analysts or even economists.

SPECIFYING THE OBJECTIVES

I want to turn now to planning and forecasting within the company. I start from the assumption that every company, large or small, has certain objectives, specified or unspecified. In my judgment the very first task in planning is to make those objectives specific.

I cannot stress this too much. Vague or undefined objectives lead to vague, undefined and unco-ordinated plans, and to decisions taken under pressure of circumstances leading to actions which are often incompatible.

Objectives, in this context, are always long term. Where does the firm want to be five years from now or even ten years from now? Just how long term the objective is depends upon the nature of the firm or of the industry within which it is operating and the technical constraints on what is practicable. For example, the electricity supply industry probably has to plan 25 years ahead, the oil industry maybe fifteen years. In case you think this starry eyed, pause and consider the plans for your own children. When they reach the age of about three or four you are already planning how best to accomplish the change from primary education seven or eight years ahead. By fifteen at the latest you are planning how best to make him or her a doctor, whether of medicine or philosophy, by the age of twenty-five. By the age of thirty most of us have made some sort of provision for endowment insurance to mature some thirty years ahead. We all do long term planning for ourselves, why do we shudder at the idea for the firm?

Now the characteristics of these objectives are that they are long range, subject to infrequent change and qualitative rather than quantitative.

Let us take it a step further. Objectives for the firm, as indeed for the individual, will be conditioned by guidelines about relationships. In other words they will be set within a moral—or immoral or amoral—framework which restricts the freedom of action in the same way that natural laws restrict freedom of action whether we realise it or not. The first essential of the plan is to agree on the fundamental philosophies and aims of the firm particularly in regard to its relationship with its shareholders, the general public, its employees and its customers.

I am confident that once the easy answer of aiming to please all of these characters has been dismissed, each of you will recognise tensions consequent upon trying to formulate a balance between the legitimate claims of all of these groups, just as in your private life you are aware of the need to reconcile the legitimate but often conflicting claims of office, family, friends, relatives and your own ideas. The point is that some sort of reconciliation must be made. The employees want high wages, the customers want low prices, the management wants a good image and the shareholders want good dividends and growth prospects.

THE ONE REALISTIC GROWTH TARGET

It is when we start to talk about growth that we come to the heart of the matter. I am firmly convinced that a firm, just like the human mind, must either grow or wither. It cannot remain static because static equilibrium is not consistent with a dynamic society.

We must change. Maybe it is just running to stay in the same place. Maybe we do not want to change, or we wish that time would stop still. It won't. Even if we do nothing our relationship with other groups changes as they move ahead. Our primary planning objective, within the philosophies and framework we have already decided is therefore growth—but growth of what?

We can talk about growth in volume of output, growth in the share of the market, growth in number of outlets, growth in number of employees, growth in turnover, growth in capital employed, even I suspect we sometimes take a perverse delight in growth of waiting time to supply a customer. What sort of growth are we planning for? I suggest that, for survival, there is only one realistic growth target—growth in total cash flow available to the company. Cash. Money in the pocket. Liquid resources to devote to re-investment, whether within the company or outside it. Growth in cash flow to offset the effects of inflation. Growth in cash flow after the money lenders and the tax gatherers have had their pound of flesh. Growth, if I may quote the scriptures, which turns the one talent into ten.

ACHIEVING THE DYNAMIC BALANCE

Well, we are making some progress with our plan. We have written down our fundamental aims and philosophies. We have recognised the problem of dynamic balance in the conflicting and legitimate claims of other people and groups in our society, and we have decided that to survive our primary objective must be to increase our cash flow within these constraints. And that is more progress in half an hour than many companies make in half a century!

I imagine that if you simply went back to your managing director and said "Sir, we have been to a conference on planning. What we have to do is to plan to maximise our cash flow within certain constraints and that is all there is to it." He might not be very impressed, and this for two reasons. In the first place, so far, he is the only one with any extra work to do as a result of our weekend in the country. He has to sit down and write out the fundamental philosophies of the firm and how he proposes to reconcile conflicting claims, for this is company policy. In the second place he has no idea what orders of magnitude you are talking about and no comprehensive plan that he can look at to see how to maximise his cash flow. Clearly something else is needed. What is it, and who will supply it?

Planning, in my judgment, starts at the marketing end of the business. The question is not what can we make, but what can we sell, and this can be sub-divided into four questions. How much can we expand sales of an existing product first in existing markets and secondly in new markets? And how much can we market of new products, first in existing markets and secondly in new markets, and by market I do not merely mean geographical territories. I also mean types of customer. Suppose that we are selling a service, window cleaning for example. We have a private household market, an office market and a factory market to name but three. The basic function is the same but both the marketing and the production techniques are different in each case.

So, remembering that we are looking at this against a basic objective of growth of cash flow, we can begin to develop our strategy. If we are in a market growing so rapidly that it is as much as we can do to expand with it and still keep our administration efficient and our costs low, the emphasis in our plan will be different from that when we are in a static market insufficient to accomodate our growth plans. But before we can make any decisions we have to develop some firm planning numbers about market size and growth, product range, profitability by market and product and so on.

WHO DOES THE PLANNING?

But although in my judgment marketing comes first it is not the only piece of the jig-saw by any means. We need finance, administration and production to say their piece and impose their constraints. It is no good planning to double the number of outlets if we cannot recruit, train and organise the salesmen for it, if we cannot finance the increased working capital or cannot obtain delivery of the necessary machinery to make the goods for another couple of years.

Company planning then is a team effort, but it obviously needs a co-ordinator. This man might be the managing director or he might be a staff man specially appointed for the job. In a small company it probably is the managing director but in a large one almost certainly a staff man will be needed. And I stress "staff". He should not have day to day responsibilities for the company's operations. He must have a detached, critical and constructive mind, so that he can take an unbiased view of the interrelationships between departments and the inevitable incompatibility of their plans. He must be able not only to suggest amendments to departmental plans but also to sell them to departmental heads so that he can produce a workable and consistent company plan. He should not get bogged down in too much detail. For one thing, if he does he will never produce any sort of plan and secondly and ideally he is not a technician, unless you call a professional administrator or manager a technician. The most successful planner the Pentagon ever found is not a military man. He is Robert MacNamara of Ford Motor Company. He probably would not pretend to know how to lead an assault platoon or dock an aircraft carrier. Those are technical tasks that he leaves to technicians. But he does know about cost effectiveness and critical path analysis. Similarly, I imagine it is a good thing that the Minister of Health is not a doctor, nor the Postmaster General a telecommunications engineer.

This is not to imply that soldiers or doctors or telecommunications engineers cannot plan. It is simply to say that just because they are soldiers or doctors or what have you they necessarily *can* plan, and to suggest that if we have a doctor who is also a good planner he will probably do better in planning a national telecommunications service than a national health service.

Let us recapitulate and then press on. By now, I hope, we have written down the philosophies and aims of the company and set a series of objectives about relationships with shareholders, the public, customers and employees. We have set ourselves a growth target expressed fundamentally in terms of cash flow. We have looked at our product range and our markets to see whether, in the external conditions expected in the future this product/market matrix will be sufficient to achieve our growth target, and whether it is or not, we have got various departmental heads thinking about whether the targets set for this product/market matrix are attainable. We have our directors of sales, finance, administration and production busily burning the midnight oil. We have in fact set the machinery in motion to answer most of the four questions we posed at the beginning. Where have we been? Where are we now? Where are we going and how do we get there?

But many fundamental questions remain, not least of which is how often do we plan and what techniques do we use. I suggest that the basic concept of the plan—the statement of aims and philosophies and relationships is pretty nearly a once for all exercise. If you like to use the term, it is the fundamental morality of the firm, and fundamental moralities do not change very quickly even in these days. When we look at the external environment of the firm, however, we must be prepared to take account of the changes which we see around us.

THE INFLUENCE OF ENVIRONMENT

When we made our first plan we made certain assumptions about the world outside the firm—at least if we did our homework properly, we did. We looked first of all at the political and social environment in which we live—and by this I do not simply mean whether it is conservative or labour, I mean the fundamental structure of the state. We live in a Welfare State; Americans do not—yet. This makes a tremendous difference to attitudes and to business decisions. In the U.K. much less of the cost of welfare is carried directly by the employer than in most European countries. This makes a difference—of which we may not be conscious—in our attitudes. In Germany there is a more modern trade union structure; in America there is much more geographical and probably more social mobility. If we are a small firm working only for the home market these factors may not be very important. If we are working for export markets, or have overseas plants or want to make international comparisons then these things become much more important. If we are constantly short of skilled personnel because of the brain drain we need to know why. What can we, as a firm, offer? It is no good reacting like the parent who says, "I can't understand him. I've given him everything he wanted including a university education and now he has just walked out on me." The firm, as well as the state, must be a bit introspective sometimes.

The next assumption we should have made is about the economic and business environment. What are the growth prospects for the economy, or for our overseas territories? Is investment likely to be encouraged or discouraged in a particular area and so on?

Thirdly there is the technological environment. Will developments in plastics or computers or hovercraft change the conditions in which you operate?

The final set of assumptions which you will have made refer to competitive actions and reactions. If I try to enter a new market what will happen? If I raise my price what will competitors do? If competitors lower their price what will I do? How would I react to a take over bid, and so on?

These assumptions need to be taken out and dusted relatively frequently, I suggest about once a year or possibly every two years. On the whole I favour the annual review, each looking five years or more ahead and revising the plan as may be necessary in the light of changing circumstances.

In the first part of my talk I tried to distinguish between plans and forecasts. If we take as a working definition that forecasts are the estimates upon which plans are based I would like to spend just a little time in conclusion in talking about forecasting techniques.

TECHNIQUES OF FORECASTING

There is an infinite number of highly sophisticated techniques of forecasting, most of which I do not understand. Forecasting will always be a mixture of science and art. If pressed you can always go and hire someone to do the science side of it for you. The art side is a little more difficult.

We have to admit, that when it comes to relevant facts we are a woefully ignorant lot. We have a lot of figures which we think we understand but which do not provide us with exactly the data we need, and which in any case come too late. We have a lot of figures which we think we understand but which we use in a way that demonstrates that we do not—and cost accountants of all people must educate management about that! We have a few figures which we do understand but which we cannot use for forecasting. Most figures we do not even pretend to understand; we do not know how to use them; they come too late and we do not know the errors contained within them or the underlying assumptions on which they are based.

To be quite honest we know very little about how the economy works and we kid ourselves a great deal once we start to put definite numbers—as distinct from ranges—on our forecasts. Just as the old fashioned airman used to fly by the seat of his pants because his instruments were inaccurate or insufficient or both so we must do the same for the same reasons. I pause simply to remind you that the fatality rate amongst early airmen was very high indeed.

I am now going to over-simplify so grossly that the purists among you may walk out. I apologise in advance.

TREND ANALYSIS

On the science side we really have two fundamental techniques for forecasting. One is trend analysis and the other is correlation analysis.

Now a trend simply says that the best guide to what will happen in the future is what has happened in the past. However sophisticated your mathematics, this is all that a trend projection is doing for you.

Of course trends come in many shapes and sizes and you can while away many a happy hour doing curve fitting to see which type of trend is tailor made for your current situation.

The great virtue of trends is that they do demonstrate that, seasonal and cyclical variations apart, the momentum of industrial production is such that very sudden and catastrophic changes in the demand for the services of a product are rare. Notice however the careful way that I put this. In my company we are selling weather-proof containers for personal transport equipment. That is a service from a product which is likely to be needed for a long time, probably much longer than the demand for steel car bodies which is what we make at the moment.

Even with this caveat, however, change does not come all that quickly. The rate of change tends to vary with the capital intensity of the industry concerned and the technical limitations upon producing substitutes. For example, it may become fashionable to eat steak rather than pork chops, but it takes time to build up sufficient herds of beef cattle. So the demand for steak becomes regulated by price. The trend is discernible long in advance; so the trend to motor cars was obvious to blacksmiths, who had at least a quarter of a century to adjust to it; the first jet engine appeared in 1936 or thereabouts, but the first jet service across the Atlantic did not start until 1957.

CORRELATION ANALYSIS

The first basic technique in forecasting then is to watch the trend. The second is to try and establish a correlation. By itself the correlation is the coward's way out, because all this says is 'MY industry reacts in sympathy with something else—the balance of payments or the weather or what have you. So what I need to do is to establish what is going to happen to something else and then the same sort of thing will happen to me.' It seems rather a long way round. In my younger days I was greatly excited to find a close correlation between the demand for commercial vehicles and equity share prices. A little reflection showed me that if I could forecast equity share prices I could earn a lot more money than forecasting commercial vehicle sales. As you know, I am still in the motor industry.

FORECASTING IN THE MOTOR INDUSTRY

I thought you might be interested if I spent a little time in elaborating the problems of forecasting and planning which we have to face in my company. I do this partly because I think you may be interested—after all most people are experts about motor cars and partly because in the discussion period afterwards I hope to pick your brains about possible solutions.

Forecasting, without doubt, is the greatest of all the types of risk which I outlined earlier. With a daring stroke of originality, I can compare forecasting to the ancient State of Gaul and say that it is divided into three parts. Long term forecasting, medium term forecasting and short term forecasting.

The most difficult of these is probably medium term forecasting—that is to say forecasting for the period six to eighteen months ahead. It is important from the capital investment point of view mostly in terms of the timing of the investment. The long term forecast, that is to say, the one which looks three to five years ahead with a glance at the period ten years ahead, is the one which most greatly influences our decisions about the volume of capital investment. Short term forecasting has relatively little influence on capital investment decisions.

LONG TERM FORECASTS

The long term forecast is the basis of planning our production facilities—factory space, machine tools and so on. We have to go through quite a long and tedious exercise to arrive at our conclusions. We try to make forecasts first about the level of demand for motor vehicles, second about the technological developments in their manufacture, and third about the availability and cost of labour. Rightly or wrongly, we have never been very much concerned about whether the money would be available to make the investments or whether the type of facility which we wanted would also be available.

Before I appear to dismiss these two problems too lightly and in order to forestall any questions, let me re-assure you—of course we do financial planning but we are realistic enough to know that over a five year period this is pretty hazardous. None the less we remain reasonably confident that we can either generate the money we need internally or we can obtain it from the market. This confidence is a direct reflection of confidence in our own ability to make our products sufficiently profitably to ensure that people are anxious to lend us money if we want to borrow it.

In regard to the second feature, the availability of the physical resources when we need them, this is not meant to imply that we do not suffer from the frustration of delayed deliveries and delayed introduction dates. Nor is it supposed to imply that we anticipate all new technological developments and are able to order these virtually straight off the drawing board. What I am saying can perhaps be illustrated by a hypothetical example. If we decided now that we need to have a new factory in operation in 1972 we can be reasonably confident that all the necessary resources will be forthcoming more or less at the required time. If we decided that we wanted a factory in 1968 we should be much less confident about their availability and this would reflect poor forward planning.

Let me return to our first aspect of forecasting; the forecast of the number of motor vehicles which will be made in 1972, and the share of the market which we hope to obtain. There is a series of fairly logical steps which we take in arriving at this figure.

Perhaps I should add here that when I talk about 1972 I am not talking about a specific year but about a representative period. We are looking at the sort of market which will exist about five years from now. We look at the way in which we shall progress towards that market and we look at the period for the five subsequent years to see whether anything is likely to happen which will influence the decisions we take about the meeting of the demand for the representative year.

PROBLEMS IN LONG TERM FORECASTING

For the moment let us just look at some of the problems of the long term forecast of volume. Basically there are two approaches which we use, starting from entirely different assumptions which we check to see whether the results are widely divergent. The first approach is through estimating what the total car population of Great Britain will be. A lot of work has been done on this and by and large we see no great virtue in trying to refine what already exists.

It is generally expected that by 1972 the number of motor cars in use will be in the order of fourteen to fifteen million. In theory, given the current car population of nine million all that we have to do is to subtract one from the other, add on the demand for replacements and subtract imported cars and this gives us the total number of vehicles which will be produced over the period.

The main problem here, as you will readily detect is what assumption one uses for the replacement element. Again, in theory, it should be relatively easy to discover what this has been in the past and then to make certain projections. The number is arrived at quite easily by going to the S.M.M.T. or other appropriate publications, looking up the car population at the end of year one subtracting from this the car population at the end of year nought and thereby arriving at the answer. If in turn you subtract this figure from the new registrations for the same period, you will find out the scrappage rate. Our confidence in this approach was considerably shaken when in some years, we found that the scrappage rate was negative, the car population had risen by more than the number of cars produced! There are all sorts of minor technical problems which give rise to this result which I won't bother you with now.

We have taken a rather cowardly approach towards our estimate of scrappage by using the much more elaborate data which is available from the United States. They have a series of actuarial tables on car life and by assuming that we shall be approximately ten years behind the United States, we can use these tables to make our forecasts. Perhaps I should interject here that the main difference in projecting the actuarial life of a car against that of a human being is that the latter tends to be largely a technical problem whereas the former is an economic one. Technically, most cars could be made to run for ever if you were prepared to spend enough money on maintaining them. Economically, of course, it just is not worth it. The repair of a motor car tends to be a labour intensive process whereas its manufacture is a capital intensive process. Therefore, the price of new cars relative to the cost of maintaining old ones tends to decrease over the long period.

To put the matter in perspective, the average life of cars in the United Kingdom today is about 14½ years. The average age is of course, appreciably lower as more cars have been built in the later years. In the U.S.A. average life is still surprisingly high, somewhere about 10 or 11 years. Now just to be quite clear, what I mean by saying that the average life of a motor car is 10 years, is that assuming an even distribution about the mean, of the cars built in 1957, one half will have survived to the present day.

We are a little bit doubtful about the growth and replacement concept taken by itself, so we use as a check our other approach, which is also very naive. It is simply a projection of the logarithmic trend of past production. By putting these two approaches together, scratching our heads a little and taking a very deep breath, we come up with the view that in 1972 the home demand for motor cars will be in the order of 1¾ to 2 million. It is possible to spend a tremendous amount of time and effort in trying to estimate this figure more closely. But, quite frankly, from our point of view it is scarcely worth it. This sort of figure is a good enough base for our facilities planning as far as the home market is concerned.

FORECASTING FOR EXPORT MARKETS

We now turn to the much more difficult problem of the export market. First let me explain a statistical quirk which can distort the historical figures quite a bit. As you know, a large and increasing proportion of vehicles is shipped abroad as components, and not as finished vehicles. If the kit of parts is valued at more than 50 percent of the cost of the complete vehicle, it is counted in the export figures as a vehicle. If the cost is less than 50 percent, it is counted as components.

With the increasing demand for local assembly in most areas of the world the number of statistical vehicles exported is unlikely to grow very much. The big markets for assembled vehicles will be Europe and North America. The so-called traditional markets of Australia, South Africa, New Zealand and so on will become less and less important. However, since one of the last things to be manufactured locally is body sets—because of the cost of tools to make them—we have to be particularly careful, in Pressed Steel Fisher, in looking at the export figures. By and large we consider that the only satisfactory approach is to make separate estimates for each of the major markets. We feel that any attempt at a global prediction of exports is doomed to failure.

THE VOLUME FACTOR

You will readily appreciate that from the point of view of facilities planning it is largely irrelevant whether a vehicle goes on the home or export market. All that we are concerned about is the total volume. As a planning base for the mid-1970s we can see that total industry demand will be in the order of 2½ million to 3 million motor cars and this is the figure which is significant for our purposes.

THE PRODUCT RANGE FACTOR

When we have settled on the total market however, our task has only just begun. We next need to divide the market into size groups and into manufacturers' shares. You will notice that I say size groups and not price groups. To us it is immaterial whether a car is sold as a Morris 1100 or a Wolseley 1100. For practical purposes it requires the same amount of press work whatever its final price, and it is made on the same assembly track.

I would not pretend that it is easy to forecast size groups. There seems to be a tendency for cars within a group to get bigger and bigger until eventually somebody comes in at the bottom end of the scale and starts the whole cycle once more. The classic example of this, I suppose, is the Mini. Most of you will realise that what is provided in a car such as the Morris 1100 today is as much as was provided in a 1500 c.c. vehicle ten years ago.

It is pretty safe to say that a manufacturer's aim is to cover the largest possible spectrum of the market with the smallest possible number of models. Vauxhall, for example, have three models—the Viva, the Victor and the Cresta—which cover a very large proportion of the market. In effect, B.M.C. have four models—the Mini, the 1100, the 1800 and the big Austin and Wolseley range—which cover 90 percent of the market, and two sports cars which cover another 7 percent or 8 percent. Standard Triumph have introduced a third model to plug the gap between their small and medium sized cars. It is a fascinating task to speculate who is going to do what about new models in the future. Who, for example, could have predicted that Ford, straddling a large section of the market very nicely with two models would suddenly decide to cover the same sectors with four?

FORECASTING SHARE OF THE MARKET

In forecasting a manufacturer's share of the market, we have three guides. The first, and far the most important, is his present share. Over the years this will change very little unless he does one or both of two things. He may introduce a model in a section of the market where previously he did not compete, or he may increase the strength of his dealer organisation. If he does the first, he must do the second if he is to gain any success at all, but the converse is not necessarily true. Whenever an addition to a range is made it is a fair rule of thumb that it will compete most effectively with other models of the same manufacturer. B.M.C. for example were honest enough to state publicly that they did not expect the new Riley and Wolseley 1100s significantly to increase their total volume of sales.

Considerable problems of subjective judgment arise about the impact on existing models of all manufacturers of the introduction of a new model by any manufacturer, and a lot of emotion is involved. In making forecasts, one makes the basic assumptions that, over a period, a manufacturer will maintain his competitive position, both in respect of product and dealer outlets, so his market share will not alter dramatically.

So with decreasing degrees of confidence, from the total car population to the home market demand for motor cars, to the export market demand for motor cars, to the size of motor cars and to the manufacturer's share of the total market, we finally arrive at a figure upon which we base our future plans for production requirements.

THE TECHNOLOGICAL CHANGE FACTOR

To those of you who are still with me, however, I must now begin to elaborate the problem that I referred to earlier, i.e. that of technological change.

By and large technological change takes place slowly but it takes place just the same. For example, it is most improbable that over the next ten years gas turbine motor cars will be a significant proportion of the total. Speaking personally, I do not think that they will be a very significant proportion of the total within the next twenty years, but fortunately we do not have to take any decisions about that, so it does not matter how much we speculate. Again, over the next ten years, I am pretty confident that most car bodies will be made mostly in steel.

You will notice that this statement is much more cautious than the previous one. We know a good deal about the possibilities of incorporating plastics into cars and we know enough about their technical and economic problems to have some idea of where we are likely to be going over the next ten years. It is no secret that we and other people in the industry are constantly experimenting with plastics. Their potential is obviously very great and obviously can be grossly exaggerated, particularly in terms of the rapidity of change. However, one can foresee that the proportion of steel in a motor car will tend to diminish over time.

The second and perhaps the most important change that we have to foresee is the ability to design work out of the manufacture of a car. For example, we can design labour out of the assembly of a car by putting in expensive multi-welding equipment. But we can also design it out of a car by making sure that the number of pieces to be assembled, and consequently the number of times we have to change the dies on our presses, gets less and less. Hence we shall be able to make the same number of cars with fewer presses. These factors have a big influence on facilities planning and also on manpower planning. If we can progressively lessen the work content in a motor car, we are making a significant contribution towards the growth target formulated in the National Plan. The industry has been most successful in the past in doing this. For example, over the period 1960–64 output of the industry went up by more than 27 percent whereas employment went up by 10 percent. We shall hope to improve on this in the future.

If you have not already guessed it, let me stress that there is a wide degree of imprecision in making forecasts about facilities required.

Fortunately, in any industry showing a long term secular growth, such as the motor industry, this has not proved too great a problem in the past, for if we have made mistakes by over-providing facilities the industry has only had to mark time until demand caught up with it. This, however, is an expensive method of carrying on a business and since the war many motor firms have gone out of business because they were unable to carry for a sufficient length of time the heavy overheads involved.

SEARCH FOR A CYCLICAL PATTERN

The question of timing of investment brings me on to this problem of marrying up the medium and long term forecasts. In this country, and to the best of my knowledge, in no other major motor car manufacturing country in the world, there has developed since the end of the war a very marked cycle of approximately five years' duration in the output of motor cars. Strangely enough, this is true, even if you go back to the period 1948/50 when one would have supposed that the world shortage of cars was such that anything produced anywhere would easily have been snapped up. However, this cycle exists and the fluctuations have been very wide.

For example, in 1960 the motor industry produced 1,350,000 cars. In 1961 it produced only 1,000,000 cars—nearly 30 percent drop. It did not regain the 1960 level until 1963, reached a peak in 1964, and then fell off in 1965. In 1950 the industry produced 523,000 cars. In 1951 it dropped to 476,000. A fall of about 10 percent and once again the 1950 levels were not regained until 1953, and a peak was reached in 1955.

Into the area of uncertainty which I have already outlined to you, you therefore have to add this further one about the uncertainty of the cyclical pattern and yet the cyclical pattern can provide the golden opportunity either of making a fortune or bankrupting the company. This is particularly the case when one is concerned with replacing existing facilities on the existing site.

To replan the layout of a factory is a major operation which involves very considerable interruption to production, besides costing a lot of money. Now if one could say that, for certain, demand in 1967 would be 15 percent below that of 1966, it would obviously be a very good opportunity to change the existing layout and substitute for it a more efficient one.

However, if the forecast proves wrong lots of people are going to have red faces explaining to the manufacturers that they are unable to supply bodies for the next three months as they have just used a bulldozer to knock down the press shop.

We have covered a fairly wide field tonight and I fear that in so doing I may have led you to suppose that planning and forecasting are things only for the large firms and the specialist departments. Believe me they are not. Because the large firm has far greater totals at risk it can afford to spend more on working out its plans, but the relative risks involved are often much greater for the small firm than for the larger one.

THE CASE FOR PROFESSIONAL MANAGEMENT TEAMS

In stating the case for planning and forecasting I am really only stating the case for professional management. For most firms today, the era of the eccentric genius who invented, designed, productionised, purchased, financed and marketed all by himself has passed. Management control is a team effort so far as providing and analysing the data is concerned, even though the final decisions in reality are the responsibility of one man. Where a firm does not possess the necessary expertise in a particular field, or may not need it full time it can always hire it. There are market research firms, computer bureaux, consultants, and so on, all only too anxious to help. And help they will, but simply to call them in neither solves your problems nor absolves you from responsibility.

In the end, whatever the size of organisation, and whether it's in business or government or social service, its chief executive is responsible to shareholders and to the public and to the nation at large to see that the resources which he commands are used effectively and efficiently to achieve the objectives which have been agreed. Inspired amateurism or the ability to improvise are no substitutes for a managerial professionalism which will minimize the number of occasions upon which improvisation is necessary. It is in the nature of life that we have short term crises. It is also in the nature of life that these are generally better solved by the application of already accepted principles, harmonised into a unified philosophy and tested against previously agreed objectives than by what is currently called pragmatism but which in reality is very often an excuse for not having done our homework.

Let me remind you of the questions which we set out to answer:

Where have we been?
Where are we now?
Where are we going?
How do we get there?

I hope that I have been able to shed a little light at least on the last of these. The first three you must all answer for yourselves. And just in case I have led anyone to suppose that all that is needed to succeed in planning is bigger and better computers let me conclude with my one and only quotation from Shelley:

What were our hopes in this world
And what were our aspirations beyond
If poetry did not ascend to pluck light and fire
From those eternal regions to which
The owl winged faculty of calculation could
never soar.

F

Finance and Accounting

The author defines the role of the controller and chief financial officer, and points out ways in which this role has changed.

23

CONTROLLERSHIP IN ACTION

Alexander L. Stott

You may notice that this article has a dangerous title—Controllership in Action. I'd just like to emphasize it's a three-word title—the *in* and *action* are separate words—because I can assure you I'm not referring to inactive financial managers.

I don't know that I can conceive of an inactive financial manager in today's world: a world wherein the scale and complexity of business operations are growing rapidly, wherein competition is worldwide, wherein fast-moving technological change may greatly increase the risk of large capital commitments; a world wherein international political pressures may have a decisive influence on the future of a business in Denver, or Seattle, or Chicago, or any city in the United States.

Today's controller stands face to face with the fact that changing technology, the long intervals between the raw materials and the finished product, and management's urgent need for pertinent information are forcing new responsibilities and new opportunities on him. The factors, both economic and social, that influence each business decision have multiplied many times, while the margin for error has greatly diminished.

The role of the controller has expanded far beyond the bounds of the traditional duties of the corporate controller: To record the transactions of the business; to audit the accounts; to authorize the payments of bills; to issue reports; and to see to it that sound accounting practices are followed. There is a new awareness in corporate headquarters that

Reprinted from *Financial Executive*, September 1964, pp. 30–35, by permission of the publisher.

the controller is emerging as a center of information and as an important contributor to over-all financial policy decisions.

The real contribution that a financial manager brings to the job is a different viewpoint. What we are looking for in the financial manager is an imaginative and searching viewpoint. I suggest that the energies of the entire financial department—from the controller down to the youngest trainee—will more and more consist of forays into new areas. There will be searching out methods for more accurate financial planning, for more accurate controls, for better measures of performance, for better operating procedures, and for more relevant analysis of the information required for sound decisions—all these looking forward toward improving the profits, performance and products of the business.

In this new role, the controller must be a doer of new things. He must be a leader, not a follower, and he must take advantage of every opportunity.

LET'S BRING THIS DOWN TO WORKABILITY

In my company one of our three top officers, the vice chairman of the Board, is also our chief financial officer. Both the treasurer and I report to him.

My department is made up of six divisions. Three are concerned with the traditional duties of the controller, although each carries on work related to his new and expanded functions.

One division covers the professional accounting areas, including accounting classifications, cost allocations, auditing and protection of assets and revenues. Another handles security issues and taxes. And the third deals with records, reports, analysis of financial information, budgets and financial requirements. I might add that the operations of all three of these divisions have been radically changed in recent years as a result of the expanding scope of the work and the introduction of new and improved techniques.

The remaining three divisions are more oriented to the new and developing needs of the business. They carry on economic and market research; develop measures of performance; provide and analyze information for decision-making and conduct studies of organization structure. They use computers to help solve operating problems. They develop accounting procedures and methods. They undertake statistical and mathematical analyses of all types. And they carry on research in the pension and actuarial fields.

While I do not mean to discuss all of these areas, I would like to touch on a few where the enlarged role of the controller has made profound changes in our business.

MECHANIZATION

The first is the mechanization of Bell System accounting operations. As you might expect, our operations have become more and more mechanized over the years in payroll, billing of customers' accounts, the preparation of financial statements, tax returns and reports of many kinds. We began, years ago, to change a number of our activities from manual to punched card operations. This program has moved forward steadily until today many of our activities are being performed by computers.

The transition, however, has posed a number of perplexing problems—some of our own making. We have had a tendency to solve our more troublesome problems first. As a result, mechanization has proceeded piecemeal rather than aiming at a complete information system.

For instance, most companies chose to mechanize first the pricing and billing of the millions of long-distance calls made by customers each day. Prior to mechanization this was a staggering job. Telephone operators had to write the necessary information about *each* toll call on a paper slip. These slips were then processed manually by accounting clerks. The mechanization of this activity has resulted in significant cost reductions; it has increased accuracy; and it has eliminated some extremely boring and repetitive jobs which we were having difficulty in keeping filled.

Another reason for proceeding on a piecemeal basis was that we could not envision nor await the great strides that would be made in the development of computers. We simply had to use equipment that was available at the time to the best advantage. The new equipment, combined with data communications networks, makes possible for us a truly complete business information system—not the earlier step-by-step application to individual operations.

TOP-MANAGEMENT PARTICIPATION

Under such a business information system our goal is to satisfy the entire company's needs for information of any type—at the right time—in the right place—and in the right form.

This business information system would be shaped to the requirements of the operating departments of the Bell System companies. Yet since it is meant to serve all departments, each department, including my own, will have to adapt its operations and requirements to take full advantage of the computer's capabilities. This means that top management in all departments will have to participate in the introduction of this system to assure its success.

Let me give you a simplified description of how our business information system might serve a state or area operating unit.

Information will be accumulated from various operating sources and from sources outside the company. A data communications network will be used to collect essential information which will be edited, supervised and processed by a computer. The computer will develop a completely mechanized master file of information and summarize it into meaningful reports. Each level of management will receive only information pertinent to its needs for analysis, interpretation and decision-making. For the first time we will have a truly real-time data-processing arrangement.

By "real-time" I mean that requests for data and information made on demand by customers or by our own operating groups will be handled on an immediate basis. Since the computer acts in microseconds, the entire set of control operations—the retrieval, collection, processing and distribution of the data involved in every transaction—will take place *one transaction at a time,* instead of in batches. The operations will be completed at the same time as events, such as work orders or customer contacts, take place in the real world.

With such a system, physical operations should never have to wait more than a few seconds for the completion of those record and control functions which are now handled much more slowly by complex systems of paper work. As you know, paper work systems require the accumulation of batches of similar work in order to get reasonable efficiency. Many different groups of people must perform a chain of interrelated tasks because of the division of labor now required. In present systems, total transportation time between the various work stations often exceeds the actual work times themselves. Real-time systems, in effect, reduce the total "transportation time" to something close to zero and complete the various processing steps at computer speeds.

You can see that a system like this puts heavy reliance on data communications in order that widely decentralized work locations can have instant access to the centralized computers and records.

As a supplier of data communications, the Bell System has an intense interest in the development of new data services and hardware. Also, we have made a good progress in the training and education of a whole new generation of engineering, marketing, and maintenance experts in data communications techniques. We now have more than 2,000 data-phone customers using more than 7,000 sets.

Our accounting departments are customers for data communications and our Bell System controllers have sensed their deep involvement in this new art. They have sent accounting men to our most advanced data communications schools—schools run primarily for a highly select group of engineers and salesmen in an effort to anticipate future demands. Today they are committing their best talents so that tomorrow they will not be short of required skills when demands are high.

The business information system may well prove to be one of the most promising concepts that our accounting organizations have ever undertaken. Without question it will reduce costs but, even more important, it will provide far better information for decision-making at all levels of the company.

The financial executive must, of course, accept the responsibility for the business information system. He must evaluate and judge its cost against its potential benefits. He must persuade the management of its value. He must be willing to undertake necessary changes to achieve the best results.

COMPETENT PEOPLE ARE NECESSARY

In the difficult and demanding art of translating the concepts of a business information system into the hard realities of equipment, procedures and training, we can never have enough competent people. If anything, their numbers will set the limit on how fast progress will be achieved. As controllers, we must insure that a new personnel breed is brought into our organizations.

These people will be additions, rather than substitutions, for we must still get our former work done, and handle its increased demands. The new personnel will be men and women disciplined in the arts of engineering, systems analysis, statistics and programming design. Together with our traditional forces, they will forge the hard-hitting groups which will help create a new world of business.

In this new world, the art of model simulation has an intriguing potential for improving management decisions. In its old form it was used to try out model planes in wind tunnels and model ships in test basins. Complex designs could be tested in artificial environments at relatively low cost before huge capital expenditures were committed for actual construction. The point is that simulation offers the opportunity to test many approaches to a problem at little cost.

A SIMULATION PROGRAM

Today we are using this old idea, coupled with the newest and most powerful computers, to attack many complex problems . . . problems that in the past had to be solved by a combination of analytical methods and, hopefully, brilliant intuition. Often it was necessary to devote valuable resources over long periods of time to a proposed solution and to make improvements on an operating basis by trial and error. Now, we are learning how to test the effectiveness of various data-processing configurations for jobs such as toll billing in the computer itself. We are trying to do this by simulating the dimensions of the job and the machine arrangements in the form of digital computer programs. The procedure is to reduce the characteristics of several different machine configurations of several manufacturers to a simulation program which will determine in a few minutes of computer time answers to such vital economic questions as:

Is the machine configuration adequate?
Are bottlenecks likely to appear?
What about programming costs?
How much computer time?
What about operating costs?

The machine configurations can be varied by adding different pieces of equipment such as higher speed tape drives to the simulation program. Again, the program will determine whether bottlenecks will be eliminated and costs reduced by using additional equipment. The important point is that information as to efficient machine arrangements can be readily available for review by management before any equipment is ordered or any real programming undertaken.

EFFECTIVE OPERATING ARRANGEMENTS

This simulation technique has already made us reappraise our prior views in some areas. By simulating file and equipment layouts in business offices, we have determined more effective operating arrangements. By simulating alternate locations for supply and service centers, we have improved our supply system. We have only made a start in the use of simulation technique, and we have much to learn before this tool is fully effective. Our experience so far has been promising, however.

The application of simulation techniques to financial situations and decisions may not be as obvious. However, I think the financial executive can find many uses for it, particularly in the area of testing the feasibility of alternate projects involving large capital outlays. Simulation will give the controller better information than he has ever had to aid the management team in decision-making. I urge you to experiment with this technique and get a head start on the future.

FRAUD PREVENTION MEASURES

I would like to comment on another activity that has expanded rapidly in the Bell System in the last few years, namely, the protection of our assets and revenues. Over the years, we have always had a strong internal auditing function. In recent years, however, with the use of electronic gear in our business and with widespread general education in electronics, we have realized that our activities in fraud prevention had to be greatly expanded. We have taken positive steps to prevent and uncover fraud of all types, including coin box robberies, misuse of credit cards and the like.

Our Chairman, F. R. Kappel, pointed out that within the business those who manage have a special responsibility:

"Through their own personal conduct and through supervisory action, they must impress upon employees under their leadership, the need for the highest ethical standards."

In the Bell System, as in many of your companies, the controllers are now performing audits of the operations of all departments covering cost, quality and productivity measurements related to the work performed. Accordingly our auditing organizations were the logical groups to be given the responsibility for the security job of protecting the company's revenues and assets.

As a result, the Bell System audit organizations have been strengthened and security organizations have been created and expanded. One successful innovation has been the use of young manager-caliber people from operating departments to perform auditing and security work on a rotational-type assignment. Their familiarity with operating department jobs assist them in their audit and security work and broadens their experience in operating areas.

BUSINESS RESEARCH

I would also like to comment on the work of our statistical division. The head of this organization was, for many years, the chief statistician and his title was fairly descriptive of the division's work. This work included statistical and economic studies and, to a limited extent, applied mathematics. In recent years the work of the division has expanded into many new areas of business research and scientific management. As a result, the name of the organization was changed a few years ago from the Chief Statistician's Division to the more descriptive title of the Business Research Division.

The Business Research Division participates in customer attitude surveys, in testing new products, in market surveys, in continuing research involving economic problems, in surveys of business conditions, and in studies of population growth and change. It also carries on research in the application of economic, mathematical and statistical techniques to many problems both within and outside the business. For example, the division uses Operations Research to improve manpower scheduling, material supply and distribution, cost analysis and statistical analysis, to name only a few. The division also uses scientific sampling and probability theory in analyzing many business problems. We expect the use of such techniques to grow rapidly in importance.

LONG-RANGE FINANCIAL WELL-BEING

Another area of growing importance is the financial aspects of pension and fringe benefits. Here the financial executive has wide scope for his abilities in advising on new pension and fringe benefit plans or changing established ones. He can also play an important role in determining the costs of changes, in establishing investment policies consistent with the needs of the business and the purposes of the plan, in preparing sound funding programs, and in establishing proper accounting for pension costs. Perhaps no field of financial responsibility is, on the one hand, so little understood and, on the other hand, so important to the long-range financial well-being of the business. Clearly the financial executive has both a special responsibility and a unique opportunity to provide more enlightening information in this complex area.

The matters I have discussed so far have a clear and understandable relationship to the responsibilities of the controller. I should like to mention a few others where the relationship may not appear as direct but where I believe the controller also has a great responsibility.

CHANGES IN SOCIAL CONCEPTS

As a regulated business the Bell System is perhaps required to follow more rules of various authorities than most other businesses. For example, our system of accounts is prescribed by the Federal Communications Commission. But regulated or not, all businesses must be alert to the impact of change. All of us must be guided by "generally accepted accounting principles." All of us are subject to income tax laws. All of us are affected by the changes in the business atmosphere which may be brought about by government. All of us are subject to the pressures of changing economic theories.

For many years, controllers did not think that much could be done about these things. We simply accepted dicta handed down by various authorities—accounting, governmental, economic—as being facts of life—pleasant or unpleasant—and made the best of the situation.

I urge you to take a far more positive approach in many of these fields. As you know, accounting principles are established by the Accounting Principles Board of the American Institute of Certified Public Accountants. When a new problem arises—and in recent years the government has posed several new problems in the form of accelerated depreciation and the investment credit—the controller should speak up to insure that proper accounting principles are established. I mean principles that can stand the test of time. Similarly, if changes in social concepts or in the economy dictate the up-dating of long-accepted practices we should be in the forefront in making recommendations.

Where tax legislation is likely to have an unfair impact upon a particular industry, the financial officer has a duty to furnish legislators with his views on the matter. For the Bell System, I can mention the 10 percent excise tax on local telephone service as a case in point. We have testified before Congress and urged the repeal of this highly discriminatory tax—the only excise tax remaining on any of the household necessities. We do not hold the cynical view that temporary taxes inevitably become permanent.

I believe that the financial executive should participate fully in the development of national economic opinion. This important field in the making of public policy has tended to be dominated by college professors, government economists and professional economists. Although many controllers may not consider themselves as particularly expert in the field of economics, I am sure that they have acquired a wealth of knowledge and practical experience that should be shared. In the history of any subject, the greatest advances are made when practice and theory inform each other.

ADAPTABILITY IS THE GREATEST SKILL

Now I have been talking about computers, operations research, sampling, statistical analysis, economic analysis and the like as if these disciplines might provide all the answers for the problems of the future. Let me hasten to say that, in my opinion, they will not—they are but new and improved tools to help the managers of the future to make better decisions. No computer, however sophisticated it may be, can ever take the place of the judgment, understanding and intuition of a truly experienced financial executive. As we move forward in this rapidly changing world, I believe that the greatest asset of any business will be the abilities of its people, and particularly their abilities, to adapt to new situations. It hardly seems possible to me to develop today in our people the specific skills that they will need to manage the business even ten years from now, let alone twenty or thirty years hence. Therefore the ability to adapt—to discard the old and learn the new—may well prove to be one of the most essential skills of tomorrow's financial executive.

In developing our abilities along these lines, let us welcome today's new environment and seek to prepare ourselves for tomorrow. In this way we shall become more valuable to the management of the business and better able to accept and perform our duties. To meet our full responsibilities as financial executives, we must seek to develop the abilities of our people to be doers of new things—as administrators, researchers, problem solvers, planners and innovators—so that finally they may become top financial managers in their own right.

Do we need executives who know all the answers—who know every facet of the job? I think not, for such executives may spend too much time on details instead of reaching out for the broader challenges and responsibilities.

Certainly the financial executive must have a supporting cast of highly capable specialists who are expert in the various phases of finance. But these specialists should include a generous proportion of individuals with a wide-ranging outlook. They must be able to see the job in its entirety. They must be able to articulate their thoughts in the written and spoken word. They must be willing to stand up and be counted on controversial matters. They must not be afraid to take on new and difficult projects.

THE "EDUCATED" EXECUTIVE

Theodore O. Yntema, in an excellent talk at Wayne University several years ago, defined an executive as a man who can take on almost any job and do it well. He believes that a man is educated if "he has a sense of values thoughtfully evolved, if he has the basic skills and ability generally needed to do the world's work, if he has a fair amount of classified and ordered knowledge, if he finds satisfaction in work and play and enjoyment in the good things in life."

We all know men with these qualifications. They have the ability to shift from one position to another with little or no handicap. They are able to tackle challenging and unfamiliar problems. They are forward-looking and adaptable. They are articulate. And they have the ability to inspire and lead people. They are the men we must look for and try to develop as the leaders to meet the demands of the future in the field of finance.

Perhaps some of you, like myself, are old enough to remember the days when the New York Giants under John McGraw were the cream of the National League. A newspaper reporter asked once of McGraw's outfielders what it was like being a Giant.

He said: "It's great to be young, and a Giant."

Now, young or old, I say, "It's great to be a controller."

What Is Controllership?

The Institute's concept of the function of controllership is:

1. *Planning for Control.* To establish, coordinate and administer, as an integral part of management, an adequate plan for the control of operations. Such a plan would provide, to the extent required in the business, profit planning, programs for capital investing and for financing, sales forecasts, expense budgets and cost standards, together with the necessary procedures to effectuate the plan.
2. *Reporting and Interpreting.* To compare performance with operating plans and standards, and to report and interpret the results of operations to all levels of management and to the owners of the business. This function includes the formulation of accounting policy, the coordination of systems and procedures, the preparation of operating data and of special reports as required.
3. *Evaluating and Consulting.* To consult with all segments of management responsible for policy or action concerning any phase of the operation of the business as it relates to the attainment of objectives and the effectiveness of policies, organization structure and procedures.
4. *Tax Administration.* To establish and administer tax policies and procedures.
5. *Government Reporting.* To supervise or coordinate the preparation of reports to government agencies.
6. *Protection of Assets.* To assure protection for the assets of the business through internal control, internal auditing and assuring proper insurance coverage.
7. *Economic Appraisal.* To continuously appraise economic and social forces and government influences, and to interpret their effect upon the business.

The author describes the impact of the current technological revolution, including systems theory and computer development, on the accounting profession.

24

HOW DO ELECTRONIC COMPUTERS AFFECT ACCOUNTING AND AUDITING TECHNIQUES?

Max S. Simpson

The business world of today is characterized by a state of innovation and change unsurpassed in history. This is not surprising when one considers the technological revolution that has taken place in the last 20 years. While man is striving to reach the moon and beyond in space, he is to no lesser extent attempting to apply technical and scientific advancements to optimize the complex art of managing a business in a highly competitive marketplace. One of the major contributing factors in attaining this objective is the electronic computer and associated scientific devices.

What has been the impact of the computer on business management? The answer to this question is difficult and not easily visible at first glance. To say that the computer impact has been extensive is not sufficient. The possibility exists that in the decades ahead history will show that the computer, as a management tool for decision making and control, was the catalyst in revolutionizing business concepts as they are known today. An indication of this premise can be seen in examining the far-reaching effects of the computer on accounting and auditing techniques.

Long-established accounting theory has not been altered by the computer impact; rather, the effect has been in the area of the changed

Reprinted from *Financial Executive,* February 1966, pp. 38–45, by permission of the publisher.

implementation practices of this theory. Specifically, these machines have provided an environment where not only has labor saving justified their existence, but it has also become possible to service larger geographical areas out of a centralized location and to generate more detailed, accurate information for business management purposes. Further, standardization of accounting procedures and of accounting classification has been stimulated by the centralization of the accounting function, and accelerated processing of data has substantially shortened the accounting cycle.

COMPUTER EVOLUTION

The emergence of these activities has occurred during the past 10 years. From the computer standpoint, this decade was marked by an evolutionary machine development which saw significant advances in higher processing speeds, greater and more flexible storage capacity, and the emergence of communications capability. For little or no increase in equipment costs, speeds and capacities are increasing at a geometric rate as computer improvements continue to be generated. The computers available today can even process various major programs concurrently on a time-shared basis in a communications-oriented data-processing environment.

Along with the development of improved computers, tremendous strides have been taken in knowledge of how to exploit the speeds, versatility, and capacities of the modern computers.

Concurrently with computer improvements, significant advances were taking place in the development of related scientific devices: that is, a large array of communications equipment and computer input/output devices without which a modern computer cannot function. In the communications area, telephone and telegraph lines and microwave circuits are used for the transmission of business data, and the use of satellites is in the foreseeable future. In addition, there are about 50 different types of computer input/output devices ranging from such ordinary equipment as punchcard readers and conventional printers to some highly sophisticated and scientific instruments, such as remote console devices, cathode ray tube terminals, and audio-response devices.

Now computer-communication-oriented concepts for the processing of the business and scientific information flow are a practical and highly desirable objective. The most sophisticated examples of this type of processing are generally associated with real-time systems where there is instantaneous response to any physical transaction at the time of occurrence. An example of this in the commercial area is seen in the more advanced current airline reservation systems, in the scientific area in the control of missiles, and in space exploration activities.

ADVANCES IN SYSTEMS INTEGRATION

The accountant and the auditor should be familiar with the current developments in the area of systems integration. Certain companies have attempted with varying degrees of success to integrate the data flow from an initial point-of-sale inquiry to the sending of the material ordered by the customer. For example, one of the leading manufacturers of electrical equipment in the United States has in operation an integrated nationwide message switching and order-processing center, which for certain of its product lines permits automatic triggering from sales inquiry to sales order to shipment of material along with the necessary recording of inventory changes and issuance of re-stocking orders. Also, standard accounting applications such as invoicing, accounts receivable, and sales statistics are automatically spun off from this integrated system. In this example, everything we need to know about a customer's order is generated by the system whether it be concerned with aspects of marketing, distribution, inventory, or accounting—all without human intervention. The extension of this conceptual approach may be further characterized by a company having the capability of updating all records on an as-occur basis, culminating theoretically in an ability to project control statements even to profit and loss on an as-required basis. While this concept is somewhat esoteric in nature and may not be obtainable or economical within the near future, a conceptual direction definitely has been started.

The centralization of the accounting function even in a decentralized company environment has been prompted by cost and control advantages. The computer as a management tool permits large-volume accounting applications to be maintained and processed at a centralized location. Accounting application examples include payroll, accounts receivable, accounts payable, credit accountability, fixed assets, and associated summary and analytical evaluation reports. With the inherent records being maintained and processed in this manner, operating divisions are relieved of the administration of these arduous tasks and are permitted to concentrate their energies on other pertinent areas of responsibility. The bringing together of these accounting applications facilitates the standardization and integration of accounting applications.

The computer impact on standardization and integration of accounting applications is already discernible. The standardization provided to a large American steel company by a single wage payroll system affords uniform interpretation of labor contracts with standardized audit procedures regardless of the number of processing locations. The increased control, accuracy, and monetary savings of this approach have been confirmed.

An interesting example of accounting application integration is being implemented by a large banking organization in the United States involving the consolidation of payroll, personnel records, expense distribution, and work measurement standards. Not only can an employee be properly selected for a job but he can also be paid, evaluated, and have his benefits controlled from a composite data base.

Also, through adoption of a uniform chart of accounts, monthly closings processed in a communications-oriented data-processing system can provide for the preparation of financial statements at a much earlier data than was formerly possible. The management benefits involved are significant in providing more timely, accurate information for over-all planning and decision making.

MANAGEMENT CONSIDERATIONS

Such business intelligence systems will go far beyond the limits of classical accounting procedures to process and analyze a broad range of information—both financial and other decision-making data—that are needed by management to run the business. The ultimate achievement would be a system that not only encompasses all information handling requirements but processes each piece of information instantaneously.

Management would be notified on an "exception" basis of any irregular behavior of business performance requiring immediate action. The environmental aspects would depict a management "control center" where, through the use of graphic displays, pertinent information could be recalled from the computer system and exhibited in chart form for management decision making.

As an accompanying development, operations research techniques would be employed to permit the structuring of composite company profit plans in the form of a "profit model" whereby management could evaluate alternative profit forecasts prior to final selection of the most appropriate profit plan.

A progressive example of current activity in this area is the Financial Executives Institute Research Project, "Impact of Computers on Management and Organization." The project's main objective is to present for general management the constructive uses of computer utilization. Emphasis is being directed towards computer system definition—present and planned, influence of the computer on decision making, management's part in today's and tomorrow's system, and the influence of the computer on organization.

CHANGING ROLE OF THE ACCOUNTANT

The underlying significance for the accountant in this changing business environment is his emergency in a new role. Traditionally the accountant has dealt with historical facts. The accountant of tomorrow, however, will have the ability to deal with current information at time of occurrence, and with computer-generated projections, so that his services to management can be infinitely greater than was possible with the old tools. The accountant must not only accept and understand the new techniques, he also must take the lead in designing systems which fully exploit the computer and its related sciences. His task then will be adapting to a new profession rather than continuing an old one.

AUDIT CONTROLS

Insofar as the auditor is concerned, it can be stated that his basic objectives and responsibilities are not altered by the installation of a computer system. The nature of the "control" problem for a computer system is different from other systems, however, and this not only requires new audit techniques but also substitutes new areas of control that must be examined. Since the computer offers a system that replaces manual activities, the auditor will now be more concerned with testing the controls over the system than with controls designed to prevent human error. Although valid for all computer systems, these requirements are intensified in a real-time or on-line data-processing environment.

The American Institute of Certified Public Accountants has recognized the necessity for exploring in depth the computer impact on accounting and auditing techniques. Recently a project has been initiated to develop an applied research and education program in computer technology. Particular attention is being directed toward the capabilities of information processing systems as they relate to accounting, auditing, tax work, and management sciences. The research findings will be used in organizing an expanded educational program to service the needs of the Certified Public Accountant on the latest developments of computer technology.

Another perspective of the computer impact on auditing, however, is represented by the use of the computer to conduct various comparisons and tests involved in an audit in a faster and more economical manner than manual methods which would otherwise be employed by the auditor. In this context, reference is made to the use of the computer to facilitate an audit, rather than to problems posed the auditor by the existence of a computerized accounting system. The computer has provided for the auditor centralized control and information accuracy previously not available.

For electronic data processing systems, it is common to designate three areas of control with which the auditor must be concerned:

1. Controls over the movement of data into and out of the computer operations, commonly referred to as "input/output controls."
2. Administrative controls over the organization and operating procedures of the computer department itself.
3. Controls incorporated in the computer programs—that is, built into the sequence of instructions followed by the computer in processing data.

Input/output controls are usually handled by a control section which monitors all data into and out of the computer system. Specific functions would include the monitoring of source data, the processing of rejects and errors due to incorrect input data, and insuring accuracy of final output reports.

Administrative controls over the computer operation include the separation of functions that is so important for effective control, such as the separation of the programming section from the operating section of the computer function (Exhibit 24–A, "Organization of Functions for Control of EDP Data Flow"). Other controls include the requirement that procedures and operation instructions be fully documented, with flow charts describing each application; also, that log sheets be maintained to account for all computer operating time.

Controls incorporated into computer programs are of many types. Examples of controls that may be used—such as "zero balance" checks, reasonableness checks, sequence checks, self-checking numbers, and feedback controls—are generally well described in the many books and articles on the subject, such as Felix Kaufman's *Electronic Data Processing and Auditing.*

CONDUCT OF AN AUDIT

The conduct of an audit should certainly cover a thorough review and testing of the first two areas of control as described above; that is, evaluation of the input-output controls and of the administrative controls over the computer operation itself. The techniques involved in the audit of these two areas are not particularly technical and, indeed, no unusual training is required once the auditor has familiarized himself with the nature of these areas of control. Actual input controls can be compared against a list of those generally acceptable; organization must be reviewed

EXHIBIT 24–A.

ORGANIZATION OF FUNCTIONS[a] FOR CONTROL OF EDP DATA FLOW

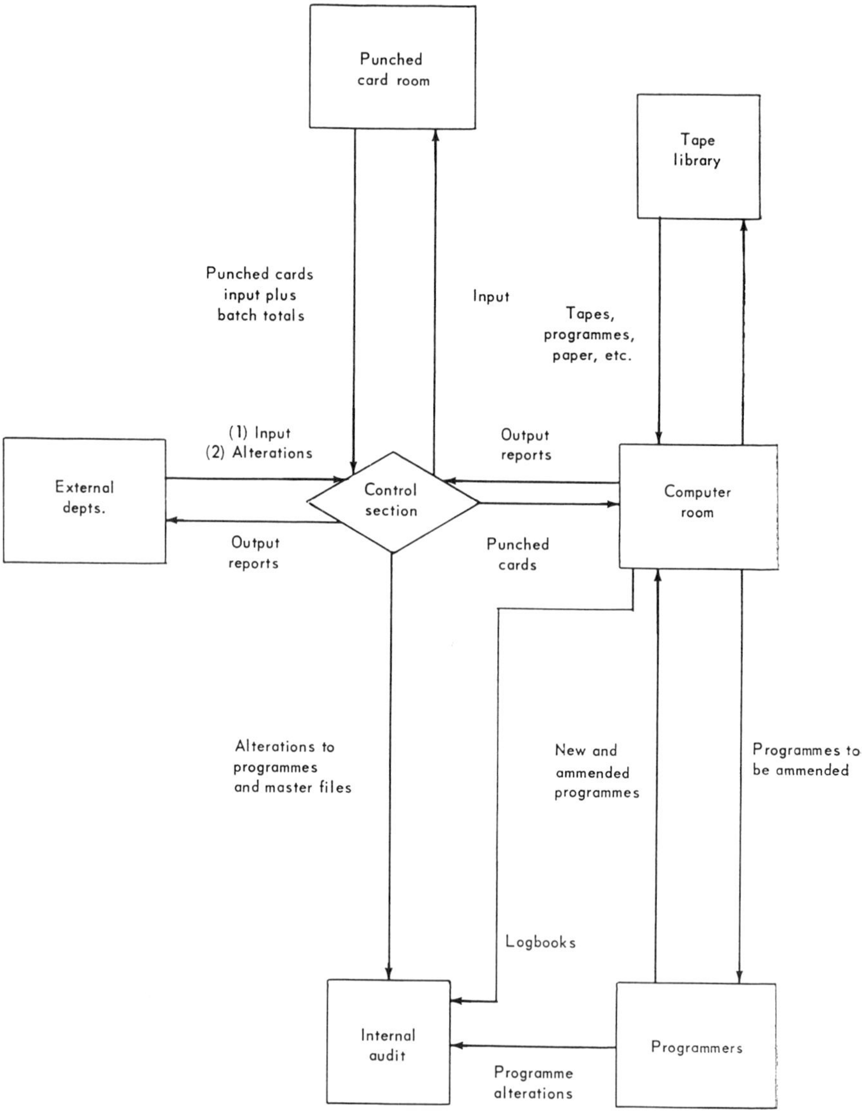

(a) Source: The Impact of Computers on Accounting, by T.W. McRae

for proper separation of duties; procedures employed must be written and understood.

It is in the third area—controls over actual computer programs—that the auditor generally experiences difficulty. In the past, a technique was employed which involved taking a sample of computer input and manually checking the validity of the output in terms of the pertinent input data. If the sample of output data was correct, the auditor assumes that all of the processing procedures were also correct and that they had sufficient control features.

With the growing complexity of computer programs, the greater use of exception reporting, and the trend toward integrated processing without separate printout between operations, it is necessary that the auditor now assume a direct responsibility for auditing the adequacy of the computer programs themselves. To an increasing degree, relying only upon the evaluation of an input-output sample will not represent an efficient or adequate check of the operating controls involved.

AUDIT REVIEW AND TESTS

The best time for initial audit review of computer programs is while the programs are being designed. In this manner the auditor may make suggestions for improved controls to be built into these programs—suggestions which could be extremely expensive to implement were they to be developed after the program was in operation. Some large companies, in addition to developing training programs and manuals for computer auditing, have established procedures whereby agreed-upon program documentation of all new computer accounting applications is forwarded to the internal audit department for evaluation of control requirements. Principal elements in this documentation generally consist of a flow chart showing the flow of data through the various processing steps, and a narrative description of the system, including the various control procedures over the processing within the computer.

In addition to evaluating controls incorporated in computer programs, the auditor needs techniques for testing transactions to insure that the programs, as written, are producing accurate and complete results in actual operation. The two techniques that have so far been found to be most practicable are sample testing (perhaps using the more refined statistical sampling techniques) and simulation. Indeed, statistical sampling can be aided by designing a computer program to select the proper sample.

For the auditor who has sufficient computer knowledge, probably the most desirable technique is simulation, using what are commonly referred to as "test decks." These "test decks" of punched cards or magnetic tape simulate actual transactions involved in the system's processing. They can be introduced into the system like actual transactions and are a relatively inexpensive method of testing transactions since no programming requirements are involved. The system, in effect, checks itself to insure that the necessary outputs are reliable, accurate and appropriate.

The computer also presents the auditor with a unique opportunity to use its services in performing many of the time-consuming tasks normally involved in an audit. Computer programs can be designed which will test the records maintained on magnetic tape and which will select data from a tape file and print it out for audit. Other computer programs can be designed which will perform such functions as comparison of activity between periods, measure actual versus budget figures, or material on hand versus normal stock levels.

One of the international oil companies has developed a computerized payroll audit program which prints out for the auditor all changes since the previous audit in master payroll tapes and also develops a statistical sample of those items to be given detailed audit verification. This same program also makes certain comparisons to test for such cases as salary or overtime outside of normal limits, incompatibility between base pay and income tax deductions, or between base pay and employee savings deductions.

CHALLENGES AND OPPORTUNITIES

In review, ours is a changing world, changing at a technological rate that challenges comprehension. One of the prime motivators of this revolution has been the computer. The computer impact has been significant on business practices, and specifically on the accountant and auditor and the techniques utilized in the administration of their functions.

The accountant must accept the challenges posed by his changing environment. He must adapt to a new profession rather than continue an old one. He must provide management with unbiased, timely recommendations on day-to-day business activities and future predictions to optimize long-range plans and goals. If the accountant does not accept this premise or is not up to this responsibility, he runs the risk of being relegated to a restricted role as various organizations are formed to carry out these "management service" functions. Certainly these functions must be performed if the company is to wage a successful battle in the increasingly competitive worldwide marketplace.

Similarly, the auditor must recognize the full impact of the computer revolution. He must view a computer as a centralized tool of control previously not available to accomplish his objectives. A "through the computer" approach must be adopted along with necessary knowledge involved to insure that factors of reliability, timeliness, and control inherent in computer systems are realized.

Finally, the years ahead will be marked by opportunity. The accountant and the auditor have an unparalleled opportunity to exploit the utilization of the computer as the prime tool in servicing management's needs. This opportunity must be seized eagerly but with intelligence, lest we forget that the computer must supplement and complement, though not pre-empt, man's role in achieving his business objectives. As Gilbert Burck states in *The Computer Age:* "The machines compel men to formulate their problems so much more intelligently and more thoroughly than they ever have that men can hardly be unaware of the shortcomings of their programs. . . . Nothing would make a company more vulnerable to smart competitors than to abdicate responsibility to the neat, clean, consistent judgments of a machine."

By keeping this belief basic to our professional philosophy, we can successfully respond to the changing accounting and auditing techniques demanded by the computer and other scientific devices.

The author expands the concept of budgetary control to include many of the management control principles discussed earlier in this book.

25

THE BUDGETARY CONTROL FUNCTION

Ernest I. Hanson

The process of budgeting and its product, the budget, are extremely useful in assisting management to fulfill its functions of planning, coordinating, and controlling enterprise activities. Although it is difficult to isolate these interdependent functions, they are usually so categorized when portraying the budgetary process. This paper will focus on the control function. The conventional concept of control will be expanded as consideration is given to the factors which influence the nature of the responses of employees performing within the sphere of the budgeting process.

BUDGETS AND CONTROL: CONVENTIONAL CONCEPT

A budget is a formal statement by management of its plans for a given time period which will be used as a guide during that period. The view of the budget as a blueprint for action gives rise to the typical role attributed to it in the control function. It is portrayed as a type of "yardstick" against which preformance is measured. An evaluation of this measurement then determines what corrective action is necessary.

Without management's implementing the yardstick qualities of the budget through measurement, the budget is not considered to be useful as a control device. The control process starts after the budget has been adopted. A diagrammatic representation of this control function is shown in Exhibit 25–1.

Reprinted from *The Accounting Review,* April 1966, pp. 239–243, by permission of the publisher.

EXHIBIT 25–1

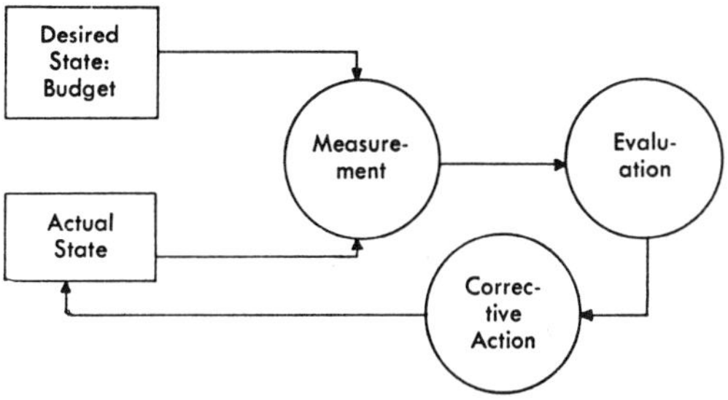

The representation of the budget as a desired state follows from the fact that it is a management plan designed to provide direction to the entity concerned. Since effective planning requires the existence of entity objectives, it is apparent that the fulfillment of corporate plans will move the enterprise nearer to its over-all goals.

The conventional concept of control is not complete. It is incomplete since it explains control through budgeting as a mechanistic, responsive action without recognizing that it is to some degree a self-governing action. Responding to measured differences between budgeted and actual performances, the corrective actions will always be applied after performances creating the differences have taken place. The corrective actions can in no way control these past activities.

BUDGETS AND CONTROL: EXPANDED CONCEPT

The typical control concept does delineate the objective of the control process, namely, to carry out plans with a minimal divergency between budgeted and actual activities. In addition to the sporadic corrective actions, there are certain attributes of the control process which operate continuously to bring about congruity between the planned and actual performance. The formulation of a more comprehensive concept requires the explicit recognition of these self-governing characteristics.

The expanded concept considers the fact that the control function necessarily involves the direction of people. Accordingly, it is appropriate to view the business enterprise within which budgeting takes place

> . . . as a miniature society in which traditional social controls over the individual appear in sharp focus. The organization draws upon the accumulated learning and experience of the individual, who brings to it certain socially inculcated attitudes that encourage a satisfactory accommodation to the organization's major values and expectations.[1]

[1] Robert V. Presthus, "Toward a Theory of Organizational Behavior," *Administrative Science Quarterly,* 3 (June 1958), p. 49.

The additional areas of control which become relevant with this perspective of a business organization may be categorized as follows:

1. The nature of authority and the budget.
2. The degree of employee identification with budget goals.
3. The degree of attainability of budget goals.

These intangible aspects of control precede the measurement and evaluative activities of the conventional model. They are complementary to the responsive and corrective actions focused on in the typical concept. These attributes are functioning at all times to reduce divergencies between actual performance and desired performance.

THE NATURE OF AUTHORITY AND THE BUDGET

Authority is the power to make decisions which guide the actions of another. Authority establishes superior-subordinate relationships. A business organization, a system of structured interpersonal relationships, contains many of these superior-subordinate relationships.

Custom may be the most important basis for the acceptance of the superior-subordinate role by the respective parties.[2] The many authoritative situations that an individual confronts, and accommodates to, prior to entering a business organization possibly explain why this relationship is accepted within an enterprise as a matter of custom.[3] In any event, deference to authority is one of the "socially inculcated attitudes" brought into the organization by an individual.

An important condition for the creation of an authoritative relationship is that the superior's decisions be communicated to subordinates. Without communication effective authority does not exist. Since the budget is a formal statement of management's plans, its role in the control function is evident. It is a vehicle used to convey the wishes of management. The budget acquires an authoritative aspect once it is communicated to those to whom it pertains. The customary tendency to defer to authority suggests that the individuals to whom the budget is communicated will undertake appropriate actions to meet the budget requirements. Authority, therefore, is a major control mechanism in a business firm. A budget, as it achieves authoritative characteristics, thus also serves as an effective control mechanism.

This conception of the budget as a control device remains completely detached from the manner in which it is administered. The budget is often pictured as a pressure device. In contrast, the reasoning developed thus

[2] Herbert A. Simon, *Administrative Behavior*, 2d ed. (Macmillan Company, 1957), p. 130.

[3] Presthus, *op. cit.*, p. 57.

far leads to a different conclusion. The budget acts as a *pressure-reducing device* since it provides individuals with a knowledge of actions necessary in order for them to meet the approval of their superiors.

THE DEGREE OF IDENTIFICATION WITH BUDGET GOALS

The communication of budget requirements to an individual does not assure that his responses will be entirely in accord with those desired, even given the tendency to defer to the authoritative nature of the budget. There is a reciprocal aspect to authority such that a subordinate may choose not to abide by the communicated budget.[4] There is a continuum of responses available, some of which are clearly more appropriate than others in meeting the budget requirements. The more closely an individual identifies himself with budget goals, the more appropriate will be his responses to the budget. Another significant aspect of the control function, then, centers on the degree of identification with budget goals.

There are numerous procedures available which serve to increase employee identification with budget objectives. One procedure directly associated with budgeting is the use of a participative budgeting process.[5] Meaningful involvement in the budgeting process at the lower operating levels is a useful principle to employ in the planning function of a budgetary system. Those who are going to have the responsibility for the performance of certain cost and profit centers should be fully involved in the planning of the expected performances.

The control aspects of participative budgeting are equally as important as its planning advantages. By becoming involved in the creation of the budget, the members of the organization associate themselves more closely with and become better acquainted with the budget goals. Thus, the participative process, which precedes the execution of plans, works as a control mechanism once the budget is implemented since it encourages identification with the budget objectives.

The existence of an evaluation system is an additional influence affecting the identification with budget goals. Under the conventional concept of the control function, the measurement and evaluation of performance provide the basis for formulating corrective actions. Inherent in this process, however, is an element of control influencing the actions of employees as they perform. This is noted in the following remark:

[4] Chester I. Barnard, *The Functions of the Executive* (Cambridge, Mass.: Harvard University Press, 1938), p. 163.

[5] For a consideration of the applicability of participation to different types of business environments see Selwyn Becker and David Green, Jr., "Budgeting and Employee Behavior," *The Journal of Business,* October 1962, pp. 392–402; and Andrew Stedry, "Budgeting and Employee Behavior: A Reply," *The Journal of Business,* April 1964, pp. 195–202.

> . . . there is another, more subtle way in which cost reports influence performance, and indeed influence the very performance being reported on. Advance knowledge of the fact that a report on performance is going to be prepared can be an important stimulus to good performance on the part of the person being judged.[6]

Many of the procedures thus develop employees' identification not only with budget objectives but also with all organizational goals. A company's selective recruiting and hiring process must contain some judgment as to how well a potential employee's interests and motivations will mesh with the organization's needs and objectives. Training programs, whether of the formally structured type or of the continuous on-the-job type, are designed to hasten one's inculcation of the enterprise's values. The involvement of the individual in peripheral company activities, such as participation in company recreational functions, also serves to strengthen the identification process.

An organization's system of rewards and penalties fulfills a function of maintaining an individual's identification with company goals, or, perhaps, even increasing the degree of identification by a more direct means than the procedures discussed up to now. Examples of positive sanctions available to a business entity include periodic pay raises, commissions, pensions, stock options, promotions, and bonuses. Negative sanctions include pay cuts or no increases, demotions or no advancement, and the possibility of losing the job.

The authoritative nature of the budget and the receptiveness of employees to communicated budget goals are important factors controlling the action-responses to a budget. Yet these items are not enough if the objective of control is to reduce the divergencies between actual and desired performances.

THE DEGREE OF ATTAINABILITY OF BUDGET GOALS

A third critical area involves the attainability of the budget goals. If budget standards are not reasonably attainable, there may be much inefficient and frustrating employee performance. On the other hand, budget standards that are too easily attainable are also impractical. To obtain efficient and productive performance, budget goals must be attainable and yet challenging.

Since the attainability of budget goals is significant, a sound system of control must include mechanisms designed to prevent too unfavorable a gap from developing. One mechanism, a participative budgeting proc-

[6] Robert N. Anthony, "Cost Concepts for Control," *The Accounting Review,* April 1957, p. 233.

ess, has already been discussed. Two other techniques are flexible budgeting and establishing a range of performance levels for each goal.

A flexible budget is intended to provide attainable goals regardless of the operating level. Under a fixed budget, attainability of goals becomes meaningless as soon as the operating level varies from the level assumed.

Creating a range of expected performances for any given level is another budget approach. One author has suggested gradations of excellent, good, fair, and poor in the expected levels of performance.[7] Obviously, some performances within this range are more desirable than others. Yet this multi-goal approach does act as a hedge against the creation of a situation wherein the individual is faced with a single unattainable goal.

Closely related to the importance of attainable budget goals is the concept of responsibility accounting. An individual should not be expected to achieve certain budget objectives unless he has the responsibility for whatever performances are necessary to reach the goals. The absence of such responsibilities may cause the budget requirements to appear unattainable. Formulating a budget in terms of responsibility centers therefore helps to increase the effectiveness of the budgeting control function. This means the budget system must be individually tailored to each organization.

Also relevant to this discussion is the suggestion that more frequent comparisons of actual and budgeted performance should be made and communicated to the employees.[8] The objective of such a recommendation is to obtain information so that budget goals may be adjusted, if necessary, to keep them rigorous yet achievable. Success in achieving goals generally leads to a rising aspiration level and failure to a lowering aspiration level.

SUMMARY

The objective of any control system is to reduce to a minimum the difference between actual conditions and desired conditions. The conventional concept of the budgeting control system emphasizes the process whereby management's attention is directed mainly to differences which have arisen. This concept, however, fails to give express recognition to the intangible and self-governing elements which serve to reduce the number and the magnitude of these differences.

The budget itself controls as soon as it achieves its authoritative

[7] Chester H. Sneider, "Setting Operating Goals and Measuring Achievements," *N.A.A. Bulletin,* July 1958, p. 27.

[8] Becker and Green, *op. cit.,* p. 402.

characteristics through approval by high management and communication to subordinates. All factors which increase employee identification with budget goals are control elements. These include a participative budgeting process, advance knowledge of performance evaluations, hiring and training programs, involvement in extra-organizational activities, and a system of sanctions. Attainability is a third attribute of good control by budgetary means. For this purpose, flexible budgets, multi-goal performance levels, and responsibility accounting are leading methods of implementation. To the extent that authority, identification, and attainability are properly applied, the effectiveness of budget control should be increased.

The author describes how "return on investment" can be used both as a test of the effectiveness of planning and as a measure of performance.

26

RETURN ON INVESTMENT: AN ANALYSIS OF THE CONCEPT

Maurice S. Newman

Effective use of capital is vital to a company's success. Measuring that success by "earnings per share" is not always satisfactory on a short-term basis, but there is a highly persuasive presumption in favor of the use of this standard on a long-term basis. The cost of capital must be recognized, and capital must be used where it will produce the best possible return on the investment.

Return on investment is employed as a measure of performance in two broad areas. The phrase is used to refer to the overall return on the overall investment in a company, division, or product group and also to the specific return on a specific investment in merchandise, buildings, or other types of assets.

The first area, which embraces the second, is the one in which the term "return on investment" or "return on capital employed" was first applied. It reconciles the financial or accounting viewpoint with the operating or engineering viewpoint and thus contributes to unified effort toward the achievement of overall company objectives.

Use of the term "return on investment" in the second area is semantically correct, but the area is of interest only to those with a specific problem. The introduction of actuarial principles and "cost of money" in these latter calculations often makes it difficult to relate the indicated

Reprinted from *Management Services,* July–August 1966, pp. 15–23, by permission of the author and the publisher.

return on a specific investment to the subsequent transactions appearing in the financial statements and accounting records because the premises are different. In this article, unless otherwise indicated, the term will be used in the broader sense.

Return on investment is being used increasingly as an objective test of planning and as a measure of performance. Its use has been given a substantial boost by the trends toward diversification through mergers and acquisitions and toward the decentralization of profit responsibility.

One of the reasons for its widespread application is that it translates a financial objective into such operating terms as selling prices, profit margins, sales turnover, production costs, and capital equipment, which are easily understood by sales and production personnel. However, return on investment is not always easy to calculate. When two businesses are operating independently, the income of each can be matched with the investment in each to give a reasonable indication of the return on investment. If these entities are merged and various administrative functions are shared jointly, it becomes more difficult to determine the contribution of each to the overall profits of the company. The same is true when there are various divisions or product groups within a company competing for the available capital resources.

Thus, there is a considerable difference of opinion on exactly how and where the return on investment concept should be applied. Nevertheless, there is a fairly general agreement that it is a useful measure of management stewardship at various levels.

"My Years with General Motors" by Alfred P. Sloan, Jr. (parts of which were published in *Fortune*) gives a good perspective on this concept and its working. The return on investment approach was brought to a high degree of development within General Motors Corporation by Donaldson Brown as a result of Mr. Sloan's stress on incentive compensation and the consequent need to determine the effectiveness of the various operating segments of the corporation.

Other companies—for example, DuPont and Monsanto—also have refined the return on investment concept to the point where it has become a highly effective management tool. The DuPont reporting system was described in the published *Proceedings* of the annual conference of the National Association of Accountants held in June, 1952. Shortly thereafter a similar treatment of Monsanto's reporting system was published by the American Management Association. Other articles on this subject have appeared in various accounting publications. Many of these articles deal with the practical problems encountered in applying this logical analysis to the financial and operating statements of individual companies.

UNDERLYING LOGIC

The beauty of the return on investment concept lies in the pure simplicity of its logical accounting analysis as shown in the exhibit on page 336. By exploding the end result into the many business components that influence the final answer, it clearly relates the earnings to the manifold operations of the business. Step by step, it shows how the return on stockholder investment can be affected not only by the amount of net income but also by the amount of equity.

For instance, if the earnings after preferred dividends are retained in the business illustrated in the exhibit rather than paid out in common dividends, the equity would increase to $8,250,000. For the rate of return to remain the same the following year, the net income would have to increase by $75,000. If the additional funds are required in the business and can earn at least the same return on equity that the funds already invested in the business are earning, it would be in the interest of the stockholders to have the funds remain there. If the funds are not needed or cannot produce a comparable return, dividends paid to the stockholders will have a favorable influence on the rate of return.

It should be emphasized that the rate of return on equity may not be the same as the rate of return on a single stockholder's investment. Most stocks are traded in the market at prices that are entirely different from their book values.

Nor is the rate of return on equity the same as the rate of return on assets employed. Essentially the difference is represented in the accounting equation of "Assets = Liabilities plus Equity." An adjustment to the righthand side alone, such as increasing liabilities and reducing equity by the same amount, or vice versa, would not affect the return on assets but would affect the return on equity.

This is the domain of the financial officer, who, given the same operating income, may influence the return on equity favorably by several different actions. Among these would be redeeming preferred stock, buying in common stock, using cash balances effectively, deferring taxes, and paying larger dividends. Some of these actions would increase income or reduce expenses; other actions would reduce the equity. To the extent that funds were made available when needed to carry out operations and that excess funds were converted into earning assets when not required elsewhere, any of these actions would have a favorable effect on the return on equity and yet might affect the rate of return on assets employed only slightly or not at all.

It should also be noted that the return of 17 percent on assets employed is a product of two other factors: the percentage of operating

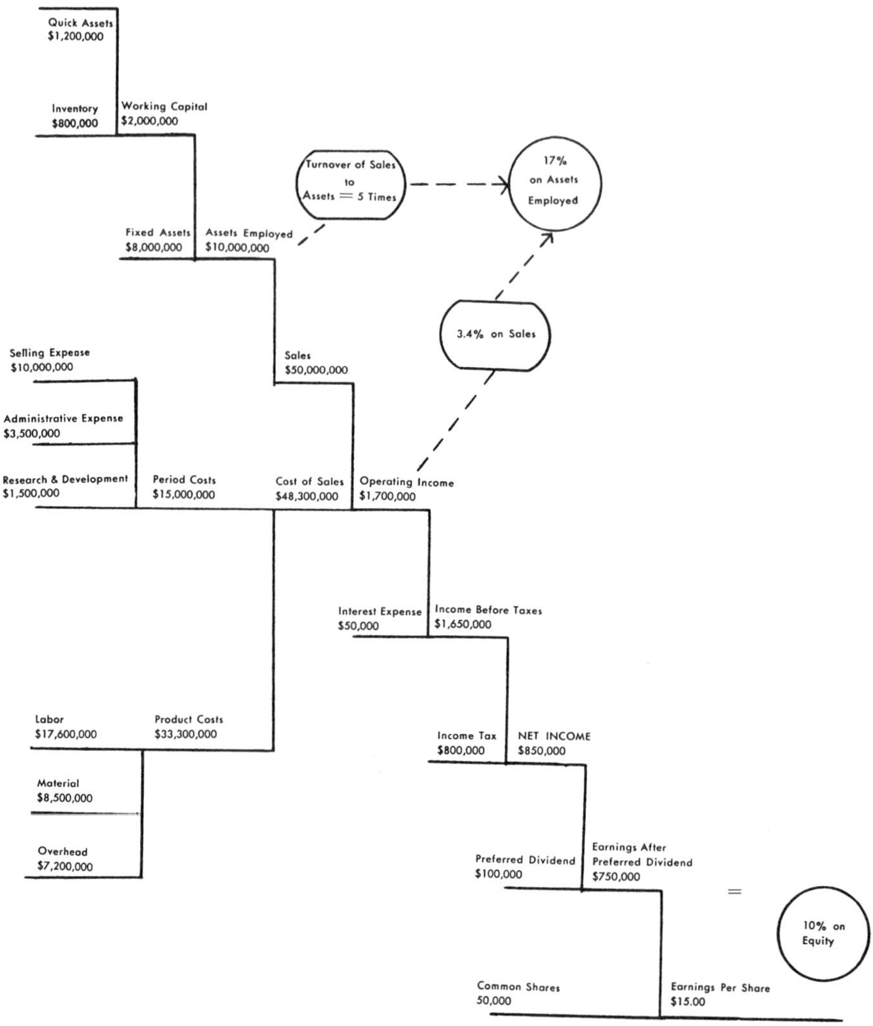

COMPONENTS OF RETURN ON INVESTMENT

Assets		Liabilities	
Cash	$ 500,000	Current Liabilities	$ 600,000
Accounts Receivable	700,000	Note Payable	900,000
Inventory	800,000	Preferred Stock	1,000,000
Fixed Assets	8,000,000	Common Equity	7,500,000
	$10,000,000		$10,000,000

income to sales and the sales volume in relation to the total investment. A glance at the equation (5 times 3.4 percent = 17 percent) makes it quite clear that a change in either component will affect the result. While this is axiomatic, it is surprising how much attention is given by most managements to the "percentage on sales" and how little to the turnover of investment. As the exhibit indicates, reduction of any component of the investment would have just as favorable an effect on the rate of return as would an increase in sales or in the profit margin.

Any $1,000 reduction of expenses would be equivalent to a $30,000 increase in sales, which might be harder to get. Considerable attention has been paid to the "product cost" component of the "cost of sales." However, a reduction in "period costs" would have an equally favorable effect on the rate of return. Furthermore, this reduction might be easier to accomplish.

It is up to each member of the management group to consider just what he can do to influence the overall return on the overall investment. Inventories could be reduced; accounts receivable could be collected more promptly; capital expenditures could be made prudently—all of which would tend to minimize the investment. These are areas to which the average production manager or marketing manager often fails to pay sufficient attention even if he holds stock options that may be adversely affected.

There are distinct advantages to using the return on investment concept in planning the future performance of a company. Changes in any one of a number of factors can have an effect on net earnings. By planning with all of these factors in mind and then measuring performance against the plans, a management may see where to take action that will increase net earnings. Furthermore, the return on investment concept allows management to plan and measure performance in a way that is understandable to the bankers and investors from whom the company must seek the capital required to finance growth.

Setting aside for the moment the complications that arise in actually applying "return on investment" principles to financial statements and management reports, the value of the concept is that it is clear and easy to understand. It reflects a basic responsibility that executive management has to its stockholders for an adequate return on the capital invested by them. This responsibility is keenly felt, as was indicated by a survey conducted some years ago. The executive officers of more than 200 companies were asked what single financial indicator they regarded as most symptomatic of the basic present fortunes of their companies. To this question more than half replied, "Net return on equity."

If this is accepted by a majority of chief executives as the basic measure of their performance, it would seem no more than reasonable to use this same criterion for planning operations on both a companywide and a divisional basis and also as a measurement of divisional performance.

CAPITAL EMPLOYED

There is general agreement that the performance of operating management should be measured by the return on the total capital employed rather than on stockholder equity, which involves financial management. There is less agreement, however, on how to compute capital employed. For instance, should fixed assets be valued at original cost, at estimated replacement value, or at their depreciated book value? Although undepreciated cost or replacement values might be more realistic, depreciated book values are often used since they are reflected in the financial statements and thus are more readily accepted by those whose profit performance will be judged. Questions can also be raised on the consideration to be given to such items as LIFO inventory values, current liabilities, and leased equipment in computing the amount of capital employed.

An essential tenet of the return on investment concept is that, in total, there should be a reasonable return on the total amount of the business investment in tangible and intangible assets. A company may be required to make certain expenditures from which no income will be received except perhaps in terms of employee morale or well-being. These expenditures are nevertheless part of the total investment, and the income from the remaining assets will have to be a little higher to offset the lack of income from the nonearning assets.

On a short-term basis, money spent for buildings and equipment or research and development may not begin to produce profits immediately but may assure adequate profits in later years. Similarly, amounts spent for preventive maintenance may reduce the present earnings but may at the same time lead to greater earnings in future years. The need for adjustment in these areas does not invalidate the concept but emphasizes that it needs to be carefully applied to individual situations.

OUTSIDERS' VIEW

Bankers, financial analysts, and company treasurers are primarily concerned with the return on equity. Financial analysts work generally from the published financial statements or similar sources. They are interested in such matters as debt service, cash flow, dividends paid, and the utilization of retained earnings.

Adjustment may have to be made before the return on investment of one company can be compared to that of another. One company may price its inventory on a LIFO basis, valuing it considerably below its market value in a period of rising prices, whereas another company may use FIFO, with the opposite result. One company may lease a considerable portion of its assets; another may own them. It could be argued that some capital assets held for future income such as undeveloped land or growth stocks should be eliminated from the capital employed base before any comparisons are made. Depreciation policies vary from company to company, and this factor must be considered. Unusual capital gains or losses on nonrecurring items have to be allowed for in any comparison.

MANAGEMENT'S VIEW

When a company is measuring its performance against its own predetermined standards, it has more freedom in the choice of ways of making this measurement, and its management may change any of the factors involved to what it considers to be a realistic measure of operating performance. Management is interested not only in the financial aspects of the situation but also in the comparative performance of various operating divisions of the company. While this operating performance will eventually be reflected in the financial statements, certain financial factors can be separated out so that the performance reports may be more easily understood by operating personnel.

For instance, it is a fairly general practice for companies to use income before taxes in calculating the return on investment so as to avoid the effect of such tax adjustments as carrybacks, carry forwards, and the investment credit. Some companies add back depreciation to the operating income when gross assets are used for assets employed. Interest on funded debt or other long-term obligations may also be excluded from consideration since operating management has little to do with such financial matters.

Similarly, total assets, rather than total stockholder invested capital, are often used for internal measurement purposes, and this is sometimes referred to as "total capital employed." The theory is that divisional managements have been provided with certain assets on which to earn profits and it is of no concern to them whether these are being financed by creditors, bondholders, or investors in common stock.

There is, however, much less agreement on whether the assets should be valued at book value, at original cost, or at replacement value. Replacement value is rarely used because of the difficulty of determining such a figure, although some companies use insurance appraisal figures for this purpose and others adjust their fixed asset and depreciation reserve values by the use of index numbers. Of the various methods, replacement value would probably be the most useful if a realistic figure could be obtained, but in practice the choice is usually narrowed down to either book value or original cost. For internal measurement of the performance of a company as a whole as against divisional performance measurement, it appears that the most common practice is to use net book value as it appears in the financial statements.

Although it is not accepted practice for a company to write up its assets in its financial statements, it may be useful to include certain assets in the investment base of an operating division at current market value. This is helpful for two purposes: one, measuring the operating department against realistic standards and, two, indicating those situations where alternative decisions might be made, for example, where valuable land and depreciated buildings might be sold and a new plant constructed elsewhere on less valuable land. There are many operations that earn a fairly good return on the book value, because the property was purchased many years ago, but earn a negligible return on the current market value.

The elimination from the operating reports of financial matters beyond the control of plant and division managers will make the reports more appropriate for these managers, who must deal with the situations they reveal. It is fundamental that these people should understand the computation of the rate of return if their performance is to be measured by it. It is fundamental that they should be charged only with the capital and those costs over which they have direct control. If for other purposes allocations are made of administrative expense over which they have no control, it may be desirable to compute the operating return both before and after such charges.

What is a reasonable rate of return for a company to adopt as a predetermined standard? This depends upon the nature of the business, the risk of capital employed, the investment basis used, and many other factors, but several manufacturing companies have established a return of 20 percent before taxes as a reasonable objective.

There seems to be a fairly general assumption that if a company is to earn over-all, say, 20 percent before taxes, each division should also earn a 20 percent return on the capital employed. This may be true where the operating divisions are similar in nature, but it is not always possible in a highly diversified organization. After all, a lower return should be expected where there is little risk entailed and a higher return where the hazards of capital loss are greater.

DIVISIONAL ANALYSIS

Applying the return on investment concept to operating divisions of the company is a different problem and often calls for a different type of measurement. The emphasis is more likely to be on operating performance and on comparison with other divisions.

This can be accomplished, in an accounting sense, by setting up a separate corporate division to carry the various investments and long-term liabilities and receive interest, dividends, or other income of a like nature as well as to absorb interest expense and other miscellaneous expenses. Such a division might possibly rent buildings and equipment to the operating divisions. This would avoid the problem that may arise when some divisions are housed in leased buildings and others are quartered in company-owned buildings. A higher return could normally be expected from a division that leased real property than from a division that owned a considerable amount of real property since lower rates are usually available on capital secured by real estate than on other risk capital. Management should review each situation objectively and arrive at rates of return for the divisions that will produce, on a composite basis, the desired overall company return.

Standards also need to be set for such things as preventive maintenance and the size of inventories. A plant manager who understands the basis on which he is being measured might embark on a program of cost cutting or inventory reduction that could have a spectacular short-term effect on his return on investment but start a long-range decline in the division's operating efficiency. If such reductions can be made wisely, however, everything possible should be done to encourage them.

One of the first questions that arise in divisional analysis is once again the valuation to be placed on the fixed assets. There seems to be fairly general agreement among those companies using return on investment to measure divisional performance that gross assets should be used as to value the investment. This avoids the variations in net return that may occur when one division has a brand new plant and another has one that is almost fully depreciated; in such circumstances the return may range widely. A further argument for using gross assets is the fact that when plants are built they are expected to produce income over their entire life expectancy. Furthermore, since companies have various depreciation policies at their disposal and different procedures may be used in various divisions, stating assets at net book value would certainly complicate relative comparisons unless corrective adjustments were made.

One of the arguments for using gross assets cited in most of the literature on this subject is that this value is closer to replacement value than the depreciated book value. This would seem to indicate that these authors would prefer to use replacement value if they could but have found considerable difficulty in determining it—whereas original cost is usually available from the books of record. These assets will eventually have to be replaced, if the business is to survive, at much higher prices. Using gross assets in the capital employed base provides one way of injecting a higher return into the pricing formulas to provide sufficient capital for the eventual replacement of these assets. This could also be accomplished by planning for a higher return on depreciated original cost, but there is always the possibility that the problem of replacement in an inflation-ridden economy will be overlooked.

If a company can develop fairly reliable present values, such as can be derived from insurance appraisals or from construction indices, there is considerable advantage to using such values, particularly in making divisional analyses. There is movement in this direction. In some utility rate hearings regulatory commissions have authorized rate increases that would produce a rate of return of approximately 6 percent on an investment based on current dollars, even though this would be equivalent to a higher return based on original cost.

Obviously the use of replacement values in divisional performance measurement would present problems if these values were not generally accepted by division managers. However, it would seem that management planning would be on a sounder basis if some approximation of replacement value could be used for the valuation of fixed assets in measuring company and divisional performance.

The real difficulty, of course, lies in the fact that the mechanical application of index numbers, price indices, or appraisal figures will rarely give the desired economic result. What is actually needed is the theoretical investment required to maintain the present capability of the existing plant and equipment, assuming that this can be defined in terms of units of physical output or other appropriate measurement. Since very few companies would be interested in identical replacement of their present plant and equipment, for the purpose of determining return on investment the replacement value of the existing plant could be quite meaningless. A possible compromise would be to use historical cost as the basis of computing the return at the level of operating responsibilities and then, in recognition of the price level problem, make a second computation on the basis of present values, dealing with this as a general policy matter.

Another question about which a difference of opinion may develop in divisional analysis is whether the total assets should be used with or without any allowance for current liabilities. In most cases it does not appear to make too much difference since liabilities are usually incurred more or less proportionately by the operating divisions, but there are certain businesses whose inventories are almost entirely financed by their suppliers; in these cases it does make a difference. When one division is in a business of this type and the others are not, it would seem necessary to give that division full credit for the working capital so obtained. This might be effected by reducing, by this amount, the value of the inventories included in the total assets.

Questions also may arise concerning plant and equipment not yet in full production, real estate held for future growth, and other such items on which a satisfactory current return cannot always be expected.

Whereas financial statements are prepared for financial purposes and must conform to generally accepted accounting principles, operating statements should be prepared for operating purposes and should be based on sound operating principles, even though these may seem to conflict with generally accepted accounting principles. Operating results should not be obscured by entries made primarily for tax accounting purposes, such as the use of LIFO valuation for inventories.

Eliminating this type of accounting entry from the operating statements prepared for the divisions and putting greater emphasis on measuring assets at their current market values, to the extent that these can be determined, might enable the division managers to concentrate more heavily on other factors, such as sales volume, prices, and product mix, which could materially improve the return on the assets entrusted to them.

EQUIPMENT REPLACEMENT

There has been considerable semantic difficulty in the application of the return on investment concept to capital equipment replacement. The most important goal of capital planning is an adequate return on the total investment. It is possible to use the return on investment concept as a guide in selecting those projects for which capital expenditures will be made. Confusingly, however, there are other methods for computing the expected return on the amount of capital invested in individual projects.

The traditional favorite is the payout method, by which the number of years required to recoup the original investment is determined. More recently the "discounted cash flow" concept has been advocated for this purpose; although it is rather complicated, it has considerable merit. The formula developed by the Machinery and Allied Products Institute, which has come to be known as the MAPI formula, takes certain actuarial factors into consideration in determining whether equipment that may have outlived its economic life but may still appear to have a useful physical life should be replaced.

The discounted cash flow concept is based on the actuarial formula for determining the rate of an annuity with a stated present value and certain specified payments. In other words, if we expect from our initial investment certain annual cash returns, which may vary from time to time, and if we know the present cost of the investment, what will the effective interest rate be? If this rate should prove to be 7 percent, we would then, under this concept, have a 7 percent return on the investment in the equipment. If this rate of return is higher than the cost of the capital required for this investment, it would presumably be advantageous to spend the money in this way—although whether the company should purchase or lease the asset is another factor to be considered.

There is a significant difference between the discounted cash flow concept and the return on investment concept as generally expressed in financial statements. The latter concept does not give weighted consideration to the time period in which the money is returned. This is a characteristic—perhaps a weakness—of the usual pro forma financial projections; they are on an annual basis and do not usually take into consideration the years in which profits will probably accrue. A dollar earned this year is given no more weight than a dollar earned two years from now. Obviously, if the same amount of cash is to be returned over a period of, say, five years, the investment that would return the greater part of the amount in the earlier years should be preferable to one that would return the greater part of the amount in later years. As a practical matter, however, most investments do tend to return cash fairly evenly over a long period so that the differences between the discount theory and the financial statements may be more theoretical than practical.

PRODUCT PROFITS

Another valuable use of the return on investment concept is in pricing individual products or product groups for a profit. It is true that sales prices are often determined by competitive conditions. However, a company does not have to promote actively the sales of any product that it cannot make and sell at a fair profit; it would perhaps be better advised to use the capital elsewhere.

The concept can be applied both to manufactured products and to products purchased and resold. A different approach may be required in each case, but with a reasonable amount of effort some valuable conclusions can be drawn from such an application.

The significant thought added to product profitability analysis by the return on investment concept is the effect of capital turnover. When products are turned over more rapidly, a somewhat lower percentage of profit on sales can be justified. This, in turn, may be effective in increasing the turnover. Just what constitutes capital investment in a particular product may be somewhat hard to define, but in product profitability studies this is generally a relative problem. So long as the same basis is applied consistently to each product, the relative percentages of return on investment will tend to highlight the more profitable products.

For manufactured products generally, the capital employed would normally be the various inventories, such as raw materials, work in process, and finished goods, together with the accounts receivable and such plant and equipment as can be readily attributable to the product. In retailing, a very satisfactory result can be obtained by using just inventories and receivables. Mathematical formulas can be developed for making such profit analyses, on an individual product basis, with the aid of electronic computers. Calculations of the profitability of individual products can be improved if the product gross profits are reduced by standard allowances for warehousing costs and selling commissions.

Product profitability analysis is a relatively unexplored area and one in which much might be done to increase a company's overall profits. The effect of turnover on profits is not well understood by many company managers. In addition to sales volume and sales price, there are many other factors, such as product design and mix, material and labor rates, administrative costs, and equipment replacement, that can have a considerable effect on the profitability of individual products or product groups.

This article has reviewed a number of ways in which the return on investment concept can be applied to assist company management in intelligent planning and in performance measurement. The concept can be used for measuring the performance of a company against that of others with which it can be usefully compared, and it can be used within a company for measuring the performance of the company as a whole and the performance of the separate divisions. It can be used in planning for the use of capital—both of the total amount to be spent in any given period and of the way in which the total should be distributed, as among divisions or products. It can also be used to evaluate the use of capital for individual equipment purchase commitments or for the establishment of higher inventory levels.

It is not necessary to use the same bases for all these purposes; both the bases and the definition of return can be adjusted to suit the individual circumstances. In external comparisons it is desirable to stay fairly close to the published financial statements, both in the definition of return and of investment. For internal company comparisons it may be desirable to eliminate certain items of a financial or miscellaneous nature. For divisional purposes it may be logical to use operating profit rather than net profit and gross assets rather than net assets. In product profitability studies gross profit may be used instead of operating profit, and certain assets may be eliminated from the investment base. Finally, in retail product profitability studies the investment may be reduced to a bare minimum of the inventory and accounts receivable applicable to each product.

There are many ways in which the return on investment concept may be applied, and there are no hard and fast rules about the choice of method, particularly when the comparisons are used for internal purposes. When relative, rather than absolute, measurements are sought, the results are useful whatever the bases used. There is no question that return on investment analysis is a valuable tool for managerial purposes and that it will be used in many more companies and in many more applications by progressive company managers of the future.

G

Management Control Reporting

The author discusses ways in which management control reports can be made more effective.

27

FINANCIAL REPORTS AIMED AT MANAGEMENT ACTION

Thomas B. Neff

Opinions as to how business enterprises should be run and what data are required to run them effectively vary considerably among operating managers. No two managers run their companies in exactly the same way nor do two managers often agree on the details of what constitutes a good report. This makes the financial executive's job more difficult if he is to serve his management properly. Each of us is a product of his own environment. A manager who has "grown up" in one company will, in all probability, prefer his company's reporting system. If he should join another company, he would probably attempt to convert their system to the one with which he is familiar.

Despite the disagreement among executives as to what constitutes an ideal report, they will all agree that the real measurement of performance in any type of business enterprise is financial. We analyze financial data to tell where the company has been, how it stands at present, and where it is going.

The day when a business could be run efficiently by "seat of the pants" management is long past. But utilization of scientific management techniques in decision making is impossible for the modern executive unless he is provided with adequate financial data upon which to base his decisions. The mere existence of basic information in corporate books or voluminous reports is not enough for good management control. The

Reprinted from *Financial Executive*, January 1967, pp. 20–26, by permission of the publisher.

information necessary for good decision making must be presented to management in time for corrective action to be taken and in a form which assists management in making the proper decision.

Decision making is the distinguishing characteristic of top executives. Decisions must be based on facts which have been considered objectively. Some executives, however, have difficulty in making decisions because they receive too much data. Absorbing and arranging vast quantities of data into an information system useful to management is a problem which we all recognize. The advent of computers has made so much more data available that reports on trivia are rapidly strangling us. The faster the machine, the more we feed it and the more trivia we have to wade through to get to the basics of the business.

FULFILLING BASIC FUNCTION

Most people today who have the responsibility for providing management with timely, accurate, and concise financial reports are not doing their job as effectively as they should. In general, the reporting of financial data to management is not effective because it is too late, too voluminous, not properly interpreted or analyzed, not distributed to persons who can use it, and not economic. In plain words, I contend that the average financial executive is not doing his job. He deserves the charge that "with a firm eye on the past he backs courageously into the future." He complains that he is frequently left off the management team, and yet he fails to earn his place on that team by his failure to fulfill the basic function of his position: to report and to interpret properly financial results for other members of management.

TYPES OF CONTROLLERS

Since most financial reports to management today are prepared under the direction of an executive with the word "controller" in his title, we will generalize, for purposes of this dissertation, by referring to the originator of financial reports as a "controller." The controller measures performance against his company's objectives by utilizing the accounting system which he has devised and implemented. If his system does not produce the kind of analyses which will permit management, with his assistance, to spot weaknesses and opportunities for profit improvement, the controller is not doing his job. Due to the tremendous increase in business in recent years and the increasing complexities of business, competent financial executives and controllers are at a premium. As a result, some of the incumbents of such positions are less competent than we would like. We might classify today's controllers into several categories on the bases of their attitudes, philosophies, and competence.

Traditional

First, there is the "traditional" controller, who generates information just because it is required by accounting tradition. He is enamored of accounting for accounting's sake and becomes gleefully excited when a 28-column work sheet "foots" and "cross foots." His reports are accurate to the cent but they are delivered at least a month after they have lost their usefulness to management, and are useful to the controller solely as historical documents or to fill surplus file drawers or waste baskets.

Auditor

Second, there is the "auditor" controller, whose greatest thrills come from surprise audits of $25 petty cash funds maintained by frightened female clerks. He visualizes himself as the president's police chief and top spy rolled into one. He is never a member of the top team because his role as "devil's advocate" prevents him from agreeing with anything or cooperating with anyone.

Executive

Then we have the "executive" controller, who sits in his swivel chair all day, every day, dictating memoranda of little significance, shuffling papers, and holding lengthy conferences which tie up his staff, thus making them, as well as himself, unavailable for useful service to management. He has not seen the inside of a factory since he received his title and does not recognize his company's products until he reads their labels.

Independent

Our fourth controller type is the "independent" controller who pleads innocent to all charges, shirks all responsibility and keeps reminding his listeners that he is "only the recorder" of the results of operations and not responsible for such results. While he may recognize a variance if he trips over it, he states quite strongly that "operating management" must tell him why they are "over budget."

Computer

The "computer" controller visualizes himself as a scientist whose greatest ambition is to produce longer reports in greater quantity than anyone else. To him, effective reports are the ones that weigh the most, and we suspect that he spends his free time in writing anonymous letters to government agencies suggesting their need for more and lengthier and more complicated reports from the business community.

Systems

Then we have the "systems" controller, who sincerely believes that people can be motivated and directed only by lengthy, detailed written instructions, practices, procedures, and policies. Even his decisions are flow-charted and he spends considerable time in a semi-annual revision of the expense account forms. His daily production of instructions, practices, directives, and other dicta, if used as fuel, would be adequate to heat the headquarters building.

Political

The "political" controller resembles C. Wright Mills' "Maybe-Man". He covers up his lack of ability and lack of performance by good fellowship. He speaks in the "rich round voice" and does not confuse his superior with details. He speaks like the "quiet competent man of affairs" and never personally says "no." "He is the tolerant maybe-man." He practices softening "the facts into the optimistic, practical, forward-looking, cordial, brisk view." He caricatures what he is supposed to be but he never lets his brains show. He thrives in the highly profitable, marketing-oriented environment but cannot exist long in the profit-oriented, highly competitive environment.

Professional

Finally, we have the "professional" controller, the one whom management recognizes as a member of the team and whose opinions management honors. Our professional controller's major contribution is in assisting top management to make decisions based upon economic evaluations accurately prepared and properly presented. He provides management with an intelligence agency, but he does not stop at providing intelligence. He influences line management in considering the information which he has provided so that proper actions are taken to achieve maximum operating effectiveness.

"KEY FACTORS" TO KEEP "ON TARGET"

While it is true that specific management reports must vary with the nature of the business and the *modus operandi* of its management, in every company there are certain "key factors" which determine the success or failure of the business and which must be carefully watched and controlled by its top management. Even in ITT, with its more than 200 thousand employees working in 53 countries in such diverse activities as telecommunications manufacture, car rentals, steel fabrication, operation of telephone companies, pump and boiler manufacture, etc., there are certain common denominators (our so-called "key factors") which permit management to meet its operating objectives *if it is provided with effective reports.*

I have seven key factors which are watched constantly to ensure that we will meet our principal objectives. If we are "on target" in these seven basic areas of measurement, the company is likely to meet its objectives. The key factors are: SALES, PROFITS, ORDER RECEIPTS, ORDER BACKLOG, RECEIVABLES, INVENTORIES, and MANPOWER. From each company I receive a weekly statistical report which shows these data for the current month, the year to date, and the present outlook for the year in comparison with the budget and the last previous report. This weekly "key factors" statistical report is accompanied by textual explanations of significant variances from budget and from the last report.

In addition to the seven key factors, I watch special problem areas and receive daily, weekly, or monthly reports until the problems are solved. These special reports are constantly changing, but they have covered such areas as cash balances, collections, overtime, paid absences, lost discounts, marketing costs per average order, marketing costs per dollar of order receipts, and sales value of production.

In a single company I would expect my controller to provide me with the key factors reports. However, in our organization, in order to ensure that each company general manager recognizes his problems and stays on top of the key factors which determine the success or failure of his performance, I insist that these reports come from him. Of course, he relies upon his controller to supply the basic data and, together they work out the forecast portions and the variance analyses.

REPORTS READY FOR SERVICE OR ACTION

I have used the expression "effective reports" several times in this dissertation. But just what is an "effective report"? Webster defines "effective" as "producing a desired effect; ready for service or action." Are your reports "ready for service or action," and do they "produce the desired effect"? To meet these criteria they must be: TIMELY, FACTUAL, READABLE, CONSISTENT, PROPERLY INTERPRETED, ECONOMIC, DRAMATIC, and READY FOR ACTION. Therefore, an effective report is:

Timely

A stale report is as non-saleable as a stale loaf of bread. A report on historical performance is useful as an historical record for reporting to stockholders or to government agencies but has little value as a management tool unless it indicates adverse trends quickly enough to permit management to take action which will affect the future results of operations. Use of pre-printed forms and the insertion of previously known data, such as budget figures, in advance of the time that variable data are known are techniques which will aid in early reporting.

Factual

The level of accuracy required in a good control report depends to some extent upon its intended use. Seldom is accuracy to the cent necessary; most reports can be rounded to the nearest thousand dollars. However, accuracy as to reported *facts* is essential. A good example is the variance analysis which tells management "why" the results were what they were.

Several months ago Mr. Harold Geneen, chairman and president of ITT, wrote a memorandum on "facts" from which I would like to quote. Mr. Geneen said:

> Yesterday we put in a long, hard, driving meeting, mostly seeking the facts on which easy management decisions could then be made. I think the important conclusion to be drawn is simple.
>
> There is no word in the English language that is more intended to convey the intent of incontrovertibility—final and reliable reality—as the word "fact." However, no word is more honored by its breach in actual usage. For example, there are, as we saw yesterday, apparent facts, assumed facts, reported facts, hoped-for facts, accepted facts, and many others.
>
> In most cases these were not the real facts at all. In many cases in daily life this point may not be too important. But in this area of management decision, it is all important! Whole trains of events and decisions can be put in motion for an entire management in the wrong direction—with the inevitable loss of money, time, and morale—by one "unfactual fact" accepted by or submitted by—you—however unintentional.
>
> The highest art of professional management requires the literal ability to smell a "real fact" from all others and to have, moreover, the temerity, intellectual curiosity, guts and/or plain impoliteness, if necessary, to be sure what you do have is indeed what we will call an unshakeable fact. So let me invite you and at the same time insist that you now become a connoisseur of all these kinds of facts—so that you can then tell a genuine snapping turtle from the others—and so that you can learn to force to the surface and deal only with unshakeable facts in the future.
>
> You will hear a lot more of this term "unshakeable facts" as we go forward. It is a never ending discipline and one that we need. So, good luck with them—and start now—*is it a fact?* but more importantly, *is it an "unshakeable fact"?*

P.S. No matter what you think, try "shaking it"—to be sure!
P.P.S. Send this message down the line.

Properly Interpreted

The reporter who recognizes the possible consequences of misinterpreted data will be most careful to ensure that he not only reports the facts but that he accurately advises the reader regarding the meaning of such facts. Based upon his report, management may decide to drop a product line, to dissolve a company, to enter into a long-term arrangement, or to take other actions which could lead to lost opportunities or to unnecessary costs. The proper interpretation of financial reports is the characteristic which most distinguishes the bookkeeper from the financial executive.

Readable

A good report must be concise, legible, and easily understood. It should be as short as possible, yet contain all essential information. Highlights and summaries should be used where possible. While the report need not be typewritten, it should be easy to read and in simple language. Accounting and other technical jargon should be avoided. If management more easily understands an "upside down" profit and loss statement, by all means turn it upside down.

Consistent

Inconsistency in financial reporting will more easily confuse the management reader than anything else. Consistency in language, descriptions of events, previously reported figures, and, particularly, format is highly desirable.

Economic

Financial reports to management should be evaluated continually as to effectiveness and cost. The financial executive should look periodically at each report published by his organization in terms of dollars and cents. Is the use to which it is put worth the cost? Is it distributed to persons who cannot use it? Can it be prepared more cheaply by using different procedures and techniques? Can the basic data be obtained in a less costly manner?

Dramatic

All financial managers must be salesmen. Their product is the financial report. To be saleable, this product must not only be a quality product but it must be attractively packaged and presented. It must contain attention-getters and attention-holders to ensure its acceptability to the reader. The use of colors, charts, drawings, and different type sizes and styles will enhance its saleability. Do not be afraid to create and to pioneer.

Ready for Action

The most important characteristic of an effective report is that it be *ready for action.* A report that does not leave the reader with a clear understanding of the problem and the recommended solution is worse than useless because it has wasted the time of both the writer and the reader.

CONCENTRATE ON THE FUTURE

The science of management is developing more rapidly than the development of control and reporting systems necessary for good decision making. Whereas we are on the verge of substantial changes in the way that decisions are made, the average manager is still receiving from his financial staff data which are not adequate as useful tools in the decision-making process. The three principal complaints are that the data are supplied too late, are too voluminous, and lack proper interpretation. To solve this major problem, the financial executive must work closely with operating management. He must give his management the "prime time." He must look at the development of effective control reports from the general management viewpoint and not from the restricted viewpoint of the financial manager. He should use history as a bench mark but concentrate on the future. His most valuable contribution is not in telling management where they have been but in telling them where they are going. He must dramatize his services to make them more saleable. Finally, he must discard his accounting blinders in favor of the broader vision of professional financial management. Only if he does these things will he produce effective financial reports for his management.

The author gives some guidelines for more effective management control reporting.

28

POWER, INFLUENCE, PERSUASION AND MANAGEMENT REPORTS

Arthur B. Toan, Jr.

If asked to make a list of the ten most powerful people in the world today, most would put the President of the United States at, or near, the top of the list. He has powers and responsibilities with an awesomeness of which we are reminded virtually every day. It comes, therefore, as something of a surprise to see how political scholars view the nature of the power which the President can bring to bear. One highly respected scholar, for example, speaking from the joint viewpoint of professorship in a major university and prior service on the White House staff, has this to say:

The President of the United States has an extraordinary range of powers and authority arising in statute law and the Constitution and in the customs of our government and of politics. He does not, however, obtain results merely by giving orders. Despite his powers, he does not get action without argument. His strength or weakness turns on his capacity to influence the conduct of the men who make up government. Presidential power is the power to persuade. (RICHARD NEUSTADT—Presidential Power.)

The power of the financial executive also lies in his power to persuade. The financial executive can give orders to relatively few. He cannot directly make the really crucial management decisions—selecting the product line, the marketing strategy and the manufacturing techniques.

Reprinted from *Financial Executive,* August 1965, pp. 11–17, by permission of the publisher.

The power of the financial executive lies in and is measured by his willingness and ability to influence, by persuasion, the other officers and key employees of his company whose combined power provides direction to the enterprise. It is the financial executive's ability to convince these men of the validity of financial data and of the financial point of view which, in the long run, will establish the value of his contribution to the company and will measure him as an individual who was "strong" or "weak."

Properly performing the housekeeping functions assigned to the financial department, properly safe-guarding the corporate assets, properly developing financial data for internal use, and fairly and fully reporting to stockholders are obviously important. Those functions must be carried out—efficiently and well. They are not, however, enough. The inherent need of a company for sound financial management and for the incorporation of sound financial policies in corporate decisions and actions requires that the financial executive add to the satisfactory fulfillment of his other responsibilities both a *willingness* and an *ability* to persuade.

Management reports can help to accomplish this result. For the financial executive to fail to use them for this purpose is for him to deprive himself of one of the most valuable and readily available forms of persuasion. How management reports can be used effectively in this role is the subject of our discussion tonight.

THE ROLE OF FINANCIAL REPORTS

What are a financial executive's management reports? They are not, as one disgruntled executive is rumored to have said, *"a set of inaccurate figures, intentionally designed to conflict with information supplied in some other way, submitted in a somewhat unintelligible manner, too late to be useful, to a set of executives who are too busy to look at them and probably wouldn't let them change what they intended to do anyway."*

These management reports are something quite different. They are to be sure, a set of statements containing many figures, showing the position and progress of the business. More than that, however, they are one of the major ways in which a financial executive speaks to management. They are one of the major methods and techniques by which a smart financial executive makes the financial man's philosophy, and the financial man's point of view, felt in the policies, decisions and actions of the company. They are one of the major ways by which the financial man influences the course of future events.

FINANCIAL CONTROLS AT GENERAL MOTORS

Alfred Sloan, in describing his years with General Motors, often talks of the role played by financial methods and philosophies in the emergence of that company from near disaster to a position of strength and highly disciplined power. At one point, for example, he says: *"General Motors' progress was largely the result of advances which the corporation made in the development of financial controls, along with those in organization and product policy. Our modern financial policies, like those in organization, came out of the ruins of 1920."* [1]

Mr. Sloan obviously attaches great importance to the way in which financial ideas and techniques, many of them drawn from the DuPont experience, were developed to meet the needs of the General Motors Corporation and then were effectively promulgated throughout it. There is no question but that Alfred Sloan himself came to understand financial policy, philosophy and technique, and that he was strongly influenced by financial concepts. As he says at one point: *"My experience was mainly from the operating side. My responsibility involved the application of financial method, for finance could not exist in a vacuum but to be effective had to be integrated with operations."*

Financial methods and policies quite clearly helped to shape, by influence and persuasion, the course of development of that very successful company. The financial executives' management reports, one can see from a reading of Mr. Sloan's book, played an important part in getting the message across.

THE IDEA OF "MESSAGE"

Having a message—a financial message—and then getting that message across are the factors under discussion. They are key elements in many aspects of the financial executive's job; they are *crucial* when it comes to his management reports.

The importance of both of these elements was reemphasized for me by a recent event which could have occurred in any of thousands of communities. However, it actually took place in my own. At a meeting of one of our community organizations, a gentleman, usually tolerated because of his age and obvious sincerity, arose to speak on the subject at issue. The usual torrent of words came forth in a somewhat formless manner, leaving everyone wondering just what point he was trying to make.

[1] The Neustadt and Sloan quotations have been slightly edited.

One of the members of the audience, whose patience was ultimately exhausted, finally broke in: *"Message,"* he said, *"what is the message?"*

This is not an inappropriate question to ask about many of the management reports financial executives prepare. Is there a clear-cut message we are trying to impart to other members of management? Are we supplying the audience with words and figures whose meaning is not quite clear? Stated in other terms, do financial executives have a fundamental financial philosophy? Is this financial philosophy clarified, reenforced and made effective by our management reports?

A FINANCIAL PHILOSOPHY

Why do we need the financial message? The reason is quite clear.

Most companies choose a course of action which is the result of the combined impact of many factors. Some of these impacts are external, such as the action of competitors or the course of general economic conditions. Others are internal, reflecting the resources available to the company, the desire and abilities of key executives, and certain seemingly inexorable rules of common sense and reality as to what is necessary to keep a company healthy and prosperous over a long period of time. Many of the voices heard reflect, in more than a minor degree, the convictions, interests, backgrounds and business objectives of the various officers involved. It is right and natural that their point of view—the point of view of sales, of manufacturing, of research, of personnel, of general management—be expressed. It is also right and necessary that the point of view of the financial executive be clearly enunciated and clearly heard. If he does not do this, should he expect others to do it for him? Should the relative objectivity and breadth of view of the financial executive be lost?

The answer, quite clearly, is *"no."*

Most, if not all, of the elements of the financial philosophy appropriate for a particular company already exist. They are not, in fact, particularly earthshaking to people like ourselves. They might, for example, include the following:

1. Financial planning is serious and "for real."
2. Budgets are to be considered a matter of both corporate and personal responsibility.
3. The return made on the corporate investment is a most significant measure of corporate health.
4. The function of goals, standards and budgets is to inspire improvement as well as to measure performance.
5. There must be a balance between current profitability and future growth.

6. The evaluation of capital and similar expenditures should recognize risk and the cost of money, as well as the amount or rate of return.

7. Pricing is a matter requiring consideration of the behavior of costs and profits as well as sales.

Other elements would, of course, be added or substituted as the circumstances of the company and the industry might dictate. What was appropriate for a bank, an oil company, a public utility, or a defense contractor might well *not* be appropriate for the others. The important points are that an appropriate financial philosophy should be created, that this *can* be done and that it should be reflected in the *message* contained in the management reports.

THE UNAVOIDABLE MESSAGE

Is there a message in your present reports? There is. Of that you can be sure, for it is impossible not to have some kind of a message in them, even though it may be weak and confused—or not what was intended at all. As soon as there is a selection of what data are to be presented, of what relative emphasis is to be given to the various items reported upon and of what bases of comparison are to be used, the character of the message has been substantially formed. When, for example, a selection is made of the data to be presented, a judgment is made as to what is important for the management of the company. When a decision is made as to the relative emphasis to be given to different kinds of information in the reports, the relative attention which that information will receive from management is further established. When bases for comparison are selected, a system of values is established which, because it forms the basis for judging good and bad performance, will influence and persuade.

No set of management reports can, in other words, be completely objective or neutral, since all require judgments which cannot be made in accordance with some set of completely unbiased, universal truths. All reports are, in at least some respects, subjective. The financial officer should recognize this and see that a sound system of values is employed—and that, in establishing this system of values, the financial man's point of view is clearly expressed.

THE FINANCIAL PHILOSOPHY AND SALES REPORTS

Perhaps I should indicate what I mean in more concrete terms. Take the simple matter of reporting sales. A very neutral but most uninformative manner of reporting sales would be merely to list them in alphabetical order by product with nothing shown but the dollars and quantities sold. About the only message which such a statement would have is that sales must be sufficiently important so that they should be brought to management's attention and that there are variations in the quantities and dollars of the different products sold. Most would readily agree that this is not message enough and choose something additional. What that "something additional" is depends upon the individual system of values as expressed in the bases of comparison used. It is suggested that there should be a financial influence present when these bases of comparison are established.

What is the message the financial executive is trying to get across? Consider these as a few possibilities:

1. Is he saying there should be a relationship between sales, sales effort and the relative profitability of individual products?—if so, one kind of information should be shown.
2. Is he saying he wants high, or higher, sales per dollar of investment in inventories, receivables and fixed assets?—if so, he needs another.
3. Is he saying he should carefully watch sales of products with rising or declining growth trends, and that he should apply different judgments in these two sets of circumstances?—if so, he needs a third.
4. Is he saying he should particularly watch sales of products developed from the R&D program to see how effective that program is?—if so, he needs still another.
5. Is he saying some of the sales are in products presently vulnerable to technological advances being made by competitors and that the company should be prepared?
6. Is he saying that some sales require a very high level of credit risk and support?
7. Is he saying that he judges the quality of sales performance against what was done last year, what he said he would do this year, his share of the market or what—if so, this is what his reports should show.

What goes into those seemingly routine sales reports says a lot more than just what sales were made. It tells what judgments are to be made, what is important, and how strong the financial influence is to be. The information those reports contain, and the managerial and financial philosophy which those reports reflect, become part of the basis for future decisions which help to shape the future of the company. Even the very fact of their submission to the managerial group is a form of influence. For, by so doing, the reports themselves become some part of the reward/penalty system on which personal performance is judged.

THE FINANCIAL PHILOSOPHY AND BUDGETS AND GOALS

Here is another illustration of how the financial executive can influence the message which comes through. Take the matter of looseness in goals—how easily attainable should the standards or the budgets which the financial reports contain actually be? What these reports show is important, for what we are really saying is "how competitive should we be internally?" Should we pit the efforts of departments and divisions and plants against a tough set of standards or not? Or, selecting another form of competition, should we pit one branch or division or unit intensively against another and reward the one which excels and penalize the one which does not? Should we, in other words, choose to develop through reports what Dr. Martin Luther King calls "creative tension" to bring about the results we would like to attain? I believe we should, but this is beside the point. What is clearly on the point is that the financial executive can influence the degree of "creative tension" which exists by the nature of his reports. How?

1. By the amounts and kinds of allowances built into the cost system.
2. By the degree of difficulty built into budgets and other financial plans.
3. By the kind of price used when goods and services are purchased by one division from the other.
4. By the manner in which good and poor performance is highlighted in reports.
5. By the criteria used to judge whether performance has been good or bad.
6. By many more devices and techniques of which we are both aware.

Let us take a more detailed example of this point and see what would happen if we were reporting on profits by branches. Let us watch how the tension is heightened as we move progressively through the following five approaches:

1. The branches are listed in alphabetical order,
2. they are rearranged in order of relative profitability,
3. they are arranged in order of relative profitability and unexplained lines are drawn across the schedule below the first and second thirds,
4. a caption is placed above the bottom third reading "substandard branches,"
5. that caption is changed to another reading "branches whose manager might be replaced."

The point has been somewhat exaggerated to make it evident. The reports measure and record, certainly—but they also influence and persuade.

THE FINANCIAL PHILOSOPHY AND DIVISIONAL RESULTS

Here is a final example of how the influence of the financial executive can be made significant in his reports—this time in distinguishing between corporate and divisional results. A great deal of *managerial* philosophy is reflected in, influenced by, and perhaps even determined by, how the financial executive chooses to report on divisional or other sub-unit results. How does this come about? It comes about in the process of determining:

1. Whether a unit is to be a profit center at all?
2. How transfer prices are to be established when interdivisional relationships are involved?
3. How headquarters costs are to be handled?
4. Whether each unit is to be judged individually, or only as part of the company as a whole?
5. How bonuses and extra compensation are to be determined?
6. Whether the adequacy of divisional results is to be judged in terms of
   —total profits alone?
   —the rate of return on the investment it employs?
   —its rate of growth?
   —or other measurements?

The decision made in response to each of these questions involves more than the financial man's point of view. Yet, in all of them, the influence of the financial man will be paramount or close to paramount. What he reports will be most significant. What he reports will strongly reflect (although not necessarily be identical with) his point of view. Therefore, consciously having and expressing a sound financial philosophy is very, very significant.

What is our message to this point? Essentially this:

The financial executive who makes the kind of contribution to the effective management of his company which a modern financial executive should make will do so only if he develops a sound financial message, based on a sound financial philosophy supported by sound financial information.

This he can do, using tools and ideas which are already available to him. The financial executive should recognize that his reports to management do contain a message. He should make sure that it is the message he would really like to see delivered.

GETTING THE MESSAGE ACROSS

If *having* a sound message is important, so too is *getting the message across*. Let us, therefore, turn our attention in that direction and consider the second topic—*getting the message across.*

How the financial man "speaks" has a great deal to do with how well the financial message will be heard.

A FEW PRINCIPLES OF COMMUNICATION

Anyone who has studied the art of communication will remember certain cardinal principles which seem to be as sound in communicating one kind of message as another. Once we accept the idea that the fundamental purpose of management reports is to communicate financial ideas and facts, we can see that these principles apply to them, and to the message they contain. It might be well, therefore, to turn to a few of these principles for they have a great deal to do with how clearly the message is heard and understood.

1. The simpler the message, the more readily it will be understood. A complex idea is hard to understand. When you can find a simple idea, use it. When you can give a set of complex factors a single, simple focus—as return on investment and some other financial ratios so beautifully do—*use* that focus. Thereby, you will increase the chance that the idea and the actual measurement will be understood. Strive for *sharply-focused simplicity.*

2. The fewer the messages, the more likely that *all* will be remembered. As the *Saturday Review* recently noted, *"plunging necklines make it more difficult to remember pretty faces."* One could add, plunging necklines, short skirts and pretty faces make it rather difficult to have a clear notion about *anything*. Financial messages are much the same. *Be selective and hammer the fewer messages home.*

3. The more frequently repeated the message, the more certain that it will sink in. Most significant concepts and facts are neither understood nor absorbed through one or two exposures. The reiteration of ideas, in a manner which continues to draw attention, is what ultimately gets the message across. Maybe you can't set your message to music, *but* you can say it more than once. *Repetition pays.*

4. If you are going to make a change, you need not make it all at once. Almost any major change, by the very fact that it constitutes a threat

to the *status quo,* seems to arouse an emotional response. The chance of acceptance will improve if the change is gradual or the recipient is, in some other manner, gradually introduced to the idea. A change in reports —as in the items to be reported or the criteria to be used or in the tightness of goals and objectives with which results are to be compared—will be more apt to succeed *when the reader is prepared.*

5. The better the idea is dramatized, the greater the chances it will "take." Dramatization, or in terms appropriate for your city—*showmanship,* is what gives a competitive edge to the ideas you expound and the facts you present in the face of other influences being exerted on your associates in management. A report, by itself, can contain a high degree of dramatic punch if words are chosen with care, if criteria for comparison are carefully selected, and the form of presentation is visually and psychologically sound. Strive for such reports. There is no need, however, to rely solely on an inanimate object to produce results. *Use the force and personality of yourself and other key financial executives as part of the program to get the ideas across.*

6. The more deeply imbedded the message, the more likely it will be applied. Most executives are forced to reach more of their conclusions and decisions when specific financial facts are *not* at hand than when the reverse is the case—either because the specific facts have never been developed about the immediate situation, or because the facts are, at that time, physically available only at some other place. There is no reason why these decisions and conclusions cannot be reached within the framework of a sound financial philosophy, however, for if the financial executive has done his job properly, key financial principles and facts will be deeply imbedded in the executive's mind. These, the executive will carry with him no matter where he goes. Strive for a "take it with you" kind of financial knowledge.

7. The probability that one single approach will effectively reach all members of the audience is small. Any advertiser will tell you that you will get the best results if you carefully select the method by which you will reach your audience. He will also point out that it is extremely unlikely that one method, or one media, will get the story across to all. Given the diversity of interests, backgrounds and knowledge of finance apt to be represented in any group of executives, it seems most unlikely that any one method will reach all of them. Least of all, will reports. The job of the financial executives is, therefore, to use management reports in a total campaign which includes oral presentations, personal contacts, participation with other executives in applying financial concepts in situations with which they are faced, and other techniques. It is a campaign which should make more understandable and vital the ideas and data contained in management reports at the same time it is making the

financial influence felt in decisions and plans which are made. Thus, *vary your approach.*

8. If you have to choose between influencing the many and the important few—those with informed opinions who *can* and *will* do something about them—make your maximum efforts in the direction of the few. As Elmo Roper said recently in talking about advertising in the 1970's, *"Today we exist in an era of advertising overkill, in which the public is often treated as if it were one vast, all-inclusive entity. There are many publics, important at different times and to different companies and groups. The important thing is to pinpoint the relevant public."* In a corporate enterprise, the most relevant group—the active, articulate and power-possessing group is high level management and the maximum effort should be made to see that this group is well and correctly informed. *Concentrate time and effort on the influentials in your group.*

9. A financial way of thinking may be at least as important as concentration on a specific set of facts. I recently discussed the effectiveness of management reports with a highly respected financial vice president of a major company. In the course of this discussion, I expressed the opinion that "financial information is used a lot less by presidents and other operating executives to run their companies than most financial executives would like to believe." His response was "that may be, but these same executives also use financial information a lot more than they think they do." This, I think, should be the goal of the financial executive—*so to drive the basic financial philosophy and the basic financial information into the minds of executives that it is a part of their way of thinking about a problem or an opportunity or a decision whether they have a report in front of them or not.*

The chances are, in fact, that the more familiar and comfortable the nonfinancial executive becomes with financial data and methodology, the more he will want to use them when important decisions must be made. The chances also are that, without this fundamental financial understanding, specific financial data will howl as a wind, unheard and unmissed.

SUMMARY

The financial executive has a choice to make. He can be a recorder of plans and facts, a housekeeper, a guardian of corporate assets. He can also be something more—*the effective voice of financial principles and methodology as a member of management.*

To seize this latter opportunity requires from him a willingness and an ability to develop a sound financial philosophy and then to communicate this message effectively where it counts the most. Management reports, while far from the sole method of communication, can play a significant part in this.

The financial executive can avail himself of a variety of techniques for getting his message across—simplification, selection, repetition, dramatization, the penetration of basic ideas—to cite a few.

The financial executive's effectiveness in using his power lies in his ability to influence management—getting them to accept the validity of financial ideas and facts. The power of persuasion resting in management reports can take these reports from the end of the accounting process and place them near the core of the management process itself.

III

APPLICATIONS OF MANAGEMENT CONTROL PRINCIPLES AND TECHNIQUES

The readings in Part III are extensions of the material in the earlier parts. In many instances the articles differ only in emphasis, by devoting more space to the applications of management control principles and techniques than to their development. The selections included here give perspective and dimension to these principles and techniques and explore ways in which these control concepts can be used for more effective management.

These readings represent only a small portion of the material available in this area. Space limitations permitted the inclusion only of articles of special interest from the fields of marketing, manufacturing, organization, and accounting and finance.

A

Marketing

After defining management control and the steps in planning for control, the author shows how they can be profitably applied to product development programs.

29

PLANNING FOR CONTROL IN DEVELOPMENT PROGRAMS

Joseph Freitag, Jr.

The onrush of technological advancement and competitive pressures has fostered the creation of product-oriented organizations within multiproduct companies. In some cases these product organizations have been self-contained—in that all personnel, all resources, and all the facilities required for the particular product development have been part of the same organization. In other cases, an organization called "product (or project) management" is created for the purpose of steering, guiding, and coordinating product development through "skill centers" of the company. These skill centers are responsible for making their contribution of specific skills, where needed, to the development of all products within the company.

Under either of these situations, the management job of product development is complex. Management's responsibility concerning the product development is to ensure that within the limits of company environment and appropriated resources, a product evolves which satisfies a set of given requirements. The emphasis implied in this statement of principles is upon management of productive effort.

Its inherent complexity arises from our inability to define exactly what the management job entails. To some, it means administration; to others it means accounting, while still others think of management as the possession of, or access to, a reservoir of data and experience as a basis

Reprinted from *Financial Executive,* August 1964, pp. 22–28, 47–48, by permission of the publisher.

for decision-making. Although each of these factors is important as a *subsidiary* function of management, under today's circumstances—which require that a rapidly advancing technology be applied effectively to product development, *despite* schedule and budget limitations—the primary task for management is *control.*

DEFINING MANAGEMENT CONTROL

In a majority of the meanings currently in vogue in the business world, control has the connotation of domination. This misconception results from historical events in which the empires that were established by *controlling* civilization, crumbled by the self-evident truth that men are endowed with certain inalienable rights which are not controllable. Equally misleading in trying to understand management control is the fact that current control practices include government control which *regulates,* in part, human behavior; airport control which is pilot *instruction* oriented; and scientific control which involves a data comparison. In sports, a basketball player has control if he sinks a high percentage of foul shot attempts.[1]

Too little has been written to explain management control in terms of its scope, locus, and philosophy. Perhaps this accounts for the difficulty (which arises today because of decentralization and product orientation) that management has in deciding what philosophy of control provides the roots of success and what philosophy establishes a base of failure. The guidelines and structure of this article embody the following philosophies:

Effective management control exists when operating people *understand* the differences between "planned" and "actual performance" and endeavor to incorporate corrective measures in the applicable areas of importance.

Ineffective management control exists when operating people conceive of it as something *restrictive, domineering,* or concerned with *punishment.*

Unfortunately, the establishment of effective management control has been considered to be, at best, a systematic process rather than one in which analytical evaluation was possible. Most management information systems—like the by-now familiar PERT-based systems—have been designed to include a definite planning period. Unfortunately, the concept of *planning for control* has not been the fundamental planning criterion, probably because it has traditionally been assumed that management will know what to do if status reports adequately and accurately reflect the real situation. Herein lies a delusive aspect, because standards for ade-

[1] See Donald G. Malcolm, and Alan J. Rowe (eds.), *Management Control Systems* (New York: John Wiley & Sons, Inc., 1960).

EXHIBIT 29–1

ALL MANAGEMENT INFORMATION SYSTEMS MUST MEET THE CRITERIA OF

ADEQUACY	ACCURACY
1. The system must be product or project oriented.	1. Realistic estimates must be provided.
2. The output must be operational, *not* presentational.	2. The output must reflect the true problems of the job.
3. Limitations of the information system must be isolated in order to provide dovetails for other systems.	3. The system must have a feature for compensation of human errors.
4. The system must be adaptable to program changes.	4. The operation must approach real time requirements.
5. Management information needs during various project stages must be met.	5. The output must be used by working groups up through top management.

quacy and accuracy as outlined in Exhibit 29–1 are not considered. Generally, today's reports are not adequate and/or accurate because key steps of planning for control have been missed in the original planning. Hence, the shape of the problem, and the control action it requires is confused by a redundant proliferation of data. If left to traditional devices, managerial efficiency is inhibited by the necessity to merely discover what information in the data is of significance and consequence. It is, therefore, the purpose of this discussion to provoke some thought towards implementation of the technique in a manner that will foster greater efficiency of management control . . . the end to which any management system *should* be directed.

PRODUCT CONTROL TODAY

Obviously, all companies must exercise controlling functions. The differences in the character of these functions at different companies arise as a result of varying emphasis placed on different areas of business by each company—which, in turn, stem from differences among customers; the products being built; the method of doing business; the business climate; and the organizational structure of the company.[2]

In the aerospace business, emphasis is generated by the customers the company is (or anticipates) serving; broad product lines; operational direction in conflict with program direction; and operating departments, satisfying program departments.

Bringing an analytical attitude to bear upon the role of the function of control parallels the evolutionary change in professional orientation

[2] See Bruce Payne, "How to Set Realistic Profit Goals," *Harvard Business Review*, September–October 1958, p. 100.

that took place in broadening the function of bookkeepers until they became accountants. In that instance, evolution occurred as management realized that the historical process of simply recording financial information for statements did not meet the increasingly complex needs brought about by government regulations, tax problems, and stockholder interests. These factors added requirements for a more detailed and specialized account structure than was previously needed, and the accountant came into his own.

In the parallel case of program management, the process of evolution is not yet complete but the inevitable results can be clearly discerned. With the ever-increasing technical complexity and the insecurities brought about by fierce market-place competition, many companies have sought to participate in several distinct areas and thereby broaden their product base. Resultant problems of administration and customer "wants" coordination become highlighted because it has become increasingly difficult to find anyone in the participating skill centers of each company who has access to, or can understand, the entire "story." Consequently, separate *project* organizations have been set up to handle all the necessary administrative details and market-place coordination for each specific project.

At first, these functions were performed according to standard accounting procedures, which dictated a more-or-less fixed set of accounts reconciled to a high degree of accuracy and completeness. Naturally, dissatisfaction has followed because of the requirements for flexibility of cost accumulation, time lags in accumulating data suitable for an accounting entry, and finally the growing realization that this *kind* of information does not provide management with the data actually required for program control. Why? Because the data actually required for program control has to be oriented to the goals of that specific program and each program has slightly different goals! This latter realization, more than anything else, ushered in the proliferation of the PERT-based management systems.

Almost everyone involved with these PERT-based methods has praised his own system as the long-awaited panacea for all management control ills. As a result, the ambitious efforts of many of those involved have been concentrated upon the *machinery* of implementing, without a real understanding of the exact need that this concept *could* satisfy. The cry has been "exception reporting" [3] without realizing that an exception report was only as good as the input information—which in turn reflected the quality of the original plan. Consequently, the objective of *planning for control* was lost in many cases, and the PERT-based technique turned into the prolific generation of processed, uncoordinated,

[3] See Gilbert Stillian, "PERT, A New Management Planning and Control Technique," *AMA Management Report,* New York: American Management Association, p. 13.

unrelated data. Efforts to reduce the sheer volume of this proliferation have centered on unselective bulk reduction—the "management summary" type of report which must still rely upon an analyst's skill in selecting the summarized items of *significance* and *consequence*. Under such circumstances, how could the PERT-based methods result in anything except an expensive paper-shuffling technique?

At best, the PERT-based systems are a technique that reflects, by a comparison with an established plan, the risks, the decisions, and the application of resources that will be entailed in accomplishing the goals that comprise the program objectives. It is a *work-oriented, time network,* which provides *cost summarizations.* To be effective, it requires attitudes [4] of acceptance and cooperation among all participants and firm, unequivocal goals with assignments of responsibilities throughout the entire managerial hierarchy. Experience has demonstrated time and again that when responsibilities for task assignment are accepted by a specific capable human being, things get done. These results can only be expected if an attitude of *planning for control* exists throughout the company.

Very often, the PERT-based systems become coordinating schemes endeavoring to meld together the status reports of the various skill centers involved in each monitored project. Problems of adequacy and accuracy are not considered, task responsibility is not accepted, and management control is not evident. Contrary to this is the *planning for control* goal for management. The object is to provide conditions such that the energies of the operating people will be devoted to a continual job-focused reappraisal—which will be easily distinguished from a limited accounting attitude that asks only "What has happened?"—to a more realistic attitude which asks, in terms of what is happening, "How should we adjust our original plans to meet the project objectives ahead of us?"

THE FOUNDATIONS OF PLANNING FOR CONTROL

It is easy enough to accept the principle that the control function exists and is exercised because operating people feel responsible for that which is being done; however, it is important to provide an approach to building responsibilities into the plan. Responsibilities are not hung on people or loosely assigned. Each individual has his own purposeful goal and the key to success is to match individual goals with the responsibility assignments that are an inextricable necessity to any goal-oriented program plan. The question that remains is: *How do you get to the part of a plan where responsibilities are assumed?*

Exhibit 29–2 is a list of nine steps that are followed in providing

[4] See James L. Peirce, "The Budget Comes of Age," *Harvard Business Review*, May–June 1954 (Vol. 32, No. 3), p. 58.

a management information system. A list such as this is basic to any implementation effort. Unfortunately, this approach during planning neglects many of the practical problems encountered in such an implementation. If the plans are not explicit, mutually understood, and accountable to the individual doers of the work, control will not be exercised and the original plans will be interpreted as intentions which are not realistic.

During the execution of the steps shown in Exhibit 29–2, it must be kept in mind that the planning must be designed and/or revised within the planning for control concept. What is this concept? Essentially, *planning for control* embodies the philosophy that the operating personnel will be *job* focused and not organization or man focused. When thought of in terms of the data flow for program status information, this may sound like the project operates for the purpose of supplying data to the management information system. In fact the opposite is true because the *planning for control* concept proposes to fulfill the information needs of the business. Unless the program is designed to provide proper data—the feedback loop breaks down, and valuable time is lost, or a duplicate overlapping and perhaps conflicting information system has to be provided to obtain program status data.

Because the flow of information provides an intelligence system for each project and serves as a nerve center for the company, it behooves the general management of a company to direct efforts to the following implementation procedural analysis if the *planning for control* concept is to succeed:

1. An understanding of the needs for *planning for control,* not an interpretation of the PERT-type requirements, is fundamental.
2. A determination of how the information system would fit into company, group, or division procedures is necessary.
3. An assessment of tailoring or special adjustments that would be necessary to satisfy the needs.
4. A procedure for developing networks or phasing plans, time estimates, and cost estimates in order to integrate the three.
5. For output reports, a determination of project type and functional type as well as summarization requirements.
6. The formation of a strong staff devoted and directed to the purpose of the management system rather than technique refinement.

PLANNING NEEDS

Earlier the idea was introduced that management control depends upon plans that are explicit, mutually understood, and accountability is assumed by the individual doers of the work. Naturally, those operating

EXHIBIT 29–2

The development of a product management information system

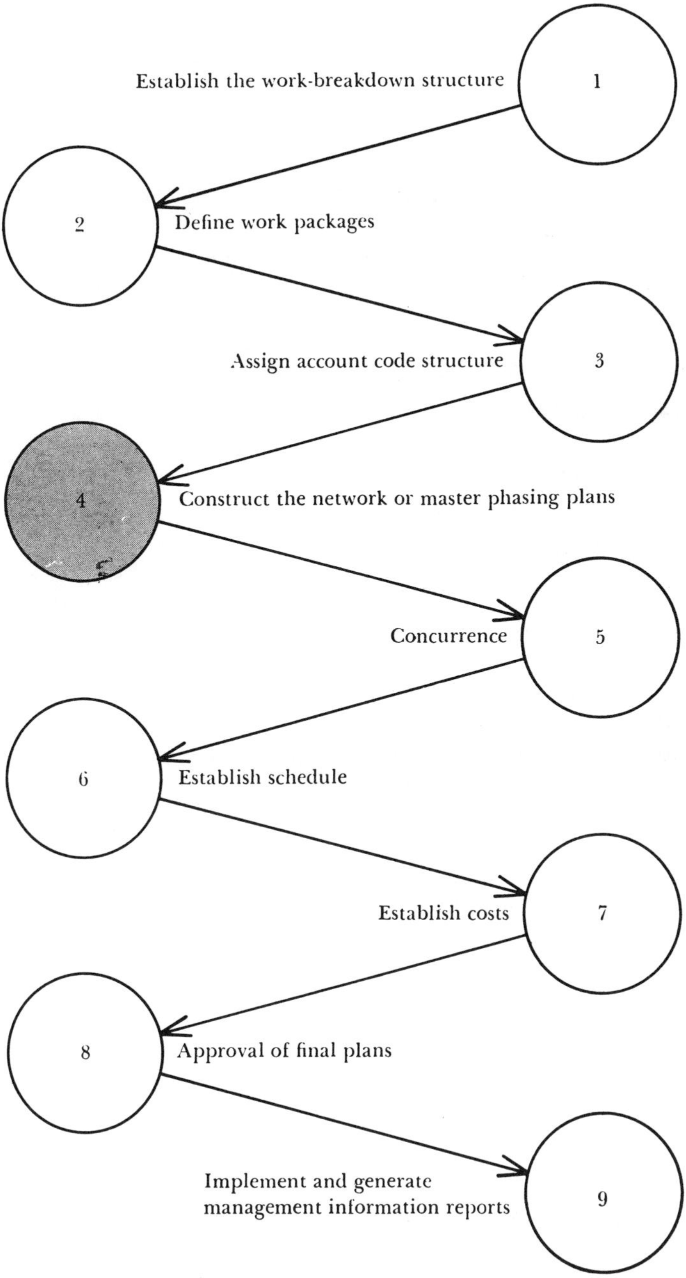

personnel who have identified their individual goals with those of the company will incorporate valuable actions in their daily routine if they know what is expected of them, because they will be anxious to show their capacity to perform.

The remaining task of this article is to demonstrate how the steps shown in Exhibit 29–2 can be achieved such that control will be planned into the management information system. Three principal areas characterize the management participation that is required during the planning phase. It is the completeness to which management satisfies the subquestions in these areas that will distinguish this phase as one of leadership and rules to be referred to in the future as opposed to a mere statement of intentions.

More often than not, the success or failure of a program can be linked with the top-management participation, commitment and dedication to:

1. Determining the Goal(s) of the Program

What should be done?
How does this goal support over-all objectives?
What is the scope of these goals within the company?
What kind of answers are required? When?

Once the goals are established the technical configuration can be expressed in a work-breakdown structure. A management goal might be to avoid research expenditures and this decision would therefore require a configuration of known products and processes. Because technical risks to be taken and resources to be allocated to the program are necessary parts of the goal determination, the preliminary versions of work package and account code structure can be prepared and revised to a final form during the second planning phase:

2. Sequence of Events

How should the work be done?
What alternatives exist?
What are the uncertainties with this approach?

This step establishes the network or master program plan content including dependency relationships and constraints as reflected by some of the specified goals. This is a significant period in the *planning for control* process. It is at this point that the management which established the goals for the program will be able to identify the operating personnel that are control oriented. Those operating personnel that identify their individual goals with the program goals will distinguish themselves with networks or plans that reflect their desires and express their conviction. Those who have not planned their tasks to meet organizational goals are probably not management control oriented. Finally, incentive-type events and monitoring events can be selected while the last phase of planning begins:

3. Organize

What is needed to do that which has to be done?
Who will be committed? Answerable? Responsible?
What is it that shall be measured?
What yardsticks should be used?

To determine what is needed is a job for operating personnel. How can they become management control oriented if they don't have the opportunity to choose the items that will come under review? It is these steps that will conclusively indicate whether or not the operating personnel selected for the program are focused on the goals, and therefore are good choices for the program. If top management has any misgivings about the attitude of proposed operating personnel, now is the time to make the necessary adjustments. Only after operating personnel assignments are firm should detail estimates and pricing be completed.

Measurements are generally neglected because of the stickiness that is involved in establishing them at the time of greatest excitement—full speed ahead on the job. It has been observed and submitted here for consideration that, once what shall be measured and what the yardsticks of measurement shall be are determined, what one pays attention to will be determined. It will make the invisible visible; the neglected will be cared for. Responsibilities will be assumed and the operating personnel will know what they are responsible for and strive to achieve what they consider personal goals. In other words, the things in the measurement become relevant while that which has been omitted is out of sight and out of mind. This concept tends to maximize the effectiveness of individual judgments and participation throughout the program because decisions will be made using a greater amount of factual knowledge.[5]

But this does not convey the idea of which items of objectivity and performance of a plan are to be measured. The aim of the future control aspect will be to provide some factual tools, to communicate to all levels the status of the project. What are the areas of objectivity and performance to which yardsticks should be applied? Obviously, contract coverage, schedule and budget standing, quality performance, and technical progress denote objectivity of the efforts to achieve the specified goals. The measurements should be made in the most convenient applicable unit be it dollars, days, or rejects. Yardsticks of acceptable performance is another matter that is an individual decision for each project because yardsticks

[5] See Edmund Learned, David Ulrich, and Donald Booz, *Executive Action* (Boston: Division of Research, Graduate School of Business Administration, Harvard University, 1951), pp. 121–137.

or standards of performance are difficult to establish as fair. The yardsticks will only be effective when they are incorporated at the working level in the daily routine. It is submitted as a conclusion that this can only happen when the standards meet the expectations and habits of the working level judged by those standards. After all, the workers are the ones who exist in the environment that applies resources to the product such that it will meet the requirements. To achieve cooperation in establishing standards requires higher management support. Obviously management's presence will influence attitudes and provide the motivation required. In fact, their presence and participation give rise to a serious review and assume accurate inputs. This is the incentive necessary to accept as the ultimate goal, that profit is the final test of business performance. Each product will be different and will therefore dictate different items to be measured as significant with different yardsticks to measure effectiveness. As an introduction, Exhibit 29–3 lists some of the significant areas that should be constantly measured and compared to an agreed-upon yardstick.

EXHIBIT 29–3

INFORMATION OF SIGNIFICANCE
(YARDSTICKS AND MEASUREMENTS ARE APPLICABLE)

Schedule	Funding
Budget	PROFIT
Value of work performed	Quality
Contract coverage	

EXHIBIT 29–4

INFORMATION OF CONSEQUENCE

Major technical problems	Faults or failures
Engineering changes	Customer-requested changes

But the best-laid plans are limited by the unforeseen and problems do occur which threaten the way the plan is being executed.[6] Therefore, management must be prepared to collect information of consequence like that shown in Exhibit 29–4. This procedure will direct attention to reversals, limiting factors, changes in alternate solutions. Anything that is or might cause a departure from the original plan is an item of *consequence* because in this area, profit—the ultimate test of business per-

[6] See John G. McLean, "Better Reports for Better Control," *Harvard Business Review,* May–June 1957, p. 101.

formance—will be affected. Yardsticks or other performance indicators cannot be established because these items of consequence are the contingencies which were expected during the scope of event definition and because of inexperience were never defined. They are in part caused by:

Technical challenges of the job or the uncertainty associated with meeting performance specifications when the application is on the edge of the art.

Resource applications might be marginal in those tasks that are new and original undertakings because of the lack of estimating experience.

THE CONTROL ACTIVITY

The control cycle commences as soon as work along the planned program begins. In simplicity, this cycle consists of following the plan, noting the deviations, and taking corrective action. This is the point where human problems are usually born. Anyone who has observed the efforts of contributing groups participating in a common effort recognizes this period as a buck-passing, finger-pointing, and other-guy's-fault rodeo. The reasons for this attitude are rooted in the fact that this cycle is a measuring and reporting activity against the original plan. If the plan was not explicit, mutually understood, or individual doers of the work did not assume the responsibility, the utility of the control activity will be substantially reduced. During the execution of the work, the doers will declaim the plans as intentions which are not realistic, and eventually the control cycle will become a series of adjustments based upon each new experience that develops—rather than adjustments referenced to the original plan.

If, however, the plans are explicit, mutually understood, and answerability exists, then the control cycle can provide valuable actions which the doers will incorporate in their daily routine—because they will know what is expected of them and they will be anxious to demonstrate their capacity to perform.

The scope of control is greater than the check against plan. While this function is primary as well as mandatory, recognition of the extent and effectiveness of the plan, in order to merit-rate the plan itself, is a latent advantage to the formulators of the plan. In other words, the events of the control cycle can provide some checks as to how well the planners understood the locus of each planning area. It is this response that has been neglected by most control philosophers and consequently omitted by product-planning organizations. The omission of this facet of effective management control reduces the over-all activity to a finger-crossing, hope-for-the-best type of systematic process. This is indeed unfortunate when, in fact, the process can be an analytical evaluation for the planners themselves.

During product development, the predicament facing the management-oriented operating personnel resembles the navigational problem of a ship. Throughout the life of a program as well as during a voyage, a major intent is to discover where we are, where we are going, and what should be done if that is not the way we want to go. In order to rechart the remainder of a voyage, you must know where you are presently and the forces that caused the deviations from the plan. It follows that the first function is:

Measurement

How much should have been done during this period?
What is the status of the program today (i.e. what in fact was done)?
What is changing?
What are the explanations?

The point to be made here is that all operating personnel must know *in advance* what it is that they are to accomplish during a specified period and this implies that a plan existed. The key to success in this phase is incremental breakouts of the total plan in order to provide periodic measurements. The hallmark of achievement is the willingness and participation of operating personnel to quantify the period by measuring the progress and comparing this progress with the standard or yardstick that was established.

The evaluation of achievement is an obligation of the plan formulators. The analytical appraisal that is possible makes direct reference to the decisions that were made during the organization phase of the planning period. Such questions as, Was that which was needed enough? and Are the measures adequate? provide the basis for growth and experience to those concerned with the planning function.

A continuing but distinct task of the control activity is the analyzation phase which interprets the measurements that were taken as follows:

Analyzation

How well is the job going?

What is it that requires management attention?

Where should rewards and penalties be made and to what extent should they be made?

Are the standards or yardsticks to measure performance still meaningful?

Does common sense indicate that this is the time for a departure from the original plan?

What are the downstream trends or impending situations?

Although these questions are easy reading and glittering with dynamism, conscientious attention to the answers that are demanded requires a disciplined attentive attitude. In many cases the reward for such an effort is a lesson and experience in humility because the product will be negative, ego-breaking, and worst of all, pessimistic. However, the ability to look ahead, and make value judgments about timing a departure from the plan for the benefit of the product development, can be the restoring factor of optimism for the future.

Equally important benefits of this process are the reflections which should be made by program formulators. The opinions reached by the analyzers have a direct bearing on the judgments that were made during the event-sequencing of the planning activity:

Were the correct alternatives chosen?

Of the uncertainties that were predicted, are we reducing the unknowns to manageable tasks? And finally,

What are the implications for future planning efforts, of the departures that have been taken?

Finally, we come to that so-much-talked-about but so-little-understood pièce de résistance—the decision-making process. Very often writers and philosophers on the management information system bent have implied that status information was sufficient for business decisions. Nothing could be farther from reality. The fact is that decision-making is not an act but rather an environment which consists of not only the *status information* of the plan but *intelligence information*, which might include knowledge of the environment external to the product being developed, and *policy information,* which might limit the choices that a decision-maker has.

It is within this total environment that the decision-making process exists and, although timing is important, it is an arduous if not an impossible thing to stipulate. Basically, two types of decisions are made: The first is to continue to collect information and the second is to act. In the first instance—the reluctance to make a decision might be couched in the excuse of a desire for better status information. In reality, the constraints might be the result of intelligence information or policy information. If on the other hand, the selection of a decision is imminent because a specific incident has been churned through the control activity, then the attitudes of the decision process must be:

Decision Process

What is the next step?
Why is action required?
What action will be taken and with what resources?

The decision phase, by nature, will be the "agonizing reappraisal" of the goals that were outlined in the initial planning phases. Consequently, this phase is a management obligation which reflects the continuity of management interest and support in the project. A result of this management action will be the communication and reinforcement of management needs to the operating personnel. Attention will be focused on the unsatisfied or redefined needs of the program and the operating personnel will be assured of the management interest in the product that is being developed.

The purpose of this past section of the article was to show what *planning for control* can do to strengthen the management technique during new product development. The strength of this approach lies in the integration of each sequential step as well as the analytical appraisal which program formulators can use to evaluate themselves. The complete structure is represented in Exhibit 29–5.

THE MANAGEMENT ATTITUDES NECESSARY IN PLANNING FOR CONTROL

Looking at Exhibit 29–5 it would appear as though all the requirements of program implementations are clear. However, the root of the planning for control argument must be nourished by an understanding of what it is that makes this approach work effectively as well as what the major root-choking weeds are. Naturally, the greatest sustenance is derived from the attitude management exhibits toward the product development. Nothing can replace or come close to the effect produced by top-management support.

In the form of explanation, it is necessary to understand that support will at times require participation because *planning is predetermination* for the product, for higher profits, for the company. As such, this predetermination process must include:

Goals which support over-all accepted objectives;

Management leadership that will influence attitudes as well as stimulate motivation;

Management participation in plan formulation;

Serious reviews for accuracy;

Commitment from the operating personnel;

An appraisal of whether the information generated for status purposes will be adequate; and

An evaluation of how good the plan is.

On the other side, *control* is a state of being which serves to stimulate and maintain responsibility during product development. A healthy attitude towards control will be reflected by the behavior of operating personnel who ask themselves: In terms of what is happening, how should we adjust our original plans to meet the project objectives ahead of us?

EXHIBIT 29–5

THE STRUCTURE OF A PLANNING FOR CONTROL SYSTEM

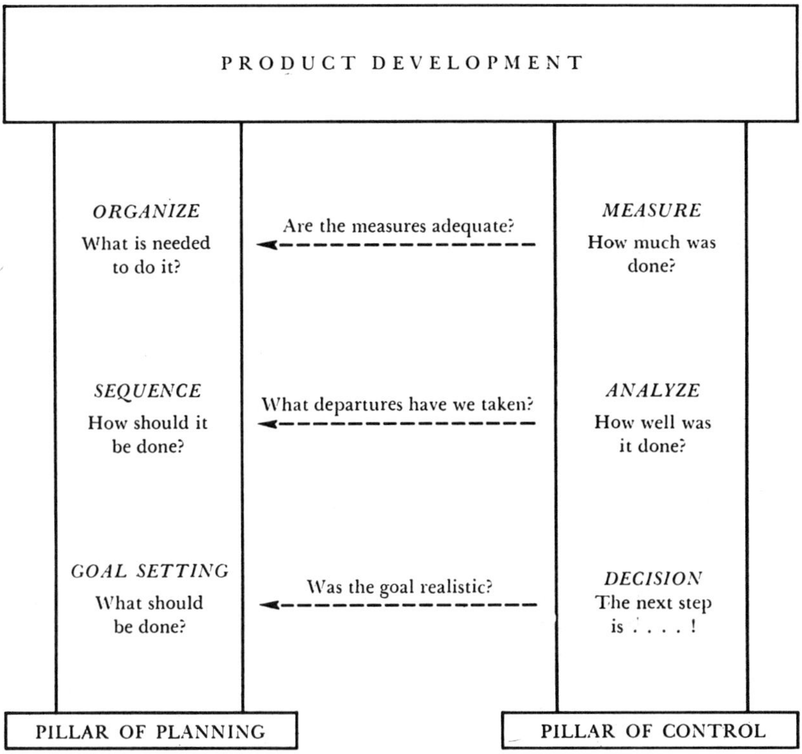

The control exercise is devoted to the task of following the plan and correcting deviations from the plan. It is here that human problems are born but they can be subdued provided the intent is to generate realistic, explicit, and mutually agreed-to plans. Naturally too much procedure and not enough control activity can cause the cycle to break down. It is for this reason that the control activity content must provide:

Quick check-ups;
Signals for significant departures from exceptions;
A requirement for explanation of noted deviations;
Answerability from the responsible person to stop buck-passing;
A system of rewards and penalties the extent of which depend upon the circumstances;
Regular check-ups; and
The ability to take departures from the plan when common sense indicates it.

The preceding paragraphs are generalities which, when understood, provide a basis for top-management thought and action toward a *planning for control* environment throughout the company. The items that have been mentioned in subparagraphs are check points that can be used to evaluate any *planning for control* system that is tailored for a particular product-development effort.

RECOGNIZING NOISE IN THE SYSTEM

It is generally much easier to discuss all the things that should be done and, in fact, these are the items that have, in part, been discussed throughout the article. An equally important if not greater challenge is to foresee the obstacles or recognize the situations that will destroy the framework and provide reams of data which are of little utility to management. Listed below are the situations that are common to product-planning. If recognized at the outset of a project, they can be managed by confinement, reduction, or elimination.

1. The job of planning is never approached with any depth because it requires determination, cooperation from many, sacrifices from all, and compromises among the participants.
2. The goals don't relate to company objectives. For example, if we state that we are in the electronics business rather than the type of product sold, type of selling done, growth expected of this product, and so on, the significance of each product development will be confused in a multiproduct plant and the search will always be toward glamour areas.
3. Staff control vs. line control. Either the planning control system is so complicated that staff people have to run it or the line people feel that the planning did not consider them. The conclusion is disaster in either case because the information system will not resemble the work that is being done.
4. The planning control system becomes a club instead of a tool. This is a natural consequence of having yardsticks which are unrealistic to the doers or generating reports that are not useful at the working level.
5. Project budgets get mixed with responsibility budgets. Without accountability assigned, no one feels identified with deviations from the plan and energy to correct the situation is as difficult to muster as finding out who is responsible when the buck is being passed.
6. Failure to distinguish level of effort. Is what is being done expected, above average, or below average? Without this minimum yardstick, rewards and punishments for performance are impossible.
7. The dilemma of dealing with deviations. Management must not only recognize deviations, but in fact see to it that action to correct

deviations is taken. The techniques are varied and individual but they can be classified as explanation, instruction, decision, argument, and discipline.

The ability to recognize these situations and deal with them expeditiously is a mark of the professional manager. It is indeed a challenge to filter out these kinds of noise. The result of such effort provides a crisp attitude toward the job of product development because operating personnel are not tempted to generate excuses which can be substantiated by organizational idiosyncrasies.

CONCLUSION

When referring to our civilization, historians will no doubt point out the growth of the multiproduct companies that characterize our industrial scene. No matter how they describe it, we know today that the management problem associated with multiproduct development programs is complex. Management control is the technique that must be applied to product development. To be effective, it must be accepted through all levels of the company but especially, the operating personnel must accept control as their obligation. Consequently, the objective for effective product development is *planning for control.*

Management implementation of a planning-for-control system is a task that requires perseverance and self-discipline. However, these attributes are necessary if the concept of *planning for control* is to be acknowledged by the product-development participants. Diligence on the part of management during the implementation phase requires an understanding of the steps involved as well as a base of experience to accept the predetermination obligations of the planning period. Finally management must accept the professional challenge to recognize the organizational idiosyncrasies and correct them as a symbol to operating personnel, of the commitment to *planning for control.* The results of this kind of thinking will be a handsome payoff of a management information system which will record trends, evaluate current situation, and direct attention to those areas that are producing trouble.

The framework proposed segregates the planning activity from the control activity. The strength of this approach lies in the integration of each sequential step as well as the analytical appraisal which program formulators can use to evaluate themselves. Teamwork is fostered by the fact that both top management and operating personnel must interact during the process. For example, goal determination lies within the realm of top management while sequencing the events is an operating personnel obligation and the organization is a joint responsibility. It is in this last area that we set what shall be measured and what the yardsticks of measurement should be. If the measurement is incorporated in the daily routine of the operating personnel, then the planning was effective because it showed them what was expected of them, and allowed them to show their capacity to do it.

This pattern allows information to be summarized in terms of what is *significant* (i.e. yardstick and measurements are applicable) and what is of *consequence* (i.e. contingencies).

To maintain this system and display, management will be called on to make decisions that change the original goals. However, the *planning-for-control* system provides status information and in some cases this may not be enough to substantiate a departure from the original goals. Intelligence and policy information must be considered too because in some cases these factors will be overriding considerations.

The most important ingredient to a successful implementation is top-management participation. Nothing can replace or come close to the effect produced by top-management support. It is precisely this participation that keeps the cycle alive, maintains direction, and allows operating people something to measure themselves against. However, those elements of top management that concern themselves with objective and goal-setting for the company in the business environment, must also evaluate themselves during the control cycle in relation to the original criteria established in the planning phases.

The author describes specific mathematical tools available to the marketing executive, and then develops five mathematical models useful in solving typical marketing problems.

30

THE USE OF MATHEMATICAL MODELS IN MARKETING

Philip Kotler

The modern marketing man has to be multilingual, for he obtains his material from many disciplines.

He must be able to converse with *economists* about marginal analysis, elasticity, and diminishing returns; with *psychologists* about projective techniques, latent needs, and nonrational behavior; with *sociologists* about acculturation, social norms, and subcultures; and with *statisticians* about standard error, least squares, and correlation.

Now another language—that of higher mathematics—is needed in marketing. Many marketing men are uncomfortable about this. They do not look askance at mathematical concepts, but they are a bit anxious because of a "language barrier." Fortunately, however, the language barrier is not insurmountable. Linear programing, waiting-line theory, and the like are simply unfamiliar names for some significant ideas.

The purpose of this article is to reduce some of the "mysticism" of the new mathematics by defining its vocabulary and illustrating its central ideas in the context of marketing.

DECISION MAKING

Quantitative analysis is not alien to the field of marketing. For many decades marketing research departments have conducted consumer sur-

Reprinted from *Journal of Marketing,* Vol. 27, No. 4, October 1963, pp. 31–41, by permission of the publisher, The American Marketing Association.

veys, prepared sales forecasts, and analyzed sales reports. A few practitioners have even used higher mathematics for complex problem-solving in marketing. But until recently the mathematical "sophistication" underlying the typical research project could be found between the covers of a textbook in elementary statistics. And much of the research has amounted to routine information gathering.

Today the emphasis is changing. The focus of research is on *decision making,* and not fact gathering for its own sake. The belief is spreading that models can be built which identify and relate the key factors in a problem situation, and which offer explicit directions for decision making.

Today's marketing executive is asked to distinguish carefully between alternative strategies in making a major decision. Each strategy will lead to one of several outcomes, depending in part upon events beyond the firm's control; and the possible outcomes for each strategy must somehow be weighed, to achieve an estimated value for that strategy. The values of the various strategies must be compared, and the executive must then attempt to select the strategy promising the highest value or payoff.[1]

THE TOOLS OF MATHEMATICS

The mathematician carries in his attaché case four basic tools, plus a *potpourri* of special models. His basic tools are *matrix algebra, calculus, probability theory,* and *simulation.*

Matrix Algebra

One tool is *matrix algebra,* by which large arrays of numbers in the form of *vectors* and *matrices* can be manipulated by rules similar to those found in ordinary algebra.

As a miniature example, suppose (6,000, 3,200, 5,000) is a *vector* (for our purposes, a single array of numbers) whose component numbers represent sales targets in three geographical markets—(say) East, West, and South respectively. Past records show that on the average it takes ½ hour of sales effort and $1 of advertising expenditure to produce a sale in the first market; ¼ hour of sales effort and $2 of advertising expenditure to produce a sale in the second market; and ⅕ hour of sales effort and $3 of advertising expenditure to produce a sale in the third market. This information can be summarized in a *matrix* (for our purposes a rectangular array of numbers):

[1] Two excellent articles illustrating this approach are Robert D. Buzzell and Charles C. Slater, "Decision Theory and Marketing Management," *Journal of Marketing,* Vol. 27 (July 1962), pp. 7–16; and Paul E. Green, "Bayesian Decision Theory in Pricing Strategy," *Journal of Marketing,* Vol. 28 (January 1963), pp. 5–14.

$$
\begin{array}{lcc}
 & \textit{Sales effort (in hours)} & \textit{Advertising expenditure (in dollars)} \\
\text{East} & \frac{1}{2} & \$1 \\
\text{West} & \frac{1}{4} & \$2 \\
\text{South} & \frac{1}{5} & \$3
\end{array}
$$

To find the total hours of sales effort and dollars of advertising expenditure required to achieve the geographical sales targets, we multiply the vector by the matrix:

$$(6{,}000,\ 3{,}200,\ 5{,}000) \begin{pmatrix} \frac{1}{2} & 1 \\ \frac{1}{4} & 2 \\ \frac{1}{5} & 3 \end{pmatrix}$$

For example, we can call the vector A and the matrix B, and we then proceed to find their product, that is, $A \cdot B$.

There are definite rules for the multiplication of a vector by a matrix (and for that matter, for the multiplication of two vectors or two matrices, etc.). In the example above, the product $A \cdot B$ is $(6{,}000 \times \frac{1}{2} + 3{,}200 \times \frac{1}{4} + 5{,}000 \times \frac{1}{5},\ 6{,}000 \times 1 + 3{,}200 \times 2 + 5{,}000 \times 3)$ or, collecting terms, (4,800, \$27,400). This new vector is the solution; and it means that the company must have enough salesmen to make 4,800 hours of calls, and also an advertising budget of at least \$27,400.

Matrix algebra is essentially a symbolic shorthand for the manipulation of large arrays of data. It affords the advantage of economy in quantitative expression.

Calculus

The second tool which the mathematician brings to marketing is *calculus.* Using *differential calculus,* the mathematician can, among other things, determine what combination of inputs will maximize some output.

A marketing mix is a combination of inputs, such as price and advertising. Suppose that it were possible experimentally to vary the price input and the advertising input while controlling other factors. The effect of these variations on sales could then be recorded, and the profit implied by each level of sales estimated.

The task is to find an equation which best describes how profit varies with variations in price and advertising. A form for such an equation as well as a method of estimating the coefficients (usually "least squares" regression) must be decided upon. Suppose the following equation is found to give a good fit to the data:

$$I = 320 - 2P^2 - 3P + 4\,PA - 7A^2 + 60A$$

On the left side of the equation is profit (represented by I). Profit is treated here as the *dependent variable,* because its value is conceived to depend upon the values taken on by variables listed on the right side of the equation. These *independent variables* are price (P) and advertising (A). The particular numbers in the equation are constants and coefficients, which are estimated by an appropriate statistical method.

If such an equation can be found, what unique mix of price and advertising would maximize profit? The nonmathematician can use trial and error to arrive at the profit-maximizing mix, but this will be frustrating and time consuming. The mathematician can determine this mix in a very short time by using calculus. Although this is not the place to explain the procedure, his calculations will show that the optimum price is $4.95, and the optimum advertising budget is $5.7 (in some appropriate unit).

The chief contribution of differential calculus to marketing is to enable a direct determination of optimal action where differentiable functions are involved. In fact, *marginal analysis* which is applied by economists to all kinds of decision situations—such as determination of the best price, or the number of salesmen—actually is a gross application of differential calculus.

Integral calculus, representing the other branch of calculus, is not used to find the maximum and minimum values of a function, but rather the *area* under a function, among other things. An area can have a meaningful marketing interpretation.

Suppose on a particular billing date that a department store ranks all of its charge accounts by dollar size. These charge accounts range from $0 to $198. The frequency distribution of all the accounts by dollar size is shown in Figure 30–1. The shaded area under the curve between $50 and $150 represents the percentage of all accounts falling in this range. How can this area be measured? It does not have the simplicity of a rectangle, triangle, or circle. This area, or other areas under the curve, can be readily measured through integral calculus, provided that the frequency distribution can be represented by a mathematical equation with certain properties.

Probability Theory

The third important tool of the mathematician for use in marketing is *probability theory.*

How should the marketing man handle the uncertainty that surrounds legislation, consumer intentions, and competitors' acts? He can try to list all the possible consequences of a business move, along with their probabilities. The probabilities can be based on the frequency distribution of past outcomes for similar business moves, or on personal

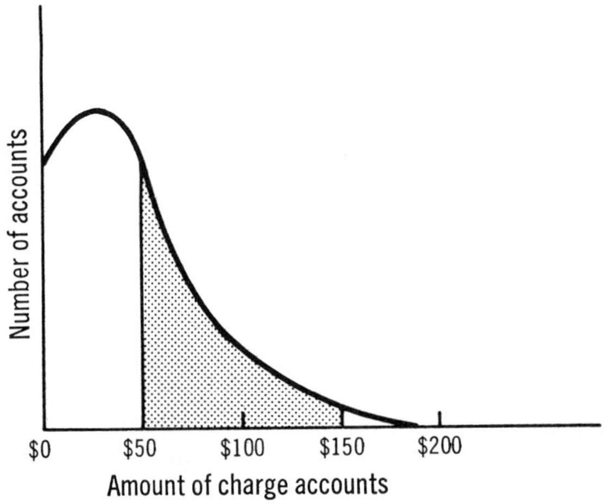

Figure 30–1. Frequency distribution of charge accounts

judgment. The assigned probability numbers must satisfy only two requirements:

1. The probability that a particular consequence will occur is given numerically by some number between 0 and 1 inclusive.
2. The sum of the probabilities of all possible consequences is 1.

Probability numbers can serve as "weights" for appraising various money (or utility) outcomes. Suppose a manufacturer has developed a new product and must hire and train a special sales force to sell it. The number of salesmen to hire will depend upon his estimate of market potential, among other things.

Suppose that he is uncertain whether there is a potential of 2,000, 3,000, or 4,000 units, and he is trying to decide whether to hire 60 or 70 salesmen. Too few salesmen will mean that some potential sales are never realized, and too many salesmen will mean that excess selling costs are incurred. It would help to estimate the profits under different assumptions as to market potential and sales-force size. The estimates will depend upon an appropriate set of assumptions concerning product price, production costs, the effect of the number of salesmen on sales, and selling costs. A hypothetical set of profit estimates is shown in Table 30–1.

If market potential is 2,000 units, the manufacturer will lose \$20,000 with 60 salesmen and \$40,000 with 70 salesmen. If market potential is 3,000 units, the manufacturer will earn \$50,000 with 60 salesmen, and \$40,000 with 70 salesmen. Finally, if market potential is 4,000 units, he will earn still larger profits. In this last case, the profit is higher with 70 salesmen because 60 salesmen are inadequate to tap the full potential.

TABLE 30–1
ESTIMATED PROFITS FOR DIFFERENT COMBINATIONS OF MARKET POTENTIAL AND SALES-FORCE SIZE

		Market potential		
		2,000 units	3,000 units	4,000 units
Decision ?	60	–$20,000	$50,000	$60,000
	70	–$40,000	$40,000	$70,000

Should the manufacturer hire 60 or 70 salesmen? By hiring 70, he has the opportunity to gain more but also to lose more. His decision will depend upon the personal probabilities he assigns to the three estimates of market potential. Suppose he quantifies his beliefs as follows: there is a .2 probability that the market potential is 2,000 units, a .3 probability that it is 3,000 units, and a .5 probability that it is 4,000 units. If this were a game of chance which the manufacturer could play repeatedly facing the same payoffs and the same probabilities, and if he had adequate funds, it would be easy to define a good decision rule: choose the act which has the highest *expected monetary value* (EMV). EMV is a weighted average of the alternative profit consequences of an act, the weights being the probabilities assigned to the alternatives. For the example we have:

$$\text{EMV (60)} = -\$20{,}000 \times .2 + \$50{,}000 \times .3 + \$60{,}000 \times .5 = \$41{,}000$$
$$\text{EMV (70)} = -\$40{,}000 \times .2 + \$40{,}000 \times .3 + \$70{,}000 \times .5 = \$39{,}000$$

The results present an interesting paradox. The manufacturer is optimistic about the market potential, and yet EMV is higher with 60 salesmen. His optimism is not quite strong enough.

The use of EMV as a decision criterion in a once-only decision is generally acceptable, if the best consequence is not too great nor the worst consequence too bad. Were the money stakes unusually high for the decision maker, it would be necessary to employ a utility index instead of a money index. This utility index can be constructed from preferences expressed by the decision maker between given sums of money and certain gambles. Instead of the maximization of EMV, the decision criterion would be the maximization of expected utility.[2]

Simulation

The great majority of marketing problems probably will remain intractable to ordinary mathematical solution. For example, the correct

[2] Robert Schlaifer, *Probability and Statistics for Business Decisions* (New York: McGraw-Hill Book Company, 1959), Chapter 2.

price to charge depends upon such elements as the future sales outlook, the possible reactions of competitors, the time lags of these reactions, the intended level of advertising support, ad infinitum. A complex phenomenon is characterized by feedbacks, distributed lags, uncommon probability distributions, and other features which render exact mathematical solutions difficult or impossible. But mathematicians are undaunted: "When all else fails, *simulate*!"

A simulation is essentially a hypothetical testing, as opposed to a field testing, of the consequences of alternative business decisions. The first step is the construction of a model which spells out how the key variables interact in the situation. The second step is the testing of alternative decisions on the model. Simulations can range from simple paper-and-pencil exercises to full scale computer analyses. The purpose is to speculate on the consequences of changing a price, or dropping small distributors, or introducing a new pattern of trade deals, before risking the irrevocable judgment of the marketplace.

The model used in the simulation may be *exact* or *probabilistic.* In an exact model, the effect of one variable upon another is known with certainty. In a probabilistic model, one of several effects might take place, and we presume to know only their respective probabilities.

Retail inventory control can be used to illustrate a probabilistic model. The problem is to adopt purchasing rules which will balance inventory losses against sales losses. Suppose a supermarket wishes to reconsider its present purchasing policy with respect to one product—for example, eggnog. The daily demand for eggnog fluctuates, and each day of the week has its own demand distribution. Suppose that on a sample of past Tuesdays the number of quarts demanded has varied between 0 and 4, according to the probabilities shown in Table 30–2.

The third column of Table 30–2 consists of an allocation of 100 2-digit numbers (between 00 and 99) to all possible events in propor-

TABLE 30–2
PROBABILITY DISTRIBUTION OF DEMAND FOR EGGNOG ON TUESDAYS

Number of quarts demanded	*Probability*	*Monte Carlo numbers*
0	.07	00-06
1	.20	07-26
2	.22	27-48
3	.33	49-81
4	.18	82-99
	1.00	

tion to their probabilities. Thus, on 7% of the Tuesdays no eggnog will be demanded; so we assign 7 different 2-digit numbers (00 to 06 inclusive) to this event. Likewise, we assign 20 different 2-digit numbers (07 –26 inclusive) to the event of 1 quart being demanded, etc.

We now go to a table of *random* digits. The digits are listed in this table in no apparent pattern. The fact is that each of the digits had the same chance of appearing on each trial. While there is no pattern, we know that all the digits will be approximately *equally* represented in a large sample of such digits.

We draw 2 digits at a time. If the first 2-digit number is 43, this can be looked up in the Monte Carlo column in Table 30–2 and would be interpreted as 2 quarts. In other words, on this Tuesday the demand at the supermarket is 2 quarts. By repeatedly drawing 2-digit random numbers, we can generate a characteristic picture of demand for a succession of Tuesdays.

We can use a different demand distribution, based on store records, for each day of the week. Then we can make assumptions about supply, such as a delivery period every other day and a decision rule to purchase (say) 3 quarts each time. With this information, we can manually or mechanically generate daily demand-and-supply quantities to learn the likely magnitude and frequency of excess inventories and shortages. We compare the average losses incurred under different purchasing rules and choose the loss-minimizing rule.

The probabilistic feature provides realism and has given rise to the name of *Monte Carlo* simulation. In the more complex simulations, a computer is used to produce the random numbers, interpret the events, make the necessary computations, and summarize the results. Computer simulation has been conducted on such marketing problems as media selection; department-store ordering and pricing; site location for retail outlets; and customer facility planning in retail outlets.

THE MAJOR MODELS

The tools of matrix algebra, calculus, probability theory, and simulation are fundamental in setting up and solving many of the models which have been developed to aid marketing executives in decision making. Some of these models are designed for *normative decision making,* and others for the *analysis of a process.* Most of them originated out of operations research activities.

The following models appear particularly "ripe" for marketing application:

1. Allocation models
2. Competitive strategy models

3. Brand-switching models
4. Waiting-line models
5. Critical-path scheduling models.

Some of the examples below may seem too simple, if not contrived. However, the examples are illustrative only. Model building is not just a "fun" exercise for those who like to solve puzzles, but can be a serious attack on decision making in business.

Actually the final model for a real decision problem can be quite elaborate and represent a "hooking together" of several elementary models and techniques.

1. Allocation Models

The economic aspect of business decision making is the "allocation of scarce resources to competing ends." In marketing, the scarce resources may be salesmen who are too few to make all the desirable contacts, or advertising dollars which are too limited to produce adequate exposure, or many other possibilities. Nevertheless, a decision must be made on how to allocate or *program* these limited resources to territories, classes of customers, and product lines.

Take, for example, the development of a media plan. The number of available media vehicles is very great. But when any particular product is considered, there are a number of constraints which severely delimit the range of media choice.

First, the advertising budget is finite. Second, the message must be directed at specific market segments (such as mothers in the case of a baby lotion); and certain media vehicles are more effective than others in reaching these segments. Third, the geographical distribution of the market segments imposes restrictions on the choice of media. Finally, the media vehicles or the advertiser, or both, may impose restrictions.

Nevertheless a large number of different media plans would satisfy all the constraints. Of these, which plan will be the most effective? An *effectiveness criterion* needs to be developed against which every feasible plan can be rated. In media selection, the criterion is the number of of the mathematical models that can be used for the discovery of an expected effective exposures, or some variant of this. *Programing* is one exposure-maximizing media plan.

As an example, a media plan is to be prepared consisting of the purchase of X_1 advertising units of medium 1 and X_2 advertising units of medium 2. Table 30–3 indicates the relevant characteristics of the two media.

TABLE 30–3

SELECTED CHARACTERISTICS OF TWO MEDIA

	Medium 1	*Medium 2*
Cost of an advertising unit	$ 2,700	$ 900
Maximum number of units	12	40
Minimum number of units	0	9
Total number of effective exposures per unit	720,000	360,000
Number of effective exposures in region 1 per unit	60,000	100,000
Number of effective exposure in region 2 per unit	660,000	260,000
Number of exposures to single women per unit	100,000	80,000
Number of exposures to college educated women per unit	400,000	40,000

The following constraints are made explicit in a discussion between the media planner and the advertiser:

1. The total advertising budget is $39,600.
2. At least 1,800,000 exposures are to be achieved in region 1, and 7,280,000 in region 2.
3. No more than 2,400,000 exposures are to take place among single women.
4. At least 2,000,000 exposures are to take place among college educated women.

The problem is to find the number of issues of the two media which would maximize the total number of effective exposures subject to the various constraints. A mathematical statement of the problem is given in Table 30–4.

Each constraint has been expressed as a mathematical inequality.

TABLE 30–4

MATHEMATICAL STATEMENT OF MEDIA PROBLEM

Maximize		$720{,}000X_1 + 360{,}000X_2$	
subject to	1	$2{,}700X_1 + 900X_2 \leq 39{,}000$	budget constraint
	2	$X_1 \leq 12$	individual medium usage constraints
	3	$X_2 \leq 40$	
	4	$X_1 \geq 0$	
	5	$X_2 \geq 9$	
	6	$60{,}000X_1 + 100{,}000X_2 \geq 1{,}800{,}000$	regional constraints
	7	$660{,}000X_1 + 260{,}000X_2 \geq 7{,}280{,}000$	
	8	$100{,}000X_1 + 80{,}000X_2 \leq 2{,}400{,}000$	customer characteristics constraints
	9	$400{,}000X_1 + 40{,}000X_2 \geq 2{,}000{,}000$	

For example, the budget constraint reads: The number of advertisements purchased in medium 1 (X_1) times their unit cost ($2,700), plus the number purchased in medium 2 (X_2) times their unit cost ($900), must be less than or equal to the budget of $39,600.

The second constraint reads: The number of advertisements placed in medium 1 must not exceed 12. The other inequalities are similarly interpreted.

The constraints have the effect of eliminating most combinations of X_1 and X_2 but there are still a large number of remaining combinations which would satisfy all the inequalities. But only one of these (usually) will also maximize the total number of effective exposures. Mathematical programing is the technique for finding the best solution.

In this simple case, the inequalities could be drawn on graph paper; and this would help to delimit the set of media plans (points) which would satisfy all of the constraints. Then there is a procedure for locating the best plan, the details of which are beyond the scope of this article.

The best plan calls for 8 advertisements in medium 1, and 20 advertisements in medium 2. This plan will cost exactly $39,600 and yield 12,960,000 exposures.

There are several types of mathematical programing. *Linear programing* implies that the criterion and the constraints in the problem can be represented by straight-line segments. The essence of a straight line is that the slope is constant, which means that the ratio of a change in one variable to a change in the other is constant. For example, a linear cost function means that the cost of an additional unit is constant; and a linear exposure function means that the effect of an additional advertising exposure is constant. In other words, diminishing or increasing returns are ruled out in strictly linear models.

Since the assumption of constant marginal returns and costs is patently false in many situations, what explains the popularity of *linear programing models?* The answer is largely that the linear assumption is the easiest to work with and solve. As an additional consideration, many important functions are linear or nearly linear over much of their range.

A number of techniques are available for solving a linear programing problem, once it has been expressed mathematically. *Graphical solutions* are possible when the number of variables is not more than three. Alternatively, the *simplex algorithm* is an all-purpose method. The word "simplex" has nothing to do with "simple"; the *simplex* is a well-defined mathematical concept which has a geometric interpretation. An *algorithm* is a systematic method for testing various solutions; it guarantees that each successive solution will represent an improvement until the best solution is reached.

The term *non-linear programing* is reserved for a problem formulation where either some constraint(s) or the effectiveness criterion, or both, are not linear. One example is *quadratic programing,* which was a second-degree curve for some of the constraints or effectiveness criterion, or both.

Integer programing is a variant so named because the optimal solution is constrained to consist of whole numbers. For example, suppose X_1 represents how many salesmen should be hired. If the answer is *not* constrained to be an integer, it could be a mixed decimal such as 9.4. What does it mean to hire 9.4 salesmen? Should the answer be "rounded" to 9 salesmen or 10 salesmen? The solution is not obvious, and the decision may involve a difference of many thousands of dollars. Integer programing is a way of avoiding the ambiguities of fractional answers.

Dynamic programing, the most complicated of the programing variants, is applied to problems where a series of consecutive *interdependent* decisions have to be made. Purchasing decisions, for example, must be made throughout the year; and today's decision must be made in terms of what it implies for the decision choices in the next period, which in turn will affect the decision choices in the following period, and so on.

In summary, a programing model is applied to problems where there seem to be many different ways to allocate resources. Constraints (usually in the form of mathematical inequalities) are introduced to reduce the number of admissible solutions. Then a search is made for that solution among the feasible set which is optimal in term of some effectiveness criterion. The programing model holds great promise for aiding in the solution of such important marketing problems as media selection; allocation of sales force; determination of the best product line in terms of a firm's resource base; site location, and selection of channels of distribution.

There are some specialized versions of the programing model which are useful in a marketing context. One of these is the *transportation model,* which defines the existence of several *origins* (such as warehouses) and *destinations* (such as retail stores), and the unit cost of shipping from every origin to every destination. Furthermore, the amount of goods available for shipment from each warehouse and the amount of goods ordered by each retail store are specified. Under the given constraints, the problem is to find which warehouses should ship their supplies to which stores, in order to minimize total transportation costs.

A sample problem is shown in Table 30–5—try to find the least-cost shipping allocation by trial and error. Mathematical analysis would show that there is a shipment allocation which would cost only $5,800. It is possible to convert this problem into a standard linear programing problem and then solve it by the simplex method. Alternatively, special techniques have been developed to solve the problem directly, using the format in Table 30–5.

TABLE 30–5
UNIT SHIPPING COSTS FROM VARIOUS WAREHOUSES TO VARIOUS STORES

Warehouse	Store 1	Store 2	Store 3	Warehouse availabilities
A	$5	$3	$6	300
B	$2	$9	$4	200
C	$3	$7	$8	600
D	$6	$1	$4	500
Store requirements	200	1,000	400	1,600

The transportation model has been used for a number of years in some large companies to develop shipping schedules. It has a useful variant, called the *assignment model,* with promising applications to other problems than transportation. In the assignment model, the number of origins *equal* the number of destinations; and each origin is to be associated with *only one* destination.

As an example, suppose 4 salesmen are to be *assigned* to 4 territories. The salesmen have differing skills, and the territories are in different stages of development. The sales manager makes an estimate of the expected annual sales that would result from each man being assigned to each territory. This information is summarized in Table 30–6.

TABLE 30–6
ESTIMATED ANNUAL SALES FROM THE ASSIGNMENT OF DIFFERENT SALESMEN TO DIFFERENT TERRITORIES

Salesman	Territory 1	Territory 2	Territory 3	Territory 4
A	$90,000	$57,000	$82,000	$45,000
B	$73,000	$75,000	$40,000	$51,000
C	$60,000	$30,000	$51,000	$75,000
D	$92,000	$95,000	$75,000	$70,000

There are 24 (4x3x2x1) different possible assignments. Because this is a small-scale example it is not difficult to arrive at the total sales maximizing assignment by trial and error—A3; B1; C4; D2; total sales, $325.

In more complex examples, the number of possible solutions increases factorially, and a mathematical analysis is necessary. Incidentally, the model could be used for assignment of salesmen to other than territories, to different company products, or to different types of customers, for example.

Another problem is known as the *"traveling-salesman" problem.* Although not involving allocation, it has certain similarities to an assignment problem. A salesman must make calls in *n* cities. This means that there are *n* factorial possible routes. One of these routes would minimize the total travel *cost;* and another route (possibly the same) would minimize the total travel *time.* The problem is to find the "best" route in terms of whichever is the stated objective. To date, general solutions are lacking, but certain important theorems have been discovered, such as the fact that the best route never involves any crossing of paths; and mathematical solutions are available where special simplifying assumptions are made. A simulation approach also can be used to search for a reasonable solution.

2. Competitive Strategy Models

Profit outcomes are not only a function of the decision of a firm, but of this decision in conjunction with the decisions made by competitors. A marketing decision must be based on an estimate of what competitors are likely to do, even though their intentions may not be known in advance.

Game theory is the name given to the systematic investigation of rational decision making in the context of uncertainty concerning the moves of competitors. As an example, suppose Row and Column are the managers of two competing supermarkets. Every week, each of the managers chooses some item to promote as the "Special of the Week." Neither manager knows in advance what the other is going to feature. However, each can estimate the approximate profit that would result from every pair of possible choices. Suppose Row estimates the payoffs shown in Table 30–7.

TABLE 30–7
PAYOFFS RESULTING FROM VARIOUS STRATEGY COMBINATIONS

Row	*Column*	
	Flour	Coffee
Sugar	4	1
Tea	6	–2

The table is interpreted as follows. If Row featured sugar and his competitor featured flour, Row would gain 4 (say in hundreds of dollars); that is, more of the marginal customers will "flow" to his store, and the profit derived from this extra trade is estimated as 4. And Column will lose 4.

If Row featured sugar and his competitor featured coffee, Row would gain only 1 on Column. If Row featured tea and his competitor featured flour, then Row would gain 6. However, if Row featured tea and Column featured coffee, Row would lose 2.

The problem is whether Row should adopt one item and feature it week after week (a *pure strategy*), or choose an item randomly each week according to a constant though not necessarily equal set of probabilities (a *mixed strategy*).

If Row is to use a pure strategy, should it be sugar or tea? According to one doctrine, he should make the move which would minimize his maximum possible loss (the *minimax rule*). Tea would lead both to the largest possible gain and the largest possible loss, whereas sugar at least guarantees to Row a small but steady gain of 1.

Furthermore, Column can minimize his maximum loss by featuring coffee, and he undoubtedly will. This is a stalemated game where, so long as the same payoffs persist, Row will feature sugar and Column will feature coffee; and it would not be to either's advantage to make a surprise change. On the other hand, there are other payoff matrices which possess no such equilibrium solution, and where a mixed random strategy could be employed to advantage.

The Row-and-Column example illustrates one of the simplest types of games: *a 2-person, zero-sum game*. Only two players are involved, and they transfer a fixed sum of money between each other. The term "zero-sum" is used because in each play the sum of one player's gain (positive) and the other player's loss (negative) is zero.

More interesting, but at the same time more mathematically difficult, are the *3-or-more person,. non-zero-sum games*. The 3-or-more-person feature allows the formation of coalitions where certain players can gain more by not acting independently. The non-zero-sum feature refers to the fact that competitive actions may expand the size of the market (that is, the total stakes) in addition to shifting market shares.

Game models have been designed for a variety of military and political situations, but some have interesting marketing possibilities. One is a game of timing involving two duelists (competitors) who at a signal are to begin approaching each other at some constant uniform rate. Each has only one available bullet (a new product) and is free to fire it whenever he wishes, with the knowledge that his chance of hitting the opponent improves as the distance narrows. When should the duelist fire?

Another game involves distributing an army over several battlefields, with the knowledge that each battlefield is "won" by the side which has disposed more troops in that battlefield. How should an army distribute its troops (or a company distribute its salesmen) in this situation?

Another game, "gambler's ruin," involves two competitors with different initial endowments of capital. A coin is tossed repeatedly with a probability p that competitor A will win and a probability $1\text{-}p$ that competitor B will win. The game ends when the capital of one competitor is exhausted. Given specific data, it is possible to estimate such things as the probability of "ruin" for each gambler, and the likely duration of the game.

Although to date game models do not seem to have much predictive power, they do suggest a useful analytical approach to such competitive problems as pricing, sales-force allocation, and advertising outlays. They may help to clarify the strategic implications of such moves as surprise, threat, and coalition.[3]

Finally, game theory should be distinguished from *operational gaming*. The latter term describes the modeling of a game around a realistic situation, where the participants actually make decisions (often in teams), and where the results of their interacting decisions are reported and become the data inputs for the next round of decisions. A large number of management and marketing games have been developed and used both in formal management-training programs and in research settings.[4]

3. Brand-switching Models

Marketing executives must watch their *market share* just as much as their profits. Present customers can never be taken for granted.

The attitude of marketing executives toward brand switching is quite simple: the switching-out rate must be slowed down, and the switching-in rate must be increased. The factors affecting brand choice must be analyzed, and this knowledge applied where possible in order to alter existing brand-switching rates.

Switching rates can be estimated from data showing the individual brand choices made over time by a representative panel of consumers. Suppose three brands are involved, A, B, and C. We can ask what proportion of those who bought A in the last period purchased A again, and what proportions switched to B and C. These proportions for each product can be conveniently exhibited in matrix form. Table 30–8 is a hypothetical example.

Note that each row adds up to 1.00. The first row reads: Of those who purchased brand A in the last period, 70% bought A again, 20% bought B, and 10% bought C. Thus, A retained 70% of its previous

[3] R. Duncan Luce and Howard Raiffa, *Games and Decisions* (New York: John Wiley & Sons, Inc., 1957); Martin Shubik, *Strategy and Market Structure* (New York: John Wiley & Sons, 1959).

[4] J. F. McRaith and Charles R. Goeldner, "A Survey of Marketing Games," *Journal of Marketing*, Vol. 26 (July 1962), pp. 69–72.

TABLE 30–8
HYPOTHETICAL BRAND-SWITCHING MATRIX

		To		
		A	*B*	*C*
	A	.70	.20	.10
From	B	.17	.33	.50
	C	.00	.50	.50

customers and lost 30%, with twice as many of its previous customers going to B as C. This means that B poses a more competitive threat to A than does C. The other two rows are interpreted similarly.

We have seen where A's ex-customers go. Where do new customers come from? This is revealed by column A, rather than row A. Note that A picks up 17% of the customers lost by B, and none lost by C. This is further evidence that A and B are in close competition.

The brand-switching matrix provides information about:

1. The *repeat-purchase rate* for each brand, indicated by the principal diagonal numbers. Under certain assumptions, the repeat purchase rate can be interpreted as a measure of brand loyalty.
2. The *switching-in and switching-out rate* for each brand, represented by the off-diagonal numbers.

But this is not all. If the switching rates are likely to remain constant, at least for the short run, the matrix becomes a useful tool in forecasting both the magnitude and speed of change in future market shares on the basis of the present market shares. Even where the switching rates change, if they change in a predictable way, a forecast of market shares is possible.

In this connection, important research has taken place to determine how switching rates are affected by price and promotion changes. Some of the products which have been studied in terms of brand switching rates are margarine, frozen orange juice concentrate, and instant and regular coffee.[5]

4. Waiting-line Models

Waiting appears in many marketing situations—customers wait for service, and companies wait for both customers and deliveries. Waiting is of interest because it imposes a cost. The customer who waits in a supermarket line bears a cost in terms of more desirable alternative

[5] Lester G. Telser, "The Demand for Branded Goods as Estimated from Consumer Panel Data," *Review of Economics and Statistics,* Vol. 44 (August 1962), pp. 300–324; Alfred A. Kuehn, "A Model for Budgeting Advertising," in reference 2.

uses of her time. If she regards the waiting time as excessive, she may leave and buy elsewhere, and the cost of her waiting would be shifted to the supermarket.

While waiting time imposes a cost, so does the effort to reduce waiting time. The supermarket might reduce waiting time by adding more counters or personnel, or both. The decision problem is one of balancing the cost of lost sales against the cost of additional facilities. In marginal terms, the supermarket should increase its servicing facilities up to the point where the cost of an additional facility would just overtake the profits lost due to customer impatience.

The decision problem is illustrated graphically in Figure 30–2. The higher the average waiting time in the system, the greater the cost of lost sales (2), but the lower the cost of facilities and personnel (1). The two cost curves are added vertically to derive a combined cost curve (3). The lowest point on this combined cost curve indicates the average waiting time, W_1, which will minimize combined costs. The implied investment in service facilities is F_1. The lowest point on (3) can be found graphically, or through differential calculus if appropriate cost equations can be found.

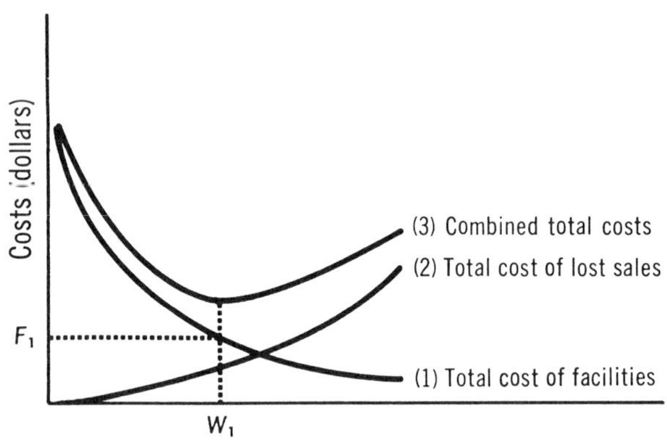

Figure 30–2. Costs as related to average waiting time

The cost of additional facilities is not difficult to measure; but it is very difficult to measure the value of lost sales which take place due to customer impatience. People vary considerably in their attitudes toward waiting; and customer impatience is also a function of the difference between anticipated and actual waiting time, and anticipated waiting varies by situations. Also, customers who feel impatient may decide not to "abandon" the store if they think that alternative stores are no better.

Waiting line theory, also called *queuing theory,* is not designed to answer how much waiting time should be built into a system. This is primarily an economic question as shown in Figure 30–2.

The theory is designed instead to handle two preliminary questions: What amount of waiting time may be expected in a particular system? How can this waiting time be altered?

The waiting time depends on four dimensions of the system:

1. *The inter-arrival time.* The time between arrivals into the system has a probability distribution which can be estimated from frequency data. The mean, standard deviation, and other characteristics of inter-arrival time can then be derived from the probability distribution.
2. *The service time.* The time between the initiating of a service and its completion can also be viewed as having a probability distribution.
3. *The number of service facilities.* The number affects the amount of waiting time.
4. *The service method.* Usually customers are serviced in the order in which they arrive (called first-in, first-out). But other methods are to give service to the most "important" customers first; to service the shortest orders first; and to service at random.

When these four dimensions are specified for a particular system, it is possible to estimate queuing characteristics, such as expected waiting time, expected queue length, and the variability of waiting time and queue length. For certain simple queuing situations, it is possible to derive these answers mathematically; but for more complicated systems, estimates can be derived through *simulation.*

If the system breeds long queues, the decision maker can simulate the effects of different hypothetical changes. In the case of a supermarket with a serious queuing problem on Saturday, four possible attacks are indicated by the dimensions. The supermarket can try to influence its customers to do their shopping on other days—this would have the effect of increasing the time between arrivals on Saturdays. Or the supermarket can decrease the service times, as by employing baggers to aid the cashiers. Or more service channels can be added. Or some of the channels can be specialized to handle smaller orders.

Most of the literature about queuing deals with facility planning for telephone exchanges, highways and toll roads, docks, and airline terminals. Yet retailing institutions such as supermarkets, filling stations, and airline ticket offices also face critical queuing problems; and marketing executives of such organizations can be expected to show increased interest in waiting line models.

5. Critical-path Scheduling Models

A technique called PERT (*Program Evaluation and Review Technique*) deals with the tactical questions of managing a complex project. As an example, consider new-product development.

Suppose that management has just finished reviewing and approving ideas for a new product. Some important tactical questions are: (1) What is the one best way to sequence the various activities which must be performed? (2) With normal departmental resources, how long will it be before the product is ready for sale? (3) What extra resources would be necessary to complete the project x weeks earlier?

Each new product will require the starting and completion of hundreds of different activities. The completion of an *activity* is called an *event*. As a simplified illustration, suppose the following six events must take place:

A. Corporate approval granted
B. Engineering and styling completed
C. Marketing analysis completed
D. Advertising campaign plans completed
E. Manufacturing preparation completed
F. Market testing completed

After these events are identified, a PERT analysis consists of three steps:

1. *Preparing a Program Network*. In what order should the above events take place? Certain events will be in a *priority* relationship, and others in a *concurrent relationship.*

The best way to see this distinction is to work backward from the terminal event. Before a market test can be started, let alone completed, two prior events must take place. The advertising campaign plans must be completed and the product must be manufactured.

But these two prior events are themselves in a concurrent relationship—the activities leading to the completion of each can be carried on concurrently. The next step would be to examine each of these events separately, to determine what events must precede each. When there are hundreds of events, the task of preparing a "network" for these events is neither easy nor free from ambiguity. But for the six events listed above, the most efficient network is fairly straightforward. By representing the events as circles and the activities as arrows connecting the circles, we would prepare the network shown in Figure 30–3.

2. *Estimating Activity Times*. The department responsible for each activity is asked to estimate the *most likely time* to complete that activity, given the department's normal resources. This estimate is supplemented by both an optimistic and pessimistic estimate, again assuming normal departmental resources. For convenience, the three estimates are connected by commas and placed along side the activity arrows. (See Figure 30–3.) As an example, the department responsible for event B

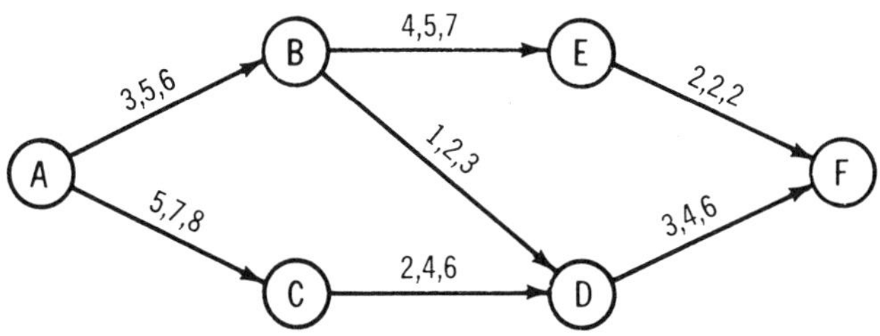

Figure 30–3. A PERT network

estimates that it will take between 3 and 6 weeks, with the most likely time being 5 weeks.

3. *Finding the Critical Path.* What is the earliest time the market test could be completed? It is necessary to trace back through all the paths which must be traveled, and the total time each will take.

There are three paths leading to the market test: ABEF, ABDF, and ACDF. On a *most likely time basis* (a different measure is used in practice), path ABEF will take $5 + 5 + 2 = 12$ weeks; path ABDF will take $5 + 2 + 4 = 11$ weeks; and path ACDF will take $7 + 4 + 4 = 15$ weeks. This last path is, therefore, considered the *critical path;* since it must be traversed and it consumes the greatest sum of time, it sets the earliest most likely time for completion.

What is equally interesting is that events along a noncritical path, such as ABEF, can take place later than estimated without necessarily delaying the 15-week estimate for the project as a whole. In other words, activities along noncritical paths have some "slack" in their required completion time.

In actual applications, the network will be extremely complicated, and its characteristics would be very time-consuming to discern through manual calculations. However, a computer can be used to estimate the likely completion date and the slack times associated with the noncritical activities. Every few weeks a new computation is made, to reflect new information affecting the completion date. Alternative decisions about shifting resources can be simulated to see what effect they would have on completion time.[6]

PERT offers a number of benefits. It forces the various participants in the planning process to make careful estimates of activity completion time; it affixes responsibility; it highlights subtle interdependencies in the planning process; it suggests where resources may be shifted to

[6] Robert W. Miller, "How to Plan and Control with PERT," *Harvard Business Review,* Vol. 40 (March–April, 1962), pp. 93–104. For an alternative model to PERT, see Borge M. Christensen and J. R. Greene, "Planning, Scheduling, and Controlling the Launching of a New Product Via CPM," in reference 1.

shorten completion times; and it quantifies an estimate of meeting scheduled dates.

PERT will undoubtedly play an increasing role as a scheduling-and-control technique in the development of new products. It will also aid in the planning of other complex marketing projects such as advertising campaigns, special promotions, new-store development, and salesmen-training programs.

IMPLICATIONS

Operations researchers have developed a number of other models to analyze special situations—such as replacement models and sequencing models—but the ones described here have the most relevance for marketers. The major purpose served by these models is to "organize our ignorance."

Yet model-building is only half the task. The other half is to find the necessary data. Sophistication in model building must be matched by further refinement in marketing research procedures.

A more quantitative approach is needed for adequate decision making in marketing. Nonetheless, there are clear limitations. Many of the known variables cannot be handled mathematically, and all the variables are never known. Intuition and experience and judgment can not be transplanted into a machine.

There is the danger also that mathematics might be used by some to lend authority to some essentially ill-conceived decisions.

Marketing men will be subject to further mathematical name-dropping in written reports and at their conventions—cybernetics, information theory, econometrics, distributed lags, Bayesian decision theory, and so forth. Although these terms stand for perfectly good ideas, they should be viewed as part of a larger plan to advance knowledge, and not just represent verbal glibness.

Following is a list of some significant collections of readings and references on model building in marketing:

Alderson, Wroe, and Shapiro, Stanley, eds., *Marketing and the Computer,* New York, Prentice-Hall, Inc., 1962.

Bass, Frank M., and others, eds., *Mathematical Methods and Models in Marketing,* Homewood, Ill., Richard D. Irwin, Inc., 1961.

Buzzell, Robert D., ed., *A Basic Bibliography on Mathematical Methods in Marketing,* Chicago, American Marketing Association, 1962.

Frank, Ronald, and others, eds., *Quantitative Techniques in Marketing,* Homewood, Ill., Richard D. Irwin, Inc., 1962.

Miller, David W., and Starr, Martin K., *Executive Decisions and Operations Research,* New York, Prentice-Hall, Inc., 1960, especially Chapter 9.

The author tells how several companies have applied the systems approach to improve marketing performance.

31

SYSTEMS APPROACH TO MARKETING

Lee Adler

More and more businessmen today recognize that corporate success is, in most cases, synonymous with marketing success and with the coming of age of a new breed of professional managers. They find it increasingly important not only to pay lip service to the marketing concept but to do something about it in terms of (a) customer orientation, rather than navel-gazing in the factory, (b) organizational revisions to implement the marketing concept, and (c) a more orderly approach to problem solving.

In an increasing number of companies we see more conscious and formal efforts to apply rational, fact-based methods for solving marketing problems, and greater recognition of the benefits these methods offer. While these benefits may be newly realized, there is nothing new about the underlying philosophy; in the parlance of military men and engineers, it is the systems approach. For, whether we like it or not, marketing is, by definition, a system, if we accept Webster's definition of system as "an assemblage of objects united by some form of regular interaction or interdependence." Certainly, the interaction of such "objects" as product, pricing, promotion, sales calls, distribution and so on fits the definition.

There is an expanding list of sophisticated applications of systems theory—and not in one but in many sectors of the marketing front. The construction of mathematical and/or logical models to describe,

Reprinted from *Harvard Business Review,* May–June 1967, pp. 105–118, by permission of the publisher.

quantify, and evaluate alternate marketing strategies and mixes is an obvious case in point. So, too, is the formulation of management information systems[1] and of marketing plans with built-in performance measurements of predetermined goals. But no less vital is the role of the systems approach in the design and sale of products and services. When J. P. Stevens Company color-harmonizes linens and bedspreads, and towels and bath mats, it is creating a product system. And when Avco Corporation sells systems management to the space exploration field, involving the marriage of many scientific disciplines as well as adherence to budgetary constraints, on-time performance, and quality control, it is creating a *service* system.

In this article I shall discuss the utilization of the systems concept in marketing in both quantitative and qualitative ways with case histories drawn from various industries. In doing so, my focus will be more managerial and philosophical than technical, and I will seek to dissipate some of the hocus-pocus, glamor, mystery, and fear which pervade the field. The systems concept is not esoteric or "science fiction" in nature (although it sometimes *sounds* that way in promotional descriptions). Its advantages are not subtle or indirect; as we shall see, they are as real and immediate as decision making itself. The limitations are also real, and these, too, will be discussed.

PROMISING APPLICATIONS

Now let us look at some examples of corporate application of the systems approach. Here we will deal with specific parts or "subsystems" of the total marketing system. Exhibit 31–1 is a schematic portrayal of these relationships.

Products and Services

The objective of the systems approach in product management is to provide a complete "offering" to the market rather than merely a product. If the purpose of business is to create a customer at a profit, then the needs of the customer must be carefully attended to; we must, in short, study what the customer is buying or wants to buy, rather than what we are trying to sell.

In the consumer products field we have forged ahead in understanding that the customer buys nutrition (not bread), beauty (not cosmetics), warmth (not fuel oil). But in industrial products this concept has been slower in gaining a foothold. Where it has gained a foothold, it expresses

[1] See, for example, Donald F. Cox and Robert E. Good, "How to Build a Marketing Information System," *Harvard Business Review*, May–June 1967, pp. 145 ff.

EXHIBIT 31–1

MARKETING SUBSYSTEMS AND THE TOTAL SYSTEM

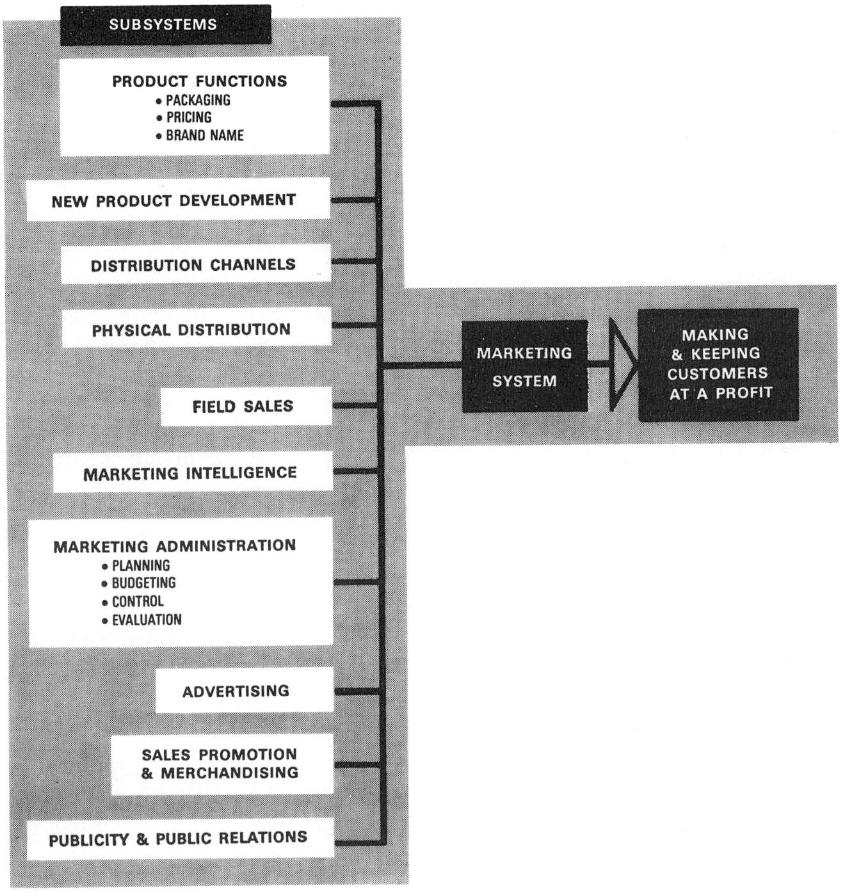

itself in two ways: the creation of a complete product system sold (1) as a unit, or (2) as a component or components which are part of a larger consumption system.

Perhaps the most eloquent testimony to the workability and value of the systems approach comes from companies that have actually used it. For a good example let us turn to the case of The Carborundum Company. This experience is especially noteworthy because it comes from industrial marketing, where, as just indicated, progress with the systems concept has generally been slow.

Birth of the concept. Founded in 1894, the company was content for many years to sell abrasives. It offered an extremely broad line of grinding wheels, coated abrasives, and abrasive grain, with a reputed capacity for 200,000 different products of varying type, grade, and formulation. But the focus was on the product.

In the mid-1950's, Carborundum perceived that the market for abrasives could be broadened considerably if—looking at abrasives through customers' eyes—it would see the product as fitting into *metal polishing, cleaning,* or *removal systems.* Now Carborundum is concerned with all aspects of abrading—the machine, the contact wheel, the workpiece, the labor cost, the overhead rate, the abrasive, and, above all, the customer's objective. In the words of Carborundum's president W. H. Wendel:

> That objective is never the abrasive per se, but rather the creation of a certain dimension, a type of finish, or a required shape, always related to a minimum cost. Since there are many variables to consider, just one can be misleading. To render maximum service, Carborundum (must offer) a complete system.[2]

Organizational overhaul. To offer such a system, management had to overhaul important parts of the organization:

1. The company needed to enhance its knowledge of the total system. As Wendel explains:

> We felt we had excellent knowledge of coated abrasive products, but that we didn't have the application and machine know-how in depth. To be really successful in the business, we had to know as much about the machine tools as we did the abrasives.[3]

To fill this need, Carborundum made three acquisitions—The Tysaman Machine Company, which builds heavy-duty snagging, billet grinding, and abrasive cut-off machines; Curtis Machine Company, a maker of belt sanders; and Pangborn Corporation, which supplied systems capability in abrasive blast cleaning and finishing.

2. The company's abrasive divisions were reorganized, and the management of them was realigned to accommodate the new philosophy and its application. The company found that *centering responsibility for the full system in one profit center* proved to be the most effective method of coordinating approaches in application engineering, choice of distribution channels, brand identification; field sales operations, and so forth. This method was particularly valuable for integrating the acquisitions into the new program.

3. An Abrasives Systems Center was established to handle development work and to solve customer problems.

[2] "Abrasive Maker's Systems Approach Opens New Markets," *Steel,* December 27, 1965, p. 38.

[3] *Ibid.*

4. Technical conferences and seminars were held to educate customers on the new developments.

5. Salesmen were trained in machine and application knowledge.

Planning. A key tool in the systems approach is planning—in particular, the use of what I like to call "total business plans." (This term emphasizes the contrast with company plans that cover only limited functions.) At Carborundum, total business plans are developed with extreme care by the operating companies and divisions. Very specific objectives are established, and then detailed action programs are outlined to achieve these objectives. The action programs extend throughout the organization, including the manufacturing and development branches of the operating unit. Management sets specific dates for the completion of action steps and defines who is responsible for them. Also, it carefully measures results against established objectives. This is done both in the financial reporting system and in various marketing committees.

Quantitative methods. Carborundum has utilized various operations research techniques, like decision tree analysis and PERT, to aid in molding plans and strategies. For example, one analysis, which concerned itself with determining the necessity for plant expansion, was based on different possible levels of success for the marketing plan. In addition, the computer has been used for inventory management, evaluation of alternate pricing strategies for systems selling, and the measurement of marketing achievements against goals.

It should be noted, though, that these quantitative techniques are management tools only and that much of the application of systems thinking to the redeployment of Carborundum's business is qualitative in nature.

Gains achieved. As a consequence of these developments, the company has opened up vast new markets. To quote Carborundum's president again:

> Customers don't want a grinding wheel, they want metal removed. . . . The U.S. and Canadian market for abrasives amounts to $700 million a year. But what companies spend on stock removal—to bore, grind, cut, shape, and finish metal—amounts to $30 billion a year.[4]

Illustrating this market expansion in the steel industry is Carborundum's commercial success with three new developments—hot grinding, an arborless wheel to speed metal removal and cut grinding costs, and high-speed conditioning of carbon steel billets. All represent con-

[4] "Carborundum Grinds at Faster Clip," *Business Week*, July 23, 1966, pp. 58, 60.

versions from nonabrasive methods. Carborundum now also finds that the close relationship with customers gives it a competitive edge, opens top customer management doors, gains entree for salesmen with prospects they had never been able to "crack" before. Perhaps the ultimate accolade is the company's report that customers even come to the organization itself, regarding it as a consultant as well as a supplier.

Profitable Innovation

The intense pressure to originate successful new products cannot be met without methodologies calculated to enhance the probabilities of profitable innovation. The systems approach has a bearing here, too. Exhibit 31–2 shows a model for "tracking" products through the many stages of ideation, development, and testing to ultimate full-scale commercialization. This diagram is in effect a larger version of the "New Product Development" box in Exhibit 31–1.

Observe that this is a logical (specifically, sequential), rather than numerical, model. While some elements of the total system (e.g., alternate distribution channels and various media mixes) can be analyzed by means of operations research techniques, the model has not been cast in mathematical terms. Rather, the flow diagram as a whole is used as a checklist to make sure "all bases are covered" and to help organize the chronological sequence of steps in new product development. It also serves as a conceptual foundation for formal PERT application, should management desire such a step, and for the gradual development of a series of equations linking together elements in the diagrams, should it seem useful to experiment with mathematical models.

Marketing Intelligence

The traditional notion of marketing research is fast becoming antiquated. For it leads to dreary chronicles of the past rather than focusing on the present and shedding light on the future. It is particularistic, tending to concentrate on the study of tiny fractions of a marketing problem rather than on the problem as a whole. It lends itself to assuaging the curiosity of the moment, to fire-fighting, to resolving internecine disputes. It is a slave to technique. I shall not, therefore, relate the term *marketing research* to the systems approach—although I recognize, of course, that some leading businessmen and writers are breathing new life and scope into the ideas referred to by that term.

The role of the systems approach is to help evolve a *marketing intelligence* system tailored to the needs of each marketer. Such a system would serve as the ever-alert nerve center of the marketing operation. It would have these major characteristics:

- Continuous surveillance of the market.
- A team of research techniques used in tandem.
- A network of data sources.
- Integrated analysis of data from the various sources.
- Effective utilization of automatic data-processing equipment to distill mountains of raw information speedily.
- Strong concentration not just on reporting findings but also on practical, action-oriented recommendations.

Concept in use. A practical instance of the use of such an intelligence system is supplied by Mead Johnson Nutritionals (division of Mead Johnson & Company), manufacturers of Metrecal, Pablum, Bib, Nutrament, and other nutritional specialties. As Exhibit 31–3 shows, the company's Marketing Intelligence Department has provided information from these sources:

—A continuing large-scale consumer market study covering attitudinal and behavioral data dealing with weight control.

—Nielsen store audit data, on a bimonthly basis.

—A monthly sales audit conducted among a panel of 100 high-volume food stores in 20 markets to provide advance indications of brand share shifts.

—Supermarket warehouse withdrawal figures from Time, Inc.'s new service, Selling Areas-Marketing, Inc.

—Salesmen's weekly reports (which, in addition to serving the purposes of sales management control, call for reconnaissance on competitive promotions, new product launches, price changes, and so forth).

—Advertising expenditure data, by media class, from the company's accounting department.

—Figures on sales and related topics from company factories.

—Competitive advertising expenditure and exposure data, supplied by the division's advertising agencies at periodic intervals.

—A panel of weight-conscious women.

To exemplify the type of outputs possible from this system, Mead Johnson will be able, with the help of analyses of factory sales data, warehouse withdrawal information, and consumer purchases from Nielsen, to monitor transactions at each stage of the flow of goods through the distribution channel and to detect accumulations or developing shortages. Management will also be able to spot sources of potential problems in time to deal with them effectively. For example, if factory sales exceed consumer purchases, more promotional pressure is required. By contrast, if factory sales lag behind consumer purchases, sales effort must be further stimulated.

Similarly, the company has been able to devise a practical measure-

EXHIBIT 31–2

WORK FLOW AND SYSTEMS CHART FOR MANAGEMENT OF NEW PRODUCTS

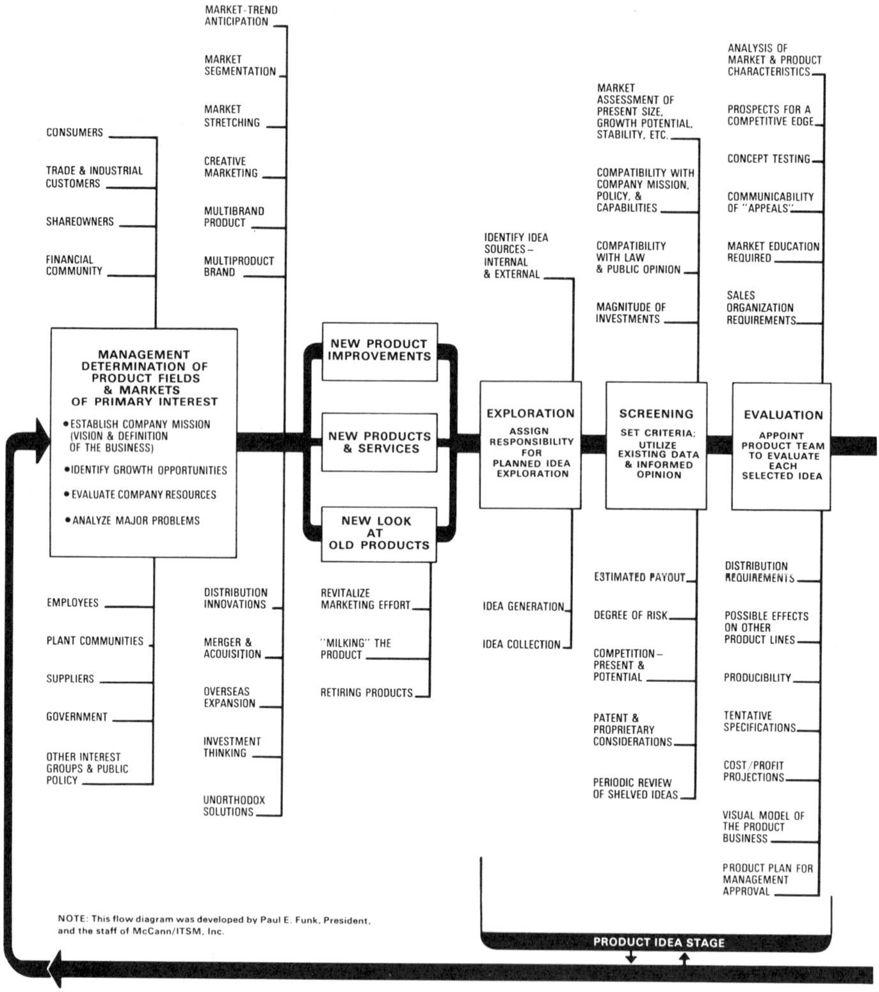

NOTE: This flow diagram was developed by Paul E. Funk, President, and the staff of McCann/ITSM, Inc.

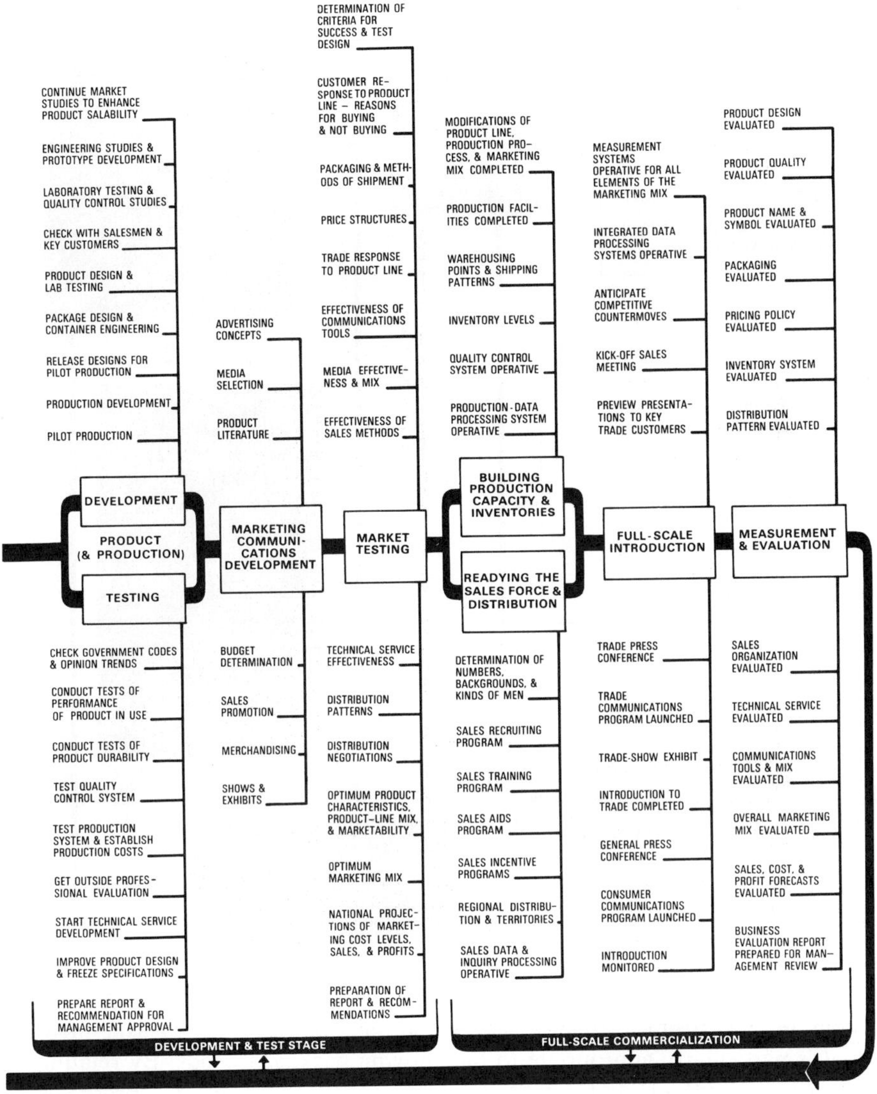

CONTINUE MARKET STUDIES TO ENHANCE PRODUCT SALABILITY
ENGINEERING STUDIES & PROTOTYPE DEVELOPMENT
LABORATORY TESTING & QUALITY CONTROL STUDIES
CHECK WITH SALESMEN & KEY CUSTOMERS
PRODUCT DESIGN & LAB TESTING
PACKAGE DESIGN & CONTAINER ENGINEERING
RELEASE DESIGNS FOR PILOT PRODUCTION
PRODUCTION DEVELOPMENT
PILOT PRODUCTION
DEVELOPMENT
PRODUCT (& PRODUCTION)
TESTING
CHECK GOVERNMENT CODES & OPINION TRENDS
CONDUCT TESTS OF PERFORMANCE OF PRODUCT IN USE
CONDUCT TESTS OF PRODUCT DURABILITY
TEST QUALITY CONTROL SYSTEM
TEST PRODUCTION SYSTEM & ESTABLISH PRODUCTION COSTS
GET OUTSIDE PROFES-SIONAL EVALUATION
START TECHNICAL SERVICE DEVELOPMENT
IMPROVE PRODUCT DESIGN & FREEZE SPECIFICATIONS
PREPARE REPORT & RECOMMENDATION FOR MANAGEMENT APPROVAL
ADVERTISING CONCEPTS
MEDIA SELECTION
PRODUCT LITERATURE
MARKETING COMMUNI-CATIONS DEVELOPMENT
BUDGET DETERMINATION
SALES PROMOTION
MERCHANDISING
SHOWS & EXHIBITS
DETERMINATION OF CRITERIA FOR SUCCESS & TEST DESIGN
CUSTOMER RE-SPONSE TO PRODUCT LINE – REASONS FOR BUYING & NOT BUYING
PACKAGING & METH-ODS OF SHIPMENT
PRICE STRUCTURES
TRADE RESPONSE TO PRODUCT LINE
EFFECTIVENESS OF COMMUNICATIONS TOOLS
MEDIA EFFECTIVE-NESS & MIX
EFFECTIVENESS OF SALES METHODS
MARKET TESTING
TECHNICAL SERVICE EFFECTIVENESS
DISTRIBUTION PATTERNS
DISTRIBUTION NEGOTIATIONS
OPTIMUM PRODUCT CHARACTERISTICS, PRODUCT–LINE MIX, & MARKETABILITY
OPTIMUM MARKETING MIX
NATIONAL PROJEC-TIONS OF MARKET-ING COST LEVELS, SALES, & PROFITS
PREPARATION OF REPORT & RECOM-MENDATIONS
MODIFICATIONS OF PRODUCT LINE, PRODUCTION PRO-CESS, & MARKETING MIX COMPLETED
PRODUCTION FACIL-ITIES COMPLETED
WAREHOUSING POINTS & SHIPPING PATTERNS
INVENTORY LEVELS
QUALITY CONTROL SYSTEM OPERATIVE
PRODUCTION-DATA PROCESSING SYSTEM OPERATIVE
BUILDING PRODUCTION CAPACITY & INVENTORIES
READYING THE SALES FORCE & DISTRIBUTION
DETERMINATION OF NUMBERS, BACKGROUNDS, & KINDS OF MEN
SALES RECRUITING PROGRAM
SALES TRAINING PROGRAM
SALES AIDS PROGRAM
SALES INCENTIVE PROGRAMS
REGIONAL DISTRIBU-TION & TERRITORIES
SALES DATA & INQUIRY PROCESSING OPERATIVE
MEASUREMENT SYSTEMS OPERATIVE FOR ALL ELEMENTS OF THE MARKETING MIX
INTEGRATED DATA PROCESSING SYSTEMS OPERATIVE
ANTICIPATE COMPETITIVE COUNTERMOVES
KICK-OFF SALES MEETING
PREVIEW PRESENTA-TIONS TO KEY TRADE CUSTOMERS
FULL-SCALE INTRODUCTION
TRADE PRESS CONFERENCE
TRADE COMMUNICATIONS PROGRAM LAUNCHED
TRADE-SHOW EXHIBIT
INTRODUCTION TO TRADE COMPLETED
GENERAL PRESS CONFERENCE
CONSUMER COMMUNICATIONS PROGRAM LAUNCHED
INTRODUCTION MONITORED
PRODUCT DESIGN EVALUATED
PRODUCT QUALITY EVALUATED
PRODUCT NAME & SYMBOL EVALUATED
PACKAGING EVALUATED
PRICING POLICY EVALUATED
INVENTORY SYSTEM EVALUATED
DISTRIBUTION PATTERN EVALUATED
MEASUREMENT & EVALUATION
SALES ORGANIZATION EVALUATED
TECHNICAL SERVICE EVALUATED
COMMUNICATIONS TOOLS & MIX EVALUATED
OVERALL MARKETING MIX EVALUATED
SALES, COST, & PROFIT FORECASTS EVALUATED
BUSINESS EVALUATION REPORT PREPARED FOR MAN-AGEMENT REVIEW
DEVELOPMENT & TEST STAGE
FULL-SCALE COMMERCIALIZATION

EXHIBIT 31–3

MEAD JOHNSON'S MARKETING INTELLIGENCE SYSTEM

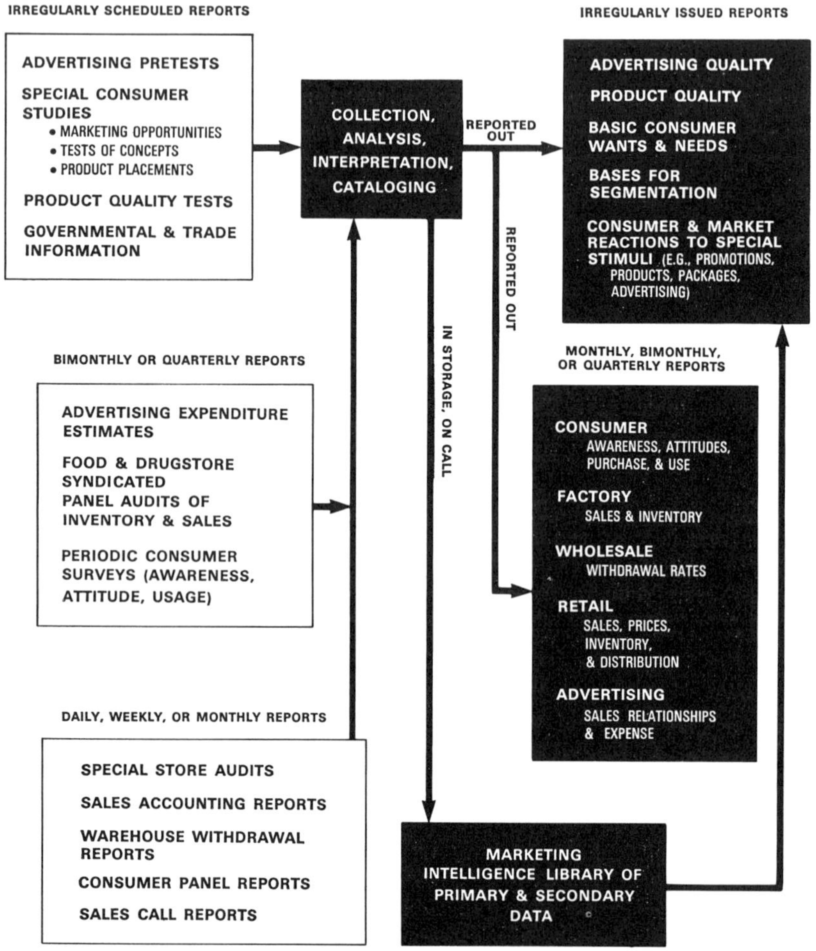

ment of advertising's effectiveness in stimulating sales—a measurement that is particularly appropriate to fast-moving packaged goods. By relating advertising outlays and exposure data to the number of prospects trying out a product during a campaign (the number is obtained from the continuing consumer survey), it is possible to calculate the advertising cost of recruiting such a prospect. By persisting in such analyses during several campaigns, the relative value of alternative advertising approaches can be weighed. Since measurement of the sales, as opposed to the communications, effects of promotion is a horrendously difficult, costly, and chancy process, the full significance of this achievement is difficult to exaggerate.

Benefits realized. Mead Johnson's marketing intelligence system has been helpful to management in a number of ways. In addition to giving executives early warning of new trends and problems, and valuable insights into future conditions, it is leading to a systematic *body* of knowledge about company markets rather than to isolated scraps of information. This knowledge in turn should lead ultimately to a theory of marketing in each field that will explain the mysteries that baffle marketers today. What is more, the company expects that the system will help to free its marketing intelligence people from fire-fighting projects so that they can concentrate on long-term factors and eventually be more consistently creative.

Despite these gains, it is important to note that Mead Johnson feels it has a long road still to travel. More work is needed in linking individual data banks. Conceptual schemes must be proved out in practice; ways must still be found to reduce an awesome volume of data, swelled periodically by new information from improved sources, so as to make intelligence more immediately accessible to decision makers. And perhaps the biggest problem of the moment, one underlying some of the others, is the difficulty in finding qualified marketing-oriented programmers.

Physical Distribution

A veritable revolution is now taking place in physical distribution. Total systems are being evolved out of the former hodgepodge of separate responsibilites, which were typically scattered among different departments of the same company. These systems include traffic and transportation, warehousing, materials handling, protective packaging, order processing, production planning, inventory control, customer service, market forecasting, and plant and warehouse site selection. Motivating this revolution are the computer, company drives to reduce distribution costs, and innovations in transportation, such as jet air freight, container ships, the interstate highway network, and larger and more versatile freight cars.

Distribution is one area of marketing where the "bread-and-butter" uses of the computer are relatively easily deployed for such functions as order processing, real-time inventory level reports, and tracking the movements of goods. Further into the future lie mathematical models which will include every factor bearing on distribution. Not only will packaging, materials handling, transportation and warehouse, order processing, and related costs be considered in such models; also included will be sales forecasts by product, production rates by factory, warehouse locations and capacities, speeds of different carriers, etc. In short, a complete picture will be developed for management.

Program in action. The experiences of the Norge Division of Borg-Warner Corporation point up the values of the systems approach in physical distribution. The firm was confronted externally with complaints from its dealers and distributors, who were trying to cope with swollen inventories and the pressures of "loading deals." Internally, because coordination of effort between the six departments involved in distribution was at a minimum, distribution costs and accounts receivable were mounting persistently.

To grapple with this situation, Norge undertook a comprehensive analysis of its distribution system. Out of this grew a new philosophy. A company executive has described the philosophy to me as follows:

> An effective system of physical distribution cannot begin at the end of the production line. It must also apply at the very beginning of the production process—at the planning, scheduling, and forecasting stages. Logistics, in short, is part of a larger marketing system, not just an evaluation of freight rates. We must worry not only about finished refrigerators, but also about the motors coming from another manufacturer, and even about where the copper that goes into those motors will come from. We must be concerned with *total flow*.

To implement this philosophy, the appliance manufacturer took the following steps:

1. It reorganized the forecasting, production scheduling, warehousing, order processing, and shipping functions into *one* department headed by a director of physical distribution.
2. The management information system was improved with the help of EDP equipment tied into the communications network. This step made it possible to process and report data more speedily on orders received, inventory levels, and the actual movement of goods.
3. Management used a combination of computer and manual techniques to weigh trade-offs among increased costs of multiple warehousing, reduced long-haul freight and local drayage costs, reduced inventory pipeline, and the sales value of an improved "total" product offering. Also assessed were trade-offs between shorter production runs and higher inventory levels, thereby challenging the traditional "wisdom" of production-oriented managers that the longer the run, the better.
4. The company is setting up new regional warehouses.

As a result of these moves, Norge has been able to lower inventories throughout its sales channels and to reduce accounts receivable. These gains have led, in turn, to a reduction of the company's overall investment and a concomitant increase in profitability.

It is essential to note that even though Norge has used operations research as part of its systems approach, many aspects of the program are qualitative. Thus far, the company has found that the development of an all-encompassing model is not warranted because of (a) the time and cost involved, (b) the probability that the situation will change before the model is completed, (c) a concern that such a model would be so complex as to be unworkable, and (d) the difficulty of testing many of the assumptions used. In addition, management has not tried to quantify the impact of its actions on distributor and retailer attitudes and behavior, possible competitive countermoves, and numerous other factors contributing to results.

Toward Total Integration

The integration of systems developed for product management, product innovation, marketing intelligence, physical distribution, and the other functions or "subsystems" embraced by the term *marketing* creates a total marketing system. Thus, marketing plans composed according to a step-by-step outline, ranging from enunciation of objectives and implementational steps to audit and adjustment to environmental changes, constitute a complete application of systems theory. Further, as the various subsystems of the overall system are linked quantitatively, so that the effect of modifications in one element can be detected in other elements, and as the influences of competitive moves on each element are analyzed numerically, then the total scheme becomes truly sophisticated.

PLUSES AND MINUSES

Two elements underlie the use and benefits of systems theory—order and knowledge. The first is a homely virtue, the second a lofty goal. Marketing is obviously not alone among all human pursuits in needing them; but, compared with its business neighbors, production and finance, marketing's need is acute indeed. The application of the systems concept can bring considerable advantages. It offers:

- A methodical problem-solving orientation—with a broader frame of reference so that all aspects of a problem are examined.
- Coordinated deployment of all appropriate tools of marketing.
- Greater efficiency and economy of marketing operations.
- Quicker recognition of impending problems, made possible by better understanding of the complex interplay of many trends and forces.
- A stimulus to innovation.
- A means of quantitatively verifying results.

These functional benefits in turn yield rich rewards in the marketplace. The most important gains are:

A deeper penetration of existing markets—As an illustration, the Advanced Data Division of Litton Industries has become a leader in the automatic revenue control business by designing systems meshing together "hardware" and "software."

A broadening of markets—For example, the tourist industry has attracted millions of additional travelers by creating packaged tours that are really product-service systems. These systems are far more convenient and economical than anything the consumer could assemble himself.

An extension of product lines—Systems management makes it more feasible to seek out compatibilities among independently developed systems. Evidence of this idea is the work of automatic control system specialists since the early 1950's.[5] Now similar signs are apparent in marketing. For example, Acme Visible Records is currently dovetailing the design and sale of its record keeping systems with data-processing machines and forms.

A lessening of competition or a strengthened capacity to cope with competition—The systems approach tends to make a company's product line more unique and attractive. Carborundum's innovation in metal-removal systems is a perfect illustration of this.

Problems in Practice

Having just enumerated in glowing terms the benefits of the systems approach, realism demands that I give "equal time" to the awesome difficulties its utilization presents. There is no better evidence of this than the gulf between the elegant and sophisticated models with which recent marketing literature abounds and the actual number of situations in which those models really work. For the truth of the matter is that we are still in the foothills of this development, despite the advances of a few leaders. Let us consider some of the obstacles.

Time and manpower costs. First of all, the systems approach requires considerable time to implement; it took one company over a year to portray its physical distribution system in a mathematical model before it could even begin to solve its problems. RCA's Electronic Data Processing Division reports models taking three to five years to build, after which holes in the data network have to be filled and the model tested against history. Add to this the need for manpower of exceptional intellectual ability, conceptual skills, and specialized education—manpower that is in exceedingly short supply. Because the prob-

[5] See *Automatic and Manual Control: Papers Contributed to the Conference at Cranford, 1951,* edited by A. Tustin (London: Butterworth's Scientific Publications, 1952).

lems are complex and involve all elements of the business, one man alone cannot solve them. He lacks the knowledge, tools, and controls. And so many people must be involved. It follows that the activation of systems theory can be very costly.

Absence of "canned" solutions. Unlike other business functions where standardized approaches to problem solving are available, systems must be tailored to the individual situation of each firm. Even the same problem in different companies in the same industry will frequently lead to different solutions because of the impact of other inputs, unique perceptions of the environment, and varying corporate missions. These factors, too, compound time and expense demands.

"Net uncertainties." Even after exhaustive analysis, full optimization of a total problem cannot be obtained. Some uncertainty will always remain and must be dealt with on the basis of judgment and experience.

Lack of hard data. In the world of engineering, the systems evolved to date have consisted all or mostly of machines. Systems engineers have been wise enough to avoid the irrationalities of man until they master control of machines. Marketing model-builders, however, have not been able to choose, for the distributor, salesman, customer, and competitor are central to marketing. We must, therefore, incorporate not only quantitative measures of the dimensions of things and processes (e.g., market potential, media outlays, and shipping rates), but also psychological measures of comprehension, attitudes, motivations, intentions, needs—yes, even psychological measures of physical behavior. What is needed is a marriage of the physical and behavioral sciences—and we are about as advanced in this blending of disciplines as astronomy was in the Middle Ages.

Consider the advertising media fields as an instance of the problem:

A number of advertising agencies have evolved linear programming or simulation techniques to assess alternate media schedules. One of the key sets of data used covers the probabilities of exposure to all or part of the audience of a TV program, magazine, or radio station. But what is exposure, and how do you measure it? What is optimum frequency of exposure, and how do you measure it? How does advertising prevail on the predispositions and perceptions of a potential customer? Is it better to judge advertising effects on the basis of exposure opportunity, "impact" (whatever that is), messages retained, message comprehension, or attitude shifts or uptrends in purchase intentions? We do not have these answers yet.

Even assuming precise knowledge of market dimensions, product performance, competitive standing, weights of marketing pressure exerted by direct selling, advertising and promotion, and so on, most marketers do not yet know, except in isolated cases, how one force will affect another. For instance, how does a company "image" affect the setting in which its salesmen work? How does a company's reputation for service affect customer buying behavior?

Nature of marketing men. Man is an actor on this stage in another role. A good many marketing executives, in the deepest recesses of their psyches, are artists, not analysts. For them, marketing is an art form, and, in my opinion, they really do not want it to be any other way. Their temperament is antipathetic to system, order, knowledge. They enjoy flying by the seat of their pants—though you will never get them to admit it. They revel in chaos, abhor facts, and fear research. They hate to be trammeled by written plans. And they love to spend, but are loathe to assess the results of their spending.

Obviously, such men cannot be sold readily on the value and practicality of the systems approach! It takes time, experience, and many facts to influence their thinking.

Surmounting the Barriers

All is not gloom, however. The barriers described are being overcome in various ways. While operations research techniques have not yet made much headway in evolving total marketing systems and in areas where man is emotionally engaged, their accomplishments in solving inventory control problems, in sales analysis, in site selection, and in other areas have made many businessmen more sympathetic and open-minded to them.

Also, mathematical models—even the ones that do not work well yet—serve to bolster comprehension of the need for system as well as to clarify the intricacies among subsystems. Many models are in this sense learning models; they teach us how to ask more insightful questions. Moreover, they pinpoint data gaps and invite a more systematized method for reaching judgments where complete information does not exist. Because the computer abhors vague generalities, it forces managers to analyze their roles, objectives, and criteria more concretely. Paradoxically, it demands more, not less, of its human masters.

Of course, resistance to mathematical models by no means makes resistance to the systems approach necessary. There are many cases where no need may ever arise to use mathematics or computers. For the essence of the systems approach is not its techniques, but the enumeration of options and their implications. A simple checklist may be the only tool needed. I would even argue that some hard thinking in a quiet room may be enough. This being the case, the whole trend to more analysis and logic in management thinking, as reflected in business periodicals, business schools, and the practices of many companies, will work in favor of the development of the systems approach.

It is important to note at this juncture that not all marketers need the systems approach in its formal, elaborate sense. The success of some companies is rooted in other than marketing talents; their expertise may lie in finance, technology, administration, or even in personnel—as in the case of holding companies having an almost uncanny ability to hire brilliant operating managers and the self-control to leave them alone. In addition, a very simple marketing operation—for example, a company marketing one product through one distribution channel—may have no use for the systems concept.

APPLYING THE APPROACH

Not illogically, there is a system for applying the systems approach. It may be outlined as a sequence of steps:

1. *Define the problem and clarify objectives.* Care must be exercised not to accept the view of the propounder of the problem lest the analyst be defeated at the outset.

2. *Test the definition of the problem.* Expand its parameters to the limit. For example, to solve physical distribution problems it is necessary to study the marketplace (customer preferences, usage rates, market size, and so forth), as well as the production process (which plants produce which items most efficiently, what the interplant movements of raw materials are, and so forth). Delineate the extremes of these factors, their changeability, and the limitations on management's ability to work with them.

3. *Build a model.* Portray all factors graphically, indicating logical and chronological sequences—the dynamic flow of information, decisions, and events. "Closed circuits" should be used where there is information feedback or go, no-go and recycle signals (see Exhibit 31–2).

4. *Set concrete objectives.* For example, if a firm wants to make daily deliveries to every customer, prohibitive as the cost may be, manipulation of the model will yield one set of answers. But if the desire is to optimize service at lowest cost, then another set of answers will be needed. The more crisply and precisely targets are stated, the more specific the results will be.

5. *Develop alternative solutions.* It is crucial to be as open-minded as possible at this stage. The analyst must seek to expand the list of

options rather than merely assess those given to him, then reduce the list to a smaller number of practical or relevant ones.

6. *Set up criteria or tests of relative value.*

7. *Quantify some or all of the factors or "variables."* The extent to which this is done depends, of course, on management's inclinations and the "state of the art."

8. *Manipulate the model.* That is, weigh the costs, effectiveness, profitability, and risks of each alternative.

9. *Interpret the results, and choose one or more courses of action.*

10. *Verify the results.* Do they make sense when viewed against the world as executives know it? Can their validity be tested by experiments and investigations?

Forethought and Perspective

Successful systems do not blossom overnight. From primitive beginnings, they evolve over a period of time as managers and systems specialists learn to understand each other better, and learn how to structure problems and how to push out the frontiers of the "universe" with which they are dealing. Companies must be prepared to invest time, money, and energy in making systems management feasible. This entails a solid foundation of historical data even before the conceptual framework for the system can be constructed. Accordingly, considerable time should be invested at the outset in *thinking* about the problem, its appropriate scope, options, and criteria of choice before plunging into analysis.

Not only technicians, but most of us have a way of falling in love with techniques. We hail each one that comes along—*deus ex machina.* Historically, commerical research has wallowed in several such passions (e.g., probability sampling, motivation research, and semantic scaling), and now operations research appears to be doing the same thing. Significantly, each technique has come, in the fullness of time, to take its place as one, but only one, instrument in the research tool chest. We must therefore have a broad and dispassionate perspective on the systems approach at this juncture. We must recognize that the computer does not possess greater magical properties than the abacus. It, too, is a tool, albeit a brilliant one.

Put another way, executives must continue to exercise their judgment and experience. Systems analysis is no substitute for common sense. The computer must adapt itself to their styles, personalities, and modes of problem solving. It is an aid to management, not a surrogate. Businessmen may be slow, but the good ones are bright; the electronic monster, by contrast, is a speedy idiot. It demands great acuity of wit from its human managers lest they be deluged in an avalanche of useless paper. (The story is told of a sales manager who had just found out about the impressive capabilities of his company's computer and called for a detailed sales analysis of all products. The report was duly prepared and wheeled into his office on a dolly.)

Systems users must be prepared to revise continually. There are two reasons for this. First, the boundaries of systems keep changing; constraints are modified; competition makes fresh incursions; variables, being what they are, vary, and new ones crop up. Second, the analytical process is iterative. Usually, one "pass" at problem formulation and searches for solutions will not suffice, and it will be necessary to "recycle" as early hypotheses are challenged and new, more fruitful insights are stimulated by the inquiry. Moreover, it is impossible to select objectives without knowledge of their effects and costs. That knowledge can come only from analysis, and it frequently requires review and revision.

Despite all the efforts at quantification, systems analysis is still largely an art. It relies frequently on inputs based on human judgment; even when the inputs are numerical, they are determined, at least in part, by judgment. Similarly, the outputs must pass through the sieve of human interpretation. Hence, there is a positive correlation between the pay-off from a system and the managerial level involved in its design. The higher the level, the more rewarding the results.

Finally, let me observe that marketing people merit their own access to computers as well as programmers who understand marketing. Left in the hands of accountants, the timing, content, and format of output are often out of phase with marketing needs.

CONCLUSION

Nearly 800 years ago a monk wrote the following about St. Godric, a merchant later turned hermit:

> He laboured not only as a merchant but also as a shipman . . . to Denmark, Flanders, and Scotland; in which lands he found certain rare, and therefore more precious, wares, which he carried to other parts wherein he knew them to be least familiar, and coveted by the inhabitants beyond the price of gold itself, wherefore he exchanged these wares for others coveted by men of other lands. . . .[6]

How St. Godric "knew" about his markets we are not told, marketing having been in a primitive state in 1170. How some of us marketers today "know" is, in my opinion, sometimes no less myste-

[6] *Life of St. Godric,* by Reginald, a monk of Durham, c. 1170.

rious than it was eight centuries ago. But we are trying to change that, and I will hazard the not very venturesome forecast that the era of "by guess and by gosh" marketing is drawing to a close. One evidence of this trend is marketers' intensified search for knowledge that will improve their command over their destinies. This search is being spurred on by a number of powerful developments. To describe them briefly:

• The growing complexity of technology and the accelerating pace of technological innovation.

• The advent of the computer, inspiring and making possible analysis of the relationships between systems components.

• The intensification of competition, lent impetus by the extraordinary velocity of new product development and the tendency of diversification to thrust everybody into everybody else's business.

• The preference of buyers for purchasing from as few sources as possible, thereby avoiding the problems of assembling bits and pieces themselves and achieving greater reliability, economy, and administrative convenience. (Mrs. Jones would rather buy a complete vacuum cleaner from one source than the housing from one manufacturer, the hose from another, and the attachments from still another. And industrial buyers are not much different from Mrs. Jones. They would rather buy an automated machine tool from one manufacturer than design and assemble the components themselves. Not to be overlooked, in this connection, is the tremendous influence of the U.S. government in buying systems for its military and aerospace programs.)

The further development and application of the systems approach to marketing represents, in my judgment, the leading edge in both marketing theory and practice. At the moment, we are still much closer to St. Godric than to the millenium, and the road will be rocky and tortuous. But if we are ever to convert marketing into a more scientific pursuit, this is the road we must travel. The systems concept can teach us how our businesses really behave in the marketing arena, thereby extending managerial leverage and control. It can help us to confront more intelligently the awesome complexity of marketing, to deal with the hazards and opportunities of technological change, and to cope with the intensification of competition. And in the process, the concept will help us to feed the hungry maws of our expensive computers with more satisfying fare.

B

Manufacturing

The authors describe how a computer model was developed to control a manufacturing operation.

32

PRODUCTION AND INVENTORY CONTROL BY COMPUTER–A UNIVERSAL MODEL

Karl E. Korn
James H. Lamb

The production-control function of a 175-man part shop making metal pieces, at the Kansas City Works of the Western Electric Company has been fully computerized. The system of computer programs corresponds precisely to a shop together with its finished-parts storeroom. The system controls the inventory of finished goods through automatic generation of replenishment orders. Determination of stock-on-hand status is not included in the model, but rather is independently provided by a works-wide stock-status system.

On a weekly basis, the computerized model of production and inventory control issues the following information:

1. The start date and size of each new lot to be produced and assembled.
2. All paperwork necessary to initiate movement of raw material and components to the proper shop area in order to start a lot.
3. A forecast by time periods of raw material quantitities required.

On a daily basis, the system issues a work list for each of the five

Reprinted with permission from *Computers and Automation,* May 1967, pp. 23–29, copyright 1967 by and published by Berkeley Enterprises, Inc., 815 Washington St., Newtonville, Mass. 02160.
Based on an article in *The Western Electric Engineer* for July 1966.

shop sections. Operations to be performed on the lots are listed in priority sequence.

The production control system is a product of the Engineering Research Center and is currently operated and maintained by personnel at a pilot installation in the Kansas City Works. The computer configuration is an IBM 1410 with an 80,000-character memory, six magnetic tape-drives and a disk file.

ENVIRONMENT

The Works is divided into a hierarchy of assembly shops and associated storerooms, as shown in Figure 32–1. The levels are arranged so that the demand on any module (shop and storeroom combined) must come from a higher level. Generally speaking, demand flows in a direction opposite to the flow of product.

Demand on each module is determined on a plant-wide basis in a

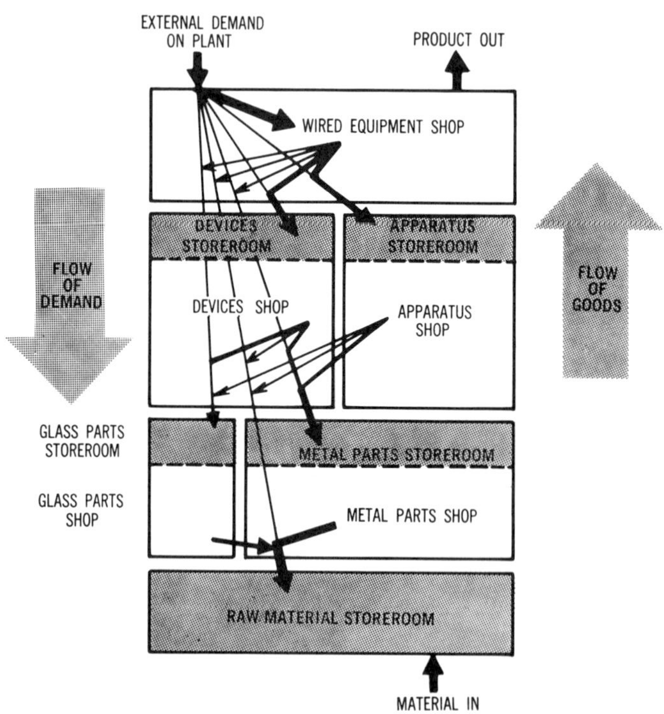

Figure 32–1. The plant is divided into a hierarchy of assembly shops and associated storerooms. Demand on a shop-storeroom module can come from external demand on the plant or from any higher-level module.

level-by-level explosion. Note that the demand on any storeroom in a module can come from all higher levels. The arrows in Figure 32–1 show the path of demand explosion through the plant hierarchy.

REQUIREMENTS FILE

Demand for the entire works is stored on a single magnetic tape file, called the requirements file. Requirements consist of weekly quantities, varying from twenty weeks into the future for piece-parts and up to forty weeks into the future for wired equipment and raw material. For shops producing non-stocked items, requirements constitute demand on the shop; for shops producing stocked items, requirements constitute demand on the storeroom.

There is an important reason why each storeroom is grouped with the shop which feeds it. Such a grouping permits fast response to unexpected demand. In this model, demand for any finished item is considered inviolable. Thus, each such module has the responsibility of satisfying all requirements for its finished products, and also has the responsibility of providing its suppliers (at lower levels within the hierarchy) with a stable demand.

A module, which has various internal assembly levels, receives external demand for its finished goods at all internal assembly levels. These levels are identified by a numerical "lowest-level code." Demand from within the shop, internal demand, is distinct from external demand and must be calculated separately by the system model. Internal demand is the demand for lower internal assembly-level items which are manufactured in, and re-enter the same shop for use in higher-level assemblies. A typical shop module is shown in Figure 32–2.

SCHEDULING BY FEEDBACK

Considering the constant changes in demand for product, any detailed production schedule deteriorates as time passes. A schedule made to a lesser degree of detail but remade at relatively frequent intervals can be adjusted to the variations and thus can be more realistic. The degree of detail for a schedule may be selected as a function of the time range, the frequency at which the schedule will be remade, and the expected variation between predicted and actual operation times. The more detailed schedules generally have shorter horizons and a higher frequency of rescheduling.

As shown in Figure 32–3, the system realizes feedback on two levels—daily and weekly.

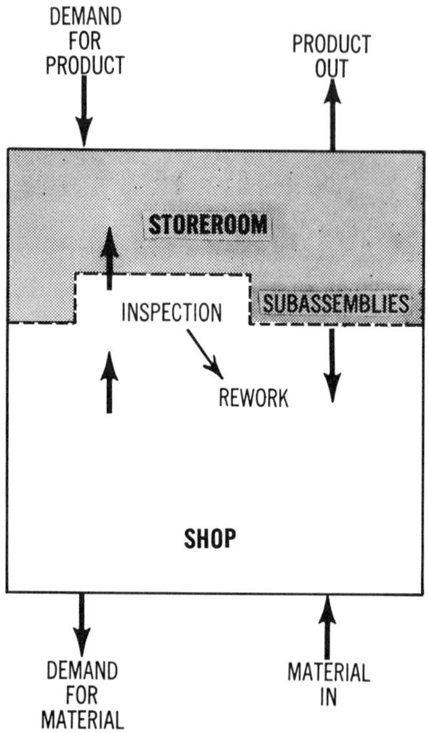

Figure 32–2. A typical shop-storeroom module

APPROXIMATIONS

Every week the system produces a twenty-week schedule for the shop by disregarding machine-capacity limitations and calculating a start and due date for each operation of each lot.

This first approximation schedule is improved by the machine-loading function of the system. Although at this time machine loading is not used at the Kansas City Works, the model is designed to adjust the schedule to meet manpower and machine capacity constraints. Each operation for each lot is loaded into a matrix of machine-time periods, as shown in Figure 32–4. If insufficient manpower or machine time is encountered, earlier dates are specified for the operation, the schedule of the lot is expanded, and an earlier lot start date is established.

Since the scheduling is repeated once a week, only those lots [1]

[1] There are three categories of lots: planned lots, lots to be started this week, and lots in the shop. The planned lots are completely recalculated each week based on the new demand pattern, the existing shop lots and the existing stock position. A planned lot becomes an actual lot when it is released to the shop.

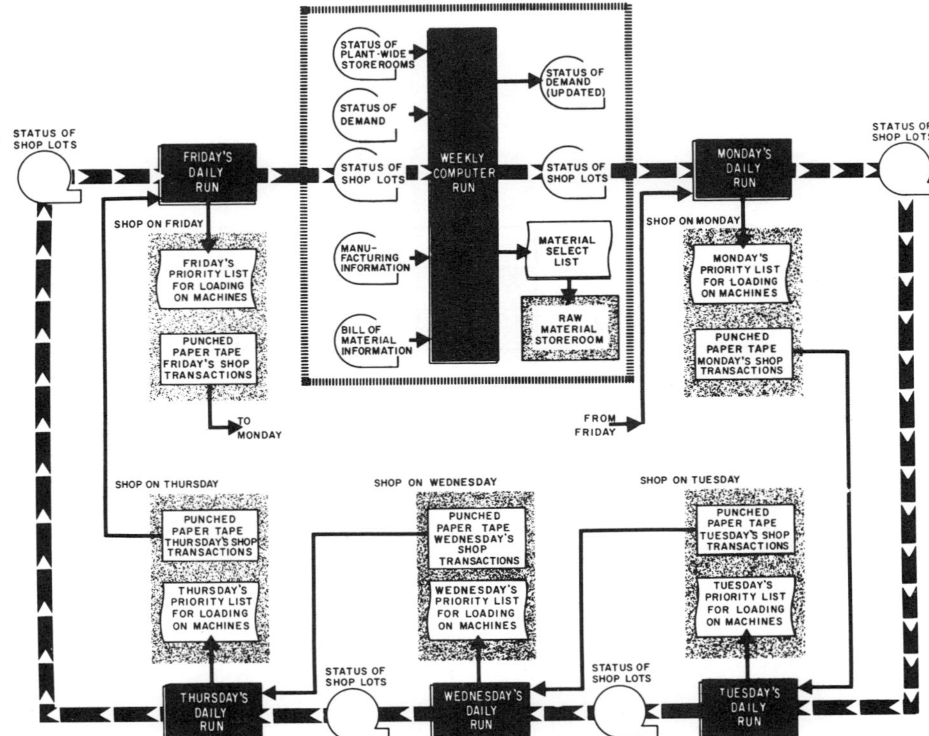

Figure 32–3. Feedback to the system occurs on a weekly and a daily basis. Once each week, a new schedule is determined from current demand and storeroom data, and the lot-status tape is updated. Each day, the shop transactions for the previous day are used to update the lot-status tape, and a new priority loading list is generated.

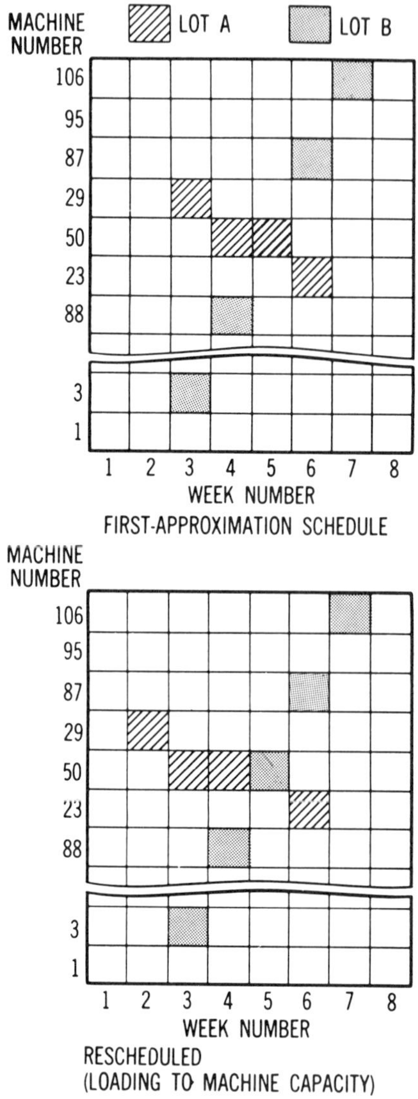

Figure 32–4. After all lots have been scheduled, each operation is loaded into a machine-week matrix, and conflicting lots are rescheduled. In this example, lot A is rescheduled a week earlier to avoid the conflict on machine 50 in week 5.

which have a start date within a specified short-range limit (normally two weeks) are released to the shop. The remaining lots are used for predicting future raw-material demand and estimating future shop and storeroom inventories. Many of these lots will never really exist, since the work will be scheduled again the following week.

ADJUSTING SHOP STATUS RECORD

The daily feedback occurs through shop-generated messages which indicate the progress of each lot during its manufacturing operations. Special telephone dialers for message input are conveniently located within the shop premises. The input messages are punched into a paper tape that becomes the input to the daily portion of the system. Once a day, the daily portion of the system, using the punched paper tape, adjusts the record of shop status. An updated priority list for the next day is then prepared and printed. A lot increases its priorities whenever an operation falls behind its scheduled date.

As shown in Figure 32–5, the transaction messages to the system are of three types: information pertaining to operations, information pertaining to lots, and inspection information. A priority loading list, showing the dispatching priority for each lot, is calculated from the computer-scheduled date for the next unfinished operation. For flexibility, short-interval (rush) orders may be introduced daily, if desired.

The Shop Status File Tape contains the status of all lots and is used

MESSAGES FROM
THE SHOP FLOOR

Operation Information

1. Setup started
2. Setup completed
3. Run started
4. Run completed
5. Work stopped
6. Work resumed
7. Rework started
8. Rework completed

Lot Information

1. Renumber the lot
2. Split the lot quantity
3. Merge two lots
4. Change lot quantity

Inspection Information

1. Accept the completed lot
2. Voided (previously accepted) completed lot message

Figure 32–5. Transaction messages inform the system of the daily progress of production lots.

and updated by both the daily and weekly portions of the system and thus forms the link between them.

SYSTEM DESIGN POLICIES

Major policies that affected the design of the system and thus produced significant system characteristics are as follows:

1. The model must be universal (repetitively applicable to all stocked shops in a manufacturing complex.)
2. Finished goods storeroom demand must be satisfied.
3. Uncompleted parts may not leave shop control, i.e., any part which has not been completed may not be stocked.
4. Investment in labor and raw material is to be made as late as possible.
5. Outside supplier lots (on parts which are also made in house) must be ordered by the model.
6. The use of historical data is avoided. The decisions made during the current computer run are maximally independent of last week's computer run. The latest status information is used in calculating the current week's decisions. Demand on the storeroom is considered deterministically dependent upon a high-level forecast.
7. The arrival of raw material to the shop floor is determined by the model. *Initiating a lot is not a manual decision.*
8. The size of the lot on the shop floor may only decrease. Messages describing increases in lot sizes from the shop floor (through a data collection device) are not accepted.
9. Rush jobs may be introduced manually.
10. Shop made subassembly (lower-generation) parts must be considered as and stored as finished goods.

THE COMPUTERIZED MODEL

The production control model consists of six major functions:

1. Netting the demand.
2. Forming economic size lots.
3. Scheduling machine operations (calculating start and due dates.)
4. Calculating lower generation demand.
5. Rescheduling to capacity constraints.
6. Producing outputs for accounting, storeroom and shop.

The structure of the system is such that each major function is a separate program. In this way program maintenance is simpler, and new or improved functions can be easily added to the system. A general flow diagram of the weekly portion of the system is given in Figure 32–6. A description of each section follows.

HOUSEKEEPING

The first program formats the disk file tracks. The second establishes the date of the computer run and accepts values of significant system constants.

CONSTRUCTING THE MASTER FILE

The primary purpose of this loader program is to bring together, each week, current information on an individual part number, for the convenience of subsequent computer programs in the weekly system. Data for one part usually occupies a single disk track of 2,800 characters. Only those parts which are subject to manufacture in the piece-part shop and which may be required by subsequent programs, are loaded onto the disk file. (Manufactured parts which are exclusively purchased are handled the same as raw material.) The loader program also performs certain miscellaneous functions. It data-protects the system by examining critical values for reasonableness. It issues a discrepancy report of missing records and certain unreasonable data values and counts the quantity of different part numbers actually loaded, the corresponding number of disk tracks utilized, the number of unfinished lots in the shop, the monetary value of completed lots, and the like.

NETTING THE DEMAND

The primary purpose of the netting program is the conversion of estimated demand (by part, by week), called "gross requirements on storeroom," into the corresponding estimated net demand on the shop facilities. This conversion takes into account the gross storeroom demand values for twenty weeks into the future, the total quantity already committed (but not withdrawn), the amount on hand, the predetermined safety stock, and lots in the shop which have not yet been received into the storeroom. A numerical example illustrating a simplified netting algorithm is given in Figure 32–7.

A refinement to the estimate, called soft netting,. permits the use of planned safety stock to meet sudden short-range increases in the demand on the shop. This refinement, not shown in the example, reduces the number of new lots that would otherwise be released on a rush basis.

All parts in the reference files have a numerical code corresponding to the lowest subassembly level in which the parts appear. It is important

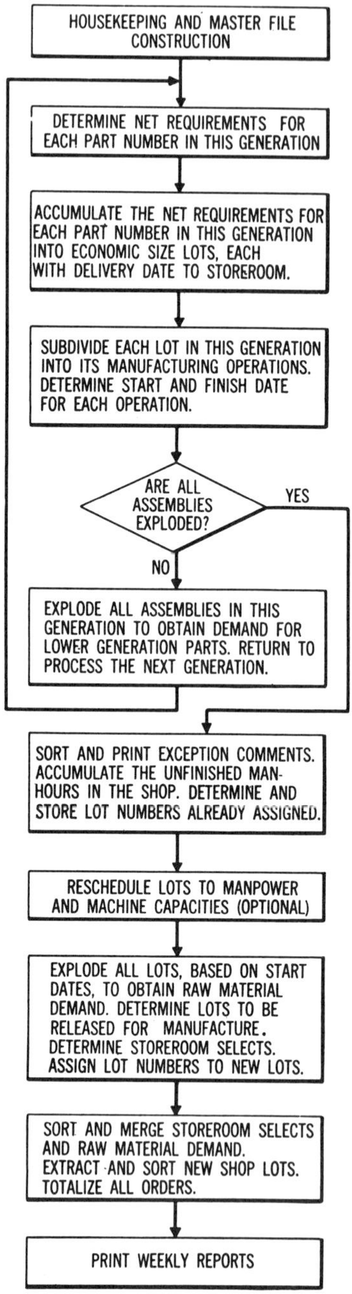

Figure 32–6. A simplified flow diagram of the weekly portion of the system. Each block represents one or more programs and contains a brief description of the major functions of that section of the system.

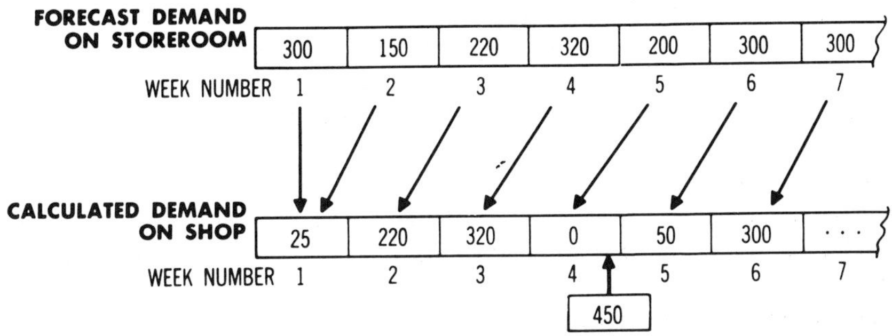

Figure 32–7. For this example of netting, 1,000 units are on hand in the storeroom, a safety stock of 450 units is required, and 125 units are committed but not yet withdrawn from the storeroom. A lot of 450 units is in shop and due in the storeroom on Friday, week 4

to note that the gross requirements for a multiple-use subassembly cannot be considered complete as long as any lots of the higher-level assemblies (in the list of parts) have yet to be scheduled and exploded. Therefore, netting, forming lots, and scheduling are delayed until the gross requirements for the sub-items are complete. The computer program utilizes the random access feature of the disk file while processing lower-generation parts, in preference to passing the entire file of parts sequentially.

DECIDING THE LOT SIZE

The Wagner and Whitin [2] dynamic programming model is one of the two methods utilized to determine the lot sizes and their delivery dates into the storeroom. With the policy that the storeroom demand on the shop must be satisfied, the shop may deliver the net requirements earlier, but not later, than the times specified. Consequently, some of the net requirements are combined into one lot, provided the saving in setup cost exceeds the penalty of the earlier investment. When the relative setup cost is sufficiently high, a single lot is produced to cover an economical time period exceeding the twenty-week horizon of demand, but limited to a year's supply as a maximum.

SCHEDULING MACHINE OPERATIONS

After a lot quantity and its delivery date into the storeroom have been specified, the individual operations required for manufacturing this lot

[2] Wagner and Whitin, "Dynamic Version of the Economic Lot Size Model," *Management Science* (October 1958).

are assigned due dates and start dates (calendar day numbers). This is done by using the required delivery date into the storeroom and providing sufficient time for the last operation, previous operation, etc., until the start date for the first operation is calculated. For each manufacturing operation, the queue time and setup time are added to the calculated make time to produce the total scheduled time for the operation. (Inspection is treated in a manner similar to a manufacturing operation.) This produces a first approximation schedule for the manufacturing operations and also results in a tentative lot start-date. Holidays, weekends, and vacation shut-downs are avoided.

CALCULATING LOWER-GENERATION DEMAND

The primary purpose of the lower-generation explosion program is to produce the total demand (quantities by weeks, twenty weeks into the future) on all lower-generation parts. These total requirements represent the total expected stores withdrawals resulting from external demand by other users and internal demand by the make shop itself for use in higher-level assemblies.

In the first pass through the list of parts, the demand for the second-generation parts is produced. The complete demand for these parts is not known until the pass is completed. The demand for the third (and subsequent) generation parts is unavailable because the second-generation lots have not yet been established at this point, their gross demand having just become available. After the first pass through this program, the total demand for all second-generation parts is known and has been up-dated on the disk file.

The computer then returns to the netting program, which converts gross demand on the storeroom into demand on the shop for the second-generation parts. For each such generation, lots are then formed, operations scheduled and, except for the lowest generation, demand for the next lower-generation components is determined.

To automatically maintain the lowest level code assignments, the system issues a correction card to the reference files in the event that an error in the lowest-level code assignment is detected.

REPORTING INVENTORY EXCEPTIONS

This program prepares and prints reports of abnormal inventory or scheduling situations, for example, those parts that have an excessive quantity on hand in the storeroom and in lots in the shop. Following this, the program totals and lists the planned man-hours scheduled for the shop over the twenty-week period. In addition, the program determines reassignable lot numbers presently in use, permitting subsequent number assignments to the new lots by computer.

RESCHEDULING TO CAPACITY CONSTRAINTS

A linear programming solution provides a forecast of smoothed manpower as an optional addition to the existing system. Input consists of weekly man-hour requirements for the planned lots and the unfinished portion of the shop lots. Output consists of the total shop smoothed manpower, a forecast by weeks, and the value of allowable overtime work. The program cost constraints include such costs as hiring, layoff, overtime, straight-time, and inventory. The machine loading program loads to weekly manpower and machine limitations and computes new operation dates when capacity for the week has been reached.

PRODUCING OUTPUTS

For each lot to be released (within a specified short range limit), a lot number is assigned, and a storeroom material-select list specifying delivery of sub-assemblies and raw materials is produced. Also, the raw material demand information for all lot start dates outside the specified short-range release limit (usually two weeks) is provided as an input to the plant-wide material ordering system. This demand is obtained by exploding shop lots to required lower generation quantities, and planned lots to required lower generation and raw material quantities. The raw material forecast, storeroom select, and lots to be released are determined after any possible change in lot start dates (caused, for example, by insufficient man or machine power capacities).

SYSTEM PERFORMANCE

With minor exceptions, the system functions as designed and is trouble-free for extended periods. The system itself is a product of the Engineering Research Center; the pilot installation is operated and maintained by the Kansas City Works operating personnel. The daily portion of the system, including the data collection hardware system, was installed in October 1963. The weekly portion of the system was installed in September 1964. The weekly portion operates the 175-man shop with no manual inputs.

The net savings of the system have been calculated to be $300,000

SHOP STATISTICS	
Number of Employees	175
Number of Machines	233
Number of Homogeneous Machine Groups	100
Number of 8-Hour Shifts	3
Number of New Lots Per Week	300
Average Number of Operations Per Lot	6
Average Time Per Operation (approx. hrs.)	4
Number of Lots in Shop	1,600
Number of Parts on File	1,800
Average Number of Active Parts	1,200
Routing Through Shop	Random

Figure 32–8. Shop statistics show the scope of the pilot installation.

per year in the pilot installation obtained from reductions in inventories and manpower requirements. The scope of the pilot installation is indicated by the shop statistics given in Figure 32–8. Including problem definition, system design, file formation, programming, coding, "debugging," and cutover, the total expended technical effort was about 20 man years.

The designers of the system have made a concerned effort to maximize both the structural nature of the system and the ease of revision. The bulk of the computer coding (in Fortran II language) was done by the designers. Autocode subroutines for character manipulation, tape records up to 2800 characters in length, and revisions to IBM software providing forward-alpha characters within words were provided by Autocoder specialists. The daily portion of the system was written in Autocoder.

Due to system complexity, multiple applications have not yet been widespread. Although the system is large and complex, almost all revisions are additive in terms of both size and complexity.

FUTURE WORK

Work is continuing on improvements to the system. The Loading Preference Factor (LPF) [3] for the machine-loading scheme is being investi-

[3] The LPF is a priority number assigned to each lot to denote its relative sequence in the loading process.

gated. A method for applying it is also under study. The LPF work should improve scheduling by determining priority equations for loading each lot into the machine matrix.

As shown by the backlog syndrome,[4] the amount of backlog interacts with the productive efforts of an individual. Specifically, the individual works best when a backlog of jobs exists, and he tends to create a backlog if one does not exist. Such shop conditions need to be considered in future improvements.

In addition, the system could be used to handle storeroom receipt of finished goods, eventually obviating the need for reporting storeroom inputs through the plant-wide stock status system.

Currently, revisions are made to the system by engineers at the Works and frequently include contact with the designers of the system. A formal revision procedure is being considered for future use.

CONCLUSIONS

In summary, a large manufacturing complex containing a hierarchy of manufacturing shops and intermediate storerooms can be subdivided in such a manner as to allow production control by a universal model, which is incorporated into a system of computer programs. The corresponding physical module is a shop together with its stored finished goods. It is dissociated from its raw material storeroom, provided shop-made subassembly parts are considered as finished goods. The boundaries of the system of computer programs should be as described herein and limited to correspond to the boundaries of one shop and its storeroom, in order that the system of programs remain repetitively applicable to each shop-storeroom combination.

Progress of the lots within the shop (down to the specific machine operation on each lot) is continuously recorded on paper tape and batched daily by computer in the pilot application described. However the system of computer programs which operates weekly and establishes the flow of goods produced within the module can be designed omitting per-operation control.

REFERENCES

Demczynski, S. "Production Control and Machine Loading in a Jobbing Shop," *Control,* October–December 1961, pp. 94–96, 102–104, 109–110.

Gomersall, E. R., "The Backlog Syndrome," *Harvard Business Review,* September–October 1964, pp. 105–115.

[4] E. R. Gomersall, "The Backlog Syndrome," *Harvard Business Review.* (September–October 1964), pp. 105–115.

Wagner and Whitin, "Dynamic Version of the Economic Lot Size Model," *Management Science,* October 1958.

Ackerman, S. S. "Even-Flow, A Scheduling Method for Reducing Lateness in Job Shops," *Management Technology,* Vol. III, No. 1, May 1963, pp. 20–32.

Stewart, W. A., and Crankavich, J. E., "Program Change Procedures," *Datamation,* Vol. X, No. 6, June 1964, pp. 51–54.

Korn, K. E., and Lamb, J. H., "Production Control by Computer," *Control and Automation Progress,* Vol. 10, No. 100, October 1966.

The author shows how a purchasing agent can use linear programing to allocate orders among several suppliers in the most economical way.

33

HOW TO USE LINEAR PROGRAMING

Stanley E. Bryan

The purchasing agent for the Blackston Co. has to divide raw material purchases for three plants among four suppliers. Prices are the same, but each supplier has a limited capacity and cannot fill the entire requirement. Furthermore, a different freight rate applies between each supplier and each of three destinations. The P.A.'s problem: What is the most economical way to allocate these purchases?

Linear programing is the tool that can help the P.A. make decisions such as this. It shows how to set up the problem, and how to solve it in a direct, systematic way.

In this hypothetical case, the problem is simple enough so that linear programing is not essential to reach a solution. But an actual purchasing situation is apt to be more complex.

As the problem becomes more complicated, trial and error methods become less reliable. Even in a simple case, there is no way of making sure that the apparently right trial solution is indeed the optimum one. With linear programing, however, the form of the answer flags the correct solution.

The three Blackston plants are Eastland, Westland, and Northland. Monthly raw material requirements for the plants are:

Reprinted from *Purchasing,* Vol. 59, No. 5, September 9, 1965, pp. 98–105, 172, by permission of the publisher.

Eastland	2,600 units
Westland	9,800 units
Northland	6,000 units
Total	18,400 units

In the past, Blackston has purchased the material from three suppliers up to the limit of their capacities. Now a fourth supplier has entered the market. Maximum monthly capacities of the suppliers are:

Supplier A	10,200 units
Supplier B	5,200 units
Supplier C	2,400 units
Supplier D	2,200 units
Total Supply	20,000 units

The F.O.B. shipping point price is the same for each supplier. Transportation costs, however, are high, and vary due to the distances between suppliers' plants and the destinations.

The cost of transportation in dollars per unit from each supplier to each plant is:

Supplier	Eastland	Westland	Northland
A	20	17	18
B	15	14	16
C	10	13	12
D	10	11	9

How should purchasing allocate the business among the four suppliers so that total transportation costs will be as low as possible?

To help organize the facts we can set up a matrix table in which the sum of the rows equals the sum of the columns (Table 33–1). To make the grand totals equal to the available supply, an extra column is added and designated "not needed."

The number in each square is the transportation cost in dollars per unit of material for the particular routing. For example, the 20 in the first square is the transportation cost from vendor "A" to the Eastland plant. The transportation costs in the "not needed" column are, of course, zero.

By inserting allocated amounts of material in the various squares, we can quickly calculate the total transportation costs for each possible program.

In a recent seminar on linear programing, three teams were asked to find the best allocation by trial and error. As they were limited to a set period of time in which to make their decisions, they did not all arrive at the optimum solution.

TABLE 33–1

	Eastland	Westland	Northland	Not needed	Total
Suppliers					
A	/20	/17	/18	/0	10,200
B	/15	/14	/16	/0	5,200
C	/10	/13	/12	/0	2,400
D	/10	/11	/9	/0	2,200
Plant needs	2,600	9,800	6,000	1,600	20,000

First step in solving problem of how to allocate raw materials from four suppliers among three plants is to set up table in form of matrix. Bottom row shows amounts needed by each plant. Right-hand column is capacity of each supplier. The 1,600 units in the "not needed" column are not required by any plant, but must be included to make the totals of the rows and columns add up to the 20,000 available supply. Figures in the squares are transportation costs in dollars per unit. Transportation cost of units not needed is zero.

TEAMS TACKLE PROBLEM BY TRIAL AND ERROR

Team #1 presented the buying program shown in Table 33–2. Reasoning that the lower transportation costs seemed to be associated with the routes located in the lower right section of the table, they started by supplying the Northland plant.

The total cost of transportation using Team #1's solution would be:

(2,600)	@	$20 =	$ 52,000
(4,800)	@	17 =	81,600
(1,200)	@	18 =	21,600
(5,000)	@	14 =	70,000
(200)	@	16 =	3,200
(2,400)	@	12 =	28,800
(2,200)	@	9 =	19,800
(1,600)	@	0 =	0
20,000	@		$277,000

Team #2 presented the program shown in Table 33–3, allocating purchases in the order of lowest transportation costs. The total cost of transportation for Team #2's program would be:

TABLE 33–2

Suppliers	Eastland	Westland	Northland	Not needed	Total
A	(2,600) /20	(4,800) /17	(1,200) /18	(1,600) /0	10,200
B	/15	(5,000) /14	(200) /16	/0	5,200
C	/10	/13	(2,400) /12	/0	2,400
D	/10	/11	(2,200) /9	/0	2,200
Plant needs	2,600	9,800	6,000	1,600	20,000

Total cost of transportation is $277,000.

Here are three solutions to the problem of allocating requirements of three plants among four vendors to obtain lowest transportation cost. All were reached by trial and error. Solution #1 (above) is based on plant with lowest freight rate first. Solution #2 (opposite page, top) scheduling allocates material in order of lowest freight rate, while solution #3 (opposite, bottom) makes further adjustments to eliminate high $20 rate. There's no way to make sure, however, that trial and error method has produced optimum solution to this complex problem of allocation.

(200)	@	$20 =	$ 4,000
(4,600)	@	17 =	78,200
(3,800)	@	18 =	68,400
(5,200)	@	14 =	72,800
(2,400)	@	10 =	24,000
(2,200)	@	12 =	26,400
(1,600)	@	0 =	0
20,000	@		$273,800

Team #3 presented the program shown in Table 33–4. This team followed the same principle as Team #2, but went a step further and moved some of the allocations out of the high-transportation cost squares. By trial and error in moving allocated amounts the team was able to reduce total transportation costs well below those of the competing teams. Its total transportation cost would be:

TABLE 33–3

Suppliers	Eastland	Westland	Northland	Not needed	Total
A	(200) /20	(4,600) /17	(3,800) /18	(1,600) /0	10,200
B	/15	(5,200) /14	/16	/0	5,200
C	(2,400) /10	/13	/16	/0	2,400
D	/10	/11	(2,200) /9	/0	2,200
Plant needs	2,600	9,800	6,000	1,600	20,000

Total cost of transportation is $273,800.

TABLE 33–4

Suppliers	Eastland	Westland	Northland	Not needed	Total
A	/20	(4,800) /17	(3,800) /18	(1,600) /0	10,200
B	(200) /15	(5,000) /14	/16	/0	5,200
C	(2,400) /10	/13	/12	/0	2,400
D	/10	/11	(2,200) /9	/0	2,200
Plant needs	2,600	9,800	6,000	1,600	20,000

Total cost of transportation is $266,800.

(4,800)	@	$17 =	$ 81,600
(3,800)	@	18 =	68,400
(200)	@	15 =	3,000
(5,000)	@	14 =	70,000
(2,400)	@	10 =	24,000
(2,200)	@	9 =	19,800
(1,600)	@	0 =	0
20,000	@		$266,800

Careful inspection of the various possibilities suggests that Team #3 probably achieved the objective of minimizing total transportation costs within the given limitations. But there is no real proof. There always remains some doubt whether this is really the optimum solution. The uncertainty would be even greater if the matrix were larger and the figures more complicated.

Linear programing does away with this uncertainty. Once the optimum program has been achieved it is immediately evident from the figures in the matrix of the last program.

The linear programing process applied to this problem is the so-called "transportation method." It involves these steps:

1. Allocating a limited amount of units from various sources to various needs with the objective (in the Blackston case) of minimizing total transportation costs.
2. The use of a matrix (or special table arrangement) to set up the problem and help solve it in a systematic way. (A simple matrix is illustrated by Table 33–1, and modified to make it easier to use as illustrated by Table 33–5.)
3. Starting with a feasible solution that will balance supply and demand, followed by a systematic search for the optimum solution. A feasible solution can be achieved by inspection (as was done by teams #1, #2, and #3). A systematic rule such as the "northwest corner rule" can also be used. The rule is to start in the upper left hand corner allocating total supply, row by row, regardless of transportation cost, to establish a program as an initial departure point.
4. The process of probing the established program for a more economical program (procedure explained below) and setting up successive programs and testing them until an optimum program is achieved. (This is referred to in linear programing terminology as the iteration process).
5. An analysis of the optimum program to determine if it fits the objectives and limitations initially prescribed.
6. A further analysis of factors that cannot be included in the linear program matrix process.

The transportation method of linear programing is based on mathematical assumptions which require that certain conditions be met. They are:

- Total supply and total demand (or grand total of rows and columns) must be equal. In the Blackston problem the requirement is met by adding the column designated "not needed." Sometimes a "dummy" source of supply or need is designated. Technically this is known as the slack variable.
- Allocations made in each program are placed in the appropriate routing squares in brackets. The number of bracketed figures must add up

to at least one less than the number of rows and columns. (In the Blackston problem the minimum is seven. In the language of mathematics, if there are m number of rows and n number of columns there must always be at least $m + n - 1$ brackets with allocated amounts.)

• While making allocations the number of brackets with real amounts allocated to them may be less than the number of rows and columns minus one. In such case, keep one of the prior program brackets in the program and allocate a zero amount to it (or an E to represent an insignificant real amount). This fulfills the technical requirement. The value of O (or E) will adjust itself in subsequent programs or can be ignored in the final solution.

Table 33–5 is a modified version of Table 33–1 arranged in a convenient work matrix to solve the Blackston problem. Demand figures are placed at the top of the table for convenience so that successive programs can be developed by working downward. Each program must be completed and tested before moving on to the next.

Program I is set up by the northwest corner rule, starting in the upper left hand corner of the matrix and allocating Supplier A's limited supply to the demand needs of the various plants (2,600 to Eastland, 7,600 to Westland, etc.) The resulting program is feasible but surely not the optimum program. Total transportation cost would be:

(2,600)	@	\$20 =	\$ 52,000
(7,600)	@	17 =	129,200
(2,200)	@	14 =	30,800
(3,000)	@	16 =	48,000
(2,400)	@	12 =	28,000
(600)	@	9 =	5,400
(1,600)	@	0 =	0
20,000	@		\$294,200

Program I should now be probed to see if a less costly program can be found. The probing (or testing) procedure is simple although somewhat tedious. A change in one part results in a chain reaction requiring changes in other parts to restore the balance of rows and columns.

Within the limits set by the row and column totals any amounts allocated to individual routings (squares) can be moved to other squares. To simplify the probing process it is carried on by working with only one unit of material. The question asked is: "What is the net effect of moving one unit from the present program routing to another routing?" This can be illustrated as follows. Allocate one unit to routing B-Eastland, by placing a 1 in B-Eastland square. The result affects three other routings in this case. The result, showing only the part of Table 33–5 affected, is illustrated in Table 33–6.

TABLE 33–5

How linear programming solves supply problem

		Total	Eastland	Westland	Northland	Not needed
Plant needs		20,000	2,600	9,800	6,000	1,600
Suppliers						
PROGRAM I	A	10,200	(2,600) /20	(7,600) /17	–1 /18	–10* /0
	B	5,200	–2 /15	(2,200) /14	(3,000) /16	–7 /0
	C	2,400	–3 /10	+3 /13	(2,400) /12	–3 /0
	D	2,200	0 /10	+4 /11	(600) /9	(1,600) /0
Total cost of transportation in Program I is $294,200						
PROGRAM II	A	10,200	(2,600) /20	(6,000) /17	–1 /18	(1,600) /0
	B	5,200	–2 /15	(3,800) /14	(1,400) /16	+3 /0
	C	2,400	–3* /10	+3 /13	(2,400) /12	+7 /0
	D	2,200	0 /10	+4 /11	(2,200) /9	+10 /0
Total cost of transportation in Program II is $278,200						
PROGRAM III	A	10,200	(200) /20	(8,400) /17	–1 /18	(1,600) /0
	B	5,200	–2* /15	(1,400) /14	(3,800) /16	+3 /0
	C	2,400	(2,400) /10	+6 /13	+3 /12	+10 /0
	D	2,200	0 /10	+4 /11	(2,200) /9	+10 /0
Total cost of transportation in Program III is $271,000						

A more appropriate question, in light of the objectives sought, however, would be: "What would be the net result of moving one unit to routing B-Eastland, in terms of cost?" To answer this question the cost of transportation per unit, found in the box in each square, is used. Table 33–6 shows that moving one unit to B-Eastland resulted in this chain reaction: B-Eastland, +1; A-Eastland, –1; A-Westland, +1; B-Westland, –1. Using the transportation cost for one unit in the same sequence, B-Eastland is +15; A-Eastland, –20; A-Westland, +17; B-Westland, +14.

TABLE 33–5 (*Continued*)

		Total	Eastland	Westland	Northland	Not needed
	Plant needs	20,000	2,600	9,800	6,000	1,600
	Suppliers					
PROGRAM IV	A	10,200	+2 /20	(8,600) /17	−1* /18	(1,600) /0
	B	5,200	(200) /15	(1,400) /14	(3,800) /16	+3 /0
	C	2,400	(2,400) /10	+4 /13	+1 /12	+8 /0
	D	2,200	+2 /10	+4 /11	(2,200) /9	+10 /0

Total cost of transportation in Program IV $270,600

		Total	Eastland	Westland	Northland	Not needed
PROGRAM V	A	10,200	+2 /20	(4,800) /17	(3,800) /18	(1,600) /0
	B	5,200	(200) /15	(5,000) /14	+1 /16	+3 /0
	C	2,400	(2,400) /10	+4 /13	+2 /12	+8 /0
	D	2,200	+1 /10	+3 /11	(2,200) /9	+9 /0

Total cost of transportation in Program V is $266,800

Series of linear programing matrices leads from obvious (but uneconomical) solution of allocation problem in Program I, to lowest cost answer in Program V. Supply, requirement, and transportation cost figures are the same as in previous tables. Bracketed numbers are allocations to indicated supplier for plant identified at top of column. Plus and minus figures are changes in transportation costs that result from moving one unit of material to the square.

Largest negative figure in each program (marked with asterisk) indicates area of greatest potential saving. To start next program, as many material units as possible are moved to that square, and other allocations are adjusted to make rows and columns add up to required values. Optimum solution is reached when no more negative numbers appear in matrix.

The net change in cost to make a move of one unit to B-Eastland would therefore be (+15 −20 +17 −14), or −2.

The process of probing, then, is to test each vacant suare (routing) to find what the net change in cost would be if one unit were moved to that square and the other allocations were adjusted to balance the totals. The aim is to keep the row or column totals the same so the total matrix remains in balance.

More complex is the result of testing the routing A-"not needed" by moving one unit to the A-"not needed" square. The first step, which may

TABLE 33–6

Supplier	Eastland	Westland
A	(2,599)	(7,601)
B	(1)	(2,199)

Result of changing allocation of one material unit from Supplier A-Eastland routing in Program I, to Supplier B-Eastland routing. Note that figures in adjacent squares must be adjusted to keep row and column totals equal to required values. Moving single units from one square to another and calculating resulting changes in cost is basic process in linear programing.

be bypassed once the procedure is clear, is to consider what would happen to the allocations if one were to move one unit of material to A-"not-needed" and keep the totals of row and column the same. Quantities would change as follows: A-"not-needed" (1); D-"not needed" (1,599); D-Northland (601); C-Northland (no change); B-Northland (2,999); B-Westland (2,201); A-Westland (7,599). The next step is to find out what the change in transportation cost would be of moving this one unit.

PROCESS OF BALANCING THE MATRIX

If one unit is moved to A-"not-needed" the addition to cost of that one unit would be +0. To offset this movement of one unit in the balance of the "not-needed" column one unit must be taken away from D-"not-needed" with a reduction of cost of –0. Row D has to be rebalanced by adding a unit to D-Northland which will add costs of +9. This throws Northland column out of balance which must be corrected. And so the process continues until the matrix is balanced again. The simple procedure for this is to use the brackets that will complete a circuit from the square being tested, around and back, alternatively adding and subtracting the transportation costs of one unit of transportation in each case. For testing what would happen if a unit were moved to vacant square A-"not-needed," moving in a clockwise direction the following figures pertain:

Square or Route Involved	Change In Transportation Cost
A-"not-needed"	0
D-"not-needed"	0
D-Northland	+ 9
(Skip C-Northland)	—
B-Northland	–16
B-Westland	+14
A-Westland	–17
Net change in cost	–10

The net change in cost from moving a unit to the A-"not-needed" square is thus a reduction of 10 (ten dollars). This suggests that an improvement can be made in Program I. Before making a re-allocation by moving as many units to A-"not-needed", however, every other alternate route (vacant square) should be tested in the same manner. Listed here are the changes that might be possible for other combinations of routes, showing the alternate adding and subtracting (moving in a clockwise direction) of transportation costs found in the route squares.

Route	Change in Cost						Net Change
A—Northland	+18	–16	+14	–17			= – 1
A—"not needed"	+ 0	– 0	+ 9	–16	+14	–17	= –10
B—Eastland	+15	–20	+17	–14			= – 2
B—"not needed"	+ 0	– 0	+ 9	–16			= – 7
C—Eastland	+10	–20	+17	–14	+16	–12	= – 3
C—Westland	+13	–14	+16	–12			= + 3
C—"not needed"	+ 0	– 0	+ 9	–12			= – 3
D—Eastland	+10	–20	+17	–14	+16	– 9	= 0
D—Westland	+11	–16	+16	– 9			= + 4

With the above tests, all the alternate routes (squares) have been probed. The changes in cost of moving one unit to each is recorded in the appropriate square as a positive number or a negative number. A positive number indicates that cost would increase by moving units to the route. A negative number indicates that cost would decrease by making such a move. As noted in Program I, and also above, –10 is the largest negative number. It would be logical to move as many units as possible from the associated brackets to the A-"not-needed" square in a situation of this type.

The number of units that can be moved to the alternate route is limited by the allocations in Program I. Inspection shows that 1,600 is the maximum that can be moved and still keep the totals in balance. The rule of thumb is to trace through the brackets in the circuit by which the largest negative cost was determined and to select the smallest number of units in the brackets associated with the successive negative numbers. In testing the A-"not needed" square the figures were:

Subtract Transportation Cost (in testing A-"not needed" route)	Number of Units In Brackets Related To These Subtractions
– 0	(1,600)
–16	(3,000)
–17	(7,600)

The smallest number of units in the brackets was 1,600. This is the number to move to the A-"not needed" route.

THE DEVELOPMENT OF PROGRAM II

The groundwork is now laid for developing Program II. (1,600) is allocated to route A-"not needed" as illustrated in Table 33–5. The "northwest corner rule" is exercised in allocating the remaining supply to demand. Be sure that the number of brackets equals at least one less than the sum of rows plus columns (in this case, 7).

Probe Program II for the largest negative number representing cost savings in changing to alternate routes. In this process there will be no change in portions of the table where the position of brackets remain in the same squares as in the preceding program. This cuts the repetition of test probing procedure to a considerable extent. If the circuit by which an alternate is tested remains the same in successive programs, the resulting change in cost will not vary. When the testing of Program II is completed the largest negative number is –3 in the C-Eastland square. The smallest bracket quantity associated with the circuit by which C-Eastland was tested is (2,400). This is moved to C-Eastland in Program III, which is then developed and tested.

A probe of Program III shows that –2 in the B-Eastland square is the largest negative number and that (200) is the smallest number units in the brackets associated with negative cost numbers on the test circuit. The (200) is moved to B-Eastland as Program IV, which is then developed and tested.

A probe of Program IV shows A-Northland to have the largest negative cost number and (3,800) to be the associated smallest negative number of units. The (3,800) is moved to A-Northland as Program V.

A probe of Program V shows no negative cost numbers. This is evidence that the program cannot be improved by additional changes. Program V fulfills the requirements in the problem and achieves the objective.

Program V is thus the optimum program based on minimum transportation cost. Each program was, of course, feasible from the standpoint of matching supply to demand, but only Program V provides lowest cost. Total costs of the alternate programs are:

Program I	$294,200
Program II	278,200
Program III	271,000
Program IV	270,600
Program V	265,800
Program of Team #1	277,000
Program of Team #2	273,800
Program of Team #3	266,800

Evidently, Team #3 achieved the optimum solution by trial and error alone. As was pointed out before, however, only through linear programing can we be sure that this is indeed the best solution. In many cases, of course, the systematic approach of linear programing is easier than trial and error.

Powerful tools that are creative can also be destructive when operated by unskilled operators on the wrong operations. Linear programing is essentially a roughing tool, not a finishing tool. For example, here are fundamental questions that should be asked in the Blackston Co. case:

- Why is the F.O.B. mill price exactly the same from all suppliers? What are the possibilities of negotiation?
- What can be done to develop suppliers such as D whose locations make for the low transportation costs?
- Can storage facilities be developed at the plants that will allow the company more flexibility in purchasing?
- Are there important considerations of service, assurance of supply, quality, research and development or other factors that should be given attention in the analysis?
- Are the cost factors used in the linear programing matrix realistic?
- Would the application of thorough value analysis reveal other important factors bearing upon the situation such as material substitution, production specialization, plant location, etc.?

In the last analysis, linear programing is no substitute for common sense in the decision-making process, but it is an effective aid in reaching decisions.

The author describes how one company adapted computer techniques to solve its distribution problems.

34

COMPUTER-COORDINATED DISTRIBUTION

J. K. McConnell

Adapting the modern computer to distribution problems has been attempted with varying degrees of success by an increasingly large number of large and small companies.

At Air Products and Chemicals, Inc., the computer is performing several complicated and sophisticated jobs for the Distribution Department. Specifically, we are using the computer for tactical and strategic distribution planning and control. In addition, we are using the computer to provide us with our private fleet operating data—both cost and performance—to give us effective control over this phase of Air Products' operations.

Our liquefied atmospheric gas distribution system is made up of an extremely complex production-distribution network covering a majority of the continental United States. This network is made up of many production points—air separation plants—and thousands of use points. These are served by a transportation system utilizing highway common carriers, railroads (both tank car and piggy-back), and a large private carrier motor transportation fleet.

Our computer is used for tactical and strategic distribution planning and control. The tactical approach provides us with a model of our distribution network which will give us our optimum costs. The strategic application is for the appraisal of various production and transport re-

Reprinted from *Distribution Age,* Vol. 64, No. 9, September 1965, pp. 37–41, by permission of the publisher.

strictions, and changes in customer demand to tell us when and where we need more transportation or producing capacity.

COMPUTER INPUT

In order to describe the computer model of our distribution network, we must first describe each of the inputs, and then how they are used in the computer. Briefly, we define our plants in terms of their productive capacity. We define our transport equipment in the form of a transportation capacity available. And we define our customers in terms of the quantity of product required to be delivered.

With this input, we describe the movement from the producing plant, in our various transport vehicles, to the customer in terms of linear equations. The computer then "solves" these equations. When we define the producing plant, we define its capacity in relation to the costs for producing product at various operating rates.

For tactical solutions, we consider the incremental cost situation at each of our producing plants. This definition of the production point, in effect, places restrictions on our production which cannot be violated in the solution of the linear equations described above.

We define transport capacity in terms of dollars per unit of product carried, and carrying capacity. We define the customer's demands in terms of volume of product required and request the computer to determine the optimum cost for satisfying all the customer's demands.

Mathematically speaking, all of these restrictions imposed by plant capacity, transportation capacity, and the customer's requirements, when added together, outline the set of possible solutions. There is an infinite number of solutions in this set which is known as a polyhedral convex set (see Exhibit 34–1), and all the linear programming does is to find the best solution to this polyhedral convex set.

The development of a typical equation proceeds like this:

The Quantity (Q) shipped from plant 1 to use point (${}_1Q_1$) plus the quantity shipped from plant 2 to use point 1 (${}_2Q_1$) plus quantity shipped from plant 3 to use point 1 (${}_3Q_1$) etc., must exactly equal the required quantity at use point 1 (${}_rQ_1$). Thus we get an equation like: ${}_1Q_1 + {}_2Q_1 + {}_3Q_1 + \ldots = {}_rQ_1$ for each use point.

Linear equations with restrictions on the quantity available from a plant or the customer's requirements or transport capacity mathematically outline an infinite set of possible solutions. This is known as a polyhedral convex set, and the distribution pattern producing lowest total cost is the optimum solution.

EXHIBIT 34–1

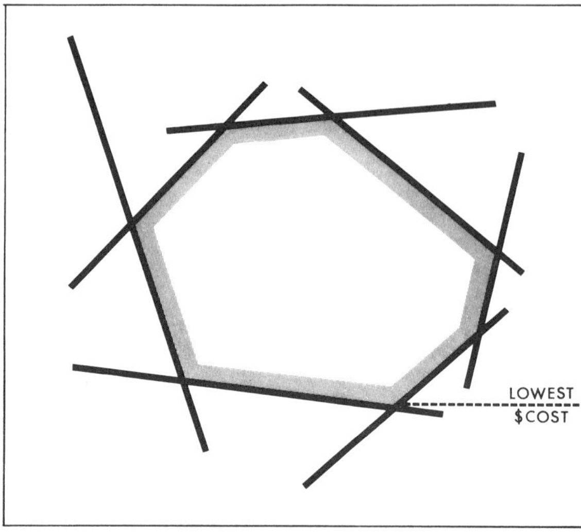

MANY-SIDED BOX

In other words, think of looking at a many-sided box. The computer will find the low point on the box, which is your minimum cost solution in this case. If, however, you are in a profit-maximization case, the computer will find the highest point on the box, which will give the maximum profits. These are optimum solutions.

After developing the restrictions for the production, transportation, and customer's requirements, we develop a large number of equations. We reduce this number by visual inspection. As an example, in the transportation equations, we obviously do not include the consideration of rail deliveries to points where we have no rail sidings. There are other shortcuts which reduce the total number of transportation equations that the computer has to solve.

In describing the demand to be fulfilled by the production and distribution system, we also take shortcuts. For example, if there are a number of accounts near one large location, we lump these destinations together and consider the demand as being at the center of gravity of the geographic area. The center of gravity is actually the physical center of gravity of the accounts, taking into consideration the distance between them.

LONG-TERM FORECASTS

Customers' requirements are defined in two ways. A sales forecast is sent in by the use point, or use group, for the tactical requirements. For strategic purposes, our long-term forecasts are prepared by geographical regions.

Now, after reducing the input to manageable proportions, the computer simultaneously solves the equations to arrive at the optimum solution. By optimum, we should make certain that it is clearly understood that we are limited by the accuracy by which the problem is described. In other words, bad meat makes bad hamburgers—inaccurate input data gives inaccurate solutions.

The results of the programming describe for us which customer should be served by what source and by what transportation method. It takes into account those plants which are overloaded and transfers some of the demand on these plants to the next most economical source. It will indicate what interplant hauling may be required, where our redistribution points get their product and by what mode of transportation.

BEST ALTERNATIVE

Now we come to another very real advantage of the computer program. If for some reason the most economical source point cannot supply the product to meet the demand, the computer gives us the next best alternative source point. It also gives us the cost penalty which is paid for exercising the option to go to that alternate source.

This, of course, is most helpful when there is an unscheduled outage, and the entire distribution network has to be juggled to supply the customer demand. Starting with the original solutions, it takes a matter of about four or five minutes of computer time to come up with a new optimum solution taking into account new circumstances or facts.

Strategic uses of linear programming cover the over-all, long-range planning of our system. In other words, where should plants be built? Where should we have redistribution centers? This requires long-range sales forecasts. These forecasts must be made a number of years in advance since the capital expenditure in a plant is something which will have an effect over many years duration.

Linear programming has also been used very successfully in this company for the purposes of business interruption-insurance cost determination. In other words, if one plant in a network is shut down as a result of some major catastrophe—which will mean the plant will be shut down

TRIP NO.
TRACTOR/TRUCK
USED IN PLACE OF
TRAILER NO.

Air Products and Chemicals INC.

TRIP REPORT

DATE
DRIVER
CLOCK NO.
PRODUCT

FROM: ______ TO: ______ RETURN: ETA ______ AM/PM DATE ______

1. RECORD SPEEDOMETER READING WHEN CROSSING A STATE BOUNDARY OR WHEN ENTERING THE N.Y. THRUWAY OR OHIO TURNPIKE—RECORD MILEAGE WHEN RETURNING TO A STATE HIGHWAY.
2. RECORD FUEL AND OIL OPPOSITE CORRESPONDING STATE.

ROW	DATE	STATE	CODE	PORT OF ENTRY CITY OR ROUTE NUMBER	SPEEDOMETER READING	FUEL GAL.	OIL QTS.
000				BEGIN READING			
010							
020							
030							
040							
050							
060							
070							
080							
090							
100				END READING			

BEGIN READING ______
TOTAL MILES ______

TRIP EXPENSES
CHARGED TOLLS ______ $ ______
CASH EXPENSES

DATE	/ /	/ /
MEALS		
MOTEL		
T-PHONE		
REPAIRS		
TOLLS		
FUEL		
TOTALS		

RECEIVED ______
APPROVED ______

ACCOUNT	AMOUNT

SHIPPER NUMBER	CUSTOMER	TIME IN	TIME OUT

OFFICE USE ONLY

DRIVER LOG NO.
TOTAL HOURS
ON-DUTY DRIVING
ON-DUTY NOT DRVG.
TOT. ON-DUTY HRS.
PAY HOURS
PAY MILES
TUBE TRAILER & PIGGYBACK
DROP TRAILER NO.
PICK-UP TRAILER NO.

TIME CLOCK
TIME IN
LEAVE PLANT
RETURN PLANT
TIME OUT

SPECIAL INSTRUCTIONS AND REMARKS

DELAY ANALYSIS

LOCATION OF DELAY	ARRIVE DATE TIME	LEAVE DATE TIME	TOTAL TIME	REASON FOR DELAY	CODE	SIGNED BY
	AM PM	AM PM				
	AM PM	AM PM				
	AM PM	AM PM				

FORM 3130

Trip report form, opposite, was specially designed to provide computer input data.

for a period of time—what is the optimum distribution pattern when this plant is shut down?

What should be our plan of attack if we were without the services of this plant? What is the increase in cost of serving our customers in this manner? This increase in cost should be the amount of business interruption insurance carried on the plant.

In addition to the distribution model, we have a trip reporting system from which data are accumulated. The data are fed into an ingenious program to develop cost, utilization and performance data for our private fleet. This program is unique in that it marries our accounting system to our distribution programs. We thus derive transportation cost and capacity inputs for our distribution model.

SELF-CHECKING SYSTEM

In addition, the program has a series of steps built into it which constitute a self-checking system for mismatches between one trip report and another. In a program of this type, where there is no balance to be struck between numbers as one would find in a bookkeeping system, this is a very significant aspect of the program.

From the trip report system data, the computer prepares a series of reports. These include:

- Vehicle utilization summaries.
- Reports for state taxing authorities covering mileage and fuel consumption.
- Performance statistics for each home terminal.
- Reports showing the location and utilization at each location for every fleet vehicle.
- Automatically prepared reports for use for verification of billings by leasing companies.
- A report showing the use of extra or spare vehicles at each terminal.
- A summary of the delay times and causes for operations out of each terminal.
- A report card for each terminal showing the trip report preparation errors.
- A recap showing the exact error detected by the computer in the trip report data submitted to the computer.

This trip reporting data processing system is tied into our bookkeeping system and the bookkeeping data is used to prepare cost and performance data on a unit-of-product-delivered basis. Maintenance expenses for each vehicle are accumulated by vehicle number from the bookkeeping system, which is handled by the computer.

The computer furnishes regular reports showing the expense by vehicle, as well as the expense by terminal for each vehicle assigned to that terminal.

These reports have been used for assisting in several significant management decisions pertaining to the selection of vehicles, the utilization of vehicles, vehicle assignments, vehicle capacity determinations, and numerous other changes resulting in improved fleet performance for the company. It has been clearly demonstrated to us that the preparation of all the information now being handled on the computer would otherwise be unavailable. This is because the cost of preparation and the clerical manpower to handle the processing of the data manually would be prohibitive.

We, at Air Products, firmly believe that the use of the computer as a tool in assisting the Distribution Department has made us more competitive, increased our profit and, most important, has put us in a position to give the best service possible to our customers.

C

Organization

The author studies the effect of the computer on three organizational levels: clerical, middle management, and top management.

35

COMPUTER SYSTEMS: HOW NOW THEIR EFFECTS ON THE ORGANIZATION?

Rudolf Borchardt

This article deals primarily with some of the current and future effects of computer systems on corporate organizational concepts and design for clerical, middle and top management levels.

In the domain of clerical organization, most of the current effects of computer systems are not only disturbing to most clerical employees, but, more often than not, downright detrimental.

Installation of a computer system causes considerable new stresses on the clerical force in that it requires ever increasing quality (especially in the area of "input data"), sets a fairly rigid working pace and accelerates the pressure by setting tougher deadlines.

Consider the hectic pressures of a conversion from a manual to an automated system. As an example, we might quickly glance at a conversion from manual to automated accounts receivable systems.

The good old ledger cards never required account numbers, but computer records cannot very well exist without them. The numerical "input data" must be accurate. Wrong account numbers, duplicated account numbers, and other "minor" errors can virtually ruin a conversion. In the "good old days," name and address on a statement only required sufficient accuracy to permit the mail carrier to deliver it to the right place. As for deadlines, filing of invoices could be delayed a day or more,

Reprinted from *Systems and Procedures Journal,* Vol. 18, No. 3, May–June 1967, pp. 27–29, by permission of the publisher and the author.

and would not even be noticed unless the monthly manual billing cycle was considerably delayed.

With a computerized system, input data has to be prepared on a daily basis to keep all the records and reports current. It is similar to billing each and every cycle each and every day, not just once a month. The resulting pressures on the clerical force are as new and unwelcome as they are terrific. You simply cannot keep a computer system waiting that costs from $300 to 600 per day and more, at least not without hearing from the boss.

WHAT HAPPENS WHEN COMPUTERS ARE APPLIED

What is happening in the automated office today is entirely similar in nature to what occurred some years ago in the automated factory. The machine and the assembly line sets the pace, and there is bound to be job displacement and job retraining among the clerical office force, just as there has been and will continue to be in the ranks of the blue collar workers.

When a computer absorbs manual clerical jobs, as it inevitably must, the first jobs that will be affected will be the simple, routine mass production jobs, usually performed by the very young employee with a very low seniority rating. While it is true that these jobs will usually be almost entirely absorbed, these younger employees have the flexibility to permit their training for other types of jobs, provided that they have sufficient schooling and intelligence to absorb such training.

Unfortunately, however, when a computer application cuts into these lower level clerical jobs, it simultaneously hits at senior clerks and lower supervisory positions usually held by persons at a somewhat higher level of seniority. This happens because these people now have fewer, if any, persons to supervise.

The problem here is that younger employees in lower level clerical jobs can usually be retrained for other types of jobs, but senior clerks and lower level supervisors have little to no flexibility to transfer to other jobs. As a result, it is not very surprising that these individuals feel threatened, and they usually show considerable resistance to the planned computer installation or new computer application.

THERE IS AT LEAST ONE WAY OUT

However, there is a way of overcoming this dilemma. It is as daring as it is progressive, and so far it appears to be working out satisfactorily. In at least one computer installation, the accounts receivable billing clerks, trained on standard bookkeeping machines, are being trained as keypunchers, and their supervisors are being taught how to run a "control center," which involves the input of controls and batches of purchases, credits and payments. Clerks used to sorting mountains of invoices, credits, payments and statements in alphabetical sequence are being taught to operate EAM sorters, collators and reproducers and to put the above punched card documents in numerical sequence. Some of these clerks are also put through computer operator school and programming school.

There are many disadvantages in going into a computer conversion with relatively "green" personnel, but there is also a tremendous advantage that must not be overlooked. These people are fully trained in the manual methods and the detailed operations of this particular business. However, the greatest advantage of all is their high level of motivation. They all recognize that management is going all out to keep them on the payroll, and that they are being trained in a new technology which would enable them to find other jobs in other corporations, should, by chance, their services be no longer required. As a result, they are willing to work day, night and weekends to accomplish successfully the conversion of "their baby" from a manual to computerized operation. This kind of motivation and dedication can never be expected from newly hired expert keypunchers and EAM operators.

ROUTE TO PROMOTION CUT OFF?

There is another personnel problem largely created by office automation which results in the frequent complaint that computer installations close down promotion opportunities for clerical workers to upper clerical and supervisory jobs. While upper level clerical jobs used to serve as a training ground for management positions, the majority of these senior clerical positions are now being eliminated through automation. The type of arguments heard, and they are difficult to deny, are that there is less opportunity for advancement, that "dead-end" jobs are on the increase and that the route of promotion and advancement is quite unclear.

It is quite true that record-keeping is more centralized in the computer; thus the various organizational line departments, like sales, finance, manufacturing, etc., have less need for their own clerical staffs. As a result, promotion within a department becomes more difficult as the bottom level clerical jobs become largely extinct.

Of course, all of this is an evolutionary process, and certainly does not happen overnight. (What sales or order entry-department, as an example, does not continue to maintain its own manual records for a while, until it fully trusts the computer output.) Until middle management becomes convinced that its jobs do not depend on the number of clerks under its supervision—indeed, that its salary increases and advancement up the ladder depend upon the number of positions it can eliminate hopefully (through attrition)—this situation of hidden, manually kept records in many clerks desks will continue.

As records become more centralized in the computer, increased numbers of keypunchers in the data processing department replace the manual clerical positions in the various line departments. As far as advancement possibilities are concerned, it is quite true that keypunch operators, no matter how expert, will find it hard to demonstrate supervisory and management potential. However, in the "good old days," was it any easier for a lowly clerical filer, sorter or record-keeper to demonstrate leadership qualities and "rise to the top"? The same qualities that deserved promotion to supervisory clerical positions in the manual clerical era should still apply in the current era of automation.

EFFECTS ON THE ORGANIZATIONAL UNITS

In the automated office the route of promotion in the systems and data processing area appears to be at least a three-step process:

1. Programmers can develop into senior and chief programmers or programming managers, and eventually could be promoted to running a computer center and becoming data processing managers. Another direction would be the route of systems analysis, where an analyst can move up to becoming data processing manager, or eventually, through continuous exposure to several different corporate divisions and departments, could transfer, for example, to the controllership, the marketing department, etc., or finally could even land a consultant's spot in the president's office.
2. Machine operators can progress from keypunching to operation of EAM equipment (sorters, collectors, reproducers, etc.) or to becoming a computer operator, and then to overall supervision of the entire computer center.
3. Administrative control clerks can move up to supervising a control section and to administering the entire massive input/output paper flow, which becomes even more voluminous as optical readers on the input side and high speed printers on the output side are installed.

In the domain of middle management organization, the effects of automation are not quite as clear cut. What is quite clear, however, is that clerical jobs diminish in number while middle management's value to the corporation changes from supervising large numbers of clerks to developing new and better ways of operating the business, resulting in new or modified computer applications. It should be safe to predict that middle management in the future will be more highly rewarded for imaginative innovation and for ability to motivate personnel who are scientifically, mathematically and systems-oriented, rather than for supervising large groups of clerical types.

EFFECTS ON THE ORGANIZATIONAL UNITS

And what effect might computer installations have on the old type line organization (i.e., sales, marketing, advertising, manufacturing, engineering, finance, etc.)? Some departmental or organizational areas will be merged, while others will be eliminated entirely. Traditional lines of authority will undergo change, and some departmental walls will give way as a result of revised information flows.

And just where should the data processing department appear on the organization chart? To whom should the systems manager, the data processing manager, the director of management information services report? It is this writer's belief that there is no simple stock answer to this question. The answer depends entirely on the individual corporate personality, on the nature of the business and on the structure and size of the organization.

As the first few computers were installed in the early fifties, they were used principally either for engineering and scientific applications (and therefore reported to the vice president of engineering), or for converting punched card payroll applications (and therefore reported to the corporate controller). Punched card systems had historically been reporting to the controller, so it was only natural that when these systems were converted to computer, the installation would continue to report to the same person on the organization chart, namely, the controller.

As it became obvious during the ensuing years that these were not just going to be ordinary computer applications, but that, in effect, corporate data banks were evolving, affecting the entire operation of the enterprise, virtually all top level corporate executives began to compete for control of what was to become the centralized computer information bank.

Business literature, computer manufacturers and management consultants helped "stir the pot" still further by proclaiming that whoever in the corporate structure finally controls the computer information system in effect ends up controlling the company. This made competition for computer control in the corporate hierarchy even more fierce.

As a result, the computer department has moved up the corporate ladder, and top-level staff positions are being created to take charge of this tool and serve *all* of the line departments. Positions have come into being such as the vice-president of administration, vice-president of management services, vice-president of information services, etc. Sometimes the corporate computer and systems department even finds itself reporting to the vice-president of planning, the vice-president of finance, and, on occasion, even to the executive vice-president, the president or the chairman of the board.

COMPUTER EVOLUTIONARY DEVELOPMENT

This type of evolutionary development is quite understandable, especially when one realizes that the expensive computer has moved from a historic record-keeping-tool to one that is planning-oriented in nature. As computer applications are growing more and more sophisticated, the computer is progressing from solely keeping track of the "past" (accounting-oriented systems), to one that not only accents current, up-to-date information, but also one that attempts to predict the future (planning-oriented systems).

As a result, it is only natural that a top-level (vice-presidential), corporate staff position, consultive and neutral in nature, had to be created and placed in charge of the computer and systems areas so that these would serve all corporate departments equally well, no matter whether their individual interests center on past, current, or futuristic types of data and information.

In large corporate entities, with multidivisions and multilocations, the question of centralization and decentralization of computer and system departments has been raised in concert with the overall corporate philosophy relating to this subject. This topic has recently become increasingly popular, since the advances in data communications hardware, circuits, etc., have been catching up with computer technology. The belated appearance of relatively cheap random access mass storage computer capability (i.e., "cells"), coupled with remotely located satellite computers or terminals, giving ready access via high speed communications links to a centralized data bank, has made time-sharing network concepts extremely attractive to the larger corporate entities.

This sort of concept requires a high degree of standardization throughout the network and calls for skilled centralized corporate systems staffs of specialists in systems planning, operations research and programming. It also requires local systems and programming personnel for each of the satellite computer installations in the network to handle applications peculiar to the particular corporate division concerned, but operating within the established corporate standards.

The successful establishment of such corporate computer networks usually requires a fairly high degree of centralized management to institute and control corporate standards and procedures throughout the various divisions and departments.

Strongly decentralized organizations requiring multi-computer installations will almost surely find each of these individual computers operating independently from one another. They are most likely not compatible with one another, making communication difficult, if not impossible. This approach appears more expensive and wasteful in the long run, and will not be able to take full advantage of the latest developments in computer and communications technology.

It therefore appears most likely that centralized administrative management will grow stronger in the future to develop and institute in concert with all corporate divisions and departments the standards and procedures for computer networks that will be adhered to throughout the entire organization. (This would not in any way prevent a corporate division general manager from running his division as he sees fit.)

In summary, then, in the future, we can look for increased centralized systems planning, but a variety of degrees in centralized and decentralized operating management philosophies.

The author discusses how more precise and predicative organization models can be formulated.

36

MODEL-BUILDING AND ORGANIZATIONS

Warren B. Brown

Until recent years, studies of organizational behavior which used mathematical or computer models have been rather scarce. Two of the main reasons seem to be (1) the very complexity of organizations, involving a rich variety of interacting elements, including both human and non-human factors, and (2) a lack of persons trained both in organization theory and the uses of mathematics and/or computers. The area of organization theory consequently has been characterized by verbal theories, allowing other fields with more easily quantifiable variables—such as economics, production, and finance—to lead the way in the use of mathematics and models generally. However, as our knowledge of organizational behavior develops there is a natural tendency to strive for fuller, more precise explanations of organizational phenomena and for better predictions;[1] model-building is a general method for accomplishing these goals. Examples of this development can be seen in areas such as organizational growth, structural ramifications of shifts in authority, and organizational adaptation to external competitive pressures. The purpose of this paper is to examine techniques of theory development and model-building for organizational analysis, focusing on some specific differences of common interest among languages and types of models.

Reprinted from *Academy of Management Journal,* June 1967, pp. 169–178, by permission of the publisher.

[1] Bernard S. Phillips, *Social Research* (New York: Macmillan Co., 1966), Chapter 3.

Theories of organizational behavior involve sets of statements or propositions about organizational phenomena.[2] These statements involve relationships among variables which presumably reflect real-world processes. The organization analyst uses the theory to communicate to others his ideas concerning both the understanding and prediction of organizational behavior. It should be noted in passing that these two happy results of a good theory are not logically the same:[3] for prediction we need to establish only that a hypothesis be more credible (i.e., providing convincing evidence) than any comparable alternative, while an explanation must establish the hypothesis as more credible than its negation. The latter is of course a stiffer test for the theory.

For organizations, the languages with which we develop theories often are verbal, sometimes mathematical, and in recent years they may also take the form of computer programs. There are various advantages and disadvantages to each of these language types. Let us look at the differences between verbal and mathematical theories first since they have been somewhat controversial.

VERBAL AND MATHEMATICAL THEORIES

The analyst of organizations typically will be interested in behavior which involves subtle and complex relationships; because of this it can be argued that such descriptions are best characterized by a verbal language, replete with many specialized adjectives and terms. These have the advantage of allowing the theorist to describe a wide range of subtle activities. The verbal language also allows him to keep a broad field of vision and yet maintain nuances and complex qualifications.

Yet, there is a serious problem of clarity with verbal theory. The insights and broad viewpoints which are afforded us by a verbal theory need to be coupled with clear logic and a format of presentation which will permit ease of manipulation of the variables;[4] this will allow us to better understand the model and to make predictions. Mathematical models serve us better in these latter respects than do verbal ones. They help to clarify our thoughts by forcing us to define our variables and to be explicit about their relationships. They also give us the opportunity to generate deductions which flow logically from the model and the requirements imposed on it. In this fashion we can test our ideas in abstract form,

[2] Hans L. Zetterberg, *On Theory and Verification in Sociology,* 2nd ed. (Totowa, N.J.: Bedminister Press, 1963).

[3] Olaf Helmer and Nicholas Rescher, "On the Epistemology of the Inexact Sciences," *Management Science,* VI, No. 1 (October 1959).

[4] Martin Shubik (ed.), *Game Theory and Related Approaches to Social Behavior* (New York: John Wiley & Sons, Inc., 1964), Chapter 1.

manipulate the model's parameters, and analyze the results, all often at relatively low cost compared to obtaining similar results by real-world experimentation.

One of the more well-known sociological examples is Simon's formalization [5] of Homans' theory of small groups.[6] Through Homans uses a wider variety of concepts, Simon's model simplifies the description of the social group to a model with only four variables, all functions of time:

I (t) – the intensity of interaction among the group members;
F (t) – the level of friendliness among the members;
A (t) – the amount of activity carried on by members within the group;
E (t) – the amount of activity imposed on the group by the external environment (the external system).

In accordance with some postulated dynamic relationships among the variables, the model becomes:

$$(1.1) \quad I(t) = a_1F(t) + a_2 A(t)$$

$$(1.2) \quad \frac{dF(t)}{dt} = b\,[I(t) - \beta F(t)]$$

$$(1.3) \quad \frac{dA(t)}{dt} = c_1\,[F(t) - \gamma A(t)] + c_2\,[E(t) - A(t)]$$

By substitution one obtains two simultaneous differential equations in three variables. These are solved to give A and F as functions of E at an equilibrium point (where $\frac{dF}{dt} = \frac{dA}{dt} = 0$). The result is:

$$(1.4) \quad A = \frac{C_2\,(\beta - a_1)\,E}{(C_1\gamma + C_2)\,(\beta - a_1) - (c_1a_2)}$$

$$(1.5) \quad F = \frac{c_2a_2\,E}{(c_1\gamma + c_2)\,(\beta - a_1) - (c_1a_2)}$$

The conditions for a stable equilibrium also are investigated; these are found to be:

$$(1.6) \quad \beta > a_1$$

and $(1.7) \quad c_1\gamma + c_2 + b\,(\beta - a_1) > 0$

As illustrated by this example, with its simplifications and lack of operational definitions, the more ardent proponents of mathematical

[5] H. A. Simon, "A Formal Theory of Interaction in Social Groups," *American Sociological Review* (April 17, 1952), pp. 202–211.
[6] George C. Homans, *The Human Group* (New York: Harpers, 1950).

models are often accused of tunnel vision and that the analytic power and relative precision of their models is achieved only by dangerous oversimplification. The elegance of the model may itself lead to a blind belief in its accuracy, though in fact it may seriously misrepresent the real phenomenon with which it is associated. Again there is a counterargument, pointing out that while simplification may indeed be necessary, the resultant power of analysis which permits us to follow long chains of reasoning is more than worth the cost. Further, all types of theories, including both verbal and mathematical theories, are subject to misrepresentation.[7] Regardless of the language used there is always the possibility that (1) the theory does not tell the whole truth (a type I error), or (2) that it makes statements that are false (a type II error).

ANALOGIES AS THEORIES

Analogies, including those in the form of computer programs, also have been used as theories. Although they may be particularly prone to errors of misrepresentation, analogies can aid us nonetheless in conceptual understanding and in formulating our ideas. Systems theory relies heavily on this technique: a selected class of elements is considered to have a correspondence with the elements of another class, e.g., when one relates the elements of an organism to the elements of an organization to examine an apparently common phenomenon such as growth.[8] If the theory for one system is highly advanced, it is tempting and sometimes successful to apply it to another, analogous system. An example would be Haberstroh's application of feedback control models from engineering to the analysis of information flows in organizations.[9] His model focuses on the control pattern for the safety function of a manufacturing organization; a block diagram for the structure is shown below.

[7] Herbert A. Simon and Allen Newell, "Models: Their Uses and Limitations," *The State of the Social Sciences*, ed. Leonard D. White (Chicago: University of Chicago Press, 1956), pp. 67–83.

[8] *Ibid.*

[9] Chadwick J. Haberstroh, "Control as an Organizational Process," *Management Science*, VI, No. 2 (January 1960). Reprinted in M. K. Starr (ed.), *Executive Readings in Management Science* (New York: Macmillan Co., 1965).

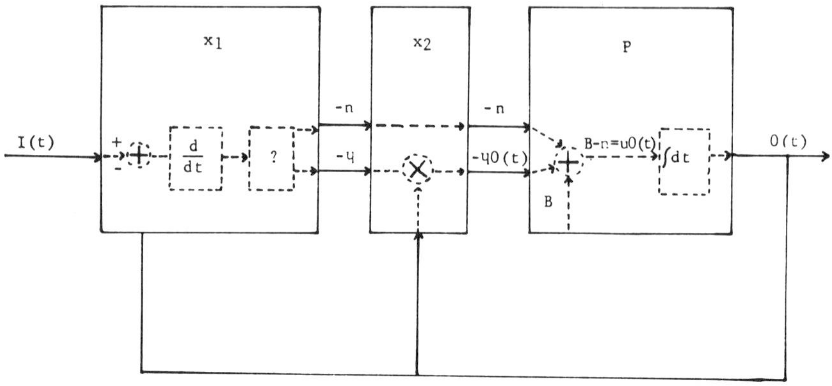

where I(t) – the annual safety objective
O(t) – safety performance of the plant
μ – the intensity of executive response to injuries
η – the level of independent safety activity
β – an exogenous load of new hazards
X_1 – the nonroutine control function
X_2 – the routine control function
P – the "program" operator which relates the control activities to the actual performance of the plant.

With an assumption μ and η are constant parameters, the injury rate is given by:

$$(2.1)\quad O(t) = \int[\beta - \eta - \mu O(t)]\, dt$$

Solving,

$$(2.2)\quad O(t) = \frac{\lambda}{\mu} + [\hat{O} - \frac{\lambda}{\mu}]\, e^{-\mu t}$$

where $\lambda = \beta - \eta$ and $\hat{O}$ is the initial level of the injury rate. His performance data for the years in question are fairly consistent with this equation.

Computer programs as analogies also have proven themselves to be quite useful for theory generation. Research at Carnegie Tech and Rand Corporation has led to a program called the "General Problem Solver" in which ill-structured problems are broken down into goals and subgoals, and the means related to the ends. This type of research will hopefully lead us to better theories regarding complex real-world problems such as the formulation of corporate policies.

An example of a computer flow chart to represent elementary social behavior is shown below. It is the first part of the Gullahorns' program [10]

[10] John T. Gullahorn and Jeanne E. Gullahorn, "A Computer Model of Elementary Social Behavior," *Behavioral Science,* VIII, No. 4, (October 1963).

which simulates the relatively simple interaction sequence between two persons, called Ted and George. The program is based on some of Homans' propositions concerning social exchange,[11] and it traces the dynamic implications of these propositions.

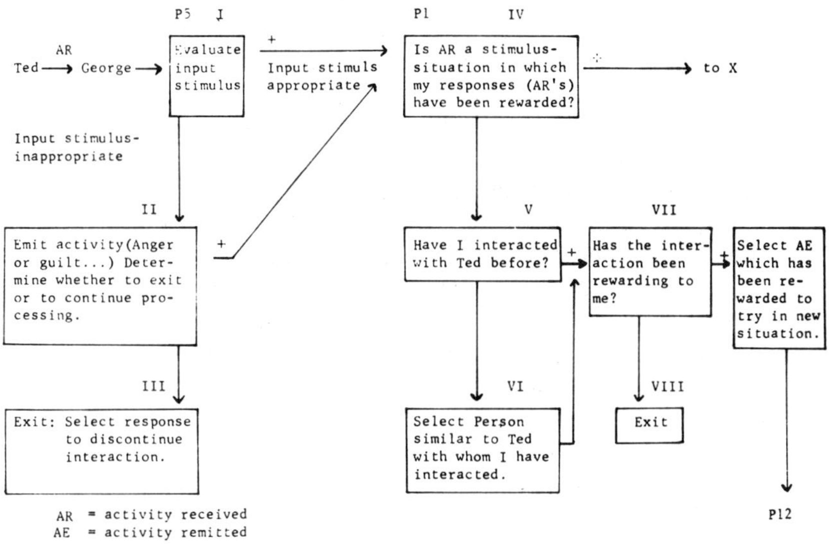

Other examples of model-building using computer programs which have generated a continuing line of research are the heuristic programs by which a computer can simulate cognitive properties.[12] This type of theory description, especially where many variables and/or details are involved, can be a great help in introspecting about the real processes involved. In addition, a computer model might stimulate the creation of models couched in other languages, e.g., a computer model of organizational adaptation might generate a mathematical description of the same process.

CHOOSING THE FORM OF EXPRESSION

The choice among languages for theory development thus depends simply on which one best fits one's area of interest and also permits the logical content to be manipulated and analyzed. Since there is a tendency for

[11] George C. Homans, *Social Behavior: Its Elementary Forms* (New York: Harcourt, Brace, 1961).

[12] Edward A. Feigenbaum and Julian Feldman (eds.), *Computers and Thought* (New York: McGraw-Hill Book Company, 1963).

people to use those tools (languages) with which they are most familiar, this means that organization analysts increasingly will need more proficiency in more than one of the languages just mentioned to stay abreast of the field.

When we test our theories of organizational behavior to determine their powers of explanation and prediction, we typically use somewhat simplified descriptions of the phenomena under observation. Although these are only approximations to the real-world, if the test results seem satisfactory we may accept the descriptions and the theory as idealized general statements and cease our experimentation in that area. When widely accepted by people working in the same field, we honor these paradigms with the name "scientific laws."

In our strivings to develop such paradigms through the use of model-building we find that several broad types of strategies are available to us (we will focus here on mathematical and computer models). In fact, it often is far more clear when one begins to create an abstraction of some selected organizational phenomenon which type of representation to use. One of the fundamental differences between types of mathematical models is whether they are deterministic or probabilistic.[13] With a deterministic model, if one knows enough about the history of the system, the future can be precisely predicted. Newton's famous laws are a classic example of this. Probabilistic models, which seem more currently popular for analyzing social processes, give us the probabilities of events occurring. Their popularity is based on the arguments that (1) social or psychological processes are in fact probabilistic, and/or (2) probabilistic models best fit the present evidence. Consequently, although we may not be able to predict any one person's behavior in a given setting, we may be able to make rather accurate predictions as to the way a percentage of persons will behave in that same situation. Models of learning and choice behavior typically are probabilistic for this reason.

An illustration is the stochastic model of freely-forming social groups which recently has been discussed by Horvath.[14] The model assumes that the distribution of the number of groups, by group size, is the equilibrium outcome of a stochastic process. The following 3 assumptions are made: (1) the probability of an individual joining a group is independent of the number of members in the group, (2) the probability of a member leaving a group is proportional to the number of members in that group, and (3) that members leave and join independent of any other person's decisions. Then, let

[13] James S. Coleman, *Introduction to Mathematical Sociology* (Glencoe, Ill.: Free Press, 1964), p. 526.

[14] William J. Horvath, "Stochastic Models of Behavior," *Management Science,* XII, No. 12, (August 1966).

α be the rate at which individuals join groups,
β be the rate at which individuals leave groups,
n_j be the number of groups of size j.
$A = \Sigma^{\circ}{}_1{}^{\circ}\ n_j$ is the total number of groups.
$N = \Sigma^{\circ}{}_1{}^{\circ}\ jn_j$ is the total number of individuals.

For equilibrium, the change in the number of groups of size j per unit time must be zero, i.e., $dn_j/dt = 0$.

Therefore,

$$(3.1)\quad \alpha n_{j-1} + \beta(j+1)n_{j+1} - \alpha n_j - \beta j n_j = 0$$

The distribution function is then derived:

$$(3.2)\quad n_j = (\alpha/\beta)^{j-1}\, n_1/j!$$

where n_1 is the number of isolates. Replacing α/β by k, we get:

$$(3.3)\quad n_j = k^{j-1}\frac{n_1}{j!}$$

In terms of A and k, the distribution function becomes:

$$(3.4)\quad n_j = \frac{k^j A}{j!\,(ek-1)}$$

To evaluate k in terms of N and A, the following transcendental equation is derived:

$$(3.5)\quad \frac{N}{A} = \frac{k}{1-e^{-k}}$$

Since N and A are known this equation may be solved for k. The expected values are then compared with the observed values; from data obtained by Coleman and James [15] for 23 different social gatherings, acceptable fits were found for 18 of them.

It should be noted that models are not necessarily true or false.[16] A model which attempts to describe some administrative phenomena such as influence relationships may be "sometimes-true"; the exact process or context of the situation may vary enough to make the description represented by the model inaccurate, at least at times. Social diffusion processes are often of this type: for example, the diffusion of an innovative idea through a large organization or social system may occur by means of a chain reaction process, or directly from a central information point, or in stages from a central source to staging points, and from these directly

[15] J. S. Coleman and J. James, "The Equilibrium Size Distribution of Freely-Forming Groups," *Sociometry*, XXIV (1961), pp. 36–45.
[16] Coleman, *op. cit.*, p. 561.

to the individuals. There may be combinations of these processes, and there may be variations of them based on such factors as a limited time-span of influence for a given individual in the diffusion chain, or competition among two or more new ideas which arise in the organization at approximately the same time. The result is that any one model may be true for a specific instance, but it may not hold true for all the variations of the basic type of process. It is a task for the analyst (and /or administrator!) to decide which of the many possibilities is a valid description in a given setting, or, put in a different way, what are the postulates which best describe the behavior in question.

It is also useful to distinguish among our models by their levels of abstraction. This distinction can be made either in terms of deterministic of probabilistic formulations. A model of a relatively specific concept relating to organizational behavior will be closely tied to the measurement of the particular phenomenon, whereas very abstract concepts often have only tenuous connections with actual experiences. An illustration can be found in the differences between theories of a person's mental states, involving concepts which are not directly measurable, and theories regarding the number of customers who wait in line for service from the organization, involving observable quantities. Consequently the lower level theories may have specific applications but are difficult to generalize, while the higher level theories may be broadly applied but are difficult to use to obtain detailed results in a specific instance. We must note, however, that as one's concepts become more abstract and the models describing them have a relatively wider scope, one gains potentially greater power for prediction of behavior. Significantly, it is at this level that major additions and changes in the construction of organizational paradigms occur.

In the beginning of an analysis of complex phenomena, our efforts can sometimes be made more effective by deliberately reducing the level of abstraction at first and building several models to explain the various observations. The concept of closure is relevant here; Phillips defines this as "the degree to which the boundaries which define the investigator's focus of attention include those factors which affect the phenomena under investigation." [17] Though our models will not include all possible factors which affect the variables even in a simple situation, we can obtain a high degree of closure nonetheless by accounting for the significant factors. Thus while no model representing real organizational phenomena can claim complete closure, good representations may still be obtained by relatively simplified abstractions, i.e., where primary factors are brought into the model and their interactions are accurately described.

[17] Phillips, *op. cit.*, p. 45.

GAME THEORY

Some specific models of interest to the organization analyst have been derived from the theory of games. Shubik comments on this theory as follows: "Game theory is a method for the study of decision making in situations of conflict. It deals with human processes in which the individual decision-unit is not in complete control of other decision units entering into the environment. It is addressed to problems involving conflict, cooperation, or both, at many levels. The decision unit may be an individual, a group, a formal or an informal organization, or a society."[18] Although rather wide-ranging in some applications, this theory is somewhat limited due to its highly normative flavor (as opposed to descriptive theories). The models tell us how games (conflict situations) should be played rather than how they actually are played in reality. Consequently, though this type of theory may serve as a useful model for the rational selection of a strategy given some alternatives, it has the drawback of leaving people out of the theory. In actual organizations, of course, the achievement of organizational strategies requires not only a knowledge of non-human factors (such as expected monetary payoffs for potential investments), but also a detailed knowledge of the way the people in the organization behave.

Computer simulation techniques provide us with another general strategy. In the broad sense a simulation is the same thing as a model, i.e., it purports to represent some real-world phenomenon. In the physical sciences, simulation—both with and without computers—has had a long tradition of use, as illustrated by physical models of airfoils and mathematical models of gas dynamics. For convenience with experimentation and manipulation of the variables, the mathematical models are often translated into computer models. In the field of organizational behavior, we are interested in using computers to aid us in building operating models of social processes and man-machine systems. These models enable us to reproduce (at least in part) the dynamics of a social process and to generate information about the changes taking place within the system over time.

Simulations also allow us to experiment with the variables in a system, a fact of particular value when it is too costly, undesirable, or impossible to work on the real system. Such experimentation may be a great help in organization design, for example in anticipating overload problems in organization communication channels and at decision centers. Several computer simulations have been designed as educational devices. There are a variety of management games available for business students

[18] Shubik, *op. cit.,* p. 8.

and executives to use, and for analysing certain kinds of international problems there is Guetzkow's internation simulation.[19]

Another grouping of models derives from the applications of cybernetic principles to organizations. Goal-directed, purposive behavior in organizations involves information feedback loops to maintain equilibrium values.[20] Models which represent this behavior can be used to analyze problems or organizational adaptation, indicating patterns of internal stress caused by external forces on the system. Cybernetic models can also be used to illustrate organizational goal selection on the basis of equilibrium conditions, and may even provide for learning by changing the probabilities of selected responses on the basis of past payoffs.

CONCLUSION

In conclusion, we find that model-building for organizational analysis is a relatively new and growing area, but one which holds out much promise for better organization theory. It must be emphasized, however, that the models in themselves do not give us good descriptions of organizational behavior, i.e., a model may be good mathematics but bad organization theory. The models themselves are basically tools for better understanding. Further, as we have noted, model-building has several dangers, such as over-simplifications, premature closure of a theory, and the generation of mystical beliefs in formulas. Despite such problems, however, model-building has already proven itself useful for theory development in several areas of organizational behavior, and it is certain that formal models will help us with additional studies. The dissatisfactions that have been expressed regarding older frameworks for administrative and organizational problems are well-known;[21] if new paradigms are to be created, based on validated hypotheses, it seems a safe bet that model-building will play a major role.

[19] Harold Guetzkow (ed.), *Simulation in Social Science: Readings* (Englewood Cliffs, N.J.: Prentice-Hall, Inc., 1962), Chapter 7.

[20] Stafford Beer, *Cybernetics and Management* (New York: John Wiley & Sons, Inc., 1959).

[21] Herbert A. Simon, *Administrative Behavior,* 2nd ed. (New York: Macmillan Co., 1959), especially Chapter 11, and Harold Koontz, "Making Sense of Management Theory," *Harvard Business Review* (July–August 1962) and "The Management Jungle," *Academy of Management Journal* (December 1961).

D

Finance and Accounting

The author describes ways in which the computer can be utilized in accounting procedures.

37

WHAT THE COMPUTER MEANS TO THE ACCOUNTING PROFESSION

Edwin T. Boyle

The computer presents two sides to CPAs: a side that threatens our existence as a profession and a side that promises dynamic opportunity.

The computer confronts us as a profession with a situation as basic as the discovery of nuclear energy. If we don't master the computer, it could destroy us. If we do master the computer, it will give us an abundantly creative instrument with which to work. But whatever we do with it, things are never going to be the same again.

I strongly believe that unless we overcome the *threat* of the computer, we shall never have a chance to realize its opportunities.

I would like to cover four basic points as they relate to this problem:

First—the threat itself

Second—the opportunities (Here I would like to present specific examples of services we are already performing for clients on our EDP equipment and some exciting potentials for new services.)

Third—some of the basic economics of computer practice

Fourth—the responsibility that we have to the business public, our staffs, and to ourselves as professionals

Reprinted from *The Journal of Accountancy,* Vol. 121, No. 1, January 1966, pp. 56–67, by permission of the author and the publisher.

I. THE THREAT

The banks, the service bureaus, the manufacturers and others who have entered the financial reporting and advisory fields are not just providing perfunctory write-up services, but often fairly sophisticated levels of management services.

These agencies provide package programs for financial management, which inevitably involves them in making choices on principles of accounting. Service centers are offering to convert present systems of accounting, such as are now set up in our clients' offices, to computerized systems. Clearly, these service centers are engaged in systems work—and they don't charge for it.

It's possible that in the future these service centers will add systems specialists to their staffs, including CPAs—and that they will use as a cogent sales argument the desirability of having the systems design work performed by those who own or control the hardware, of having systems specifically designed around the configurations of their own machines.

Atrophy could afflict the profession if CPAs become less and less engaged in this systems design work.

The attest function itself may also be vitally affected. An automated system generates more information, and faster, than the accountant can by wading through papers to prepare analyses of his client's accounts. The computer can automatically prepare balance sheets and income and expense statements, *both fully backed up* with detailed listings such as agings of receivables and payables, expenses, etc.

How much auditing will the client want for himself when he can see all the details of each account?

How much auditing will the banks insist on, if they themselves are preparing the data—especially when their systems will automatically provide a listing of all the components in an account?

Conceivably, the services provided by these agencies could destroy our local firms by taking over the lion's share of accounting work for all small and medium-size businesses. Loss of these clients, which provide a substantial share of the national firm's revenues, would hit even the largest CPA firms with a crippling blow.

II. THE OPPORTUNITIES

These threats make the computer sound like a potent machine.

What makes this machine so powerful an accounting implement—either for us, or for the other agencies who may utilize it?

We all know computers can add, subtract, multiply, divide and print—but so can many other accounting machines. The computer has more important capabilities that separate it from the posting machine category—capabilities that are all important to us as accountants and that make the computer an effective tool in our professional work.

This paper discusses the computer as a means of marrying two talents in our professional work—the marriage of management services with financial reporting.

Physically, this is what the computer can do:

The machine has a tremendous capacity to store information in its memory for subsequent recall. It can store in its memory such elements as price lists, cost factors, rates, descriptive data, equations and sequential order of working with that data. The computer will carry out programed instructions and print out the results at speeds that start at rates of 400 to 500 lines per minute.

Computers, once programed, can relate financial information in an infinite number of ways, far more effectively and with greater speeds than we, as accountants, can do it.

Computers have the ability to make calculations without the need for reprocessing cards, as was necessary under earlier types of tabulating equipment.

They can perform a sequence of operations without the input of new cards or tape to activate new calculations. Results obtained are held in abeyance pending further calculation. The information may be retained by the machine until further call, according to the programed instructions.

Under the conventional written system, because of the limitations of distribution columns, we normally recorded the amount of the transaction without all the collateral information. In order to analyze the different functions and facets of a business, we had to search through the files and through the basic records for much of the information that is provided for us automatically under computer systems of accounting.

Under computer systems, we may analyze sales separate and apart from the other functions of the business without scrounging through files and original records. We can separate sales by employee, by geographical area, by department, by product.

In studying labor costs, we can examine labor costs per hour, per unit, per classification of labor; we can analyze whether it is seasonal, fixed, etc. If we place in the machine's memory constant factors of cost and then later place the operating variables—as these variables become known—an infinite number of operating relationships may be developed and studied. Just think what opportunities this offers to CPAs in the future—to be able to obtain *currently* the basic data which are so necessary for management analyses.

By recording financial data with all the collateral information such as quantity, types, descriptive material, etc., we are able to record a financial transaction in its full environment for later retrieval. By recording transactions in terms of their lowest common denominators, we can correlate factors according to cause and effect relationships that exist in business situations. We can relate hours worked to labor costs, production units to manufacturing costs—all as a routine rather than an exceptional procedure.

It is *not* the ability of the machine to write up volumes of information with great speed that is important to us as professionals; this is a negligible aspect of computer operation as it relates to us. Rather, the computer affords us the means of carrying out many sophisticated, new, creative ideas in management services.

And if, when we are designing systems, we are able to anticipate factors that are important in solving problems, we can build these factors into the system, so that later they can be retrieved with minimum cost to the client—and these factors will be of tremendous importance to us in doing creative work for the client.

The type of information that we seek and what we do with it is limited only by our imagination and our resourcefulness.

A few examples of work being done on computers today (and remember, this is probably kindergarten work compared with the work that will be done in the next few years) will show how the computer benefits the profession.

Payroll Job

Preparation of a payroll is a time-consuming but routine job, which can be performed by the computer. And if we add the slight additional input information of how the employees spent their time, the computer can correlate this with production data and give management valuable cost and efficiency analyses.

To set up the basic payroll preparation job on the computer, the complete environment of an employee's pay and all the collateral information about him is fed into the computer's memory by means of punched cards, paper or magnetic tape. This information would include the employee's name, address, identifying number, base pay, overtime rate, premium pay, deductions, number of tax exemptions, method of computing unemployment tax, and other factors about pay and deductions. The same type of information is stored for all employees.

After the computer is fed the employee's weekly hours worked and his identifying number, it searches out his name and number and calculates his base pay, overtime, premium pay, total pay, withholding tax, unemployment deductions and other deductions and figures his net pay. It also updates this information and prints it out in a statement.

If the employee is paid by check, the computer writes the check in full, ready for signature—if in cash, it figures how many $20's, $10's, $5's and coins are needed.

But suppose not only the total number of hours an employee worked during the week was put into the computer, but also the time spent on different operations in a 48-hour work week. For example, if the employee worked 20 hours on operation A, 18 hours on operation B, and 10 hours on operation C, the computer could determine the rate per hour by computing the total pay and dividing by the number of hours worked during the week. By multiplying the hours worked on different operations by the cost per hour figure, the computer could print out, at the end of the payroll, the cost for each operation.

If the hours worked on these different operations, according to different locations or branches of the company, were fed into the computer, data on operational costs per branch would be printed out. If productive units were introduced into this calculation, data costs per productive unit, per branch, per operation and so forth would turn up.

The payroll job gives a good example of how you can take a routine task, add a little forethought as to what cost relationships may be significant, and produce reports as simultaneous by-products which have real value to management.

Budget Accounting

Budget accounting is another example of a computer application. The title of the budget accounts and the dollar amount of the annual appropriation can be stored in the memory unit. During the period under review, charges to the accounts are recorded not only in dollar amount, but with all the peripheral information relating to that dollar amount.

When preparing a periodic budget report, the computer lists the title of the budget account. In the first money column the amount of the appropriation is shown, in the next column the amount expended to date, and in the next column the unexpended balance. If the transactions of the preceding year are programed, the machine will then compare the unexpended balance remaining for the current year with the amount actually expended during the same remaining months of the preceding year. For example, if a report for the period ended July 31, 1965, were running it would show the budget account title, the amount of the appropriation, the amount spent for the seven months ended July 31, the unexpended balance left in the appropriation account and the amount expended from August 1 until December 31 of the preceding year. In this way a measure of the adequacy of the unexpended balance—by account—is obtained.

Furthermore, many of the budget accounts as shown in the summary report are broken into sub-accounts in a detailed report, so that it is possible to highlight the financial condition of each component of the budget.

In addition, the machine may list in full detail the descriptive matter in full support of each charge in the respective budget accounts. Copies of these reports are then distributed to the individuals responsible for the expenditure of funds.

This type of report makes additional auditors of the people who are responsible for the expenditure of funds. It places information that normally would be lost in the records up on the table for management to see—and at the proper time.

It brings to bear on a problem the vast storehouse of collateral information that management knows about the transaction, not just the cold final-figure results.

Inventory Control

Inventory is the heart of many businesses. It represents a substantial part of the capital investment in a business—not only in the cost of the inventory items themselves, but also the cost of housing them, financing them, etc.

Inventory items that do not move are of great cost to a business. Items that turn quickly are a great boon to a business. Yet many of the pulsations as they take place in the inventory account are unknown to management until they are too late for use. Automation is able to assist materially in this area.

For example, consider a client in the retail business with approximately 30,000 different items in its stock. We have converted their inventory control system from a manually posted card system to automation. Here is what we now provide to this client.

Each week we list, on a cyclical basis, by department, every item of stock in inventory—and its location. The client has numerous locations.

From "inventory outs," we can tell the client the "hot" items of merchandise that are selling. Since the date is shown for each inventory purchase, he knows the items that have not moved in 30 days, 60 days, 90 days.

On the basis of this information he is able to plan periodic sales of slow-moving stock.

The client receives an inventory summary showing inventory at the beginnning, purchases to date, sales at retail, sales at cost, gross profit on each item of sale, gross profit by category, open-to-buy quantities, and, by annualizing the cost of goods sold, the rate of inventory turn on each item of merchandise is computed.

When the buyers go to market, the information by factory and also by description of item is available to them.

Automation again gets the vital information up on the table where it can do the most good—and at a time when it is not merely historical in nature but when it can be used for management planning and decision-making.

Buying Decisions

One manufacturer of computer hardware recently conducted an experiment for a CPA's client, who is a wholesale distributor, to determine whether a computerized system could be designed to provide for automatic "buying."

At the time this was considered a difficult computer application, since many buyers feel that purchasing is based upon a sixth sense which only they possess, and that the reasoning used in determining a proper purchase could not be defined. Nevertheless, the experiment was started.

The buyers were first asked which basic data they considered in determining a proper purchase. Based upon their answers, the relevant data were programed into the machines. The machines then came up with their first tentative purchase order.

The buyers disagreed with some of the purchases. The reason for the difference was pursued, and the machine was then instructed to consider these additional factors in determining future purchase orders. This process continued until the machine finally came up with results, still different from the buyers, but which the buyers, upon reflection, admitted were probably more prudent purchases than theirs.

Do not forget, the machine was using the buyers' judgment—not its own. The machine was merely applying to a problem everything that the buyers said was important in solving that problem.

But, unlike humans, once a machine is programed to apply certain considerations to a set of data, all these instructions will be applied to all future problems without exception. The machines will not forget any one of these considerations and as more experience is gained and more factors added, the answers will become continually more refined and more reliable.

Furthermore, these instructions are applied to problems at a rate of thousands per minute.

Cash Flow

Just recently, my office worked on a cash projection for each month of an ensuing year. We did this cash projection by the familiar long method. On the first schedule, in addition to the opening cash balance, we anticipated the predictable receipts, other than operating income, and the reasonably anticipated disbursements, other than operating expenses.

On another schedule we listed items of income in varying amounts from 90 percent down to 30 percent. Correlated with that, we listed variable expenses that fluctuated between the 90 percent and 30 percent. From this format we were able to show the cash surplus or deficit which would be created each month, depending upon whether or not the revenue was 90 percent, 80 percent, 70 percent and so on down to 30 percent.

The cumulative cash balances at the end of each month were also shown. The preparation of these schedules was a long, arduous process. Also, we realized that if one of these figures were changed at any time subsequent to the preparation of the statements, the whole report would become obsolete.

After this report was prepared, we programed the same basic data into the computer so as to duplicate the original long method report.

There are different work potentials in the two reports. First, in the computer report all headings were stored in the computer's memory so that for all time in the future these same headings will appear; therefore, the reprinting of this particular report would be automatic at 600 lines per minute.

Second, under the computer system, if any of the receipts or disbursements were changed, or any item of revenue or expenses changed, by merely inserting the changed figures for each month of the year we could completely update the report in a matter of three to four minutes.

But, far more important, we are able to show on a continuing basis the various financial results that might obtain at the various levels of sales, with full consideration given to the costs and expenses that correlate with those various levels.

By showing the range of the information and calling management's attention to the critical point of operations, management can then devote its full attention to avoiding that critical level. Or if a proper level of sales cannot be maintained, expenses may be cut at the appropriate time. The cloth can be cut to fit the pattern!

Estate Planning

In estate planning the computer is a valuable instrument in dealing with thousands of facts that ordinarily tie up a considerable amount of an adviser's time. A great deal of information relative to a client's estate can be punched and placed in computers.

In one estate planning operation known to the author, 80,000 instructions guide the computer in relating such information as assets held, property owned individually, in joint tenancy, or in tenancy by entirety; number of testator's children, and their ages, marital status, etc.

This particular program stores 15,000 footnotes or references based upon results obtained after applying 80,000 instructions to data. And if one of the footnotes or instructions needs to be changed, it is a simple matter to add the change into the program. For example, if a person's estate is of a certain size and he has not taken the lifetime exemptions concerning gifts, there may be a footnote to consult with his attorney. There also may be a footnote to consider changing title to his residence.

An adviser might think of every significant factor of a client's case except that contained in instruction No. 72,004—the computer will not forget it. The adviser may customarily think of footnote No. 9,268, but forget to apply it in a particular case; the computer will always remember it. Thus the estate planning program will continually be refined, and will permanently retain all refinements.

The machine does not have judgment, but it does catalogue and apply all considerations that we are able to define in forming our judgments. It certainly narrows the judgment area. And if a new idea or a new instruction must be added to the program in the distant future, that too will be automatically applied to all future problems.

Historical Statements

Many CPAs in public accounting practice today know that as their firms grow, it becomes more and more difficult to maintain close contact with clients. It is possible, however, to stay close to a client's figures.

Today, automation makes it possible to record all the significant items of the balance sheet and income and expense statement of clients in a format that compares his figures for past years.

For clients without automation equipment, balance sheet and income and expense items may be recorded according to codes established in the computer program.

To the right of the money columns, as they appear in the balance sheet, we show the percentage that each component is of the total assets. For example, cash may be 5.2 cents of each dollar, accounts receivable 13.4 cents, and so forth—these figures are shown next to comparable items of prior years. This also applies to liabilities.

The percentage that each item of cost is to the sales figure may be shown in the income statement—and again next to figures of the prior three years.

In planning the job program, CPAs can decide which information is important to us and to management, so that this information will be called to our attention currently with each new report. This information includes current working-capital comparisons, net ratios, cost comparisons relative to sales, inventory turns, number of days' sales in accounts receivable, and other relationships that might be suggested.

Once these ratios and relationships are defined they may be programed so that the machines will automatically compute and update the reports with every new set of figures—prepared at calculation and print-out speeds of hundreds per minute.

Once an accumulation of back data is stored in the machine, this information may be used in numerous calculations and comparisons at no extra cost to the management.

And these back figures often bring to bear on a problem valuable information which, because of age, would have been completely disregarded in the consideration of the problem. They add a new dimension to the study of trends, ratios and comparisons and thereby make more scientific our interpretation and diagnosis of the financial story.

Family Costing: Cause/Effect Relationships

As automation develops, it's quite probable a completely new type of report will evolve that will be used quite extensively in future financial reporting. This will be a report that shows not only dollar amounts, but cause and effect relationships that also exist in a business. A simple example of the nature and importance of this type of report will clarify this point further.

Assume in the construction business that costs of a number of 3½-ton tractors are compared: Equipment A spent $1,200 for gasoline during the current year, equipment B spent $850. Naturally, in comparing the two, the question arises: "So what, how many miles did equipment A travel and how many miles did equipment B travel?" The wages for the operator chargeable to equipment A might have been $2,000; equipment B, $2,200. Again, "So what, how many hours did the operators work on the respective pieces of equipment?" The same question may be asked for each expense chargeable to the individual pieces of equipment.

For a construction company we have designed a format that brings these cause and effect relationships into focus.

The usual conventional dollar amounts of the transactions are at the top of the report. At the bottom are shown the miles traveled, the number of gallons of gasoline consumed, the miles per gallon, the operator hours. By dividing hours worked into the cost of wages, the cost per hour for the operator can be computed. The total cost of operating the equipment can be divided by days worked, by miles, or by hours—by whatever divisors seen significant. We can show the number of units delivered by each piece of equipment. The machine computes these costs per unit for each piece of equipment at speeds of hundreds a minute.

Family Costing: Comparison of Components

All of the above information is of extreme interest to this particular company—but still, it is not the full story. Next, they would like to be able to compare how one 3½-ton tractor compares with another, not only in total costs but for all of the component relationships as well.

We therefore inform the machine that equipment No. 102 is a 3½-ton tractor, No. 105 is a 3½-ton tractor, No. 182 is a 5-ton tractor, No. 240 is a 3,000-gallon trailer. We identify the family to which each numbered piece of equipment belongs. We now run a report which shows in the total column all the dollar amounts and also the cause and effect relationships for the total family of equipment, and, as a spread, these same component figures for each piece of equipment within the family.

This report shows very clearly the inefficient equipment and also the cause of the inefficiency: The piece that may be inefficient from the point of view of gasoline economy may be efficient from the point of view of cost per productive unit because of its larger productive capacity. This report permits a comparison of likes with likes.

Family Costing: Retrieval Possibilities

And the report can also be expanded. In the construction business one piece of equipment may have a complete overhaul at the end of the second year of operation; another piece may have an overhaul at the start of its third year of operation. One year's figures are not adequate in arriving at comparable costs of operating equipment. Our firm has therefore tried to get away from period accounting for one year and to show for each piece of equipment the costs and components described above which are applicable for the three preceding years, in addition to those of the current year. This furnishes management with valuable information.

We can now divide overhaul costs by miles and come up with a significant figure. This figure might not have been accurate had it been done for one year alone. Labor dollars can be divided by numbers of hours and productive units to get unit costs, costs which might have been distorted in one particular period. We can see the ranges of costs—the high figure, low figure, average figure—and this is done not only per piece of equipment but also according to family and according to location of the respective units. This report assists management in formulating its equipment replacement policy. While depreciation costs go down as the equipment gets older, operating costs in all probability go up. Immediately evident are the miles per gallon per piece of equipment relative to its age. The Fords may be compared with the Dodges, with the Macks; truck costs can be compared according to their efficiency while under control of different operators. The retrieval information possibilities are almost infinite.

Now that we have this information on hand, all the cost data necessary are available to store standard costs in the machine's memory. Hourly labor cost per operator, per helper, are known and, where applicable, according to geographical areas.

We know the direct cost of operating the different pieces of equipment.

We decide which is the significant factor in cost calculations—the mileage figure, hours worked by the equipment, or days on the job—and use any one of them. Only cost components that are pertinent are stored in the computer.

If at the end of a day an operator reports that he worked five hours, and the equipment traveled 140 miles and worked for five hours, the machine will seek out the cost per hour for the operator according to his location and multiply out the labor cost. It will seek out the family to which the piece of equipment belongs and its location, multiply the hours worked by the cost per hour or by the miles traveled, whichever figure is deemed appropriate. If material were used on the job, by merely reporting the type material and the quantity, the machine will seek out the cost of the material and compute its cost.

In addition to the above direct costs, the computer's memory may store the burden that applies to the different direct costs and compute the total cost of the job and the resulting profit or loss for the element involved.

If the income is reported daily on this basis, it is possible to come up with complete income and expense statements daily, per piece of equipment and per contract, with little difficulty.

If the coding system is designed to separate the costs according to the breakeven concept of accounting, it prepares breakeven results automatically. Once cost factors are stored in the computer and identified, the machine will make all the necessary calculations upon introduction of the variable information.

"Explosion Report"

This report is one in which we record financial data in one particular way, prove it to a known total, and then explode out results in completely different arrangements of the figures. For example, in connection with banking we have an expense report in which the items that are to be apportioned are listed in varying percentages.

The methods of apportionment have been predetermined and have been written into the computer program. Let us say that the amount of

SCHEDULE NO. 1

Tank Trucks

Family 03–1000-1400 Gallons
Location—Plant No. 3

Equipment Costs *(Exclusive of Operating Labor)*		*Total Family Cost*	*Equipment No. 157*	*Equipment No. 158*	*Equipment No. 207*
Gasoline	(1)	xxxxxx	xxxxx	xxxxx	xxxxx
Oil		xxxxx	xxxx	xxxx	xxxx
Tires		xxxxx	xxxxx	xxxxx	xxxxx
Overhaul work:					
Parts and service	(2)	xxxxxx	xxxxx	xxxxx	xxxxx
Labor	(2)	xxxxxx	xxxxx	xxxxx	xxxxx
Miscellaneous repair parts	(2)	xxxxx	xxxxx	xxxxx	xxxxx
Miscellaneous repair labor	(2)	xxxxx	xxxxx	xxxxx	xxxxx
License plates		xxxxx	xxxx	xxxxx	xxxxx
Insurance		xxxxx	xxxxx	xxxxx	xxxxx
Depreciation		xxxxxx	xxxxx	xxxxx	xxxxx
Total direct expense		xxxxxx	xxxxxx	xxxxxx	xxxxxx
Shop overhead (XXXX%)	(2)	xxxxxx	xxxxx	xxxxx	xxxxx
Total equipment expense		xxxxxxx	xxxxxx	xxxxxx	xxxxxx
Cost per hour:					
Equipment hours worked		xxxx	xxxx	xxxx	xxxx
Cost per hour		xxx	xxx	xxx	xxx
Cost per mile:					
Miles traveled		xxxxx	xxxxx	xxxxx	xxxxx
Cost per mile		xxx	xxx	xxx	xxx
Cost per day:					
Days worked		xxx	xxx	xxx	xxx
Cost per day		xxxx	xxxx	xxxx	xxxx
Units delivered:					
Quantity		xxxxxx	xxxxxx	xxxxxx	xxxxxx
Cost per unit of measure		xxx	xxx	xxx	xxx
Gasoline consumption		xxxx	xxxx	xxxx	xxxx
Miles per gallon		xx	xx	xx	xx
Units delivered per hours worked		xxx	xxx	xxx	xxx

Explanatory Notes—Schedule No. 1

Gasoline costs (1) are developed by the computer itself by multiplying the number of gallons of gasoline consumed, as taken from an operating report, by the cost of gasoline per gallon. The rate per gallon is stored in the machine's memory according to the status of the equipment.

Shop Overhead. In applying a burden to represent shop overhead, the computer singles out and accumulates certain specific items of cost chargeable to each piece of equipment such as repair labor, parts, etc., and multiplies this total by a predetermined burden rate stored within the machine. See (2). Items of cost such as license plates, insurance, etc. are disregarded in this calculation.

Cause and Effect Relationships. Distortions in operating ratios may have many different causes. The piece of equipment with the best gasoline efficiency (as shown in miles per gallon ratio) may have the highest cost per hour (as a result of a major overhaul performed during the current period) and the lowest unit cost per quantity delivered (because of the capacity of the unit).

Cause and effect ratios for any one piece of equipment while under the control of different drivers can readily be shown.

A significant distortion in any one of the ratios leads to further inquiry or further refinement of the figures. The computer can do the latter with ease.

SCHEDULE NO. 2

History of Equipment Costs

Equipment No.: 157
Equipment Make: Ford; Year: 1964
Family 03—Tank Trucks 1000-1400 Gallons

Equipment Costs (Exclusive of Operating Labor)	*Year to Date*	*1964*	*Accumulation for Period*
Gasoline	xxxxx	xxxxx	xxxxxx
Oil	xxxx	xxxx	xxxxx
Tires	xxxxx	xxxxx	xxxxx
Overhaul work:			
Parts and service	xxxxx	xxxxx	xxxxxx
Labor	xxxxx	xxxxx	xxxxxx
Miscellaneous repair parts	xxxxx	xxxxx	xxxxx
Miscellaneous repair labor	xxxxx	xxxxx	xxxxxx
License plates	xxxx	xxxx	xxxxx
Insurance	xxxxx	xxxxx	xxxxxx
Depreciation	xxxxx	xxxxx	xxxxxx
Total direct expense	xxxxxx	xxxxxx	xxxxxxx
Shop overhead—apportioned	xxxxx	xxxxx	xxxxxx
Total equipment expense	xxxxxx	xxxxxx	xxxxxxx
Cost per hour:			
Equipment hours worked	xxxx	xxxx	xxxx
Cost per hour	xxx	xxx	xxx
Cost per mile:			
Miles traveled	xxxxx	xxxxx	xxxxx
Cost per mile	xxx	xxx	xxx
Cost per day:			
Days worked	xxx	xxx	xxx
Cost per day	xxxx	xxxx	xxxx
Units delivered:			
Quantity	xxxxxx	xxxxxx	xxxxxxx
Cost per unit of measure	xxx	xxx	xxx
Gasoline consumption:	xxxx	xxxx	xxxx
Miles per gallon	xx	xx	xx
Units delivered per hour worked	xxx	xxx	xxx
Tire cost per mile	xx	xx	xx

NOTE: Above piece of equipment owned since 1964; therefore spread of costs limited to two years.

Explanatory Notes—Schedule No. 2

This schedule shows the highs, the lows, the averages for each piece of equipment over a period of at least three years. Distortions which may be induced in the figures for a particular year have little effect on the accumulation for the full period covered.

If desired, the computer will update the gasoline expense of prior years to reflect the current prices of gasoline.

Through the use of index numbers, other components of cost (such as labor costs, insurance, shop overhead) could readily be updated to reflect current costs.

the expense is $2,452. This same figure totaling $2,452 is exploded out by branch, and immediately following that we explode out the same $2,452 by Federal functions. Thus we have the original transaction according to the general ledger code of the particular bank, according to branch accounting, and according to Federal function.

This is very useful in other types of industry as well. For example, consider the item of labor costs: This expense can be classified according to seasonal, fixed, casual labor, etc., and then this same total may be exploded out in many different cost relationships.

How does this work with regard to sales analysis? Take a company in the plant-mix business. We list various products sold during a specified period by ton and dollar amount. Each one of these products has a different formula and a different mix of ingredients. After listing the sales analysis by finished product, the ingredients that went into that particular product according to the standard bill of material that makes up the end product are exploded out. In this way it is possible to control costs of the ingredients at the source.

Annualization of Statements

In a seasonal business it is often normal to have losses occur in the off-season. Whether or not these losses are of significant concern to the management depends upon their comparison with prior years. These losses may be greater than the norm or they may be less than the norm. The loss alone is not sufficient to judge how well the company is doing during the current year.

Many of these companies find it necessary to combine the actual operating results for a part of the year with estimates for the remainder of the year based upon prior years' figures.

One method by which this type of statement may be prepared on a routine basis with automatic data processing equipment is to present statements for a five-month operating period ended, say, on May 31 on a normal basis. The income and expense statement would start with sales, then show the components of expenses, and finally the profit or loss for the period ended May 31.

From the prior year it would be relatively easy to take May 31 results for that year and subtract that figure from the December 31 figures in order to get a basis for estimating the period from May 31 to December 31.

This deduction of May figures from December 31 figures could be performed merely by placing in the machine the figures of the previous year for May 31 and the figures for December 31 and programing the machine to subtract one figure from the other.

To continue, if labor costs were up 5 percent for the current period as compared to the preceding year, the labor cost representing the period from May 31 to December 31 could be multiplied by 1.05 within the machine.

If material costs were up 12 percent, the material costs as developed for the remaining period could be multiplied by 1.12 with little effort. If administrative salaries were up $3,000 per month, this increase in dollar amount could be programed into the machine with little difficulty.

This same principle could be applied to the income account taking into account product mix. One particular product might be selling for 6 percent more than during the previous year; one could be selling for 3 percent under the average selling price for the preceding year.

By computing as a base the remainder of the preceding year, and applying to it the new conversion ratios for each one of these figures, it may be seen readily that information could be converted each month from the remaining period of the preceding year or years to a revised estimate for the current year.

At the end of the six-month period this same principle could be applied; that is, the six-month actual report plus a six-month converted estimate for the year.

After seven months it could be seven months actual plus five months remaining, converted on the basis of the new ratios within each one of the accounts. In other words, we would be telescoping in on the annual figures and removing the surprises from the company's figures—which is one of the objectives of financial planning.

The annualization of statements could be produced by the machine with little effort and become as routine as the normal monthly trial balance. If it were desired to take the last three years as a base, compute an average and apply a percentage to that average, that could also be done within the machine's programing. If you can do it in your head, the machine will do it merely by carrying out your instructions according to the sequence of calculations you would use in performing this task by the long method.

III. THE CPA AND COMPUTER ECONOMICS

The above cases indicate that they have a consistent theme throughout. In each of them the computer has been used as a means to make possible the marriage of two professional talents: management advisory services and financial recording techniques.

We have not been looking primarily at examples of the ability of the computer to process mass quantities of data at rapid speeds; we have been seeing it combine the accountant's skills in management services with his skills in financial recording.

At this point many will be wondering how this marvelous—and fairly expensive—tool will fit in the economic framework of a customary accounting practice.

Naturally, it is very difficult to generalize in this area because of the various degrees to which a CPA may become involved in the computer business. He may rent or own his own equipment; he may work through the service bureaus or through the banks; he may combine with other CPAs in a pooled operation; or he may join with other CPAs in a membership-type program.

The costs incurred in computer practice, therefore, will depend on which mode of operation an individual chooses. The important point is that one or more of these modes is within the economic range of every CPA firm.

Even though it is difficult to put a figure on the economics of computer practice without knowing specifics, there is one basic point that I would like to stress: This concerns the income potential that exists in this practice. The increased depth of the services performed in a computer practice means a higher base amount of fees.

It is not unusual that sophisticated computer work for one client will total fees of $2,000 to $3,000 per month. These fees naturally must be justified in the opinion of the client's management or, as we all know, they never would be accepted.

When management does the work in their own offices, their costs run at least as large as our fees and most times larger—for computer services—and they do not get all the collateral benefits that are byproducts of a CPA's computer service.

In my office we use a rule of thumb that we can do the work for the client at a cost no greater than that currently incurred by him. And for the same cost he gets infinitely more significant information than he could from a noncomputerized system.

IV. THE CPA'S RESPONSIBILITIES

Accountants should be extremely active in the development of computer systems. We owe it to our clients, ourselves and our staffs. We are completely familiar with accounting proofs and accounting controls, with methods and systems, with business reporting, with costs, breakeven figures, pro formas. We have become more or less the business doctors—we are eminently qualified to be the main participants in this field. But are we assuming our full and proper role in its development? How many of us are aware of the great potential offered us?

Accountants must decide today: Who are the leaders going to be in the development of this new field—who will the prime movers be?

SCHEDULE NO. 3

Contract Income and Expense Report Period: ______________

Key to Cost Codes: M = Material; E = Equipment; F = Foremen; O = Operator; H = Helper; L = Laborers; S = Sundry

				Income			Direct Costs					Burden			
Date	Cust. Name	Job No.	Type Matl.	Quantity	Unit Price	Income	Cost Code	Equip. No.	Quantity	Rate*	Total	Rate*	Amount	Total Cost	Profit or Loss
07-01-65	Smith	8060		Contract Price		1,600.00									
07-01-65	Smith	8060	A				M		58.29	20.00	1,165.80	6.05	70.53		
07-01-65	Smith	8060					E	177	10.50 hrs	8.05	84.53	4.25	3.59		
07-01-65	Smith	8060					O		10.50 hrs	4.20	44.10	24.75	10.91		
07-01-65	Smith	8060					H		10.50 hrs	4.00	42.00	19.62	8.24		
			Job Totals			1,600.00†					1,336.43†		93.27†	1,429.70†	170.30†
07-02-65	Brown	8092	C	75.02	13.25	994.02									
07-02-65	Brown	8092	C				M		75.02	8.00	600.16	6.05	36.31		
07-02-65	Brown	8092					E	224	8.67 hrs	6.72	58.26	4.25	2.48		
07-02-65	Brown	8092					O		8.67 hrs	4.20	36.41	24.75	9.01		
07-02-65	Brown	8092					H		5.00 hrs	4.00	20.00	19.62	3.92		
07-02-65	Brown	8092					L		24.00 hrs	3.90	93.60	15.45	14.46		
07-02-65	Brown	8092													
			Job Totals			994.02†					808.43†		66.18†	874.61†	119.41†
	Total All Contracts					2,594.02†					2,144.86†		159.45†	2,304.31†	289.71†

Cost "Explosion" ______________

Material A	1,165.80	
Material C	600.16	
Equipment	142.79	
Operators	80.51	
Helpers	62.00	
Laborers	93.60	
Matl. Burden		106.84
Equipment Burden		6.07
Operators Burden		19.92
Helpers Burden		12.16
Laborers Burden		14.46
	2,144.86†	159.45†

*Stored in memory.
†Dagger designates totals.

Explanatory Notes—Schedule No. 3

All rates shown on this schedule are stored in the computer's memory.

By introducing the variable information, as it becomes known, the computer will do the rest: compute costs, profit or loss, components of cost—by day, by job, by location, etc.

In future years, these same variables could be used to recompute job costs on the basis of cost levels at that time. Thus, job experience of the past that normally would become obsolete because of changes in labor rates, material cost, etc., may now as a routine matter be restored to management for use in current bidding. Furthermore, if a change in volume of business were being considered, the rates correlating with the contemplated change could be stored in memory and its effects shown. During the course of a current year, as new cost standards become known, all job costs for the current year may be computed retroactively on the basis of the new standards, merely by inserting new rate cards in memory, and reprocessing the variables for the year.

Will it be the engineers, who certainly are qualified in scientific methods?

Will it be the mathematicians and physicists, who are extremely sophisticated in the use of computers? They have done the programing for the missile age—their work in operations research has important business applications.

Will it be the bankers? They have the money, they have the hardware. In addition, they have a captive audience. They have been making great strides of late with the business public.

Or shall we be able to retain our present position of prominence in the business advisory areas—and if so, how? It has to be more than self-preservation—it must be based upon good solid business reasons.

And what should we, as practitioners, be doing about it today? How do we participate meaningfully in this new field?

First, we must improve our own skills. This may be accomplished through educational courses designed to train us in scientific techniques of solving problems. We must study causal relationships in business, and learn what operations research is all about when applied to business problems. We must further our studies in the management sciences. By broadening our base, we will know what additional information we want to retrieve from computer systems.

The American Institute has already taken an active role in the indoctrination of the regular practitioner in this new computer field. Professional development courses will be presented in computer science. These courses need not at first be at a highly sophisticated level—that can come later. Articles have been, and I am sure will continue to be, featured in *The Journal of Accountancy* concerning the roots of the problem. By this I do not mean the mechanics of programing: In my opinion, programing is a technique for the specialist, not necessarily for the general practitioner.

But the professional CPAs must gain overall control and direction of some equipment. They must band together to share the resources of the computer. With improved communication providing for direct input to machines it will be no problem for CPA firms in widely separated locations to utilize centralized computer facilities.

There must be a complete interchange of ideas by accountants among themselves as they develop computer concepts and methods. This kind of exchange is vital to the future of any profession.

The present situation calls for a very large, concerted, all-out effort by accountants. We cannot afford to be like the oldtime barber who explained the origin of the stripes on the barber pole. He noted that the stripes date back to the time when barbers did the blood-letting and were the surgeons; then he said, regretfully, "We never should have let it get away from us." This is the position of the accounting profession today.

Let's not let it get away from us.

Fortunately, the clients are still ours.

The authors describe one company's experiments in simulating the financial structure of the entire enterprise.

38

SIMULATION IN FINANCIAL PLANNING

E. N. Khoury
H. Wayne Nelson

Simulation, the mathematical representation of a system in order to see how a change in one of its elements will affect the others, is—at least potentially—one of the most powerful tools of operations research. It is finding increasing use in the solution of military and production problems.

In the financial area its application is less well known. Simulations of economic and financial processes have been employed mainly as research and teaching aids. Little has been done to develop simulation techniques to improve precision and response in the financial planning process within the corporate structure.

At Burroughs we have been experimenting with a simulation of the financial structure of the entire company. Our experience thus far has convinced us that this technique can provide management with an effective new planning tool.

This article, based on that experience, discusses the development of a financial simulation model structured around traditional accounting reporting practices. It emphasizes (1) the understanding of the business processes necessary to structure a useful model, (2) the model as a mirror of corporate policy, (3) the values and pitfalls in the use of a simulation model, and (4) certain methodological issues involved.

Reprinted from *Management Services,* March–April 1965, pp. 13–21, by permission of the authors and the publisher.

SIMULATION

Whenever the logical relations between the elements in a structure or a system can be quantified or expressed in measurable terms, a mathematical representation of these relationships can be formulated. The set of all these formal statements is then a model of the system. When we manipulate this model, the technique is called simulation. (This definition lacks the precision that the professional operations researcher would require, but it is adequate for the needs of the financial executive.)

As a tool applied to management problems, simulation is comparatively new. Its development and application are closely tied to the development and application of computer technology. It has been used to study complex problems in military strategy, traffic control, machine loading, and process control that do not lend themselves to solution by mathematical programing and other optimization techniques.

Because simulation has generally been applied to the nonfinancial aspects of business, many financial executives are as yet unaware of it. Yet simulation has proved to be a powerful tool when applied to the planning process.

In almost everything we do, the ultimate test of the adequacy of our decisions is the test of reality. But today business can seldom afford the luxury of testing the consequences of major decisions in the real world. Rather than determining the flight characteristics of a proposed missile by building and launching it, we now first simulate its performance on the basis of its design characteristics. In this way we can experiment without incurring the full cost of failure.

Similarly, in his role as planner, the executive is well aware of the magnitude of his investment decisions and the difficulty (sometimes the impossibility) of systematically evaluating all alternatives available to the company. He is also aware that he has at his disposal finite resources that have to be allocated among competing demands. Simulation techniques allow the businessman to examine the probable consequences of his decisions without the risk of real-life experimentation. They allow him to test the effects of his decisions on the whole corporation before these decisions are implemented.

Computers shorten the computational time period and thus permit repetitive use of the simulation model. This ability of the computer to compress the time needed to test the results of decisions makes experimentation much easier.

MANAGEMENT SCIENCE

Simulation is, of course, only one of a number of new mathematical techniques whose use has been facilitated by the availability of computers. During the past decade we have seen a growing recognition by management of its need for newer and more sophisticated planning tools. Operations research and other techniques now frequently referred to as management science have emerged to help satisfy that need. They are contributing new skills to aid management in meeting the complexities of the decision making process.

Not too long ago it was unusual to find a mathematician or statistician working in management. We had grown accustomed to his presence in the engineering department or the research laboratory, but we were surprised when we found him attacking such operational problems as production scheduling or inventory control. Now we even see him contributing to the financial planning function in such areas as capital budgeting, sales forecasting and investment analysis. We see operations research and management science departments on the organization charts of many of our more progressive companies.

These professions, like all others, have developed their own characteristic approaches, methodology, tools, and techniques—decision theory, information theory, linear and dynamic programing, and network analysis as well as simulation. These are now being applied to an increasing array of complex business problems.

Many of these techniques offer significant potential for use in financial planning. Simulation is particularly useful in this area because it can be applied to problems that are too complex and have too many variables to be reduced to optimization formulas. That is the reason we chose the simulation approach at Burroughs. It seemed to us the only means by which we could cope with the complexity of the financial planning process in the level of detail deemed essential while retaining the inherent flexibility needed to accommodate change.

SIMULATION MODEL

A financial simulation model can be defined as a formal statement of the relationships among the elements of a company's financial structure. The diagram on page 516 illustrates what we term the "accounting dependencies" within the corporate structure of Burroughs. It has some similarity to our organizational pattern in that the elements on the chart represent units of management responsibility and managerial control, but

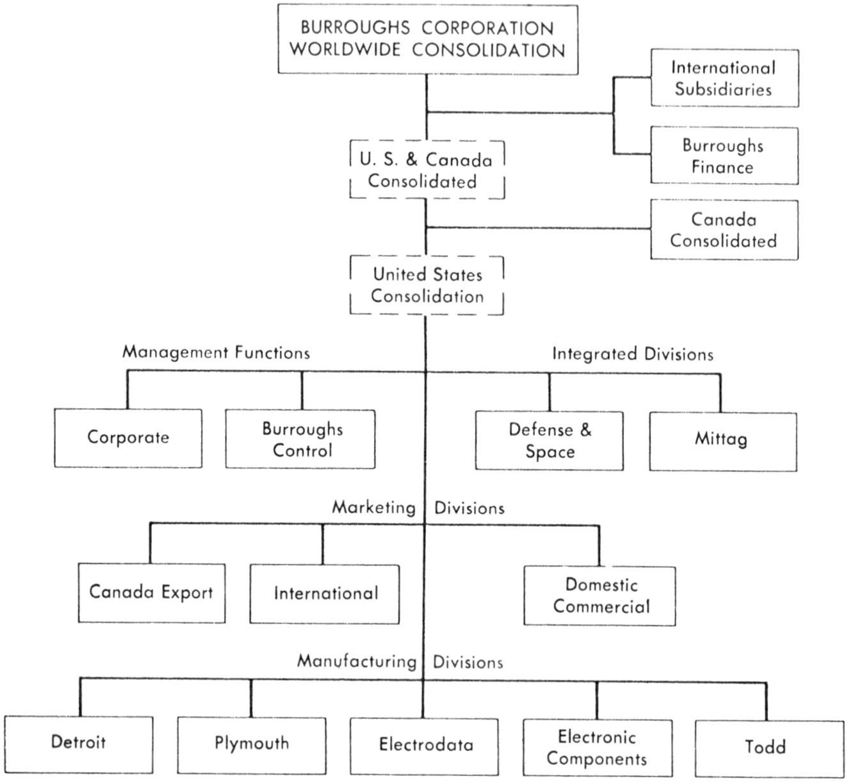

The "accounting dependencies" diagramed above define the framework of the model.

they are not necessarily described in their organizational hierarchy. The figure reflects one aspect of our accounting practice—the way we consolidate. As such, it defines the framework of our financial model.

Two key points in our concept of financial simulation are illustrated by this figure. The first is the concept of modular construction. The total Burroughs model is actually a set of sub-models, one for each of the management units shown. Specifically, we constructed individual models for each of these management units, expressing their output in accounting terms, and aggregated this output to produce the accounting consolidations indicated.

This design gives us the ability to identify and summarize the activities of each major corporate management unit. In addition, we can vary the form and level of detail between organizational units as a function of their inherent characteristics and their contribution to the planning process. Finally, the modular construction provides us with great model flexibility; it facilitates the introduction of worthwhile change to the program.

The second point we mean to illustrate in the figure is that there is a logical sequence that must be followed. This sequence depends on the structure of the business. The output of certain models forms the input for others. The relationship thus created reflects the interplay between divisions. The ordering of the models is of prime importance.

If the model is to be an effective planning tool, it must explicitly reflect cause and effect both within the specific business process and between the business and the market in which it participates. In defining cause and effect in the model there are two considerations—the inter-model relationships and the intra-model detail. The former refers to the explicit identification of the cause and effect factors that determine the relationship and thus the ordering between the sub-models. The latter refers to the level of detail essential in structuring one of the sub-models per se. Let us discuss each of these factors.

CAUSE AND EFFECT RELATIONS

The importance of the inter-model relationship can be illustrated by discussing the relationship of demand to production in the total model complex. The marketing division models constitute the primary demand source within the total corporate model. The manufacturing divisions constitute the principal production source and capability since we make what we sell. Because the marketing divisions are organized on a geographic basis and within their respective marketing areas handle the full product line, there is no direct inter-divisional relationship influencing the ordering of the marketing models. On the other hand, the stimulus for the manufacturing division models is the output of the marketing models. Here—given policy as to desired inventory and capacity constraints—production levels and manufacturing expenses are determined. The cost penalties of constraints (and of constraints masquerading as policies) can also, often, be determined. This creates opportunity to assess the value of making changes. The models must specifically describe the form in which marketing demands are translated into production requirements both as a direct functional relationship, acknowledging the explicit interplay of company policy, and in terms of the time transformation represented in this relationship. The output of both the marketing models and the manufacturing models provides input to the "management" model where we determine financial capacity, taxes, etc.

A complex interaction exists among our various manufacturing facilities. While they are each primarily identified with a specific product, each acts as a sub-contractor for assemblies, sub-assemblies, or parts to the other manufacturing facilities. Obviously, with this type of interaction any decisions made by the marketing organizations which affect demand rate will influence in varying degrees each of the manufacturing divisions, even though the decision might affect only one product in a wide product line. In order to create a useful planning tool, the development of the sub-models must explicitly include a formal statement of this inter-model cause-effect relationship.

In the Burroughs Financial Simulation Model the manufacturing inter-divisional relation is accomplished by having the demand for all product lines carried to each manufacturing unit, even though they are primarily product organized, in order to acknowledge this inter-divisional relationship. The model itself does not allocate total capacity among products so as to maximize production efficiency. In other words, the production sites for the various products have been predetermined for any simulation run. If capacity of a given producing unit will not satisfy the generated demand, both primary and secondary, we do not automatically adjust the demand. Rather we determine the imbalance and generate a report which states the deficiency in terms of demand lost or added capacity required to satisfy the demand input.

During the development of our model we found it expedient to view the cause-effect relationship we have just illustrated in a serial fashion. A better understanding is obtained by viewing the process as continuous rather than as sequential. The marketing demand interacts in the manufacturing sectors with capacity constraints and inventory policy to generate a production requirement. When this production requirement is accepted and met, goods are provided to marketing to satisfy the demand. Pricing and other marketing policies then determine revenue potential. This, in turn, affects the capital position and debt level of the firm. The capital position in turn defines the limits for the marketing activity. The financial simulation model must reflect this feedback relationship explicitly or have some check and balance features incorporated to assure reasonable constraint.

EFFECTS OF INPUT CHANGE

To illustrate the level of detail which we felt necessary to reflect in the simulation structure, we will trace the impact of a hypothetical change in input to our simulation model. Assume that we desire to evaluate the aggregate impact of a change in sales manpower in one of our marketing divisions. We have structured our demand forecast to be a function of the amount of direct sales manpower and a productivity function. In addition to evaluating the impact of the proposed manpower change through the relationship just identified, we explicitly evaluate the impact of the demand change on equipment and services revenue, cost of sales, and finished goods inventory. The impact of the demand change together with an inventory policy allows us to determine the resultant production requirement. This production requirement is an input in determining the in-process inventory. The determination of the production in-process activity provides the necessary stimulus for the determination of the sub-assembly and part manufacturing requirements, which in our model interact throughout the whole manufacturing sector. We must further relate this activity to its effect on variable, semi-variable, and fixed costs of manufacturing, which collectively affect the burden absorption functions. Marketing expenses and commissions, freight and shipping costs, and interest expense will be affected. The change will affect the tax provision, after-tax profits, accounts receivable, and liabilities. It will affect the equity section since dividends and retained earnings are both functions of net income. Indeed, it will be essential to evaluate the magnitude of funds required to carry out the suggested program which in itself has a feedback to marketing, where we began the illustration.

PROCESS VS. POLICY

Two categories of causative action are involved—one a function of the physical process, the other a matter of corporate policy. The establishment of an appropriate training pipeline to support a desired sales force represents a cause-effect relationship that is related to the "physical process" of the operation of the corporation; it also illustrates the introduction of a balancing and control mechanism on the marketing assumption. On the other hand, the inventory policy, which affects production requirements, is a reflection of corporate policy.

There is no pat answer to the choice of level of detail which must or should be represented within the simulation model. Nevertheless it is important that those specific considerations to which system performance is sensitive be separately identified and treated within the models. Certainly, all aspects of policy should be separately identified. The aggregation of details not only masks their individual impact but makes it difficult to use the results of the simulation; through lack of detail, precise responsibility for a change is unknown. Either condition makes it difficult to interpret an output of a simulation run for planning purposes. In creating a useful planning model prudence cautions against presenting too much detail, but an excess of detail is preferable to over-aggregation.

We have discussed the kinds of effects on the corporate plan caused by introducing a single change of input to the marketing division submodel. We have mentioned the complex functional relationships that are affected throughout the system. It is important to re-emphasize that the complexity of this relationship is not only a functional interaction but is also compounded by a time dimension; the nature of the relationship explicitly changes as time passes. For example, expenditures for research and development are not expected to produce revenue in the same period. These expenditures are investments in future revenue. We could term R&D a "lead" factor. It is important that we know, or make assumptions about and test the sensitivity to, the exact form of this time translation. On the other hand, administrative expenses may follow changes in revenue and thus, in certain instances, could be classed as a "lag" function. In many situations the semi-variable costs in the manufacturing sector show "asymmetric" properties relative to changes in production volume. That is, changes in semi-variable costs may lead changes in production volume when they are increasing but lag changes in production volume in a down trend. These relationships must be derived. Their specific form is in most instances unique to a particular firm. It is essential that the relationships used in the model be adequately representative of the corporation's own processes.

A financial simulation model must not only reflect cause and effect within the firm and between the firm and its market. It must also be logically consistent with the financial practices of the firm and be a true representation of management policies and plans. These relationships are not simple—they are not God-given. To establish an adequate representation that will assure an effective planning tool requires a rigorous and continuous study program within the firm.

So far in our discussion we have used some language that may be peculiar to Burroughs' operations. It is not our intent, however, to emphasize our unique operating characteristics. The most important point is this: Since we have unique characteristics in our operations, our model must be structured to acknowledge and represent them. Furthermore, we are not unlike any other dynamic organization. The interactions within our corporate structure are complex. The relationships are varied. The importance of the planning process to our operations forced us to seek new tools. In order to use simulation techniques effectively, we had to establish a program which would result in a better understanding of our business in order that we could identify and quantify the essential cause-effect relationships and assure a realistic representation of management policies and their effect on the firm.

USES OF THE MODEL

Because of the complexity of the interactions that take place within the firm, it is difficult if not impossible for a human to think through all of the ramifications in the systematic form demanded for proper planning. Without the assistance of the simulation technique, we would have an overwhelming computational task and a very nasty communications problem in trying to respond to today's demands for planning information. The simulation model lessens the communications problem through the definition and quantification of the relationships within the system. We cannot emphasize too strongly that you must be honest with yourself; you must learn about yourself and the way you do business; you must explicitly define and quantify the relationships applicable to your operation and your business. Otherwise a simulation model will produce uninteresting irrelevant or erroneous information.

Our experience has verified that financial simulation can add a new dimension to the planning process. Simulation provides flexibility by making it possible to generate a number of different plans quickly, easily, and cheaply. By forcing management to define and to quantify the relationships existing within the system and the interactions among its elements, it brings into clearer focus the hidden determinants of policy and practice. By making automatic the process of tracing the effects of decisions throughout the system, it solves the problems of communication that exist within any dynamic and diversified organization. By integration with management information systems, it provides the potential for the development of feedback control systems. The following are some examples of the uses we have made of our financial simulation model:

At the division level

1. To learn the combined influence of independent decisions
2. To improve decision making ability:
   a. To enforce discipline through formal relationships
   b. To allow the testing of independent decisions
   c. To point out problem areas
   d. To point out some inconsistent areas in decision making
3. To allow divisions to make several test runs before preparing their detailed forecasts

At the corporate level

1. To learn the effect on the corporation of a proposed divisional plan
2. To evaluate divisional "profit plans" and study alternative plans with respect to:

   a. Growth objectives
   b. Asset management
   c. Profit maximization
   d. Cash flow
3. To evaluate corporate decision alternatives
4. To prepare long-range financial and debt management plans

Clearly, financial simulation increases the effectiveness of the financial analyst. The responsible analyst has, of course, always been aware of the interactions among elements in the system and has considered these in the development of his projections. At the same time, however, he has been hampered by the restrictions placed on him by computational limitations. He has had to ignore variables and relationships that he knew were important, simply because they could not be considered with the time and manpower resources he had available. He has been curious about the effects of altering certain basic assumptions but has never been able to test more than a few alternatives.

Today, burdened by increasing demands from top management, faced with more complex systems to analyze, and operating within the complex organizational and communications structure of a diversified corporation, the financial analyst needs the assistance that the technique of simulation can give him. Through the use of simulation, he acquires the potential for doing his job the way he has always wanted to do it.

DOS AND DON'TS

Now that we have examined the concepts of a financial model and seen how financial simulation contributes to the planning process, it may be helpful to summarize what we have learned about setting up a simulation program and the steps that must be taken in its implementation.

Construction of a model is an expensive, time-consuming process and requires the cooperation of middle and some lower management across the organization. Without the active interest and participation of top management, the project is doomed to failure from the start. This fact is of primary importance.

A second ingredient essential to the success of the project is the joint participation of the operations research or management science staff and the corporate financial analysis group in the development of the model. This inter-disciplinary approach is necessary to provide a balance between simulation technique on the one hand and financial logic and knowledgeability on the other. In our case the operations research man acted as the hub of the simulation team. At the same time, participation by financial analysis guaranteed that the operations research techniques were not applied in a vacuum but were kept within the bounds of logical and meaningful financial relationships.

A fine measure of success of a financial simulation program is its actual use by management in the planning process. If executives' participation has been enlisted in the development of the model, they will become knowledgeable concerning the nature and use of the approach. They will understand how the model works, how to use the model to simulate various policies and plans, and how to interpret its output. This understanding on the part of managers and their willingness to participate adds realism to the model and facilitates its acceptance as an official corporate planning tool.

In developing a model, it is necessary to examine a multitude of data. Sound research and financial logic are required in order to extract from the total information stream those data that reflect cause and effect. Initial efforts should be directed toward examining past research and making use of relationships previously developed and tested. Where previous research has not provided an adequate base for model design a research program must be initiated. If historical data are inadequate or judged not to be indicative of the future, one is forced to depend upon estimated relationships. Here the judgment of the informed manager is of great value in developing the necessary estimates.

After this approach has created an initial model, the model should be tested with actual data to measure the reasonability of its results. It is then modified and re-tested in a process continued until a simulation close enough to reality is obtained. No generalized criteria can be provided. What we are in fact doing is engaging in a formal validation procedure, to ensure that the model actually mirrors the corporate financial structure and that it truly reflects the effects of policies, plans, and actions.

A financial model must be dynamic in nature. It must be periodically reworked in order to improve the precision with which functional relationships are stated, to incorporate the organizational changes that occur in any dynamic organization, and to reflect changes in accounting practice which could lead either to changes in established relationships or changes in the accounting structure of the model.

A simulation model, like anything else in life, can always be improved. We can simulate, test, modify, and simulate again, until we get as close to reailty as we wish. However, in expending this effort, we should try to strike a happy and acceptable balance between realism on the one hand and cost, time, and complexity of the model on the other.

In guarding against over-simulation, however, we should not go to the other extreme of oversimplification. For then the accuracy and the realism of the model are destroyed, and the effort expended becomes a costly exercise in futility.

THE PLANNING PROBLEM

The effort is worthwhile, for corporate planning—in particular, long-range planning—is a complex and difficult task. It requires sophistication and know-how on the part of the corporate executive who must formulate the corporate policies and plans that determine the future course of his organization.

The planning function is, first of all, a complex process. The executive is seeking to identify the alternatives available and assess their relative worth. The identification of reasonable alternatives is in itself a time consuming task, requiring the executive to sift through and analyze volumes of information. The determination of the relative desirability of these alternatives is made more difficult because of the element of uncertainty about the future within which each has been cast.

Uncertainty and change must be acknowledged as paramount forces to be coped with in the planning process. The balance between the need to make decisions and take action and the need for flexibility to permit adaptation to change remains a matter of judgment.

Changes are not only external. The organization, through expansion and diversification, may become more complicated as well. The economic environment, the acceptance of the company's product in the market place, and the company's cost of doing business are all affected in subtle but powerful ways by the complex interactions taking place between the enterprise on the one hand and government, labor, competition, and consumer demand on the other.

In addition to being complex, the planning process is a difficult one increasingly so because of the shrinkage of time allowed the executive for response. As he attempts to cope with the complexities of his environment, the executive finds that his traditional patterns of decision making are breaking down in the face of ever increasing demands for faster reaction times. He recognizes the need for new planning tools to assist him in his planning role.

Traditionally, management has relied upon the financial segment of the organization for counsel in formulating plans. All activities have cost consequences. Hence, regardless of who else takes part in planning, the financial staff is an essential participant.

Top executives recognize the importance of the financial ramifications of planning. They are aware that decisions on budgets, appropriations, new product development, plant acquisition, and resource allocations made anywhere within the corporate structure have a far-reaching effect on the total fabric of the organization. They realize that policies and plans to achieve desired corporate objectives are embodied in these decisions.

Today we find the role of the financial manager in a corporation to be of primary importance. The financial manager is being asked to share the increased planning burden, to produce more planning exercises, to explore more alternatives, to provide information in greater detail, and, most significantly, to respond more rapidly.

The financial manager enjoys the confidence of top management because of his contribution to the planning process. The financial people have dedicated themselves to the development of technical competence and the accumulation of the experience necessary to act as consultants and advisors to top management. They have evolved accounting systems and analytic tools to aid them in performing this function.

The pressures under which the financial manager must now operate are obviously not due to any decrease in his capability. Instead, they stem from the increased demands now being put upon him by top management. The problem facing the financial manager, then, is only in relatively small part that of developing new theory, for the existing body of theory has proved generally adequate. Instead, he must acquire new tools, tools that are appropriate to his changing planning environment, tools that permit him to respond more quickly, more flexibly, and with greater accuracy and precision to requests from top management.

An attempt to use the traditional management structure of the corporation for financial planning creates significant communications problems that do not satisfy the executive response requirements. If management finds it necessary to communicate with all echelons and activities in order to determine the ramifications of a single "I wonder what would happen if" condition, the planning potential of the organization is limited. Yet relying solely on the experience of executives around the board room table does not satisfy today's need for explicit and systematic testing of the impact of change.

In financial simulation we have the potential for an effective solution to this problem. If a sound program—based upon top management participation, an interdisciplinary approach, and a thorough preliminary study phase—is established, this potential can be realized.

The structuring of a financial model is a difficult and sensitive task. We must learn and understand a great deal about the behavior of our organizations before we can produce workable and meaningful models. There is no cheap way to buy the tool. There is no such thing as a general financial simulation model that will act as an effective planning tool for a specific organization. There are no general equations applicable to every organization. While some equations in functional form can be expressed so as to be universal, their real value is in providing a guide for study and development. Even if our study provides a validation of their applicability we have, in fact, developed our own.

Thus, Burroughs' experience and Burroughs' model are hardly to be taken as universal. Indeed, our experience may not even provide an adequate sample from which to state a set of hard and fast rules. However, our experience has been sufficient to identify some important do's and don't's. And this description of the relationships and circumstances that have produced an effective planning model may be useful as a general to those interested in applying the technique.

The author describes how an economic simulator in a computer program can reduce the cost of evaluating and developing credit policies.

39

CREDIT ANALYSIS BY COMPUTER

Joel Zelnick

The complex business of extending credit, which depends heavily on intuition, has long posed some difficult managerial problems. These problems are primarily concerned with making sure that all credit risks are evaluated with some sort of consistency and in accordance with management's credit policy.

Because management has had no explicit way (with numbers, for example) of expressing its cerdit policy and has been able to provide little in the way of rules for credit decision to guide those implementing its policy, this policy is exposed to a broad range of subjective interpretations. Consequently, the definition of "good" and "bad" credit risks tends to vary from city to city, office to office, and even interviewer to interviewer. What is more, there is no real way for management to monitor the evaluation process and ensure that decisions made are in accordance with established policy. There is simply no way to distinguish between a right and wrong decision except in the relatively rare case of obvious poor judgment.

For example, if management decides to tighten credit, it is unable to express the new policy to individual credit interviewers in a way that provides either the interviewers with some objective criteria for judging credit risks or management with criteria against which the individual implementation of its policy can be measured. The result is that each credit interviewer interprets "tighten" in his own way, leading either to gross inconsistencies in the implementation of the credit

Reprinted from *Financial Executive,* June 1966, pp. 26–31, by permission of the publisher.

policy or to an increase in the number of credit decisions that are referred to management for action. These circumstances generally leave much room for improvement in both the operating efficiency and income-producing effectiveness of the credit operation.

CONVENTIONAL WEIGHTED SCORING SYSTEM

During the past couple of years, attempts have been made to introduce some degree of scientific method into the credit-evaluation process by using weighted application forms. These forms differ from conventional forms only in the fact that numerical weights are assigned to each personal characteristic of the applicant. In order to score the applicant, these weights are totalled by the credit interviewer, who takes the first step in coming to a decision by comparing this score against a scale of average good- and bad-risk scores. This does not mean that the need for human judgment is completely eliminated by statistical techniques. Although minimum judgment is required for the obviously good and bad risks, there is an area between the two extremes in which considerable human judgment must be applied.

Despite bringing a measure of consistency to the credit-evaluation process, the scoring system described above suffers from being too intuitive and general, and from not going as far as modern statistical techniques now enable us to go. The weights used in such a system are usually determined purely on the basis of intuitive judgment rather than by any scientific statistical analysis. In many cases, the scoring system developed for one customer group is used across the board, with no allowances for the significant socio-economic differences that exist in the population groups of different neighborhoods, cities, and regions.

The disadvantages of generalized scoring systems of the type described, as compared to customized scores based upon the specific history of a particular area, were shown in a study conducted by a national finance company. The study showed that a generalized scoring system applied to all the company's offices would produce a saving of $25,000, whereas a saving of $270,000 would result if a customized scoring system were developed for each office. The customized scoring system would save $245,000 more than the generalized approach. Obviously, there is much to be said in favor of customized scoring systems.

The other shortcoming of the scoring systems currently in use is that they do not help the credit manager to choose the "passing" score that will give him the desired economic results. He is forced to rely solely upon his intuition. This shortcoming exists in the intuitive, generalized weighting systems because they lack a sound statistical base for predicting the results of specific adjustments in the "passing" score.

ECONOMICS OF DOING BETTER

Until recently there have existed valid economic reasons for not pushing statistically based scoring systems further in credit operations. Because it might require up to two years to develop the proper techniques for generating statistically valid weights, it is easy to understand why companies have been willing to settle for the lesser benefits offered by intuitive, generalized systems.

Predicting the result of changes in the "passing" score poses the same type of economic problem, because it requires the development of a computer-simulation model. An extensive study would be necessary to define the variables and their interrelationships, diagram the procedures, and collect the data.

COMPUTER PROGRAMS CHANGE THE ECONOMICS

In recent months the economics of developing a statistically based scoring system for credit evaluation have changed radically. The statistical techniques needed to generate scientific weights on the basis of the historical performance of a specific population and to simulate the economics of various "passing" scores have been developed and put into the form of computer programs. These computer programs significantly reduce the cost of developing a scientific weighting system. Once the required historical data have been gathered, a series of computer analyses can determine the optimum weights to be used, predict the economic results of various "passing" scores, and generate a reasonably accurate estimate of the financial savings the weighting system can be expected to produce in the credit operation.

This formalization of statistical techniques in computer programs, which can be applied at relatively low cost, not only makes it practical to consider statistically based weighting systems as an alternative to intuitive methods, but also to consider developing individual weighting systems that take into account the difference between customer groups.

A particularly important part of this computer-program package is the economic simulator, which shows the credit manager beforehand how large an increase in income to expect from loosening or tightening credit by a given number of points.

NO NEED FOR MAJOR SYSTEM REVISION

This computer-program package provides a way of placing a scientific base under an existing manual system; it is not a replacement for an existing system. In this sense, it is really a set of tools or techniques that can be used to improve an existing system—and it can be applied with considerably less effort, expense, and operational disruption than is normally associated with development of new systems.

Application of this credit-evaluation tool begins with the gathering of a statistically significant and representative sample of past accounts. This information is then analyzed by a computer to find the defining characteristics of "good" and "bad" risks and to determine the relative importance of each characteristic. The characteristics are then weighted according to importance.

One possible result of this analysis is the shortening of the credit-application form. Often the analysis shows that some of the information requested on the form is not relevant in evaluating the applicant as a good or bad risk.

Major products of such analyses are a statistically based system of weighting the relevant characteristics of applicants, and a scoring scale.

The scale defines the scoring range within which a breakpoint between "good" and "bad" risks must be established. This range is developed by applying the weights to a proper sample of good and bad past accounts. The results can be plotted on two separate curves, showing the distribution of bad and good risks and the scoring range of each (Figures 39–1 and 39–2). If these two curves are put together (Figure 39–3), there is an area in the scoring range where the two curves overlap. This is the area governed by management policy. Management must decide which point in this range should be designated as the breakpoint between

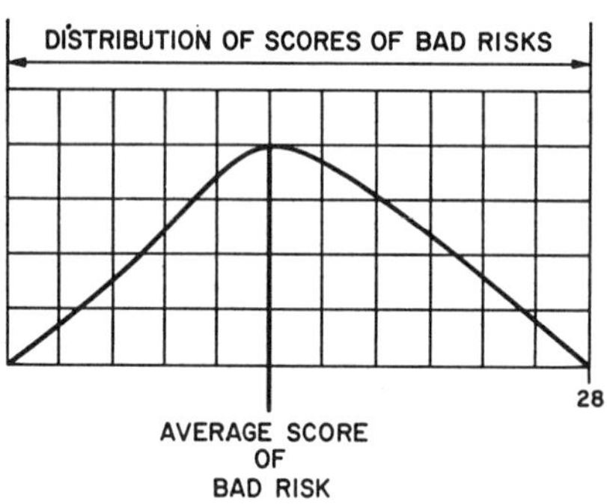

Figure 39–1

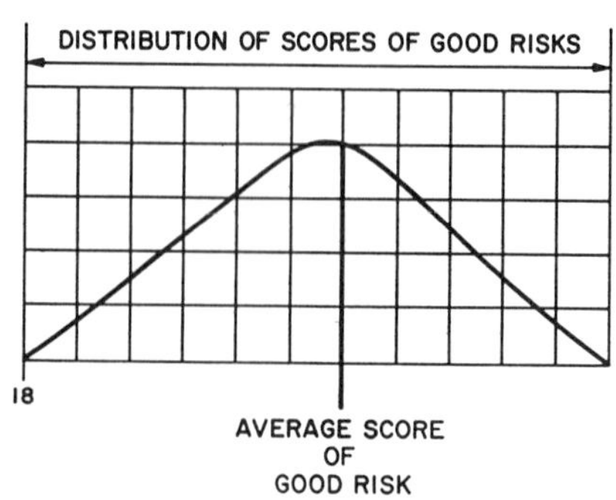

Figure 39–2

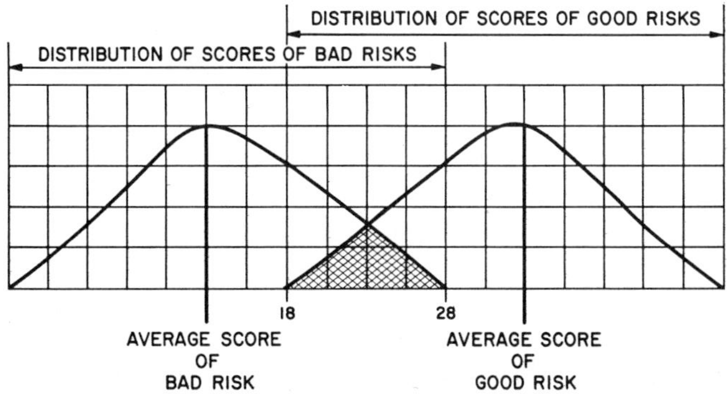

Figure 39–3

good and bad risks. A tradeoff must be made between added income and added risk. This decision cannot be generalized, because it depends upon the specific factors and objectives of each individual manager. Nor, of course, can the breakpoint be permanent; it must be revised periodically in accordance with the fluctuations in economic factors and the changing objectives of the manager's operation.

ECONOMIC SIMULATOR FOR CREDIT OPERATIONS

Setting credit policy is, of course, one of the credit manager's most crucial functions. The economic simulator included in the new package of computer programs for credit evaluation allows the credit manager to simulate the economic performance of his credit operation at given breakpoints and to predict the results which different breakpoints will produce. To perform this simulation, the credit manager needs only to provide figures on the current status of his interest income and writeoff expenses. Once these figures are added to the computer program, alternative breakpoints can be tested in a series of short computer runs, which will give the manager the kind of information shown in Figure 39–4.

In the hypothetical situation pictured in Figure 39–4, a breakpoint of 35 would increase costs (loss) by $50,000, while a breakpoint of 20 would increase income (gain) by $100,000. Information such as this enables management to evaluate alternative credit policies scientifically to see which one is most likely to produce the desired results.

MORE EFFECTIVE CREDIT MANAGEMENT

The real value of this new set of computer programs for credit operations lies in helping credit managers achieve more effective control over

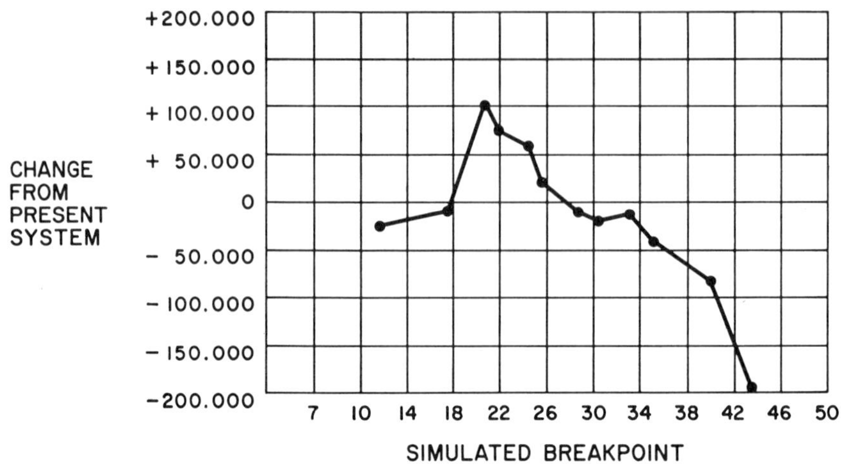

Figure 39–4

operations and better decision making. A purely objective, carefully customized weighting system of the type described enables him to express his credit policy in very concrete numerical terms, to supply his interviewers with consistent evaluation criteria, and to obtain criteria for measuring his interviewers' performance. Beyond that, testing alternative credit policies inexpensively and easily by economic simulations will assist the manager in improving his own performance in a key decision-making area.